The Holt, Rinehart and Winston Accuracy Commitment: From Manuscript to Bound Book

As a leading textbook publisher in foreign languages since 1866, Holt, Rinehart and Winston recognizes the importance of accuracy in foreign language textbooks. In an effort to produce the most accurate introductory foreign language program available we have added two new stages to the development of *Wie geht's?*, Sixth Edition—**double proofing** in production and a **final accuracy check** by experienced teachers.

The outline below shows the unprecedented steps we have taken to ensure accuracy:

Author	Writes and proofs first draft.
1st Round of Reviews	Review of first draft manuscript. Independent reviewers check for clarity of text organization, pedagogy, content, and proper use of language.
Author	Makes corrections/changes.
2nd Round of Reviews	Review of second draft manuscript. Independent reviewers again check for clarity of text organization, pedagogy, content, and proper use of language.
Author	Prepares text for production.
Production	Copyediting and proofreading. The project is **double-proofed**—at the galley proof stage and again at the page proof stage.
Final Accuracy Check	The entire work is read one last time by experienced instructors, this time to check for accurate use of language in text, examples, and exercises. The material is read word for word again and all exercises are worked to ensure the most accurate language program possible. The accompanying workbook/lab manual, tapescript, and video are proofed simultaneously.
Final Textbook	Published with final corrections.

Holt, Rinehart and Winston would like to acknowledge the following instructors who, along with others, participated in the final accuracy check for *Wie geht's?*, Sixth Edition: Francis Brévart, University of Pennsylvania; Richard Ruppel, University of Wisconsin; John Jeep, Miami of Ohio; Elfriede Smith, Drew University; Gabriela Appel, Pennsylvania State University; Monika Nenon, University of Memphis; Virginia Lewis, Drake University; Bettina Cothran, Georgia Institute of Technology; Elio Brancaforte, Harvard University; Rolf Goebel, University of Alabama; Robert Rymer, University of North Carolina at Charlotte; Jutta Arend, College of the Holy Cross; Joseph Brockington, Kalamazoo College; George Evertte, University of Mississippi; Marilya Veteto-Conrad, Northern Arizona State University; Heidi Schlipphacke, University of Illinois at Chicago; Cordelia Stroinigg, University of Cincinnati; Elke Hatch, University of Dayton; Gamin Bartle, University of Alabama; and Christine Castle, MIT.

EUROPA und NORDAFRIKA
Hauptstadt
Landeshauptstadt
Stadt
ISLAND
Reykjavik
Arctic Circle
der ATLANTIK
die NORDSEE
NORWEGEN
SCHWEDEN
FINNLAND
Oslo
Stockholm
Helsinki
St. Petersburg
Tallinn
ESTLAND
RUSSLAND
LETTLAND
Riga
Moskau
SCHOTTLAND
NORDIRLAND
Edinburgh
Belfast
Dublin
IRLAND
GROSSBRITANNIEN
DÄNEMARK
Kopenhagen
die OSTSEE
Königsberg
LITAUEN
Wilna
Minsk
(ZU RUSSLAND)
BELARUS
WALES
ENGLAND
Cardiff
London
die NIEDERLANDE
Amsterdam
Den Haag
Berlin
POLEN
Warschau
der ÄRMELKANAL
Brüssel
Bonn
BELGIEN
DEUTSCHLAND
Kiew
LUXEMBURG
Luxemburg
Paris
Prag
die UKRAINE
TSCHECHIEN
die SLOWAKEI
FRANKREICH
LIECHTENSTEIN
Wien
Pressburg
MOLDAU
Bern
Vaduz
ÖSTERREICH
Budapest
Chisinau
die SCHWEIZ
SLOWENIEN
UNGARN
Laibach
Zagreb
RUMÄNIEN
KROATIEN
Belgrad
Bukarest
BOSNIEN-HERZEGOWINA
das SCHWARZE MEER
PORTUGAL
Madrid
Sarajevo
SERBIEN
BULGARIEN
ITALIEN
Lissabon
KORSIKA
Sofia
SPANIEN
MONTENEGRO
Skopje
Istanbul
Rom
MALLORCA
Tirana
MAKEDONIEN
ALBANIEN
SARDINIEN
die TÜRKEI
die STRASSE von GIBRALTAR
GRIECHENLAND
Rabat
Algier
SIZILIEN
Athen
Tunis
das MITTELMEER
MAROKKO
ALGERIEN
TUNESIEN
KRETA
Tripoli
Meilen
0
400
LIBYEN
Kilometer
0
400
AFRIKA

ÖSTERREICH
Hauptstadt
Landeshauptstadt
Stadt
Berg
Tunnel/Pass
TSCHECHIEN
DEUTSCHLAND
Passau
der Inn
NIEDERÖSTERREICH
die SLOWAKEI
die Donau
Linz
Melk
WIEN
Pressburg
OBERÖSTERREICH
St.Pölten
Wien
Steyr
Salzburg
Wiener Neustadt
Eisenstadt
der Bodensee
die ZUGSPITZE 2.963 m
Kitzbühel
die Enns
BURGENLAND
der Neusiedler See
Bregenz
VORARLBERG
A L P E N
die Salzach
der DACHSTEIN 2.995m
Leoben
Vaduz
der Inn
Innsbruck
SALZBURG
STEIERMARK
TIROL
LIECHTENSTEIN
der GROSSGLOCKNER 3.798 m
der TAUERN TUNNEL
Graz
der BRENNER PASS
die Mur
UNGARN
die SCHWEIZ
(Zu Tirol)
KÄRNTEN
Lienz
der Worther See
Villach
Klagenfurt
die Drau
Meilen
0
50
Kilometer
0
50
ITALIEN
SLOWENIEN

die Schweiz
Hauptstadt
Landeshauptstadt
Stadt
Berg
Tunnel/Pass
der Rhein
DEUTSCHLAND
SCHAFFHAUSEN
Schaffhausen
der Bodensee
BASEL-STADT
Frauenfeld
Basel
Liestal
AARGAU
ZÜRICH
THURGAU
die Aare
Winterthur
St. Gallen
Delémont
BASEL-LAND
APPENZELL AUSSERRHODEN
JURA
Aarau
Zürich
Herisau
Appenzell
SOLOTHURN
die
der Zürichsee
APPENZELL INNERRHODEN
FRANKREICH
Solothurn
Zug
SANKT GALLEN
LIECHTENSTEIN
Biel
der Bieler See
BERN
LUZERN
SCHWYZ
ZUG
Vaduz
ÖSTERREICH
Schwyz
Glarus
NEUENBURG
Neuenburg
Bern
Luzern
GLARUS
der Neuenburger See
die Aare
Sarnen
Stans
der Vierwaldstätter See
NIDW.
Altdorf
Chur
Freiburg
UNTERWALDEN OBW.
URI
der Rhein
Davos
Thun
GRAUBÜNDEN
WAADT
Interlaken
der Inn
FREIBURG
der Thuner See
Grindelwald
A L P E N
Lausanne
der ST. GOTTHARD TUNNEL
die JUNGFRAU 4.158 m
St. Moritz
der Genfer See
Montreux
TESSIN
die Rhône
ITALIEN
der SIMPLON TUNNEL
GENF
WALLIS
Bellinzona
Sion
Locarno
Genf
Saas Fee
Meilen
das MATTERHORN 4.478 m
Zermatt
der Lago Maggiore
Lugano
0
40
Kilometer
der MONT BLANC 4.807 m
0
40
FRANKREICH
ITALIEN

Elevation in meters
2000+
500–2000
200–500
0–200
Sea Level
DÄNEMARK
die Ostsee
Flensburg
Rügen
Helgoland
die Nordsee
Kiel
Stralsund
Rostock
SCHLESWIG-
HOLSTEIN
Lübeck
MECKLENBURG-
VORPOMMERN
die Ostfriesischen Inseln
Schwerin
Bremerhaven
HAMBURG
Hamburg
Neubrandenburg
die NIEDERLANDE
Oldenburg
BREMEN
Bremen
die Elbe
BRANDENBURG
die Oder
POLEN
die Ems
NIEDERSACHSEN
die Havel
BERLIN
Berlin
der Mittelland kanal
Hannover
Wolfsburg
Potsdam
Frankfurt
Braunschweig
Hildesheim
die Weser
Hameln
Magdeburg
der Teutoburger Wald
Münster
SACHSEN-
ANHALT
der HARZ
Wittenberg
Dessau
Cottbus
der Rhein
Dortmund
Göttingen
die Spree
die Neiße
Essen
die Ruhr
Halle
Leipzig
die Elbe
Düsseldorf
Kassel
NORDRHEIN-
WESTFALEN
THÜRINGEN
die Saale
Dresden
Köln
SACHSEN
Eisenach
Weimar
Erfurt
Jena
HESSEN
Aachen
Chemnitz
Marburg
der THÜRINGER WALD
Bonn
der Rhein
die Fulda
die Lahn
die Werra
das ERZGEBIRGE
die Elbe
BELGIEN
Koblenz
der TAUNUS
die Mosel
Wiesbaden
Frankfurt
LUXEMBURG
Mainz
der Main
TSCHECHIEN
Bayreuth
Würzburg
Trier
RHEINLAND-
PFALZ
Mannheim
Fürth
Nürnberg
SAARLAND
Ludwigshafen
der BÖHMERWALD
Saarbrücken
Heidelberg
Rothenburg
die FRÄNKISCHE ALB
Karlsruhe
BADEN-
WÜRTTEMBERG
Regensburg
die Saar
der BAYERISCHE WALD
Stuttgart
die Donau
Tübingen
die SCHWÄBISCHE ALB
BAYERN
die Isar
Passau
FRANKREICH
der Rhein
der SCHWARZWALD
Landshut
die Donau
Ulm
Augsburg
der Inn
die VOGESEN
der Neckar
ÖSTERREICH
München
Freiburg
Meilen
0
80
der Chiemsee
Friedrichshafen
Konstanz
Lindau
Kilometer
0
80
der Rhein
der Bodensee
A L P E N
die ZUGSPITZE
2.963 m
Garmisch-Partenkirchen
die SCHWEIZ

DIE WELT

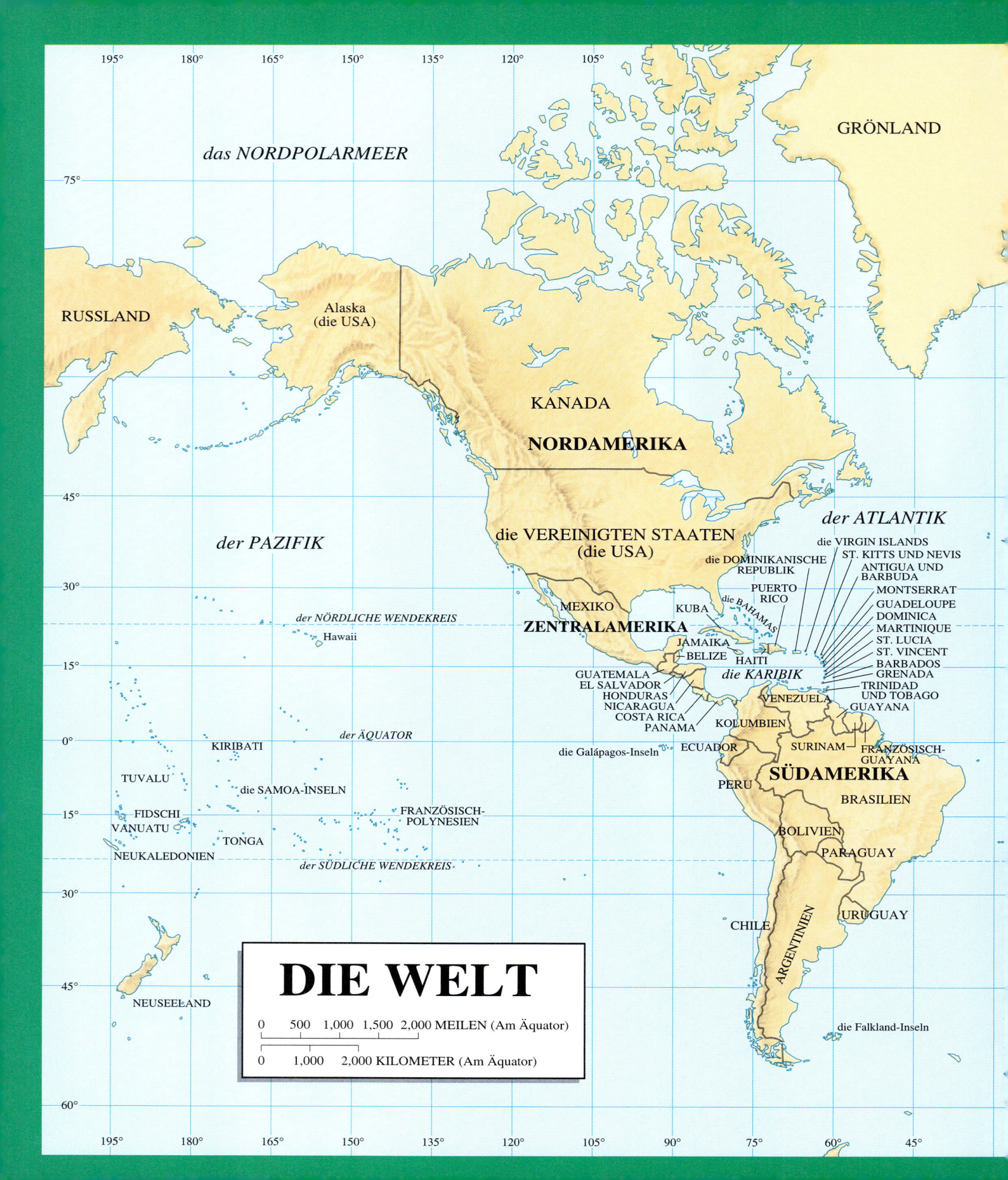

Weltkarte

das NORDPOLARGEBIET

die NORDSEE

- ISLAND
- NORWEGEN
- SCHWEDEN
- FINNLAND
- das VEREINIGTE KÖNIGREICH
- IRLAND
- DEUTSCHLAND
- **EUROPA** *
- ÖSTERREICH
- die SCHWEIZ
- RUSSLAND (die RUSSISCHE FÖDERATION)
- ASERBAIDSCHAN
- GEORGIEN
- ARMENIEN
- SYRIEN
- ZYPERN
- LIBANON
- ISRAEL
- IRAK
- **der NAHE OSTEN**
- IRAN
- KASACHSTAN
- USBEKISTAN
- TURKMENISTAN
- KIRGISTAN
- TADSCHIKISTAN
- AFGHANISTAN
- die MONGOLEI
- **ASIEN**
- CHINA
- NORD-KOREA
- SÜD-KOREA
- JAPAN
- BHUTAN
- NEPAL
- PAKISTAN
- INDIEN
- LAOS
- MYANMAR
- TAIWAN
- BANGLADESCH
- SRI LANKA
- THAILAND
- VIETNAM
- die PHILIPPINEN
- KAMBODSCHA
- BRUNEI
- MALAYSIA
- SINGAPUR
- INDONESIEN
- PAPUA-NEUGUINEA
- die KANARISCHEN INSELN
- MAROKKO
- TUNESIEN
- ALGERIEN
- WESTSAHARA
- MAURETANIEN
- LIBYEN
- ÄGYPTEN
- KATAR
- SAUDI-ARABIEN
- JEMEN
- OMAN
- die VEREINIGTEN ARABISCHEN EMIRATE
- KUWAIT
- JORDANIEN
- GUINEA-BISSAU
- SENEGAL
- GAMBIA
- MALI
- NIGER
- **AFRIKA**
- TSCHAD
- ERITREA
- DSCHIBUTI
- BURKINA FASO
- GUINEA
- SIERRA LEONE
- LIBERIA
- die ELFENBEINKÜSTE
- GHANA
- TOGO
- BENIN
- NIGERIA
- KAMERUN
- GABUN
- REP. KONGO
- ÄQUATORIALGUINEA
- die ZENTRALAFRIKANISCHE REPUBLIK
- SUDAN
- ÄTHIOPIEN
- SOMALIA
- UGANDA
- RUANDA
- DEMOKRATISCHE REPUBLIK KONGO
- BURUNDI
- KENIA
- TANSANIA
- MALAWI
- SAMBIA
- ANGOLA
- NAMIBIA
- SIMBABWE
- BOTSUANA
- MOSAMBIK
- MADAGASKAR
- SÜDAFRIKA
- SWASILAND
- LESOTHO
- AUSTRALIEN
- Tasmanien

der ÄQUATOR

der INDISCHE OZEAN

das SÜDPOLARGEBIET

* See European map for detailed country listings.

Wie geht's?

Sixth Edition

HOLT RINEHART WINSTON *soon to become*

Harcourt College Publishers
A Harcourt Higher Learning Company

Soon you will find **Holt, Rinehart & Winston's** distinguished innovation, leadership, and support under a different name . . . a new brand that continues our unsurpassed quality, service, and commitment to education.

We are combining the strengths of our college imprints into one worldwide brand: **Harcourt** Our mission is to make learning accessible to anyone, anywhere, anytime—reinforcing our commitment to lifelong learning.

We'll soon be Harcourt College Publishers. Ask for us by name.

**One Company
"Where Learning Comes to Life."**

Wie geht's?
An Introductory German Course

Sixth Edition

Dieter Sevin
Vanderbilt University

Ingrid Sevin

Holt, Rinehart and Winston
Harcourt College Publishers
Fort Worth Philadelphia San Diego New York Orlando Austin San Antonio
Toronto Montreal London Sydney Tokyo

Publisher	Phyllis Dobbins
Acquisitions Editor	Jeff Gilbreath
Market Strategist	Kenneth S. Kasee
Project Editor	Katherine Dennis
Art Director	Garry Harman
Production Manager	Cindy Young

Cover image provided by Christie's Images/Super Stock. Artist: Ernst Ludwig Kirchner
Work Title: Eisbahn mit Schlittschuhlaufern

ISBN: 0-03-021444-0
Library of Congress Catalog Card Number: 99-62169

Copyright © 2000, 1995, 1991, 1988, 1984, 1980 by Harcourt Brace & Company

All rights reserved. No part of this publication may be reproduced or transmitted in any form or by any means, electronic or mechanical, including photocopy, recording, or any information storage and retrieval system, without permission in writing from the publisher.

Requests for permission to make copies of any part of the work should be mailed to: Permissions Department, Harcourt Brace & Company, 6277 Sea Harbor Drive, Orlando, FL 32887-6777.

Copyrights and Acknowledgments appear on page P-1, which constitutes a continuation of the copyright page.

Address for Domestic Orders
Holt, Rinehart and Winston, 6277 Sea Harbor Drive, Orlando, FL 32887-6777
800-782-4479

Address for International Orders
International Customer Service
Holt, Rinehart and Winston, 6277 Sea Harbor Drive, Orlando, FL 32887-6777
407-345-3800
(fax) 407-345-4060
(e-mail) hbintl@harcourtbrace.com

Address for Editorial Correspondence
Harcourt Brace College Publishers, 301 Commerce Street, Suite 3700, Fort Worth, TX 76102

Web Site Address
http://www.hbcollege.com

Harcourt Brace College Publishers will provide complimentary supplements or supplement packages to those adopters qualified under our adoption policy. Please contact your sales representative to learn how you qualify. If as an adopter or potential user you receive supplements you do not need, please return them to your sales representative or send them to: Attn: Returns Department, Troy Warehouse, 465 South Lincoln Drive, Troy, MO 63379.

Printed in the United States of America

0 1 2 3 4 5 6 7 8   048   9 8 7 6 5 4 3 2
Holt, Rinehart and Winston
Harcourt Brace College Publishers

To the Student

Welcome to *Wie geht's?*, a program for Introductory German that focuses on all four skills—listening, speaking, reading, and writing—and promotes cultural proficiency.

ORGANIZATION OF *WIE GEHT'S?*

The main text is divided into five pre-units *(Schritte)*, fifteen chapters *(Kapitel)*, five review sections *(Rückblicke)*, and an Appendix.

The Pre-Units

The purpose of the pre-units is to acquaint you with the German language and the language learning process by focusing on listening and speaking. When you have completed the last pre-unit, you should be able to greet others, describe your classroom and your clothes, use numbers, discuss the weather, and tell time, all in German.

The Fifteen Chapters

Each chapter opens with a summary of the learning objectives *(Lernziele)* for that chapter. This is followed by a cultural preview in English *(Vorschau)* that provides you with background information on the chapter topic. The first section of the learning material itself is called *Gespräche*. It includes one or two dialogues that focus on the chapter topic and function as models for conversation. For your reference, English translations for these dialogues can be found in the Appendix.

Next comes *Wortschatz 1*, which contains most of the new chapter vocabulary; it is arranged thematically, with nouns listed in alphabetical order according to gender. The vocabulary list is followed by exercises and activities *(Zum Thema)* that foster communication and help you to learn the new words and expressions. A pronunciation section *(Aussprache)* is included as well and is coordinated with more extensive practice in your Lab Manual. At the end of *Zum Thema*, and again after the reading text, you will find an activity *(Hören Sie zu!)* that will help improve your listening comprehension. To complete it, you will need to listen to the CD that accompanies the book.

The following *Struktur* section introduces two or three major points of grammar. A variety of exercises *(Übungen)* provides practice of the principles presented.

The grammar explanations and activities are followed by a reading section, *Einblicke*. An introductory passage in English first introduces the reading topic. This is followed by a brief pre-reading section *(Vorm Lesen)* that includes an activity and, under the rubric *Was ist das?*, a list of cognates and other easily recognized words that will appear in the reading. Other words that are not part of the active vocabulary are translated in the margin of the reading text. Those few additional words that must be mastered actively are listed in *Wortschatz 2;* they will recur in later chapters. The reading passage itself features one or more cultural aspects related to the chapter topic. It offers additional examples of the new grammar and a review of the chapter vocabulary. The reading text is followed by exercises and activities *(Zum Text)* that check comprehension and provide additional grammar, writing, and speaking practice. They are followed by a second listening activity *(Hören Sie zu!)*.

Cultural notes *(Fokus)* are interspersed throughout every chapter, as well as the pre-units; they point out or explain differences between life in North America and in countries where German is spoken. Beginning with Chapter 8, the last *Fokus* section will include a poem in German, for your enrichment and enjoyment.

Finally, the speaking situations *(Sprechsituationen)* at the end of the pre-units and each chapter list and practice expressions that are useful in social situations, such as extending, accepting, or declining invitations.

Each chapter also includes a *Web-Ecke* ("web corner") referring you to Holt, Rinehart and Winston's web site, where you will find on-line activities related to the chapter topic. Using them will open new vistas of direct contact in Germany and enrich your language learning and cultural insights.

Review Sections

After the pre-units and Chapters 3, 7, 11, and 15, you will find review sections *(Rückblicke)* that summarize the grammatical structures you have learned. Correlating review exercises can be found in the Workbook *(Zu Hause)*, with answers given in an answer key *(So geht's)*.

The Appendix

The Appendix includes information on predicting the gender of some nouns, a grammar summary in chart form, tables of all basic verb forms, lists of irregular verbs, translations of dialogues, supplementary charts for the "information-gap" activities in each chapter *(Hoppla, hier fehlt 'was!)*, a German–English and English–German vocabulary, and a grammar index.

Visual Icons for *Wie geht's?*

This icon designates an activity where you'll be working with a partner.

Activities marked with this icon are designed for work in small groups of perhaps 3–5 students.

This icon indicates an "information-gap" activity. Here, you work with a partner, compiling information that each of you has but the other does not, in order to complete a chart or find out certain information.

This denotes the listening activity that appears twice in each chapter. To complete the activity, listen to the CD that accompanies the book.

This icon indicates a writing activity.

This symbol marks the *Web-Ecke*.

Used in the *Struktur* section, this icon indicates vocabulary that must be memorized.

This icon will also appear from time to time in a *Struktur* section; it identifies grammar points where you should watch out that your knowledge of English doesn't interfere with the point under discussion.

This icon appears with each *Fokus* section, where you'll find cultural information about the German-speaking countries and things German.

STUDENT PROGRAM COMPONENTS

- *Wie geht's?* comes packaged with **a free audio CD** that contains thirty-one listening texts *(Hören Sie zu!):* one for the pre-units and two for each regular chapter.
- The **tape or CD program** and the **Workbook/Lab Manual** *(Im Sprachlabor und zu Hause)* provide additional practice in listening, speaking, and writing.

    On the tapes or CDs you will find the dialogues and reading texts, supplementary grammar activities, listening-comprehension exercises, and pronunciation practice.

    The Lab Manual section *(Im Sprachlabor)* is correlated to the tape or CD program; it contains instructions and examples for the recorded activities, as well as a worksheet that enables you to check your progress. Preceding the main section is a complete pronunciation guide with brief explanations of correct sound production; corresponding exercises are available on a separate pronunciation tape or CD.

    The Workbook section *(Zu Hause)* focuses on vocabulary building, structure, and cultural enrichment. Extensive review exercises that correlate with the review chapters *(Rückblicke)* of the main text have an answer key in the back, so that you can check your answers.

- The student **video manual** provides activities that are correlated to the *Wie geht's?* video, newly filmed for this edition and correlated to the textbook.
- A text-specific **CD-ROM** offers interactive activities that will help to improve your listening comprehension skills and provide further exposure to the culture of the German-speaking countries.
- Taking advantage of the new possibilities of the Internet, the sixth edition of *Wie geht's?* offers a new feature, the *Web-Ecke*. Near the end of each chapter, this section refers you to the ***Wie geht's?* World Wide Web site,** where you'll find **on-line activities** specifically tailored to the book. Go to http://www.hrwcollege.com/german/sevin/.
- The **PC and Macintosh tutorial software** lets you practice and review most of the exercises in the book on your own; error analysis will guide you to correct answers.

We hope that you will find the *Wie geht's?* program enjoyable. You will be surprised at the rapid progress you will make in just one year. Many students have been able to study abroad after only two years of studying German!

ACKNOWLEDGMENTS

We would like to thank the following colleagues who reviewed the manuscript during its various stages of development for the sixth edition:

Gabriela Appel, Pennsylvania State University
Jutta Arend, Holy Cross College
Gamin Bartle, University of Alabama
Elio Brancaforte, Harvard University
Francis Brévart, University of Pennsylvania
Joseph L. Brockington, Kalamazoo College
Roger S. Brown, University of New Hampshire at Durham
Raymond L. Burt, University of North Carolina at Wilmington
Belinda Carstens-Wickham, Southern Illinois University at Edwardsville
Christine Castle, MIT
Maurice W. Conner, University of Nebraska at Omaha
Bettina Cothran, Georgia Institute of Technology
Charlotte M. Craig, Kutztown University
Thomas G. Evans, Towson University
George Everett, University of Mississippi
Larry L. George, Southwest Missouri State University
Rolf Goebel, University of Alabama at Huntsville
Elke Hatch, University of Dayton
Kent Hooper, University of Puget Sound
John Jeep, Miami University of Ohio
Robert J. Joda, Marquette University
Virginia Lewis, Drake University
Laurie Ann McLary, University of Mississippi
George Mower, Community College of Allegheny County
Monika Nenon, University of Memphis
Louise Rozier, University of Arkansas
Richard Ruppel, University of Wisconsin
Robert Rymer, University of North Carolina at Charlotte
Heidi M. Schlipphacke, University of Illinois at Chicago
Elfriede W. Smith, Drew University
Robert Stanley, University of Tennessee at Chattanooga
Cordelia Stroinigg, University of Cincinnati
Barry Thomas, Ohio University
Klaudia Thompson, Salisbury State University
Katherine Tosa, Muskegon Community College
Marilya Veteto-Conrad, Northern Arizona State University
Allan P. Weirick, University of Georgia

We are grateful to the following of Holt, Rinehart and Winston: Chris Carson and Phyllis Dobbins, Publishers; Jeff Gilbreath, Acquisitions Editor; Ken Kasee, Marketing Strategist; Joan Schoellner, Developmental Editor; Katherine Dennis, Project Editor; Cindy Young, Production Manager; and Biatriz Chapa and Garry Harman, Art Directors. We would also like to thank Judy Mason for her work on the photo program and Mary K. Coman for managing the project during development.

Last but not least, we would like to express our appreciation to our co-author of previous editions, Katrin T. Bean, whose valuable contribution continues to be an integral part of this text.

Contents

KAPITEL	VORSCHAU	GESPRÄCHE AND WORTSCHATZ
Schritte **WIE GEHT'S?** *p. xxiv*	The German language *p. 1*	1. Greetings and good byes, *p. 2* 2. Colors and the classroom, *p. 5* 3. Clothing, numbers, and opposites, *p. 10* 4. The year and the weather, *p. 15* 5. Telling (informal) time, *p. 19*
Rückblick: Schritte *p. 27*		
Kapitel 1 **FAMILIE, LÄNDER, SPRACHEN** *p. 32*	Spotlight on Germany *p. 33*	Your family, yourself, and the countries of Europe *p. 34*
Kapitel 2 **LEBENSMITTEL UND GESCHÄFTE** *p. 54*	Shopping and store hours *p. 55*	Food and shopping *p. 56*

STRUKTUR	EINBLICKE	FOKUS	SPRECHSITUATIONEN
		• Coming and going, *p. 3* • Trendsetters of the fashion world, *p. 12* • The benefits of learning German, *p. 26*	• Greetings and saying good-byes, *p. 24* • Useful classroom expressions, *p. 24*
		• The German Climate, *p. 31*	

• Present tense of regular verbs, *p. 40*
• Nominative case, *p. 43*
• Sentence structure, *p. 45*
  • Position of subject
  • Linking verbs
  • Predicate adjectives
• Compound nouns, *p. 46*
	• German in Europe, *p. 49*
	• Germany and its neighbors, *p. 50*
		• The Goethe Institute, *p. 34*
		• **Du** or **Sie**, *p. 36*
		• Frankfurt am Main, *p. 47*
		• German throughout the world, *p. 51*
			• Making small talk, *p. 53*
			• Asking for personal information, *p. 53*

• Present tense of **sein** and **haben**, *p. 61*
• Accusative case and n-nouns, *p. 61*
• Sentence structure, *p. 66*
  • Verb complements
  • Negation
  • Coordinating conjunctions
	• Pedestrian areas, *p. 71*
	• Stores and shopping, *p. 73*
		• Weights and measures, *p. 57*
		• Breads, sausages, and cheeses, *p. 60*
		• Flower power, *p. 69*
		• Regensburg, *p. 74*
			Making a purchase, *p. 76*

KAPITEL	VORSCHAU	GESPRÄCHE AND WORTSCHATZ
Kapitel 3 **IM RESTAURANT** *p. 78*	Eating in and out *p. 79*	Meals and restaurants *p. 80*
Rückblick: Kapitel 1–3 *p. 104*		
Kapitel 4 **FESTE UND DATEN** *p. 108*	Holidays and vacations *p. 109*	Celebrations and the calendar *p. 110*
Kapitel 5 **IN DER STADT** *p. 134*	Spotlight on Austria *p. 135*	City life and directions *p. 136*
Kapitel 6 **WOHNEN** *p. 158*	Housing *p. 159*	Housing and furniture *p. 160*
Kapitel 7 **AUF DER BANK UND IM HOTEL** *p. 184*	The story of the *Deutsche Mark* *p. 185*	(Formal) time, banking, and hotel accommodations *p. 186*
Rückblick: Kapitel 4–7 *p. 208*		

STRUKTUR	EINBLICKE	FOKUS	SPRECHSITUATIONEN
• Verbs with vowel changes, *p. 84* • Dative case, *p. 86*	• Regional specialties, *p. 93* • You are what you eat, *p. 94*	• Where to eat, *p. 82* • Friends and acquaintances, *p. 94* • Cafés and coffee houses, *p. 96* • Table manners, *p. 98* • Wines from Germany, Austria, and Switzerland, *p. 99*	• Choosing and ordering a meal, *p. 100* • Expressing likes and dislikes, *p. 100*
• Present perfect with **haben**, *p. 116* • Present perfect with **sein**, *p. 119* • Subordinating conjunctions, *p. 121*	• Traditions, *p. 126* • German holidays, *p. 127*	• Congratulations, *p. 111* • German Christmas, *p. 124* • Wine festivals, harvest time, and traditional garb, *p. 131*	• Offering congratulations and best wishes, *p. 132* • Expressing surprise and gratitude, *p. 132*
• Personal pronouns, *p. 140* • Modal auxiliary verbs, *p. 142* • **sondern** vs. **aber**, *p. 147*	• Vienna, *p. 150* • Greetings from Vienna, *p. 151*	• Viennese landmarks, *pp. 136, 146* • Jugendstil, *p. 148* • Heurigen wine, *p. 153*	• Getting someone's attention, *p. 156* • Asking for directions, *p. 156* • Understanding directions, *p. 156*
• Two-way prepositions, *p. 165* • Imperative, *p. 170* • **Wissen** vs. **kennen**, *p. 171*	• Public transportation and city life, *p. 175* • Work hard, save money, build a house, *p. 176*	• Shared living arrangements, *p. 161* • Homes and houses, *p. 162* • Friedensreich Hundertwasser, *p. 172* • High German and dialects, *p. 179*	• Describing locations, *p. 182* • Offering apologies, *p. 182* • Expressing forgiveness, *p. 182*
• **Der-** and **ein-** words, *p. 191* • Separable-prefix verbs, *p. 193* • Flavoring particles, *p. 197*	• Accommodations and tourist information, *p. 199* • Hotels, youth hostels, and other lodging, *p. 201*	• Exchange offices and credit cards, *p. 187* • Hotel names, *p. 197* • Youth hostels, *p. 204* • Luxembourg, *p. 205*	• Telling and asking about time, *p. 206* • Expressing disbelief, *p. 206* • Giving a warning, *p. 206*

KAPITEL	VORSCHAU	GESPRÄCHE AND WORTSCHATZ
Kapitel 8 **POST UND REISEN** *p. 214*	Spotlight on Switzerland *p. 215*	Postal service and travel *p. 216*
Kapitel 9 **HOBBYS** *p. 238*	Sports and clubs in the German-speaking countries *p. 239*	Physical fitness and leisure time *p. 240*
Kapitel 10 **UNTERHALTUNG** *p. 264*	The magic of the theater *p. 265*	Entertainment *p. 266*
Kapitel 11 **BEZIEHUNGEN** *p. 288*	Women and society *p. 289*	Relationships and character traits *p. 290*
Rückblick: Kapitel 8–11 *p. 314*		
Kapitel 12 **WEGE ZUM BERUF** *p. 320*	German schools and vocational training *p. 321*	Professions and education *p. 322*

STRUKTUR	EINBLICKE	FOKUS	SPRECHSITUATIONEN

• Genitive case, *p. 221*
• Time expressions, *p. 224*
• Sentence structure, *p. 226*
   • Types and sequence of adverbs
   • Position of **nicht**
	• Switzerland and its languages, *p. 230*
	• Tourists in Switzerland, *p. 231*
		• Phoning and postal services, *p. 217*
		• Train travel, *p. 218*
		• Car travel, *p. 220*
		• William Tell, *p. 233*
		• Switzerland's mountain world, *p. 234*
		• Hermann Hesse: "Im Nebel", *p. 235*
			• Expressing sympathy/lack of sympathy, *p. 236*
			• Expressing empathy, *p. 236*
			• Expressing relief, *p. 236*

• Endings of preceded adjectives, *p. 245* • Reflexive verbs, *p. 249* • Infinitive with **zu,** *p. 252*	• Vacationing, *p. 255* • Leisure time—Pleasure or frustration, *p. 256*	• Telephone courtesies, *p. 240* • Animal and food talk, *p. 244* • *Schrebergärten, p. 248* • Rose Ausländer: "Noch bist du da", *p. 260*	• Speaking on the telephone, *p. 261* • Extending, accepting, declining an invitation, *p. 261*
• Verbs with prepositional objects, *p. 271* • **Da-** and **wo-** compounds, *p. 273* • Endings of unpreceded adjectives, *p. 275*	• German television, *p. 279* • Choosing isn't easy, *p. 280*	• German film, *p. 267* • The world of music, *p. 270* • The art scene, *p. 273* • German cabaret, *p. 284* • Wolf Biermann: "Ach, Freund, geht es nicht auch dir so?", *p. 285*	• Expressing satisfaction/dissatisfaction, *p. 286* • Expressing anger, *p. 286*
• Simple past, *p. 296* • Conjunctions **als, wann, wenn,** *p. 300* • Past perfect, *p. 301*	• The Brothers Grimm and their fairy tales, *p. 305* • *Rumpelstilzchen, p. 306*	• Love and marriage, *p. 291* • Liechtenstein, *p. 310* • Eva Strittmatter: "Werte", *p. 312*	• Expressing admiration, *p. 313* • Telling a story, *p. 313* • Encouraging a speaker, *p. 313*

• Comparison of adjectives and adverbs, *p. 327*
• Future tense, *p. 331*
• Nouns with special features:
   • Predicate nouns, *p. 333*
   • Adjectival nouns, *p. 333*
	• Hard times and social policy, *p. 337*
	• Choosing a profession, *p. 338*
		• Women in business and industry, *p. 323*
		• Gender bias and language, *p. 324*
		• Foreign workers in Germany, *p. 335*
		• Writing a résumé, *p. 341*
		• Suna Gollwitzer: "Totales Versagen", *p. 342*
			• Expressing agreement/disagreement, *p. 343*
			• Expressing hesitation, *p. 343*

KAPITEL	VORSCHAU	GESPRÄCHE AND WORTSCHATZ
Kapitel 13 **DAS STUDIUM** *p. 346*	German universities *p. 347*	University study and student life *p. 348*
Kapitel 14 **EINST UND JETZT** *p. 372*	Chronicle of German history since World War II *p. 373*	A visit to Berlin *p. 374*
Kapitel 15 **DEUTSCHLAND, EUROPA UND DIE ZUKUNFT** *p. 398*	The path to a united Europe *p. 399*	Nature and environmental protection *p. 400*

Rückblick: Kapitel 12–15
p. 422

Appendix
p. A-0

Vocabularies
   1. German–English, *p. V-1*
   2. English–German, *p. V-39*

Photo and Illustration Credits
p. P-1

Index
p. I-1

STRUKTUR	EINBLICKE	FOKUS	SPRECHSITUATIONEN
• Subjunctive mood, *p. 352* • Present-time general subjunctive (Subjunctive II), *p. 353* • Past-time general subjunctive, *p. 359*	• Studying in Germany, *p. 363* • A year abroad, *p. 364*	• Red tape, *p. 348* • Writing letters, *p. 367* • Bertolt Brecht: "1940", *p. 369*	• Giving advice, *p. 370* • Asking for permission, *p. 370* • Granting/denying permission, *p. 370*
• Relative clauses, *p. 379* • Indirect speech, *p. 384*	• Berlin's past, *p. 390* • Berlin, a gate to the world, *p. 391*	• Berliners, *p. 375* • Berlin today, *p. 378* • Berlin, a multicultural melting pot, *p. 384* • Erich Kästner: "Fantasie von übermorgen", *p. 395*	• Expressing doubt and uncertainty, *p. 396* • Expressing probability and possibility, *p. 396* • Expressing concern, *p. 396* • Drawing conclusions, *p. 396*
• Passive voice, *p. 405* • Review of the uses of **werden,** *p. 410* • Special subjunctive (Subjunctive I), *p. 410*	• In search of an identity, *p. 414* • The wind knows no borders, *p. 415*	• Cultural capital Weimar, *p. 401* • The German spelling reform, *p. 417* • Goethe: "Erinnerung", Schiller: "Ode an die Freude", *p. 419*	• Describing objects, *p. 420*

Wie geht's?

Sixth Edition

PRE-UNITS

Schritte

WIE GEHT'S?

Wie geht's? — Danke, gut.

LERNZIELE *(Learning objectives)*

The pre-units will help you take your first steps in German. You will learn to . . .

- introduce yourself and say hello and good-bye
- say the alphabet and spell in German
- describe your classroom and name various colors
- talk about articles of clothing and use adjectives to describe them
- use numbers
- discuss the calendar and the weather
- tell time
- understand some basic classroom expressions.

VORSCHAU *(Preview)*
- The German language

SPRECHSITUATIONEN *(Communication)*
- Greetings and good-byes
- Useful classroom expressions

FOKUS *(Focus on cultural information)*
- Coming and going
- Trendsetters of the fashion world
- The benefits of learning German
- The German climate

VORSCHAU

The German Language

More than 100 million people speak German as their native tongue. It is the official language in Germany, Austria, Liechtenstein, and large areas of Switzerland. It is also spoken in parts of Luxembourg, Belgium, France (Alsace), and Italy (South Tyrol), and by some of the German minorities in Poland, Romania, and a few of the republics of the former Soviet Union. Canada, the United States, and some South American countries have significant German-speaking populations.

German belongs to the Germanic branch of the Indo-European language family and is closely related to Dutch, English, the Scandinavian languages, Flemish, Frisian, Yiddish, and Afrikaans. For various political, literary, and linguistic reasons, we speak of Germans and the German language as dating from around the year 800. At that time, at least six major dialects and numerous variations of them were spoken. During the twelfth and thirteenth centuries, efforts were made to write a standardized form of German; thus, the period from 1170 to around 1250 became one of great literary achievements. Afterwards, however, this literary language declined and, with few exceptions, Latin was used in writing; it remained the sole language of instruction at German universities until the 1700s. Luther's translation of the Bible coupled with the invention of the Gutenberg printing press in the sixteenth century was a major influence on the development of a common written German language. Because of political fragmentation, a standard language was slow to develop in Germany. As late as the early 1900s, most people spoke only their regional dialects. First, newspapers and magazines, then radio and television, fostered the use of standard German; but regional accents are still common.

Because German and English are members of the same branch of the Indo-European language family, they share a considerable amount of vocabulary. Some of these related words, called cognates, are identical in spelling (e.g., **der Arm, die Hand, der Finger**), and others are similar (e.g., **der Vater, die Mutter, das Haus**). As the two languages developed, certain cognates acquired different meanings, such as **die Hose** *(pair of pants)* versus "hose" *(stockings)*. Differences between English and German cognates developed quite systematically; here are a few examples:

	English	German
t > z	*ten*	zehn
	salt	Salz
p > pf	*pound*	Pfund
	apple	Apfel
t > ss	*water*	Wasser
	white	weiß
p > f	*ship*	Schiff
	help	helfen
k > ch	*book*	Buch
	make	machen
d > t	*bed*	Bett
	dance	tanzen
th > d	*bath*	Bad
	thank	danken

Lippe Rose bitter Ring Nest Gold mild Sack Witz sitzen Land Pfanne Hammer Plan Seite Ellbogen warm Fuß Pfeife Milch Silber dick weiß Storch danken gleiten

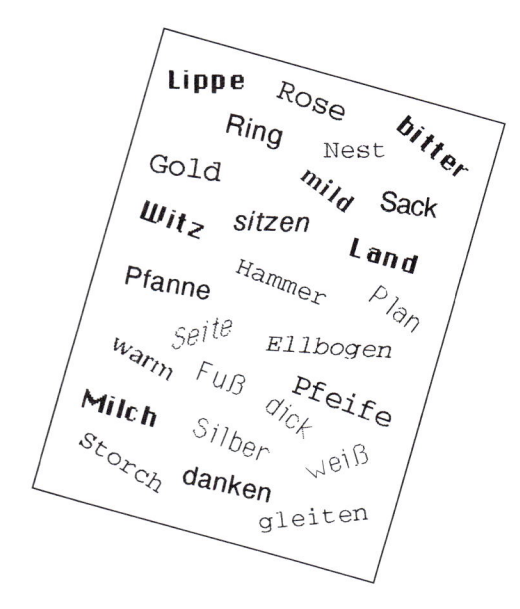

Schritt 1 / Step 1

Guten Tag!

> Read the following dialogues aloud until you can do so fluently, and be prepared to answer questions about them. If necessary, you may consult the translations in the Appendix.

HERR SANDERS	Guten Tag!
FRAU LEHMANN	Guten Tag!
HERR SANDERS	Ich heiße Sanders, Willi Sanders. Und Sie, wie heißen Sie?
FRAU LEHMANN	Mein Name ist Erika Lehmann.
HERR SANDERS	Freut mich.
HERR MEIER	Guten Morgen, Frau Fiedler! Wie geht es Ihnen?
FRAU FIEDLER	Danke, gut. Und Ihnen?
HERR MEIER	Danke, es geht mir auch gut.
HEIDI	Hallo, Ute! Wie geht's?
UTE	Tag, Heidi! Ach, ich bin müde.
HEIDI	Ich auch. Zu viel Stress. Bis später!
UTE	Tschüss!

WORTSCHATZ (Vocabulary)

> You are responsible for knowing all the vocabulary of the *Wortschatz* (literally "treasure of words"), including the headings. Be sure to learn the gender and plural forms of nouns! Words and phrases listed under *Zum Erkennen* are intended for comprehension only; you will not be asked to produce them actively.

- In German, all nouns are capitalized.
- The pronoun **ich** *(I)* is not capitalized unless it occurs at the beginning of a sentence. The pronoun **Sie** *(you)* is always capitalized.

der Herr, die Herren *(pl.)*	*Mr.; gentleman*
die Frau, die Frauen *(pl.)*[1]	*Mrs., Ms.; woman; wife*
Guten Morgen![2]	*Good morning.*
Guten Tag![2]	*Hello.*
Tag![2]	*Hi! (casual)*
Guten Abend![2]	*Good evening.*
Wie heißen Sie?	*What's your name? (formal)*
Mein Name ist . . .	*My name is . . .*

---

[1] In modern German the title **Frau** is generally used for all adult women, regardless of a woman's age or marital status. The title **Fräulein** *(Miss)* has more or less disappeared, though some people, especially in southern Germany, still use it to address young females under age 18.

[2] **Guten Morgen** is generally used until about 10:00 A.M., **(Guten) Tag** between then and early evening, and **Guten Abend** from about 5:00 P.M. on.

heißen	to be called
ich heiße . . .	my name is . . .
Sie heißen . . .	your name is . . . (formal)
Freut mich.	Pleased to meet you.
Wie geht es Ihnen?	How are you? (formal)
Wie geht's?	How are you? (casual)
wie?	how?
Es geht mir gut.[3]	I'm fine.
gut / schlecht	good, fine / bad(ly)
wunderbar	wonderful(ly), great
Ich bin müde.[3]	I'm tired.
ja / nein	yes / no
danke / bitte	thank you / please
auch	also, too
nicht	not
und	and
Auf Wiedersehen!	Good-bye.
Tschüss! (colloquial)	Good-bye. Bye.

[3] **Es geht mir** gut (schlecht, wunderbar). BUT **Ich bin** müde.

Zum Erkennen: *(For comprehension only):* Hallo! *(Hi! Hello!);* ach *(oh);* ich auch *(me too);* zu viel Stress *(too much stress);* Bis später! *(See you later!);* Buchstabieren Sie auf Deutsch! *(Spell in German!)*

Coming and Going — FOKUS

When you ask **Wie geht's?** or **Wie geht es Ihnen?**, expect a detailed answer about the other person's well-being. In this sense, the question is different from the casual English expression *How are you?* and should be directed only to people you already know. The parting expression **Tschüss!** is more informal than **Auf Wiedersehen!**

Aussprache *(Pronunciation):* a, e, er, i, o, u

The words listed below are either familiar words, cognates (words related to English), or proper names **(Erika, Amerika).** A simplified phonetic spelling for each sound is given in brackets. The colon *(:)* following a vowel means that the vowel is long. Pay particular attention to word stress as you hear it from your instructor or the tape. For a while, you may want to mark words for stress.

Hören Sie gut zu und wiederholen Sie! *(Listen carefully and repeat.)*

[a:]   **A**bend, T**a**g, B**a**n**a**ne, N**a**me, j**a**
[a]   **A**nna, **A**lbert, w**a**s, H**a**nd, d**a**nke
[e:]   **E**rika, P**e**ter, Am**e**rika, g**e**ht, T**ee**
[e]   **E**llen, H**e**rmann, **e**s, schl**e**cht

[ə]	*(unstressed e)* Ut**e**, dank**e**, heiß**e**, Ihn**e**n, Gut**e**n Morg**e**n!
[ʌ]	*(final -er)* Diet**er** Fiedl**er**, Rain**er** Mei**er**, Wern**er** Schneid**er**
[iː]	**Ih**nen, Mar**i**a, Sab**i**ne, w**ie**, S**ie**
[i]	**i**ch b**i**n, b**i**tte, n**i**cht, Schr**i**tt
[oː]	M**o**nika, H**o**se, s**o**, w**o**, Z**oo**
[o]	**O**skar, **o**ft, M**o**rgen, S**o**mmer, k**o**sten
[uː]	**U**te, G**u**drun, g**u**t, N**u**del, Sch**uh**
[u]	**u**nd, w**u**nderbar, Ges**u**ndheit, H**u**nger, B**u**tter

- As you may have noticed, double vowels (**Tee, Boot**), vowels followed by **h** (**geht, Schuh**), and the combination **ie** (**wie, Sie**) are long. Vowels followed by double consonants (two identical consonants as in **Anna, Sommer**) are short.

Mündliche Übungen *(Oral exercises)*

A. Mustersätze *(Patterns and cues)*

> These patterns give you a chance to practice phrases from the dialogues and the vocabulary of each *Schritt*. Listen carefully and repeat the sentences until you can say them fluently.

1. Willi Sanders: **Ich heiße** Willi Sanders.
   Hugo Schmidt, Gudrun Kleese, Anna Peters
2. Erika Lehmann: **Heißen Sie** Erika Lehmann?
   Monika Schulz, Wolfgang Friedrich, Hermann Lorenz
3. Hugo Schmidt: **Ja, ich heiße** Hugo Schmidt.
   Hans Holbein, Brigitte Fischer, Simone Holtkamp
4. Oskar Meier: **Nein, ich heiße nicht** Oskar Meier.
   Gustav Mahler, Clara Schumann, Wolfgang Amadeus Mozart
5. Frau Fiedler: **Wie geht es Ihnen,** Frau Fiedler?
   Frau Lehmann, Herr Sanders, Herr und Frau Bauer
6. gut: **Es geht mir** gut.
   auch gut, nicht schlecht, wunderbar

B. Das Alphabet
1. **Lesen Sie laut!** *(Read aloud.)*

a	ah	**g**	geh	**m**	emm	**s**	ess	**y**	üppsilon
b	beh	**h**	hah	**n**	enn	**t**	teh	**z**	tsett
c	tseh	**i**	ih	**o**	oh	**u**	uh	**ä**	äh (a-umlaut)
d	deh	**j**	yot	**p**	peh	**v**	fau	**ö**	öh (o-umlaut)
e	eh	**k**	kah	**q**	kuh	**w**	weh	**ü**	üh (u-umlaut)
f	eff	**l**	ell	**r**	err	**x**	iks	**ß**	ess-tsett

For capital letters say **Großes A (B, C . . .)**. For further explanation of the **ß**-sound, see III A.6 in the pronunciation section of the Workbook.

2. **Buchstabieren Sie auf Deutsch!** *(Spell in German.)*
   BMW, VW, AUDI, UPS, USA; ja, gut, müde, danke, schlecht, heißen, Name, wunderbar, Autobahn, Kindergarten, Gesundheit

Aufgaben *(Assignments)*

Prepare all assignments so that you can answer fluently in class.

A. Buchstabieren Sie Ihren Namen auf Deutsch! *(Spell your name in German.)*

B. Was sagen Sie? *(What do you say? Read the cue lines and prepare appropriate responses. Be ready to enact the scene with a partner.)*

S1	Guten Tag!
S2	. . .
S1	Ich heiße . . . Und Sie, wie heißen Sie?
S2	Ich heiße . . .
S1	Freut mich.
S2	Wie geht es Ihnen?
S1	. . . Und Ihnen?
S2	. . .
S1	Auf Wiedersehen!

LERNTIPP — What's It Like to Learn a Language?

Learning another language is much like learning a musical instrument or a sport. Just as you can't learn to play the piano or swim by reading about it, you can't learn a foreign language by thinking or reading about it. You must practice. Listen to your instructor, to tapes, to the answers of your fellow students. Speak German every chance you get. Whenever possible, read the language aloud and write it.

Remember also that you are still improving your English; therefore don't expect perfection in another language. You made mistakes while learning English; when you are learning a foreign language, mistakes are also inevitable. With daily practice, however, your fluency in German will rapidly increase.

Was und wie ist das?

Schritt 2

DEUTSCHPROFESSORIN	Hören Sie jetzt gut zu und antworten Sie auf Deutsch! Was ist das?
JIM MILLER	Das ist der Bleistift.
DEUTSCHPROFESSORIN	Welche Farbe hat der Bleistift?
SUSAN SMITH	Gelb.
DEUTSCHPROFESSORIN	Bilden Sie einen Satz bitte!
SUSAN SMITH	Der Bleistift ist gelb.
DEUTSCHPROFESSORIN	Ist das Heft auch gelb?
DAVID JENKINS	Nein, das Heft ist nicht gelb. Das Heft ist hellblau.
DEUTSCHPROFESSORIN	Gut!
SUSAN SMITH	Was bedeutet *hellblau*?
DEUTSCHPROFESSORIN	*Hellblau* bedeutet *light blue* auf Englisch.
SUSAN SMITH	Und wie sagt man *dark blue*?
DEUTSCHPROFESSORIN	*Dunkelblau.*
SUSAN SMITH	Ah, der Kuli ist dunkelblau.
DEUTSCHPROFESSORIN	Richtig! Das ist alles für heute. Für morgen lesen Sie bitte das *Gespräch* noch einmal und lernen Sie auch die Wörter!

WORTSCHATZ

- In English the DEFINITE ARTICLE has just one form: *the*. The German singular definite article has three forms: **der, das, die.** Some nouns take **der** and are called MASCULINE; some take **das** and are called NEUTER; and some take **die** and are called FEMININE. This is a grammatical distinction and has little to do with biological sex, although it is true that most nouns referring to females are feminine and most referring to males are masculine.

    der Herr, **die** Frau, BUT **das** Kind *(child)*

    Inanimate objects such as *table, book,* and *blackboard* can be of any gender.

    der Tisch, **das** Buch, **die** Tafel

    Because the gender of many nouns is unpredictable, you must always learn the article with the noun.

- In German the plural of nouns is formed in various ways that are often unpredictable. You must therefore learn the plural together with the article and the noun. Plurals are given in an abbreviated form in vocabulary lists and in dictionaries. These are the most common plural forms and their abbreviations.

Abbreviation	Listing	Plural Form
-	das Fenster, -	die Fenster
¨	der Mantel, ¨	die Mäntel
-e	der Tisch, -e	die Tische
¨e	der Stuhl, ¨e	die Stühle
-er	das Bild, -er	die Bilder
¨er	das Buch, ¨er	die Bücher
-en	die Frau, -en	die Frauen
-n	die Farbe, -n	die Farben
-nen	die Professorin, -nen	die Professorinnen
-s	der Kuli, -s	die Kulis

NOTE: The plural article for all nouns is **die.** In this book, when the noun is not followed by one of the plural endings, it either does not have a plural or the plural is rarely used.

Die Farbe, -n *(color)*

blau   rot   orange   gelb

grün

braun   grau   rosa   schwarz   weiß

Das Zimmer, - *(room)*

der Bleistift, -e	*pencil*	das Heft, -e	*notebook*
Kuli, -s	*pen*	Papier, -e	*paper*
Stuhl, ̈e	*chair*	die Kreide	*chalk*
Tisch, -e	*table*	Tafel, -n	*blackboard*
das Bild, -er	*picture*	Tür, -en	*door*
Buch, ̈er	*book*	Wand, ̈e	*wall (inside)*
Fenster, -	*window*		

Weiteres *(Additional words and phrases)*

auf Deutsch / auf Englisch	*in German / in English*
für morgen	*for tomorrow*
hier / da	*here / there*
noch einmal	*again, once more*
richtig / falsch	*correct, right / wrong, false*
Was ist das?	*What is that?*
Das ist (nicht) . . .	*That is (not) . . .*
Welche Farbe hat . . . ?	*What color is . . . ?*
Was bedeutet . . . ?	*What does . . . mean?*
Wie sagt man . . . ?	*How does one say . . . ?*
Wo ist . . . ?	*Where is . . . ?*
antworten	*to answer*
fragen	*to ask*
hören	*to hear*
lernen	*to learn; to study*
lesen	*to read*
sagen	*to say*
wiederholen	*to repeat*
sein	*to be*
ich bin	*I am*
es ist	*it is*
sie sind	*they are*
Sie sind	*you (formal) are*

Zum Erkennen: *(For comprehension only):* Hören Sie gut zu! *(Listen carefully!);* Bilden Sie einen Satz! *(Form a sentence.);* hell(grün) / dunkel(blau) *(light [green] / dark [blue]);* Das ist alles für heute. *(That's all for today.)*; das Gespräch, -e *(dialogue)*; das Wort, ̈-er *(word)*; der Artikel, - (von); das Beispiel, -e *(example)*; zum Beispiel *(for example)*; der Plural (von); Alle zusammen! *(All together!)*

Aussprache: ä, ö, ü, eu, äu, au, ei, ie

Hören Sie gut zu und wiederholen Sie!

[e:]   Erika, Käthe, geht, lesen, Gespräch
[e]   Ellen Keller, Wände, Hände, hängen
[ö:]   Öl, hören, Löwenbräu, Goethe, Österreich
[ö]   Ötker, Pöppel, Wörter
[ü:]   Tür, für, Stühle, Bücher, müde, grün, typisch
[ü]   Jürgen Müller, Günter, müssen, tschüss
[oi]   Deutsch, freut, Europa, Löwenbräu
[au]   Frau Paula Bauer, auf, auch, blaugrau
[ai]   Rainer, Kreide, weiß, heißen, nein

- Pay special attention to the pronunciation of **ei** and **ie** (as in *Einstein's niece*):

    [ai]   heißen, Heidi Meier, Heinz Beyer
    [i:]   Sie, wie, Dieter Fiedler, Wiedersehen
    [ai / i:] Beispiel, Heinz Fiedler, Heidi Thielemann

Mündliche Übungen

A. **Mustersätze**
   1. der Tisch: **Das ist** der Tisch.
      das Zimmer, die Tür, der Stuhl
   2. das Papier: **Wo ist** das Papier? **Da ist** das Papier.
      der Kuli, die Kreide, das Bild
   3. das Buch: **Ist das** das Buch? **Ja, das ist** das Buch.
      der Bleistift, das Fenster, die Tür
   4. die Tafel: **Ist das** die Tafel? **Nein, das ist nicht** die Tafel.
      der Tisch, das Papier, der Stuhl
   5. schwarz: **Das ist** schwarz.
      rot, gelb, weiß
   6. der Bleistift: **Welche Farbe hat** der Bleistift?
      der Kuli, das Buch, die Tafel
   7. lesen: Lesen **Sie bitte!**
      antworten, hören, fragen, lernen, wiederholen

B. **Fragen und Antworten** *(Questions and answers)*
   1. Ist das Papier weiß? **Ja, das Papier ist weiß.**
      Ist das Buch gelb? die Tafel grün? die Kreide weiß? der Kuli rot?
   2. Ist die Kreide grün? **Nein, die Kreide ist nicht grün.**
      Ist die Tafel rot? der Bleistift weiß? das Buch rosa? das Papier braun?
   3. Die Kreide ist weiß. Ist das richtig? **Ja, das ist richtig.**
      Das Heft ist schwarz. Ist das richtig? **Nein, das ist nicht richtig.**
      Das Papier ist weiß. Die Tür ist orange. Der Kuli ist blau. Das Buch ist rosa. Der Tisch ist braun.

C. **Wiederholung** *(Review)*
   1. **Was sagen sie?** *(What are they saying?)*

   a.   b.   c.

   2. **Buchstabieren Sie auf Deutsch!**
      Elefant, Maus, Tiger, Löwe, Katze, Hund, Giraffe, Hamster, Ratte, Goldfisch, Dinosaurier, Känguru
   3. **Was buchstabiere ich?** *(Think of any German word or name and spell it in German without saying the word. Let others write it down and read it back to you.)*

Aufgaben

Fragen und Antworten
1. Was ist der Artikel? **Tür → die Tür**
   Zimmer, Bleistift, Bild, Kreide, Kuli, Stuhl, Tafel, Buch, Tisch, Fenster, Farbe, Papier, Wand, Heft, Wort, Herr, Frau
2. Was ist der Plural? **Kuli → die Kulis**
   Tür, Bild, Bleistift, Buch, Heft, Tisch, Fenster, Tafel, Stuhl, Wort, Farbe
3. Welche Farben hat das Deutschbuch?

LERNTIPP **How to Get Organized**

Take a few minutes to get acquainted with your textbook. Read the table of contents, then find the index, the vocabulary lists, and the Appendix. Find out how each chapter is organized. Familiarize yourself with the Workbook, too. See how the lab work and the supplementary exercises are arranged. Learn whether the language lab is set up to duplicate tapes, and what other support is available to you.

In addition, find out whether you have access to the text-specific software. It features the exercises in the book and can be particularly useful if you have not been able to attend class or if you want to review lessons before a test. A CD-Rom with supplementary exercises is also available. For Internet activities, see the *Web-Ecke* at the end of each chapter.

After each class, make it a habit to divide your assignments into small units. Since it is highly impossible to cram in a foreign language course, don't fall behind. Study and review daily.

Schritt 3

Im Kaufhaus

VERKÄUFERIN	Na, wie ist die Hose?
CHRISTIAN	Zu groß und zu lang.
VERKÄUFERIN	Und der Pulli?
MAIKE	Zu teuer.
CHRISTIAN	Aber die Farben sind toll. Schade!
VERKÄUFERIN	Guten Tag! Was darf's sein?
SILVIA	Ich brauche ein paar Bleistifte und Papier. Was kosten die Bleistifte?
VERKÄUFERIN	Fünfundneunzig Pfennig (0,95 DM).
SILVIA	Und das Papier hier?
VERKÄUFERIN	Vier Mark achtzig (4,80 DM).[1]
SILVIA	Gut. Ich nehme sechs Bleistifte und das Papier.
VERKÄUFERIN	Ist das alles?
SILVIA	Ja, danke.
VERKÄUFERIN	Zehn Mark fünfzig (10,50 DM) bitte!

[1] One euro equals just under two marks, e.g., DM 4,80 are approximately € 2,40.

WORTSCHATZ

Die Kleidung (clothing)

das T-Shirt, -s
der Mantel, ⸗
das Hemd, -en
die Jeans, -(pl)[1]
die Hose, -n[1]
die Bluse, -n
der Schuh, -e
das Sweatshirt, -s
die Jacke, -n
das Kleid, -er
der Pullover, -
der Pulli, -s
der Rock, ⸗e

[1] Note that **die Hose** is singular in German; **die Jeans,** however, is plural.

Die Zahl, -en *(number)*

1	eins	11	elf	21 einundzwanzig	0	null
2	zwei	12	zwölf	22 zweiundzwanzig	10	zehn
3	drei	13	dreizehn	30 drei**ß**ig	100	hundert
4	vier	14	vierzehn	40 vierzig	101	hunderteins
5	fünf	15	fünfzehn	50 fünfzig	200	zweihundert
6	sechs	16	se**chz**ehn	60 se**ch**zig	1 000	tausend
7	sieben	17	sie**bz**ehn	70 sie**b**zig	1 001	tausendeins
8	acht	18	achtzehn	80 achtzig	10 000	zehntausend
9	neun	19	neunzehn	90 neunzig	100 000	hunderttausend
10	zehn	20	zwanzig	100 hundert	1 000 000	eine Million

As a memory aid, note these similarities between English and German:

> **-zehn** = *-teen*   **vierzehn** = *fourteen*
> **-zig** = *-ty*   **vierzig** = *forty*

- 21–29, 31–39, and so on to 91–99 follow the pattern of "four-and-twenty (**vierundzwanzig**) blackbirds baked in a pie."
- German numbers above twelve are seldom written out, except on checks. When they are written out, however, they are written as one word, no matter how long:

    234 567
    zweihundertvierunddreißigtausendfünfhundertsiebenundsechzig

- German uses a period or a space, where English uses a comma, and vice versa:

    2,75 DM   BUT $2.75
    1 600,00 DM (or 1.600,00 DM)   BUT $1,600.00.

- The numbers 1 and 7 are written differently:

Das Gegenteil, -e *(opposite)*

dick / dünn	*thick, fat / thin, skinny*
groß / klein	*tall, big, large / short, small, little*
lang / kurz	*long / short*
langsam / schnell	*slow(ly) / fast, quick(ly)*
neu / alt	*new / old*
sauber / schmutzig	*clean, neat / dirty*
teuer / billig	*expensive / inexpensive, cheap*

Weiteres

aber	*but, however*
oder	*or*
zu	*too (+ adjective or adverb)*
wie viel? / wie viele?	*how much / how many?*
kosten	*to cost, come to (a certain amount)*
Was kostet / kosten . . . ?	*How much is / are . . . ?*
Das kostet . . .	*That comes to . . .*
brauchen	*to need*
nehmen	*to take*

1 EINS
7 SIEBEN

zählen	*to count*
ich zähl**e**	*I count*
wir ⎫	*we count*
sie ⎬ zähl**en**	*they count*
Sie ⎭	*you (formal) count*
ein Pfennig (zehn Pfennig)	*one pfennig (ten pfennigs)*
eine Mark (zwei Mark)[1]	*one mark (two marks)*

---

[1] **eins** BUT **eine** Mark!

Zum Erkennen: im Kaufhaus *(in the department store);* der Verkäufer, — / die Verkäuferin, -nen *(sales clerk);* na *(well);* toll *(super);* Schade! *(Too bad!);* Was darf's sein? *(May I help you?);* ein paar *(a couple of);* Ist das alles? *(Is that all?);* von . . . bis *(from . . . to);* plus / minus; die Seite, -n *(page);* der Preis, -e *(price)*

Aussprache: l, s, st, sp, sch, f, v, z

Hören Sie gut zu und wiederholen Sie!

[l]	**l**ernen, **l**esen, Pu**ll**over, to**ll**, Mante**l**, Tafe**l**
[z]	**s**ie **s**ind, **s**ieben, **s**auber, lang**s**am, Blu**s**e, Ho**s**e
[s]	Profe**ss**orin, hei**ß**en, Prei**s**, wei**ß**, gro**ß**, alle**s**
[st]	Fen**st**er, ko**st**en, i**st**
[št]	**St**efan, **St**uhl, **St**ein, Blei**st**ift
[šp]	**Sp**ort, Bei**sp**iel, Ge**sp**räch, Au**sp**rache
[š]	**sch**nell, **sch**lecht, **sch**warz, **sch**ade, fal**sch**
[f]	**f**ünf, **f**ünfzehn, **f**ünfzig, **f**ünfhundert**f**ünfund**f**ünfzig
[f]	**v**ier, **v**ierzehn, **v**ierzig, **v**ierhundert**v**ierund**v**ierzig
[ts]	**Z**immer, **Z**ahl, **z**ählen, **z**wei, **z**ehn, **z**wölf, **z**wanzig, **z**weiund**z**wanzig, schmu**tz**ig, Sa**tz**
[z / ts]	**s**ieben, **s**ieb**z**ig, **s**iebenund**s**ieb**z**ig, **s**iebenhundert**s**iebenund**s**ieb**z**ig

FOKUS: Trendsetters of the Fashion World

German fashion has always been known for outstanding quality and workmanship, but it is also beginning to have more of an impact on international fashion trends. Today, Jil Sander, Joop, and Hugo Boss are well-known names in every major city. Fresh ideas are also coming from the German "eco-fashion" scene: Britta Steilmann, for example, has explored new and interesting directions with her collections made of environmentally friendly materials. Twice a year, fashion takes center stage in the trade fair metropolises of Berlin, Düsseldorf, Cologne, and Munich. There, international designers and manufacturers meet with retail buyers to set the latest styles for the coming season.

Mündliche Übungen

A. Mustersätze
1. der Schuh: **Das ist** der Schuh.
   die Jacke, das Hemd, der Mantel, der Pulli
2. die Jacke / grau: **Ist** die Jacke grau? **Ja,** die Jacke **ist** grau.
   die Hose / braun; der Rock / blau; die Bluse / rosa; der Pullover / rot

3. der Mantel / lang: **Ist** der Mantel lang? **Nein,** der Mantel **ist nicht** lang.
   das Hemd / schmutzig; das Kleid / neu; der Pulli / dick; das Sweatshirt / teuer
4. Schuhe / groß: **Sind** die Schuhe groß? **Nein,** die Schuhe **sind nicht** groß.
   die Röcke / kurz; Mäntel / dünn; T-Shirts / blau; Jeans / schwarz
5. das Papier: **Was kostet** das Papier?
   das Heft, der Mantel, die Jacke, der Pulli
6. Bleistifte: **Was kosten** die Bleistifte?
   Kulis, Bücher, Bilder, Schuhe, Jeans

B. **Hören Sie gut zu und wiederholen Sie!**
1. Wir zählen von eins bis zehn: eins, zwei, drei, vier, fünf, sechs, sieben, acht, neun, zehn.
2. Wir zählen von zehn bis zwanzig: zehn, elf, zwölf, dreizehn, vierzehn, fünfzehn, sechzehn, siebzehn, achtzehn, neunzehn, zwanzig.
3. Wir zählen von zwanzig bis dreißig: zwanzig, einundzwanzig, zweiundzwanzig, dreiundzwanzig, vierundzwanzig, fünfundzwanzig, sechsundzwanzig, siebenundzwanzig, achtundzwanzig, neunundzwanzig, dreißig.
4. Wir zählen von zehn bis hundert: zehn, zwanzig, dreißig, vierzig, fünfzig, sechzig, siebzig, achtzig, neunzig, hundert.
5. Wir zählen von hundert bis tausend: hundert, zweihundert, dreihundert, vierhundert, fünfhundert, sechshundert, siebenhundert, achthundert, neunhundert, tausend.

C. **Zahlen**
1. **Seitenzahlen** *(page numbers)*. Lesen Sie laut auf Deutsch!

   Seite 1, 7, 8, 9, 11, 12, 17, 21, 25, 32, 43, 54, 66, 89, 92, 101

2. **Preise.** Lesen Sie laut auf Deutsch!

   0,25 DM; 0,75 DM; 1,10 DM; 2,50 DM; 8,90 DM; 30,00 DM
   45,54 DM; 80,88 DM; 99,60 DM; 100,00 DM

3. **Inventar** *(With an employee, played by a partner, take inventory of the items you have in stock in your store.)*

   BEISPIEL: Jacke / 32
   Wie viele Jacken? — Zweiunddreißig Jacken.

   a. Pullover / 42   d. Kleid / 19   g. Sweatshirt / 89
   b. Rock / 14   e. Hose / 21   h. T-Shirt / 37
   c. Hemd / 66   f. Jeans / 102   i. Schuh / 58

4. **Sonderangebote** *(Specials. In small groups, ask each other about prices of the items shown below.)*

SONDERANGEBOTE!

Damen		Herren	
Röcke	115.- 50.-	Sweat-Shirt	90.90 69.90
Blusen	90.90 69.90	Leder-Strick-Blouson	625.- 399.-
Hosen	145.- 99.90	Hosen	139.- 79.-
Blazer	285.- 199.-		

Buschfort
BERO-Einkaufszentrum
Telefon 2 27 27

Kombi-Mode
Composé-Kostüm auch in Schwarz/Weiß, Rot/Schwarz, Marine/Weiß, Gr. 38–52, 19–25
99.-

Polo-Pullover auch in Grau, Beige oder Schwarz, Gr. S–XXL
39.90

BEISPIEL: Was kosten die Damenhosen *(. . . for ladies?)*
Die Damenhosen kosten 99,90 DM.

D. Wiederholung
1. **Fragen**
   a. Wie geht es Ihnen? Sind Sie müde?
   b. Wie heißen Sie? Heißen Sie . . . ?
   c. Was ist das? Ist das . . . ? *(Point to items in the classroom.)*
   d. Welche Farbe hat der Tisch? die Tafel? . . .
   e. Was ist auch grün? blau? . . .

2. **Buchstabieren Sie auf Deutsch!**

   Mozart, Beethoven, Strauß, Schönberg, Dürer, Barlach, Kandinsky, Goethe, Nietzsche, Aichinger, Wohmann, Einstein, Röntgen, Zeppelin, Schwarzenegger

Aufgaben

A. Fragen
1. Was ist der Artikel von Mantel? Kleidung? Pulli? Bluse? Hemd? Rock? Hose? Kleid? Jacke? Schuh? T-Shirt?
2. Was ist der Plural von Schuh? Jacke? Rock? Kleid? Hemd? Bluse? Pullover? Mantel?
3. Sprechen Sie langsam oder schnell? Hören Sie gut oder schlecht? Sind Sie groß oder klein? Sind die Schuhe sauber oder schmutzig?
4. Was ist das Gegenteil von richtig? alt? schlecht? schnell? billig? dick? da? nein? danke?

B. Beschreiben Sie bitte! *(Describe some of your clothing or one or two items you have with you.)*
BEISPIEL: Die Hose ist blau. Die Schuhe sind . . .

C. Wie viel ist das? *(How much is that? Read aloud in German.)*
BEISPIEL: 4 + 4 = 8   Vier plus vier ist acht.
8 − 4 = 4   **Acht minus vier ist vier.**

3 + 2 = 5   8 + 1 = 9   8 − 2 = 6
7 + 3 = 10   10 − 2 = 8   7 − 6 = 1
1 + 1 = 2   9 − 4 = 5   5 − 5 = 0

D. Wie geht's weiter? *(What comes next?)*
100 − 10 = 90   90 − 10 = 80   80 − 10 = ? . . .
70 − 7 = 63   63 − 7 = 56   56 − 7 = ? . . .

E. Was sagen Sie? *(Read the dialogue in the left-hand column below. Then be prepared to enact a similar one with a partner, based on objects in the classroom.)*

S1	Ist das die Tafel?	S1	Ist das . . . ?
S2	Nein, das ist nicht die Tafel. Das ist die Wand.	S2	Nein, das ist nicht . . . Das ist . . .
S1	Wo ist die Tafel?	S1	Wo ist . . . ?
S2	Da ist die Tafel.	S2	. . .
S1	Welche Farbe hat die Tafel?	S1	Welche Farbe hat . . . ?
S2	Die Tafel ist grün.	S2	. . . ist . . .
S1	Was ist auch grün?	S1	Was ist auch . . . ?
S2	Das Buch ist auch grün.	S2	. . . ist auch . . .
S1	Wie ist das Buch? Ist das Buch alt?	S1	Wie ist . . . ?
S2	Nein, das Buch ist neu.	S2	. . .

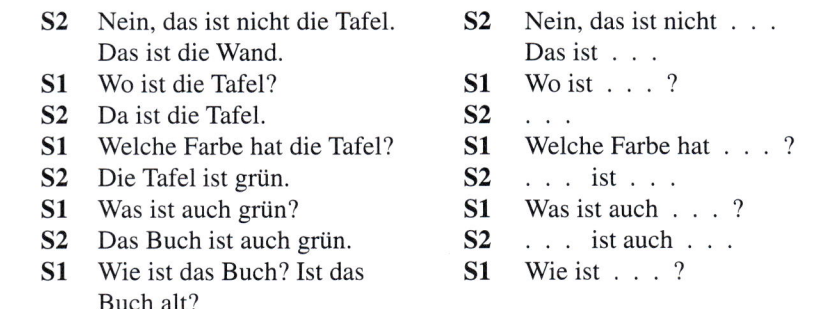

LERNTIPP **Developing Listening Comprehension**

Being able to understand spoken German is probably your most important skill. Without it, you can't learn to speak. Use class time well; listen carefully to the instructor and your classmates. Play the tape that comes with this book as often as you need in order to understand the dialogues and anecdotes and to complete the exercises correctly. Use the tape program in the lab, at home, or in the dormitory, and be sure to listen to the reading texts with the book closed. Take advantage of opportunities to hear German in the German Club or German House, if there is one on your campus. Listen to tapes and watch plays or movies (some can be rented in video stores). Even if you can't understand much of it in the beginning, you will be able to pick out key words and learn to "tune in" to German.

Das Wetter im April

Schritt 4

NORBERT	Es ist schön heute, nicht wahr?
JULIA	Ja, wirklich. Die Sonne scheint wieder!
RUDI	Nur der Wind ist kühl.
JULIA	Ach, das macht nichts.
NORBERT	Ich finde es toll.

HANNES	Mensch, so ein Sauwetter! Es schneit schon wieder.
MARTIN	Na und?
HANNES	In Mallorca ist es schön warm.
MARTIN	Wir sind aber hier und nicht in Mallorca.
HANNES	Schade!

DOROTHEA	Das Wetter ist furchtbar, nicht wahr?
MATTHIAS	Das finde ich auch. Es regnet und regnet!
SONJA	Und es ist wieder so kalt. Nur 7 Grad!
MATTHIAS	Ja, typisch April.

WORTSCHATZ

Das Jahr, -e *(year)*

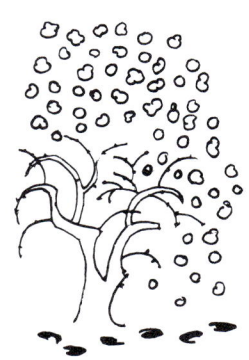

der Frühling   der Sommer   der Herbst   der Winter

Der Monat, -e *(month)*[1]
Die Woche, -n *(week)*
Der Tag, -e *(day)*

der Montag	*Monday*[1]	der Januar	*January*
Dienstag	*Tuesday*	Februar	*February*
Mittwoch	*Wednesday*	März	*March*
Donnerstag	*Thursday*	April	*April*
Freitag	*Friday*	Mai	*May*
Samstag[2]	*Saturday*	Juni	*June*
Sonntag	*Sunday*	Juli	*July*
		August	*August*
		September	*September*
		Oktober	*October*
		November	*November*
		Dezember	*December*

Das Wetter *(weather)*

Es ist . . .	*It's . . .*	heiß / kalt	*hot / cold*
Es regnet.	*It's raining.*	warm / kühl	*warm / cool*
Es schneit.	*It's snowing.*	furchtbar	*awful, terrible*
Die Sonne scheint.	*The sun is shining.*	prima	*great, wonderful*
		schön	*nice, beautiful*
		super	*superb, super*
		toll	*great, terrific*
		windig	*windy*

Weiteres

Die Woche hat [sieben Tage].	*The week has [seven days].*
heute / morgen	*today / tomorrow*
nur	*only*
sehr	*very*
(schon) wieder	*(already) again*
wirklich	*really, indeed*
Schade!	*Too bad!*
nicht wahr?	*isn't it? isn't this true?*
Wann sind Sie geboren?	*When were you born?*
Ich bin im Mai[3] geboren.	*I was born in May.*
finden	*to find*
Ich finde es . . .	*I think it's . . .*
Das finde ich auch.	*I think so, too.*

---

[1] Note that the days, months, and seasons are all masculine!

[2] People in northern and central Germany prefer **Sonnabend**, those in southern Germany **Samstag** (derived from the Hebrew word *Sabbat*).

[3] **Im** is used with the names of the months and seasons: **im Mai, im Winter.**

Zum Erkennen: der Wind; Das macht nichts *(It doesn't matter; That's okay.)*; Mensch, so ein Sauwetter! *(Man, what lousy weather!)*; Na und? *(So what?)*; wir sind *(we are)*; Grad *(degrees)*; typisch; die Jahreszeit, -en *(season)*

Aussprache: r; p, t, k; final b, d, g; j, h

Hören Sie gut zu und wiederholen Sie!

- [r] **r**ichtig, **r**egnet, **r**ot, **r**osa, b**r**aun, g**r**ün, F**r**eitag, le**r**nen, hö**r**en
- [ʌ] wi**r**, vi**er**, nu**r**, od**er**, ab**er**, saub**er**, teu**er**, Wett**er**, Somm**er**, Wint**er**
  BUT [ʌ / r] Tü**r** / Tü**r**en; Papi**er** / Papi**er**e; Jah**r** / Jah**r**e
- [p] **P**ulli, **P**lural, **p**lus, **p**rima
  AND [p] Her**b**st, Jako**b**, gel**b**, hal**b**
  BUT [p / b] gel**b** / gel**b**e; hal**b** / hal**b**e
- [t] **Th**eo, **T**ür, Doro**th**ea, Ma**tth**ias, bi**tt**e
  AND [t] un**d**, tausen**d**, Bil**d**, Klei**d**, Hem**d**, Wan**d**
  BUT [t / d] Bil**d** / Bil**d**er; Klei**d** / Klei**d**er; Hem**d** / Hem**d**en; Wan**d** / Wän**d**e
- [k] **k**ühl, **k**urz, **K**uli, dan**k**e, Ja**ck**e, Ro**ck**
  AND [k] sa**g**t, fra**g**t, Ta**g**
  BUT [k / g] sa**g**t / sa**g**en; fra**g**t / fra**g**en; Ta**g** / Ta**g**e
- [j] **j**a, **J**ahr, **J**anuar, **J**uni, **J**uli
- [h] **h**ören, **h**eiß, **h**at, **h**eute
- [:] z**äh**len, ne**h**men, I**h**nen, St**uh**l, Sch**uh**

Mündliche Übungen

A. **Hören Sie gut zu und wiederholen Sie!**
   1. Das Jahr hat vier Jahreszeiten. Die Jahreszeiten heißen Frühling, Sommer, Herbst und Winter.
   2. Das Jahr hat zwölf Monate. Die Monate heißen Januar, Februar, März, April, Mai, Juni, Juli, August, September, Oktober, November und Dezember.
   3. Die Woche hat sieben Tage. Die Tage heißen Montag, Dienstag, Mittwoch, Donnerstag, Freitag, Samstag und Sonntag.

B. **Mustersätze**
   1. schön: **Es ist heute** schön.
      kalt, kühl, heiß, warm
   2. sehr kalt: **Es ist** sehr kalt.
      sehr heiß, schön warm, furchtbar kalt
   3. toll: **Ich finde es** toll.
      gut, prima, wunderbar, furchtbar
   4. Juli: **Ich bin im** Juli **geboren**.
      Januar, März, Sommer, Winter
   5. 19: **Ich bin** neunzehn.
      16, 20, 27, 31

C. **Wiederholung**
   1. **Antworten Sie mit JA!**
      BEISPIEL: Wiederholen Sie das noch einmal?
      Ja, ich wiederhole das noch einmal.
      a. Lesen Sie das auf Deutsch?   c. Brauchen Sie das Buch?
      b. Lernen Sie das für morgen?   d. Nehmen Sie das Heft?
   2. **Antworten Sie mit NEIN!**
      BEISPIEL: Ist das die Kreide?
      Nein, das ist nicht die Kreide.
      a. Ist das die Wand?   c. Sind das die Schuhe?
      b. Ist das der Pulli?   d. Sind das die Klassenzimmer?

BEISPIEL: Ist die Kreide gelb?
Nein, die Kreide ist nicht gelb.

e. Ist die Antwort richtig?   g. Ist das Wetter schön?
f. Ist die Farbe gut?   h. Ist das typisch?

3. **Zahlen**
   a. **Lesen Sie laut auf Deutsch!**

   101 / 315 / 463 / 1 110 / 20 000 / 88 888 / 267 315
   100,10 DM / 212,25 DM / 667,75 DM / 1 920,- DM / 9 999,99 DM

   b. **Was ist Ihre Telefonnummer?** *(What's your phone number? Ask other students.)*

   BEISPIEL: Was ist Ihre Telefonnummer?
   Meine Telefonnummer ist 646-0195.
   (sechs vier sechs, null eins neun fünf)

4. **Gegenteile** *(Tell which adjectives best describe each pair.)*

Aufgaben

A. Geben Sie Befehle! *(Give commands, but politely.)*

BEISPIEL: antworten
Antworten Sie bitte!

fragen, wiederholen, lesen, buchstabieren, zählen

B. Fragen
1. Wie ist das Wetter hier im Winter? im Sommer? im Frühling? im Herbst?
2. Was ist der Artikel von Montag? September? Herbst? Juni? Monat? Jahr? Woche?
3. Welcher Tag ist heute? morgen?
4. Wie viele Tage hat die Woche? Wie heißen die Tage?
5. Wie viele Tage hat der September? der Oktober? der Februar?
6. Wie viele Monate hat das Jahr? Wie heißen die Monate?
7. Wie viele Wochen hat das Jahr?
8. Wie viele Jahreszeiten hat das Jahr? Wie heißen die Jahreszeiten?

9. Wie heißen die Wintermonate? die Sommermonate? die Herbstmonate?
10. Wie ist das Wetter heute? Scheint die Sonne oder regnet es?

C. Temperaturen

> European thermometers use the Celsius scale. On that scale water freezes at 0°C and boils at 100°C. Normal body temperature is about 37°C, and fever starts at about 37.6°C. To convert Fahrenheit into Celsius, subtract 32, multiply by 5, divide by 9. To convert Celsius into Fahrenheit, multiply by 9, divide by 5, add 32.

1. **Wie viel Grad Celsius sind das?** *(How many degrees Celsius? Use the thermometer as a reference.)*
   BEISPIEL: 32°F = 0°C
   Zweiunddreißig Grad Fahrenheit sind null Grad Celsius.

   100°F, 96°F, 84°F, 68°F, 41°F, 23°F, −4°F, −13°F

2. **Wie ist das Wetter?** *(What's the weather like?)*
   BEISPIEL: 12°C (zwölf Grad Celsius)
   Es ist kühl.

   21°C, 0°C, 30°C, 38°C, −10°C, −25°C

LERNTIPP **Learning Vocabulary**
To remember vocabulary, you must use it. Name things as you see them in the course of your day. Label objects in your room or home, using index cards. Practice new words aloud—the use of your auditory and motor memory will quadruple your learning efficiency. Be sure to learn the gender and plural with each noun. For some, the gender and plural are predictable; study Part 1 in the Appendix.

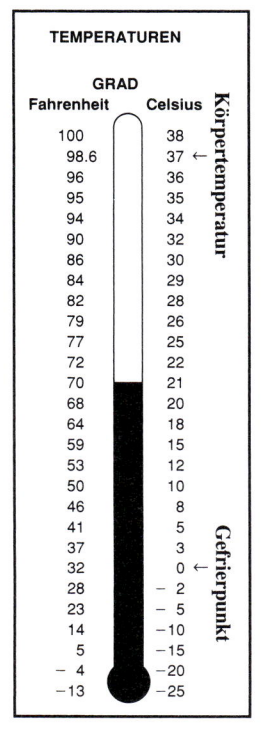

Wie spät ist es?

Schritt 5

RITA   Hallo, Axel! Wie spät ist es?
AXEL   Hallo, Rita! Es ist zehn vor acht.
RITA   Oje, in zehn Minuten habe ich Philosophie.
AXEL   Dann mach's gut, tschüss!
RITA   Ja, tschüss!

PHILLIP   Hallo, Steffi! Wie viel Uhr ist es denn?
STEFFI   Tag, Phillip! Es ist halb zwölf.
PHILLIP   Gehen wir jetzt essen?
STEFFI   O.K., die Vorlesung beginnt erst um Viertel nach eins.

HERR RICHTER   Wann sind Sie heute fertig?
HERR HEROLD   Um zwei. Warum?
HERR RICHTER   Spielen wir heute Tennis?
HERR HEROLD   Ja, prima! Es ist jetzt halb eins. Um Viertel vor drei dann?
HERR RICHTER   Gut! Bis später!

SCHRITT 5

WORTSCHATZ

- German has a formal (see Chapter 7) and informal way of telling time. The informal system is used in everyday speech and varies somewhat from region to region. The system below is a compromise, but certain to be understood everywhere.

Wie spät ist es? *(How late is it? What time is it?)*
Wie viel Uhr ist es?

die Minute, -n	minute	morgens	in the morning
Sekunde, -n	second	mittags	at noon
Stunde, -n[1]	hour	nachmittags	in the afternoon
Uhr, -en	watch, clock; o'clock	abends	in the evening
Zeit, -en	time		

Es ist ein Uhr. / Es ist eins.

Es ist zwei Uhr. / Es ist zwei.

Es ist Viertel nach zwei.

Es ist halb drei.

Es ist Viertel vor drei.

Es ist zehn (Minuten) vor drei.

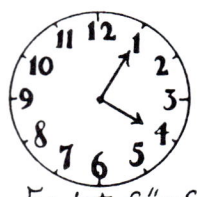

Es ist fünf nach vier.

Es ist zwanzig (Minuten) nach sieben.

Weiteres

der Student, -en	student (male)
die Studentin, -nen	student (female)
der Kurs, -e	course
die Vorlesung, -en	lecture, (university) class

Es ist ein Uhr (zwei Uhr).[2]	It's one o'clock (two o'clock).
Es ist eins (zwei).	It's one (two).
(um) eins[2]	(at) one o'clock
(um) Viertel nach eins	(at) quarter past one

---

[1] **Stunde** refers to duration or a particular class: **Die Deutschstunde ist von acht bis neun. Eine Stunde hat 60 Minuten. Uhr** refers to clock time: **Es ist 9 Uhr.**

[2] **um ein Uhr** BUT **um eins.**

(um) halb zwei, 1.30[3]	(at) half past one, 1:30
(um) Viertel vor zwei, 1.45	(at) quarter to two, 1:45
fertig	finished, done
jetzt	now
Bitte!	here: *You're welcome.*
beginnen	to begin
essen	to eat
gehen	to go
Tennis spielen	to play tennis
haben	to have
ich habe	*I have*
es hat	*it has*
wir ⎫	*we have*
sie ⎬ **haben**	*they have*
Sie ⎭	*you (formal) have*
Ich habe eine Frage.	*I have a question.*
Ich habe keine Zeit.	*I don't have time.*
Bis später!	*See you later!*

---

[3] Note the difference in punctuation between English *(1:30)* and German **(1.30)**.

Zum Erkennen: Oje! *(Oh no! Oops!)*; Dann mach's gut! *(Then take care!)*; denn *(flavoring particle used for emphasis)*; erst *(only, not until)*; warum? *(why?)*; die Uhrzeit *(time of day)*

Aussprache: ch, ig, ck, ng, gn, kn, qu, pf, ps, w

Hören Sie gut zu und wiederholen Sie!

- [k] **Ch**ristine, **Ch**ristian, **Ch**aos
- [x] a**ch**t, a**ch**thundert**ach**tunda**ch**tzig, au**ch**, brau**ch**en, Wo**ch**e, Bu**ch**, Ba**ch**arach
- [ç] i**ch**, ni**ch**t, wirkli**ch**, wel**ch**e, schle**ch**t, Gesprä**ch**e, Bü**ch**er
- [iç] richt**ig**, wind**ig**, bill**ig**, fert**ig**, sechz**ig** Pfenn**ig**
- [ks] se**chs**, se**chs**undse**chs**zig, se**chs**hundertse**chs**undsechzig
- [k] Ja**ck**e, Ro**ck**, Pi**ck**nick, di**ck**
- [ŋ] I**ng**e La**ng**e, Wolfga**ng** E**ng**el, E**ng**lisch, Frühli**ng**, la**ng**
- [gn] re**gn**et, resi**gn**ieren, Si**gn**al
- [kn] **Kn**irps, **Kn**ie, **Kn**ut **Kn**orr
- [kv] **Qu**alität, **Qu**antität, **Qu**artett, Ä**qu**ivalent
- [pf] **Pf**ennig, **Pf**efferminz, Dummko**pf**, **pf**ui
- [ps] **Ps**ychologie, **Ps**ychiater, **Ps**ychoanalyse, **Ps**eudonym
- [v] **W**illi, **W**olfgang, **W**and, **W**ort, **w**ie, **w**as, **w**o, **w**elche, **V**olvo, **V**ase

Mündliche Übungen

A. **Wie spät ist es?**
  1. 1.00: **Es ist** ein **Uhr.**
     3.00, 5.00, 7.00, 9.00, 11.00
  2. 1.05: **Es ist** fünf **nach** eins.
     3.05, 9.10, 11.10, 4.20, 8.20
  3. 1.15: **Es ist Viertel nach** eins.
     2.15, 4.15, 6.15, 8.15, 10.15

4. 1.30: **Es ist halb** zwei.
   2.30, 4.30, 6.30, 8.30, 10.30
5. 1.40: **Es ist** zwanzig **vor** zwei.
   5.40, 9.50, 1.50, 12.55, 4.55
6. 1.45: **Es ist Viertel vor** zwei.
   3.45, 5.45, 7.45, 9.45, 12.45

B. **Wann ist die Vorlesung?** *(When is the lecture?)*
   1. 9.00: **Die Vorlesung ist um** neun.
      3.00, 1.00, 9.15, 12.15, 1.30, 3.30, 9.45, 12.45
   2. 5: **Die Vorlesung beginnt in** fünf **Minuten.**
      2, 10, 12, 15, 20
   3. morgens: **Die Vorlesung ist** morgens.
      nachmittags, abends, um acht, um Viertel nach acht, um halb neun, um Viertel vor neun.

C. **Mustersätze**
   1. essen: Essen **Sie jetzt? Ja, ich** esse **jetzt.**
      gehen, fragen, lernen, antworten, beginnen
   2. heute: **Ich spiele** heute **Tennis.**
      jetzt, morgens, nachmittags, abends, wieder
   3. Sie: **Wann** sind Sie **heute fertig?**
      Horst, ich, Rolf und Maria, sie *(pl.)*
   4. ich: Ich habe **keine Zeit.**
      wir, Maria, Maria und Rita

D. **Wiederholung**
   1. **Wie ist das Wetter?**

   a.   b.   c.   d.

   2. **Was sagen Sie?** *(Talk about the weather with a classmate.)*

      S1 Wie ist das Wetter heute?
      S2 . . .
      S1 Wie finden Sie das Wetter?
      S2 . . .
      S1 Typisch . . . , nicht wahr?
      S2 . . .

   3. **Wie fragen Sie?** *(Formulate the questions for these answers.)*
      BEISPIEL: Ja, ich bin müde.
                 Sind Sie müde?

a. Danke, gut.
b. Das Buch ist grau.
c. Nein, ich heiße nicht Fiedler.
d. Da ist die Tür.
e. Ja, ich spreche langsam.
f. Das Papier kostet 1,50 DM.
g. Heute ist es furchtbar heiß.
h. Ich finde das nicht schön.
i. Fünf plus sechzehn ist einundzwanzig.
j. Nein, heute ist Dienstag.

4. **Und Sie?** *(Answer, then ask someone else.)*
   a. Wie alt sind Sie? (**Ich bin _____. Und Sie?**)
   b. Wo sind Sie geboren? (**Ich bin in _____ geboren. Und Sie?**)
   c. Wann sind Sie geboren? (**Ich bin im _____ geboren. Und Sie?**)

5. **Was tun Sie wann?** *(What do you do when? Use the drawings to discuss with other students what you like to do in various months and seasons.)*

   BEISPIEL: Was tun Sie im Sommer?
   Im Sommer spiele ich Tennis. Und Sie?

Aufgaben

Ski laufen, angeln, segeln, campen, joggen, reiten, schwimmen, Golf spielen, Tennis spielen

A. Fragen und Antworten
1. Wie viele Stunden hat der Tag? Wie viele Minuten hat die Stunde? Wie viele Sekunden hat die Minute?
2. Wie spät ist es? (8.45, 9.30, 10.15, 1.05, 2.20, 2.45, 6.59)
3. Wann essen Sie morgens? mittags? abends?

B. Meine Kurse *(Read the cue lines below, then use them to ask about your partner's schedule and to relate your own.)*

Biologie, Chemie, Deutsch, Englisch, Französisch *(French)*, Geographie, Geologie, Geschichte *(history)*, Informatik *(computer science)*, Kunst *(art)*, Latein, Mathe(matik), Musik, Philosophie, Physik, Politik, Psychologie, Soziologie, Spanisch, Sport

S1 Welche Kurse haben Sie heute?
S2 . . .
S1 Und morgen? Welche Kurse haben Sie morgen?
S2 . . .
S1 Wann haben Sie . . . ?
S2 Ich habe . . . um . . . und . . . um . . .
S1 Wie heißt der/die . . .professor(in)?
S2 . . .
S1 Ist der . . .kurs gut?
S2 . . .
S1 Wann sind Sie heute fertig?
S2 Ich bin heute um . . . fertig.

SPRECHSITUATIONEN

> These sections focus on practical language functions. In German as in English, there are many ways to say the same thing, but which one you choose depends on the circumstances. You already know most of these words; here, they are grouped for specific situations. New words or expressions are translated. Your instructor will indicate which of them you will need to learn.

Greetings and good-byes

1. In formal situations or when speaking with strangers, you can use these expressions:

   Guten Tag!
   Guten Morgen! *(until about 10:00 A.M.)*
   Guten Abend! *(from about 5:00 to 10:00 P.M.)*
   Wie geht es Ihnen?
   Auf Wiedersehen!

   German speakers usually shake hands whenever they meet, not only for the first time.

2. Here are some greetings and ways to say good-bye in casual situations or with friends:

Hallo!	Wiedersehen! Tschüss!
Tag! Wie geht's?	Mach's gut!
Morgen! Abend!	Bis später!

   Other casual ways of saying *Hi!* are **Grüß dich!, Grüß Gott!** *(lit.: Greetings in the name of God!)* and **Servus!** in southern Germany or Austria; and **Grüezi!** in Switzerland and Liechtenstein. **Gute Nacht!** *(Good night!)* is normally used to wish someone who lives in the same house a good night's sleep.

3. Here are some responses to **Wie geht es Ihnen?** or **Wie geht's?**

   Gut, danke.
   Sehr gut, danke.
   Prima! Super!
   Es geht mir gut / nicht gut.
   Es geht mir schlecht / nicht schlecht.

4. To introduce yourself, you should say:

   Mein Name ist . . .
   Ich heiße . . .

5. When meeting someone for the first time, you can use the following expressions:

(Es) freut mich!	*(I'm) pleased to meet you.*
(Es) freut mich auch.	*Pleased to meet you, too. Same here.*

Useful classroom expressions

You should be able to use and understand the following phrases:

Ich habe eine Frage.	*I have a question.*
Ich verstehe (das) nicht.	*I don't understand (that).*
Wie bitte?	*What did you say, please?*
(Sagen Sie das) noch einmal bitte!	*(Say that) again, please.*
Wiederholen Sie bitte!	*Please repeat.*

Was bedeutet . . . ?	*What does . . . mean?*
Wie sagt man . . . ?	*How do you say . . . ?*
Ich weiß nicht.	*I don't know.*
Passen Sie auf!	*Pay attention!*
Hören Sie zu!	*Listen!*
Öffnen Sie das Buch auf Seite . . . !	*Open the book to (literally on) page . . . !*
Lesen Sie bitte!	*Please read!*
Lesen Sie laut!	*Read aloud!*
(Sprechen Sie) langsam bitte!	*(Speak) slowly, please!*
Gehen Sie an die Tafel!	*Go to the board!*
Schreiben Sie bitte!	*Please, write!*
Das ist alles.	*That's all.*

Mündliche Übungen

A. Was sagen sie? *(What are they saying?)*

B. Was sagen Sie? *(What would you say in response to these statements?)*
1. Mein Name ist Dinkelacker, Horst Dinkelacker.
2. Guten Morgen! Wie geht es Ihnen?
3. Auf Wiedersehen!
4. Sprechen Sie langsam bitte!
5. Dort drüben ist die Straßenbahnhaltestelle.
6. Tag! Wie geht's?

C. **Was sagen Sie dann?** *(What would you say in these situations?)*
   1. You got called on in class and didn't hear the question.
   2. You were unable to follow your instructor's explanation.
   3. You have to ask your instructor to repeat something.
   4. You want to say good-bye to the host after an evening party.
   5. You want to say good-bye to some friends.
   6. You are staying with the family of a friend in Austria. What do you say as you go to bed?
   7. You have asked a native of Hannover for directions and she is speaking much too fast.
   8. In a conversation the word **Geschwindigkeitsbegrenzung** keeps coming up. You want to ask for clarification.

D. **Kurzgespräche** *(With a partner, practice the following conversations in German until you are fluent in both parts. Eventually you'll want to include additional phrases of your own.)*
   1. S1 Hi! How are you?
      S2 Great!
      S1 That's wonderful.
      S2 And how are you?
      S1 Not bad, but I'm very tired.
      S2 See you later!
      S1 Bye!
   2. S1 Hello! My name is . . . What's yours?
      S2 My name is . . .
      S1 Pleased to meet you.
      S2 Pleased to meet you, too.

The Benefits of Learning German

Learning German will bring you benefits you may not have thought of before. In professional terms, you will be at an advantage regardless of whether your interests are in business, law, or academics. After all, the German economy is the strongest in Europe. Germany and Austria are active partners in the European Union, and many fields (such as music, art, literature, archaeology, philosophy, physics—to name just a few) reflect the creative work of artists and researchers from the German-speaking world. In personal terms, knowing German will open the doors to another culture. Because German and English are closely related Germanic languages, it is probable that in the course of your studies you will gain new insights into your own language as well.

Rückblick: Schritte

By now you know quite a few German words and a number of idiomatic expressions. You have learned how to pronounce German and to say a few things about yourself. You also have learned a good deal about the structure of the German language.

I. Nouns

1. German has three genders: MASCULINE, NEUTER, and FEMININE. Nouns are distinguished by **der, das,** and **die** in the singular. In the plural there are no gender distinctions; the article **die** is used for all plural nouns:

der Herr, der Bleistift	Herren, Bleistifte
das Bild	**die** Bilder
die Frau, die Tafel	Frauen, Tafeln

2. There are several ways to form the plural of nouns. You have learned how to interpret the most common plural abbreviations found in dictionaries and vocabulary lists:

das Fenster, **-**	Fenster
der Mantel, **⸚**	M**ä**ntel
der Tag, **-e**	Tage
der Stuhl, **⸚e**	St**ü**hle
das Kleid, **-er**	Kleid**er**
das Buch, **⸚er**	B**ü**ch**er**
die Uhr, **-en**	Uhr**en**
die Sekunde, **-n**	Sekunde**n**
die Studentin, **-nen**	Studentin**nen**
der Kuli, **-s**	Kuli**s**

3. When you learn a noun, you must also learn its gender and plural form.
4. All nouns are capitalized.

    Ich brauche **B**leistifte, **K**ulis und **P**apier.

II. Pronouns

You have used the following pronouns:

ich	*I*	Ich heiße Sanders.
es	*it*	Es regnet.
wir	*we*	Wir zählen von eins bis zehn.
sie	*they*	Sind sie müde?
Sie	*you (formal)*	Wann sind Sie heute fertig?

- The pronoun **ich** is not capitalized unless it stands at the beginning of a sentence.
- The pronoun **Sie** (when it means *you*) is always capitalized; **Sie** is used in all formal relationships, and always when others are addressed with such titles as **Herr** and **Frau**. It is used to address one or more persons.

    Frau Thielemann, verstehen **Sie** das?

    Frau Thielemann und Herr Fiedler, verstehen **Sie** das?

Rückblick: Schritte

III. Verbs

1. You have noticed that German verbs have different endings—that is, they are INFLECTED, or CONJUGATED. You have used the following verb endings:

ich	-e	Ich brauche Papier.
wir	-en	Wir brauchen Papier.
sie, Sie	-en	Sie brauchen Papier.

2. **Sein** *(to be)* and **haben** *(to have)* are two important verbs. As in English, their forms are not regular.

ich	bin	Ich bin müde.
es	ist	Es ist spät.
sie, Sie	sind	Sie sind schnell.

ich	habe	Ich habe Zeit.
es	hat	Es hat Zeit.
sie, Sie	haben	Sie haben Zeit.

IV. Sentence structure

You have encountered three basic sentence types: STATEMENTS, QUESTIONS, and IMPERATIVES. In all of them, verb position plays a significant role.

1. Statements

   One of the most important observations you will make is that the verb is always the second element in a statement. (As you see from the examples, a SENTENCE ELEMENT can consist of more than one word.)

   Mein Name **ist** Dieter Schneider.
   Gerda und Dorothea **sind** hier.
   Ich **finde** das schön.
   Der Rock und die Bluse **kosten** 150,- DM.

2. Questions

   You have practiced two types of questions: INFORMATION QUESTIONS and QUESTIONS THAT ELICIT YES / NO ANSWERS.

   a. Information questions begin with a question word or phrase and ask for specific information: *what, where, how.* In information questions, too, the verb is the second element. You have learned the following question words and phrases. Note that all question words begin with a **w**!

   Wer Wie Wo Was ?

   Wann **haben** Sie Deutsch?
   Was **kostet** das?
   Wo **ist** der Stuhl?
   Wie **geht** es Ihnen?
   Welche Farbe **hat** das Buch?
   Wie viel Uhr **ist** es?
   Wie viele Tage **hat** die Woche?

b. Questions eliciting a yes / no response, on the other hand, begin with the verb.

Haben Sie Zeit?
Regnet es morgen?
Spielen wir heute Tennis?
Ist das richtig?

3. Imperatives

   Imperatives (commands, requests, suggestions) also begin with the verb. Note that they usually conclude with an exclamation mark.

   Antworten Sie bitte!
   Nehmen Sie die Kreide!
   Öffnen Sie das Buch!
   Sagen Sie das noch einmal!
   Zählen Sie von zwanzig bis dreißig!

Rückblick: Schritte

HÖREN SIE ZU!

Twice in every chapter, you will find listening comprehension exercises, like the one below, for the CD that comes with the textbook. These exercises provide you with an opportunity to listen to conversations that are as close to native speech as possible. You may want to listen to them several times. Note that it is not essential to understand every word in order to comprehend the meaning of the dialogue. However, when the passage includes vocabulary items that you have not yet learned, they are listed after the instructions, for recognition only. Additional listening exercises are included in the tape program in the section called *Verstehen Sie?*

Das Klassenzimmer *(Listen to the description of this class and classroom. Then select the correct response from those given below.)*

1. Das Klassenzimmer ist _____.
   a. kühl   b. groß   c. schmutzig

2. Das Zimmer hat _____ Fenster.
   a. vier   b. fünf   c. sieben

3. Die Wände sind _____.
   a. grau   b. blau   c. schwarz

4. Die _____ sind rot.
   a. Türen   b. Bücher   c. Stühle

5. Der Professor heißt _____.
   a. Theo Seidl   b. Oskar Thieme   c. Otto Brockmann

6. Die Bilder sind _____.
   a. alt   b. schön   c. furchtbar

7. Die Studenten lernen _____.
   a. Deutsch   b. Spanisch   c. Englisch

Rückblick: Schritte

Wiederholung

A. Zahlen und Zeiten

1. **Wie geht's weiter?** *(Add to or subtract from the previous sum. Continue from one person to another.)*

   BEISPIEL: 7 + 5 = 12 + 9 = 21 − ? = ? . . .

2. **Was kostet das?** *(A student writes prices on the board for others to read aloud.)*

3. **Was ist die Telefonnummer?** *(Ask each other for the telephone number of persons listed below.)*

   BEISPIEL: Was ist die Telefonnummer von *(of)* Karl-Heinz Kuckuck?
   Die Nummer ist 74 88.

Fischer Ulrich Berliner-1	71 29	**Harms Ralf** (Du)	18 93	**Jung Detlef**	73 35	**Kreissparkasse Alfeld Leine**	
Fittje Herta Heinsen 4B	67 44	Alte Mühlen-8		Heinrich-Sohnrey-Weg 13		Geschäftsstellen	
Fientje Isabella Alte-12	74 99	**Harstick Alfred** Landw. (Du)	5 98	−**Walter**	73 24	Duhnser-1	64 01
Flor Andrea Heinser-4	65 74	Deinsen		Heinrich-Sohnrey-Weg 11		Deilmissen	71 00
Forstverwaltung		−**Werner** Landw. (Du)	5 08	**Junge Kurt** Alte-1	65 00	Deinsen (Du)	5 28
		Deinsen 14		−**Rolf** Betriebswirt Am Knick 78	76 45	**Krempig Dieter** Dunser-13	63 64
○ Staatl. Revierförsterei (Du)	5 92	**Hartig Jürgen** KfzRep. Dorf-36	72 71	−**Wilhelm** RohrMstr.	61 36	**Kreth Erich** Am Knick 33	71 17
Deinsen		**Hartmann Helene**	64 94	Am Knick 78		−**Harald** Kampweg 6	76 85
Freimut Ella Breslauer-1	71 45	Schachtweg 30		**Kahle Wolfgang** (Du)	12 86	−**Hugo** Königsberger-7	72 87
Freund Achim Im Külfeld 6	62 40	**Haushaltswaren- und**	66 63	Lange-22		**Kreutz Kurt** Drogerie Haupt-1	66 08
−**Friedrich** Haupt-49	61 39	**Geschenkartikel-Vertriebs**		**Kaiser Rolf** Bantelner-12	65 69	**Kreybohm Erich** (Du)	14 03
−**Helga** Fußpflege Am Knick 32	65 97	**GmbH** Haupt-17A		−**Siegfried** SparkassenOInsp.	66 82	Landw. Deinsen 23	
−**Klaus** Haupt-49	68 80	**Hausmann Christian**	61 35	Breslauer-19		**Krieter Franz** (Du)	65 85
Frie August Wassertor-18	76 54	Kampweg 5		−**Willi** Bantelner-29	68 91	Aschenkamp 3	
Friebe Martha Alte-10	74 17	−**Heinz** Schachtweg 12	74 59	**Kalkof Carsten** Mühlen-3	68 35	**Krömer Alfred**	72 41
−**Paul** Deilmissen Dorf-29	73 55	**Hebisch Ernst** Haupt-5	62 09	−**Otto** Mühlen-3	73 59	Wilhelm-Raabe-4	
Friedrich Leo Berliner-19	72 60	−**Heinrich** jun. Dunser-14	66 70	**Kanngießer Wolfgang**	63 40	**Krüger Horst** Neue-3	65 22
−**Norbert** Wassertor-22	75 13	−**Heinrich** sen. Dunser-16	68 27	Dunser-46		−**Selma** Dunser-56	73 19
Friese Horst Heinser-2	70 84	−**Karl** Deilmissen Dorf-22	69 44	**Kasper Bernhard**	72 11	**Krumfuß Anna** Haupt-30	75 92
Fritsche Herbert	62 24	−**Karl** Deilmissen Dorf-20A	71 52	Schachtweg 85		**Kube Klemens** (Du)	17 62
Unter den Tannen 9		**Hecht Friedrich W.**	62 84	**Kassebeer Horst**	65 66	Schlesierweg 102	
Frömming H.	72 06	Bantelner-6		Im Külfeld 2		**Kuchenbach Waldtraut**	73 37
Am Bahndamm 21		**Hehr W.** Gronauer-14	70 31	**Kassing Uwe**	69 88	Wassertor-9	
Frohns Gustav Landw.	68 13	**Hein Alfred** Ing. Gastst.	66 50	Unter den Tannen 10		**Kuckuck Friedhelm**	66 57
Deilmisser-6		Haupt-41		**Katt Günter** Berg-30	61 76	Kampweg 6	
Fromm Josef Berg-10	69 43	−**Günter** Neue-1	60 89	**Kaufmann Friedel**	62 55	−**Karl-Heinz** ElektroMstr.	74 88

B. Buchstabieren Sie bitte! *(Pronounce and spell these familiar words that English has borrowed from German.)*

Angst, Gesundheit, Poltergeist, Rucksack, Strudel, Zwieback

C. Wann ist was? *(At the registration desk of your school, you are giving information about the schedule of next semester's classes. Use the suggested cues from both groups.)*

BEISPIEL: 9.00: **Deutsch ist um neun.**

Politik, Musik, Spanisch, Deutsch, Geologie, Kunst *(art)*, Soziologie, Informatik *(computer science)*, Psychologie, Geschichte *(history)*, Sport, Physik, Philosophie, Biologie, Chemie

3.30, 4.00, 11.15, 10.45, 12.50, 8.30, 2.00, 5.45, 10.30

D. Das Wetter in Europa *(Looking at the map below, ask each other about the weather in various places of Europe.)*

1. Wo scheint die Sonne?
2. Wo regnet es?
3. Wie warm ist es in . . . ? Ist das heiß (schön warm, kühl) oder kalt?

The German Climate

Although Germany lies between the 47th and 55th parallel north, roughly as far north as northern New England and southern Canada, its climate is generally far milder because of the effect of the Gulf Stream. Overall, Germany enjoys a temperate climate, ample rainfall throughout the year, and an absence of extreme heat and cold. In the northwest, summers tend to be cool and winters mild. Towards the east and south, the climate becomes more continental, with greater temperature differences between day and night, and summer and winter. Average daytime temperatures in Berlin are 30°F in January and 64°F in July; in Munich they are 33°F in January and 73°F in July. Autumns are usually mild, sunny, and dryer than other seasons. Between December and March, the mountainous regions of Germany can always expect snow. At the Zugspitze, the highest point in the German Alps, snow may pile up 13 to 16 feet, in comparison to the Black Forest where it averages 5 feet.

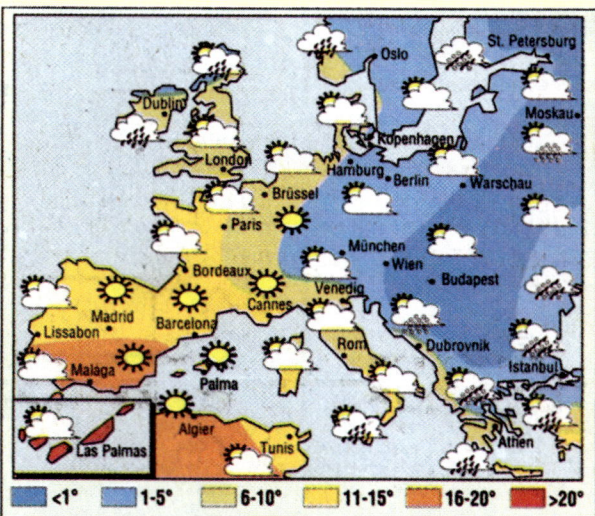

In Norwegen bringt stürmischer Wind Schnee/Regen und auch im Südosten Europas ist's winterlich. Viel Sonne steht dagegen von Warschau über Paris bis Malaga auf dem Programm – dazu in Südspanien 20°.

Wetter und Klima aus erster Hand
Deutscher Wetterdienst

Wo?
Im Internet unter:
http://www.stern.de/wetter

Frühling in Niedersachsen (*Lower Saxony*)

KAPITEL 1

FAMILIE, LÄNDER, SPRACHEN

Die Familie spielt „Mensch ärger dich nicht" ("Sorry").

LERNZIELE

■ VORSCHAU
Spotlight on Germany

■ GESPRÄCHE AND WORTSCHATZ
Your family, yourself, and the countries of Europe

■ STRUKTUR
Present tense of regular verbs
Nominative case
Sentence structure: position of subject; linking verbs and predicate adjectives
Compound nouns

■ EINBLICKE
German in Europe
Germany and its neighbors

■ FOKUS
The Goethe Institute
Du or **Sie?**
German throughout the world
Frankfurt/Main

■ WEB-ECKE

■ SPRECHSITUATIONEN
Making small talk
Asking for personal information

VORSCHAU

Spotlight on Germany

Size: Approximately 135,800 square miles, comparable to the size of Montana; would fit twenty times into the area of the continental United States. Divided into 16 federal states (**Länder**).
Population: About 82 million (including 7.3 million foreigners). After Russia, the most populous country of Europe, followed by Italy, the United Kingdom, and France.
Religion: 50% Protestant, 37% Catholic, 13% other.
Geography: Divided into three major regions: the flat lowlands in the north, the central mountain region, and the southern highlands including a narrow band of the Alps.
Currency: Deutsche Mark, 1 DM = 100 Pfennige. The new European currency, the euro, is being phased in, replacing the DM in the year 2002.
Principal cities: Berlin (pop. 3.9 million, capital); Bonn (pop. 300,000, former seat of government); Hamburg (pop. 1.7 million); Munich (*München,* pop. 1.3 million); Cologne (*Köln,* pop. 1 million); Frankfurt am Main (pop. 670,000); Düsseldorf (pop. 590,000); Stuttgart (563,000); Hanover (*Hannover,* 543,000); Leipzig (554,000); Dresden (519,000).

Germany's sometimes turbulent history spans nearly 2,000 years. Unlike many of its neighbors, Germany did not become a centralized state until relatively late. Initially, the population consisted of various Germanic tribes, and even now their heritage gives the different regions of Germany their particular identity. The Holy Roman Empire, a loose federation of states under an emperor, lasted from 962 to 1806. During this time, the country was divided further until there were almost 350 individual political entities, some of them minuscule. Under Napoleon they were consolidated into 32 states. In 1871, under Prussian chancellor Otto von Bismarck, Germany became a unified state for the first time. This monarchy lasted until the end of World War I, when Germany became a republic.

After the Nazi dictatorship led Germany to ruin in World War II, the country was divided into the Federal Republic of Germany, or FRG (**Bundesrepublik = BRD**), in the west, and the German Democratic Republic, or GDR (**Deutsche Demokratische Republik = DDR**), in the east. The line between the West and Communist Europe, a heavily fortified border, ran through the middle of Germany. The symbol of this division, the infamous Berlin Wall built in 1961 by the GDR, came down on November 9, 1989. On October 3, 1990, the two Germanys were officially united. Since then, Germans have been trying to overcome more than 40 years of living in diametrically opposed political and economic systems. Many Germans are still waiting for the day when "the wall in the minds" of people will finally fall. The cost of unification, both socially and economically, has been much higher than anticipated. In the East, the closing of obsolete socialist enterprises has resulted in massive unemployment; in the West, taxes have increased in order to finance the high costs of unification. However, the massive transfer of funds from West to East (about $100 billion annually since unification) is showing results. The telephone, rail, and road system of the new states has been almost completely rebuilt, and the eastern part of Germany now boasts one of the most modern infrastructures in all of Europe.

GESPRÄCHE

Am Goethe-Institut

SHARON Roberto, woher kommst du?
ROBERTO Ich bin aus Rom. Und du?
SHARON Ich komme aus Sacramento, aber jetzt wohnt meine Familie in Seattle.
ROBERTO Hast du Geschwister?
SHARON Ja, ich habe zwei Schwestern und zwei Brüder. Und du?
ROBERTO Ich habe nur eine Schwester. Sie wohnt in Montreal, in Kanada.
SHARON Wirklich? So ein Zufall! Mein Onkel wohnt auch da.

Später

ROBERTO Sharon, wann ist die Prüfung?
SHARON In zehn Minuten. Du, wie heißen ein paar Flüsse in Deutschland?
ROBERTO Im Norden ist die Elbe, im Osten die Oder, im Süden . . .
SHARON Die Donau?
ROBERTO Richtig! Und im Westen der Rhein. Wo liegt Düsseldorf?
SHARON Düsseldorf? Hm. Wo ist eine Landkarte?
ROBERTO Oh, hier. Im Westen von Deutschland, nördlich von Bonn, am Rhein.
SHARON Ach ja, richtig! Na, viel Glück!

Fragen

1. Woher kommt Roberto? 2. Woher kommt Sharon? 3. Wo wohnt Sharons Familie? 4. Wie groß ist Sharons Familie? 5. Wann ist die Prüfung? 6. Was sind die Elbe, die Oder, die Donau und der Rhein? 7. Wo ist die Elbe? die Oder? die Donau? der Rhein? 8. Wo liegt Düsseldorf?

FOKUS The Goethe Institute

The Goethe Institute is the official representative of German culture abroad. With approximately 150 branches in more than 70 countries, it offers German language courses and organizes lectures, exhibitions, film screenings, and readings by poets and authors. The combination of language instruction and lively cultural exchange makes the Goethe Institutes important intermediaries in international dialogue.

WORTSCHATZ 1

Die Familie, -n *(family)*

der Bruder, ¨	brother	die Frau, -en	woman; wife
Junge, -n	boy	Kusine, -n	cousin
Onkel, -	uncle	Mutter, ¨	mother

der Mann, ⸚er	man; husband	die Großmutter, ⸚	grandmother
Sohn, ⸚e	son	Schwester, -n	sister
Vater, ⸚	father	Tante, -n	aunt
Großvater, ⸚	grandfather	Tochter, ⸚	daughter
Vetter, -n	cousin	die Eltern *(pl.)*	parents
das Kind, -er	child	Großeltern *(pl.)*	grandparents
Mädchen, -	girl	Geschwister *(pl.)*	siblings, brothers and / or sisters

Das Land, ⸚er[1] (country, state) | Die Leute *(pl.)*[2] (people) | Die Sprache, -n[3] (language)

Deutschland	der Deutsche, -n/die Deutsche, -n	Deutsch
Frankreich	der Franzose, -n/die Französin, -nen	Französisch
Österreich	der Österreicher, -/die Österreicherin, -nen	Deutsch
die Schweiz	der Schweizer, -/die Schweizerin, -nen	Deutsch, Französisch, Italienisch
Italien	der Italiener, -/die Italienerin, -nen	Italienisch
Spanien	der Spanier, -/die Spanierin, -nen	Spanisch
England	der Engländer, -/die Engländerin, -nen	Englisch
Amerika	der Amerikaner, -/die Amerikanerin, -nen	Englisch
Kanada	der Kanadier, -/die Kanadierin, -nen	Englisch, Französisch

Weiteres

der Satz, ⸚e	sentence	die Frage, -n	question
Berg, -e	mountain	Landkarte, -n	map
Fluss, ⸚e	river	Prüfung, -en	test, exam
See, -n	lake	Stadt, ⸚e	city
		Hauptstadt, ⸚e	capital city

kommen	to come
liegen	to lie (be located)
wohnen	to live, reside
amerikanisch / kanadisch	American / Canadian
woher?	from where?
Ich bin / komme aus . . .	I'm from . . . (a native of)
im Norden / Süden / Osten / Westen[4]	in the north / south / east / west
nördlich / südlich / östlich / westlich von	north / south / east / west of
mein(e)[5]	my
dein(e) / Ihr(e)[5]	your (informal / formal)

---

[1] All countries and cities are neuter unless indicated otherwise (**die Schweiz**).

[2] Many feminine nouns can be derived from masculine nouns by adding **-in,** in which case their plurals end in **-nen** (**der Schweizer > die Schweizerin, -nen**). BUT: **der Deutsche > die Deutsche, -n; der Franzose > die Französin, -nen!**

[3] Adjectives denoting nationality are not capitalized: **Typisch deutsch!** *(Typically German!),* BUT: **Ich spreche Deutsch** *(the German language);* **Antworten Sie auf Deutsch!** *(Answer in German!)*

[4] **im** is used with months, seasons, and points of the compass (**im Mai, im Winter, im Norden**); **in** is used with names of cities, countries, and continents (**in Berlin, in Deutschland, in Europa**).

[5] **mein, dein,** and **Ihr** have no ending when used before masculine and neuter nouns that are sentence subjects: **mein Vater, dein Bruder, Ihr Kind.** Before feminine and plural nouns, **meine, deine,** and **Ihre** are used (see p. 43): **meine Mutter, deine Schwester, Ihre Eltern.**

Zum Erkennen: So ein Zufall! *(What a coincidence!);* Na, viel Glück! *(Well, good luck!)*

FOKUS *Du or Sie?*

In forms of address, German is much more formal than English. **Du**—the cognate of the archaic English word *thou*—is used primarily for addressing children, family members, and friends. **Sie** is used with adults who are not close friends or relatives. Today, young people and university students tend to address each other automatically with the informal **du**-form; but it is still extremely rude to call older people—or even work colleagues—by **du.** When in doubt, use **Sie.** The general custom is that it is up to the person of higher age or status to suggest **duzen** instead of **siezen.** Similarly, you address a German speaker "on a first name basis" only after you begin using the **du**-form. Up to that point, it's **Herr** or **Frau** to you.

Zum Thema

A. Mustersätze
  1. Ihre Familie: **Woher kommt** Ihre Familie?
     Ihr Vater, Ihre Mutter, Ihr Onkel, Ihre Tante
  2. Rom: **Ich bin aus** Rom.
     Frankfurt, Österreich, Amerika, Berlin
  3. Hamburg / Norden: Hamburg **liegt im** Norden.
     Leipzig / Osten; München / Süden; Düsseldorf / Westen; Rostock / Norden
  4. die Schweiz / südlich: Die Schweiz **liegt** südlich **von Deutschland.**
     Dänemark / nördlich; Polen / östlich; Österreich / südlich; Luxemburg / westlich
  5. Österreich / Deutsch: **In Österreich sprechen die Leute** Deutsch.
     Frankreich / Französisch; England / Englisch; Italien / Italienisch; Spanien / Spanisch.

B. Was sind sie?

CAUTION: Unlike English, German does not use an indefinite article before nationalities or references to membership in a group: **Sie ist Amerikanerin** *(an American).* **Sie ist Studentin** *(a student).* **Er ist Berliner** *(a Berliner).*

  1. BEISPIEL: Juan ist Spanier. Und Juanita?
               Juanita ist Spanierin.
     a. Antonio ist Italiener. Und Luisa?
     b. Hugo ist Österreicher. Und Lilo?
     c. Walter ist Schweizer. Und Helga?
     d. Pierre ist Franzose. Und Monique?

  2. BEISPIEL: Uwe und Margit sind aus Frankfurt.
               Uwe ist Frankfurter, und Margit ist Frankfurterin.
     a. Robert und Evi sind aus Berlin.
     b. Klaus und Inge sind aus Hamburg.
     c. Rolf und Katrin sind aus Wien.
     d. Bert und Romy sind aus Zürich.

C. **Was passt?** *(For each question or statement on the left, select one or more appropriate responses from the right-hand column, or give your own.)*

_____ 1. Woher kommst du?	a.	Sehr klein. Ich habe keine Geschwister.
_____ 2. Wie groß ist deine Familie?	b.	Am Rhein.
_____ 3. Meine Schwester wohnt in Seattle.	c.	Mein Onkel wohnt auch da.
_____ 4. Wann ist die Prüfung?	d.	Aus Seattle, und du?
_____ 5. Wo liegt Erfurt?	e.	Um Viertel nach zehn.
	f.	Im Osten von Deutschland.
	g.	In zwanzig Minuten.
	h.	Westlich von Weimar.
	i.	Ich bin aus Rom.
	j.	Wir sind sechs.
	k.	Wirklich?
	l.	Ich weiß nicht.

D. **Familien**
  1. **Elkes Stammbaum** *(Look at Elke's family tree and explain who each person is.)*
     BEISPIEL: Elke ist die Tochter von Jens und Ute.
     Elke ist Arndts Schwester.

  2. **Meine Familie** *(Draw your own family tree modeled on the one shown and name all the people on it. Then describe your family to a classmate. Take turns; don't hesitate to ask questions.)*
     BEISPIEL: Meine Familie ist groß / klein. Meine Mutter heißt . . . und ist . . . Jahre alt. Sie wohnt in . . .

E. **Fragen** *(Ask another student the following questions, then answer them in turn.)*
  1. Wie heißt du?
  2. Woher kommst du? deine Mutter? dein Vater? deine Großeltern?
  3. Wo wohnt deine Familie?
  4. Wo liegt _____ *(name of city)?* (e.g., **Santa Barbara liegt in Kalifornien.**)
  5. Wo liegt _____ *(name of state or province)?* (e.g., **Kalifornien liegt südlich von Oregon.**)

6. Wie heißt die Hauptstadt von _____ *(name of state)?* (e.g., **Die Hauptstadt von Kalifornien heißt Sacramento.**)
7. Welche Städte liegen im Norden und im Süden von _____ *(name of your city)?* (e.g., **Im Norden von Santa Barbara liegt San Francisco und im Süden Los Angeles.**)
8. Ist _____ *(name of your city)* groß oder klein? Wie viele Leute wohnen da?
9. Ist da ein Fluss, ein See, der Ozean *(ocean)?* Sind da Berge? Wenn ja *(if so),* wie heißt der Fluss, der See, der Ozean? / wie heißen die Berge?
10. Wie ist das Wetter da im Frühling? im Sommer? im Herbst? im Winter?

Stadtzentrum von Erfurt

F. Aussprache: i, a, u *(See also Section II. 1, 3–4, 11–13, 17, 19–20 in the pronunciation section of the Workbook.)*
1. [i:] **Ih**nen, l**ie**gen, w**ie**der, W**ie**n, B**e**rlin
2. [i] **i**ch b**i**n, b**i**tte, K**i**nd, Geschw**i**ster, r**i**chtig
3. [a:] Fr**a**ge, Spr**a**che, Amerik**a**ner, Sp**a**nier, V**a**ter
4. [a] St**a**dt, L**a**nd, K**a**nada, S**a**tz, T**a**nte
5. [u:] g**u**t, Br**u**der, K**u**li, Min**u**te, d**u**
6. [u] St**u**nde, J**u**nge, M**u**tter, Fl**u**ss, schm**u**tzig, k**u**rz
7. Wortpaare
   a. still / Stil   c. Kamm / komm   e. Rum / Ruhm
   b. Stadt / Staat   d. Schiff / schief   f. Ratte / rate

HÖREN SIE ZU!

Guten Morgen! *(Listen to the conversation between Hugo Schmidt and Monika Müller. Then decide whether the statements below are true or false according to the dialogue. Remember that you may listen as often as you wish.)*

Zum Erkennen: die Assistentin; die Arbeit *(work)*

_____ 1. Hugo Schmidt ist Professor.
_____ 2. Monika Müller ist Professorin.
_____ 3. Monika spricht *(speaks)* Deutsch, Englisch und Spanisch.
_____ 4. Monika ist aus Spanien.
_____ 5. Monikas Mutter ist aus Deutschland.
_____ 6. Monika ist 23.
_____ 7. Der Professor braucht Monika von 2 Uhr bis 6 Uhr.
_____ 8. Monika braucht Arbeit.
_____ 9. Monika ist zwei Monate da.

LERNTIPP

Studying Grammar

Don't let the idea of grammar scare you. It is a shortcut to learning, providing you with the patterns native speakers follow when they use the language. The fact that German and English are closely related will be very helpful. However, you must make sure to note the instances when German patterns differ from English. As a bonus, your study of German will make you more aware of the fine points of English grammar.

Hamburg und die Alster

STRUKTUR

I. Present tense of regular verbs

1. You are already familiar with some of the PERSONAL PRONOUNS; there are four others: **du, er, sie,** and **ihr.**

	singular	plural	singular / plural
1st person	ich *(I)*	wir *(we)*	
2nd person	du *(you, fam.)* informal	ihr *(you, fam.)*	Sie *(you, formal)*
3rd person	er / es / sie *(he, it, she)*	sie *(they)*	

   - **du** and **ihr** are intimate forms of address used with family members, close friends, fellow students, children up to the age of fourteen, and animals.
   - **Sie,** which is always capitalized when it means *you,* is used with strangers, acquaintances, and people addressed with a title, e.g., **Herr** and **Frau.** It is used to address one or more persons. **Sie** *(you)* and **sie** *(they,* not capitalized) can be distinguished in conversation only through context.

     Herr Schmidt, wo wohnen **Sie**? Und Ihre Eltern, wo wohnen **sie**?

     Mr. Schmidt, where do you live? And your parents, where do they live?

   - The subject pronouns **sie** *(she, it)* and **sie** *(they)* can be distinguished through the personal endings of the verb.

     Sie komm**t** im Mai, und **sie** komm**en** im Juni.

     She comes in May, and they come in June.

2. The infinitive is the form of the verb that has no subject and takes no personal ending (e.g., *to learn*). Almost every German infinitive ends in **-en: lernen, antworten.** The stem of the verb is the part that precedes the infinitive ending **-en.** Thus the stem of **lernen** is **lern-,** and that of **antworten** is **antwort-.**

   English verbs have at most one personal ending in the present tense, *-s: I (you, we, they) learn,* BUT *he (it, she) learns.* In German, endings are added to the verb stem for all persons.

   > stem + personal ending = present tense verb form

   German verb endings vary, depending on whether the subject is in the FIRST, SECOND, or THIRD PERSON, and in the SINGULAR or PLURAL. The verb must agree with the subject. You have already learned the endings used for some persons. Here is the complete list of endings:

	singular	plural	formal (sg. / pl.)
1st person	ich lerne	wir lernen	
2nd person	du lernst	ihr lernt	Sie lernen
3rd person	er / es / sie lernt	sie lernen	

   NOTE: The verb forms for formal *you* (**Sie**) and plural *they* (**sie**) are identical. The same holds true for **er / es / sie.** For that reason **Sie** and **es / sie** will not be listed in charts in future chapters.

The following verbs, which you already know from the *Schritte* and from this chapter, follow the model of **lernen.** Be sure to review them:

beginnen	*to begin*	sagen	*to say, tell*
brauchen	*to need*	schreiben	*to write*
fragen	*to ask*	spielen	*to play*
gehen	*to go*	verstehen	*to understand*
hören	*to hear*	wiederholen	*to repeat, review*
kommen	*to come*	wohnen	*to live, reside*
liegen	*to lie, be located*	zählen	*to count*

NOTE: The bar on the left of vocabulary signals that a list is important. Any new words are **boldfaced;** learn them before you do the exercises that follow!

3. When a verb stem ends in **-d** or **-t** (**antwort-, find-**), or in certain consonant combinations (**öffn-, regn-**), an **-e** is inserted between the stem and the **-st** and **-t** endings to make these endings clearly audible.

	singular	**plural**	**formal (sg. / pl.)**
1st person	ich antwort**e**	wir antwort**en**	
2nd person	du antwort**est**	ihr antwort**et**	Sie antwort**en**
3rd person	er / es / sie antwort**et**	sie antwort**en**	

These familiar verbs follow the model of **antworten:**

| finden | *to find* | öffnen | *to open* |
| kosten | *to cost* | regnen | *to rain* |

4. The **du**-form of verbs with a stem ending in any **s**-sound (**-s, -ss, -ß, -tz, -z**) adds only a **-t** instead of **-st: ich heiße, du heißt.** Thus, the **du**-form is identical with the **er**-form of these verbs: **du heißt, er heißt.**

5. German has only one verb form to express what can be said in English in several ways.

Ich wohne in Köln.
I live in Cologne.
I'm living in Cologne.
I do live in Cologne.

Wo wohnst du?
Where are you living?
Where do you live?

6. Even more than in English, in German the present tense is very frequently used to express future time, particularly when a time expression clearly indicates the future.

In dreißig Minuten **gehe** ich in die Stadt. *I'm going downtown in thirty minutes.*
Er **kommt** im Sommer. *He'll come in the summer.*

Übungen

A. ***Du, ihr* oder *Sie*?** *(How would you generally address these people—in the singular familiar, the plural familiar, or in a formal fashion?)*

BEISPIEL: your brother
(I would address him with) **du**

1. your father 2. members of your family 3. your German professor 4. a store clerk 5. two police officers 6. your roommate 7. friends of your three-year-old niece 8. your classmates 9. a group of strangers who are older than you

B. **Ersetzen Sie das Subjekt!** *(Replace the subject by using the words in parentheses.)*

BEISPIEL: Ich sage das noch einmal. (wir, Maria)
Wir sagen das noch einmal.
Maria sagt das noch einmal.

1. Wir antworten auf Deutsch. (Roberto, du, ich, die Mutter)
2. Ich wiederhole die Frage. (er, wir, ihr, Sie)
3. Ihr lernt die Wörter. (ich, du, die Kinder, wir)
4. Du öffnest das Buch auf Seite 3. (der Franzose, ich, ihr, sie / *sg.*)
5. Heidi Bauer geht an die Tafel. (ihr, sie / *pl.*, ich, du)
6. Brauchst du Papier und Bleistifte? (wir, ich, Sie, ihr)
7. Wie finden Sie das? (ihr, du, Ihre Familie, die Leute)

C. **Kombinieren Sie!** *(Create sentences by combining items from each column.)*

BEISPIEL: Er kommt aus Kanada.

1	2	3
ich	beginnen	auf Deutsch
du	brauchen	auf Englisch
er	hören	aus . . .
es	kommen	(das) nicht
sie	kosten	Deutsch
das	lernen	heute
die Deutschvorlesung	regnen	in . . .
das Mädchen *girl*	schreiben	jetzt
wir	spielen	morgen
ihr	wohnen	(nicht) gut
Sie	zählen	Tennis
sie		um . . . Uhr
		vier Mark
		von zehn bis zwanzig

D. **Was fehlt?** *(What's missing? Fill in the missing verb forms.)*

JENS Inge und Heidi, woher _____ ihr? (kommen)
HEIDI Ich _____ aus Heidelberg. (kommen)
INGE Und ich _____ aus Berlin. (sein)
JENS Wirklich? Meine Großmutter _____ auch aus Berlin. (kommen) Aber sie _____ jetzt in Hamburg. (wohnen) Wie _____ ihr es hier? (finden)
HEIDI Wir _____ es hier prima. (finden)
INGE Ich _____ die Berge wunderbar. (finden)
JENS Ich auch!

E. **Auf Deutsch bitte!**

1. We're learning German. 2. I'm counting slowly. 3. Where do you *(pl. fam.)* come from? 4. They come from Canada. 5. I'm from America. 6. Do you *(sg. fam.)* answer in English? 7. No, I'll speak German. 8. She's opening the book. 9. I do need the book. 10. What does she say? 11. Do you *(sg. fam.)* understand (that)? 12. Is she repeating that? 13. Her name is Sabrina. 14. They do live in Wittenberg.

II. Nominative case

To show the function of nouns or pronouns in a sentence, German uses a system called CASE. There are four cases in German: nominative, accusative, dative, and genitive. The NOMINATIVE CASE is the case of the subject and of the predicate noun. (The latter is discussed in Section III. 2, p. 45).

In the English sentence *The boy asks the father*, the SUBJECT of the sentence is *the boy*; he does the asking. We know that *the boy* is the subject of the sentence because in English the subject precedes the verb. This is not always true in German, where the function of a word or phrase frequently depends on its form rather than on its position. In the sentence **Der Junge fragt den Vater,** the phrase **der Junge** indicates the subject, whereas **den Vater** represents a direct object (more about this in Chapter 2). In dictionaries and vocabulary lists, nouns are given in the nominative. The nominative answers the questions *who?* for persons or *what?* for objects and ideas.

Der Junge fragt den Vater.　　*The boy asks the father.*
Der See ist schön.　　*The lake is beautiful.*

1. The forms of the INTERROGATIVE PRONOUNS are **wer?** *(who?)* and **was?** *(what?)*.

	persons	things and ideas
nom.	wer?	was?

Wer fragt den Vater? → **Der Junge.**
Who is asking the father? → *The boy.*
Was ist schön? → **Der See.**
What is beautiful? → *The lake.*

2. The nominative forms of the DEFINITE ARTICLE **der** *(the)* are already familiar. Note that the INDEFINITE ARTICLE **ein** *(a, an)* is the same for masculine and neuter nouns; it has no ending. It also has no plural: *I have a pencil,* BUT *I have pencils.*

	SINGULAR			PLURAL	
	masc.	neut.	fem.		
nom.	der	das	die	die	the
	ein	ein	eine	—	a, an
	kein	kein	keine	keine	no, not a, not any

The POSSESSIVE ADJECTIVES **mein** *(my)*, **dein** *(your)*, and **Ihr** *(your, formal)* follow the pattern of **ein** and **kein.**

Die Frau, der Junge und das Mädchen sind aus Österreich.
Mein Onkel und **meine** Tante wohnen auch da. Wo wohnen **deine** Eltern?

3. Nouns can be replaced by PERSONAL PRONOUNS. In English we replace persons with *he, she,* or *they,* and objects and ideas with *it* or *they.* In German the pronoun used depends on the gender of the noun.

Wer ist **der Mann**?　　**Er** heißt Max.　　*He's called Max.*
Wie heißt **das Kind**?　　**Es** heißt Susi.　　*She's called Susi.*
Wer ist **die Frau**?　　**Sie** heißt Ute.　　*She's called Ute.*

Wie ist **der See**?	**Er** ist groß.	*It's big.*
Wie ist **das Land**?	**Es** ist klein.	*It's small.*
Wie heißt **die Stadt**?	**Sie** heißt Ulm.	*It's called Ulm.*

- Note that German uses three pronouns (**er, es, sie**) for objects where English uses only one *(it)*.
- Note also how similar these pronouns are to the forms of the articles:

  der → er *(he, it);* das → es *(it, he, she);* die → sie *(she, it)*

- In the plural there are no gender distinctions, as the definite article for all plural nouns is **die**. The pronoun for all plural nouns is **sie**.

  die Männer
  die Kinder } **sie** *(they)*
  die Frauen

  die Seen
  die Länder } **sie** *(they)*
  die Städte

Übungen

F. Ersetzen Sie die Wörter mit Pronomen! *(Replace the nouns with pronouns.)*

  BEISPIEL: Fritz   **er**
             die Landkarte   **sie**

der Vater, der Berg, das Land, die Großmutter, der Junge, die Stadt, der Bleistift, der Pulli, Österreich, der Österreicher, die Schweiz, die Schweizerin, Deutschland, das Kind, die Geschwister, die Töchter, die Söhne

G. Die Geographiestunde

1. **Was ist das?** *(As the instructor of a geography course, describe some features of Europe to your class. Use the appropriate form of **ein**.)*

   BEISPIEL: Frankfurt / Stadt
              Frankfurt ist eine Stadt.

   Österreich / Land; die Donau / Fluss; Italienisch / Sprache; Berlin / Stadt; der Main / Fluss; das Matterhorn / Berg; Französisch / Sprache; Kanada / Land; der Bodensee *(Lake Constance)* / See; Bremen / Stadt

2. **Ist das richtig?** *(Now test your students to see what they do and don't know about Europe. Use the appropriate form of **kein**.)*

   BEISPIEL: die Donau / Land?
              Ist die Donau ein Land?
              Nein, die Donau ist kein Land. Die Donau ist ein Fluss.

   Frankfurt / Fluss; Frankreich / Sprache; Heidelberg / Berg; der Rhein / Stadt; die Schweiz / See; Spanien / Sprache; Bonn / Land

3. **Ethnisches Mosaik** *(Working in pairs, find out the ethnic background of a classmate. Use the appropriate form of **mein** and **dein**.)*

   BEISPIEL: Woher kommt dein Vater?
              Mein Vater kommt aus Salzburg.

   Woher kommt dein Vater oder dein Stiefvater *(stepfather)*? deine Mutter oder deine Stiefmutter? dein Großvater? deine Großmutter? dein Urgroßvater *(great-grandfather)*? deine Urgroßmutter?

H. Ersetzen Sie das Subjekt!

1. **Antworten Sie mit JA!** *(A curious neighbor asks you questions about the new family in the neighborhood. Answer positively, using pronouns.)*

    BEISPIEL: Die Eltern kommen aus Italien, nicht wahr?
    Ja, sie kommen aus Italien.

    a. Der Sohn antwortet auf Italienisch, nicht wahr? b. Die Tochter versteht Deutsch, nicht wahr? c. Das Kind ist fünf Jahre alt, nicht wahr? d. Die Großmutter heißt Maria, nicht wahr? e. Der Großvater wohnt auch da, nicht wahr? f. Die Familie kommt aus Rom, nicht wahr?

2. **Antworten Sie bitte!** *(Ask another student the following questions. He or she answers, using pronouns. Then change roles.)*

    BEISPIEL: Wann beginnt dein Tag?
    Er beginnt morgens um sechs.

    a. Wann beginnt die Deutschvorlesung? b. Wie heißt das Deutschbuch? c. Ist dein Kuli schwarz? d. Welche Farbe hat dein Heft? e. Welche Farbe hat deine Jacke? f. Wo ist das Fenster? g. Wie ist das Fenster? h. Wie viele Monate hat das Jahr? i. Wie viele Tage hat die Woche? j. Wie viele Stunden hat der Tag?

III. Sentence structure

1. In English the subject usually precedes the verb, and more than one element may do so.

                  1   2
    *They **are learning** German at the Goethe Institute.*
    *At the Goethe Insitute they **are learning** German.*

    As you know, in German statements and information questions the verb is always the second sentence element.

         1   2
    Sie **lernen** Deutsch am Goethe-Institut.

    In contrast to English, however, only one sentence element may precede the verb, and this element is not necessarily the subject. If an element other than the subject precedes the verb, *the verb stays* in the second position and *the subject follows* the verb. This pattern is called INVERTED WORD ORDER.

           2   1
    Deutsch **lernen** sie am Goethe-Institut.
    Am Goethe-Institut **lernen** sie Deutsch.

2. The verbs **sein** *(to be)* and **heißen** *(to be called)* are LINKING VERBS. They normally link two words referring to the same person or thing, both of which are in the nominative: the first is the subject, the other a PREDICATE NOUN.

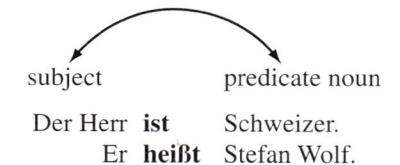

        subject   predicate noun

    Der Herr **ist**   Schweizer.
         Er **heißt** Stefan Wolf.

    The verb **sein** can be complemented not only by a predicate noun, but also by a PREDICATE ADJECTIVE. Both are considered part of the verb phrase. This is an example of a typical and important feature of German sentence structure: when the verb consists of more than one part, the inflected part (V1)—that is, the part of the verb that takes a personal ending—is the second element in the sentence, as always. However, the uninflected part (V2) stands at the very end of the sentence as a verb complement.

Stefan Wolf **ist** auch **Schweizer.**
Er **ist** heute **sehr müde.**
V1 V2

REMEMBER: In German no indefinite article is used before nationalities: **Er ist Schweizer** (*an inhabitant of Switzerland*).

Übungen

I. Sagen Sie es anders! (*Say it differently. Begin each sentence with the word or phrase in boldface.*)

BEISPIEL: Mein Vetter kommt **morgen.**
   Morgen kommt mein Vetter.

1. Ich bin **jetzt** am Goethe-Institut.
2. Die Leute sprechen **hier** nur Deutsch.
3. Wir haben **in zehn Minuten** eine Prüfung in Geographie.
4. Du findest die Landkarte **auf Seite 162.**
5. Die Donau ist **im Süden.**
6. Düsseldorf liegt **nördlich von Bonn.**
7. Es geht **mir** gut.
8. Wir spielen **um halb drei** Tennis.
9. Es regnet oft **im April.**
10. Die Sonne scheint **heute** wieder.

J. Welche Nationalität? (*Professor Händel of the Goethe Institute is determining the nationality of his summer-school students. Follow the model.*)

BEISPIEL: Pierre kommt aus Frankreich.
   Er ist Franzose.

1. Roberto kommt aus Italien.
2. Sam kommt aus Amerika.
3. Carla kommt aus Spanien.
4. James kommt aus England.
5. Maria und Caroline kommen aus Amerika.
6. Monique und Simone kommen aus Frankreich.
7. John und Donna kommen aus Kanada.

IV. Compound nouns

In German, two or three simple words are frequently combined to create a new one, like **Fingerhut** (a "hat" that protects your finger = *thimble*), **Menschenfreund** (a friend of human beings = *philanthropist*), or **Stinktier** (an animal that stinks = *skunk*). The last component determines the gender and the plural form.

das Land + die Karte = die Landkarte, -n
der Arm + das Band + die Uhr = die Armbanduhr, -en
schreiben + der Tisch = der Schreibtisch, -e
klein + die Stadt = die Kleinstadt, ⸚e

Übung

K. Was bedeuten die Wörter und was sind die Artikel? *(Determine the meaning and gender of the following words.)*

BEISPIEL: Schokoladentafel
die Schokoladentafel; *chocolate bar*

Wochentag, Neujahr, Sommerbluse, Frühlingswetter, Altstadt, Bergsee, Wörterbuch, Sprechübung, Familienvater, Jungenname, Zimmertür, Hosenrock, Hemdbluse, Hausschuh, Handschuh, Deutschstunde, Wanduhr, Uhrzeit

Frankfurt am Main FOKUS

Located on the Main River, Frankfurt is Germany's principal transportation hub. The city boasts the country's largest train station and an airport that handles more passengers than many others in Europe. Nicknamed "Mainhattan" because of its modern skyline, Frankfurt is one of Europe's leading financial centers. Some 430 banks are located there, as is the seat of the European Central Bank, whose precursor, the European Monetary Institute, was established there in 1994.

Thanks to its central location, Frankfurt has been hosting one of Germany's most important trade fairs **(Frankfurter Messe)** since the Middle Ages. Since Roman times, the city has been valued for its strategic position; and beginning in 1356, the emperors of the Holy Roman Empire were crowned there. The poet Johann Wolfgang von Goethe (1749–1832), for whom the city's university is named, was born in Frankfurt, and the first German national assembly met there in St. Paul's Church in 1848.

Zusammenfassung

> The sentences in exercise L include the material introduced in this chapter and in the *Schritte*. Watch carefully for differences between English and German patterns.

L. Sprachstudenten. Auf Deutsch bitte!

1. Tomorrow my parents are coming. 2. My father is (a) French(man), and my mother is (an) Austrian. 3. In France they speak French, and in Austria they speak German. 4. France is west of Germany, and Austria is south of Germany. 5. I do understand French and German, but I answer in English. 6. Where are you *(fam.)* from? 7. I'm from Texas. 8. There's Thomas. Thomas is (an) American. 9. He's learning Spanish. 10. I think it's beautiful here, but I am very tired.

M. Hoppla, hier fehlt 'was! *(Oops, something is missing here.)*

> This is the first of many activities in which you will try to find missing information with the help of a partner. Each of you has a chart—one appears below, the other in Section 11 of the Appendix. Each chart has information the other person needs. Do not look at your partner's chart! Instead, ask each other questions in order to complete both charts.

Wer sind sie? *(Take turns asking each other for the missing names, nationalities, places of residence, and ages of the persons listed. Follow the example.)*

S1:

Name	Nationalität	Wohnort	Alter
	Schweitzer	Bern	
	Deutsche		21
Pia		Graz	
Nicole			26
	Franzose	Dijon	52
Mario	Italiener	Rimini	
	Spanierin		17
Tom		Halifax	
	Amerikanerin		49

BEISPIEL: S1 Wer ist Schweizer?
S2 Toni ist Schweizer? Und woher kommt Toni?
S1 Toni kommt aus Bern.

LERNTIPP   Reading German Texts

First, read for general content, without worrying about unfamiliar words and phrases. Then reread carefully and always finish a paragraph, or at least a sentence, before looking up an unfamiliar word or phrase. Look up as little as possible; it is often possible to determine meaning from context. Underline and pronounce the words in question, but do not scribble the English translation into the text. It will only distract you from the German. Finally, read the text a third time, after having guessed or looked up all the underlined words. See how many of them you remember. Try to learn them now, at least passively, so as to avoid looking them up repeatedly. If a word or phrase still remains unclear, circle it and ask your instructor instead of spending more time on it.

EINBLICKE

German in Europe

Thanks to geography, history, and economics, German is one of the principal languages of Europe. Some 92 million Europeans are native speakers, and millions more speak German as a second language. In many schools in western and northern Europe—in Scandinavia and France in particular—German is a required foreign language. In Greece, Spain, and Turkey, German is widely spoken, mainly because of southern European "guest workers" **(Gastarbeiter)** who brought German back to their countries, as well as the millions of German tourists who flock to the Mediterranean every year.

Farther east, German has a long tradition. The Austro-Hungarian Empire, in which German was the official language, encompassed large areas of central and eastern Europe. Today, after decades of Russian domination, young people in Poland, the Czech Republic, Slovakia, and Hungary are rediscovering old links to German culture. Of course, the opportunities offered by the powerful economies of neighboring Austria and Germany are an added incentive. In Russia alone, 1.6 million students are learning German, and in the other countries of the former Soviet Union German is taught widely.

At the beginning of the century, German—not English—was the primary language of science, philosophy, and psychology. Although the German language has since seen growing competition from English, it will remain one of the most widely understood languages in Europe.

The reading texts expand on the chapter topic. All vocabulary that is to become active is listed under *Wortschatz 2*. Learn these words well; they will recur in future exercises and activities. Following *Wortschatz 2,* a two-part pre-reading section *(Vorm Lesen)* introduces each reading selection. The first part consists of an activity composed of all sorts of general and personal questions; the second part—*Was ist das?*—is a short set of cognates and compounds from the reading that you should be able to pronounce and recognize but do not have to master actively.

WORTSCHATZ 2

der Mensch, -en	human being, person; pl. people
Nachbar, -n / die Nachbarin, -nen	neighbor
Teil, -e	part
arbeiten	to work
so . . . wie . . .	as . . . as . . .
ungefähr	about, approximately
wichtig	important

Vorm Lesen *(Pre-reading section)*

A. Die Europakarte *(Look at the map of Europe on the inside cover of the book. Then work out the answers to the questions below.)*
1. Wie viele Nachbarn hat Deutschland? Wie heißen sie?
2. Wo liegt Dänemark? Belgien? Spanien? Frankreich? Italien? Schweden? . . .
3. Wie heißt die Hauptstadt von Deutschland? Dänemark? Belgien? Frankreich? Spanien? Italien? Finnland? Norwegen? Schweden? England? Polen?
4. Welche Sprache sprechen die Leute wo? *(See the list in exercise B.)*
5. Raten Sie *(guess):* Wo sprechen Leute Deutsch als Muttersprache? *(You'll find the answers in the reading passage.)*

_____ Deutschland	_____ Belgien	_____ Polen
_____ Bosnien	_____ Luxemburg	_____ Ungarn
_____ Österreich	_____ Liechtenstein	_____ Dänemark
_____ die Schweiz	_____ Litauen *(Lithuania)*	_____ Holland

B. Was ist das? *(As your instructor pronounces the following words, guess their meaning in English.)*

der Bankier, Europäer, Großteil, Tourismus; (das) Europa, Sprachenlernen; die Millionen, Muttersprache, Politik; die USA *(pl.)*; Belgisch, Dänisch, Finnisch, Griechisch, Holländisch, Luxemburgisch, Norwegisch, Polnisch, Portugiesisch, Schwedisch, Tschechisch, Ungarisch; studieren; europäisch, interessant, lange

Deutschland und die Nachbarn

Europa hat viele Länder und viele Sprachen. In Deutschland hören Sie natürlich° Deutsch. Aber die Nachbarn im Norden sprechen Dänisch, Schwedisch, Norwegisch und Finnisch. Die Nachbarn im Osten sprechen Polnisch und Tschechisch und im Westen sprechen sie Holländisch und Französisch. Im Süden von Europa sprechen die Menschen Italienisch, Spanisch, Portugiesisch und Griechisch; und das sind noch lange nicht° alle Sprachen!

    Deutsch ist sehr wichtig. Ungefähr 92 Millionen Europäer sprechen Deutsch als° Muttersprache: die Deutschen, Österreicher, Liechtensteiner, ein Großteil der° Schweizer und ein Teil der Luxemburger und Belgier. Viele Ausländer° arbeiten oder studieren in Deutschland, Österreich und in der° Schweiz und lernen so° auch Deutsch. Sehr viele Menschen in Europa sprechen zwei oder drei Sprachen. Sie finden das interessant und auch wichtig für Tourismus, Handel° und Politik. In Westeuropa wohnen ungefähr 350 Millionen Menschen; das sind mehr Menschen als° in den° USA und in Kanada zusammen. Die meisten° Länder sind ein Teil der° Europäischen Union (EU). Viele Europäer wohnen und arbeiten im Ausland°. Ein Beispiel ist Familie Breughel. Marcel Breughel erzählt°: „Ich bin aus Brüssel und meine Frau Nicole ist Französin. Wir sind Bankiers. Wir wohnen schon zwei Jahre in Frankfurt. Wir finden es hier sehr schön. Wir haben zwei Kinder, Maude und Dominique. Sie sprechen zu Hause° Französisch, aber in der Schule° sprechen sie Deutsch. Das finde ich toll. Das Sprachenlernen ist heute so wichtig wie nie zuvor°."

Margin glosses: of course; by far not; as; of the; foreigners; in / this way; trade; more than / in the / most of the / of the / abroad; tells; at home; in school; as never before

Zum Text

A. Richtig oder falsch?

_____ 1. In Europa hören Sie viele Sprachen.
_____ 2. Alle Europäer sprechen Schwedisch.
_____ 3. Ungefähr 920 000 Europäer sprechen Deutsch.
_____ 4. Die Liechtensteiner sprechen Deutsch als Muttersprache.
_____ 5. In Westeuropa wohnen so viele Menschen wie in Kanada und in den USA zusammen.
_____ 6. Alle Länder in Europa sind ein Teil der EU.
_____ 7. In Deutschland wohnen keine Ausländer.
_____ 8. Herr und Frau Breughel sind Bankiers.
_____ 9. Herr Breughel ist Franzose.
_____ 10. Familie Breughel wohnt schon fünf Jahre in Frankfurt.
_____ 11. Sie finden es da sehr schön.
_____ 12. Die Eltern und die Kinder sprechen zu Hause Deutsch.

B. Interview *(Imagine yourself to be Mr. or Mrs. Breughel. Respond to the reporter's questions.)*

1. Guten Tag! Woher kommen Sie? 2. Warum sind Sie hier in Frankfurt? 3. Wie heißt Ihre Frau / Ihr Mann? 4. Haben Sie Kinder? 5. Sind die Kinder auch hier? 6. Was sprechen Sie zu Hause, Deutsch oder Französisch? 7. Sprechen die Kinder noch andere *(other)* Sprachen? 8. Wie finden Sie es hier in Frankfurt?

C. Die Deutschlandkarte *(Look at the map of Germany on the inside cover of the book. Then answer the questions below.)*
1. Welche Flüsse, Seen und Berge gibt es in Deutschland?
2. Wo liegt die Nordsee? die Ostsee? die Insel *(island)* Rügen? die Insel Helgoland? Wo liegen die Ostfriesischen Inseln?
3. Wo liegt . . . ? *(Ask each other about the location of various towns in Germany.)*

German Throughout the World

Even though Germany was never an important colonial power, German language and culture have reached all regions of the globe. Looking for new opportunities, millions of Germans emigrated to the Americas, especially to the United States, Canada, Chile, Argentina, and Brazil. Nearly a fourth of the U.S. population claims German ancestry, and some 300 German-language periodicals are still published there.

In Asia, German language, literature, and philosophy continue to be popular subjects at universities; thousands of exchange scholars and students from the Far East have studied in Germany. When Japan opened up to the West in the late 1800s, it borrowed heavily from German law and science. At the turn of the century, the Chinese city of Qindao was under German administration and consequently has many German buildings—and the best beer in China.

Although Germany only briefly controlled a handful of African colonies—Togo, Cameroon, and Namibia (formerly South West Africa)—the impact of those years as well as the influence of German missionaries and doctors can still be found in some regions. German is taught at all levels throughout Africa. Worldwide, 20 million people are learning German as a second language.

D. **Wo sprechen die Leute auch Deutsch?** *(Use the information from the preceding* Fokus *section and from the pre-reading passage "German in Europe" to complete the statements about where German is spoken throughout the world.)*

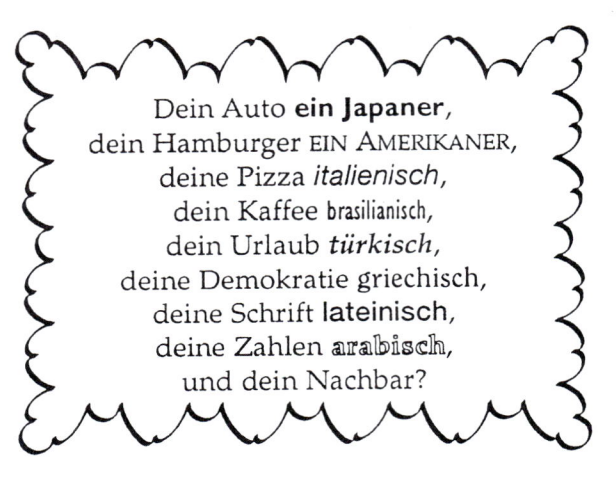

1. Ungefähr 92 Millionen _____ sprechen Deutsch als *(as)* Muttersprache.
   a. Deutsche b. Holländer c. Europäer
2. Auch in Griechenland, in _____ und in der Türkei verstehen sehr viele Menschen Deutsch.
   a. Spanien b. Sizilien c. Andorra
3. Deutsch hat auch eine Tradition in Polen und _____ .
   a. Portugal b. Irland c. Ungarn
4. In Russland allein *(alone)* _____ 1,6 Millionen Deutsch.
   a. brauchen b. lernen c. wiederholen
5. Viele Amerikaner, _____ , Chilenen, Argentinier und Brasilianer kommen ursprünglich *(originally)* aus Deutschland.
   a. Kanadier b. Schweizer c. Liechtensteiner

Dein Auto **ein Japaner**,
dein Hamburger EIN AMERIKANER,
deine Pizza *italienisch*,
dein Kaffee brasilianisch,
dein Urlaub *türkisch*,
deine Demokratie griechisch,
deine Schrift lateinisch,
deine Zahlen arabisch,
und dein Nachbar?

Deutschland

DIE ZEITSCHRIFT IN 15 SPRACHEN
• DEUTSCH
• ENGLISCH
• FRANZÖSISCH
• PORTUGIESISCH
• SPANISCH
• POLNISCH
• RUMÄNISCH
• UNGARISCH
• RUSSISCH
• UKRAINISCH
• TÜRKISCH
• IWRITH
• ARABISCH
• CHINESISCH
• JAPANISCH

AUSSERDEM IM INTERNET:
http://www.government.de
INTERNET-SERVICE IN:
• ENGLISCH
• FRANZÖSISCH
• SPANISCH

HÖREN SIE ZU!

Europäer in Deutschland *(Many foreign nationals have chosen to live in Germany. Listen to the four speakers, and then circle the letter of the response that correctly completes the statement.)*

Zum Erkennen: zuerst *(first of all)*; komisch *(strange)*

VITTORIO
1. Vittorio ist _____ .
   a. 20 b. 29 c. 21
2. Seine Eltern sind aus _____ .
   a. Portugal b. Italien c. Spanien

MANUEL
3. Manuel ist aus _____ .
   a. Spanien b. Portugal c. Italien
4. Er wohnt schon _____ Jahre in Deutschland.
   a. 34 b. 33 c. 23

MARIA
5. Maria wohnt in _____ .
   a. Frankfurt b. Dresden c. Düsseldorf
6. Sie und ihre Familie sind _____ .
   a. Griechen b. Italiener c. Türken

JOSÉ
7. José ist Professor in _____ .
   a. Frankfurt b. Bonn c. Düsseldorf
8. Seine Frau ist aus _____ .
   a. Berlin b. Erfurt c. Köln

WEB-ECKE For updates and online activities related to this chapter, visit the *Wie geht's?* homepage of Holt, Rinehart and Winston at http://www.hrwcollege.com/german/sevin/! You'll meet some real German families, visit a few German cities, check their current situation, and learn about some of Germany's neighbors and partners in the European Union.

SPRECHSITUATIONEN

Making small talk

When you meet someone for the first time, it is useful to be able to make small talk. The weather is a typical point of departure.

> Heute ist es heiß!
> Es ist wirklich schön heute, nicht wahr?
> Furchtbares Wetter heute, nicht wahr?
> Jetzt regnet es schon wieder!
> So ein Sauwetter! *(very casual)*

Asking for personal information

You have already learned many words that make it possible for you to ask questions, e.g., **was? wo? woher? wer? wann? wie? wie viel? wie viele?** Here is a list of expressions you can use to elicit personal information.

> Ich bin aus . . . Woher sind Sie / bist du?   Wo wohnt Ihre / deine Familie?
> Ach, Sie sind / du bist (auch) aus . . . !   Wie finden Sie / findest du es hier / da?
> Sind Sie / bist du auch Student(in) . . . ?   Wie alt sind Sie / bist du?
> Was studieren Sie / studierst du?   Haben Sie / hast du Geschwister?
> Wo wohnen Sie / wohnst du?

The confirmation tag **nicht wahr?**—abbreviated to **nicht?** in informal speech—is used to get someone to agree with the speaker.

> Sie lernen auch Deutsch, nicht wahr?—Ja, natürlich.
> Sie sind auch Amerikanerin, nicht?—Ja!

Kurzgespräche

> The *Kurzgespräche* sections are intended to give you an opportunity to practice conversational German. The situations presented in the book will give you a start, but you are free to elaborate on or embellish the basic structure in any way you see fit. Make use of your sense of humor, too. Take turns with your partner(s) in playing the roles suggested until you are quite fluent.

1. As you wait for a class to start, you begin a conversation with the student next to you by commenting on the weather. Then you introduce yourself, and ask what the other student is studying. You learn that he / she is also taking German. Respond appropriately.
2. You have been asked to prepare a brief background report on one of your classmates for a radio broadcast. Find a classmate you don't know well, and ask where the person comes from, what he or she is studying, etc. Inquire about his or her family as well. Prepare and present your report.

KAPITEL 2
LEBENSMITTEL UND GESCHÄFTE

Einkaufszentrum in Düsseldorf

LERNZIELE

■ VORSCHAU
Shopping and store hours

■ GESPRÄCHE AND WORTSCHATZ
Food and shopping

■ STRUKTUR
Present tense of **sein** and **haben**
Accusative case and n-nouns
Sentence structure: verb complements, negation, and coordinating conjunctions

■ EINBLICKE
Pedestrian areas
Stores and shopping

■ FOKUS
Weights and measures
Breads, sausages, and cheeses
Regensburg
Flower power

■ WEB-ECKE

■ SPRECHSITUATIONEN
Making a purchase

VORSCHAU

Shopping and Store Hours

As much as the development of American-style supermarkets and discount chains has changed the way Europeans shop, customs still differ considerably from those in North America. Many people shop daily or several times a week, frequently going on foot or by bicycle rather than by car. With competition from supermarket chains, the traditional corner grocery store **(Tante-Emma-Laden)** is disappearing rapidly. Specialty stores such as butcher shops and bakeries continue to thrive, however, and many towns have retained open-air farmers' markets. Consumers value the freshness of the products and the personal atmosphere.

Customers usually bring their own shopping bags **(Einkaufstaschen)** to stores and shops or buy reusable cloth bags or plastic bags **(Plastiktüten)** at the check-out counter. They also bag their purchases themselves. Grocery store clerks sit rather than stand when checking out customers. People generally pay in cash **(Bargeld).** Checks and credit cards are rarely accepted, although some supermarkets have introduced ATM links to their cash registers. The amount shown on the price tag always includes tax.

Recycling laws require stores to take back all packaging materials; completely recyclable products are marked with a green dot.

Until 1996, store hours in Germany were regulated by a rigid shop closing law that permitted shopping only during regular business hours and a few hours on Saturday. Despite stiff opposition from small shopkeepers and trade unions, the law was finally liberalized. Stores can now be open from 6:00 A.M. to 8:00 P.M., Monday through Friday, and until 4:00 P.M. on Saturday. There are no 24-hour supermarkets in Germany. The only place to shop after hours—and all day Sunday—is at gas stations. Airports and almost all train stations also have shops that are exempt from the normal store hours.

Es gibt immer weniger *(less and less)* Tante-Emma-Läden.

GESPRÄCHE

Im Lebensmittelgeschäft

VERKÄUFER	Guten Tag! Was darf's sein?
OLIVER	Ich hätte gern etwas Obst. Haben Sie denn keine Bananen?
VERKÄUFER	Doch, da drüben.
OLIVER	Was kosten sie?
VERKÄUFER	1,80 DM[1] das Pfund.
OLIVER	Und die Orangen?
VERKÄUFER	90 Pfennig das Stück.
OLIVER	Gut, zwei Pfund Bananen und sechs Orangen bitte!
VERKÄUFER	Sonst noch etwas?
OLIVER	Ja, zwei Kilo Äpfel bitte!
VERKÄUFER	16,20 DM bitte! Danke! Auf Wiedersehen!

In der Bäckerei

VERKÄUFERIN	Guten Morgen! Was darf's sein?
SIMONE	Guten Morgen! Ein Schwarzbrot und sechs Brötchen bitte!
VERKÄUFERIN	Sonst noch etwas?
SIMONE	Ja, ich brauche etwas Kuchen. Ist der Apfelstrudel frisch?
VERKÄUFERIN	Natürlich, ganz frisch.
SIMONE	Gut, dann nehme ich vier Stück.
VERKÄUFERIN	Ist das alles?
SIMONE	Ich möchte auch ein paar Plätzchen. Was für Plätzchen haben Sie heute?
VERKÄUFERIN	Zitronenplätzchen, Schokoladenplätzchen, Butterplätzchen . . .
SIMONE	Hm . . . Ich nehme 300 Gramm Schokoladenplätzchen.
VERKÄUFERIN	Noch etwas?
SIMONE	Nein, danke. Das ist alles.
VERKÄUFERIN	Das macht dann 18,90 DM bitte.

---

[1] Remember that one euro equals just under two marks. Therefore 1,80 DM are approximately € 0.90.

Fragen

1. Was braucht Oliver? 2. Was kosten die Bananen? die Orangen? 3. Wie viele Bananen und wie viele Orangen kauft er? 4. Was kauft er noch? 5. Was kostet alles zusammen? 6. Wie viele Brötchen möchte Simone? 7. Was ist frisch? 8. Wie viel Stück Apfelstrudel kauft sie? 9. Was für Plätzchen kauft sie? 10. Kauft sie sonst noch etwas?

LEBENSMITTEL UND GESCHÄFTE 57

Weights and Measures FOKUS

In Europe—as in most of the world—the metric system is used to measure distance, volume, and weight. One exception is the older measurement **Pfund,** which is half a kilogram (500 grams), or a little more than the U.S. pound (454 grams). When shopping for food at the market, you can ask for **100 Gramm Leberwurst, ein halbes Pfund Salami,** or **ein Kilo Äpfel.** Liquids are measured by the liter, which is a little more than a quart. In cooking or baking, scales are preferred over cups and spoons, as weighing is more precise: a cup of sugar weighs about 200 grams; a cup of flour 150 grams; a tablespoon **(Esslöffel)** 12 grams; a teaspoon **(Teelöffel)** 5 grams. One ounce equals 28.3 grams.

WORTSCHATZ 1

Die Lebensmittel *(pl.)* (groceries)

der Apfel, ⸚	apple	die Banane, -n	banana
Fisch, -e	fish	Bohne, -n	bean
Kaffee, -s	coffee	Butter	butter
Käse, -	cheese	Cola	cola drink
Kuchen, -	cake	Erbse, -n	pea
Saft, ⸚e	juice	Erdbeere, -n	strawberry
Salat, -e	lettuce, salad	Gurke, -n	cucumber
Tee, -s	tea	Karotte, -n	carrot
Wein, -e	wine	Limonade, -n = Limo, -s	soft drink
das Bier, -e	beer	Marmelade, -n	jam
Brot, -e	bread	Milch	milk
Brötchen, -	roll	Orange, -n	orange
Ei, -er	egg	Tomate, -n	tomato
Fleisch	meat	Wurst, ⸚e	sausage
Gemüse, -	vegetable(s)	Zitrone, -n	lemon
Joghurt, -s	yoghurt		
Obst	fruit		
Plätzchen, -	cookie		
Wasser	water		

Weiteres

der Markt, ⸚e	(farmers') market
Supermarkt, ⸚e	supermarket
Verkäufer, -	sales clerk
das Geschäft, -e	store
Kaufhaus, ⸚er	department store
Pfund, -e; ein Pfund[1]	pound; one pound (of)
Stück, -e; ein Stück[1]	piece; one piece (of)

---

[1] One says **ein Pfund Fleisch, zwei Pfund Fleisch; ein Stück Kuchen, zwei Stück Kuchen.** Remember also **eine Mark, zwei Mark.**

die Bäckerei, -en	*bakery*
Buchhandlung, -en	*bookstore*
alles	*everything, all*
Das ist alles.	*That's all. That's it.*
dann	*then (temporal)*
doch	*yes, sure, certainly, of course*
es gibt[2]	*there is, there are*
etwas . . .	*a little, some . . . (used with sg. collective nouns)*
frisch	*fresh*
gern[3]	*gladly*
Ich esse / trinke gern . . .[3]	*I like to eat / drink . . .*
Ich esse / trinke nicht gern . . .[3]	*I don't like to eat / drink . . .*
Ich hätte gern . . .[4]	*I would like (to have) . . .*
Ich möchte . . .[4]	*I would like (to have) . . .*
glauben	*to believe, think*
kaufen / verkaufen	*to buy / to sell*
machen	*to make, do*
suchen	*to look for*
natürlich	*of course*
was für (ein) . . . ?[5]	*what kind of (a) . . . ?*
zusammen	*together*

---

[2] See Struktur II.1d.

[3] To express that you like to do something, use **gern** with the main verb: **ich esse gern** Obst; er **trinkt gern** Cola. If you dislike something, use **nicht gern,** which normally precedes the direct object: **ich esse nicht gern** Erbsen; sie trinken **nicht gern** Milch.

[4] **möcht-** and **hätt-** are subjunctive verb forms that will be explained in Chapters 13–14: **ich möchte, du möchtest, er möchte, wir möchten, ihr möchtet, sie möchten; ich hätte, du hättest, er hätte, wir hätten, ihr hättet, sie hätten.**

[5] Treat this phrase as you would treat **ein** by itself: **Das ist ein Kuchen. Was für ein Kuchen? Das ist eine Wurst. Was für eine Wurst?** There's no **ein** in the plural: **Das sind Plätzchen. Was für Plätzchen?** Don't use **für** in answers to a **was für**-question: **Was für Obst essen Sie gern? Ich esse gern Bananen.**

Zum Erkennen: Was darf's sein? *(May I help you?);* da drüben *(over there);* Sonst noch etwas? *(Anything else?);* das Kilo / zwei Kilo; der Apfelstrudel

Zum Thema

A. Mustersätze

1. Bananen: **Ich esse gern** Bananen.
   Äpfel, Erdbeeren, Orangen, Gurken, Joghurt
2. Fisch: **Die Kinder essen nicht gern** Fisch.
   Salat, Tomaten, Karotten, Gemüse, Eier
3. Cola: **Wir trinken gern** Cola.
   Limo, Kaffee, Tee, Bier, Wein
4. Obst: **Ich hätte gern etwas** Obst.
   Brot, Fleisch, Marmelade, Käse, Wurst
5. Bananen: **Haben Sie keine** Bananen?
   Erdbeeren, Bohnen, Erbsen, Zitronen, Brötchen

B. Was passt nicht? *(Which item does not belong in each list?)*
1. die Butter — der Käse — die Wurst — die Bohne
2. das Brötchen — die Zitrone — das Plätzchen — der Kuchen
3. die Tomate — die Erdbeere — die Gurke — der Salat
4. das Gemüse — der Apfel — die Orange — die Banane
5. das Obst — das Gemüse — der Salat — der Tee
6. der Wein — das Bier — die Zitrone — die Milch
7. das Geschäft — die Lebensmittel — die Bäckerei — das Kaufhaus

C. Was bedeuten die Wörter und was sind die Artikel?

Bohnensalat, Buttermilch, Delikatessengeschäft, Erdbeermarmelade, Fischbrötchen, Kaffeemilch, Milchkaffee, Obstsalat, Orangenlimonade, Zitronenlimonade, Zitronensaft, Schreibwarengeschäft, Teewasser, Wurstbrot

D. Was passt?
1. Ich glaube, der Fisch ist nicht frisch.
2. Möchten Sie etwas Obst?
3. Die Bäckerei verkauft Wurst, nicht wahr?
4. Wir kaufen auch Kuchen.
5. Ich trinke morgens gern Cola.

a. Wirklich?
b. Wie bitte?
c. Ich nicht.
d. Ja, gern.
e. Ja, bitte.
f. Natürlich nicht.
g. Prima!
h. Wir auch.
i. Richtig.
j. Nein, danke.
k. Doch.
l. Nein, das ist alles.
m. Schade.

E. Und Sie? *(Interview a classmate to find out what foods he / she likes and what his / her eating habits are.)*
1. Was für Obst essen Sie (nicht) gern?
2. Was für Gemüse essen Sie (nicht) gern?
3. Was für Kuchen, Plätzchen, Salat essen Sie gern?
4. Was trinken Sie oft?
5. Was essen Sie morgens / mittags / abends?

F. Aussprache: e, o *(See also Section II. 2, 5, 14–16, 18, and 21 in the pronunciation section of the Workbook.)*
1. [e:]   g**e**hen, n**e**hmen, K**ä**se, G**e**genteil, Am**e**rika, **Tee**
2. [e]   **e**s, spr**e**chen, Gesch**ä**ft, M**e**nsch, **H**emd
3. [o:]   **oh**ne B**oh**nen, **o**der, gr**o**ß, **O**bst, **B**rot
4. [o]   k**o**mmen, d**o**ch, **O**sten, N**o**rden, **S**onne
5. Wortpaare
   a. *gate* / geht
   b. *shown* / schon
   c. zähle / Zelle
   d. den / denn
   e. Ofen / offen
   f. Bonn / Bann

FOKUS: Breads, Sausages, and Cheeses

When Germans think of **Brot,** they probably think first of a firm, heavy loaf of rye bread **(Schwarzbrot)** and not of the soft white bread so common in America. In Germany, white loaves and rolls are prized for their crisp crust. There are more than 300 varieties of bread in Central Europe, including bread made from a mixture of wheat and rye **(Graubrot)** or of cracked rye and wheat grains **(Vollkornbrot),** and bread with linseed **(Leinsamenbrot)** or sunflower seeds **(Sonnenblumenkernbrot).** For Germans, bread is the most important staple—on average they eat four slices of bread and one roll per day.

The traditional German supper, appropriately called **Abendbrot,** usually consists of bread with cheese, sausage, or cold cuts **(Aufschnitt).** Germany offers a wide variety of cheeses and sausages, which often carry the names of the place of origin: **Allgäuer** (cheese), **Frankfurter, Thüringer** (both sausages). Others are named after ingredients: **Butterkäse, Schimmelkäse, Leberwurst.** Many Germans also eat bread and cheese for breakfast.

Die Deutschen, Österreicher und Schweizer essen gern Brot.

HÖREN SIE ZU!

Essen und Trinken *(Listen to three students tell what they like and don't like to eat and drink. Then note which foods and beverages each student mentions; write H for Hanjo, M for Martina, and D for Dirk. Not all the available slots will be filled.)*

Zum Erkennen: also *(well);* und so weiter *(etc.);* manchmal *(sometimes);* Kartoffeln *(potatoes);* der Kakao *(hot chocolate)*

ESSEN	
gern	**nicht gern**
_____ Äpfel	_____ Gemüse
_____ Bananen	_____ Gurken
_____ Kartoffeln	_____ Karotten
_____ Kuchen	_____ Erbsen
_____ Erdbeeren	_____ Fisch
_____ Orangen	_____ Bananen
_____ Gemüse	_____ Joghurt
_____ Fisch	_____ Pizza
_____ Fleisch	_____ Käsebrot

TRINKEN	
gern	**nicht gern**
_____ Tee	_____ Kaffee
_____ Kaffee	_____ Bier
_____ Kakao	_____ Wein
_____ Milch	_____ Milch
_____ Saft	_____ Cola
_____ Bier	_____ Wasser
_____ Cola	_____ Tee
_____ Mineralwasser	_____ Kakao
_____ Limonade	_____ Eiswasser

STRUKTUR

I. Present tense of *sein (to be)* and *haben (to have)*

	sein		haben	
1st person	ich bin	wir sind	ich habe	wir haben
2nd person	du bist	ihr seid	du hast	ihr habt
3rd person	er ist	sie sind	er hat	sie haben

Übung

A. Ersetzen Sie das Subjekt!

    BEISPIEL: Haben Sie Zeit? (du)
                           Hast du Zeit?

1. Ich bin schon fertig. (er, wir, sie / *sg.*)
2. Sind Sie müde? (du, ihr, sie / *pl.*)
3. Sie hat die Landkarte. (ich, er, wir)
4. Haben Sie Papier? (sie / *sg.*, ihr, du)
5. Wir sind Amerikaner. (er, sie / *pl.*, ich)
6. Er hat eine Frage. (ich, wir, Sie)
7. Seid ihr aus Düsseldorf? (Sie, du, sie / *sg.*)
8. Er hat Orangensaft. (sie / *pl.*, ich, ihr)

II. Accusative case and n-nouns

The accusative case has two major functions: it is the case of the direct object, and it follows certain prepositions.

1. In the English sentence *The boy asks the father*, the DIRECT OBJECT of the sentence is *the father*. He is being asked; he is the target of the verb's action. We determine the direct object by asking *who or what* is directly affected by the verb's action. In other words, the person you see, hear, or ask, or the thing you have, buy, or eat is the direct object.

        Der Junge fragt den Vater.   *The boy asks the father.*
        Ich kaufe den Kuchen.   *I buy the cake.*

  a. The accusative forms of the INTERROGATIVE PRONOUN are **wen?** *(whom?)* and **was?** *(what?)*. You now know two cases for this pronoun.

	persons	things and ideas
nom.	wer?	was?
acc.	wen?	was?

        Wen fragt der Junge?   → **Den Vater.**
        Whom does the boy ask?   → *The father.*
        Was kaufe ich?   → **Den Kuchen.**
        What am I buying?   → *The cake.*

b. Of the articles, only those for masculine nouns have special forms for the accusative. In the other genders, the nominative and accusative are identical in form.

	SINGULAR masc.	SINGULAR neut.	SINGULAR fem.	PLURAL
nom.	der	das	die	die
	ein	ein	eine	———
	kein	kein	keine	keine
acc.	den	das	die	die
	einen	ein	eine	———
	keinen	kein	keine	keine

PETER Der Käse, das Obst, die Wurst und die Brötchen sind frisch.
PETRA Dann kaufe ich den Käse, das Obst, die Wurst und die Brötchen.
PETER Aber wir brauchen keinen Käse, kein Obst, keine Wurst und keine Brötchen!

- The POSSESSIVE ADJECTIVES **mein, dein,** and **Ihr** follow the pattern of **ein** and **kein:**

  Brauchen Sie mein**en** Bleistift?

  Nein danke, ich brauche Ihr**en** Bleistift nicht.

c. German has a few masculine nouns that have an **-n** or **-en** ending in all cases (singular and plural) except in the nominative singular. They are called N-NOUNS. Note how they are listed in vocabularies and dictionaries: the first ending refers to the singular for cases other than the nominative, the second one to the plural. You are already familiar with all of the n-nouns below.

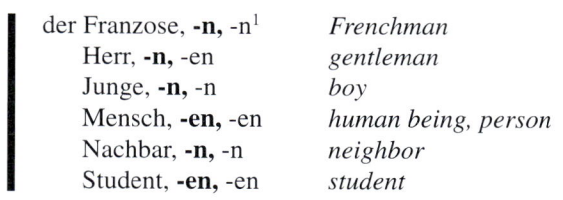

der Franzose, **-n,** -n[1]	*Frenchman*
Herr, **-n,** -en	*gentleman*
Junge, **-n,** -n	*boy*
Mensch, **-en,** -en	*human being, person*
Nachbar, **-n,** -n	*neighbor*
Student, **-en,** -en	*student*

---

[1] *REMINDER:* The bar on the left of vocabulary signals that a list is important. Any new words are **bold-faced;** learn them before you do the exercises that follow!

	singular	plural
nom.	**der Student**	**die Studenten**
acc.	**den Studenten**	**die Studenten**

Der Herr heißt Müller. Fragen Sie Herr**n** Müller!

Da kommt ein Student. Fragen Sie den Student**en**!

d. Verbs that can take accusative objects are called TRANSITIVE. (Some verbs are INTRANSITIVE, i.e., they cannot take a direct object: **gehen** *to go.*) Here are some familiar transitive verbs:

brauchen	*to need*	möcht-	*would like*
essen	*to eat*	nehmen	*to take*
finden	*to find*	öffnen	*to open*
fragen	*to ask*	sagen	*to say*
haben	*to have*	schreiben	*to write*
hören	*to hear*	sprechen	*to speak, talk*
kaufen	*to buy*	suchen	*to look for*
lernen	*to learn*	trinken	*to drink*
lesen	*to read*	verkaufen	*to sell*
machen	*to make, do*	verstehen	*to understand*
es gibt	*there is, there are*		

Sie kauft den Rock und die Bluse.

Schreiben Sie den Satz!

Ich esse einen Apfel und eine Banane.

Wir haben einen Supermarkt und ein Kaufhaus.

Das Geschäft verkauft keinen Fisch und kein Fleisch.

- The idiom **es gibt** is always followed by the accusative case in the singular or in the plural.

Es gibt hier einen Markt. *There's a market here.*

Es gibt auch Lebensmittelgeschäfte. *There are also grocery stores.*

The pronoun **es** is the subject of the sentence. What "there is," is in the accusative. **Es gibt** implies a general, unspecified existence—unlike **hier ist** or **da ist,** which points to a specific item.

Gibt es hier einen Markt? *Is there a market here (in town)?*

Ja, es gibt einen Markt. *Yes, there's a market.*

Wo ist ein Markt? *Where is a market?*

Da ist ein Markt. *There's a market. (There it is.)*

2. ACCUSATIVE PREPOSITIONS are always followed by the accusative case. Here are those used most frequently:

durch	*through*	Britta kommt **durch die Tür.**
für	*for*	Das Obst ist **für den Kuchen.**
gegen	*against*	Was hast du **gegen meinen Bruder?**
ohne	*without*	Wir essen das Brötchen **ohne den Käse.**
um	*around*	Die Kinder laufen **um den Tisch.**
	at (time)	Wir kommen **um 12 Uhr.**

- Some prepositions may be contracted with the definite article. These forms are especially common in everyday speech.

durch + das =	**durchs**
für + das =	**fürs**
um + das =	**ums**

NOTE: A sentence can contain two accusatives, one the direct object and the other the object of a preposition.

Sie kauft den Fisch für den Fischsalat.

Übungen

B. Wiederholen Sie die Sätze noch einmal mit *ein* und *kein*!

BEISPIEL: Er kauft den Bleistift, das Buch und die Landkarte.
Er kauft einen Bleistift, ein Buch und eine Landkarte.
Er kauft keinen Bleistift, kein Buch und keine Landkarte.

1. Sie möchte den Rock, das Kleid und die Bluse.
2. Du brauchst das Hemd, die Hose und den Pullover.
3. Ich esse das Brötchen, die Orange und den Apfel.
4. Wir fragen den Herrn, die Frau und das Mädchen.
5. Öffnen Sie bitte die Tür und das Fenster!
6. Kauft ihr den Kuchen, das Brot und die Brezel *(pretzel)*?

C. Einkaufen *(You're making small talk while shopping with friends. Substitute the nouns in parentheses.)*

BEISPIEL: Wir kaufen den Saft. (Salat)
Wir kaufen den Salat.

1. Möchtest du das Fleisch? (Gemüse, Obst, Schwarzbrot)
2. Die Wurst essen wir nicht. (Marmelade, Tomate, Gurke)
3. Meine Schwester trinkt keinen Saft. (Limonade, Cola, Wasser)
4. Hast du den Tee? (Saft, Milch, Käse)
5. Gibt es hier eine Buchhandlung? (Markt, Delikatessengeschäft, Kaufhäuser)
6. Fragen Sie den Herrn! (Junge, Mensch, Student, Studenten / *pl.*)
7. Den Verkäufer verstehe ich nicht! (Verkäuferin, Nachbar, Kind)
8. Haben Sie kein Joghurt? (Saft, Eier, Limo)

D. Umzug *(Moving. You are giving instructions to the movers who are bringing your belongings into your new apartment. Use the cues.)*

BEISPIEL: durch / Zimmer
Durch das Zimmer bitte!

1. gegen / Wand
2. um / Tisch
3. ohne / Bücher
4. durch / Tür
5. ohne / Tisch
6. für / Kinderzimmer *(pl.)*
7. gegen / Fenster *(sg.)*
8. um / Ecke *(f.)*

Aus der Käsetheke:
Galbani Mozzarella
italienischer Weichkäse,
45% Fett i. Tr.
100 g
1.99

Aus der Käsetheke:
Galbani Gorgonzola
50% Fett i. Tr., 100 g
1.99

E. **Sagen Sie es noch einmal!** *(Replace the noun following the preposition with another noun.)*

> BEISPIEL: Ich suche etwas für meinen Vater. (Mutter, Kind)
> **Ich suche etwas für meine Mutter.**
> **Ich suche etwas für mein Kind.**

1. Wir gehen durch die Geschäfte. (Supermarkt, Kaufhaus, Bäckerei)
2. Er kommt ohne das Bier. (Wein, Cola, Kaffee, Käsebrot, Salat)
3. Was haben Sie gegen den Herrn? (Verkäuferin, Mädchen, Junge, Nachbarin)
4. Wiederholen Sie das für Ihren Großvater! (Bruder, Schwester, Nachbar, Eltern)

F. **Kombinieren Sie!** *(You are a salesperson in a clothing store. Ask your customers what kind of items they need. Also indicate how you would address your customers if they were: [a] a friend, [b] a stranger, [c] two of your relatives.)*

> BEISPIEL: Was für einen Pullover möchten Sie?

1	2	3	4
was für (ein)	Rock	brauchen	du
	Hemd	möchten	ihr
	Jacke	suchen	Sie
	Schuhe		
	. . .		

G. **Was kaufen Sie?** *(Working with a partner, answer each question with four to six items, drawing on all the vocabulary you have had so far. Use articles whenever necessary.)*

> BEISPIEL: Sie sind im Supermarkt. Was kaufen Sie?
> **Wir kaufen einen Kuchen, eine Cola, ein Pfund Butter, ein Stück Käse, etwas Obst, etwas Joghurt . . .**

1. Sie sind in der Bäckerei. Was kaufen Sie?
2. Sie sind im Kaufhaus. Was kaufen Sie?
3. Sie sind in der Buchhandlung. Was kaufen Sie?

H. **Wie bitte?** *(Your grandfather, who is hard of hearing and forgets quickly, always wants you to repeat whatever you say. What questions does he ask?)*

> BEISPIEL: Rudi hat heute eine Prüfung.
> **Wer hat eine Prüfung?**
> **Was hat Rudi?**

1. Vater hört den Nachbarn.
2. Matthias fragt Tante Martha.
3. Die Mutter kauft Obst.
4. Die Kinder möchten einen Apfel.
5. Helga und Britta verstehen die Engländer nicht.
6. Wir lernen Deutsch.
7. Ich suche eine Landkarte.

I. **Im Kaufhaus.** Sagen Sie es auf Deutsch!

S1 Good morning! May I help you?
S2 Hi! I need a sweater for my son.
S1 The sweater here is from England. Would you like a sweater in blue **(in Blau)**?
S2 No. Don't you have any sweater in red?
S1 Of course . . . here.
S2 Fine. I think the color is very beautiful. **(Ich finde . . .)**
S1 Do you also need a shirt or (a pair of) slacks *(sg.)*?
S2 No, he doesn't need any shirt or (any) slacks. (He needs no shirt and no slacks.)

III. Sentence structure

1. Verb complements

   As you know from Chapter 1, predicate nouns and PREDICATE ADJECTIVES are verb complements (V2). Sometimes objects or another verb also become part of the verb phrase, i.e., VERB COMPLEMENTS, and in that combination they complete the meaning of the main verb (V1). Verb complements usually stand at the end of the sentence.

Sie **sprechen Deutsch.**	Wir **gehen essen.**
Sie **sprechen** gut **Deutsch.**	Wir **gehen** gern **essen.**
Sie **sprechen** wirklich gut **Deutsch.**	Wir **gehen** mittags gern **essen.**
V1 V2	V1 V2

2. Negation

   a. **Kein**

   Kein *(no, not a, not any)* is the negative of **ein** and therefore takes the same endings as **ein.** It negates nouns that in an affirmative statement or question would be preceded by **ein** or by no article at all.

   preceded by **ein:**   Hast du **einen** Bleistift?

                         Nein, ich habe **keinen** Bleistift.

                         No, I don't have a pencil.

   unpreceded: Haben Sie Geschwister?

                         Nein, ich habe **keine** Geschwister.

                         No, I don't have any brothers or sisters.

   b. **Nicht**

   Nicht *(not)* is used when **kein** cannot be used. It can negate an entire sentence, or just part of it. Its position is determined as follows:

   - When negating an entire statement, **nicht** generally stands at the end of that sentence or clause. It always follows the <u>subject and verb</u>; also, it usually follows <u>noun and pronoun objects</u> and expressions of <u>definite time.</u>

     | subject and verb: | *Sie schreiben* **nicht.** |
     | noun object: | Ich brauche *die Landkarte* **nicht.** |
     | pronoun object: | Ich brauche *sie* **nicht.** |
     | definite time: | Ich brauche sie *heute* **nicht.** |

   - When **nicht** negates a particular sentence element, it usually comes right before that element. Such elements commonly include <u>adverbs,</u> including adverbs of general time; <u>prepositional phrases</u>; and <u>verb complements (V2).</u>

     | adverbs: | Ich kaufe das **nicht** *gern.*[1] |
     | | Ich kaufe das **nicht** *hier.* |
     | | Ich kaufe das **nicht** *oft.* |
     | prepositional phrase: | Ich kaufe das **nicht** *im Geschäft.* |
     | | Ich kaufe das **nicht** *auf dem Markt.* |

---

[1] BUT: with **nicht gern** + noun, the word order is usually **Ich esse nicht gern Käse. Ich trinke nicht gern Buttermilch.**

verb complements: Ich gehe heute **nicht** *essen.*
Ich spiele heute **nicht** *Tennis.*
Ich heiße **nicht** *Beyer.*
Das ist **nicht** *mein Buch.*
Das Obst ist **nicht** billig.

- The following chart shows the most frequent pattern for the placement of **nicht:**

S	V1	O	definite time expression	other adverbs or adverbial phrases	V2.
			↑ **nicht**		

c. **Kein** vs. **nicht**

- Use **kein-** when the noun has an indefinite article or no article at all.

    noun + indefinite article: Ich kaufe *ein Brot.*
    Ich kaufe **kein** Brot.
    unpreceded noun: Ich kaufe *Milch.*
    Ich kaufe **keine** Milch.

- Use **nicht** when the noun is preceded by a definite article or a possessive adjective.

    noun + definite article: Ich kaufe *das Brot.*
    Ich kaufe *das Brot* **nicht.**
    noun + possessive adj.:   Das ist *mein Buch.*
    Das ist **nicht** *mein Buch.*

d. **Ja, nein, doch**

   COMPARE: Hast du das Buch?   **Ja!**   *Yes.*
   Nein!   *No.*
   Hast du das Buch **nicht?**   **Doch!**   *Of course I do.*

- **Doch** is an affirmative response to a negative question or statement.

    Wohnt Erika Schwarz **nicht** in Salzburg?   **Doch!**
    Haben Sie **keine** Swatch-Uhren?   **Doch,** hier sind sie.
    Ich glaube, sie wohnt **nicht** in Salzburg.   **Doch,** sie wohnt dort.

3. Coordinating conjunctions

Two independent clauses can be joined into one sentence by means of COORDINATING CONJUNCTIONS. Each of the two clauses keeps the original word order.

aber	*but, however*	Wir essen Fisch, aber sie essen Fleisch.
denn	*because, for*	Sie kauft Obst, denn es ist frisch.
oder	*or*	Nehmen Sie Brot oder möchten Sie Brötchen?
und	*and*	Ich kaufe Wurst und er kauft Käse.

Übungen

J. Die Nachbarin *(Every time you visit your elderly neighbor, she insists that you eat or drink something. Use the negative* **kein.***)*

   BEISPIEL: Möchten Sie eine Banane?
   Möchten Sie keine Banane?

1. Nehmen Sie Erdbeeren? 2. Essen Sie Gurkensalat? 3. Trinken Sie Limo? 4. Essen Sie Joghurt? 5. Möchten Sie ein Stück Brot? 6. Nehmen Sie ein Wurstbrötchen? 7. Trinken Sie ein Glas Milch? 8. Möchten Sie einen Apfel?

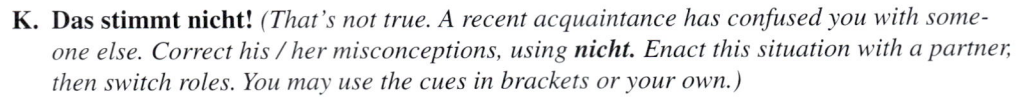

K. Das stimmt nicht! *(That's not true. A recent acquaintance has confused you with someone else. Correct his / her misconceptions, using* **nicht**. *Enact this situation with a partner, then switch roles. You may use the cues in brackets or your own.)*

BEISPIEL: Ihr Name ist [Fiedler], nicht wahr?
Nein, mein Name ist nicht [Fiedler]. Mein Name ist [Fiede].

1. Sie heißen [Watzlik], nicht wahr? 2. Sie kommen aus [Polen], nicht wahr? 3. Ihre Familie wohnt in [Mecklenburg], nicht wahr? 4. Ihr Onkel und Ihre Tante sprechen [Mecklenburgisch], nicht wahr? 5. Ihr Bruder wohnt in [Thüringen], nicht wahr? 6. Sie studieren [Musik], nicht wahr? 7. Sie trinken gern [Tomatensaft], nicht wahr? 8. Sie essen gern [Fleischsalat], nicht wahr?

L. Nein! *(To get your attention, your little brother negates everything you say. Use either* **nicht** *or* **kein**.*)*

1. Heute ist es heiß. 2. Die Sonne scheint. 3. Da drüben *(over there)* ist ein Geschäft. 4. Das Geschäft verkauft Limonade und Eistee. 5. Die Cola ist kalt. 6. Ich möchte ein Käsebrötchen. 7. Ich esse das Käsebrötchen! 8. Ich bin Vegetarier *(vegetarian)*. 9. Ich esse gern Käse. 10. Käse ist gesund *(healthy / healthful)*. 11. Wir gehen jetzt in eine Buchhandlung. 12. Vater braucht eine Landkarte und einen Stadtplan *(city map)*. 13. Er braucht die Landkarte! 14. Ich finde das Amerikabuch schön. 15. Wir haben Zeit. 16. Ich lese gern Bücher. 17. Das ist ein Spanischbuch. 18. Heinz lernt Spanisch. 19. Er studiert in Madrid. 20. Ich brauche einen Kalender *(calendar)*. 21. Ich finde den Städtekalender gut. 22. Der Kalender ist billig. 23. Ich möchte den Kalender! 24. Wir brauchen Bleistifte und Kulis.

M. *Ja, nein* oder *doch*? *(The instructor of your German class is asking questions to check how much you know about the German-speaking countries. Answer appropriately.)*

BEISPIEL: Ist der Rhein im Westen von Deutschland? **Ja!**
Ist der Rhein im Osten von Deutschland? **Nein!**
Ist der Rhein nicht im Westen von Deutschland? **Doch!**

1. Sprechen die Österreicher nicht Deutsch?
2. Hat Deutschland viele Nachbarn?
3. Ist Bonn die Hauptstadt von Deutschland?
4. Ist Wien nicht die Hauptstadt von Österreich?
5. Hamburg liegt in Norddeutschland, nicht wahr?
6. Gibt es in Deutschland keine Supermärkte?
7. Sind 600 Gramm ein Pfund?
8. Ein Viertelpfund ist nicht 125 Gramm, oder?
9. Ein Kilogramm ist ein halbes Pfund, nicht wahr?

N. Eine Postkarte *(After your first week in Bremen, you are writing a brief postcard to a friend. Join the two sentences with the conjunctions indicated.)*

Hallo Frank!
1. Ich schreibe nicht viel. Ich habe keine Zeit. *(because)*
2. Ich finde es hier schön. Ich lerne auch sehr viel. *(and)*

3. Meine Zimmerkolleginnen / Zimmerkollegen *(roommates)* kommen aus Kanada und sprechen Französisch. Sie verstehen nicht viel Deutsch. *(but)*
4. Sonntag spielen wir zusammen Minigolf. Wir gehen in die Stadt. *(or)*

Flower Power FOKUS

Germans are very fond of having fresh flowers in their homes. When invited for coffee / tea or for dinner, guests usually bring their hosts a bouquet. The flowers have to be carefully chosen, though: red roses, for example, carry the message of love, while white chrysanthemums are considered funeral flowers. The gift of flowers (or some other small present) eliminates the need for a thank-you note, but a follow-up telephone call is very much appreciated.

Blumenmarkt in Freiburg

Zusammenfassung

O. Im Lebensmittelgeschäft. Auf Deutsch bitte!

1. What would you like? 2. What kind of vegetables do you have today? 3. I think I'll take two pounds of beans. 4. The eggs are fresh, aren't they?—Of course. 5. We don't need (any) eggs. 6. But we need some fish and lettuce. 7. I'm not eating any fish. 8. Do you have any carrot juice? 9. Don't you like (to drink) carrot juice?—No! 10. Do you have any coke? I like to drink coke. 11. She's buying a coke and some orange juice. 12. Is that all?—No, I'd also like two pieces of strawberry cake.

70   Kapitel 2

P. Hoppla, hier ist 'was anders! Zwei Geschäfte *(Oops, something is different here. It's 3:00 P.M. on Saturday, and some stores are running low on supplies. You are in one store, shown below, and your partner in another, shown in Section 11 of the Appendix. Without looking at each other's pictures, find out differences between the two. Take turns asking questions, completing the charts as you do so.)*

S1:

	Gibt es hier . . . ?	**Gibt es da . . . ?**
Eier	ja	ja
Brot		
Milch		
Joghurt		
Erdbeeren		
Gurken		
Wein	nein	ja
. . .		

BEISPIEL: S1   Hier gibt es Eier. Gibt es da Eier?

               S2   Ja, hier gibt es auch Eier. — Und Wein, gibt es da Wein?

               S1   Nein, hier gibt es keinen Wein, aber es gibt . . .

EINBLICKE

Pedestrian Areas

Most European cities have developed a pedestrian area *(Fußgängerzone)* in the center of town. Since cars are prohibited, these areas are free of traffic noise and exhaust fumes—a great improvement in the quality of life in dense urban centers. During business hours, and especially on Saturday mornings, pedestrian areas are packed with shoppers. Suburban shopping malls are still the exception in Germany; most large department stores and smaller specialty shops are located in town. During the summer, cafés spill out onto the sidewalks, and street musicians add to the atmosphere. The prime real estate along pedestrian areas has provided property owners with an incentive to refurbish older buildings, which typically combine apartments in the upper stories and businesses on the ground floor.

Fußgängerzone in Heidelberg

WORTSCHATZ 2

der Durst	thirst
Hunger	hunger
das Glas, ¨er; ein Glas[1]	glass; a glass (of)
Würstchen, -[2]	hot dog
die Apotheke, -n[3]	pharmacy
Blume, -n	flower
Drogerie, -n[3]	drugstore
Tasse, -n; eine Tasse[1]	cup; a cup (of)

Ach du liebes bisschen!	Good grief! My goodness! Oh dear!
Bitte, bitte!	You're welcome.
ein paar[4]	a few, some (used with plural nouns)
montags (dienstags . . .)	on Mondays (Tuesdays, . . .)
offen / zu	open / closed
warum?	why?
Ich gehe . . . einkaufen.	I go shopping . . .
Ich habe Hunger / Durst.	I'm hungry / thirsty.

---

[1] **Möchten Sie** *ein Glas Milch* (a glass of milk) **oder** *eine Tasse Kaffee* (a cup of coffee)?

[2] All nouns ending in **-chen** are neuter. The suffix makes diminutives of nouns, i.e., it makes them smaller. They often have an umlaut, but there is no additional plural ending: **der Bruder, das Brüderchen; die Schwester, das Schwesterchen; das Glas, das Gläschen; die Tasse, das Tässchen**

[3] A **Drogerie** sells over-the-counter drugs, cosmetics, and toiletries. An **Apotheke** sells prescription and non-prescription drugs.

[4] *Ein paar* **Tomaten,** *ein paar* **Äpfel** (pl.) BUT *etwas* **Kaffee,** *etwas* **Butter** (sg. collective noun)

Vorm Lesen

A. Beim Einkaufen

1. **Die Einkaufsliste** (*In the following text you'll meet Carolyn, an American student in Germany. Consult her shopping list, where she has checked what she needs. Then complete the sentences below. Several correct answers are possible.*)

a. Was hat Carolyn und was braucht sie nicht?
   Sie hat noch etwas _____ und ein paar _____ . Sie braucht kein(e/en) _____ .
b. Was hat sie nicht und was kauft sie?
   Carolyn hat kein(e/en) _____ . Sie kauft ein paar _____ , ein Pfund _____ und etwas _____ .

2. **Lebensmittel und Geschäfte** *(As you read the text below, look for the various types of food and stores mentioned. Circle the food-related items, and underline the types of shops.)*

B. **Was ist das?**

das Auto, Café, Einkaufen, Einkaufszentrum, Spezialgeschäft; die Boutique, Medizin; romantisch

Geschäfte und Einkaufen

Carolyn ist Studentin. Sie studiert ein Jahr in Regensburg. In der Studentenheimküche° findet sie zwei Regensburger Studenten, Ursula und Peter.   *dorm kitchen*

CAROLYN	Guten Morgen! Mein Name ist Carolyn.
URSULA	Freut mich. Das ist Peter und ich heiße Ursula.
PETER	Guten Morgen, Carolyn! Woher kommst du?
CAROLYN	Ich komme aus Colorado.
PETER	Du, wir frühstücken° gerade°. Möchtest du eine Tasse Kaffee? *are eating breakfast / just now*
CAROLYN	Ja, gern. Ich habe wirklich Hunger.
URSULA	Hier hast du ein Stück Brot, etwas Butter und Marmelade.
CAROLYN	Danke!
PETER	Etwas Milch für den Kaffee?
CAROLYN	Ja, bitte.
PETER	Auch ein Ei?
CAROLYN	Nein, danke.—Mm, das Brot ist gut! Wo gibt es hier Geschäfte?
URSULA	Um die Ecke° gibt es ein Lebensmittelgeschäft, eine Metzgerei° und auch eine Drogerie. *corner / butcher shop*
CAROLYN	Prima! Ich brauche auch Medizin.
URSULA	Da findest du auch eine Apotheke.
CAROLYN	Ist das Lebensmittelgeschäft sehr teuer?
PETER	Billig ist es nicht. Wir gehen oft in die Stadt, denn da findest du alles. Da gibt es Spezialgeschäfte, Supermärkte und auch Kaufhäuser. Es gibt auch ein Einkaufszentrum.
URSULA	Regensburg ist wirklich sehr schön. Es ist alt und romantisch und um den Dom° gibt es viele Boutiquen. *cathedral*
PETER	Ich finde die Fußgängerzone prima, denn da gibt es keine Autos, nur Fußgänger. Da beobachte° ich gern die Leute. *watch*
URSULA	Du meinst° die Mädchen. *mean*
PETER	Na und°! *So what!*
URSULA	Wir gehen auch manchmal in ein Café und essen ein Stück Kuchen.
PETER	Oder wir gehen an die Donau zur° „Wurstküche", essen ein paar Würstchen und trinken ein Glas Bier. *to the*

farmers	URSULA	Samstags ist Markt. Da verkaufen die Bauern° Obst, Gemüse, Eier und Blumen. Alles ist sehr frisch.
	CAROLYN	Und wann sind die Geschäfte offen?
	PETER	Die Kaufhäuser sind von morgens um neun bis abends um acht offen, ein paar Boutiquen nur bis um halb sieben.
	CAROLYN	Gut, dann gehe ich heute Abend einkaufen.
That won't work.	PETER	Das geht nicht°.
	CAROLYN	Warum nicht?
out here	PETER	Heute ist Samstag. Samstags sind die Geschäfte nur bis um vier offen und sonntags sind sie hier draußen° zu.
	CAROLYN	Aber nicht die Kaufhäuser, oder?
	PETER	Doch!
	CAROLYN	Ach du liebes bisschen! Dann gehe ich jetzt einkaufen. Danke fürs Frühstück!
	PETER	Bitte, bitte!

FOKUS Regensburg

Regensburg is one of the few larger medieval cities in Germany not seriously damaged during World War II. Founded by the Celts around 500 B.C., it was later the site of a Roman military outpost called *Castra Regina*, dating back to A.D. 179. During the Middle Ages, the imperial diet of the Holy Roman Empire held occasional sessions there. After 1663, the city was the seat of a perpetual diet, the first attempt to establish a permanent German parliament.

Today Regensburg's old center is largely intact and contains fine examples of Romanesque, Gothic, and baroque architecture. Its two most famous landmarks are the Gothic cathedral and a 12th-century stone bridge that spans the Danube. The city lives from tourism, as well as the electronics industry and a BMW plant. The university, founded in 1962, has a significant impact on the cultural and economic life of the city.

Zum Text

A. Was passt wo? *(Find the correct places for the listed words.)*

Apotheke, einkaufen, Hunger, Kaffee, Kuchen, Kaufhäuser, Lebensmittelgeschäft, samstags, Studenten, Studentin

1. Carolyn ist _____ . 2. Peter und Ursula sind auch _____ . 3. Carolyn hat wirklich _____ . 4. Um die Ecke gibt es ein _____ und eine _____ . 5. Die Leute im Café essen _____ und trinken _____ . 6. Von Montag bis Freitag sind die _____ bis abends um acht offen. 7. _____ sind die Geschäfte nur bis um vier offen. 8. Carolyn geht jetzt _____ .

B. **Verneinen Sie die Sätze!** *(Negate the sentences.)*
   1. Sie möchte ein Ei.
   2. Sie möchte Milch für den Kaffee.
   3. Die Kaufhäuser sind samstags zu.
   4. Verkauft die Drogerie Medizin?
   5. Das Lebensmittelgeschäft ist billig.
   6. Gibt es da Autos?
   7. Das glaube ich.
   8. Die Blumen sind frisch.
   9. Ich brauche Blumen.

C. **Was bedeuten die Wörter und was sind die Artikel?**

   Söhnchen, Töchterchen, Stühlchen, Tischchen, Heftchen, Flüsschen, Mäntelchen, Höschen, Stündchen, Teilchen, Blümchen

D. **Interviews**
   1. **Einkaufen in . . .** *(Ask a partner about the stores in his / her native town and his / her shopping habits.)*
      a. Welche Geschäfte sind billig? teuer?
      b. Gibt es hier eine Fußgängerzone? ein Einkaufszentrum? Was für Kaufhäuser gibt es?
      c. Gibt es hier einen Markt? Wo? Was kaufen die Leute da?
      d. Wann sind die Geschäfte da offen? Sind sonntags die Geschäfte zu?
      e. Gehst du gern einkaufen? Was kaufst du oft? Kaufst du auch Blumen?

   2. **Einkaufen in Regensburg** *(On your first day in Regensburg, you find out about shopping from a fellow student who answers your questions.)*

      You want to know . . .

      a. where stores are   b. when they are open   c. if the grocery store is expensive
      d. where the drugstore is   e. if the department store is closed on Sundays   f. if there is a pedestrian area   g. if the city is very beautiful   h. if there is a (farmers') market and when   i. what they sell there

HÖREN SIE ZU!

Neu in Regensburg *(Listen to the conversation between two students. Then decide whether the statements below are true or false according to the information in the dialogue.)*

Zum Erkennen: Sag mal! *(Say);* nachher *(afterwards)*

_____ 1. Ursula wohnt schon zwanzig Jahre in Regensburg.
_____ 2. Claudia ist aus Passau.
_____ 3. Claudia braucht Schuhe.
_____ 4. Ursula geht heute nachmittag einkaufen.
_____ 5. Sie geht um drei Uhr.
_____ 6. Ursula braucht Jeans und ein Sweatshirt.
_____ 7. Dann gehen sie ein paar Würstchen essen.

WEB-ECKE For updates and online activities, visit the *Wie geht's?* homepage at http://www.hrwcollege.com/german/sevin/! You visit a German supermarket and an Austrian clothing store and go on a virtual shopping tour, purchasing items and converting marks into dollars and euros. You'll also tour Regensburg, take a closer look at a German map, and convert kilometers into miles.

SPRECHSITUATIONEN

Making a purchase

Here are some useful phrases for shopping.

1. Salesclerks offer assistance, saying:

   Was darf's sein? *(May I help you?)*
   Ja, bitte?

   You may respond with:

   Ich brauche . . .   Haben Sie . . . ?
   Ich möchte . . .   Gibt es . . . ?
   Ich hätte gern . . .   Was kosten / kostet . . . ?
   Ich suche . . .   Ich nehme . . .

2. After you have made a selection, you may hear the following and respond accordingly:

   Sonst noch (et)was? *(Anything else?)*   Ja, ich brauche (auch) noch . . .
                                             Nein, danke! (Das ist alles.)
   Ist das alles?   Ja, danke! (Das ist alles)
                                             Nein, ich brauche (auch) noch . . .

   After adding up the bill, the salesclerk might say:

   Das macht (zusammen) . . .

   When you get your change back, you may hear:

   Und . . . Mark zurück *(back)*.

Übungen

A. **Wir kaufen ein Buch.** *(Organize the sentences below in proper sequence.)*

   _8_ Ist das alles?
   _6_ 35,—DM.
   _2_ Ich suche ein Bilderbuch von Österreich für meinen Großvater.
   _12_ Auf Wiedersehen!
   _4_ Ach, es ist wirklich sehr schön.
   _10_ Das macht dann 35 Mark.
   _1_ Guten Tag! Was darf's sein?
   _5_ Was kostet es?
   _3_ Wie finden Sie das Buch hier?
   _7_ Gut, ich nehme es.
   _11_ Vielen Dank! Auf Wiedersehen!
   _9_ Ja, danke.

B. Im Lebensmittelgeschäft *(With a partner, enact the following conversation. You may discuss the items shown or any others you would like.)*

S1   Guten Tag! Was darf's sein?
S2   Ich brauche . . . und . . . Was kosten / kostet . . . ?
S1   . . .
S2   Und was kosten / kostet . . . ?
S1   . . .
S2   Gut, dann nehme ich . . . und . . .
S1   Sonst noch etwas?
S2   . . .
S1   . . . DM bitte!

Frische Vollmilch
3,5% Fettgehalt
1-l-Packung
-.99

ebner
DIE BÄCKEREI · DAS BROT
Kleine Baguettes   2.20
2 Stück
Sonnenblumenbrot   3.60
ofenfrisch
750-g-Stück
Mohnschnecken   4.35
mit bester Butter
gebacken
3 Stück

Dr. Oetker Zitronen Kuchen
Dr. Oetker Kuchenmischung
versch. Sorten, jede Packung
real spezial 3,33

Knorr Feinschmecker Blumenkohl-Broccoli-Suppe
Knorr Feinschmecker Suppen und Saucen oder Spaghetteria Pasta Saucen
versch. Sorten, jeder Beutel
real spezial 1,19

C. Kurzgespräche

1. You want to buy an item of clothing in a department store. Describe to the salesclerk what you are looking for. After viewing and commenting on several items the clerk has shown you (e.g., one is too small, one too big, one too expensive, etc.), decide whether or not to buy one. If you do not buy it, explain your reasons. If you do buy it, of course you must pay before you leave!

2. At the beginning of the semester you want to organize a welcome party for your new roommate. At the grocery store, buy cookies, the ingredients for a fruit salad, soft drinks, etc. Always ask the clerk for the price of each item to make sure that anything you are buying is within your limited budget. Try to include phrases like "half a pound, a quarter of a pound, a kilo," and "a dozen" (**ein halbes Pfund, ein Viertelpfund, ein Kilo, ein Dutzend**).

KAPITEL 3

IM RESTAURANT

Guten Appetit!—Danke gleichfalls.

LERNZIELE

■ VORSCHAU
Eating in and out

■ GESPRÄCHE AND WORTSCHATZ
Meals and restaurants

■ STRUKTUR
Verbs with vowel changes
Dative case

■ EINBLICKE
Regional specialties
You are what you eat

■ FOKUS
Where to eat
Friends and acquaintances
Cafés and coffee houses
Table manners
Wines from Germany, Austria, and Switzerland

■ WEB-ECKE

■ SPRECHSITUATIONEN
Choosing and ordering a meal
Expressing likes and dislikes

VORSCHAU

Eating In and Out

Until the end of World War II, cooking in the German-speaking countries varied substantially from region to region, as each region's cuisine was noticeably influenced by its neighbors. Austrian cooking, for example, absorbed a strong Hungarian component, whereas Bavarian cooks in turn borrowed from Austria. Swiss-German cuisine incorporates many aspects of French and Italian culinary arts. Although retaining its regional differences, German cooking has meanwhile been influenced by the cuisines from around the world. Overseas travel and a large number of foreign residents have brought all kinds of culinary delights to markets and restaurants.

Germans are sometimes said to be especially fond of heavy, rich foods. However, compared to the lean postwar period, when only quantity mattered, Germans have developed a sophisticated taste and a sharp awareness of variety and quality in their diet. Health-food shops **(Reformhäuser)** and organic food stores **(Bio-Läden)** can be found almost everywhere.

Food preparation is no longer the sole domain of women. More and more German men have ventured into the kitchen, and many assume responsibility for shopping and cooking on weekends. Those Germans who prefer to eat out can choose from a wide range of restaurants, including Italian, Thai, Spanish, Chinese, and, most recently, Tex-Mex. Fast food also has gained great popularity. Pizza delivery and American hamburger outlets are available in most cities, and Turkish snack bars can be found even in small towns. Traditional German **Imbiss** continues, of course, to offer a quick sausage with fries **(Bratwurst mit Pommes)**.

Restaurant customs in Germany, Austria, and Switzerland differ somewhat from those of North America. Guests usually seat themselves, and if the restaurant is crowded, it is acceptable to share a table with strangers after asking for permission: **Entschuldigen Sie, können wir uns dazusetzen?** Before eating, diners usually wish each other a pleasant meal **(Guten Appetit!)**. The appropriate response is **Danke, gleichfalls.** Salads are not eaten before but with the main course. Germans, like most Europeans, don't drink coffee with a meal, only afterwards. Also, water is never served automatically; diners are expected to order mineral water or another beverage. A service charge **(Bedienung)** of 10 to 15 percent and the value-added tax **(Mehrwertsteuer)** are always included in the price of the meal. Although a tip **(Trinkgeld)** is not necessary, it is customary to add a small amount to round up the total. After asking for the bill, **(Zahlen, bitte!),** diners give the money, including the tip, directly to the server. Often diners are asked if they want to pay the whole bill **(Zusammen . . .)** or go Dutch treat **(. . . oder getrennt?)**. Most restaurants do not accept credit cards.

GESPRÄCHE

Im Restaurant

AXEL	Herr Ober, die Speisekarte bitte!
OBER	Hier bitte!
AXEL	Was empfehlen Sie heute?
OBER	Die Menüs sind alle sehr gut.
AXEL	Gabi, was nimmst du?
GABI	Ich weiß nicht. Was nimmst du?
AXEL	Ich glaube, ich nehme Menü 1: Schnitzel und Kartoffelsalat.
GABI	Und ich nehme Menü 2: Rindsrouladen mit Kartoffelklößen.
OBER	Möchten Sie etwas trinken?
GABI	Ein Glas Apfelsaft, und du?
AXEL	Mineralwasser. *(Der Ober kommt mit dem Essen.)* Guten Appetit!
GABI	Danke, gleichfalls . . . Mm, das schmeckt.
AXEL	Das Schnitzel auch.

Später

GABI	Wir möchten zahlen bitte!
OBER	Ja, bitte. Alles zusammen?
GABI	Ja. Geben Sie mir die Rechnung bitte!
AXEL	Nein, nein, nein!
GABI	Doch, Axel! Heute bezahle ich.
OBER	Also, einmal Menü 1, einmal Menü 2, ein Apfelsaft, ein Mineralwasser, zwei Tassen Kaffee. Sonst noch etwas?
AXEL	Ja, ein Brötchen.
OBER	Das macht 60,60 DM bitte.
GABI	*(Sie gibt dem Ober 70,– DM)* 62,00 Mark bitte.
OBER	Und acht Mark zurück. Vielen Dank!

Fragen

1. Wer bringt die Speisekarte? 2. Was empfiehlt der Ober? 3. Was bestellen Gabi und Axel? 4. Was trinken sie? 5. Was bringt der Ober am Ende? 6. Wer zahlt? 7. Was kostet alles zusammen? 8. Wie viel Trinkgeld *(tip)* gibt *(gives)* Gabi dem Ober? Ist das viel? 9. Wie viel Trinkgeld geben Sie normalerweise *(normally)*? **(Ich gebe normalerweise . . . Prozent.)**

WORTSCHATZ 1

Das Restaurant, -s *(restaurant)*

der Kellner, -[1]	waiter	die Bedienung[1]	server; service
Ober, -[1]		Gabel, -n	fork
Löffel, -	spoon	Mensa	student cafeteria
Teller, -	plate	Rechnung, -en	check / bill
das Café, -s	café	Serviette, -n	napkin
Messer, -	knife	Speisekarte, -n	menu

Das Essen *(food, meal)*

der Nachtisch	dessert	die Pommes (frites) *(pl.)*	*(French) fries*
Pfeffer	pepper	Suppe, -n	soup
Pudding	pudding	das Eis[2]	ice cream
Reis	rice	Salz	salt
Zucker	sugar	Frühstück	breakfast
die Kartoffel, -n	potato	Mittagessen	lunch, midday meal
Nudel, -n	noodle	Abendessen	supper
Pizza, -s	pizza		

Weiteres

Herr Ober![1]	Waiter!
Was gibt's zum Frühstück (Mittagessen . . .)?	What's for breakfast (lunch . . .)?
Guten Appetit!	Enjoy your meal!
Danke, gleichfalls!	Thanks, the same to you!
Das schmeckt (gut)!	That's good. That tastes (good)!
etwas (zu essen)	something (to eat)
nichts (zu trinken)	nothing (to drink)
noch ein(e)	another
viel / viele[3]	much / many
wie viel? / wie viele?[3]	how much? / how many?
zu Hause / nach Hause[4]	at home / (toward) home
bestellen	to order
(be)zahlen	to pay (for)
bleiben	to remain, stay
bringen	to bring
empfehlen	to recommend
frühstücken	to eat breakfast

Zum Erkennen: das Menü, -s *(dinner, daily special);* das Schnitzel *(veal cutlet);* der Kartoffelsalat; die Rindsroulade *(stuffed beef roll);* der Kloß, ⸚e *(dumpling);* das Mineralwasser; einmal *(once);* zurück *(back)*

---

[1] **Herr Ober!** is used to address a waiter, while **der Ober** and **der Kellner** are job descriptions, usually for someone working in a fancy restaurant. **Bedienung** refers to waiters and waitresses in a regular restaurant as well as their service. Waitresses are no longer summoned by calling **Fräulein!** *(Miss!)* Now diners usually use **Entschuldigen Sie!**, **Hallo!**, or a hand signal to catch a server's attention.

[2] **Eis** means both *ice* and *ice cream.* If you ask for **Eis** in a restaurant, you will get ice cream. Ice water is not served in German-speaking countries.

[3] **viel** Obst *(sg. collective noun),* **Wie viel** Obst? BUT **viele** Äpfel *(pl.),* **Wie viele** Äpfel?

[4] Ich bin **zu Hause** BUT Ich gehe **nach Hause**. (See Struktur II. 3.)

Where to Eat

In smaller towns, hotels are often the best place to eat. A **Gasthof, Gasthaus,** or **Gastwirtschaft** is—or includes—a restaurant serving complete meals. Since many restaurants serve hot food only at lunch and dinner times, the selection in the afternoon or late at night is usually limited. Whereas older people still take **Kaffee und Kuchen** in cafés, young people flock to pubs **(Kneipen)** for a drink or small meal. To avoid fancy places with astronomical prices, check the menus that are usually posted outside the entrance.

Zum Thema

A. Mustersätze
1. die Speisekarte: **Herr Ober,** die Speisekarte **bitte!**
   ein Glas Mineralwasser, eine Tasse Kaffee, ein Stück Kuchen, ein Eis, die Rechnung
2. eine Tasse: **Ich brauche** eine Tasse.
   einen Teller, einen Löffel, ein Messer, eine Gabel
3. ein Glas Mineralwasser: **Ich möchte noch** ein Glas Mineralwasser.
   eine Tasse Kaffee, eine Tasse Tee, ein Glas Limonade, einen Teller Suppe
4. gut: **Das Schnitzel schmeckt** gut.
   auch gut, wunderbar, nicht schlecht, furchtbar
5. ein Eis: **Zum Nachtisch nehme ich** ein Eis.
   Schokoladenpudding, etwas Käse, ein Stück Apfelkuchen, ein paar Erdbeeren

B. Was passt nicht?
1. der Teller—das Messer—die Speisekarte—die Gabel
2. das Frühstück—der Nachtisch—das Mittagessen—das Abendessen
3. das Salz—der Zucker—der Pfeffer—die Serviette
4. die Rechnung—die Kartoffeln—die Nudeln—der Reis
5. das Café—der Appetit—das Restaurant—die Mensa
6. bestellen—empfehlen—sein—zahlen

C. Was bedeuten die Wörter und was sind die Artikel?

Frühstückstisch, Kaffeetasse, Fleischgabel, Buttermesser, Teelöffel, Suppenlöffel, Suppenteller, Kartoffelsuppe, Schokoladenpudding, Joghurteis

D. Was passt?

_____ 1. Die Suppe ist eiskalt.
_____ 2. Der Kartoffelsalat schmeckt prima.
_____ 3. Möchten Sie etwas zum Nachtisch?
_____ 4. Guten Appetit!
_____ 5. Möchtest du nichts trinken?

a. Danke schön!
b. Wirklich?
c. Freut mich.
d. Das finde ich auch.
e. Ja, bitte.
f. Ja, wirklich.
g. Doch!
h. Nein, danke.
i. Ja, sie schmeckt furchtbar.
j. Ja, gern.
k. Natürlich.
l. Danke, gleichfalls.

E. **Was noch?** *(What else? In groups of two to four students, see how many items you can find for each word or phrase below. The group with the largest number of items wins.)*

BEISPIEL: ein Stück . . .
  Ich möchte ein Stück Brot.

1. ein Stück . . .
2. ein Glas . . .
3. eine Tasse . . .
4. ein paar . . .
5. etwas . . .
6. ein Pfund . . .
7. viel . . .
8. viele . . .

F. **Persönliche Fragen** *(Work in pairs: At the exit of your cafeteria a marketing specialist, who is studying what college students eat and drink, asks you to answer some questions. Play each role in turns.)*
1. Wann frühstücken Sie? Was essen Sie zum Frühstück (zum Mittagessen, zum Abendessen)?
2. Trinken Sie morgens Kaffee, Tee, Milch oder Kakao? Trinken Sie Ihren Kaffee schwarz oder mit *(with)* Milch? mit oder ohne Zucker?
3. Was essen Sie gern zum Nachtisch? Essen Sie oft Nachtisch? Wann?
4. Essen Sie schnell oder langsam?
5. Trinken Sie Wein oder Bier? Wenn *(if)* ja, wann? Wenn nicht, was trinken Sie auf *(at)* Partys?

G. **Aussprache: ü** *(See also II. 22–28 in the pronunciation section of the Workbook.)*
1. [ü:] über, Tür, für, Frühling, Prüfung, Gemüse, südlich, grün, natürlich, müde
2. [ü] Flüsse, Würste, Stück, Jürgen Müller, München, fünf, fünfundfünfzig
3. Wortpaare
   a. vier / für
   b. missen / müssen
   c. Stuhl / Stühle
   d. Mutter / Mütter
   e. fühle / Fülle
   f. Goethe / Güte

HÖREN SIE ZU!

Im Gasthaus *(Find out what Jürgen, Helga, and Michael are ordering for dinner. Put their initials by the foods and beverages they order, then add up their total bill to see whether the waitress calculated it correctly.)*

Zum Erkennen: früh *(early)*; das Getränk, -e *(beverages)*; einmal *(one order of)*

Getränke	Essen	Nachtisch
_____ Limonade	_____ Schnitzel	_____ Apfelkuchen
_____ Apfelsaft	_____ Rindsroulade	_____ Vanilleeis
_____ Bier	_____ Pizza	_____ Reispudding
_____ Mineralwasser	_____ Würstchen	_____ Schokoladenpudding
_____ Cola	_____ Fisch	_____ Käsekuchen

Das kostet:

_____   _____   _____
_____   _____   _____
_____   _____   _____

  Alles zusammen: _____ DM

STRUKTUR

I. Verbs with vowel changes

Some very common verbs have a STEM-VOWEL CHANGE in the SECOND and THIRD PERSON SINGULAR. These changes will be clearly noted in all vocabulary lists like this: **sprechen (spricht)**.

	e > i **sprechen** *to speak*	e > ie **sehen** *to see*	a > ä **fahren** *to drive*	au > äu **laufen** *to walk, run*
ich	spreche	sehe	fahre	laufe
du	**sprichst**	**siehst**	**fährst**	**läufst**
er	**spricht**	**sieht**	**fährt**	**läuft**
wir	sprechen	sehen	fahren	laufen
ihr	sprecht	seht	fahrt	lauft
sie	sprechen	sehen	fahren	laufen

Siehst du Dresden auf der Landkarte?

Dieter **fährt** nach Dresden.

A few verbs in this group have additional, consonant changes:

	nehmen *to take*	**werden** *to become, get*
ich	nehme	werde
du	**nimmst**	**wirst**
er	**nimmt**	**wird**
wir	nehmen	werden
ihr	nehmt	werdet
sie	nehmen	werden

You need to know the following common verbs with stem-vowel changes:

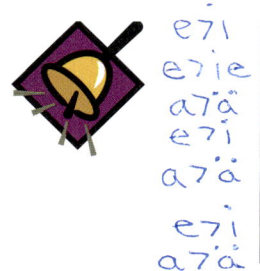

essen	**isst**	*to eat*	lesen	**liest**	*to read*
empfehlen	**empfiehlt**	*to recommend*	nehmen	**nimmt**	*to take; to have (food)*
fahren	**fährt**	*to drive*			
geben	**gibt**	*to give*	sehen	**sieht**	*to see*
gefallen	**gefällt**	*to please, be pleasing*	sprechen	**spricht**	*to speak*
			tragen	**trägt**	*to carry; to wear*
helfen	**hilft**	*to help*	werden	**wird**	*to become, get*
laufen	**läuft**	*to walk, run*			

Note that the second and third person singular forms of **essen** and **lesen** are identical (**du liest, er liest**). As you know from Chapter 1, the **du**-form of verbs with a stem ending in any s-sound (**-s, -ß, ss, -tz, -z**) adds only a **t**-ending instead of an **-st**: lese > du liest; heißen > du heißt.

Übungen

A. Ersetzen Sie das Subjekt!

   BEISPIEL: Der Ober trägt die Teller. (ich)
   Ich trage die Teller.

1. Fahren Sie zum Kaufhaus? (wir, er, ihr, du)
2. Wir nehmen Nudelsuppe. (er, ich, sie / *pl.,* du)
3. Ich werde müde. (das Kind, wir, sie / *sg.,* sie / *pl.*)
4. Sie empfehlen das Schnitzel. (der Ober, ich, du, Axel)
5. Sehen Sie die Apotheke nicht? (du, ihr, er, die Leute)
6. Sprechen Sie Deutsch? (er, du, sie / *pl.*)
7. Hilfst du heute nicht? (ihr, Sie, sie / *sg.*)
8. Lesen Sie gern Bücher? (du, ihr, er, sie / *pl.*)

B. **Was tun sie?** *(Answer logically, telling what others do. Use pronouns and stem-changing verbs.)*

   BEISPIEL: Ich esse schnell. Und Ihr Großvater?
   Er isst sehr langsam.

   1. Ich helfe gern. Und Ihr Nachbar?
   2. Ich nehme Apfelstrudel. Und Gabi?
   3. Ich empfehle den Schweinebraten *(pork roast)*. Und der Ober?
   4. Ich laufe langsam. Und Ihr Bruder oder Ihre Schwester?
   5. Ich lese gern. Und Ihre Mutter?
   6. Ich fahre im Sommer nach Deutschland. Und Ihre Familie?
   7. Ich sehe alles. Und Ihre Nachbarin?
   8. Ich gebe gern Hausaufgaben. Und Ihr(e) [Englisch]professor(in)?

C. **Und du?** *(Choose a classmate whom you don't know well, and find out what he / she likes. Follow the model and try to vary your responses.)*
   1. **Was isst du gern?**

      BEISPIEL: S1   Ich esse gern Fischbrötchen. Und du, isst du gern Fischbrötchen?
      S2   Ja, ich esse auch gern Fischbrötchen. (Nein, ich esse nicht gern
           . . . Nein, ich hasse *[hate]* . . .)
      S1   Was isst du auch (nicht) gern?

2. **Was trägst du gern?**

   BEISPIEL: S1 Ich trage gern Jeans. Und du, trägst du auch gern Jeans?
                  S2 Natürlich trage ich Jeans.
                  S1 Was trägst du noch gern? (Was trägst du nicht gern?)

II. Dative case

The dative case has three major functions in German: it is the case of the INDIRECT OBJECT, it follows certain verbs, and it follows certain prepositions.

1. In English the INDIRECT OBJECT is indicated in two ways:
   - through word order: *The boy gives **the father** the plate.*
   - with a preposition: *The boy gives the plate **to the father**.*

   In German this function is expressed through case and word order. You can determine the indirect object by asking for whom or in reference to whom (or occasionally what) the action of the verb is taking place.

       Der Junge gibt **dem Vater** den Teller. *The boy gives the father the plate.*

   a. The dative form of the INTERROGATIVE PRONOUN is **wem?** *(to whom?)*.

	persons	things and ideas
nom.	wer?	was?
acc.	wen?	was?
dat.	wem?	—

       Wem gibt der Junge den Teller? → **Dem Vater.**
       To whom does the boy give the plate? → *To the father.*

   b. The dative forms of the DEFINITE and INDEFINITE ARTICLES are as follows:

	SINGULAR masc.	SINGULAR neut.	SINGULAR fem.	PLURAL
nom.	der / ein / kein	das / ein / kein	die / eine / keine	die / — / keine
acc.	den / einen / keinen	das / ein / kein	die / eine / keine	die / — / keine
dat.	dem / einem / keinem	dem / einem / keinem	der / einer / keiner	den / — / keinen

   Der Ober empfiehlt **dem** Vater, **der** Mutter und **den** Kindern das Schnitzel. Er bringt **dem** Kind einen Löffel, aber er gibt **einem** Kind **kein** Messer und **keine** Gabel.

   - The POSSESSIVE ADJECTIVES **mein, dein,** and **Ihr** follow the pattern of **ein** and **kein:**

     Was empfiehlt er Ihr**em** Vater und Ihr**er** Mutter?

     Er empfiehlt mein**em** Vater und mein**er** Mutter den Fleischsalat.

- In the dative plural all nouns add an **-n** ending, unless the plural form already ends in **-n** or **-s.**

    die Väter / den Väter**n**

    die Kinder / den Kinder**n**

    die Äpfel / den Äpfel**n**

    BUT: die Eltern / den Eltern

         die Mädchen / den Mädchen

         die Kulis / den Kulis

- N-nouns also have an **-n** or **-en** ending in the dative singular, as they do in the accusative singular:

    Das Eis schmeckt dem Herr**n** und dem Student**en.**

c. Many verbs can have both accusative and dative objects. Note that the direct object is usually a thing and the indirect object a person.

     Der Ober bringt dem Kind den Kuchen.
     The waiter brings the child the cake.

     Er empfiehlt der Studentin den Fisch.
     He recommends the fish to the student.

Note the difference in meaning:

Der Onkel trägt der Tante die Lebensmittel.   BUT   Der Onkel trägt die Tante.

d. In sentences with two objects, the direct object, <u>if it is a noun,</u> generally follows the indirect object.

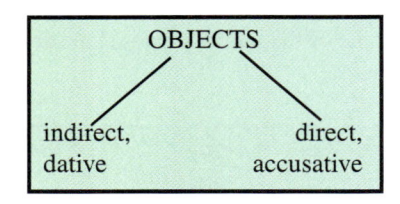

OBJECTS

indirect,   direct,
dative   accusative

Der Kellner bringt dem Herrn den Tee.

2. Dative verbs

   Some verbs take only dative objects; a few such verbs are:

antworten	to answer	**gehören**	to belong to
danken	to thank	glauben	to believe
gefallen	to please, be pleasing	helfen	to help

Der Bruder antwortet der Kusine.	The brother answers (gives an answer to) the cousin.
Alex dankt der Kellnerin.	Alex thanks (gives thanks to) the waitress.
Der Mantel gehört dem Mädchen.	The coat belongs to the girl.
Ich glaube dem Jungen.	I believe the boy.
Ich helfe dem Nachbarn.	I'm helping (giving help to) the neighbor.
Die Mensa gefällt den Studenten.	The students like the cafeteria (the cafeteria pleases the students).
Die Salate gefallen den Studenten.	The students like the salads (the salads are pleasing the students).

3. Dative prepositions

   These prepositions are always followed by the dative case:

aus	out of	Sie kommt **aus** dem Geschäft.
	from (a place of origin)	Er ist **aus** Berlin.
außer	besides	**Außer** dem Café ist alles zu.
bei	at, for (a company)	Sie arbeitet **bei** VW.
	near, by	Die Drogerie ist **beim** Markt.
	at the home of, with	Er wohnt **bei** Familie Angerer.
mit	with	Ich schreibe **mit** einem Kuli.
	together with	Alex kommt **mit** Gabi.
nach	after (time)	Kommst du **nach** dem Mittagessen?
	to (cities, countries, continents)	Fahrt ihr auch **nach** Österreich?
	to (used idiomatically)	Gehen Sie **nach** Hause!
seit	since	Sie wohnen **seit** Mai in Ulm.
	for (time)	Sie wohnen **seit** drei Tagen da.[1]
von	of	Das Gegenteil **von** billig ist teuer.
	from	Wir fahren **von** Ulm nach Hamburg.
	by (origin)	Das Bild ist **von** Albrecht Dürer.
zu	to (in the direction of)	Sie fährt **zum** Supermarkt.
	at (used idiomatically)	Sie sind **zu** Hause.
	for (purpose)	Was gibt es **zum** Nachtisch?

---

[1] **seit** translates as *for* in English when it expresses duration of time (three minutes, one year) that began in the past and still continues in the present: *They have been living there for three days.*

- In everyday speech, some of the dative prepositions are usually contracted with the definite article.

bei + dem = **beim**	zu + dem = **zum**
von + dem = **vom**	zu + der = **zur**

- Pay particular attention to the contrasting use of these pairs of prepositions:

  Sie fährt **zum** *(to the)* Supermarkt.

  Fahrt ihr **nach** *(to)* Deutschland?

  Wir fahren **von** *(from)* Salzburg nach München.

  Er kommt **aus** *(from)* Salzburg.

  Gehen Sie **nach** Hause *(home)*!

  Sie sind nicht **zu** Hause *([at] home)*.

Übungen

D. Sagen Sie die Sätze im Plural! *(Restate the sentences below, making the phrases in boldface plural.)*

BEISPIEL: Wir sprechen mit **dem Kanadier.**
Wir sprechen mit den Kanadiern.

1. Er lernt seit **einem Jahr** Deutsch. (drei)
2. Das Restaurant gehört **dem Schweizer.**
3. Sie kommen aus **dem Geschäft.**
4. Nach **einem Monat** bezahlt er die Rechnung. (zwei)
5. Ich gehe nur mit **dem Kind.**
6. Die Stadt gefällt **dem Engländer.**
7. Der Ober kommt mit **der Serviette.**
8. Wir sprechen mit **dem Nachbarn.**
9. Das Geschäft ist bei **dem Restaurant.**
10. Der Kuchen schmeckt **dem Studenten.**

E. Ersetzen Sie das Dativobjekt!

BEISPIEL: Die Bedienung bringt dem Kind ein Eis. (Großvater)
Die Bedienung bringt dem Großvater ein Eis.

1. Die Kellnerin empfiehlt dem Vater die Rouladen. (Bruder, Spanier, Schweizer)
2. Der Junge gibt der Mutter ein Bild. (Schwester, Studentin, Frau)
3. Der Ober bringt den Eltern das Essen. (Leute, Amerikaner / *pl.*, Studenten / *pl.*)
4. Die Drogerie gehört meiner Großmutter. (Großvater, Eltern, Familie)
5. Axel dankt dem Bruder. (Schwester, Vater, Leute)
6. Meine Großmutter hilft meinem Vater. (Mutter, Kusinen, Vettern)

F. Sagen Sie es noch einmal! *(Replace the nouns following the prepositions with the words suggested.)*

BEISPIEL: Eva geht zum Lebensmittelgeschäft. (Apotheke)
Eva geht zur Apotheke.

1. Paula kommt aus dem Kaufhaus. (Drogerie, Café, Mensa)
2. Seit Sonntag ist er wieder hier. (zwei Tage, eine Stunde, ein Monat)
3. Wir sprechen mit dem Großvater. (Frau, Mädchen, Großeltern)
4. Ich wohne bei meinen Eltern. (Bruder, Schwester, Familie)
5. Er möchte etwas Salat zu den Rouladen. (Schnitzel, Suppe, Würstchen / *pl.*, Fleisch)
6. Nach dem Mittagessen spielen sie Tennis. (Frühstück, Kaffee, Deutschstunde)
7. Außer meinem Bruder sind alle hier. (Vater, Mutter, Nachbar, Studentin)
8. Tante Liesl bleibt bei den Kindern. (Vetter, Kusine, Töchter)

G. **Wer, wem oder was?** *(At your friend's graduation party you are talking to a friend. Because of the loud music, you can't hear him / her. Ask what he / she said.)*

BEISPIEL: Oskar gibt dem Bruder die Bücher.
   Wer gibt dem Bruder die Bücher? — Oskar!
   Wem gibt Oskar die Bücher? — Dem Bruder!
   Was gibt Oskar dem Bruder? — Die Bücher!

1. Der Nachbar verkauft Onkel Willi den BMW.
2. Onkel Willi gibt dem Jungen den BMW.
3. Großmutter empfiehlt Irene ein paar Tage Ferien *(vacation)*.
4. Die Kinder zahlen der Mutter die Hotelrechnung.
5. Der Vater glaubt den Leuten die Geschichte *(story)* nicht.

H. **Hoppla, hier fehlt 'was!** Was gehört wem? *(You and your partner are helping another friend unpack after a family move. Work together to figure out what belongs to whom. One of you looks at and completes the chart below, the other the chart in Section 11 of the Appendix.)*

S1:

	Bruder	**Schwester**	**Mutter**	**Vater**	**Großeltern**
Bild	x				
Bücher					
Tennishose				x	
Hausschuhe					
Pulli		x			
Ringe *(pl.)*			x		
T-Shirts					
Mantel					
Messer *(sg.)*					
Gläser					x

BEISPIEL: S1 Wem gehören die Hausschuhe?
   S2 Die Hausschuhe gehören dem Vater. Und wem gehört das Bild?
   S1 Das Bild gehört dem Bruder.

I. **Was gefällt wem?**
1. **Ersetzen Sie das Dativobjekt!**
   a. Das Restaurant gefällt dem Onkel. (Tante, Großmutter, Kinder, Geschwister, Student, Studentin, Studenten)
   b. Aber die Preise gefallen der Familie nicht. (Frau, Leute, Nachbar, Herren)

2. **Auf Deutsch bitte!**

   BEISPIEL: My cousin likes Hamburg.
      Hamburg gefällt meinem Vetter.

   a. Ms. Bayer likes the country. b. My father likes the city. c. My mother likes the South. d. My sister likes the lakes. e. My brothers and sisters like the mountains. f. My grandparents like the student. g. The student likes my grandparents. h. I like German **(mir).**

J. Was kaufen wir wem? (*The Christmas season is approaching, and you and your roommate are coming up with ideas for presents. Working with a classmate, form sentences using one word from each list. Follow the model.*)

Was?: der Kaffee; Kalender, -; (Ohr)ring, -e; Tee; Wein, -e . . .
    das Kochbuch, ¨er; Portemonnaie, -s *(wallet);* Schreibpapier; Taschenmesser, -
        (pocket knife) . . .
    die Blumenvase, -n; Kassette, -n; Kette, -n *(necklace);* Kleidung; Krawatte, -n *(tie);*
        Tasche, -n *(handbag);* Schokolade . . .

Wem?: Bruder, Schwester, Geschwister, Mutter, Vater, (Groß)eltern, Onkel, Tante,
    Freund(in) *(friend)*

BEISPIEL: S1 Braucht deine Mutter Schreibpapier?
         S2 Nein. Sie hat Schreibpapier. Ich kaufe meiner Mutter keine Schreibpapier.
         S1 Gefallen deinem Vater Kochbücher?
         S2 Ja, sehr. Gut, ich kaufe meinem Vater ein Kochbuch.

K. Was fehlt?

1. *Nach Hause* **oder** *zu Hause?*
    a. Heute essen wir _____.
    b. Jürgen ist nicht _____.
    c. Er kommt oft spät _____.
    d. Morgen bleibt er _____.
    e. Wir arbeiten gern _____.
    f. Geht ihr um sechs _____?
    g. Bringst du die Großeltern _____?

2. **Die Präpositionen** *mit, bei, aus, von, nach* **und** *zu.* (*Use contractions when appropriate.*)
    a. Gehst du _zu der_ Buchhandlung? — Nein, ich gehe _aus dem_ Kaufhaus. *(to the / to the)*
    b. Das Kaufhaus ist _bei_ Café Kranzler. *(by)*
    c. Christl arbeitet _bei_ VW. *(at)*
    d. Julia fährt heute _nach_ Leipzig und Philipp _nach_ Dresden. *(to)*
    e. Sind Sie auch _aus_ Norddeutschland? *(from)*
    f. Antonio kommt _aus_ Rom und wohnt _bei_ Familie Dinkelacker. *(from / at the home of)*
    g. Herr Dinkelacker fährt morgen _von_ Frankfurt _nach_ Stuttgart. *(from / to)*
    h. Er fährt _mit_ der Familie. *(together with)*
    i. Der Hund *(dog)* bleibt _bei_ den Nachbarn. *(at the home of)*

LERNTIPP **Reviewing For Tests**

If you have taken full advantage of all class sessions, kept up with your work, and reviewed regularly, you should not have to spend much time preparing for tests. Concentrate on the areas that give you the most trouble. Use the *Rückblicke* sections in this text and in the Workbook for efficient reviewing. Go over the vocabulary lists of the chapters that will be covered by the test; make sure you know genders and plurals of nouns. Mark any words you seem to have trouble remembering; review them again. Begin your review early enough so that you can clear up any questions with your instructor.

Zusammenfassung

L. Bilden Sie Sätze!

BEISPIEL: das / sein / für / Onkel
Das ist für den Onkel.

1. Ober / kommen / mit / Speisekarte
2. Mutter / kaufen / Kind / Apfelsaft
3. Student / empfehlen / Studentin / Apfelkuchen
4. er / sehen / Großvater / nicht
5. kommen / du / von / Mensa?
6. Familie / fahren / nicht / nach Berlin
7. arbeiten / du / auch / bei / Delikatessengeschäft Dallmayr?
8. die Mutter / kaufen / Kinder / schnell / ein paar / Pommes (frites)

M. Guten Appetit! Was fehlt?

1. Zu____ Essen braucht man ein____ Messer und ein____ Gabel. 2. Suppe isst man mit ein____ Esslöffel *(tablespoon)* und für ____ Kaffee braucht man ein____ Kaffeelöffel. 3. Wir haben kein____ Messer, kein____ Gabel und kein____ Löffel *(sg.)*. 4. Gibt es hier kein____ Salz und kein____ Pfeffer? 5. Doch, d____ Salz steht bei d____ Pfeffer. 6. Jetzt habe ich alles außer ein____ Speisekarte. 7. Der Ober empfiehlt d____ Studentin d____ Schweinebraten *(pork roast, m.)*. 8. Nach d____ Essen bringt er ein____ Eis und ein____ Kaffee. 9. D____ Restaurant gefällt d____ Studenten *(pl.)*. 10. Aber sie haben etwas gegen d____ Preise *(pl.)*. 11. Wir sprechen von d____ Professor und von d____ Prüfung. 12. Ich bestelle noch ein____ Cola. 13. Hier trinke ich d____ Cola aus ein____ Glas, aber zu Hause aus ein____ Flasche *(f., bottle)*. 14. Da kommt der Ober mit d____ Rechnung. 15. Ohne d____ Rechnung geht's nicht. 16. Danke für d____ Mittagessen!

N. In der Mensa. Auf Deutsch bitte!

1. We're going with the students through the cafeteria. 2. They're from Hamburg. They're Hamburgers. 3. Paul lives with *(at the home of)* a family, and Helga lives at home. 4. Helga, what are you having? 5. I think I'll take the roast **(der Braten)**, peas and carrots, and a glass of juice. 6. Would you *(formal)* like a piece of cake for dessert? 7. No, I'm not eating any cake because it's fattening **(dick machen)**. 8. I have no knife, no fork, and no spoon. 9. Paul brings the student *(f.)* a knife, a fork, a spoon, and (some) ice cream. 10. Whose ice cream is that? (To whom does the ice cream belong?) 11. Would you *(fam.)* like some ice cream with a cookie? 12. She thanks the student. 13. Who's paying for (the) lunch?

EINBLICKE

Regional Specialties

"Food and drink are the glue that keep body and soul together," claims an old Viennese saying. The sentiment is popular in all of the German-speaking countries.

German cooking has many regional specialties. In addition to excellent hams and sausages, there are numerous fish dishes, such as Helgoland lobster, **Hamburger Matjestopf** *(pickled herring with sliced apples and onion rings in a sour-cream sauce)*, Berlin eel soup, or Black Forest trout. Other regional dishes include **Sauerbraten** *(marinated pot roast)* from the Rhineland, **Kasseler Rippchen** *(smoked loin of pork)*, or Bavarian **Leberkäs** *(meat loaf made from minced pork)*. In the South, dumplings and pasta dishes (e.g., **Spätzle**) are popular. Germany also boasts a large variety of pastries, such as **Schwarzwälder Kirschtorte, Frankfurter Kranz** *(a rich cake ring decorated with whipped cream and nuts)*, or **Thüringer Mohnkuchen** *(poppy-seed cake)*. A favorite summer dessert is **Rote Grütze** *(berries and their juices thickened with sago starch and served with vanilla sauce or cream)*.

Most famous among Austrian dishes are **Schnitzel, Gulasch,** and a variety of salted and smoked meats, as well as dumplings. But desserts like **Strudel, Palatschinken** *(dessert crêpes)*, or **Sachertorte** delight visitors even more. Swiss cooking has also developed many specialties of its own, such as **Geschnetzeltes** *(minced veal in a cream sauce)*, **Berner Platte** *(dish with a variety of hams and sausages)*, or **Rös(ch)ti** *(fried potatoes with bacon cubes)*. The most famous Swiss dish is probably the cheese fondue **(Käsefondue),** a reminder that Switzerland produces a great variety of excellent cheeses (e.g., **Gruyère, Emmentaler, Appenzeller**).

Mecklenburger Rippenbraten

WORTSCHATZ 2

der Freund, -e	(a close) friend; boyfriend
die Freundin, -nen	(a close) friend; girlfriend
Flasche, -n; eine Flasche . . .	bottle; a bottle of . . .
Hand, ¨e	hand
besonders	especially
gewöhnlich	usual(ly)
man	one (they, people), you
manchmal	sometimes
nicht nur . . . sondern auch	not only . . . but also . . .
überall	everywhere
vielleicht	perhaps
dick machen	to be fattening
schlafen (schläft)	to sleep

FOKUS Friends and Acquaintances

Germans consciously distinguish between friends **(Freunde)** and acquaintances **(Bekannte).** This is based on the belief that there are only a few real friends among so many people. Genuine friendships are considered special and often last for a lifetime.

Vorm Lesen

A. Wie ist das hier?

1. Beginnen wir hier den Tag mit einem guten Frühstück? 2. Was isst man hier zum Frühstück? Was trinkt man? 3. Essen hier viele Leute mittags zu Hause? 4. Was gibt es hier zum Mittagessen / zum Abendessen? Was trinkt man zum Essen? 5. Was isst oder trinkt man hier nachmittags / abends mit Freunden? 6. Welche Spezialitäten aus Deutschland, Österreich oder der Schweiz kennen Sie *(do you know)*? Machen Sie eine Liste!

B. Was ist das?

der Kaffeeklatsch; das Omelett; die Bratwurst, Großstadt, Pasta, Schule, Spezialität; *(pl.)* Kartoffelchips; relativ, voll

Man ist, was man isst.

<small>good</small> Die Deutschen, Österreicher und Schweizer beginnen den Tag gewöhnlich mit einem guten° Frühstück. Zum Frühstück gibt es Brot oder Brötchen, Butter, Marmelade, vielleicht auch ein
<small>whole-grain granola / With it</small> Ei, etwas Schinken oder Käse und manchmal auch etwas Joghurt oder Müesli°. Dazu° trinkt man Kaffee, Milch, Obstsaft, Tee oder Kakao.

Gemütlich frühstücken ist wichtig.

Mittags isst man warm. Um die Zeit sind die Schulen aus und die Kinder kommen zum Mittagessen nach Hause. Manche Büros° machen mittags zu. Viele Leute essen mittags zu Hause. Andere° gehen nicht nach Hause, sondern in die Kantine° oder in ein Restaurant. Im Restaurant gibt es gewöhnlich ein Tagesmenü. Das ist oft besonders gut und billig. Außer Bratwurst, Omelett oder Hühnchen° findet man natürlich auch Lokalspezialitäten, wie zum Beispiel Berliner Aal grün° oder in Bayern Schweinshax'n° mit Knödeln°. Zum Mittagessen trinkt man gern Saft, Mineralwasser, Limonade, Bier oder Wein, aber kein Leitungswasser° und auch keinen Kaffee. Kaffee trinkt man manchmal nach dem Essen. Egal wo°, überall findet man etwas Besonderes°. Probieren° Sie die Spezialitäten! Nehmen Sie auch das Messer in die rechte° Hand und die Gabel in die linke° Hand, und dann Guten Appetit! Noch etwas: Manchmal sitzen° auch andere Leute bei Ihnen am° Tisch. Das ist oft sehr interessant. Fürs Mittagessen braucht man gewöhnlich Zeit. Leute mit nur wenig° Zeit gehen zur Imbissbude°. Da gibt es Bratwurst, Fischbrötchen, Pizza, Pasta, Schaschlik° oder auch Hamburger mit Pommes (frites). In Großstädten findet man gewöhnlich auch McDonald's oder Burger King. Schnell essen ist manchmal nicht schlecht, aber ein Mittagessen ist das für die meisten° Leute nicht.

Nachmittags sieht man viele Menschen in Cafés. Da sitzen sie gemütlich° bei einer Tasse Kaffee und reden°. Kaffeeklatsch gibt es aber nicht nur im Café oder einer Konditorei°, sondern auch zu Hause. Besonders sonntags kommt man oft mit Freunden zusammen zu einer Tasse Kaffee und einem Stück Kuchen.

Abends isst man gewöhnlich kalt und nicht so viel wie mittags. Man sagt: Mit einem vollen Bauch° schläft man schlecht; und was man abends isst, macht dick. So gibt es nur etwas Brot mit Quark° oder Käse, Wurst oder Fisch, ein paar Tomaten oder saure Gurken. Dazu gibt es vielleicht eine Tasse Tee oder ein Bier. Abends öffnet man auch gern eine Flasche Wein für Freunde. Dazu gibt es Salzstangen° oder Kartoffelchips.

Den meisten Deutschen, Österreichern und Schweizern ist wichtig, was sie essen. Wie bei uns° essen sie relativ viel Obst, Salat und Gemüse. Auch haben sie etwas gegen Farbstoffe° und Konservierungsmittel°. Sie glauben: „Man ist, was man isst."

---

some offices
Others / company cafeteria

chicken
eel in herb sauce / pig's knuckles / dumplings / tap water
no matter where
something special / try
right / left
sit / at the
little / snack bar
shish kebabs

most

leisurely
talk / pastry shop

full stomach
curd cheese

pretzel sticks

as we do here / artificial colors
preservatives

Zum Text

A. Welche Antwort passt? *(Fill in the correct answer according to the text.)*

1. Zum Frühstück gibt es _____.
   - a. Sauerbraten
   - b. Kuchen und Plätzchen
   - c. viel Obst und Gemüse
   - d. Brot, Butter und Marmelade
2. Mittags essen die Schulkinder _____.
   - a. in der Schule
   - b. zu Hause
   - c. im Restaurant
   - d. etwas Besonderes
3. Zum Mittagessen trinkt man gern _____.
   - a. Kaffee, Milch oder Tee
   - b. Eiswasser
   - c. Mineralwasser, Bier oder Wein
   - d. Kakao
4. Zum Abendessen isst man gewöhnlich _____.
   - a. Kaffee und Kuchen
   - b. Brot, Wurst und Käse
   - c. Suppe, Fleisch und Gemüse
   - d. Salzstangen und Kartoffelchips
5. Die Deutschen, Österreicher und Schweizer essen _____ Obst und Gemüse.
   - a. nicht viel
   - b. kein
   - c. nur
   - d. gern

FOKUS: Cafés and Coffee Houses

Cafés and **Konditoreien** *(pastry shops)* are favorite places for conversation or for breaks in shopping excursions. They serve coffee, tea, and hot chocolate, along with a great variety of delicious cakes and pastries. In Austria, many people have a favorite café **(das Kaffeehaus)**, where they can relax over such items as **Kaffee mit Schlag** *(coffee with whipped cream)* or a piece of **Linzertorte** *(jam-filled tart)*. The tradition of the coffee house goes back to the early 1700s, when it was the preferred meeting place not only of the literati, reformers, artists, and philosophers, but also of middle-class society.

Mm, da bekommt man Appetit.

B. Guten Appetit! Was fehlt?

1. Ich beginne den Tag gewöhnlich mit ein_____ guten Frühstück: mit ein_____ Brötchen, ein_____ Ei und ein_____ Tasse Tee. 2. Gehst du mittags _____ Hause? 3. Ja, _____ Hause ist es nicht so teuer. 4. Bei d_____ Preisen *(pl.)* esse ich gern _____ Hause. 5. Warum gehst du nicht zu_____ Mensa? 6. D_____ Essen schmeckt nicht. 7. Manchmal gehe ich zu ein_____ Imbissbude *(f.)*. 8. Dann esse ich nichts außer ein_____ Bratwurst und die Cola trinke ich schnell aus d_____ Flasche. 9. Oft habe ich kein_____ Hunger. 10. Dann esse ich nur ein_____ Apfel oder ein_____ Banane. 11. Möchtest du etwas Brot mit ein_____ Stück Käse? 12. Es ist von d_____ Bio-Laden und hat kein_____ Konservierungsmittel *(pl.)*!

C. Vergleichen Sie! *(With a classmate, make two lists that compare German and North American food and drink preferences.)*

	Zum Frühstück isst / trinkt man . . .	**Zum Mittagessen** isst / trinkt man . . .	**Zum Abendessen** isst / trinkt man
In den deutschsprachigen Ländern			
In Nordamerika			

Zum Erkennen:
der Hamburger, -; Honig *(honey);* Krapfen, - *(doughnut);* Pfannkuchen, - *(pancake);*
  Schinken, - *(ham);* Senf *(mustard);* Speck *(bacon)*
das belegte Brot / Brötchen, - *(open-faced sandwich);* Toastbrot, -e; gekochte Ei *(boiled egg);*
  Rührei, -er *(scrambled egg);* Spiegelei, -er *(fried egg);* Müesli *(whole-grain granola)*
die Cornflakes *(pl.);* Waffel, -n

D. Die Pizzeria

1. Wie heißt die Pizzeria? 2. Wo ist sie? 3. Was ist die Telefonnummer? Faxnummer? 4. Was ist der Minimumbestellwert *(minimum order)?* 5. Was macht das Pizza-Taxi? 6. Wer sitzt und wer flitzt *(is rushing)?* 7. Von wann bis wann sind sie offen? 8. Haben Sie einen Ruhetag *(a day when they're closed)?* 9. Bestellen Sie manchmal auch Pizza? Wenn ja, wo? 10. Von wann bis wann sind sie offen? 11. Was für Pizza bestellen Sie gern? 12. Was kostet eine Pizza? Gibt es einen Minimumbestellwert?

FOKUS Table Manners

Whenever Europeans eat something that needs to be cut, they hold the knife in the right hand and the fork in the left throughout the meal—rather than shifting the fork to the right hand after cutting. (It is said that American spies during World War II could be identified by their different food-cutting habits.) If no knife is needed, the left hand rests on the table next to the plate, not in the lap. To signal that a person is finished eating, the knife and fork are placed parallel and diagonally on the plate.

Beim Mittagessen

E. **Wie isst man das?** *(Show how you would eat the following foods.)*

Suppe, Salat, Bratwurst, Hühnchen, Putenfleisch *(turkey meat)*, Sauerbraten, Schnitzel, Spaghetti, Erbsen, Spargel *(asparagus)*, Kartoffelbrei *(mashed potatoes)*, Fondue, Eis, Erdbeeren

F. **Schreiben Sie!** Essgewohnheiten *(Eating habits. Write eight to ten sentences, describing when you eat, what you eat and drink at various meals, and what you like and dislike.)*

HÖREN SIE ZU!

Gäste zum Wochenende *(Listen to Kai and Gerda's plans for their weekend guests, Ruth and Uwe. Then read the questions below and select the correct response.)*

Zum Erkennen: die Forelle *(trout)*; genug *(enough)*

1. Ruth und Uwe kommen am _____ .
   a. Sonntag um vier   b. Samstag Nachmittag   c. Sonntag zum Kaffee
2. Gerda macht einen _____ .
   a. Quarkkuchen   b. Apfelkuchen   c. Erdbeerkuchen
3. Zum Abendessen gibt es _____ .
   a. Kartoffelsalat und Würstchen   b. Fondue, Brot und Wein
   c. Eier, Wurst und Käse
4. Uwe isst gern _____ .
   a. Joghurt   b. Schwarzbrot   c. Erdbeerkuchen
5. Zum Mittagessen machen sie _____ .
   a. eine Nudelsuppe   b. Fleisch und Gemüse   c. Fisch mit Kartoffelsalat

6. Zum Nachtisch gibt's _____ .
   a. Äpfel und Orangen   b. Quark   c. Obstsalat
7. Kai fährt _____ .
   a. zum Supermarkt   b. zum Markt   c. zur Bäckerei
8. Gerda kauft Eier, _____ .
   a. Joghurt und Kaffee   b. Obstsalat und Plätzchen
   c. Gemüse und Blumen

Wines from Germany, Austria, and Switzerland

All in all, there are 13 German wine-growing regions, but most of Germany's wine is produced in western and southwestern Germany. Especially the wines from the Rhine and Moselle rivers (**Rheinwein** and **Moselwein**) are famous around the world. In Switzerland, 18 of the 23 cantons grow wine, which leads one to believe that wine is to the Swiss what beer is to the Bavarian. In Austria, there are excellent vineyards along the Danube around Vienna. Wines are classified as **Tafelwein** *(table or ordinary wine)*, **Qualitätswein** *(quality wine)*, and **Qualitätswein mit Prädikat** *(superior wine)*.

WEB-ECKE For updates and online activities, vist the *Wie geht's?* homepage at http://www.hrwcollege.com/german/sevin/! You'll visit several different restaurants and cafés in Germany and Austria. In addition, a few "extra links" will expose you to some of the subtleties of dining out in Germany.

SPRECHSITUATIONEN

Choosing and ordering a meal

To order a meal, you can use the following expressions:

> Herr Ober, die (Speise)karte bitte!
> Ich möchte bestellen.
> Was empfehlen Sie?
> Was ist heute besonders gut?
> (Ich glaube,) ich nehme . . .
> Ich möchte . . .
> Ich hätte gern . . .
> Bringen Sie mir bitte . . . ! (Please, bring me . . .)

To request the bill, you may say:

> Herr Ober / Entschuldigen Sie / Hallo, ich möchte zahlen!
> Zahlen bitte!
> Die Rechnung bitte!

Expressing likes and dislikes

1. Likes

   > Ich esse / trinke gern . . .
   > Ich finde . . . gut.
   > . . . schmeckt wunderbar / ist prima.
   > . . . gefällt mir. *(I like . . .)*
   > Wie gefällt Ihnen / dir . . . ? (How do you like . . . ?)

2. Dislikes

   > Ich esse / trinke nicht gern . . .
   > Ich finde . . . nicht gut.
   > . . . schmeckt nicht gut (furchtbar).
   > . . . ist zu heiß / kalt, zu teuer / billig, . . .
   > . . . gefällt mir nicht.

CAUTION: **Gefallen** is usually not used to talk about food, but rather to say that a city, a picture, an item of clothing, or a person is pleasing to you. **Schmecken** is used with food and beverages.

Übungen

A. **Wie gefällt dir das?** *(In pairs, ask each other about three likes and three dislikes, using various expressions, e.g.,* **gern** + *verb,* **gefallen, schmecken, finden.** *You might ask about people, places, restaurants, food and beverages, clothing, books, and so on.)*

BEISPIEL: Wie gefällt es dir hier? Was schmeckt dir besonders gut? Was für Obst isst du gern? Wie findest du Fisch? usw.

B. **Im Ratskeller**

1. **Die Speisekarte** *(Look for the following words on the menu and match them with the listing in English.*

    _____ 1. Kalbsleber   a. *beverages*
    _____ 2. Putensteak   b. *calves' liver*
    _____ 3. Champignons   c. *cherry cake*
    _____ 4. Mais   d. *a rich chocolate cake*
    _____ 5. Preiselbeeren   e. *compote made of raspberries, etc.*
    _____ 6. Zwiebeln   f. *corn*
    _____ 7. Spätzle   g. *cranberries*
    _____ 8. Kartoffelbrei   h. *cucumber salad*
    _____ 9. Weinsoße   i. *lentil soup*
    _____ 10. Linsensuppe   j. *mashed potatoes*
    _____ 11. Gurkensalat   k. *mushrooms*
    _____ 12. Getränke   l. *onions*
    _____ 13. Apfelkompott   m. *stewed apples*
    _____ 14. Rote Grütze   n. *tiny (Swabian) dumplings*
    _____ 15. Kirschtorte   o. *turkey steak*
    _____ 16. Sachertorte   p. *whipped cream*
    _____ 17. Schlagsahne   q. *wine sauce*

Schweizer Fondue schmeckt besonders gut.

Ratskeller

Tagesmenü:
    I. Nudelsuppe, Schnitzel und Kartoffelsalat, Eis   DM 24,20
    II. Gemüsesuppe, Rindsrouladen mit Kartoffelklößen, Eis   27,60

Tagesspezialitäten:

Bratwurst und Sauerkraut	12,50
Hering mit Zwiebeln, Äpfeln, Gurken und Kartoffeln	13,90
Omelett mit Schinken, Salat	14,00
Putensteak mit Mais und Preiselbeeren	16,80
Kalbsleber, Erbsen und Karotten, Pommes frites	18,75
Hühnchen mit Weinsoße, Reis, Salat	21,00
Schweinebraten, Kartoffelbrei, Salat	22,40
Sauerbraten, Spätzle, Salat	23,75
Gemischte Fischplatte, Kartoffeln, Salat	26,25

Suppen:

Gulaschsuppe, Bohnensuppe, Erbsensuppe, Linsensuppe, Kartoffelsuppe, Tomatensuppe	4,50

Salate:

Grüner Salat, Tomatensalat, Gurkensalat, Bohnensalat	4,80

Getränke:

Mineralwasser	1,80	Tee	3,00
Apfelsaft	2,75	Kaffee	3,50
Limonade	2,75	Espresso	4,00
Cola	3,20	Cappuccino	5,50
Bier (0,2 l)[1]	2,40		
Wein (0,2 l)	3,20		

Nachtisch:

Schokoladenpudding	2,80	Käsekuchen	4,55
Apfelkompott	2,80	Apfelstrudel	4,80
Vanilleeis mit Erdbeeren	5,00	Kirschtorte	5,60
Rote Grütze mit Sahne	6,50	Sachertorte	5,80

---

[1] A liter is a little more than a quart. 0,2 l therefore is approximately three-fourths of a cup.

2. **Wir möchten bestellen!** *(In groups of two to five students, take turns ordering from the menu.)*

3. **Zahlen bitte!** *(Ask for the check. Tell the server what you had, e.g.,* **Einmal Bratwurst** *. . . , and let him / her figure out what you owe. Round up your bill to include an appropriate tip.)*

C. **Kurzgespräche**
   1. You have just met another student in the cafeteria for the first time and inquire how he / she likes it here. Very much, he / she answers. The other student then asks you whether the soup tastes good. You reply that it is not bad, but too hot. You ask how your fellow student likes the chicken. He / she replies that it doesn't taste particularly good and is cold. You say the food is usually cold.

   2. You and a friend are in a German restaurant. The server asks what you would like, and you ask what he / she recommends. He / she mentions a particular dish. Both you and your friend order, each choosing a soup, a main dish, and a salad. The server asks what you would like to drink, and you order beverages. Use the menu from exercise B.

Rückblick: Kapitel 1–3

The review sections give a periodic summary of material that has been introduced in the preceding chapters. They are intended for reference and as a preparation for quizzes, tests, and finals. Review exercises for both vocabulary and structure can be found in the Workbook, with a corresponding answer key in the back.

I. Verbs

1. Forms: PRESENT TENSE

    p. 40 a. Most verbs inflect like **danken:**

singular	plural
ich dank**e**	wir dank**en**
du dank**st**	ihr dank**t**
er dank**t**	sie dank**en**

    p. 41 b. Verbs whose stem ends in **-d, -t,** or certain consonant combinations inflect like **antworten,** e.g., arbeiten, bedeuten, finden, kosten, öffnen, regnen.

singular	plural
ich antwort**e**	wir antwort**en**
du antwort**est**	ihr antwort**et**
er antwort**et**	sie antwort**en**

    p. 84 c. Some verbs have vowel changes in the second and third person singular, e.g., essen, geben, helfen, nehmen, werden; empfehlen, lesen; gefallen, tragen.

	e > i **sprechen**	e > ie **sehen**	a > ä **fahren**	au > äu **laufen**
ich	spreche	sehe	fahre	laufe
du	**sprichst**	**siehst**	**fährst**	**läufst**
er	**spricht**	**sieht**	**fährt**	**läuft**

    pp. 61, 84 d. Some verbs are irregular in form:

	haben	**sein**	**werden**	**essen**	**nehmen**
ich	habe	**bin**	werde	esse	nehme
du	hast	**bist**	wirst	isst	**nimmst**
er	hat	**ist**	wird	isst	**nimmt**
wir	haben	**sind**	werden	essen	nehmen
ihr	habt	**seid**	werdet	esst	nehmt
sie	haben	**sind**	werden	essen	nehmen

Rückblick:
Kapitel 1–3

2. Usage
   a. German has only one verb to express what English says with several forms:

   p. 41

   Er **antwortet** meinem Vater. ⎧ He **answers** my father.
   ⎨ He **is answering** my father.
   ⎩ He **does answer** my father.

   b. The present tense occasionally expresses future time.

   Im Mai **fährt** sie nach Aachen. ⎧ She **is going** to Aachen in May.
   ⎩ She **will be going** to Aachen in May.

II. Nouns and pronouns

1. You have learned three of the four German cases.

   pp. 43–44, 45

   a. The NOMINATIVE is the case of the subject:

   Da kommt **der Ober. Er** bringt das Essen.

   It is also used for PREDICATE NOUNS following the linking verbs **heißen, sein,** and **werden.**

   Der Herr **heißt** Oskar Meyer.
   Er **ist** Wiener.
   Er **wird** Vater.

   b. The ACCUSATIVE is the case of the direct object:

   pp. 61–63

   Wir fragen **den Freund.**

   It follows these prepositions: durch, für, gegen, ohne, um

   c. The DATIVE is the case of the indirect object:

   pp. 86–88

   Rotkäppchen bringt **der Großmutter** den Wein.

   It follows these prepositions: aus, außer, bei, mit, nach, seit, von, zu
   It also follows these verbs: antworten, danken, gefallen, gehören, glauben, helfen.

   Nouns in the dative plural have an **-n** ending unless the plural ends in **-s:**

   die Freunde / den Freunde**n**   BUT   die Kulis / den Kulis

   d. N-nouns

   pp. 62, 87

   Some masculine nouns have an **-n** or **-en** ending in all cases (singular and plural) except in the nominative singular.

   der Franzose, **-n, -n**   der Mensch, **-en, -en**
   der Herr, **-n, -en**   der Nachbar, **-n, -n**
   der Junge, **-n, -n**   der Student, **-en, -en**

   Der Junge fragt den Nachbar**n.** Der Nachbar antwortet dem Junge**n.**

Rückblick: Kapitel 1–3

2. These are the case forms of the DEFINITE and INDEFINITE ARTICLES.

pp. 43, 62, 86

	SINGULAR			PLURAL
	masc.	neut.	fem.	
nom.	der ein kein	das ein kein	die eine keine	die — keine
acc.	den einen keinen	das ein kein	die eine keine	die — keine
dat.	dem einem keinem	dem einem keinem	der einer keiner	den — keinen

Mein, dein, and **Ihr** follow the pattern of **ein** and **kein**.

pp. 43, 61, 86

3. These are the case forms of the INTERROGATIVE PRONOUNS.

	persons	things and ideas
nom.	wer?	was?
acc.	wen?	was?
dat.	wem?	—

III. Sentence structure

1. Verb position

pp. 28, 45

a. In a German statement the verb must be the second GRAMMATICAL ELEMENT. The element before the verb is not necessarily the subject.

               1   2
Ich **sehe** meinen Vater morgen.
Morgen **sehe** ich meinen Vater.
Meinen Vater **sehe** ich morgen.

pp. 46, 66

b. A verb phrase consists of an INFLECTED VERB and a COMPLEMENT that completes its meaning. Such complements include predicate nouns, predicate adjectives, some accusatives, and other verbs. When the verb phrase consists of more than one part, the inflected part (V1) is the second element in a statement, and the other part (V2) stands at the very end of the sentence.

Das **ist**   meine Schwester.
Du **bist**   prima.
Er **spielt** sehr gut   Tennis.
Jetzt **gehen** wir schnell **essen.**
     V1   V2

2. Negation
   a. nicht + (ein) = kein

   Möchten Sie **ein** Eis?   Nein, ich möchte **kein** Eis.
   Möchten Sie Erdbeeren?   Nein, ich möchte **keine** Erdbeeren.

   b. S V1 0 definite time expression   other adverbs or adverbial phrases   V2.
                                    ↑
                                  nicht

   Wir spielen heute **nicht** mit den Kindern Tennis.

3. Clauses

   Coordinate clauses are introduced by COORDINATING CONJUNCTIONS: aber, denn, oder, und
   Coordinating conjunctions do not affect the original word order of the two sentences.

   Ich bezahle den Kaffee **und** du bezahlst das Eis.

Übung macht den Meister.
Practice makes perfect.

KAPITEL 4

FESTE UND DATEN

Festzug in Bad Ems. Eine Eisenbahn *(train)* mit Blumen dekoriert.

LERNZIELE

- **VORSCHAU**
  Holidays and vacations

- **GESPRÄCHE AND WORTSCHATZ**
  Celebrations and the calendar

- **STRUKTUR**
  Present perfect with **haben**
  Present perfect with **sein**
  Subordinate clauses

- **EINBLICKE**
  Traditions
  German holidays

- **FOKUS**
  Congratulations
  German Christmas
  Wine festivals, harvest time, and traditional garb

- **WEB-ECKE**

- **SPRECHSITUATIONEN**
  Offering congratulations and best wishes
  Expressing surprise and gratitude

VORSCHAU

Holidays and Vacations

One of the most pleasant aspects of life in Germany, Switzerland, and Austria is the large number of secular and religious holidays **(Feiertage)** that are celebrated. There are, for example, two holidays each on Christmas, Easter, and Pentecost. In combination with a weekend and a couple of vacation days, these holidays make it easy to visit family in other parts of the country, to go skiing, or to go to the countryside for a few days in the sun.

Secular holidays include New Year's Eve and New Year's Day **(Silvester** and **Neujahr)**, May Day or Labor Day **(Maifeiertag** or **Tag der Arbeit)**, and national holidays, marked by parades, speeches, and fireworks. On October 3 **(Tag der deutschen Einheit)**, Germany commemorates its reunification in 1990. Austria, in turn, celebrates its independence from the Allied occupation in 1955 on October 26 **(Nationalfeiertag)**. Switzerland's **Bundesfeiertag** on August 1 is based on the country's founding in 1291. Besides Christmas **(Weihnachten)**, Good Friday, and Easter **(Karfreitag, Ostern)**, religious holidays include Ascension Day **(Christi Himmelfahrt)** and Pentecost **(Pfingsten)** throughout Germany, Austria, and Switzerland. Additional religious holidays, such as Epiphany **(Heilige Drei Könige)**, Corpus Christi **(Fronleichnam)**, and All Saints' Day **(Allerheiligen)**, are observed only in those states and areas where the majority of the population is Catholic.

The combination of very generous vacations **(Urlaub)**—up to six weeks for wage earners—and of the many holidays has reduced the average number of working days in Germany to about 190 per year, compared with 230 in the United States and 260 in Japan. Germans feel that frequent holidays and generous vacations improve efficiency and productivity. Recently, however, some concerns have arisen about the competitiveness of German workers in the global economy, especially as some unions have been able to reduce the work-week to less than 40 hours.

German enthusiasm for vacation travel has created some problems, such as overcrowding on highways when school vacations **(Ferien)** begin and end. To alleviate this situation, a system of rotating and staggered school vacations was developed in the various federal states, so that no state—with the exception of Bavaria—always has very late or very early vacations.

Lebkuchenherzen als Geschenk für den Freund oder die Freundin

GESPRÄCHE

Am Telefon

CHRISTA Hallo, Michael!

MICHAEL Hallo, Christa! Wie geht's dir denn?

CHRISTA Nicht schlecht, danke. Was machst du am Wochenende?

MICHAEL Nichts Besonderes. Warum?

CHRISTA Klaus hat übermorgen Geburtstag und wir geben eine Party.

MICHAEL Super! Aber bist du sicher, dass Klaus übermorgen Geburtstag hat? Ich glaube, sein Geburtstag ist am siebten Mai.

CHRISTA Quatsch! Klaus hat am dritten Mai Geburtstag. Und Samstag ist der dritte.

MICHAEL Na gut. Wann und wo ist die Party?

CHRISTA Samstag um sieben bei mir. Aber nichts sagen! Es ist eine Überraschung.

MICHAEL O.K.! Also, bis dann!

CHRISTA Tschüss! Mach's gut!

Klaus klingelt bei Christa

CHRISTA Grüß dich, Klaus! Herzlichen Glückwunsch zum Geburtstag!

KLAUS Wie bitte?

MICHAEL Ich wünsche dir alles Gute zum Geburtstag.

KLAUS Tag, Michael! . . . Hallo, Gerda! Kurt und Sabine, ihr auch?

ALLE Wir gratulieren dir zum Geburtstag!

KLAUS Danke! So eine Überraschung! Aber ich habe heute nicht Geburtstag. Mein Geburtstag ist am siebten.

CHRISTA Wirklich?—Ach, das macht nichts. Wir feiern heute.

Richtig oder falsch?

_____ 1. Michael hat Geburtstag.
_____ 2. Klaus hat vor einem Monat Geburtstag gehabt.
_____ 3. Am 3. Mai gibt es eine Party.
_____ 4. Klaus hat am 7. Mai Geburtstag.
_____ 5. Die Party ist bei Christa.
_____ 6. Zum Geburtstag sagt man „Grüß dich!"
_____ 7. Klaus gratuliert zum Geburtstag.
_____ 8. Alle gratulieren.

Congratulations

Herzlichen Glückwunsch! or **Alles Gute zum Geburtstag!** are the most accepted and popular ways of saying *Happy birthday!* The first two words (or the plural, **Herzliche Glückwünsche**) suit almost any occasion, be it a birthday, an engagement, a wedding, the birth or christening of a baby, church confirmation or communion, or an anniversary. Germans make a lot of fuss over the celebration of birthdays. Quite contrary to American custom, the "birthday kid" in Germany is expected to throw his/her own party. Surprise parties, however, are popular with students. Coming-of-age and special birthdays (25, 30, 40, 50, etc.) are considered particularly important—the older you get, the more elaborate the celebration.

WORTSCHATZ 1

Das Fest, -e *(celebration, festival)*

der Feiertag, -e	*holiday*	die Ferien *(pl.)*	*vacation*
Geburtstag, -e	*birthday*	Party, -s	*party*
Sekt	*champagne*	Überraschung, -en	*surprise*
das Geschenk, -e	*present, gift*		
bekommen	*to get, receive*	singen	*to sing*
dauern	*to last (duration), take*	tanzen	*to dance*
denken	*to think*	tun[1]	*to do*
feiern	*to celebrate, party*	überraschen	*to surprise*
schenken	*to give (a present)*		

Die (Ordinal)zahl, -en *(ordinal number)*

1. **erste**[2]
2. zweite
3. **dritte**
4. vierte
5. fünfte
6. sechste
7. **siebte**
8. **achte**
9. neunte
10. zehnte
11. elfte
12. zwölfte
13. dreizehnte
14. vierzehnte
15. fünfzehnte
16. **sechzehnte**
17. **siebzehnte**
18. achtzehnte
19. neunzehnte
20. zwanzigste
21. einundzwanzigste
22. zweiundzwanzigste
30. dreißigste

Das Datum, die Daten *(calendar date)*

Welches Datum ist heute?	*What's the date today?*
Heute ist der erste Mai (1.5.).[3]	*Today is the first of May (5/1).*
Wann haben Sie Geburtstag?	*When is your birthday?*
Ich habe am ersten Mai (1.5.) Geburtstag.[3]	*My birthday is on the first of May.*
Wann sind Sie geboren?	*When were you born?*
Ich bin 1960 geboren.[4]	*I was born in 1960.*
Ich bin am 1.5. 1960 geboren.	*I was born on May 1, 1960.*
Die Ferien sind vom . . . bis zum . . .	*The vacation is from . . . until . . .*

Weiteres

am Wochenende	on the weekend
gerade	just, right now
noch	still; else
sicher	sure(ly), certain(ly)
vor einer Woche[5]	a week ago
vorgestern	the day before yesterday
gestern / morgen	yesterday / tomorrow
übermorgen	the day after tomorrow
Wie lange?	How long?
Mach's gut!	Take care.
(zu) Ostern	(at / for) Easter
(zu) Weihnachten	(at / for) Christmas
(zu) Silvester	(at / for) New Year's Eve
zum Geburtstag	(on / for) the birthday
Alles Gute zum Geburtstag!	Happy birthday!
Herzlichen Glückwunsch zum Geburtstag!	Congratulations on your birthday!
Ich gratuliere dir / Ihnen zum Geburtstag!	

Zum Erkennen: nichts Besonderes *(nothing special);* Quatsch! *(Nonsense!);* na gut *(all right);* klingeln *(here: to ring the doorbell);* Grüß dich! *(Hi! Hello!);* So eine Überraschung! *(What a surprise!)*

---

[1] The present tense forms of **tun** are: **ich tue, du tust, er tut, wir tun, ihr tut, sie tun.**

[2] From 1 to 19, the ordinal numbers have a **-te(n)** ending. Starting with 20, they end in **-ste(n)**. Note the irregularities within the numbers.

[3] In writing dates, Americans give the month and then the day: *5/1 (May 1), 1/5 (January 5).* Germans give the day first and then the month. The ordinal number is followed by a period: **1.5. (1. Mai), 5.1. (5. Januar).** Thus **1.5.** reads **der erste Mai,** and **5.1.** reads **der fünfte Januar.** Note the **-en** after **am, vom,** and **zum:** am ersten Mai, vom neunten Juli bis zum achtzehnten August.

[4] German traditionally does not use a preposition when simply naming a year: Ich bin **1960** geboren. *I was born in 1960.*

[5] **vor** meaning *ago* is PREpositional rather than POSTpositional as it is in English: **vor einem Monat** *(a month ago),* **vor zwei Tagen** *(two days ago).*

Zum Thema

A. Sagen Sie das Datum!

1. **Welches Datum haben wir?** *(Chain reaction. Start with any date, then name the next two.)*

    BEISPIEL: Heute ist der 2. Juli.
    Morgen ist der 3. Juli und übermorgen ist der 4. Juli.

2. **Nationalfeiertage in Europa** *(Say when these European countries celebrate their national holidays.)*

   BEISPIEL: Irland (3.3.)
   Der Nationalfeiertag in Irland ist am dritten März.

   a. Griechenland (25.3.)   b. England (23.4.)   c. Italien (2.6.)   d. Dänemark (5.6.)
   e. Portugal (10.6.)   f. Luxemburg (23.6.)   g. Frankreich (14.7.)   h. Belgien (21.7.)
   i. Deutschland (3.10.)   j. Spanien (12.10.)

B. **Was spielt wann?** *(You work at the box office of the theater. Give patrons information about dates and times of the upcoming performances. Read aloud!)*

   BEISPIEL: Am zweiten um halb acht spielt *Vor Sonnenaufgang* von Hauptmann.

Datum	Uhrzeit	Titel
Montag, 2.3.	19.30 Uhr	Gerhart Hauptmann, ***Vor Sonnenaufgang***
Dienstag, 3.3.	20.00 Uhr	Brecht / Weill, ***Die Dreigroschenoper***
Mittwoch, 4.3.	19.30 Uhr	Carl Zuckmayer, ***Der Hauptmann von Köpenick***
Donnerstag, 5.3.	19.00 Uhr	Shakespeare, ***Hamlet***
Freitag, 6.3.	19.30 Uhr	Franz Xaver Kroetz, ***Nicht Fisch noch Fleisch***
Samstag, 7.3.	19.30 Uhr	Botho Strauss, ***Der Park***
Sonntag, 8.3.	17.30 Uhr	Anton Chekhov, ***Drei Schwestern***

C. **Tierkreiszeichen** *(Signs of the zodiac. Ask each other your birthdays, and find out what sign of the zodiac you are.)*

   BEISPIEL: Wann hast du Geburtstag und was bist du?
   Ich habe am 25. Dezember Geburtstag. Ich bin Steinbock.

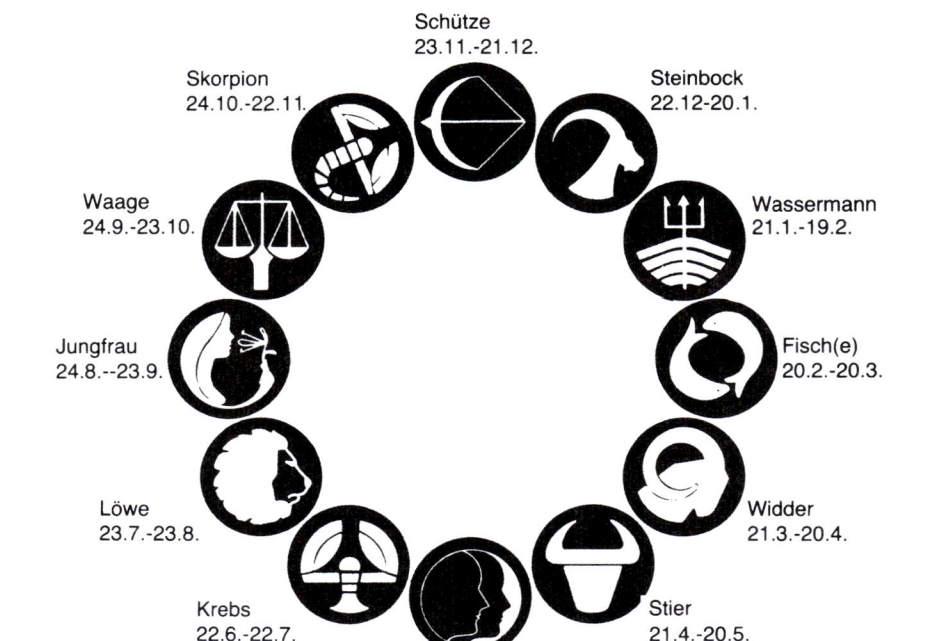

Schütze 23.11.-21.12.
Skorpion 24.10.-22.11.
Steinbock 22.12-20.1.
Waage 24.9.-23.10.
Wassermann 21.1.-19.2.
Jungfrau 24.8.-23.9.
Fisch(e) 20.2.-20.3.
Löwe 23.7.-23.8.
Widder 21.3.-20.4.
Krebs 22.6.-22.7.
Stier 21.4.-20.5.
Zwilling(e) 21.5.-21.6.

D. Geburtstage *(Ask each other about your birth dates and the birth dates of other family members.)*

BEISPIEL: S1 Wann bist du geboren?
               S2 Ich bin am 12.6. 1962 geboren. Und du?
               S1 Ich bin am 1.9. 1965 geboren.
               S2 Wann ist . . . (dein Vater, deine Mutter . . .) geboren?
               S1 Mein . . . ist am . . . geboren und meine . . . am . . .

E. Deutsche Länder und Hauptstädte *(Look at the map of the various federal states of Germany. Then take turns asking each other questions about their location and their respective capitals.)*

F. Ferienkalender
1. Was für Ferien gibt es in Deutschland?
2. Von wann bis wann sind die Osterferien in Bayern? die Pfingstferien *(Pentecost holidays)* in Baden-Württemberg? die Sommerferien in Berlin und in Schleswig-Holstein? die Herbstferien in Niedersachsen? die Weihnachtsferien in Hessen? . . .

Schulferien

Land	Sommer	Herbst	Weihnachten	Ostern	Pfingsten
Baden-Württemberg	11.7.-24.8.	25.10.-30.10.	23.12.- 4.1.	13.4.-25.4.	1.6.-5.6.
Bayern	25.7.- 9.9.	28.10.- 2.11.	23.12.- 7.1.	13.4.-25.4.	9.6.-20.6.
Berlin	4.7.-17.8.	26.10.- 2.11.	23.12.- 6.1.	4.4.-25.4.	6.6.- 9.6.
Brandenburg		21.10.-25.10.	23.12.- 3.1.	14.4.-16.4.	5.6.- 9.6.
Bremen	4.7.-17.8.	14.10.-19.10.	23.12.- 6.1.	1.4.-21.-4	–
Hamburg	1.7.-10.8.	7.10.-19.10.	23.12.- 4.1.	9.3.- 21.3. 16.4.-21.4.	29.5.
Hessen	1.7.-10.8.	7.10.-18.10.	23.12.-11.1.	3.4.-22.4.	–
Mecklenburg-Vorpommern		21.10.-25.10.	23.12.- 3.1.	15.4.-21.4.	5.6.- 9.6.
Niedersachsen	4.7.-14.8.	10.10.-19.10.	21.12.- 6.1.	1.4.-21.4.	6.6.- 9.6.
Nordrhein-Westfalen	18.7.-31.8.	21.10.-26.10.	23.12.- 6.1.	6.4.-25.4.	9.6.
Rheinland-Pfalz	20.6.-31.7.	21.10.-26.10.	23.12.- 8.1.	6.4.-25.4.	9.6.
Saarland	18.6.-31.7.	7.10.-19.10.	23.12.- 6.1.	13.4.-27.4.	–
Sachsen		14.10.-18.10.	23.12.- 3.1.	16.4.-24.4.	4.6.- 9.6.
Sachsen-Anhalt		21.10.-25.10.	23.12.- 6.1.	13.4.-21.4.	4.6.-10.6.
Schleswig-Holstein	28.6.-10.8.	14.10.-26.10.	23.12.- 6.1.	9.4.-25.4.	–
Thüringen		21.10.-25.10.	23.12.- 3.1.	13.4.-16.4.	5.6.- 9.6.

3. Was für Ferien gibt es hier (in den USA, in Kanada . . .)? Wann sind sie? Wie lange dauern sie?
4. Wann beginnen die nächsten *(next)* Ferien? Wann enden sie? Was tun Sie dann?

G. **Aussprache: ch, ck** *(See also III. 13–15 in the pronunciation section of the Workbook.)*
 1. [ç] i**ch**, ni**ch**t, fur**ch**tbar, vielle**ich**t, man**ch**mal, spre**ch**en, Re**ch**nung, Mäd**ch**en, Mil**ch**, dur**ch**, gewöhnli**ch**, ri**ch**tig, wi**ch**tig
 2. [x] a**ch**, a**ch**t, ma**ch**en, Weihna**ch**ten, au**ch**, brau**ch**en, Wo**ch**e, no**ch**, do**ch**, Bu**ch**, Ku**ch**en, Ba**ch**ara**ch**
 3. [ks] se**chs**, se**chs**te
 4. [k] di**ck**, Zu**ck**er, Bä**ck**er, Ro**ck**, Ja**ck**e, Frühstü**ck**, schme**ck**en
 5. Wortpaare
    a. mich / misch   c. nickt / nicht   e. Nacht / nackt
    b. Kirche / Kirsche d. lochen / locken   f. möchte / mochte

HÖREN SIE ZU!

Die Geburtstagsparty *(Listen to the conversation between Anke and Paul. Then answer the questions below by jotting down key words.)*

Zum Erkennen: Gute Idee! *(That's a good idea!);* es geht sicher *(it's probably all right)*

1. Wer hat am 10. Oktober Geburtstag? _____
   Wer hat am 12. Oktober Geburtstag? _____
2. Was möchte Paul machen? _____
3. Was tut Claire samstags bis um drei? _____
4. Wo wollen sie feiern? _____
5. Was bringt Paul? _____ und _____
   Was bringt Klaus? _____
6. Wer telefoniert mit Peter und Claire? _____
7. Wann beginnt die Party? _____

STRUKTUR

I. Present perfect with *haben*

1. The German PRESENT PERFECT corresponds closely in form to the English present perfect. In both languages it consists of an inflected auxiliary verb (or "helping verb") and an unchanging past participle.

    *You **have learned** that well.*   Du **hast** das gut **gelernt.**
    *She **has brought** the books.*   Sie **hat** die Bücher **gebracht.**
    *We **haven't spoken** any English.*   Wir **haben** kein Englisch **gesprochen.**

2. In the use of this tense, however, there is a considerable difference between English and German. In everyday conversation English makes more use of the simple past, whereas German prefers the present perfect.

    Du **hast** das gut **gelernt.**   *You **learned** that well.*
    Sie **hat** die Bücher **gebracht.**   *She **brought** the books.*
    Wir **haben** kein Englisch **gesprochen.** *We **didn't speak** any English.*

    The German present perfect corresponds to four past-tense forms in English:

    Wir haben das gelernt.
    { *We have learned that.*
      We learned that.
      We did learn that.
      We were learning that. }

3. Most German verbs form the present perfect by using the present tense of **haben** (V1) with the past participle (V2). The past participle is placed at the end of the sentence or clause.

ich	**habe**	... gelernt	wir	**haben**	... gelernt
du	**hast**	... gelernt	ihr	**habt**	... gelernt
er	**hat**	... gelernt	sie	**haben**	... gelernt

4. German has two groups of verbs that form their past participles in different ways:

    - T-VERBS (also called "WEAK VERBS") with the participle ending in **-t (gelernt)**
    - N-VERBS (also called "STRONG VERBS") with the participle ending in **-en (gesprochen).**

    Any verb not specifically identified as an irregular t-verb or as an n-verb can be assumed to be a regular t-verb.

    a. The majority of German verbs are regular t-verbs. They form their past participles with the prefix **ge-** and the ending **-t.** They correspond to such English verbs as *learn, learned,* and *ask, asked.*

    ge + stem + t   lernen →   ge lern t

    Verbs that follow this pattern include: brauchen, danken, dauern, feiern, fragen, glauben, hören, kaufen, machen, sagen, schenken, spielen, suchen, tanzen, wohnen, zählen.

- Verbs with stems ending in **-d, -t,** or certain consonant combinations make the final **-t** audible by inserting an **-e-**.

  > ge + stem + et   kosten →   ge kost et

  Other verbs that follow this pattern include: antworten, arbeiten, bedeuten, öffnen, regnen.

- A few t-verbs are IRREGULAR (MIXED VERBS), i.e., they usually change their stem. They can be compared to such English verbs as *bring, brought,* and *think, thought.*

  > ge + stem (change) + t   bringen →   ge brach t

  Here are the participles of familiar irregular t-verbs:

bringen	**gebracht**
denken	**gedacht**
haben	**gehabt**

b. A smaller but extremely important group of verbs, the N-VERBS, form their past participles with the prefix **ge-** and the ending **-en.** They correspond to such English verbs as *write, written,* and *speak, spoken.* The n-verbs frequently have a stem change in the past participle. Their forms are not predictable, and therefore must be memorized. (Many of them also have a stem change in the second and third person singular of the present tense: **sprechen, du sprichst, er spricht.** *NOTE:* Those that do have this change are always n-verbs.)

  > ge + stem (change) + en   geben →   ge geb en
  >   finden → ge fund en

  You will need to learn the past participles of these n-verbs:

essen	**gegessen**	schlafen	**geschlafen**
finden	**gefunden**	schreiben	**geschrieben**
geben	**gegeben**	sehen	**gesehen**
heißen	**geheißen**	singen	**gesungen**
helfen	**geholfen**	sprechen	**gesprochen**
lesen	**gelesen**	tragen	**getragen**
liegen	**gelegen**	trinken	**getrunken**
nehmen	**genommen**	tun	**getan**
scheinen	**geschienen**		

5. Two groups of verbs have no **ge-**prefix.

   - Inseparable-prefix verbs

     In English as in German, many verbs have been formed by the use of inseparable prefixes, e.g., *to belong, to impress, to proceed.* In both languages the stress is on the verb, not on the prefix. The German inseparable prefixes are **be-, emp-, ent-, er-, ge-, ver-,** and **zer-.** Note: These verbs do <u>not</u> have a **ge-** prefix.

     > bestellen → be stell t
     > verstehen → ver stand en

     Familiar t-verbs that also follow this pattern include: bezahlen, gehören, verkaufen, überraschen, wiederholen. *NOTE:* **über-** and **wieder-** are not always inseparable prefixes.

You will need to learn the past participles of these familiar n-verbs:

beginnen	**begonnen**	gefallen	**gefallen**
bekommen	**bekommen**	verstehen	**verstanden**
empfehlen	**empfohlen**		

- Verbs ending in **-ieren** (all of which are t-verbs):

| gratulieren | **gratuliert** |
| studieren | **studiert** |

Übungen

A. Geben Sie das Partizip!

   BEISPIEL: fragen **gefragt**

1. dauern, feiern, danken, wohnen, tanzen, antworten, bedeuten, kosten, öffnen, regnen, verkaufen, bezahlen, gratulieren, denken, bringen, studieren
2. essen, finden, tun, helfen, lesen, heißen, trinken, schlafen, scheinen, singen, bekommen, empfehlen, beginnen, gefallen, verstehen

B. Geben Sie den Infinitiv!

   BEISPIEL: gebracht **bringen**

begonnen, bekommen, bezahlt, empfohlen, geantwortet, gedacht, gefallen, gefeiert, gefunden, gegessen, geglaubt, gehabt, geholfen, gelegen, genommen, geschienen, geschrieben, gesprochen, gesucht, gesungen, getan, getrunken, gratuliert, überrascht, verkauft, verstanden

C. Ersetzen Sie das Subjekt!

   BEISPIEL: Ich habe eine Flasche Sekt gekauft. (er)
   Er hat eine Flasche Sekt gekauft.

1. Du hast nichts gesagt. (ihr, man, ich)
2. Ich habe auf Englisch geantwortet. (wir, du, er)
3. Er hat Klaus Geschenke gebracht. (ihr, sie / *pl.*, ich)
4. Sie haben nur Deutsch gesprochen. (du, ihr, Robert und Silvia)

D. Was habt ihr gemacht? *(Tell your roommate what happened at Klaus' party.)*

   BEISPIEL: Ich habe Klaus ein Buch gegeben. (schenken)
   Ich habe Klaus ein Buch geschenkt.

1. Wir haben viel gefeiert. (tanzen, spielen, essen, tun, servieren)
2. Christa und Joachim haben Kuchen gekauft. (bestellen, nehmen)
3. Susanne hat Klaus gratuliert. (danken, glauben, helfen, überraschen, suchen)
4. Klaus hat viel gegessen. (arbeiten, trinken, singen, bekommen)
5. Wie gewöhnlich hat Peter nur gelesen. (schlafen, lernen, sprechen)
6. Sabine hat Helmut nicht gesehen. (fragen, antworten, schreiben)

E. Auf Deutsch bitte!

1. She was still sleeping. 2. They helped, too. 3. Have you (3 x) already eaten? 4. Did you *(formal)* find it? 5. I didn't understand that. 6. Have you *(sg. fam.)* read that? 7. I repeated

the question. 8. Who took it? 9. They bought winter coats. 10. My aunt recommended the store. 11. Did you *(pl. fam.)* sell the books? 12. I was paying the bills.

II. Present perfect with *sein*

Whereas most German verbs use **haben** as the auxiliary in the perfect tenses, a few common verbs use **sein**. You will probably find it easiest to memorize **sein** together with the past participles of those verbs requiring it. However, you can also determine which verbs take **sein** by remembering that they must fulfill two conditions:

- They are INTRANSITIVE, i.e., they cannot take an accusative (direct) object. Examples of such verbs are: **gehen, kommen,** and **laufen.**
- They express a CHANGE OF PLACE OR CONDITION. **Sein** and **bleiben** are exceptions to this rule.

Wir **sind** nach Hause **gegangen.**	*We went home.*
Er **ist** müde **geworden.**	*He got tired.*
Ich **bin** zu Hause **geblieben.**	*I stayed home.*

CAUTION: A change in prefix or the addition of a prefix may cause a change in auxiliary because the meaning of the verb changes.

Ich **bin** nach Hause **gekommen.**	*I came home.*
Ich **habe** ein Geschenk **bekommen.**	*I received a present.*

The present perfect of the following verbs is formed with the present tense of **sein** (V1) and the past participle (V2). They are all n-verbs, although some t-verbs also take **sein**.

sein	ist gewesen	kommen	ist gekommen
bleiben	ist geblieben	laufen	ist gelaufen
fahren	ist gefahren	werden	ist geworden
gehen	ist gegangen		

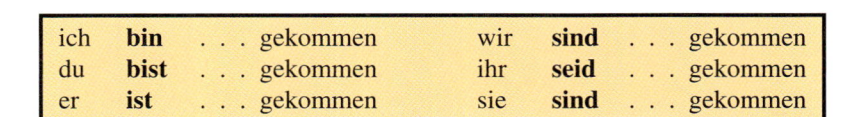

ich	bin	. . . gekommen	wir	sind	. . . gekommen
du	bist	. . . gekommen	ihr	seid	. . . gekommen
er	ist	. . . gekommen	sie	sind	. . . gekommen

Occasionally **fahren** takes an object. In that case, the auxiliary **haben** is used:

Sie **sind** nach Hause **gefahren.**	*They drove home.*
Sie **haben** mein Auto nach Hause **gefahren.**	*They drove my car home.*

Übungen

F. *Sein* oder *haben?* Geben Sie das Partizip und das Hilfsverb *(auxiliary)!*

BEISPIEL: empfehlen **hat empfohlen**
gehen **ist gegangen**

essen, bringen, werden, sein, gefallen, bleiben, liegen, sprechen, laufen, helfen

G. Hoppla, hier fehlt 'was! Wie ist das gewesen? *(How was it? Yesterday's party went very late, and you don't remember all the details. With a partner, piece together the picture. One of you looks at and completes the chart below, the other the chart in Section 11 of the Appendix.)*

S1:

	Max	Stefan	Petra	Ute	du	wir	mein(e) Freund(in) und ich
die Party gegeben							
mit dem Essen geholfen							
Getränke gebracht	x	x					
viel getanzt							x
laut gesungen							
viel getrunken					x		
sehr müde gewesen							
bis um zehn geschlafen						x	
zu lange geblieben							
nicht da gewesen				x			
nach Hause gelaufen							
mit Max gefahren			x				

BEISPIEL: S1 Wer hat die Party gegeben?
                S2 Petra hat die Party gegeben. Wer hat die Getränke gebracht?
                S1 Max und Stefan haben die Getränke gebracht.

H. Auf Deutsch bitte!
1. Have you *(pl. fam.)* eaten?—No, we haven't had time till now.
2. Uncle Georg, did you like the restaurant?—Yes, the food tasted good.
3. Andrea, where have you been?—I drove to the supermarket.
4. Mom (**Mutti**), did you buy the book?—No, the bookstore was closed.
5. Kirsten, what did you get for your birthday?—My parents gave me a watch.
6. When did you *(pl. fam.)* get home?—I don't know. It got very late.

I. Sommerferien *(Michael is explaining what he did during his last summer vacation. Use the present perfect. In each case decide whether to use the auxiliary **haben** or **sein**.)*

BEISPIEL: Im August habe ich Ferien.   **Im August habe ich Ferien gehabt.**

1. In den Ferien fahre ich nach Zell.
2. Ich nehme zwei Wochen frei *(take off)*.
3. Ich wohne bei Familie Huber.
4. Das Haus liegt direkt am See.
5. Zell gefällt mir gut.
6. Nachmittags laufe ich in die Stadt.
7. Manchmal gehen wir auch ins Café.
8. Das Café gehört Familie Huber.
9. Mittwochs hilft Renate da.
10. Renate bringt oft Kuchen nach Hause.
11. Ich bekomme alles frei.
12. Sie empfiehlt die Sahnetorte.
13. Die schmeckt wirklich gut.
14. Den Apfelstrudel finde ich besonders gut.
15. Renate ist in den Sommerferien bei uns.
16. Wir werden gute Freunde.
17. Leider regnet es viel.
18. Wir lesen viel und hören Musik.

J. Interview *(Find out the following information from a classmate and then tell the class what he / she said.)*
1. wann er / sie gestern ins Bett *(to bed)* gegangen ist
2. ob *(if)* er / sie viel für die Deutschstunde gelernt hat

3. wie er / sie geschlafen hat und wie lange
4. was er / sie heute zum Frühstück gegessen und getrunken hat
5. wie er / sie zur Uni(versität) gekommen ist, ob er / sie gelaufen oder gefahren ist
6. wie viele Kurse er / sie heute schon gehabt hat und welche

III. Subordinating conjunctions

You already know how to join sentences with a coordinating conjunction. Clauses can also be joined with SUBORDINATING CONJUNCTIONS. Subordinating conjunctions introduce a subordinate or dependent clause, i.e., a statement with a subject and a verb that cannot stand alone as a complete sentence.

because it's his birthday

that they have left already

While coordinating conjunctions do not affect word order, subordinating conjunctions do. German subordinate clauses are always set off by a comma, and the inflected verb (V1) stands at the very end.

1. Six common subordinating conjunctions are:

bevor	*before*
dass	*that*
ob	*if, whether*[1]
obwohl	*although*
weil	*because*
wenn	*if, when(ever)*[1]

Ich ⃞kaufe⃞ ein Geschenk.
Ich frage Helga, **bevor** ich ein Geschenk **kaufe**.
I'll ask Helga before I buy a present.

Klaus ⃞hat⃞ Geburtstag.
Sie sagt, **dass** Klaus morgen Geburtstag **hat**.
She says that Klaus has a birthday tomorrow.

⃞Ist⃞ sie sicher?
Ich frage, **ob** sie sicher **ist**.
I ask whether she is sure.

Sie ⃞hat⃞ nicht viel Zeit.
Sie kommt zur Party, **obwohl** sie nicht viel Zeit **hat**.
She's coming to the party although she doesn't have much time.

Er ⃞trinkt⃞ gern Sekt.
Wir bringen eine Flasche Sekt, **weil** er gern Sekt **trinkt**.
We are bringing a bottle of champagne because he loves to drink champagne.

Ich ⃞habe⃞ Zeit.
Ich komme auch, **wenn** ich Zeit **habe**.
I'll come, too, if I have time.

---

[1] When it is possible to replace *if* with *whether*, use **ob**; otherwise use **wenn**.

NOTE: The subject of the dependent clause almost always follows the subordinating conjunction. When a sentence with inverted word order becomes a dependent clause, the subject moves to the position immediately after the conjunction.

Morgen hat **Klaus** Geburtstag.

Ich glaube, dass **Klaus morgen** Geburtstag hat.

2. Information questions can become subordinate clauses by using the question word (**wer? was? wie? wo?** etc.) as a conjunction and putting the verb last.

   Wie schmeckt der Salat?
   Sie fragt, **wie** der Salat **schmeckt**.
   She asks how the salad tastes.

   Wo sind die Brötchen?
   Sie fragt, **wo** die Brötchen **sind**.
   She asks where the rolls are.

   Note the similarity with English:

   Where are the rolls?
   She asks **where** the rolls **are**.

3. Yes / no questions require **ob** as a conjunction.

   Schmeckt der Salat gut?
   Sie fragt, **ob** der Salat gut schmeckt.
   She asks whether the salad tastes good.

   Sind die Würstchen heiß?
   Sie fragt, **ob** die Würstchen heiß sind.
   She asks whether the franks are hot.

4. Subordinate clauses as the first sentence element

   If the subordinate clause precedes the main clause, the inflected verb of the main clause—the second sentence element—comes right after the comma. In that case, the entire subordinate clause is the first sentence element.

            1   2
   Ich **komme,** wenn ich Zeit habe.
   Wenn ich Zeit habe, **komme** ich.

5. The present perfect in subordinate clauses

   In subordinate clauses in the present perfect, the inflected verb **haben** or **sein** (V1) stands at the end of the sentence.

   Er hat eine Geburtstagskarte bekommen.

   Er sagt, **dass** er eine Geburtstagskarte bekommen **hat.**

   Er ist überrascht gewesen.

   Er sagt, **dass** er überrascht gewesen **ist.**

LERNTIPP **Having the Last Word**

When listening or reading, pay special attention to the end of the sentence, which often contains crucial sentence elements. As Mark Twain wrote in *A Connecticut Yankee in King Arthur's Court:* "Whenever the literary German dives into a sentence, that is the last we are going to see of him till he emerges on the other side of the Atlantic with his verb in his mouth."

Übungen

K. **Verbinden Sie die Sätze!**

  BEISPIEL: Eva geht zur Bäckerei. Sie braucht noch etwas Brot. *(because)*
  Eva geht zur Bäckerei, weil sie noch etwas Brot braucht.

  1. Der Herr fragt die Studentin. Kommt sie aus Amerika? *(whether)*
  2. Die Stadt gefällt den Amerikanern. Sie ist alt und romantisch. *(because)*
  3. Eine Tasse Kaffee tut gut. Man ist müde. *(when)*
  4. Rechnen Sie alles zusammen! Sie bezahlen die Rechnung. *(before)*
  5. Wir spielen nicht Tennis. Das Wetter ist schlecht. *(if)*
  6. Sie hat geschrieben. Sie ist in Österreich gewesen. *(that)*
  7. Ich habe Hunger. Ich habe gerade ein Eis gegessen. *(although)*
  8. Ich arbeite bei Tengelmann. Ich brauche Geld. *(because)*

L. **Sagen Sie die Sätze noch einmal!**

  1. **Er sagt, dass . . .** *(A friend has just come back from Luxembourg. Tell the class what he has observed. Follow the model.)*

     BEISPIEL: Luxemburg ist wirklich schön.
     Er sagt, dass Luxemburg wirklich schön ist.

     a. Die Luxemburger sprechen Französisch, Deutsch und Letzeburgisch.
     b. Letzeburgisch ist der Luxemburger Dialekt.
     c. Er hat den Geburtstag auf einer Burg *(in a castle)* gefeiert.
     d. Das ist einfach toll gewesen.
     e. In Luxemburg gibt es viele Banken.
     f. Den Leuten geht es wirklich sehr gut.
     g. Überall sieht man BMWs und Citroëns.

  2. **Sie fragt, . . .** *(Your mother wants to know about Carla's graduation party. Follow the model.)*

     BEISPIEL: Wer ist Carla?
     Sie fragt, wer Carla ist.

     a. Wo wohnt Carla? b. Wie viele Leute sind da gewesen? c. Wie lange hat die Party gedauert? d. Was habt ihr gegessen und getrunken? e. Mit wem hast du getanzt? f. Wie bist du nach Hause gekommen?

  3. **Sie fragt, ob . . .** *(Your parents are celebrating their 30th anniversary and your sister is in charge of the party. Now she asks whether you and your brothers have completed the tasks she assigned a week ago.)*

     BEISPIEL: Hast du Servietten gekauft?
     Sie fragt, ob du Servietten gekauft hast.

     a. Seid ihr gestern einkaufen gegangen? b. Hat Alfred Sekt gekauft? c. Haben wir jetzt alle Geschenke? d. Habt ihr den Kuchen beim Bäcker *(baker)* bestellt? e. Hat Peter mit den Nachbarn gesprochen? f. Hat Alfred die Kamera gefunden?

M. Beginnen Sie mit dem Nebensatz! *(Begin with the subordinate clause.)*

BEISPIEL: Ich trinke Wasser, wenn ich Durst habe.
Wenn ich Durst habe, trinke ich Wasser.

1. Ich habe ein Stück Käse gegessen, weil ich Hunger gehabt habe.
2. Ich verstehe nicht, warum die Lebensmittel Farbstoffe brauchen.
3. Ihr habt eine Party gegeben, weil ich 21 geworden bin.
4. Ich finde (es) prima, dass ihr nichts gesagt habt.
5. Ich bin nicht müde, obwohl wir bis morgens um sechs gefeiert haben.

FOKUS: German Christmas

In the German-speaking countries, Christmas Eve **(Heiligabend)** is at the center of the Christmas celebration. A late-afternoon or midnight church service is held on this day, and gifts are exchanged in the evening. In southern Germany, the **Christkind** brings the **Christbaum** and gifts, whereas in the North, the **Weihnachtsmann** is responsible for delivering the **Weihnachtsbaum** and presents. Many Germans also observe **St. Nikolaustag** on December 6 with the exchange of smaller gifts and goodies.

Nuremberg's outdoor **Christkindlmarkt** is the most famous German Christmas market. In the months before Christmas, more than 2 million visitors stroll by the market's booths, which offer Christmas decorations, candy, and toys. The smell of hot punch, roasted almonds, and roasted chestnuts is in the air as well as the festive music of choirs and instrumentalists. Nuremberg is home to the fancy gingerbread called **Nürnberger Lebkuchen.** The traditional **Weihnachtsplätzchen** and **Stollen**—a buttery yeast bread filled with almonds, currants, raisins, and candied fruit—are other favorites at Christmas.

Abends auf dem Christkindlmarkt in Nürnberg

Zusammenfassung

N. Schreiben Sie! Was haben Sie gestern gemacht? (8–10 Sätze im Perfekt)
BEISPIEL: Ich habe bis 10 Uhr geschlafen. Dann . . .

O. Die Abschlussparty
1. **Wir planen eine Abschlussparty.** *(With one or several partners, work out a plan for your cousin's graduation party. Be prepared to outline your ideas.)*
Sagen Sie, . . . !

a. wann und wo die Party ist b. wie lange sie dauert c. wer kommt d. was Sie trinken und essen e. was Sie noch brauchen

2. **Wie ist die Party gewesen?** *(Describe what happened at the party.)*

P. **Die Geburtstagsparty.** Auf Deutsch bitte!

1. The day before yesterday I gave a birthday party. 2. Did Volker and Bettina come? 3. Yes, they came, too. 4. My friends brought presents. 5. My father opened a bottle of champagne. 6. How long did you *(pl. fam.)* celebrate? 7. Until three o'clock. We danced, ate well, and drank a lot of Coke. 8. The neighbors said that the music was too loud **(laut)**. 9. Did you *(sg. fam.)* hear that? 10. Yesterday a neighbor came and spoke with my parents. 11. I liked the party.

EINBLICKE

Traditions

Germany is a thoroughly modern industrial society, but it also has many traditions rooted in its long history. Some of these are carried on not only out of reverence for the past, but possibly also to foster tourism, which contributes significantly to the German economy.

Every year millions of visitors flock to Munich's **Oktoberfest,** the world's biggest beer festival. The tradition began with a royal wedding more than 150 years ago. Similar festivals on a much smaller scale take place elsewhere, with amusement park rides and game booths. In late summer and early fall, wine festivals **(Winzerfeste)** are celebrated in wine-growing regions, especially along the Rhine, Main, and Moselle rivers where wine production plays an important economic role.

Some towns attract visitors by recreating historical events in their carefully preserved surroundings. The **Meistertrunk** in Rothenburg ob der Tauber recalls an event from the Thirty Years' War (1618–1648). Landshut recruits many of its residents in the reenactment of the 1475 wedding of the son of Duke Ludwig to a Polish princess **(die Fürstenhochzeit).** The **Rattenfänger von Hameln** *(The Pied Piper of Hamelin)* commemorates the Children's Crusade of 1284, when 130 of the town's children mysteriously vanished.

Carnival time—the German version of Mardi Gras—starts in January and ends with Ash Wednesday. It has its roots in the pre-Christian era and was intended to exorcise the demons of winter. Celebrated in the South as **Fasching** and along the Rhine as **Karneval,** it ends just before Lent with parades and merry-making in the streets.

Zwei Clowns beim Karneval in Köln

WORTSCHATZ 2

das Lied, -er	*song*
die Kerze, -n	*candle*
dort	*(over) there*
eigentlich	*actual(ly)*
ein bisschen	*some, a little bit (+sing.)*
immer	*always*
laut	*loud, noisy*
lustig	*funny, amusing*
(noch) nie	*never (before)*
verrückt	*crazy*
fallen (fällt), ist gefallen	*to fall*
Glück (Pech) haben	*to be (un)lucky*
Spaß machen[1]	*to be fun*
studieren[2]	*to study a particular field, be a student at a university*

»Ich tue, was mir Spaß macht«

---

[1] Das **macht Spaß.** *(That's fun.)*; Tanzen **macht Spaß.** *(Dancing is fun.)*

[2] **Ich studiere** *(I am a student)* in Heidelberg. **Ich studiere** Kunst und Geschichte *(i.e., art and history are my majors)*. BUT **Ich lerne** Deutsch und Französisch *(i.e., I'm taking these languages)*. **Ich lerne** gerade Vokabeln *(i.e., I'm learning / studying, possibly for a test)*.

Vorm Lesen

A. Fragen

1. Welche religiösen Feste feiern wir hier (in den USA, in Kanada . . .)? 2. Gibt es hier historische Feste? Wenn ja, welche? 3. Wann gibt es hier Karussells, Buden *(booths)*, Spaß für alle? 4. Was machen die Leute hier gern am 4. Juli? Was machen Sie / haben Sie gemacht?

B. Informationssuche *(Looking for information. Skim the passage and underline all the holidays / festivals that Carolyn experienced in Germany.)*

C. Was ist das?

der Prinz, Studentenball, Vampir; das Kostüm, Musikinstrument, Weihnachtsessen, Weihnachtslied; die Adventszeit, Brezel, Flamme (in Flammen), Kontaktlinse, Konversationsstunde, Prinzessin, Weihnachtsdekoration, Weihnachtspyramide, Weihnachtszeit; Ende Juli; ins Bett fallen; authentisch, enorm viel, exakt, historisch, Hunderte von, wunderschön

Deutsche Feste

(Carolyn berichtet° für die Konversationsstunde.) — reports

Wie ihr gehört habt, habe ich gerade ein Jahr in Deutschland studiert. Ich bin erst° vor einem Monat wieder nach Hause gekommen, weil ich dort mit der Uni erst Ende Juli fertig geworden bin. Es ist wunderschön gewesen. Ich habe viel gesehen und viel gelernt. Heute habe ich ein paar Bilder gebracht. — only

Im September bin ich mit Freunden beim Winzerfest° in Bacharach am Rhein gewesen. Da haben wir Wein getrunken und gesungen. Abends haben wir von einem Schiff den Rhein in Flammen gesehen, mit viel Feuerwerk° und Rotlicht°. Ich habe immer gedacht, dass die — vintage festival / fireworks / red light of torches

128　　KAPITEL 4

stiff / them　　Deutschen etwas steif° sind. Aber nicht, wenn sie feiern! So lustig und verrückt habe ich sie°
　　noch nie gesehen. Zwei Wochen später sind wir zum Oktoberfest nach München gefahren. Im
. . . tent / for me　　Bierzelt° haben wir Brezeln gegessen und natürlich auch Bier getrunken. Die Musik ist mir°
was / parade in traditional garb　　ein bisschen zu laut gewesen. Was mir aber besonders gefallen hat, war° der Trachtenzug° zur
festival grounds　　Wies'n°.

Im Oktoberfestzelt

instead　　　Halloween gibt es in Deutschland nicht, aber dafür° gibt es im Februar den Fasching. Das
like / parades　　ist so etwas wie° Mardi Gras in New Orleans, mit Umzügen° und Kostümen. Ich bin als Vampir zu einem Studentenball gegangen. Wir haben lange getanzt und morgens bin ich dann tod-
dead-tired　　müde° ins Bett gefallen.
these / was　　　Außer diesen° Festen gibt es natürlich noch viele Feiertage. Weihnachten war° besonders
booths　　schön. Beim Christkindlmarkt in Nürnberg gibt es Hunderte von Buden° mit Weihnachtsdeko-
toys / mulled wine　　rationen, Kerzen, Spielzeug°, Lebkuchen und auch Buden mit Glühwein°. Den Weihnachtsen-
. . . angel / nutcracker　　gel° habe ich dort gekauft; der Nussknacker° und die Weihnachtspyramide kommen aus dem
　　Erzgebirge. In der Adventszeit hat man nur einen Adventskranz°. Den Weihnachtsbaum sehen
. . . wreath　　die Kinder erst am 24. Dezember, am Heiligabend. Aber dann bleibt er gewöhnlich bis zum 6.
　　Januar im Zimmer.

Nussknacker aus dem Erzgebirge

Zu Weihnachten bin ich bei Familie Fuchs gewesen. Bevor das Christkind die Geschenke gebracht hat, haben wir Weihnachtslieder gesungen. Am 25. und 26. Dezember sind alle Geschäfte zu. Die zwei Feiertage sind nur für Familie und Freunde. Das finde ich eigentlich gut. Zum Weihnachtsessen hat es Gans° mit Rotkraut° und Knödeln gegeben. Die Weihnachtsplätzchen und der Stollen haben mir besonders gut geschmeckt.

goose / red cabbage

Silvester habe ich mit Freunden gefeiert. Um Mitternacht° haben alle Kirchenglocken° geläutet° und wir haben mit Sekt und „Prost Neujahr!"° das neue Jahr begonnen.

at midnight / church bells
rang / Happy New Year!

Landshuter Fürstenhochzeit

Das Bild hier ist von der Fürstenhochzeit in Landshut. Da bin ich im Juni gewesen. Das vergesse° ich nie. Viele Landshuter haben mittelalterliche° Kleidung getragen und alles ist sehr authentisch gewesen: die Ritter°, Prinzen und Prinzessinnen, die Musikinstrumente und Turniere°. Man ist historisch so exakt, dass Leute mit Brillen° Kontaktlinsen tragen, weil es im Mittelalter° noch keine Brillen gegeben hat. Übrigens habe ich Glück gehabt, weil man das Fest nur alle° vier Jahre feiert.

forget / medieval
knights
tournaments / glasses
in the Middle Ages
every

Ich habe immer gedacht, dass die Deutschen viel arbeiten. Das tun sie, aber sie haben auch enorm viele Feiertage, viel mehr als° wir. Und Feiern in Deutschland macht Spaß.

more than

Zum Text

A. Was hat Carolyn gesagt? *(Match the sentence fragments from the two groups.)*

_____ 1. Wie ihr gehört habt, . . .
_____ 2. Ich bin erst vor einem Monat wieder nach Hause gekommen, . . .
_____ 3. Ich habe immer gedacht, . . .
_____ 4. Im Bierzelt haben wir . . .
_____ 5. Der Weihnachtsbaum bleibt . . .
_____ 6. Bevor das Christkind die Geschenke gebracht hat, . . .
_____ 7. Was mir besonders gut gefallen hat, . . .
_____ 8. Man ist historisch so exakt, . . .

a. haben wir Weihnachtslieder gesungen.
b. war der Trachtenzug in Landshut.
c. Brezeln gegessen.
d. bis zum 6. Januar im Zimmer.
e. weil ich dort mit der Uni erst Ende Juli fertig geworden bin.
f. habe ich gerade ein Jahr in Deutschland studiert.
g. dass die Deutschen etwas zu steif sind.
h. dass Leute mit Brillen Kontaktlinsen tragen.

B. Feiern in Deutschland *(Complete these sentences with the appropriate verb in the present perfect. Use each verb once.)*

bringen, fahren, feiern, gefallen, gehen, haben, kaufen, kommen, sein, studieren

1. Carolyn _____ vor einem Monat nach Hause _____. 2. Sie _____ ein Jahr in Deutschland _____. 3. Es _____ wunderbar _____. 4. Sie _____ ein paar Bilder zur Deutschstunde _____. 5. Im September _____ sie mit Freunden zum Winzerfest nach Bacharach _____. 6. Zum Fasching _____ sie als Vampir zu einem Studentenball _____. 7. Die Weihnachtszeit _____ Carolyn besonders gut _____. 8. In Nürnberg _____ sie einen Weihnachtsengel _____. 9. Sie _____ Weihnachten bei der Familie Fuchs _____. 10. Mit der Landshuter Fürstenhochzeit _____ sie Glück _____, weil man das Fest nur alle vier Jahre feiert.

C. Interview. Fragen Sie einen Nachbarn / eine Nachbarin, . . . !
1. wie und wo er / sie das (Ernte)dankfest *(Thanksgiving)* feiert
2. wie er / sie gewöhnlich Weihnachten (oder Hannukah) feiert
3. was für Geschenke er / sie gewöhnlich bekommt und was er / sie der Familie schenkt
4. wie und wo er / sie das letzte Silvester gefeiert hat
5. ob er / sie zum 4. Juli auch Kracher *(firecrackers)* gehabt oder ein Feuerwerk gesehen hat

D. Schreiben Sie! Zwei Feiertage *(Jot down some key words about two of the holidays Carolyn mentions, then write three to five sentences about each.)*

BEISPIEL: Winzerfest
Bacharach am Rhein, September, Wein, singen
Carolyn ist zum Winzerfest nach Bacharach gefahren. Bacharach liegt am Rhein. Das Winzerfest ist im September. Die Leute haben Wein getrunken, gesungen und getanzt. Es ist sehr lustig gewesen.

1. Rhein in Flammen
2. Oktoberfest
3. Fasching
4. Weihnachtszeit
5. Silvester
6. Fürstenhochzeit in Landshut

HÖREN SIE ZU!

Das Straßenfest *(Listen to what Bibi tells Matthias about their local street fair. Then select the correct response from those given below.)*

Zum Erkennen: Was gibt's? *(What's up?)*; niemand *(nobody)*; Krimskrams *(this and that)*; Spiele *(games)*; Jung und Alt *(all ages, young and old)*

1. Matthias ist bei Bibi gewesen, aber niemand hat _____ geöffnet.
   a. das Fenster   b. die Garage   c. die Tür
2. Bei Bibi hat es am _____ ein Straßenfest gegeben.
   a. Freitag   b. Samstag   c. Sonntag
3. Bibi findet das eigentlich _____ ganz gut.
   a. nie   b. immer   c. noch
4. Bibi hat mit _____ beim Straßenfest geholfen.
   a. Matthias   b. den Eltern   c. dem Bruder
5. Der Vater hat _____.
   a. Würstchen verkauft   b. mit den Kindern gespielt
   c. mit den Tischen und Stühlen geholfen
6. Abends haben die Leute ein bisschen _____.
   a. Pech gehabt   b. getanzt   c. geschlafen

Wine Festivals, Harvest Time, and Traditional Garb

- Germany's largest wine festival, the Sausage Fair **(Wurstmarkt)** in Bad Dürkheim—between Mannheim and Kaiserslautern—dates back to the year 1442 and attracts more than 500,000 visitors annually. Aside from Bacharach, big wine festivals are also held in Koblenz, Mainz, Assmannshausen, Trier, and Bingen.
- Germans don't have a Thanksgiving Holiday with traditional foods like cranberry sauce and pumpkin pie. Instead, churches and rural communities celebrate Harvest Thanksgiving **(Erntedankfest)** with special services and harvest wreaths.
- Traditional folk-style dresses **(Trachten)** are still worn in rural areas of Germany, Austria, and Switzerland, but only on church holidays, for weddings, and on similar occasions. Special clubs **(Trachtenvereine)** try to keep the tradition alive.

WEB-ECKE

For updates and online activities, visit the *Wie geht's?* homepage at http://www.hrwcollege.com/german/sevin/! You'll visit Munich and the Octoberfest, learn about German Christmas customs, and go to two different shopping sites to select presents for your friends.

SPRECHSITUATIONEN

Offering congratulations and best wishes

What do you say to wish someone well on a birthday or a similar occasion, or a special holiday? Here are some useful expressions:

Ich gratuliere dir / Ihnen zum Geburtstag.
Alles Gute zum Geburtstag!
Herzlichen Glückwunsch zum Geburtstag!

Herzliche Glückwünsche! *(Best wishes.)*
Ich wünsche dir / Ihnen . . .
Fröhliche Weihnachten!
Frohe Ostern!
Ein gutes neues Jahr!
(Ein) schönes Wochenende!
Alles Gute!
Viel Glück (und Gesundheit)!
Gute Besserung! *(Get well soon.)*

Expressing surprise

Here are a few ways to express surprise:

So eine Überraschung!
Das ist aber eine Überraschung!
Toll!
Wirklich?
Das ist ja unglaublich! *(That's unbelievable.)*
Das gibt's doch nicht! *(I don't believe it!)*

Expressing gratitude

There are many ways to express your gratitude:

Danke! / Danke sehr! / Danke schön!
Vielen Dank! / Herzlichen Dank!

Appropriate responses include:

Bitte! / Bitte bitte! / Bitte sehr! / Bitte schön!
Nichts zu danken! *(My pleasure.)*
Gern geschehen! *(Glad to . . .)*

365 Tage Gesundheit und Glück

♥ 52 Wochen Lebensfreude und Liebe

12 Monate reichlich Geld und Erfolg

Zum Geburtstag herzliche Glückwünsche

Übungen

A. Was sagen Sie? *(Use the appropriate expression for each of the following situations.)*
1. Ein Freund oder eine Freundin hat heute Geburtstag.
2. Sie haben Geburtstag. Ein Freund oder eine Freundin aus der Oberschule *(high school)* telefoniert und gratuliert Ihnen.
3. Sie schreiben Ihrer Großmutter zu Weihnachten.
4. Sie haben einen Aufsatz *(paper)* geschrieben. Sie haben nicht viel Zeit gebraucht und doch ein „A" bekommen.
5. Sie haben mit einer Freundin in einem Restaurant gegessen. Die Freundin zahlt fürs Essen.
6. Sie sind im Supermarkt gewesen und haben viel gekauft. Die Tür zu Ihrem Studentenheim ist zu. Ein Student öffnet Ihnen die Tür.
7. Ihre Eltern haben Ihnen etwas Schönes zu Weihnachten geschenkt.
8. Sie haben eine Million Dollar gewonnen.
9. Sie danken Ihrem Zimmernachbarn, weil er Ihnen geholfen hat. Was antwortet der Nachbar?
10. Ein Freund fragt, ob Sie zu einer Party kommen möchten.
11. Ihre beste Freundin sagt, dass sie im Herbst ein Jahr nach Deutschland geht.
12. Sie studieren in Deutschland. Ein Regensburger Student fragt, ob Sie Weihnachten bei seiner *(his)* Familie feiern möchten.
13. Sie haben Weihnachten bei Familie Huber gefeiert. Sie fahren wieder nach Hause. Was sagen Sie zu Herrn und Frau Huber?
14. Ihr Vetter hat die Grippe *(flu)*.

B. Kurzgespräche
1. One of your very best friends has been quite sick. You stop by to visit. Your friend expresses his / her surprise. You have also brought a little present (a book, flowers, cookies, for example). Your friend is very pleased and thanks you. You respond appropriately and wish him / her a speedy recovery.

2. Your parents call you up and ask whether you have plans for the weekend. They are driving through the town where you are studying and would like to see you (**dich**). You are surprised and pleased. It is your mother's birthday, and you wish her a happy birthday. Tell her you have bought a present and that she'll get it when they come. You conclude the conversation.

KAPITEL 5

IN DER STADT

Blick auf *(view of)* Wien vom Schloss Belvedere

LERNZIELE

▪ VORSCHAU
Spotlight on Austria

▪ GESPRÄCHE AND WORTSCHATZ
City life and directions

▪ STRUKTUR
Personal pronouns
Modal auxiliary verbs
Sondern vs. **aber**

▪ EINBLICKE
Vienna
Greetings from Vienna

▪ FOKUS
Viennese landmarks
Jugendstil
Heurigen wine

▪ WEB-ECKE

▪ SPRECHSITUATIONEN
Getting someone's attention
Asking for directions
Understanding directions

VORSCHAU

Spotlight on Austria

Area. Approximately 32,400 square miles, about the size of Maine.
Population. About 8 million. 98 percent German-speaking; ethnic minorities include some 50,000 Croats in the Burgenland, 20,000 Slovenes in southern Carinthia, and small groups of Hungarians, Czechs, Slovaks, and Italians.
Religion. 84 percent Catholic, 6 percent Protestant, 10 percent other.
Geography. The Alps are the dominant physical feature, covering all of the narrow western part of the country and much of its central and southern regions. The Danube Valley and the Vienna Basin lie in the northeastern part of the country.
Currency. Schilling, 1 ÖS = 100 Groschen. The new European currency, the euro, is being phased in, replacing the Schilling in the year 2002.
Principal cities. Vienna (*Wien,* pop. 1.6 million, capital); Graz (pop. 243,000), Linz (pop. 200,000); Salzburg (pop. 140,000); Innsbruck (pop. 120,000).

The history of Austria and that of the Habsburg family were closely linked for nearly 650 years. Rudolf von Habsburg started the dynasty in 1273, when he was elected emperor of the Holy Roman Empire (962–1806). Over the course of several centuries, the Habsburg empire grew to include Flanders, Burgundy, Bohemia, Hungary, and large areas of the Balkans. These acquisitions were made not only through war, but also through shrewdly arranged marriages (**Heiratspolitik**) with other European ruling houses. The Holy Roman Empire ended with the Napoleonic wars, yet members of the Habsburg family ruled until the end of World War I. In 1918, the defeated Austro-Hungarian Empire was carved up into independent countries: Austria, Hungary, Czechoslovakia, Yugoslavia, and Romania. In 1938, after several political and economic crises, Hitler annexed the young Austrian republic into the Third Reich. After World War II, the country was occupied by the Allies until 1955, when Austria regained its sovereignty and pledged neutrality. During the Cold War, the country belonged to neither the Warsaw Pact nor to NATO.

Since the end of World War II, Austria has been actively involved in international humanitarian efforts. Hungary's decision in 1989 to allow East German refugees to cross their border into Austria was a contributing factor to the fall of the Berlin Wall. Austria has also joined the process of European integration. In 1995, the country became a member of the European Union. Finally, there also is a domestic movement to give up neutrality and join NATO.

Panorama von Salzburg

GESPRÄCHE

Entschuldigen Sie! Wo ist . . . ?

TOURIST Entschuldigen Sie! Können Sie mir sagen, wo das Hotel Sacher ist?
WIENER Erste Straße links hinter der Staatsoper.
TOURIST Und wie komme ich von da zum Stephansdom?
WIENER Geradeaus, die Kärntner Straße entlang.
TOURIST Wie weit ist es zum Dom?
WIENER Nicht weit. Sie können zu Fuß gehen.
TOURIST Danke!
WIENER Bitte schön!

Da drüben!

TOURIST Entschuldigung! Wo ist das Burgtheater?
HERR Es tut mir Leid. Ich bin nicht aus Wien.
TOURIST Verzeihung! Ist das das Burgtheater?
DAME Nein, das ist nicht das Burgtheater, sondern die Staatsoper. Fahren Sie mit der Straßenbahn zum Rathaus! Gegenüber vom Rathaus ist das Burgtheater.
TOURIST Und wo hält die Straßenbahn?
DAME Da drüben links.
TOURIST Vielen Dank!
DAME Bitte sehr!

Fragen

1. Wo ist das Hotel Sacher? 2. Wie kommt man von der Staatsoper zum Stephansdom? 3. Wen fragt der Tourist im zweiten Gespräch? 4. Ist der Herr Wiener? 5. Wie kommt der Tourist zum Burgtheater? 6. Wo ist die Haltestelle? 7. Was ist gegenüber vom Burgtheater?

FOKUS Viennese Landmarks

- **Hotel Sacher** is probably the best-known hotel in Vienna. One of the reasons for its popularity is its famous café, for which a rich, delicious cake **(Sachertorte)** has been named.
- Vienna's Opera **(Staatsoper)**, inaugurated in 1869, was built in the style of the early French Renaissance and is one of the foremost European opera houses.

- A masterpiece of Gothic architecture, St. Stephen's **(Stephansdom)** dates from the twelfth century. Its roof of colored tile and its 450-foot-high spire make it the landmark of Vienna.

- In 1776, Emperor Joseph II declared Vienna's **Burgtheater** Austria's national theater. The Burgtheater has always been devoted to classical drama and has developed a stylized mode of diction, giving it an aura of conservatism. Most of the ensemble, numbering more than a hundred, have lifetime contracts.

Das Burgtheater

WORTSCHATZ I

Der Stadtplan, ⸚e *(city map)*

der Bahnhof, ⸚e	*train station*	die Bank, -en	*bank*
Bus, -se	*bus*	Bibliothek, -en	*library*
Dom, -e	*cathedral*	Brücke, -n	*bridge*
Park, -s	*park*	Haltestelle, -n	*(bus etc.) stop*
Platz, ⸚e	*place; square*	Kirche, -n	*church*
Weg, -e	*way; trail*	Post	*post office*
das Auto, -s	*car*	Schule, -n	*school*
Fahrrad, ⸚er	*bike*	Straße, -n	*street*
Hotel, -s	*hotel*	Straßenbahn, -en	*streetcar*
Kino, -s	*movie theater*	U-Bahn	*subway*

das Museum, Museen	museum	die Universität, -en	university
Rathaus, ⸚er	city hall	Uni, -s	
Schloss, ⸚er	palace		
Taxi, -s	taxi		
Theater, -	theater		

Weiteres

der Tourist, -en	tourist
die Dame, -n	lady
Touristin, -nen	tourist
da drüben	over there
Entschuldigen Sie!	Excuse me!
Entschuldigung! / Verzeihung!	
Es tut mir Leid.	I'm sorry.
Fahren Sie mit dem Bus!	Go by bus!
gegenüber von (+ *dat.*)	across from
(immer) geradeaus	(keep) straight ahead
in der Nähe von (+ *dat.*)	near (in the vicinity of)
links / rechts	on the left / on the right
nah / weit	near / far
sondern	but (on the contrary)
Vielen Dank!	Thank you very much!
besichtigen	to visit (palace, etc.), tour
halten (hält), gehalten[1]	to stop; to hold
zeigen	to show
zu Fuß gehen, ist zu Fuß gegangen	to walk

---

[1] When **halten** is intransitive (i.e., without an accusative object), it means *to come to a stop:* Der Bus **hält** hier. When it is transitive, it means *to hold:* **Halten** Sie mir bitte das Buch!

Zum Erkennen: hinter *(behind);* die Oper, -n *(opera house);* entlang *(along)*

Zum Thema

A. Mustersätze

1. das Theater / die Oper: **Das ist nicht** das Theater, **sondern** die Oper.
   das Rathaus / die Universität; das Museum / die Bibliothek; die Bank / die Post; die Bushaltestelle / die Straßenbahnhaltestelle
2. zur Universität: **Können Sie mir sagen, wie ich** zur Universität **komme?**
   zum Rathaus, zur Bibliothek, zum Museum, zur Schulstraße
3. erste / links: **Die** erste **Straße** links.
   zweite / rechts; dritte / links; vierte / rechts
4. die Straßenbahn: **Fahren Sie mit** der Straßenbahn!
   der Bus, das Auto, das Fahrrad, die U-Bahn, das Taxi
5. da drüben: **Die Straßenbahn hält** da drüben.
   da drüben rechts, beim Bahnhof, in der Nähe vom Park, gegenüber vom Theater

B. Was bedeuten die Wörter und was sind die Artikel?

Domplatz, Fußgängerweg, Fahrradweg, Schlosshotel, Postbus, Touristenstadt, Kirchenfest, Schulferien, Studentenkino, Bahnhofsdrogerie, Universitätsparkplatz, Parkuhr

C. **Was passt nicht?**
   1. der Bus—das Taxi—das Fahrrad—das Kino
   2. das Theater—der Weg—das Museum—die Bibliothek
   3. die U-Bahn—die Bank—die Post—das Rathaus
   4. die Straße—die Brücke—der Stadtplan—der Platz
   5. da drüben—gegenüber von—in der Nähe von—schade
   6. fahren—zu Fuß gehen—halten—laufen

D. **Wo ist . . . ?** *(Working with a classmate, practice asking for and giving directions to various places on campus or in town.)*

   S1 Entschuldigen Sie! Ist das . . . ?
   S2 Nein, das ist nicht . . . , sondern . . .
   S1 Wo ist . . . ?
   S2 . . . ist in der Nähe von . . .
   S1 Und wie komme ich von hier zu . . . ?
   S2 . . .
   S1 Wie weit ist es zu . . . ?
   S2 . . .
   S1 Vielen Dank!
   S2 . . . !

E. **Aussprache: ö** *(See also II. 29–36 in the pronunciation section of the Workbook.)*
   1. [ö:] Österreich, Brötchen, Goethe, schön, gewöhnlich, französisch, hören
   2. [ö]   öffnen, östlich, können, Löffel, zwölf, nördlich, möchten
   3. Wortpaare
      a. kennen / können   c. große / Größe   e. Sühne / Söhne
      b. Sehne / Söhne   d. schon / schön   f. Höhle / Hölle

HÖREN SIE ZU!

Touristen in Innsbruck *(Listen to this conversation between two tourists and a woman from Innsbruck. Then complete the sentences below with the correct information from the dialogue.)*

Zum Erkennen: uns *(us)*; das Goldene Dachl *(The Golden Roof, a fifteenth-century burgher house)*; das Konzert *(concert)*; erst *(only)*; Viel Spaß! *(Have fun!)*

Das Goldene Dachl

1. Die Touristen fragen, wo _____ ist.
2. Es ist _____ sehr weit. Sie können _____ gehen.
3. Bei der Brücke _____ die Fußgängerzone.
4. Da geht man _____, bis man links zum Dachl kommt.
5. Der Dom ist _____ Dachl.
6. Das Konzert beginnt _____.
7. Vor dem Konzert möchten die Touristen _____.
8. Von der Maria-Theresia-Straße sieht man wunderbar _____.
9. Sie sollen nicht *(are not supposed to)* zu spät zum Dom gehen, weil _____.

STRUKTUR

I. Personal pronouns

1. In English the PERSONAL PRONOUNS are *I, me, you, he, him, she, her, it, we, us, they,* and *them.* Some of these pronouns are used as subjects, others as direct or indirect objects, or objects of prepositions.

SUBJECT:	*He is coming.*
DIRECT OBJECT:	*I see **him.***
INDIRECT OBJECT:	*I give **him** the book.*
OBJECT OF A PREPOSITION:	*We'll go without **him.***

   The German personal pronouns are likewise used as subjects, direct or indirect objects, or objects of prepositions. Like the definite and indefinite articles, personal pronouns have special forms in the various cases. You already know the nominative case of these pronouns. Here are the nominative, accusative, and dative cases together.

	singular					plural			sg. / pl.
nom.	ich	du	er	es	sie	wir	ihr	sie	Sie
acc.	mich	dich	ihn	es	sie	uns	euch	sie	Sie
dat.	mir	dir	ihm	ihm	ihr	uns	euch	ihnen	Ihnen

SUBJECT:	**Er** kommt.
DIRECT OBJECT:	Ich sehe **ihn.**
INDIRECT OBJECT:	Ich gebe **ihm** das Buch.
OBJECT OF A PREPOSITION:	Wir gehen ohne **ihn.**

   - Note the similarities between the definite article of the noun and the pronoun that replaces it.

	masc.	neut.	fem.	pl.
nom.	der Mann = er	das Kind = es	die Frau = sie	die Leute = sie
acc.	den Mann = ihn	das Kind = es	die Frau = sie	die Leute = sie
dat.	dem Mann = ihm	dem Kind = ihm	der Frau = ihr	den Leuten = ihnen

2. As in English, the dative object usually precedes the accusative object, unless the accusative object is a pronoun. If that is the case, the accusative object pronoun comes first.

Ich gebe **dem Studenten** den Kuli.		*I'm giving the student the pen.*
Ich gebe **ihm**	den Kuli.	*I'm giving him the pen.*
Ich gebe ihn	**dem Studenten.**	*I'm giving it to the student.*
Ich gebe ihn	**ihm.**	*I'm giving it to him.*

   ```
                OBJECT
               /      \
           dative   accusative
              ←- - - - -
                pronoun
   ```

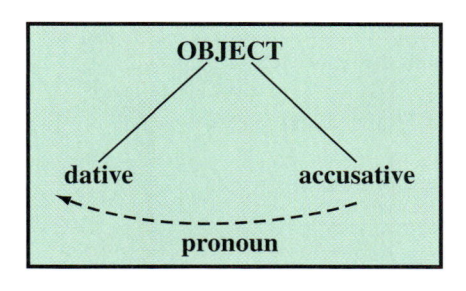

Übungen

A. Ersetzen Sie die Hauptwörter durch Pronomen! *(Replace each noun with a pronoun in the appropriate case.)*

   BEISPIEL: den Bruder   **ihn**

   1. der Vater, dem Mann, den Großvater, dem Freund, den Ober
   2. die Freundin, der Großmutter, der Dame, die Frau, der Familie
   3. die Eltern, den Herren, den Frauen, die Freundinnen, den Schweizern
   4. für die Mutter, mit den Freunden, gegen die Studenten, außer dem Großvater, ohne den Ober, von den Eltern, zu dem Mädchen, bei der Großmutter

B. Kombinieren Sie mit den Präpositionen! Was sind die Akkusativ- und Dativformen?

   BEISPIEL: ich (ohne, mit)
                ohne mich, mit mir

   1. er (für, mit)
   2. wir (durch, von)
   3. Sie (gegen, zu)
   4. du (ohne, bei)
   5. ihr (für, außer)
   6. sie / *sg.* (um, nach)
   7. sie / *pl.* (für, aus)
   8. es (ohne, außer)

C. Was fehlt?

   1. **Geben Sie die Pronomen!** *(Complete the sentences with the appropriate German case forms of the suggested pronouns.)*

      BEISPIEL: Sie kauft _____ das Buch. *(me)*
                   Sie kauft mir das Buch.

      a. Siehst du _____? *(them, him, her, me, us)*
      b. Geben Sie es _____! *(him, me, her, us, them)*
      c. Sie braucht _____. *(you / sg. fam., you / pl. fam., you / formal, me, him, them, us)*
      d. Wie geht es _____? *(him, them, you / formal, her, you / sg. fam., you / pl. fam.)*
      e. Der Ober hat _____ das Eis gebracht. *(you / sg. fam., you / pl. fam., us, him, her, me, you / formal)*
      f. Hat die Party _____ überrascht? *(you / formal, me, you / sg. fam., us, her, him, you / pl. fam.)*

   2. **Fragen und Antworten** *(Working with a partner, complete the following sentences.)*

      S1   Siehst du _____? *(them)*
      S2   Nein, aber sie sehen _____. *(us)*
      S1   Gehört das Buch _____? *(you / sg. fam.)*
      S2   Nein, es gehört _____. *(him)*
      S1   Glaubst du _____? *(him)*
      S2   Nein, ich glaube _____. *(you / pl. fam.)*
      S1   Sie sucht _____. *(you / sg. fam.)*
      S2   Ich suche _____. *(her)*
      S1   Hilft er _____? *(us)*
      S2   Nein, er hilft _____. *(them)*
      S1   Zeigst du _____ die Kirche? *(us)*
      S2   Ja, ich zeige sie _____. *(you / pl. fam.)*

D. **Antworten Sie!** Ersetzen Sie die Hauptwörter!

   BEISPIEL: Wo ist **das Hotel? Es** ist da drüben. (Bank)
              Wo ist die Bank? Sie ist da drüben.

   1. Wo ist **die Post?** Da ist **sie.** (Dom, Rathaus, Apotheke)
   2. Ist **das Museum** weit von hier? Nein, **es** ist nicht weit von hier. (Kirche, Geschäft, Platz)
   3. Zeigen Sie **der Dame** den Weg? Ja, ich zeige **ihr** den Weg. (Mann, Leute, Touristin)
   4. Helfen Sie **dem Herrn?** Ja, ich helfe **ihm.** (Kind, Damen, Touristin)
   5. Haben Sie **die Straßenbahn** genommen? Ja, ich habe **sie** genommen. (Bus, U-Bahn, Taxi)
   6. Wie hat dir **die Stadt** gefallen? **Sie** hat mir gut gefallen. (Hotel, Universität, Park)

E. **Auf Deutsch bitte!**

   1. Did you *(sg. fam.)* thank him? 2. We congratulated her. 3. I surprised them. 4. We'll show you *(pl. fam.)* the palace. 5. Did they answer you *(pl. fam.)*? 6. I wrote (to) you *(sg. fam.)*. 7. Are you *(sg. fam.)* going to give him the present? 8. She doesn't believe me.

F. **Variieren Sie die Sätze!**
   1. **Es tut mir Leid.**
      a. He's sorry. b. She's sorry. c. They're sorry. d. Are you (3 x) sorry? e. We aren't sorry. f. Why are you *(sg. fam.)* sorry? g. I was sorry. h. We weren't sorry.

   2. **Wien gefällt mir.**
      a. They like Vienna. b. Do you (3 x) like Vienna? c. He doesn't like Vienna. d. We like Vienna. e. I liked Vienna. f. How did you *(sg. fam.)* like Vienna? g. Who didn't like Vienna? h. She didn't like Vienna.

G. **Wem gibt sie was?** *(Carolyn has just cleaned out her closet and is going to give away all the souvenirs from her European trip. Explain to whom she is going to give them.)*

   BEISPIEL: ihrer Schwester / die Bilder
              Sie gibt ihrer Schwester die Bilder.
              Sie gibt ihr die Bilder.
              Sie gibt sie ihrer Schwester.
              Sie gibt sie ihr.

   1. ihrem Vater / den Stadtplan 2. ihren Großeltern / die Landkarte 3. ihrer Mutter / den Zuckerlöffel 4. ihrer Schwester / das Kleingeld *(small change)* 5. Eva / die Kassette von Udo Lindenberg 6. Markus und Charlotte / die Posters 7. dir / das T-Shirt

II. Modal auxiliary verbs

1. Both English and German have a small group of MODAL AUXILIARY VERBS that modify the meaning of another verb. Modal verbs express such ideas as the permission, ability, necessity, obligation, or desire to do something.

dürfen	to be allowed to, may	sollen	to be supposed to
können	to be able to, can	wollen	to want to
müssen	to have to, must	mögen	to like

Ich soll Sie schön grüßen...

- The German modals are irregular in the singular of the present tense:

	dürfen	können	müssen	sollen	wollen	mögen	/ möchten
ich	darf	kann	muss	soll	will	mag	möchte
du	darfst	kannst	musst	sollst	willst	magst	möchtest
er	darf	kann	muss	soll	will	mag	möchte
wir	dürfen	können	müssen	sollen	wollen	mögen	möchten
ihr	dürft	könnt	müsst	sollt	wollt	mögt	möchtet
sie	dürfen	können	müssen	sollen	wollen	mögen	möchten

- The **möchte**-forms of **mögen** occur more frequently than the **mag**-forms. **Mögen** is usually used in a negative sentence.

    Ich **möchte** eine Tasse Tee.   *I would like (to have) a cup of tea.*
    Ich **mag** Kaffee nicht.   *I don't like coffee.*

2. Modals are another example of the two-part verb phrase. In statements and information questions, the modal is the inflected second element of the sentence (V1). The modified verb (V2) appears at the very end of the sentence in its infinitive form.

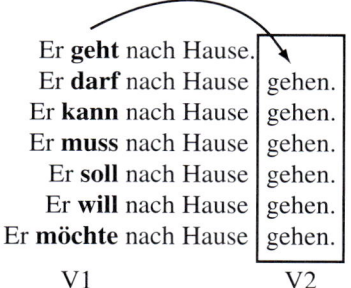

    Er **geht** nach Hause.   *He's going home.*
    Er **darf** nach Hause gehen.   *He may (is allowed to) go home.*
    Er **kann** nach Hause gehen.   *He can (is able to) go home.*
    Er **muss** nach Hause gehen.   *He must (has to) go home.*
    Er **soll** nach Hause gehen.   *He is supposed to go home.*
    Er **will** nach Hause gehen.   *He wants to go home.*
    Er **möchte** nach Hause gehen.   *He would like to go home.*
    V1   V2

CAUTION:
- The English set of modals is frequently supplemented by such forms as *is allowed to, is able to, has to*. The German modals, however, do not use such supplements. They follow the pattern of *may, can,* and *must*: **Ich muss gehen.** *(I must go.)*
- The subject of the modal and of the infinitive are always the same: **Er will nach Hause gehen.** *(He wants to go home.)* The English *He wants you (to go home)* cannot be imitated in German. The correct way to express this idea is **Er will, dass du (nach Hause gehst).**

3. Modals can be used without an infinitive, provided the modified verb is clearly understood. This structure is common with verbs of motion.

    Musst du zum Supermarkt?—Ja, ich **muss,** aber ich **kann** nicht.

4. Watch these important differences in meaning:
   a. **Gern** vs. **möchten**

    Ich **esse gern** Kuchen. BUT Ich **möchte** ein Stück Kuchen **(haben).**

   The first sentence says that I am generally fond of cake *(I like to eat cake)*. The second sentence implies a desire for a piece of cake at this particular moment *(I'd like a piece of cake)*.

b. **Wollen** vs. **möchten**

Notice the difference in tone and politeness between these two sentences:

Ich **will** Kuchen. BUT Ich **möchte** Kuchen.

The first might be said by a spoiled child *(I want cake)*, the second by a polite adult *(I would like cake)*.

5. Modals in subordinate clauses

   a. Remember that the inflected verb stands at the very end of clauses introduced by subordinate conjunctions such as **bevor, dass, ob, obwohl, wenn,** and **weil.**

   Sie sagt, **dass** du nach Hause gehen **kannst.**

   Du kannst nach Hause gehen, **wenn** du **möchtest.**

   b. If the sentence starts with the subordinate clause, then the inflected verb of the main sentence (the modal) follows right after the comma.

   Du **kannst** nach Hause gehen, wenn du möchtest.
   Wenn du möchtest, **kannst** du nach Hause gehen.

Übungen

H. Ersetzen Sie das Subjekt!

   BEISPIEL: Wir sollen zum Markt fahren. (ich)
               Ich soll zum Markt fahren.

   1. Wir wollen zu Hause bleiben. (er, sie / *pl.*, du, ich)
   2. Sie müssen noch die Rechnung bezahlen. (ich, ihr, du, Vater)
   3. Du darfst zum Bahnhof kommen. (er, ihr, die Kinder, ich)
   4. Möchtet ihr ein Eis haben? (sie / *pl.*, du, er, das Mädchen)
   5. Können Sie mir sagen, wo das ist? (du, ihr, er, die Damen)

I. Am Sonntag *(Say what these people will do on Sunday.)*

   BEISPIEL: Carolyn spricht nur Deutsch. (wollen)
               Carolyn will nur Deutsch sprechen.

   1. Volker und Silvia spielen Tennis. (wollen)
   2. Paul fährt mit ein paar Freunden in die Berge. (möchten)
   3. Friederike bezahlt Rechnungen. (müssen)
   4. Helmut hilft Vater zu Hause. (sollen)
   5. Herr und Frau Ahrendt besichtigen Schloss Schönbrunn. (können)
   6. Die Kinder gehen in den Zoo. (dürfen)

J. Besucher *(Visitors)*

   1. **Stadtbesichtigung** *(Sightseeing in town. Mitzi and Sepp are visiting their friends Heike and Dirk in Quedlinburg. Dirk tells Mitzi and Sepp what Heike wants to know.)*

   Beginnen Sie mit **Heike fragt, ob . . . !**

   a. Könnt ihr den Weg in die Stadt allein finden?
   b. Wollt ihr einen Stadtplan haben?
   c. Möchtet ihr zu Fuß gehen?
   d. Soll ich euch mit dem Auto zum Stadtzentrum bringen?
   e. Müsst ihr noch zur Bank?

2. **Fragen** *(Mitzi has several questions. Tell what she asks.)*

Beginnen Sie mit **Mitzi fragt, wo (was, wie lange, wann, wer) . . . !**

   a. Wo kann man hier in der Nähe Blumen kaufen?
   b. Was für ein Geschenk sollen wir für den Vater kaufen?
   c. Wie lange dürfen wir hier bleiben?
   d. Wann müssen wir abends wieder hier sein?
   e. Wer will mit in die Stadt?

K. **Hoppla, hier fehlt 'was!** Was tun wir? *(You, your partner, and some friends have been in Vienna for several days and you're trying to plan how to spend the rest of your time there. You've each talked with different members of the group. Work together to discuss who wants to do what. One of you looks at and completes the chart below, the other the chart in Section 11 of the Appendix.)*

S1:

	du	Thomas	Kevin + ich	Mareike	Frank und Margit
den Stadtplan nicht finden (können)					
zum Burgtheater gehen (sollen)			x		
die Hofburg besichtigen (mögen)				x	
die Uni sehen (wollen)					
durch die Kärntner Straße laufen (können)					x
noch Bilder machen (müssen)					
keinen Wein trinken (dürfen)					
Sachertorte essen (mögen)	x	x			

BEISPIEL: S1 Wer kann den Stadtplan nicht finden?
              S2 Ich kann den Stadtplan nicht finden. Und wer soll
                  zum Burgtheater gehen?
              S1 Kevin und ich, wir sollen zum Burgtheater gehen.

L. **Auf Deutsch bitte!**
   1. He wants to see the cathedral.
   2. They have to go to the post office.
   3. I can't read that.
   4. You *(pl. fam.)* are supposed to speak German.
   5. You *(sg. fam.)* may order a piece of cake.
   6. She's supposed to study **(lernen).**
   7. We have to find the way.
   8. Can't you (3 x) help me?
   9. We'd like to drive to Vienna.
   10. Are we allowed to see the palace?

M. Welches Modalverb passt? *(Work with a partner to complete the dialogue. Often several answers are possible.)*

UWE Uta, _____ du mit mir gehen? Ich _____ einen Stadtplan kaufen.
UTA Wo _____ wir einen Stadtplan bekommen?
UWE Die Buchhandlung _____ Stadtpläne haben.
UTA Gut, ich gehe auch. Ich _____ zwei Bücher für meinen Bruder kaufen.
UWE _____ wir zu Fuß gehen oder _____ wir mit dem Fahrrad fahren?
UTA Ich _____ mit dem Fahrrad fahren. Dann _____ wir noch zur Bank. Die Bücher sind bestimmt nicht billig. _____ du nicht auch zur Bank?
UWE Ja, richtig. Ich _____ eine Rechnung bezahlen.

N. Was machst du morgen? *(Using the modals, ask a partner what he / she wants to, has to, is supposed to, would like to do tomorrow. In the responses you may use some of the phrases below or choose your own expressions.)*

BEISPIEL: Was möchtest du morgen tun?
Ich möchte morgen Tennis spielen.

einen Pulli kaufen   einkaufen gehen   nach . . . fahren
Pizza essen gehen   Rechnungen bezahlen   zu Hause bleiben
viel lernen   ein Geschenk für . . . kaufen   das Schloss besichtigen
ein Buch lesen   meine Eltern überraschen

FOKUS: Viennese Landmarks *(continued)*

- The **Hofburg** is almost a self-contained city within the city of Vienna. For two-and-a-half centuries (until 1918) it was the residence of the Austrian emperors. It now houses the Museum of Art and Ethnography, the portrait collection of the National Library, the treasury, the Spanish Riding Academy, and the federal chancellor's residence.

- **Schönbrunn** was the favorite summer residence of the Empress Maria Theresa *(Maria Theresia)*, who ruled Austria, Hungary, and Bohemia from 1740 to 1780. Her daughter Marie Antoinette, who was beheaded during the French Revolution, spent her childhood there. It was Schönbrunn where Mozart dazzled the empress with his talents. During the wars of 1805 and 1809, Napoleon used it as his headquarters. Francis Joseph I, emperor of Austria from 1848 to 1916, was born and died at Schönbrunn, and Charles I, the last of the Habsburgs, abdicated there in 1918, when Austria became a republic. To this day, the parks of Schönbrunn feature some of the best-preserved French-style baroque gardens.

- The **Prater** is a large amusement park with a giant Ferris wheel and many modern rides, a stadium, fairgrounds, race tracks, bridle paths, pools, and ponds.

Das Riesenrad im Prater

III. *Sondern* vs. *aber*

German has two coordinating conjunctions corresponding to the English *but*.

aber	*but, however*
sondern	*but on the contrary, but rather*

- **Sondern** implies *but on the contrary* and occurs frequently with opposites. It must be used when the first clause is negated and the two ideas are mutually exclusive.

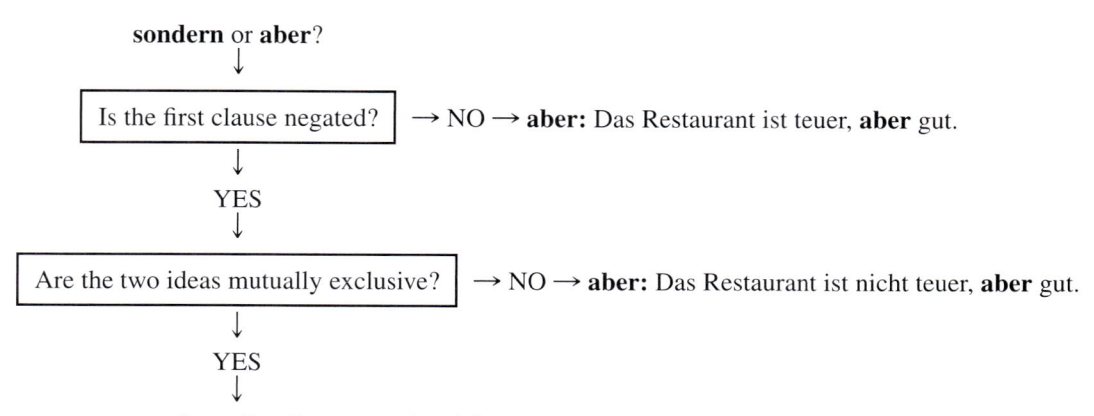

sondern or **aber**?
↓
Is the first clause negated? → NO → **aber:** Das Restaurant ist teuer, **aber** gut.
↓
YES
↓
Are the two ideas mutually exclusive? → NO → **aber:** Das Restaurant ist nicht teuer, **aber** gut.
↓
YES
↓
sondern: Das Restaurant ist nicht teuer, **sondern** billig.

- **Nicht nur . . . sondern auch . . .**

    Das Restaurant ist **nicht nur** gut, **sondern auch** billig.
    The restaurant is not only good, but also inexpensive.

Übungen

O. *Sondern* oder *aber*? *(Insert the appropriate conjunction.)*

1. Wien ist sehr schön, _____ Salzburg gefällt mir besser *(better)*.
2. Die Straßenbahn hält nicht hier, _____ gegenüber von der Post.
3. Gehen Sie beim Theater nicht rechts, _____ geradeaus!
4. Die Kirche ist nicht alt, _____ neu.
5. Das Rathaus ist nicht besonders schön, _____ sehr alt.
6. Das ist kein Museum, _____ eine Bibliothek.
7. Die Mensa ist billig, _____ nicht gut.

F⚪KUS Jugendstil

Jugendstil (*art nouveau*, *Sezessionsstil* in Austria) is a style of art that emerged toward the end of the 19th century and flourished until World War I. It broke with previous historical styles, combining romantic and almost sentimental fidelity to nature with symbolic and abstract ornamentation. The school's influence brought about changes not only in art, but in the applied arts, including fashion, architecture, jewelry, sculpture, poetry, music, the theater, and dance. Munich, Darmstadt, Brussels, Paris, Nancy, and Vienna were all centers of the movement. Gustav Klimt emerged as the leader of the "secession" in Austria.

„Der Kuss *(The Kiss)*" von Gustav Klimt

Zusammenfassung

P. Kombinieren Sie! (*Create questions by combining items from each column. Then ask different classmates and have them give you an answer, using a modal.*)

BEISPIEL: S1   Wann möchtet ihr essen gehen?
                 S2   Ich möchte jetzt gehen. Und ihr?
                 S3   Wir möchten um halb eins gehen.

1	2	3	4
wann	dürfen	du	nach Österreich fahren
warum	können	man	nach Hause gehen
was	möchten	wir	in die Stadt (Mensa . . .) gehen
wem	müssen	ihr	schön (billig . . .) essen
wen	sollen	sie	zu Fuß gehen
wer	wollen	Sie	mit dem Bus fahren
wie lange		das	jetzt tun
		. . .	schenken
			dauern
			haben
			sein
			. . .

Q. Wie geht's weiter? (*Use the statements below as models to tell a partner something about yourself. You may modify the sentences as needed. Then take turns.*)

BEISPIEL: Ich esse nicht gern Karotten, aber . . .
                Ich esse nicht gern Karotten, aber Bohnen finde ich gut.

1. Ich trinke nicht gern Cola, aber . . .
2. Wir besichtigen nicht das Museum, sondern . . .
3. Die Straßenbahn hält nicht hier, sondern . . .
4. Es gibt keinen Bus, aber . . .
5. Er kann uns heute die Stadt nicht zeigen, aber . . .
6. Ich bin nicht in Wien geblieben, sondern . . .
7. Ihr lernt nicht Spanisch, sondern . . .

R. Wo ist eine Bank? Auf Deutsch bitte!

1. Excuse me *(formal)*, can you tell me where there's a bank? 2. I'm sorry, but I'm not from Vienna. 3. Whom can I ask? 4. Who can help me? 5. May I help you? 6. I'd like to find a bank. 7. Near the cathedral (there) is a bank. 8. Can you tell me whether that's far from here? 9. You can walk (there), but the banks close (are closed) in twenty minutes. 10. Take the subway or a taxi!

Passau, an der Grenze zu Österreich, liegt an der Donau (links) und am Inn (rechts).

EINBLICKE

Vienna

Originally, Vienna **(Wien)** was a Roman settlement. The city's fate was linked to its geographical location on the Danube and at the gateway to the plains of eastern Europe. Here merchants met where ancient trade routes crossed; crusaders passed through on their way to the Holy Land; and in 1683, at the walls and gates of this city, the Turks had to abandon their hope of conquering the heart of Europe.

The center of Vienna **(die Innenstadt)** dates from medieval times. As late as the 1850s, it was surrounded by horseshoe-shaped walls. The city reached its zenith of power and wealth as the capital of the Austro-Hungarian Empire during the reign of Emperor Franz Josef (1848–1916), when it developed into one of Europe's most important cultural centers. Composers such as Haydn, Mozart, Beethoven, Schubert, Brahms, Bruckner, Johann and Richard Strauss, Mahler, and Schönberg have left a lasting imprint on the city's cultural life. The psychoanalyst Freud, the writers Schnitzler, Zweig, and von Hofmannsthal, as well as the painters Klimt and Kokoschka laid the intellectual and artistic foundation of the 20th century. Today Vienna ranks among the leading convention cities in the world and is headquarters for the International Atomic Energy Agency, the Organization of Petroleum Exporting Countries (OPEC), and the United Nations Industrial Development Organization.

Der Stephansdom

WORTSCHATZ 2

bekannt	*well-known*
Das macht nichts.	*That doesn't matter.*
einmal	*once, (at) one time*
gemütlich	*pleasant, cozy, convivial*
genug	*enough*
hoffentlich	*hopefully; I hope*
interessant	*interesting*
leider	*unfortunately*
lieb[1]	*dear*
stundenlang[2]	*for hours*
usw. (und so weiter)	*etc.*
bummeln, ist gebummelt	*to stroll*

---

[1] Lieb**e** Eltern, lieb**e** Elisabeth, lieb**er** Michael

[2] Also: **jahrelang, monatelang, wochenlang, tagelang,** etc.

IN DER STADT   151

Vorm Lesen

A. **Was machen Sie gern, wenn Sie reisen?** *(Read the list below and mark what you like to do when you travel. You may add to the list if you like. Then read the following text and mark what Michael and his friends did. Compare your tastes in travel with Michael's. What do you like to do that Michael and his friends did not do or that he did not mention? What did Michael do that would not be of interest to you?)*

	ICH	MICHAEL
durch die Innenstadt bummeln	_____	_____
Souvenirs kaufen	_____	_____
in ein paar Museen gehen	_____	_____
in die Oper gehen	_____	_____
in eine Weinstube *(small restaurant)* gehen	_____	_____
Schlösser und Kirchen besichtigen	_____	_____
ein McDonalds finden	_____	_____
tanzen gehen	_____	_____
. . .		

B. **Was ist das?**

der Sport, Stopp, Walzer; das Gästehaus; die Studentengruppe, Winterresidenz; zentral

Grüße° aus Wien greetings

Liebe Eltern!

    Jetzt muss ich euch aber wirklich wieder einmal schreiben! Ich habe so viel gesehen, dass ich gar nicht weiß, wo ich beginnen soll. Vor einer Woche war° ich mit unsrer Studentengruppe noch in Passau. Von dort sind wir mit dem Schiff die Donau hinuntergefahren°. Wir haben einen Stopp in Linz gemacht und haben die Stadt, das Schloss und den Dom besichtigt. Dann sind wir mit dem Schiff weiter bis nach Wien gefahren. Die Weinberge°, Burgen° und besonders Kloster° Melk haben mir sehr gut gefallen. Das Wetter ist auch sehr schön gewesen.

was
traveled down

vineyards / castles
monastery

Kloster Melk an der Donau

Jetzt sind wir schon ein paar Tage in Wien. Ich finde es toll hier! Unser Gästehaus liegt sehr zentral und wir können alles zu Fuß oder mit der U-Bahn erreichen°. So viel bin ich noch nie gelaufen! Am Freitag sind wir stundenlang durch die Innenstadt gebummelt. Die Geschäfte in der° Kärntner Straße sind sehr teuer, aber man muss ja° nichts kaufen. Wir haben natürlich auch den Stephansdom besichtigt und sind mit dem Aufzug° im Turm hinaufgefahren°. Von dort kann man Wien gut sehen. Am Abend haben wir Mozarts *Zauberflöte*° in der Oper gesehen.

Am Samstag haben wir die Hofburg besichtigt. Das ist einmal die Winterresidenz der° Habsburger Kaiser° gewesen. Dort ist auch die Spanische Reitschule° und man kann die Lipizzaner° beim Training sehen. Das haben wir auch getan. Wirklich prima! Da ist das Reiten° kein Sport, sondern Kunst°. Am Abend sind wir mit der Straßenbahn nach Grinzing gefahren und haben dort Marks Geburtstag mit Musik und Wein gefeiert. Die Weinstube° war sehr gemütlich.

Lipizzaner beim Training in der Spanischen Reitschule

Heute besichtigen wir das Museum für Völkerkunde° und die Sezession° und später wollen ein paar von uns noch zum Prater. Das Riesenrad° dort soll toll sein. Morgen früh wollen wir noch zum Schloss Schönbrunn, der Sommerresidenz der Habsburger; und dann ist unsere Zeit in Wien auch schon fast um°.

Wien ist wirklich interessant. Überall findet man Denkmäler° oder Straßen mit bekannten Namen wie Mozart, Beethoven, Johann Strauß usw. Aber ihr dürft nicht denken, dass man hier nur Walzer hört und alles romantisch ist. Wien ist auch eine Großstadt mit vielen Menschen und viel Verkehr°. Es gefällt mir hier so gut, dass ich gern noch ein paar Tage bleiben möchte. Das geht leider nicht, weil wir noch nach Salzburg und Innsbruck wollen. Eine Woche ist einfach° nicht lange genug für so eine Reise. Nach Budapest können wir leider auch nicht. Nun, das macht nichts. Hoffentlich komme ich im Frühling einmal nach Ungarn°.

So, jetzt muss ich schnell frühstücken und dann geht's wieder los°! Tschüss und viele liebe Grüße!

Euer Michael

Zum Text

A. *Wer, was oder wo ist das?* (Match the descriptions with the places or people in the list below.)

die Donau, Grinzing, die Hofburg, die Kärntner Straße, Linz, Melk, Passau, der Prater, Schloss Schönbrunn, die Spanische Reitschule, die Staatsoper, der Turm vom Stephansdom

1. Hier hat die Flussfahrt nach Wien begonnen.
2. Auf diesem *(on this)* Fluss kann man mit dem Schiff bis nach Wien fahren.
3. Hier haben die Habsburger Kaiser im Sommer gelebt.
4. Hier gibt es ein Barockkloster. Es ist sehr bekannt.
5. Da haben die Studenten einen Stop gemacht und die Stadt besichtigt.
6. Hier kann man schön bummeln, aber die Geschäfte sind sehr teuer.
7. Von dort kann man ganz Wien sehen.
8. Das ist einmal die Winterresidenz der *(of the)* Habsburger Kaiser gewesen.
9. Hier kann man die Lipizzaner trainieren sehen.
10. Hier kann man Mozarts *Zauberflöte* sehen.
11. Hier gibt es ein Riesenrad.
12. Dort kann man gemütlich essen und Wein trinken.

Heurigen Wine FOKUS

Located on the outskirts of Vienna, Grinzing is probably the best-known Heurigen wine village. Young, fresh wine **(der Heurige)** is sold by wine growers in their courtyards or houses, some of which have been turned into restaurants **(Weinstuben** or **Heurigenschänken).**

B. *Sondern* oder *aber?* (Insert the appropriate conjunction.)
1. Das Gästehaus ist nicht sehr elegant, _____ es liegt zentral.
2. Wir sind nicht mit dem Bus gefahren, _____ viel gelaufen.
3. Bei der Spanischen Reitschule ist das Reiten kein Sport, _____ Kunst.
4. Die Geschäfte in der Kärntner Straße sind teuer, _____ sie gefallen mir.

C. *Fahrt (trip) nach Österreich* (Mr. Schubach tells about his travel plans. Use modal verbs.)

BEISPIEL: Ihr fahrt mit uns mit dem Schiff bis nach Wien. (müssen)
Ihr müsst mit uns mit dem Schiff bis nach Wien fahren.

1. Unsere Fahrt beginnt in Passau. (sollen)
2. In Linz machen wir einen Stop. (wollen)
3. Meine Frau besichtigt Kloster Melk. (möchten)
4. Vom Schiff sieht man viele Weinberge und Burgen. (können)
5. Wir bleiben fünf Tage in Wien. (wollen)
6. Dort gibt es viel zu sehen. (sollen)
7. Man hat natürlich gute Schuhe dabei *(along).* (müssen)
8. Ich laufe aber nicht so viel. (dürfen)
9. Meine Frau bummelt gemütlich durch die Kärntner Straße. (möchten)
10. Ich sehe viele Museen. (wollen)

D. Interview. Fragen Sie einen Nachbarn / eine Nachbarin, . . . !
1. ob er / sie schon einmal in Wien gewesen ist; wenn ja, was ihm / ihr in Wien besonders gut gefallen hat (**Was hat dir . . . ?**); wenn nein, was er / sie einmal in Wien sehen möchte
2. ob er / sie in einer Großstadt oder Kleinstadt wohnt
3. ob die Stadt eine Altstadt hat und ob sie schön ist
4. ob es dort eine Straßenbahn, eine U-Bahn oder Busse gibt
5. was für Denkmäler und Straßen mit bekannten Namen es gibt
6. was ihm / ihr dort besonders gefällt und was nicht
7. ob er / sie schon einmal in einem Schloss gewesen ist; wenn ja, wo; wenn nein, welches Schloss er / sie einmal sehen möchte

E. Etwas Geographie. Sehen Sie auf die Landkarte von Österreich und beantworten Sie die Fragen! Arbeiten Sie mit einem Partner!

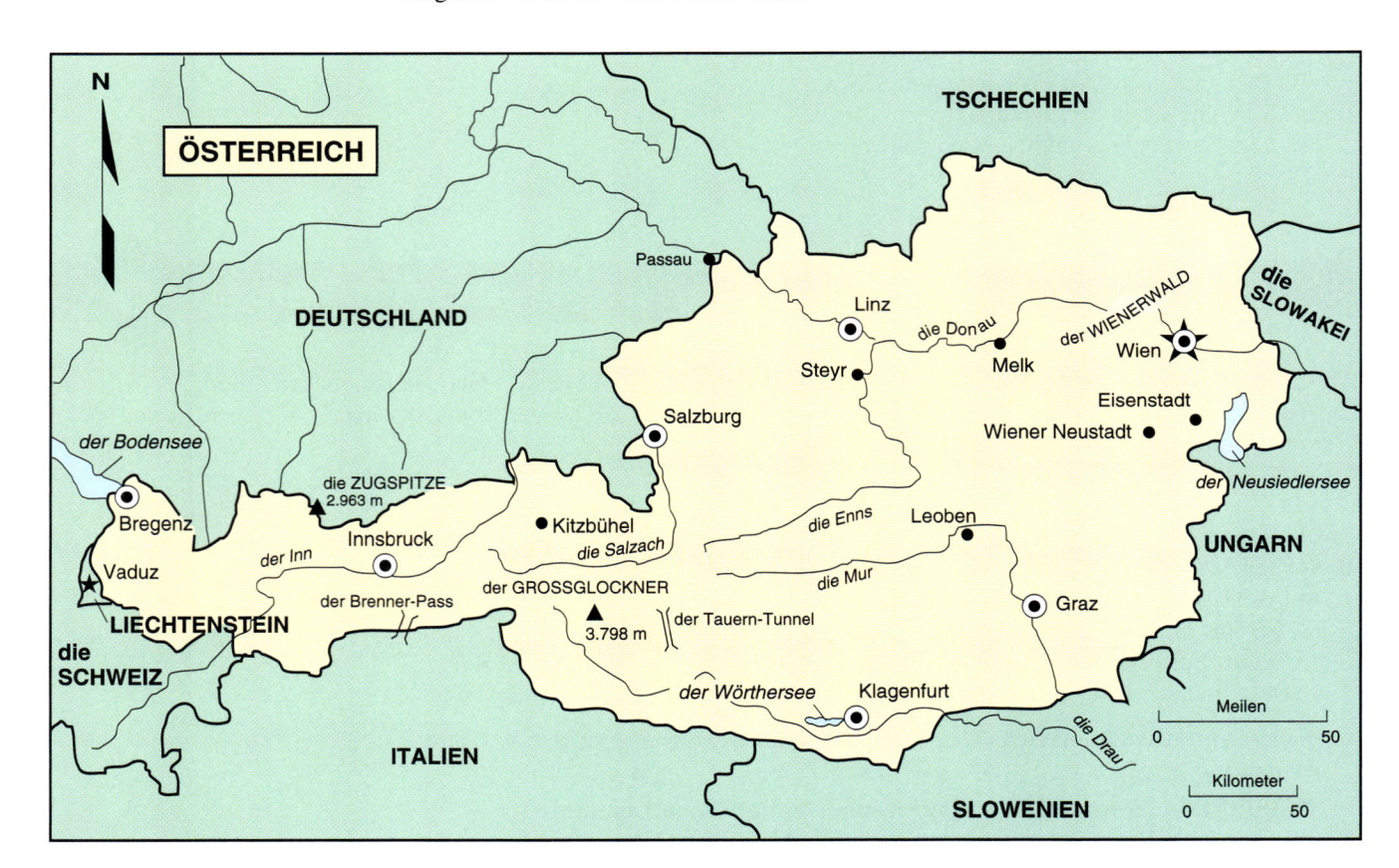

1. Wie viele Nachbarländer hat Österreich? Wie heißen sie und wo liegen sie?
2. Wie heißt die Hauptstadt von Österreich? Wie heißen ein paar Städte in Österreich?
3. Welche Flüsse gibt es in Österreich? An welchem Fluss liegt Wien? Salzburg? Innsbruck? Linz? Graz? (**. . . liegt am / an der . . .**)
4. Welcher See liegt nicht nur in Österreich, sondern auch in Deutschland und in der Schweiz? Welcher See liegt zum Teil in Österreich und zum Teil in Ungarn? An welchem See liegt Klagenfurt?
5. Wo liegt der Brenner-Pass? der Großglockner? der Tauern-Tunnel?

F. **Schreiben Sie!** Grüße von zu Hause (8–10 Sätze an Michael)

BEISPIEL: Lieber Michael! Danke für deinen Brief *(letter)!* Wie ich sehe, hast du Spaß in Wien gehabt . . . Hier zu Hause ist es kalt und es regnet viel . . . Viele liebe Grüße! Dein(e) . . .

MUSEUM FÜR VÖLKERKUNDE
A-1014 WIEN, NEUE HOFBURG
TELEFON (0222) 93 45 41

HÖREN SIE ZU!

Schon lange nicht mehr gesehen! *(Listen to the conversation between Uwe and Erika, then answer the questions. You do not need to write complete sentences.)*

Zum Erkennen: schon lange nicht mehr *(not for a long time)*; Bergwanderungen *(mountain hikes)*

1. Wo ist Uwe gewesen? _____
2. Mit wem ist er gefahren? _____
3. Wie ist das Wetter gewesen? _____
4. Wo ist Maria Alm? _____
5. Was haben sie dort gemacht? _____
6. Wo sind sie noch gewesen? _____
7. Was haben sie dort besichtigt? _____
8. Wann will Uwe nach Wien? _____
9. Warum muss Erika gehen? _____

WEB-ECKE

For updates and online activities, visit the *Wie geht's?* homepage at http://www.hrwcollege.com/german/sevin/! You'll visit Vienna, check into the Hotel Sacher, and meet the Vienna Boys' Choir and some of Austria's famous composers. You'll also visit Linz and take a trip up the Danube toward Passau, Germany.

SPRECHSITUATIONEN

When traveling or living abroad, it is very important to be able to ask for and understand directions, but first you must get someone's attention.

Getting someone's attention

Entschuldigen Sie bitte!
Entschuldigung! / Verzeihung!

Asking for directions

Bitte, wo ist . . . ?
Können Sie mir (bitte) sagen, wo . . . ist?
Ich möchte zum / zur . . .
Ich kann . . . nicht finden.
Wie kommt man (von hier) zum / zur . . . ?
Ist hier in der Nähe . . . ?
Wo gibt es hier . . . ?
Wie weit ist es (nach, bis zum / zur . . .)?

Understanding directions

Gehen Sie / Fahren Sie . . . !
(immer) geradeaus
die erste Straße links / rechts
die Hauptstraße entlang
am (Dom) / an der (Oper) vorbei *(past the cathedral / opera house)*
bis Sie zum / zur . . . kommen
bis Sie . . . sehen

Fahren Sie mit dem Auto / der Straßenbahn!
Nehmen Sie den Bus / die U-Bahn / ein Taxi!
Sie können zu Fuß gehen.
Kommen Sie! Ich kann Ihnen . . . zeigen.
Fragen Sie dort noch einmal!

Übungen

A. Fragen zum Stadtplan
1. **Wie fragt man?** *(Ask for directions to several places in Vienna, e.g., the university or the Hofburg. Use as many different ways of asking as you can.)*

2. **Wie komme ich dorthin?** *(In groups of two or three, practice asking and giving directions from one place in Vienna to another.)*

   BEISPIEL: vom Stephansdom zur Oper
   Entschuldigen Sie bitte! Können Sie mir sagen, wie ich von hier zur Oper komme?—Gern. Gehen Sie immer geradeaus die Kärntner Straße entlang! Sie sehen dann die Oper rechts.

   a. von der Oper zur Hofburg
   b. von der Hofburg zur Uni
   c. von der Uni zum Parlament
   d. vom Parlament zum Schwarzenbergplatz
   e. vom Schwarzenbergplatz zum Donaukanal
   f. vom Donaukanal zum Stephansdom

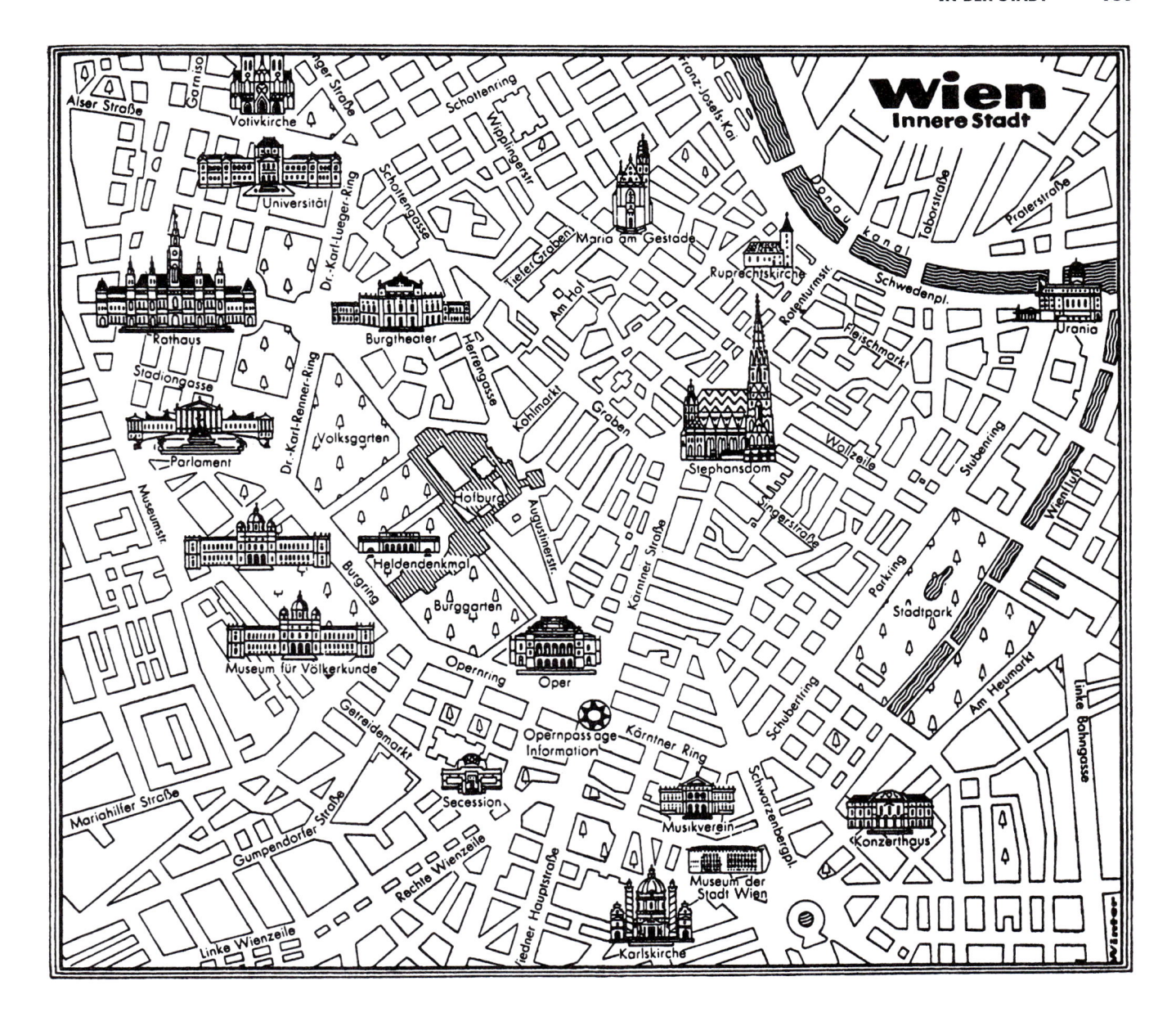

B. Kurzgespräche

1. You are new in town or on campus, and you are looking for a particular building. Ask someone, beginning *Pardon me, is that . . . ?* The stranger tells you that that's not what you are looking for but rather something else. Ask for directions, and inquire whether the building is close by or far away. Thank the person for the information.

2. You and a friend are in a Viennese coffee house. Your friend suggests visiting the *Museum für Völkerkunde.* You ask someone at the table next to yours where the museum is located. You find out that it is not too far away, but that unfortunately it is closed today. You respond politely. Your friend suggests an alternative activity (strolling along the Kärntner Straße, visiting the Riding Academy or St. Stephen's Cathedral, etc.). Discuss how to reach your destination. Then consider what you might want to do in the evening **(heute Abend):** go to Grinzing or the Prater, etc.

KAPITEL 6

WOHNEN

Moderne Wohnungen können sehr schön sein.

LERNZIELE

■ VORSCHAU
Housing

■ GESPRÄCHE AND WORTSCHATZ
Housing and furniture

■ STRUKTUR
Two-way prepositions
Imperative
Wissen vs. **kennen**

■ EINBLICKE
Public transportation and city life
"Work hard, save money, build a house"

■ FOKUS
Shared living arrangements
Homes and houses
Friedensreich Hundertwasser
High German and dialects

■ WEB-ECKE

■ SPRECHSITUATIONEN
Describing locations
Offering apologies
Expressing forgiveness

VORSCHAU

Housing

After World War II, West Germany suffered an acute housing shortage, not only because so many buildings had been destroyed, but also because of the large number of refugees who moved west. Rebuilding in the sixties and seventies created high-rise apartment clusters **(Wohnsilos)** that mushroomed around the old cities, often contrasting sharply with the traditional architecture. Fortunately, many people have rediscovered the beauty of older buildings. Along came subsidies and tax incentives that have made it possible to restore and modernize them. More recently, the new housing developments have attempted to harmonize with the landscape and to conform to local building styles. Strict zoning laws prevent the loss of open space and agricultural land, but they also make it more difficult to add housing.

With the end of the Cold War and the collapse of the eastern economies, another wave of people moved west, which again created a housing crisis. Students, young couples, large families, and foreign nationals have great difficulties finding affordable accommodations.

In the former GDR, two-thirds of the housing units dated back to the time before World War II, and they often lacked modern sanitary facilities and heating systems. Since unification, many of the old housing units have been renovated, and new modern homes and apartments are being built everywhere. Although real estate is expensive in Germany, nine out of ten Germans would prefer to own their own home or condominium **(Eigentumswohnung);** homeownership is encouraged by various forms of governmental help, such as tax incentives.

Apartments are advertised by the number of rooms. Those who want to rent a three-bedroom apartment with a living room and a dining room need a **Fünfzimmerwohnung;** bathroom and kitchen are excluded from the room count. Furnished apartments are relatively rare. "Unfurnished" is usually to be taken literally. There are no built-in closets, kitchen cabinets, appliances, light fixtures, etc. Tenants are responsible for furnishing and maintaining their apartments, including interior painting and decorating. In some buildings they are even expected to clean the stairs between floors.

Haus im Jugendstil

GESPRÄCHE

Wohnung zu vermieten

INGE	Hallo, mein Name ist Inge Moser. Ich habe gehört, dass Sie eine Zweizimmerwohnung zu vermieten haben. Stimmt das?
VERMIETER	Ja, in der Nähe vom Dom.
INGE	Wie alt ist die Wohnung?
VERMIETER	Ziemlich alt, aber sie ist renoviert und schön groß und hell. Sie hat sogar einen Balkon.
INGE	In welchem Stock liegt sie?
VERMIETER	Im dritten Stock.
INGE	Ist sie möbliert oder unmöbliert?
VERMIETER	Unmöbliert.
INGE	Und was kostet die Wohnung?
VERMIETER	1100 DM.
INGE	Ist das kalt oder warm?
VERMIETER	Kalt.
INGE	Oh, das ist ein bisschen zu teuer. Vielen Dank! Auf Wiederhören!
VERMIETER	Auf Wiederhören!

In der WG (Wohngemeinschaft)

INGE	Euer Haus gefällt mir!
HORST	Wir haben noch Platz für dich. Komm, ich zeige dir alles! . . . Hier links ist unsere Küche. Sie ist klein, aber praktisch.
INGE	Wer kocht?
HORST	Wir alle: Jens, Gisela, Renate und ich.
INGE	Und das ist das Wohnzimmer?
HORST	Ja. Es ist ein bisschen dunkel, aber das ist O.K.
INGE	Eure Sessel gefallen mir.
HORST	Sie sind alt, aber echt bequem. Oben sind dann vier Schlafzimmer und das Bad.
INGE	Nur ein Bad?
HORST	Ja, leider! Aber hier unten ist noch eine Toilette.
INGE	Was bezahlt ihr im Monat?
HORST	Jeder 400 Mark.
INGE	Nicht schlecht! Und wie kommst du zur Uni?
HORST	Zu Fuß natürlich! Es ist ja nicht weit.
INGE	Klingt gut!

Richtig oder falsch?

_____ 1. In der Nähe vom Dom gibt es eine Wohnung zu vermieten.
_____ 2. Die Wohnung hat vier Zimmer.
_____ 3. Die Wohnung ist etwas dunkel.
_____ 4. Die Wohnung liegt im Parterre.
_____ 5. Horst wohnt in einer WG.
_____ 6. Das Haus hat drei Schlafzimmer.
_____ 7. Sie fahren mit der U-Bahn zur Uni.
_____ 8. Für das Haus bezahlen die Studenten 200 DM pro Person.
_____ 9. Horst möchte, dass Inge auch dort wohnt.
_____ 10. Aber das gefällt Inge nicht.

Shared Living Arrangements — FOKUS

Students and other young people often choose to live in **WGs** or **Wohngemeinschaften** (shared housing). Moving into an apartment or house—often with complete strangers—is quite common, as rooms in dormitories **(Studentenheime)** are scarce and one-room apartments often too expensive for tight budgets.

WORTSCHATZ 1

Das Haus, ¨-er (house)
Das Studentenheim, -e (dorm)
Die Wohnung, -en (apartment)

der Balkon, -s	balcony	die Ecke, -n	corner
Baum, ¨-e	tree	Garage, -n	garage
Flur, -e	hallway, foyer	Küche, -n	kitchen
Garten, ¨-	garden, yard	Toilette, -n	toilet
das Bad, ¨-er	bathroom		
Arbeitszimmer, -	study	im Wohnzimmer	in the living room
Esszimmer, -	dining room	in der Küche	in the kitchen
Schlafzimmer, -	bedroom		
Wohnzimmer, -	living room		

Die Möbel (pl.) (furniture)

der Fernseher, -	TV set	das Bett, -en	bed
Kühlschrank, ¨-e	refrigerator	Radio, -s	radio
Schrank, ¨-e	closet, cupboard	Regal, -e	shelf, bookcase
Schreibtisch, -e	desk	Sofa, -s	sofa
Sessel, -	armchair	Telefon, -e	telephone
Stuhl, ¨-e	chair	die Kommode, -n	dresser
Teppich, -e	carpet	Lampe, -n	lamp
Tisch, -e	table		
Vorhang, ¨-e	curtain		

Weiteres

im Parterre	on the first floor (ground level)
im ersten Stock	on the second floor

im Monat	*per month*
oben / unten	*up(stairs) / down(stairs)*
hell / dunkel	*bright, light / dark*
praktisch	*practical(ly)*
(un)bequem	*(un)comfortable; (in)convenient*
sogar	*even*
ziemlich	*quite, rather*
baden	*to take a bath; to swim*
duschen	*to take a shower*
hängen, gehängt	*to hang (up)*
hängen, gehangen	*to hang (be hanging)*
kochen	*to cook*
legen	*to lay, put (flat)*
liegen, gelegen	*to lie (be lying flat)*
mieten / vermieten	*to rent / to rent out*
setzen	*to set, put*
sitzen, gesessen	*to sit (be sitting)*
stehen, gestanden	*to stand (be standing)*
stellen	*to stand, put (upright)*
waschen (wäscht), gewaschen	*to wash*
(Das) klingt gut.	*(That) sounds good.*
(Das) stimmt.	*(That's) true. / (That's) right.*
Auf Wiederhören!	*Good-bye! (on the phone)*

Zum Erkennen: renoviert *(renovated);* (un)möbliert *([un]furnished);* kalt oder warm? *(here: with or without heat);* die WG, -s / Wohngemeinschaft, -en *(shared housing);* echt *(really);* jeder *(each one)*

F●KUS Homes and Houses

When German-speakers say "first floor" (**erste Etage** or **erster Stock**), they mean what North Americans call the *second floor*. Either **das Parterre** or **das Erdgeschoss** is used to denote the ground floor, or North American first floor. In elevators, remember to press "E" (for **Erdgeschoss**) or "0" to get to the exit.

Homes and apartments usually have a foyer or hallway (**der Flur**), with doors leading to the various rooms. For privacy's sake, many Germans prefer to keep doors shut—this also holds true in the workplace and institutions like the university, where people prefer to work with doors closed. Sheer, pretty curtains (**Gardinen**) are also a typical feature that permits people to see out, but prevents others from looking in. In addition, some houses have outdoor shutters (**Rolläden** or **Rollos**) that can be rolled down vertically over the windows. Traditional half-timbered houses (**Fachwerkhäuser**) often have colorful shutters that swing shut on hinges.

WOHNEN 163

Zum Thema

A. **Mustersätze**
   1. das Haus: Das Haus **gefällt mir.**
      das Wohnzimmer, die Küche, das Bad, der Garten
   2. der Sessel: **Wie gefällt dir** der Sessel?
      das Sofa, der Teppich, das Regal, das Radio
   3. die Möbel: Die Möbel **gefallen mir.**
      Sessel, Stühle, Vorhänge, Schränke
   4. sehr praktisch: **Die Wohnung ist** sehr praktisch.
      schön hell, ziemlich dunkel, zu klein, schön sauber, sehr gemütlich, furchtbar schmutzig, wirklich bequem
   5. unten: **Die Wohnung ist** unten.
      oben, im Parterre, im ersten Stock, im zweiten Stock, im dritten Stock

B. **Beschreiben Sie die Wohnung!** *(Tell what furniture is in what rooms. You may need the optional vocabulary below.)*

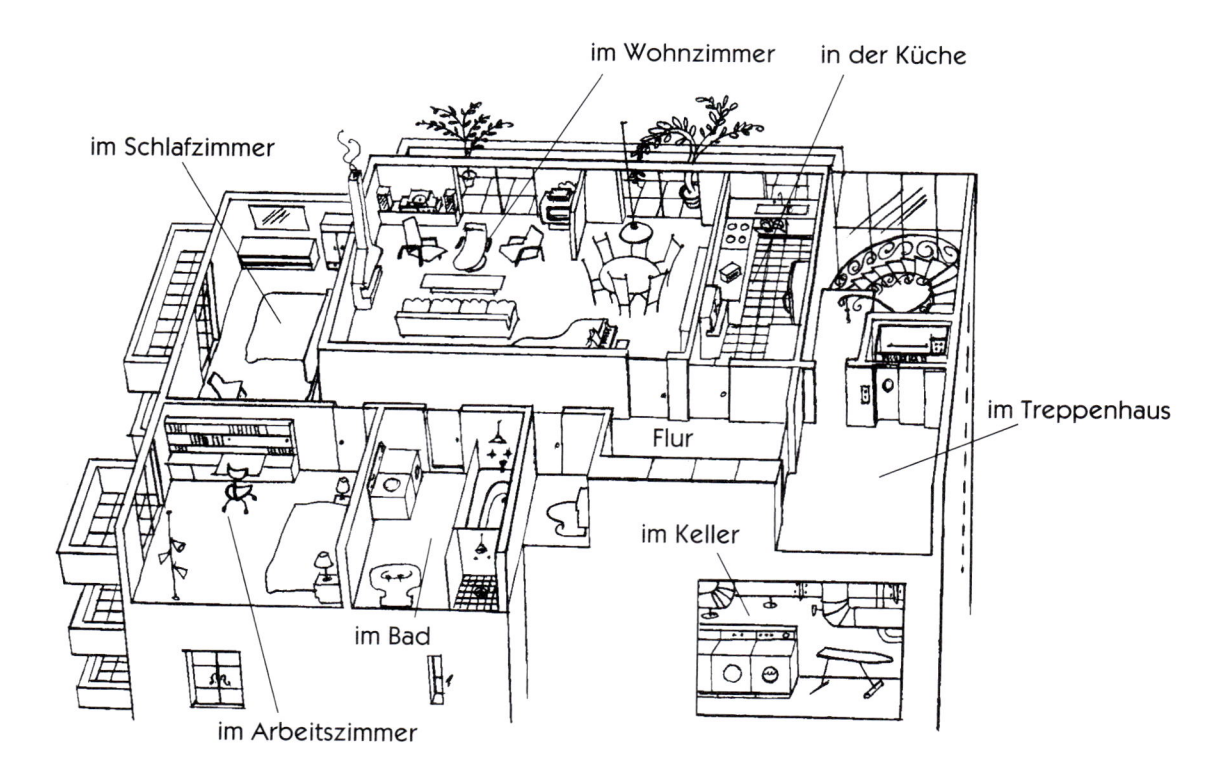

(Labels on diagram: im Schlafzimmer, im Wohnzimmer, in der Küche, im Treppenhaus, Flur, im Keller, im Bad, im Arbeitszimmer)

Zum Erkennen: der Anrufbeantworter *(answering machine)*, Aufzug *(elevator)*, CD-Spieler, Computer, Dachboden *(attic)*, Herd *(oven range)*, Kamin *(fireplace)*, Keller *(basement)*, Kleiderschrank, Kopierer, Küchenschrank, Nachttisch, Ofen, Pool, Spiegel *(mirror)*, Staubsauger *(vacuum cleaner)*, Toaster, Trockner *(dryer)*

das Büfett *(dining room cabinet)*, Faxgerät, Handy *(cellular phone)*, Klavier *(piano)*, Mikrowellengerät *(microwave oven)*, Treppenhaus *(staircase)*, Videogerät, Waschbecken *(sink)*

die Badewanne *(bathtub)*, Dusche *(shower)*, Pflanze *(plant)*, Spülmaschine *(dishwasher)*, Terrasse, Treppe *(stairway)*, Waschmaschine

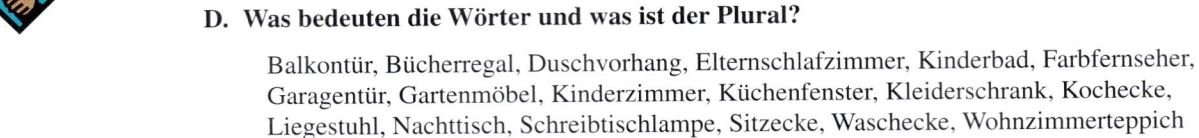

C. Kein Haus / keine Wohnung ohne Maschinen (*Working in small groups, tell what machines or appliances you have or don't have, what you need, and what you would like to have. For vocabulary, consult the list above or your instructor.*)

D. Was bedeuten die Wörter und was ist der Plural?

Balkontür, Bücherregal, Duschvorhang, Elternschlafzimmer, Kinderbad, Farbfernseher, Garagentür, Gartenmöbel, Kinderzimmer, Küchenfenster, Kleiderschrank, Kochecke, Liegestuhl, Nachttisch, Schreibtischlampe, Sitzecke, Waschecke, Wohnzimmerteppich

E. Interview. Fragen Sie einen Nachbarn / eine Nachbarin, . . . !
1. ob er / sie eine Wohnung hat oder ob er / sie zu Hause, im Studentenheim oder in einer WG wohnt; wenn nicht zu Hause, wie viel Miete er / sie bezahlt
2. ob er / sie Mitbewohner (*housemates*) hat; wenn ja, wie sie heißen
3. was für Möbel er / sie im Zimmer hat
4. ob er / sie eine Küche hat; wenn ja, was es in der Küche gibt und wer kocht
5. was man vom Zimmerfenster sehen kann
6. wie lange er / sie schon da wohnt
7. wie er / sie zur Uni kommt

F. Aussprache: ei, au, eu, äu (*See also II. 37–39 in the pronunciation section of the Workbook.*)
1. [ai]   w**ei**t, l**ei**der, **ei**gentlich, z**ei**gen, f**ei**ern, bl**ei**ben
2. [au]   **au**f, bl**au**grau, B**au**m, K**au**fhaus, br**au**chen, l**au**fen
3. [oi]   **eu**ch, h**eu**te, t**eu**er, L**eu**te, Fr**eu**nde, H**äu**ser, B**äu**me
4. Wortpaare
    a. *by* / bei   c. *mouse* / Maus   e. aus / Eis
    b. *Troy* / treu   d. Haus / Häuser   f. euer / Eier

HÖREN SIE ZU!

Hier Müller! (*Listen to the conversation between Inge and Mrs. Müller. Then decide whether the statements below are true or false according to the dialogue.*)

Zum Erkennen: Mutti (*Mom*); nett (*nice*); teilen (*to share*); na gut (*well, good*); Bis bald! (*See you soon!*)

_____ 1. Inge ist Frau Müllers Tochter.
_____ 2. Frau Müller hat ein Zimmer gefunden.
_____ 3. Das Zimmer ist in der Schillerstraße.
_____ 4. Inges Telefonnummer ist 91 68.
_____ 5. Wohnungen sind sehr teuer.
_____ 6. Inge hat Horst vor ein paar Tagen gesehen.
_____ 7. Sie teilt jetzt ein Zimmer mit Horst.
_____ 8. Inge zahlt 280 Mark im Monat.
_____ 9. Sie kann mit dem Fahrrad zur Uni fahren.
_____ 10. Am Wochenende kommt sie nach Hause.

STRUKTUR

I. Two-way prepositions

You have learned some prepositions that are always followed by the dative and some that are always followed by the accusative. You will now learn a set of prepositions that sometimes take the dative and sometimes the accusative.

1. The basic meanings of the nine TWO-WAY PREPOSITIONS are:

an	to, up to, at (the side of), on (vertical surface)
auf	on (top of, horizontal surface), onto
hinter	behind
in	in, into, inside of
neben	beside, next to
über	over, above
unter	under, below
vor	before, in front of
zwischen	between

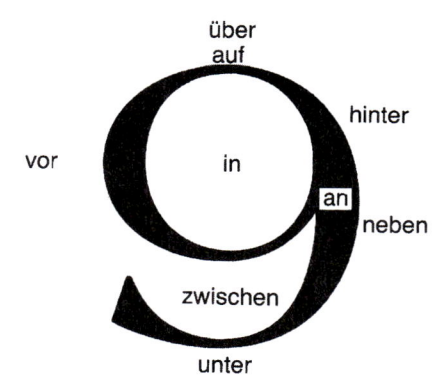

Most of these prepositions may be contracted with articles. The most common contractions are:

an + das = **ans**	in + das = **ins**
an + dem = **am**	in + dem = **im**
auf + das = **aufs**	

CAUTION: The preposition **vor** precedes a noun (**vor dem Haus**). The conjunction **bevor** introduces a clause (. . . , **bevor du das Haus mietest**).

2. **Wo?** vs. **wohin?**

   a. German has two words to ask *where*: **wo?** *(in what place?)* and **wohin?** *(to what place?)*. **Wo** asks about LOCATION, where something is, or an activity within a place. **Wohin** asks about DESTINATION OR A CHANGE OF PLACE.

   LOCATION: **Wo** ist Horst? *Where's Horst? (in what place)*
   DESTINATION: **Wohin** geht Horst? *Where's Horst going? (to what place)*

   b. The difference between location and destination also plays a role in determining the case following two-way prepositions. If the question is **wo?**, the <u>dative</u> is used. If the question is **wohin?**, the <u>accusative</u> is used.

   Wo ist Horst? → **In der** Küche. *Where's Horst?* → *In the kitchen.*
   Wohin geht Horst? → **In die** Küche. *Where's Horst going?* → *To the kitchen.*

wo?	LOCATION	→	<u>dative</u>
wohin?	DESTINATION	→	<u>accusative</u>

3. The difference lies entirely in the verb!
   - Some verbs denoting LOCATION OR ACTIVITY WITHIN A PLACE (**wo?** → dative) are: hängen, kaufen, kochen, lesen, liegen, schlafen, schreiben, sein, sitzen, spielen, stehen, studieren, tanzen, trinken, wohnen
   - Typical verbs implying DESTINATION OR A CHANGE OF PLACE OR MOTION TOWARDS one (**wohin?** → accusative) are: bringen, fahren, gehen, hängen, kommen, laufen, legen, setzen, stellen, tragen
4. Some important verb pairs

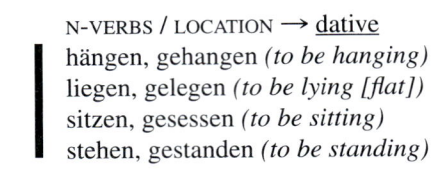

N-VERBS / LOCATION → dative	T-VERBS / CHANGE OF PLACE → accusative
hängen, gehangen *(to be hanging)*	hängen, gehängt *(to hang up)*
liegen, gelegen *(to be lying [flat])*	legen, gelegt *(to lay down, put [flat])*
sitzen, gesessen *(to be sitting)*	setzen, gesetzt *(to set down)*
stehen, gestanden *(to be standing)*	stellen, gestellt *(to put [upright])*

   - Note that the four n-verbs are all intransitive (i.e., they do not take a direct object). The four t-verbs, on the other hand, are transitive (i.e., they do take a direct object).

   Der Mantel hat **im** Schrank gehangen.

   Ich habe den Mantel **in den** Schrank gehängt.

CAUTION: Although **legen, setzen,** and **stellen** are all sometimes translated as *to put,* they are not interchangeable!

Sie **stellt** den Stuhl an die Wand. *(upright position)*

Sie **legt** das Heft auf den Tisch. *(flat position)*

Er **setzt** das Kind auf den Stuhl. *(sitting position)*

5. Summary

   WOHIN?   WO?

   WOHIN? Die Tante hängt den Teppich **über das** Balkongeländer (. . . *railing*).

   WO? Der Teppich hängt **über dem** Balkongeländer.

WOHIN?	Die Mutter stellt die Leiter *(ladder)* **an die** Wand.
WO?	Die Leiter steht **an der** Wand.
WOHIN?	Das Kind legt den Teddy **auf die** Bank *(bench)*.
WO?	Der Teddy liegt **auf der** Bank.
WOHIN?	Das Auto fährt **neben das** Haus.
WO?	Das Auto steht **neben dem** Haus.
WOHIN?	Das Kind läuft **hinter die** Mutter.
WO?	Das Kind steht **hinter der** Mutter.
WOHIN?	Der Hund läuft **vor das** Auto.
WO?	Der Hund steht **vor dem** Auto.
WOHIN?	Der Großvater nimmt die Pfeife *(pipe)* **in den** Mund *(mouth)*.
WO?	Der Großvater hat die Pfeife **in dem** Mund.
WOHIN?	Das Huhn *(chicken)* läuft **unter die** Bank **zwischen die** Bankbeine *(. . . legs)*.
WO?	Das Huhn sitzt **unter der** Bank **zwischen den** Bankbeinen.

Note also these uses of **an, auf,** and **in**! You are already familiar with most of them:

Die Stadt liegt **am** Rhein / **an der** Donau.	*The city is on the Rhine / on the Danube.*
Sie spielen **auf der** Straße.	*They're playing in the street.*
Sie leben **in** Deutschland / **in der** Schweiz.	*They live in Germany / in Switzerland.*
Sie leben **in** Stuttgart / **im** Süden.	*They live in Stuttgart / in the South.*
Sie wohnen **in der** Schillerstraße.	*They live on Schiller Street.*
Sie wohnen **im** Parterre / **im** ersten Stock.	*They live on the first / second floor.*

- With feminine or plural names of countries, **in** is used rather than **nach** to express *to*.

   Wir fahren **in die Schweiz / in die Bundesrepublik.**
   Wir fahren **in die USA / in die Vereinigten Staaten.**
   BUT: Wir fahren **nach Österreich / nach Deutschland.**

- If you plan to see a film or play, or to attend a church service, **in** must be used; **zu** implies going *in the direction of, up to,* BUT NOT *into a place.*

Wir gehen **zum Kino.**	*(just to look outside and see what's playing, or to meet somebody there)*
Wir gehen **ins Kino.**	*(to go inside and see a movie)*

Übungen

A. Sagen Sie es noch einmal! *(Replace the nouns following the prepositions with the words suggested.)*

   BEISPIEL: Der Bleistift liegt unter dem Papier. (Jacke)
   Der Bleistift liegt unter der Jacke.

1. Die Post ist neben der Bank. (Bahnhof, Kino, Apotheke)
2. Ursula kommt in die Wohnung. (Küche, Esszimmer, Garten)
3. Die Mäntel liegen auf dem Bett. (Sofa, Kommode, Stühle)
4. Mein Schlafzimmer ist über der Küche. (Wohnzimmer, Garage, Bad)
5. Willi legt den Pullover auf die Kommode. (Bett, Schreibtisch, Sessel)

B. Wo bekommt man das? *(Tell that you can get the following items where indicated, starting with the underlined phrase. Repeat the information by saying where each of the people below are going in order to get those items.)*

BEISPIEL: Frau Müller braucht etwas <u>Butter und Käse</u>. (Supermarkt)
Butter und Käse bekommt man im Supermarkt.
Frau Müller geht in den Supermarkt.

1. Erika sucht ein paar <u>Bücher</u>. (Bibliothek)
2. Stephan will ein paar <u>CDs</u>. (Kaufhaus)
3. Renate braucht <u>Parfüm</u> *(perfume)* und Shampoo. (Drogerie)
4. Willi braucht <u>Medizin</u>. (Apotheke)
5. Karin sucht ein paar <u>Schuhe</u>. (Schuhgeschäft)
6. Dieter hat viele Bücher, aber keine <u>Regale</u>. (Möbelgeschäft)
7. Oma Schütz ist müde vom Einkaufen und möchte eine Tasse <u>Kaffee und Kuchen</u>. (Café)

C. Wo sind Sie wann? *(Tell where you are at certain times. You may use the locations in the last column or come up with ideas of your own.)*

BEISPIEL: morgens
Morgens bin ich gewöhnlich in der Bibliothek.

1	2	3	4	5
morgens	fahren	gern	an	Badewanne *(f.)*
mittags	gehen	gemütlich	auf	Berge
abends	liegen	gewöhnlich	in	Bett
am Wochenende	sein	manchmal	vor	Bibliothek
(über)morgen	sitzen	nicht		Computer *(m.)*
im Sommer . . .	sprechen	oft		Fernseher
wenn ich Hunger habe	. . .	stundenlang		Garten
wenn ich faul *(lazy)* bin				Sofa
wenn ich lernen muss				Kühlschrank
wenn ich baden will				Pool
wenn ich müde bin				Kino
wenn ich keine Zeit habe				Vorlesung(en) . . .

D. Wieder zu Hause *(After you and your family come home from a camping trip, your mother has many questions. Form her questions with **wo** or **wohin**!)*

BEISPIEL: Vater ist in der Garage. **Wo ist Vater?**
Jochen geht in den Garten. **Wohin geht Jochen?**

1. Das Handy ist im Auto.
2. Der Rucksack *(backpack)* liegt im Flur.
3. Marita legt die Schlafsäcke *(sleeping bags)* aufs Bett.
4. Gabi hängt den Mantel über den Stuhl.
5. Die Regenmäntel sind auf dem Balkon.
6. Die Jacken liegen in der Ecke.
7. Gabi und Günther haben die Lebensmittel in die Küche gebracht.
8. Günther hat die Milch in den Kühlschrank gestellt.
9. Gabi hat den Schuh unterm Baum gefunden.
10. Der Hund liegt auf dem Sofa.

E. Ein paar Fragen, bevor Sie gehen! *(Before you leave on vacation, answer the questions of your house sitter.)*

BEISPIEL: Wo ist das Telefon? (an / Wand)
An der Wand!

1. Wo darf ich schlafen? (auf / Sofa; in / Arbeitszimmer)
2. Wohin soll ich meine Kleider hängen? (in / Schrank; an / Wand; über / Stuhl)
3. Wo gibt es ein Lebensmittelgeschäft? (an / Ecke; neben / Bank; zwischen / Apotheke und Café)
4. Wo können die Kinder spielen? (hinter / Haus; unter / Baum; auf / Spielplatz)
5. Wohin gehen sie gern? (in / Park; an / Fluss; in / Kino)
6. Wohin soll ich die Katze tun? (vor / Tür *[outside]*; in / Garten; auf / Balkon; in / Garage)

F. Wir bekommen Besuch. *(Tell what you still have to do; fill in the blanks with the correct form of the definite article.)*

1. Die Gläser sind in _____ Küche. 2. Ich muss die Gläser in _____ Wohnzimmer bringen und sie auf _____ Tisch stellen. 3. Der Wein ist noch in _____ Kühlschrank. 4. Wir müssen die Teller neben _____ Gläser stellen. 5. Ich muss in _____ Küche gehen und die Wurst und den Käse auf _____ Teller *(sg.)* legen. 6. Haben wir Blumen in _____ Garten? 7. Wir stellen die Blumen auf _____ Tischchen *(sg.)* vor _____ Sofa. 8. Sind die Kerzen in _____ Schrank? 9. Nein, sie sind in _____ Kommode.

G. Bei Lotte

1. **Wohin sollen wir das stellen?** *(Lotte is moving into a new house. She is telling the movers where they are supposed to put things.)*

   BEISPIEL: Schreibtisch / an / Wand
   Stellen Sie den Schreibtisch an die Wand!

   a. Computer *(m.)* / auf / Schreibtisch
   b. Schrank / in / Ecke
   c. Lampe / neben / Bett
   d. Stuhl / an / Tisch
   e. Regal / unter / Uhr
   f. Bild / auf / Regal
   g. Nachttisch / vor / Fenster
   h. Bett / zwischen / Tür / und / Fenster

2. **Was ist wo?** *(Make ten statements about the picture of Lotte's house, telling where things are standing, lying, or hanging.)*

   BEISPIEL: Der Schreibtisch steht an der Wand.

3. **Wo sind die Schlüssel?** *(Lotte has lost her keys. Looking at the drawing above, ask her about specific places she may have put them. Lotte will answer each question negatively until finally you guess right. Enact this scene with a partner. Ask at least five questions using two-way prepositions.)*

   BEISPIEL: Hast du sie auf den Schreibtisch gelegt?
   Nein, sie liegen nicht auf dem Schreibtisch.

H. Schreiben Sie! Mein Zimmer / meine Wohnung *(Describe your room / apartment in eight to ten sentences. Use a two-way preposition in each sentence. For extra vocabulary, see the list on p. 163.)*

II. Imperative

You are already familiar with the FORMAL IMPERATIVE, which addresses one individual or several people. You know that the verb is followed by the pronoun **Sie:**

Herr Schmidt, **lesen Sie** das bitte!

Herr und Frau Müller, **kommen Sie** später wieder!

1. The FAMILIAR IMPERATIVE has two forms: one for the singular and one for the plural.

    a. The singular usually corresponds to the **du**-form of the verb WITHOUT the pronoun **du** and WITHOUT the **-st** ending:

du schreibst	du tust	du antwortest	du fährst	du nimmst	du isst	du liest
Schreib!	**Tu!**	**Antworte!**	**Fahr!**	**Nimm!**	**Iss!**	**Lies!**

    NOTE: **lesen** and **essen** retain the **s** or **ss** of the verb stem. **Lies! Iss!**

    - Verbs ending in **-d, -t, -ig,** or in certain other consonant combinations USUALLY have an **-e** ending in the **du**-form.

        Finde es! **Antworte** ihm! **Entschuldige** bitte! **Öffne** die Tür!

    - Verbs with vowel changes from **a > ä** in the present singular DO NOT make this change in the imperative. Verbs that change from **e > i(e)** do retain this change, however.

        Fahr langsam! **Lauf** schnell!

        Nimm das! **Iss** nicht so viel! **Sprich** Deutsch! **Lies** laut! **Sieh** mal!

    b. The plural corresponds to the **ihr**-form of the verb WITHOUT the pronoun **ihr.**

ihr schreibt	ihr tut	ihr antwortet	ihr fahrt	ihr nehmt	ihr esst	ihr lest
Schreibt!	**Tut!**	**Antwortet!**	**Fahrt!**	**Nehmt!**	**Esst!**	**Lest!**

2. English imperatives beginning with *Let's* . . . are expressed in German as follows:

    Sprechen wir Deutsch!   *Let's speak German.*

    Gehen wir nach Hause!   *Let's go home.*

3. Here is a summary chart of the imperative.

Schreiben Sie!	Schreib!	Schreibt!	Schreiben wir!
Antworten Sie!	Antworte!	Antwortet!	Antworten wir!
Fahren Sie!	**Fahr!**	Fahrt!	Fahren wir!
Nehmen Sie!	**Nimm!**	Nehmt!	Nehmen wir!
Essen Sie!	**Iss!**	Esst!	Essen wir!
Lesen Sie!	**Lies!**	Lest!	Lesen wir!

    Frau Schmidt, **schreiben Sie** mir!
    Helga, **schreib** mir!
    Kinder, **schreibt** mir!
    Schreiben wir Lisa!

NOTE: The German imperative is usually followed by an EXCLAMATION POINT.

Übungen

I. Geben Sie den Imperativ! *(First form the singular and then the plural familiar.)*

BEISPIEL: Bleiben Sie bitte!
Bleib bitte!
Bleibt bitte!

1. Fragen Sie ihn!
2. Entschuldigen Sie bitte!
3. Bitte helfen Sie uns!
4. Zeigen Sie uns den Weg!
5. Geben Sie mir die Landkarte!
6. Fahren Sie immer geradeaus!
7. Wiederholen Sie das bitte!
8. Halten Sie da drüben!
9. Hören Sie mal!
10. Schlafen Sie gut!
11. Essen Sie einen Apfel!
12. Trinken Sie eine Cola!

J. Geben Sie Befehle! *(Form formal and familiar commands, using the phrases below.)*

BEISPIEL: an die Tafel gehen
Gehen Sie an die Tafel!
Geh an die Tafel!
Geht an die Tafel!

1. die Kreide nehmen 2. ein Wort auf Deutsch schreiben 3. von 1 bis 10 zählen 4. wieder an den Platz gehen 5. das Deutschbuch öffnen 6. auf Seite 150 lesen 7. mit dem Nachbarn auf Deutsch sprechen 8. mir einen Kuli geben 9. nach Hause gehen 10. das nicht tun

K. Was tun? *(Decide with your friend what to do with the rest of the day.)*

BEISPIEL: zu Hause bleiben   **Bleiben wir zu Hause!**

1. in die Stadt gehen 2. an den See fahren 3. durch die Geschäfte bummeln
4. eine Pizza essen 5. das Schloss besichtigen 6. ins Kino gehen

L. Noch mehr Befehle! *(Address three commands to each of the following below.)*

BEISPIEL: an einen Touristen
Fahren Sie mit dem Bus!
Gehen Sie immer geradeaus!
Fragen Sie dort noch einmal!

1. an einen Taxifahrer / eine Taxifahrerin
2. an einen Kellner / eine Kellnerin
3. an ein paar Freunde oder Klassenkameraden *(classmates)*
4. an einen Bruder / eine Schwester
5. an ein paar Kinder

III. Wissen vs. kennen

In German, two verbs correspond to the English *to know*.

kennen, gekannt	*to know (to be acquainted with a person or thing)*
wissen, gewusst	*to know a fact (the fact is often expressed in a subordinate clause)*

Whereas **kennen** is regular in the present tense, the forms of **wissen** are very similar to the forms of the modals.

ich	weiß
du	weißt
er	weiß
wir	wissen
ihr	wisst
sie	wissen

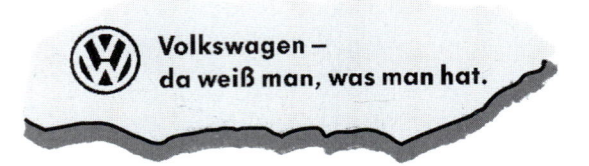

Volkswagen — da weiß man, was man hat.

Ich **kenne** das Buch.　　BUT　　Ich **weiß, dass** es gut ist.
Ich **kenne** den Lehrer.　BUT　　Ich **weiß, dass** er aus Salzburg ist.
　　　　　　　　　　　　　　　　Ich **weiß** seine Telefonnummer.

Übungen

M. *Kennen* oder *wissen*? *(Fill in the appropriate forms.)*

ANGELIKA　Entschuldigen Sie! _____ Sie, wo die Wipplinger Straße ist?
DAME　Nein. Ich _____ Wien gut, aber das _____ ich nicht.
MICHAEL　Danke! Du, Angelika, _____ du, wie spät es ist?
ANGELIKA　Nein, aber ich _____, dass ich Hunger habe.
MICHAEL　Hallo, Holger und Sabine! Sagt mal, _____ ihr Angelika?
SABINE　Ja, natürlich.
MICHAEL　Wir haben Hunger. _____ ihr, wo es hier ein Restaurant gibt?
HOLGER　Ja, da drüben ist die „Bastei Beisl". Wir _____ es nicht, aber wir _____, dass es gut sein soll.
MICHAEL　_____ ihr was? Gehen wir essen!

FOKUS Friedensreich Hundertwasser

Friedrich Stowasser, called Friedensreich Hundertwasser (born in 1928), is a well-known Austrian painter, graphic artist, and architect. In his ecologically oriented writings, he vehemently opposes contemporary architecture, which he describes as "an aesthetic void," "a desert of uniformity," and "criminal sterility." Since no straight lines exist in nature, he also rejects them in his art, referring to them as "something cowardly drawn with a ruler, without thought or feeling." His architecture echoes that conviction, as exemplified by the Hundertwasser House in Vienna and the Hundertwasser Church in Bärnbach near Graz, whose exterior is uneven and constructed of various materials to symbolize the vicissitudes of life. Its processional path leads through multiple gates that bear a variety of symbols from other religions as a mark of respect.

Hundertwasser-Haus in Wien

Zusammenfassung

N. Hoppla, wo soll das hin? Umzug *(Moving. You and a friend—your partner—have each moved into new apartments and are helping each other arrange everything. Your partner's apartment is shown below. A sketch of your apartment is depicted in Section 11 of the Appendix. First, your partner will tell you where to put everything. He / she should be as specific as possible. Follow the instructions by writing the name of that item where it should go. Then tell your partner where to put your belongings.)*

MÖBEL: Stuhl, Schreibtisch, Bücher, Computer, Telefon, Lampe, Regal, Fernseher, Radio, Klavier *(n., piano),* Kühlschrank, Kommode, Nachttisch, Schrank, Sessel, Bild, Tisch, Pflanze *(f., plant),* Spiegel *(m., mirror),* Waschmaschine, usw.

1. **Wohin soll das?**

    BEISPIEL: S1   Wohin soll der Teppich?
                     S2   Leg den Teppich ins Wohnzimmer vors Sofa!
                     S1   Und die Stehlampe?
                     S2   Stell die Lampe neben das Sofa!

2. **Ist alles da, wo es sein soll?** *(When you are through, check whether your partner has followed directions.)*

    BEISPIEL: S2   Liegt der Teppich im Wohnzimmer vorm Sofa?
                     S1   Ja, ich habe den Teppich vors Sofa gelegt.
                     S2   Steht die Stehlampe neben dem Sofa?
                     S1   Ja, ich habe die Stehlampe neben das Sofa gestellt. *(Or:* Nein, ich habe die Stehlampe . . . gestellt.*)*

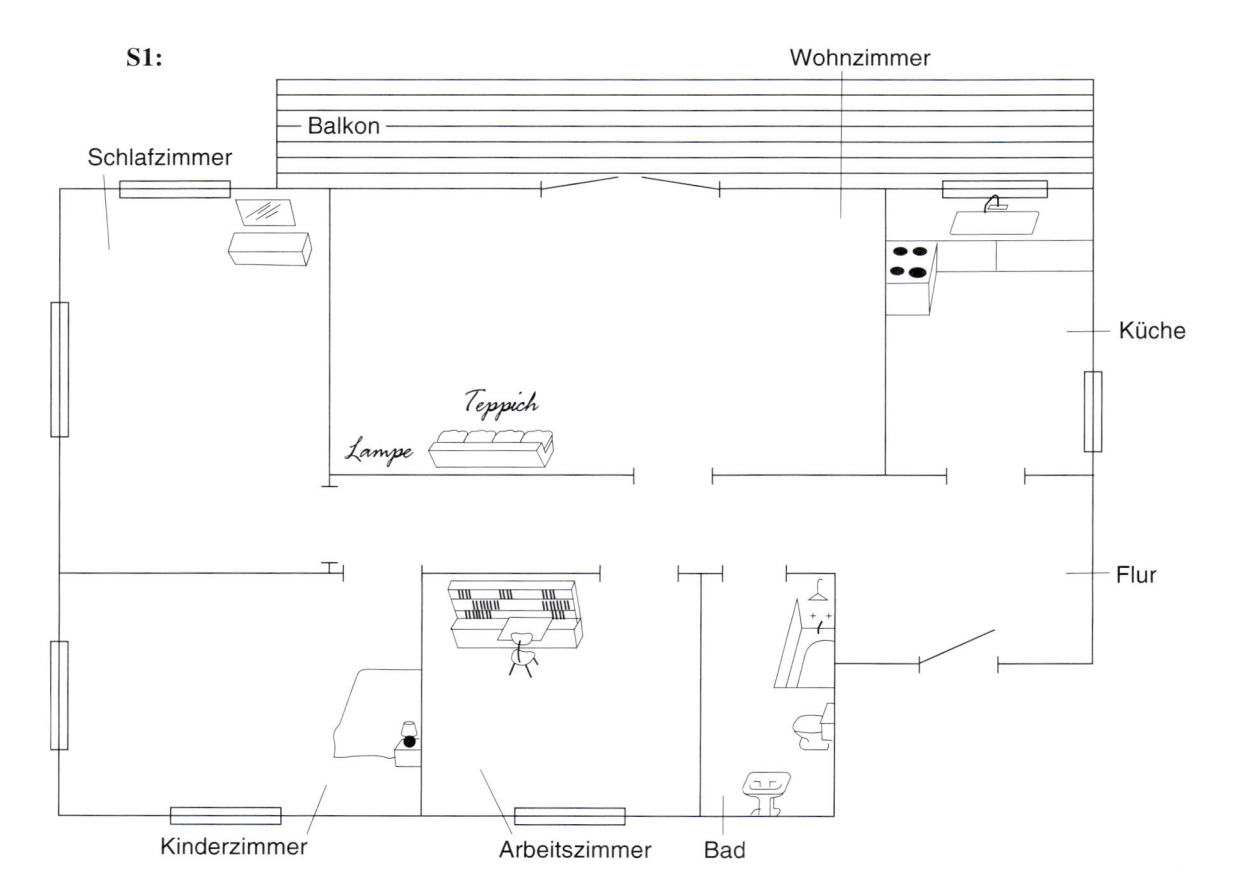

S1:

O. Zu vermieten (*For rent. Read the rental ads below, then choose one that is "yours." Your partner will inquire about it. Answer his / her questions, based on the ad. If some of the information is not given in the ad, make it up. Reverse roles.*)

S1 Ich habe gelesen, dass Sie eine Wohnung zu vermieten haben. Wo ist die Wohnung?
S2 . . .
S1 Können Sie mir die Wohnung etwas beschreiben *(describe)*?
S2 Ja, gern. Sie hat . . .
S1 Gibt es auch . . . ?
S2 . . .
S1 Wie weit ist es zu . . . ?
S2 . . .
S1 Und was kostet die Wohnung?
S2 . . .

VERMIETUNGEN
1-Zi-Whg in Uninähe, 25 qm, möbl., schön u. hell, Dushe/WC, 400,—warm. Tel. 0941/706322
1-Zi-Neubauwhg an Student/in, ca. 29 qm, teilmöbl., zentral, 450,—kalt, ab 1.1.99 Tel. 0941/42862
2 Zimmer, Altstadt, ca. 50 qm, hell, 575,— kalt, ab Februar '99. Tel. 0941/990686
2 1/2 Zi-Whg, Neubau, 60 qm, Balkon, ruhig, 560,—. Tel 0941/4636145
3 ZKB, Balkon, 72 qm, auch an WG 3 Pers., 850,—, zum 1.2.99 frei. 09401/51776
3-ZKB, Terr., 98 qm, Gäste-WC, Garage, Keller, Kaltmiete 1.080,—, inkl. NK. 0941/449869
Bungalow, 120 qm, 4-ZKB, Garten, Terr., Sauna, 1.500,—. 0941/47004
2-Zi-Whg. auf Bauernhof, 50 qm, Garten, Tiere kein Problem, geg. 10 Stunden Arbeit pro Woche. 576598

P. An der Uni. Auf Deutsch bitte!

1. Hello, Hans! Where have you been? 2. I've been in the dorm. 3. Where are you going?—To the library. 4. I'd like to live in a dorm, too. 5. Where do you live now? 6. In an apartment. Unfortunately it's over a disco *(die Disko)* and next to a restaurant. 7. Tell me, are the rooms in the dorm nice? 8. I like my room, but I don't like the furniture. 9. On which floor do you live?—On the third floor. 10. Do you know how much it costs?—350 marks a month. 11. There's Reinhart. 12. Who's that? From where am I supposed to know him? (Where am I supposed to know him from?) 13. I didn't know that you don't know him. 14. Let's say hello.

EINBLICKE

Public Transportation and City Life

Visitors from America are often astounded at the efficient and far-reaching public transportation networks in German cities. Most large cities have extensive subway lines **(U-Bahn-Linien)** that connect with suburban commuter trains **(S-Bahn).** Bikes are usually permitted on board during off-peak hours. Trains and stations are generally cleaner and safer than those in the United States.

German urban transport operates on the honor system. Passengers are required to validate their own tickets **(Fahrkarten entwerten)** by inserting them into machines that stamp the time and date. People who evade paying **(Schwarzfahrer)** have to reckon with random checks by plainclothes employees and stiff fines. Buses and streetcars complement the subway system, making for dense networks that reach outlying suburbs. At each stop a schedule is posted, and buses usually arrive within a few minutes of the given time. Most large cities also have night buses **(Nachtbusse),** which run on special routes all night long.

All cities have some form of public transportation, usually heavily subsidized in an effort to limit pollution and congestion in city centers. Monthly and yearly tickets are available with reduced rates for commuters, students, and senior citizens.

WORTSCHATZ 2

das Reihenhaus, ̈-er	townhouse
die Arbeit	work
die Eigentumswohnung, -en	condo
am Abend	in the evening
am Tag	during the day
aufs Land / auf dem Land(e)	in(to) the country(side)
ausgezeichnet	excellent
außerdem	besides (adverb)
fast	almost
leicht	easy, easily; lit.: light
schwer	hard, difficult; lit.: heavy
mitten in (+ acc. / dat.)	in the middle of
noch nicht	not yet
trotzdem	nevertheless, in spite of that
bauen	to build
leben[1]	to live
lieben	to love
sparen	to save (money, time)

Komm aufs Land!

[1] Note the difference between **leben** *(to live, literally: to be alive)* and **wohnen** *(to reside):* Dürer hat in Nürnberg **gelebt.** Er **lebt** nicht mehr. Er hat in dem Haus da drüben **gewohnt.**

Vorm Lesen

A. Fragen

1. Leben die meisten Leute *(most people)* hier in Wohnungen oder in Häusern mit Garten? 2. Wo ist Bauland *(building lot[s])* teuer? Wissen Sie, wo es nicht so teuer ist? 3. Was für öffentliche Verkehrsmittel *(public transportation)* gibt es hier? 4. Wie kommen die meisten Leute zur Arbeit? Wie kommen Sie zur Uni? Braucht man hier unbedingt *(necessarily)* ein Auto? 5. Gibt es hier Schlafstädte *(bedroom communities),* von wo die Leute morgens in die Stadt und abends wieder nach Hause fahren? 6. Wohin gehen oder fahren die Leute hier am Wochenende?

B. Was ist das?

der Arbeitsplatz, Biergarten, Clown, Dialekt, Münchner, Musiker, Spielplatz, Stadtpark, Wanderweg; das Boot, Feld, Leben, Konsulat; die Energie, Mietwohnung, Wirklichkeit; frei, idyllisch, pünktlich; Ball spielen, eine Pause machen, picknicken

Schaffen, sparen, Häuschen bauen

„Schaffe, spare, Häusle baue" ist ein Spruch° aus Schwaben°. Auf Hochdeutsch° heißt es „Schaffen°, sparen, Häuschen bauen." Der Spruch aus Schwaben ist nicht nur typisch für die Schwaben, sondern für die meisten° Deutschen, Österreicher und Schweizer.

In den drei Ländern leben viele Menschen, aber es gibt nur wenig° Land. Die meisten wohnen in Wohnungen und träumen von° einem Haus mit Garten. Für viele bleibt das aber nur ein Traum°, denn in den Städten ist Bauland sehr teuer. Es gibt auch nicht genug Bauland, weil man nicht überall bauen darf.

saying / dialect from Swabia / standard German / work hard
most
little
dream of
dream

Oft muß man an den Stadtrand° oder aufs Land ziehen°, wo mehr Platz ist und wo Land noch nicht so teuer ist. Aber nicht alle möchten so weit draußen° wohnen und stundenlang hin- und herpendeln°. Das kostet Energie, Zeit und Geld°. Abends kommt man auch nicht so leicht ins Kino oder ins Theater. Das Leben auf dem Land ist oft idyllisch, aber nicht immer sehr bequem.

to the outskirts / move
out(side)
commute back and forth / money

Haus mit Strohdach *(thatched roof)* in Schleswig-Holstein

In der Stadt kann man eigentlich sehr gut leben. Die Wohnungen sind oft groß und schön. Man braucht nicht unbedingt ein Auto, weil alles in der Nähe liegt. Fast überall gibt es Bürgersteige° und Fahrradwege, und die öffentlichen Verkehrsmittel sind ausgezeichnet. Die

sidewalks

In der Stadt ist immer etwas los.

Busse kommen relativ oft und pünktlich. In Großstädten gibt es auch Straßenbahnen, U-Bahnen und S-Bahnen. Damit° können Sie nicht nur aus der Stadt oder durch die Stadt, sondern auch mitten ins Zentrum, in die Fußgängerzone fahren, wo die Leute am Tag einkaufen und am Abend gern bummeln gehen. Man sieht ein bisschen in die Schaufenster° und geht vielleicht in eine Bar oder ein Café. Auf den Straßen ist im Sommer fast immer etwas los°. Es gibt Straßenkünstler°, Musiker und Clowns.

    Wenn man in der Stadt wohnt, kann man aber auch leicht aufs Land fahren. Viele tun das gern und oft. Am Wochenende fährt man gern einmal an die See° oder in die Berge. Überall zwischen Wäldern° und Feldern findet man Wanderwege und Fahrradwege. Dort findet man auch leicht ein Restaurant, wo man gemütlich Pause machen kann.

    Man muss aber nicht unbedingt aufs Land fahren, wenn man ins Grüne° will. Fast alle Städte, ob groß oder klein, haben Stadtparks. Die Münchner z.B. lieben ihren Englischen Garten. Dort gibt es nicht nur Wanderwege, sondern auch Spielplätze und Bänke, Biergärten, Wiesen° zum Picknicken und zum Ballspielen und einen See mit Bootchen.

    Die meisten leben eigentlich gern in der Stadt, entweder in einer Eigentumswohnung oder einer Mietwohnung. In der Stadt gibt es viel zu sehen und zu tun. Alles ist ziemlich nah, nicht nur der Arbeitsplatz, die Geschäfte und die Schulen, sondern auch die Theater, Kinos, Museen und Parks. Viele träumen trotzdem von einem Haus mit Garten. Sie wissen, dass sie schwer arbeiten und sparen müssen, wenn der Traum Wirklichkeit werden soll. Und das tun auch viele.

Im Münchner Hofgarten

Zum Text

A. Richtig oder falsch? Wenn falsch, sagen Sie warum!

_____ 1. In Deutschland, in Österreich und in der Schweiz gibt es nicht viel Bauland, besonders nicht in den Städten.

_____ 2. Die meisten Leute dort wohnen in einem Haus mit Garten.

_____ 3. Auf dem Land ist Bauland nicht so teuer wie in der Stadt.

_____ 4. Das Leben auf dem Land ist sehr bequem.

_____ 5. In allen Städten gibt es Straßenbahnen, eine U-Bahn und eine S-Bahn.

_____ 6. Mit den öffentlichen Verkehrsmitteln kann man durch die Stadt fahren.

_____ 7. Überall in Wäldern und Feldern gibt es Fahrradwege und Fußgängerzonen.

_____ 8. In der Fußgängerzone kann man am Tag einkaufen, am Abend bummeln gehen und manchmal Musik hören.

_____ 9. Im amerikanischen Konsulat in München kann man picknicken.

_____ 10. Wenn man ein Haus kaufen oder bauen möchte, muss man schwer arbeiten und lange sparen.

High German and Dialects

„Joden Dach, wie jeit es Ihne?" sagt der Kölner.

„Tachchen, wie jeht et Ihnen?" sagt der Berliner.

„Moin, moin, wie geiht Di dat?" sagt der Hamburger.

„Griaß Gott, wia geht's Eana?" sagt der Bayer.

Germany has numerous dialects. These are much older than the standard "High German" (**Hochdeutsch**) that you hear nearly everywhere today. In some regions there are movements to keep regional dialects alive. North German Radio, for example, broadcasts short daily sermons in Low German (**Plattdeutsch**), whereas some Bavarian newspapers include a regular feature in Bavarian. Some dialects are staging a comeback in song, literature, and theater. Children always learn the dialect first—automatically. However, they also need to master standard German so as not to be at a disadvantage in school and later, on the job market. "High German" is understood everywhere in Germany.

B. Haus oder Wohnung? *(Fill in the appropriate form of the article.)*

1. Die meisten wohnen in ein____ Wohnung. 2. In d____ Städten ist Bauland sehr teuer. 3. Der Traum vom Häuschen mit Garten hat viele an d____ Stadtrand *(m.)* oder auf d____ Land gebracht. 4. Zwischen d____ Wäldern und auf d____ Feldern stehen Reihenhäuser. 5. Die Reihenhäuser sind manchmal direkt an d____ Straße. 6. Morgens fahren viele in d____ Stadt. 7. Das Leben auf d____ Land kann unbequem sein. 8. Viele bleiben in d____ Stadt, weil dort alles in d____ Nähe liegt. 9. Nach d____ Arbeit fahren sie dann noch einmal in d____ Zentrum *(n.)*. 10. Mitten in d____ Zentrum ist fast immer etwas los.

C. In der Großstadt *(You have never been to Munich before. Ask questions about the city, using* **wo** *or* **wohin**.*)*

BEISPIEL: In Großstädten gibt es eine U-Bahn.
Wo gibt es eine U-Bahn?

1. Mit der U-Bahn kann man mitten in die Fußgängerzone fahren.
2. Dort kann man immer schön bummeln.
3. Abends kann man ins Kino gehen.
4. Wenn man ins Grüne will, geht man in den Park.
5. Dort gibt es überall Wege und Bänke.

D. *Kennen oder wissen?*

1. _____ Sie den Spruch „Schaffe, spare, Häusle baue"?
2. _____ Sie, wie viele Leute in Deutschland auf dem Land leben?
3. _____ Sie den Englischen Garten?
4. _____ ihr, dass es überall Fahrradwege gibt?
5. Ich habe nicht _____, dass es in der Stadt so viele Fußgängerwege gibt.
6. _____ du Herrn Jakob? Nein, aber Hans _____ ihn.
7. _____ du, dass er mit seinen 80 Jahren immer noch viel wandert?

WO BITTE GEHT'S HIER ZUR GESUNDHEIT?

IHR APOTHEKER KENNT DEN WEG.

E. Was ist typisch auf dem Land und in der Stadt? *(Work with two or three other students. Some groups list the advantages of city life and the disadvantages of country life, while the others do the reverse. Then compare; which group has the more convincing arguments?)*

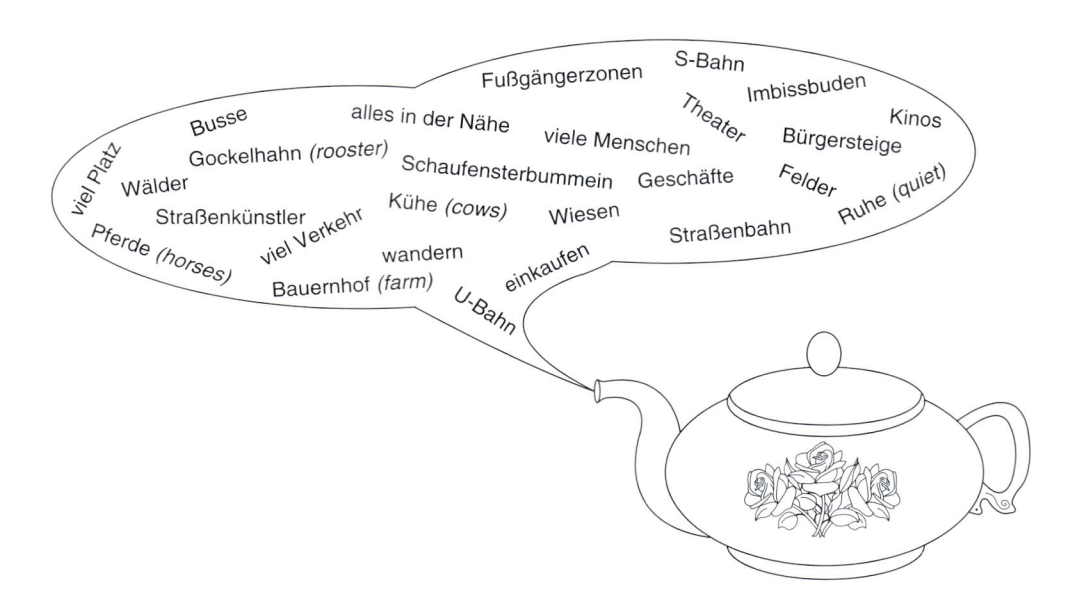

Wortschatz in der Sprechblase: viel Platz, Busse, Fußgängerzonen, S-Bahn, Imbissbuden, alles in der Nähe, Theater, Kinos, Wälder, Gockelhahn (rooster), viele Menschen, Bürgersteige, Straßenkünstler, Schaufensterbummeln, Geschäfte, Felder, Ruhe (quiet), Pferde (horses), viel Verkehr, Kühe (cows), Wiesen, Straßenbahn, Bauernhof (farm), wandern, einkaufen, U-Bahn

F. Wo möchten Sie wohnen, und warum?

1. **Schreiben Sie!** Hier wohne ich gern. *(Write three to four sentences describing where you would like to live and why. Include one phrase or word from each group below.)*

    BEISPIEL: Ich möchte in einem Reihenhaus mitten in San Francisco wohnen. Da komme ich leicht zur Arbeit und zum Ozean. Man braucht nicht unbedingt ein Auto.

1	2
in einer WG	mitten in . . .
in einer (Miet)wohnung	in der Nähe von . . .
in einer Eigentumswohnung	am Stadtrand von . . .
in einem Reihenhaus	im . . . Stock
in einem Haus mit Garten	auf dem Land . . .

2. **Meinungsumfrage** *(Opinion poll. Ask each other about your preferences now and later. Give reasons why. Your instructor then polls the entire class to determine what choices have been made.)*

    BEISPIEL: S1 Wo möchtet ihr jetzt wohnen, in der Stadt oder auf dem Land?
                    S2 Ich möchte . . . wohnen, weil . . .
                    S3 . . .
                    S1 Und wenn ihr Kinder habt?
                    S2 Dann möchte ich . . .
                    S1 Und wenn ihr alt seid?
                    S3 . . .

HÖREN SIE ZU!

Die Großeltern kommen. *(Listen to the message that Mrs. Schmidt has left for her children on the answering machine. Then indicate which chores each child has been asked to do; write S for Sebastian, M for Mareike, and J for Julia. Finally, note briefly what the children are NOT supposed to do.)*

Zum Erkennen: Vati *(Dad);* nämlich *(you know)*

1. **Wer soll was tun?**

    _____ zum Supermarkt fahren
    _____ einen Schokoladenpudding machen
    _____ Bratwurst und Käse kaufen
    _____ den Großeltern zeigen, wo sie schlafen
    _____ zum Blumengeschäft fahren
    _____ Kartoffeln kochen
    _____ Blumen ins Esszimmer stellen
    _____ 30 Mark aus dem Schreibtisch nehmen
    _____ Mineralwasserflaschen zum Supermarkt bringen
    _____ die Kleidung der *(of the)* Großeltern in den Schrank hängen
    _____ Wein in den Kühlschrank stellen

2. **Was sollen die Kinder nicht tun?**

    a. _____

    b. _____

Zum ersten Mal in Dresden und Sie kennen die Stadt wie Ihre Westentasche: Das Navigationssystem TravelPilot von Blaupunkt.

WEB-ECKE

For updates and online activities, visit the *Wie geht's?* home page at http://www.hrwcollege.com/german/sevin/! You'll have a chance to choose a German house to live in, go furniture hunting, and place the furniture throughout your new home. You will also visit Stuttgart and use its public transportation system.

SPRECHSITUATIONEN

Describing locations

You have already learned many ways of describing the locations of something, including using the two-way prepositions in this chapter. Here are a few reminders:

im Norden / nördlich von	rechts / links von	da drüben
bei	gegenüber von	hier / da / dort
in der Nähe von	an der Ecke	im Parterre / im ersten Stock
nicht weit von	Ecke Schillerstraße	am [Rhein] / an der [Donau]
mitten in	in der Schillerstraße	

Offering apologies

Entschuldigung! / Verzeihung! Es tut mir (furchtbar) Leid!
Entschuldigen Sie! Entschuldigt! Entschuldige! Leider . . .

Expressing forgiveness

(Das) macht nichts. (Es ist) schon gut. *(It's OK.)*
(Das ist) kein Problem.

Übungen

A. Straßenbild *(Make ten statements about places, vehicles, or people shown below. Use two-way prepositions, wherever possible.)*

   BEISPIEL: Der Bus hält an der Haltestelle.
   Die Leute gehen in den Bus.

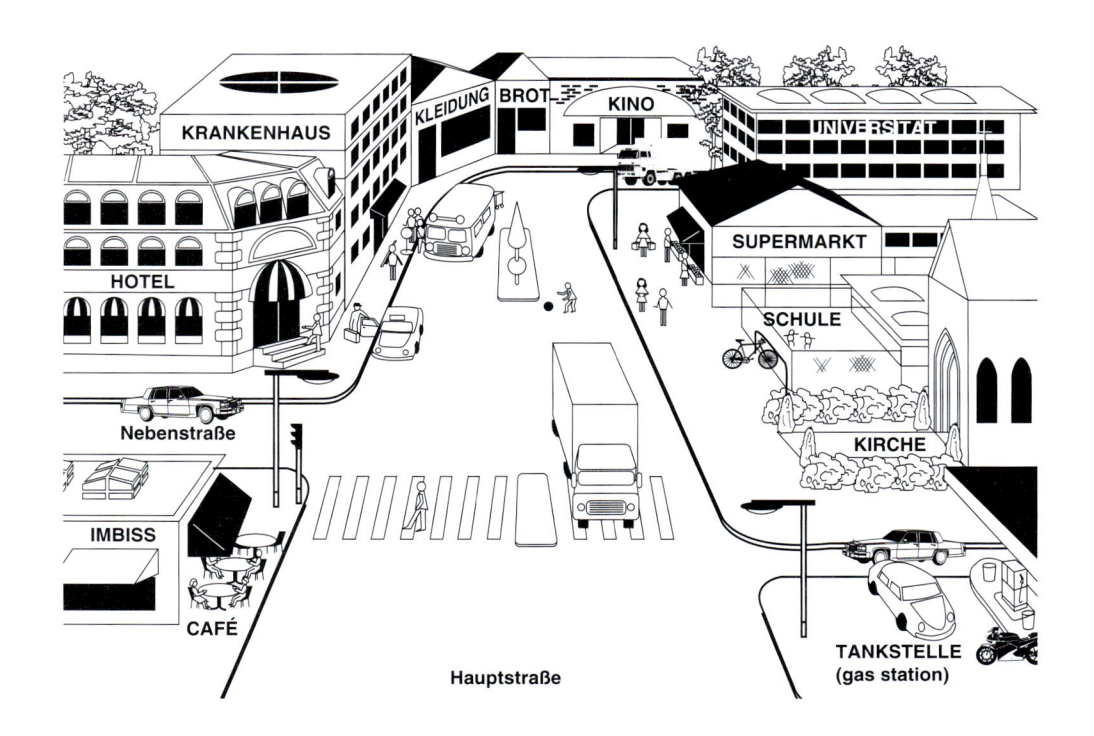

B. **Wo ist was?** *(Working with a classmate, look at the map of Germany inside the front cover of the book and write at least ten different statements about the location of various cities in Germany.)*

   BEISPIEL: Rostock liegt an der Ostsee, zwischen Wismar und Stralsund.

C. **Was sagen Sie, und was sagen die anderen?** *(Create a short exchange for each of the situations, using appropriate expressions. Work in pairs or small groups.)*
   1. Sie haben den Pullover von einem Freund getragen. Der Pullover ist schmutzig geworden.
   2. Sie haben am Samstag Plätzchen gekauft, aber am Sonntag können Sie kein Plätzchen mehr finden. Ihre Mitbewohner haben alle Plätzchen gegessen.
   3. Sie haben bei einem Professor gegessen. Ihr Glas ist vom Tisch gefallen.
   4. Eine Mitbewohnerin hat Ihre Cola getrunken.
   5. Ein Freund hat Ihnen nicht zum Geburtstag gratuliert, weil er zu viel zu tun hatte.

D. **Kurzgespräche**
   1. You have been invited to a classmate's house for dinner, but you are quite late. You introduce yourself to his / her mother, who asks you to come in **(herein)**. You apologize repeatedly for being so late, while she maintains it doesn't matter. When you hand her the flowers you have brought, she thanks you and says that dinner is ready.
   2. You are visiting Hildesheim and want to see the well-known *Knochenhauer Amtshaus,* a sixteenth-century guild house. You stop a Hildesheimer and ask where the building is. He / she replies that it is at the Marktplatz, across from city hall. Your informant asks whether you see the pedestrian area over there; he / she directs you to walk along that street and turn right at the pharmacy. The *Marktplatz* is nearby **(ganz in der Nähe)**. You thank the stranger and say good-bye.

„Der arme Poet" von Carl Spitzweg. So kann man auch wohnen.

KAPITEL 7

AUF DER BANK UND IM HOTEL

Am Bankschalter

LERNZIELE

■ VORSCHAU
The story of the *Deutsche Mark*

■ GESPRÄCHE AND WORTSCHATZ
(Formal) time, banking, and hotel accommodations

■ STRUKTUR
Der- and **ein**-words
Separable-prefix verbs
Flavoring particles

■ EINBLICKE
Accommodations and tourist information
Hotels, youth hostels, and other lodgings

■ FOKUS
Exchange offices and credit cards
Hotel names
Youth hostels
Luxembourg

■ WEB-ECKE

■ SPRECHSITUATIONEN
Telling and asking about time
Expressing disbelief
Giving a warning

VORSCHAU

The Story of the *Deutsche Mark*

Despite a West German economic boom that began in the 1950s and continued for nearly forty years, this recent prosperity has been accompanied by a fear of inflation. The concern is rooted in the conditions that plagued Germany after World War I, when it experienced what was probably the worst inflation of any modern industrialized country. The mark had so little value that people needed pushcarts to transport the piles of money needed to buy groceries, as a single loaf of bread cost billions of marks. In the aftermath of World War II, the Western Allies replaced the Reichsmark (RM) with the Deutsche Mark (DM) to hold inflation in check, to reduce the enormous war debt, and to instill economic confidence. The Soviet Union followed suit with the introduction of the Mark (M) in the Moscow-controlled East German zone. Boosted by the Marshall Plan, the West German economy experienced dramatic growth, while the Soviets stripped East German factories of machinery and shipped it east. Nevertheless, the German Democratic Republic (GDR) economy became one of the strongest in the Eastern Bloc, yet always lagged behind the capitalist West. The difference in economic efficiency accelerated in the two decades before the collapse of the GDR in 1989.

On July 2, 1990, three months before the German unification, Bonn undertook one of the biggest financial bail-outs in history with a currency union **(Währungsunion).** GDR citizens were allowed to exchange up to 6,000 Eastmark for DM at a rate of 1:1; savings above these amounts were converted at a rate of 2:1. This meant that after the exchange **(Umtausch),** the average savings of a three-member GDR household of M 27,000 became DM 16,500. The introduction of the much-desired, strong West German Mark had a devastating impact on the East German economy by driving much of the industry out of competition overnight and throwing large numbers of employees out of work. This situation required huge cash infusions from West to East, increasing inflationary pressure in all of Germany. The staunchly independent German central bank **(Bundesbank),** which is charged with ensuring monetary stability, raised interest rates to the highest level in decades. The bank reluctantly lowered them only after the worst recession since World War II hit Germany in the early 1990s.

The introduction of the euro, the new all-European currency, in 1999 for institutional transactions meant the beginning of the end of the Deutsche Mark, symbol of German economic power and stability in the second half of the 20th century. In the year 2002, the DM will be replaced by the euro in everyday transactions.

GESPRÄCHE

Auf der Bank

TOURISTIN	Guten Tag! Können Sie mir sagen, wo ich Geld umtauschen kann?
ANGESTELLTE	Am Schalter 1.
TOURISTIN	Vielen Dank! *(Sie geht zum Schalter 1.)* Guten Tag! Ich möchte Dollar in Schillinge umtauschen. Hier sind meine Reiseschecks.
ANGESTELLTE	Darf ich bitte Ihren Pass sehen?
TOURISTIN	Hier.
ANGESTELLTE	Unterschreiben Sie bitte hier, dann gehen Sie dort zur Kasse! Da bekommen Sie Ihr Geld.
TOURISTIN	Danke! *(Sie geht zur Kasse.)*
KASSIERER	324 Schilling 63: einhundert, zweihundert, dreihundert, zehn, zwanzig, vierundzwanzig Schilling und dreiundsechzig Groschen.[1]
TOURISTIN	Danke! Auf Wiedersehen!

An der Rezeption im Hotel

EMPFANGSDAME	Guten Abend!
GAST	Guten Abend! Haben Sie ein Einzelzimmer frei?
EMPFANGSDAME	Für wie lange?
GAST	Für zwei oder drei Nächte; wenn möglich ruhig und mit Bad.
EMPFANGSDAME	Leider haben wir heute nur noch ein Doppelzimmer, und das nur für eine Nacht. Aber morgen wird ein Einzelzimmer frei. Wollen Sie das Doppelzimmer sehen?
GAST	Ja, gern.
EMPFANGSDAME	Zimmer Nummer 12, im ersten Stock rechts. Hier ist der Schlüssel.
GAST	Sagen Sie, kann ich meinen Koffer einen Moment hier lassen?
EMPFANGSDAME	Ja, natürlich. Stellen Sie ihn da drüben in die Ecke!
GAST	Danke! Noch etwas, wann machen Sie abends zu?
EMPFANGSDAME	Um 24.00 Uhr. Wenn Sie später kommen, müssen Sie klingeln.

[1] One euro equals just under 14 Schilling, e.g., 324 Schilling are approximately € 23.

Fragen

1. Wer möchte Geld umtauschen? 2. Wo ist sie? 3. Wohin muss sie gehen? 4. Was muss die Touristin der Angestellten zeigen? 5. Wo bekommt sie ihr Geld? 6. Wie viel Schilling bekommt sie? 7. Was für ein Zimmer möchte der Gast? 8. Für wie lange braucht er es? 9. Was für ein Zimmer nimmt er und wo liegt es? 10. Was gibt die Dame an der Rezeption dem Gast? 11. Wo kann der Gast seinen Koffer lassen? 12. Wann macht das Hotel zu?

Exchange Offices and Credit Cards

Currency can be exchanged and traveler's checks cashed in banks and post offices. Exchange offices (**Wechselstuben**) are open daily at all major railroad stations, airports, and border crossings.

The popularity of credit cards (**Kreditkarten**) is increasing in the German-speaking countries, though many small businesses and restaurants still do not accept them. So-called eurocheques continue to be a common method of payment for Europeans. These checks are used with a special eurocheque card to withdraw cash from banks or ATMs (**Geldautomaten**) and to pay bills in shops, restaurants, and hotels throughout Europe. You can also use your Visa or American Express card in European ATMs, if you have your four-digit PIN number, but the banks will usually charge you a 2.5 percent transaction fee and the current interest rate from the date of transaction. Even though the exchange rate might be good, it is usually more advantageous to exchange traveler's checks at a bank.

WORTSCHATZ 1

Die Uhrzeit *(time of day)*

- The formal (official) time system is like the one used by the military. The hours are counted from 0 to 24, with 0 to 11 referring to A.M. and 12 to 24 referring to P.M. The system is commonly used in timetables for trains, buses, planes, etc., on radio and television, and to state business hours of stores and banks.

16.05 Uhr = sechzehn Uhr fünf		*4:05 P.M.*
16.15 Uhr = sechzehn Uhr fünfzehn		*4:15 P.M.*
16.30 Uhr = sechzehn Uhr dreißig		*4:30 P.M.*
16.45 Uhr = sechzehn Uhr fünfundvierzig		*4:45 P.M.*
17.00 Uhr = siebzehn Uhr		*5:00 P.M.*

- Note that German separates hours and minutes by a period instead of a colon: **16.05 Uhr** BUT *4:05 P.M.*

Die Bank, -en *(bank)*

der Ausweis, -e	*identification card (ID)*
Dollar, -	*dollar*
Pass, ⸚e	*passport*
Schalter, -	*counter, ticket window*
(Reise)scheck, -s	*(traveler's) check*
das Geld	*money*
Bargeld	*cash*
Kleingeld	*change*
die Kasse, -n	*cashier's window (lit. cash register)*

Hallo Pizza ist für Sie geöffnet:
Täglich
von 17.00 - 23.00 Uhr
Mindestbestellwert DM 15,- (ohne Getränke)

Das Hotel, -s *(hotel)*

der Ausgang, ⸚e	*exit*	das Einzelzimmer, -	*single room*
Eingang, ⸚e	*entrance*	Doppelzimmer, -	*double room*
Gast, ⸚e	*guest*	Gepäck	*baggage, luggage*
Koffer, -	*suitcase*	die Nacht, ⸚e	*night*
Schlüssel, -	*key*	Nummer, -n	*number*
		Tasche, -n	*bag; pocket*

Weiteres

bald	*soon*
frei	*free, available*
auf / zu \}	*open / closed*
geöffnet / geschlossen \}	
laut / ruhig	*loud / quiet(ly)*
möglich	*possible*
einen Moment	*(for) just a minute*
Wann machen Sie auf / zu?	*When do you open / close?*
einen Scheck einlösen	*to cash a check*
umtauschen	*to exchange*
wechseln	*to change; to exchange*
lassen (lässt), gelassen	*to leave (behind)*
unterschreiben, unterschrieben	*to sign*

Zum Erkennen: die Angestellte, -n *(clerk, employee, f.)*; die Empfangsdame, -n *(receptionist)*; klingeln *(here: to ring the doorbell)*

BERLINER BANK
Berlin—Düsseldorf—Frankfurt/Main—Hamburg—Hannover—
München—Stuttgart—London—Luxemburg
Jetzt auch in
Brandenburg—Cottbus—Dresden—Frankfurt(Oder)—Leipzig—
Magdeburg—Oranienburg—Potsdam—Schwerin

Zum Thema

A. Mustersätze
   1. Geld wechseln: **Wo kann ich hier** Geld **wechseln?**
      Dollar umtauschen, einen Scheck einlösen, Reiseschecks einlösen
   2. Pass: **Darf ich bitte Ihren** Pass **sehen?**
      Scheck, Reisescheck, Ausweis
   3. Dollar: **Können Sie mir das in** Dollar **geben?**
      D-Mark, Franken, Schilling, Euro, Kleingeld, Bargeld
   4. mein Auto: **Wo kann ich** mein Auto **lassen?**
      meinen Schlüssel, mein Gepäck, meinen Koffer, meine Tasche
   5. 24.00 Uhr: **Wir machen um** 24.00 Uhr **zu.**
      22.00 Uhr, 22.15 Uhr, 22.30 Uhr, 22.45 Uhr, 23.00 Uhr

B. Was bedeuten die Wörter und was sind die Artikel?

   Ausgangstür, Gästeausweis, Geldwechsel, Gepäckstück, Handtasche, Hoteleingang, Kofferschlüssel, Nachtapotheke, Nachthemd, Nachtmensch, Passnummer, Scheckbuch, Sparbuch, Taschengeld, Taschenlampe, Stehlampe, Theaterkasse

C. Ich brauche Kleingeld. *(With a partner, practice asking for a place where you can get change. Take turns, and vary your responses.)*

   S1   Ich habe kein Kleingeld. Kannst du mir . . . wechseln?
   S2   Nein, . . .

S1 Schade!
S2 Aber du kannst . . .
S1 Wo ist . . . ?
S2 . . .
S1 Danke schön!
S2 . . .

HYPO BANK

Die HYPO. Eine Bank – ein Wort.

D. Im Hotel *(With a partner, practice inquiring about a hotel room. Take turns, and be sure to vary your responses.)*

S1 Guten . . . ! Haben Sie ein . . . mit . . . frei?
S2 Wie lange wollen Sie bleiben?
S1 . . .
S2 Ja, wir haben ein Zimmer im . . . Stock.
S1 Was kostet es?
S2 . . .
S1 Kann ich es sehen?
S2 . . . Hier ist der Schlüssel. Zimmernummer . . .
S1 Sagen Sie, wo kann ich . . . lassen?
S2 . . .
S1 Und wann machen Sie abends zu?
S2 . . .

E. Wie spät ist es? *(Ralf loves his new digital watch. Kurt prefers his old-fashioned one with hands. As Ralf says what time it is, Kurt confirms it in a more casual way. Work with a classmate. Take turns.)*

BEISPIEL: 14.15 Auf meiner Uhr ist es vierzehn Uhr fünfzehn.
Ich habe Viertel nach zwei.

1. 8.05   4. 13.25   7. 19.40   10. 23.59
2. 11.10   5. 14.30   8. 20.45   11. 00.01
3. 12.30   6. 17.37   9. 22.50   12. 02.15

F. Interview. Fragen Sie einen Nachbarn / eine Nachbarin, . . . !
1. wo man hier Bargeld oder Kleingeld bekommt
2. wie er / sie bezahlt, wenn er / sie einkaufen geht: bar, mit einem Scheck oder mit einer Kreditkarte
3. wie er / sie bezahlt, wenn er / sie reist *(travels)*
4. wo man hier D-Mark, Schillinge, Franken *(Swiss currency)* oder Euros bekommen kann
5. ob er / sie weiß, wie viele Mark (Schillinge, Franken, Euro) man für einen Dollar bekommt
6. was er / sie tut, wenn er / sie kein Geld mehr hat

G. Aussprache: ei, ie (See also 11.37, 40–41 in the pronunciation section of the Workbook.)
1. [ei]   s**ei**t, w**eiß**t, bl**ei**bst, l**ei**der, fr**ei**, R**ai**ner M**ey**er, B**ay**ern
2. [ie]   w**ie**, w**ie** v**ie**l, n**ie**, l**ie**ben, l**ie**gen, m**ie**ten, l**ie**s, s**ie**h, D**ie**nstag
3. v**ie**lleicht, B**ei**spiel, bl**ei**ben / bl**ie**ben, h**ei**ßen / h**ie**ßen, W**ie**n / W**ei**n, W**ie**se / w**ei**ß
4. Wortpaare
   a. See / Sie   c. biete / bitte   e. leider / Lieder
   b. beten / bieten d. Miete / Mitte   f. Mais / mies

HÖREN SIE ZU!

Eine Busfahrt *(Listen to the discussion between these American exchange students in Tübingen and their professor before taking a bus trip early in their stay. Then complete the statements below according to the dialogue.)*

Zum Erkennen: abfahren *(to depart);* das Konto *(account);* die Jugendherberge *(youth hostel);* also *(in other words);* Briefmarken *(stamps)*

1. Der Professor und die Studenten wollen am _____ um _____ abfahren.

2. Sie sind von _____ bis _____ in der Schweiz.

3. Sie sind von _____ bis _____ in Österreich.

4. Sie sollen heute noch _____ gehen.

5. Die Jugendherbergen und _____ sind schon bezahlt.

6. Sie brauchen nur etwas Geld, wenn sie _____ oder _____ kaufen wollen.

7. _____ und _____ sind auch schon bezahlt.

8. Manchmal braucht man Kleingeld für _____.

Dieser Bankautomat ist immer offen.

STRUKTUR

I. *Der-* and *ein-*words

1. **Der**-words

    This small but important group of limiting words is called DER-WORDS because their case endings are the same as those of the definite articles **der, das, die.**

der, das, die	*the, that (when stressed)*
dieser, -es, -e	*this, these*
jeder, -es, -e	*each, every (sg. only, pl.* **alle**)
mancher, -es, -e	*many a (sg.); several, some (usually pl.)*
solcher, -es, -e	*such (usually pl.)*
welcher, -es, -e	*which*

    CAUTION: The singular of **solcher** usually is **so ein,** which is not a **der-**word but an **ein-**word: **so ein** Hotel *(such a hotel)* BUT **solche** Hotels *(such hotels).*

    COMPARE the endings of the definite article and the **der-**words!

	masc.	neut.	fem.	pl.
nom.	der dieser welcher	das dieses welches	die diese welche	die diese welche
acc.	den diesen welchen			
dat.	dem diesem welchem	dem diesem welchem	der dieser welcher	den diesen welchen

nom.	Wo ist **der** Schlüssel?—**Welcher** Schlüssel? **Dieser** Schlüssel?
acc.	Hast du **den** Kofferschlüssel gesehen?—Wie soll ich **jeden** Schlüssel kennen?
dat.	Kannst du ihn mit **dem** Schlüssel öffnen?—Mit **welchem** Schlüssel?
plural	Gib mir **die** Schlüssel!—Hier sind **alle** Schlüssel. **Manche** Schlüssel sind vom Haus, **solche** Schlüssel zum Beispiel.
BUT	Der Kofferschlüssel ist **so ein** Schlüssel. Hast du **so einen** Schlüssel?

2. **Ein**-words

    POSSESSIVE ADJECTIVES are called **ein**-words because their case endings are the same as those of the indefinite article **ein** and the negative **kein.**

mein	*my*	unser	*our*
dein	*your (sg. fam.)*	euer	*your (pl. fam.)*
sein	*his / its*	ihr	*their*
ihr	*her / its*	Ihr	*your (sg. / pl. formal)*

COMPARE the endings of the indefinite article and the **ein**-words!

	masc.	neut.	fem.	pl.
nom.	ein mein unser	ein mein unser	eine meine unsere	keine meine unsere
acc.	ein**en** mein**en** unser**en**			
dat.	ein**em** mein**em** unser**em**	ein**em** mein**em** unser**em**	ein**er** mein**er** unser**er**	kein**en** mein**en** unser**en**

CAUTION: The **-er** of uns**er** and eu**er** is not an ending!

- **Ein**-words have no endings in the masc. sing. nominative and in the neut. sing. nominative and accusative.

    nom.   Hier ist **ein** Pass. Ist das **mein** Pass oder **dein** Pass?
    acc.   Braucht er **keine** Kreditkarte?—Wo hat er **seine** Kreditkarte? Hat sie **einen** Ausweis?—Natürlich hat sie **ihren** Ausweis. Haben Sie **Ihren** Ausweis?
    dat.   In welcher Tasche sind die Schlüssel?—Sie sind in **meiner** Tasche. Oder sind die Schlüssel in **einem** Koffer?—Sie sind in **Ihrem** Koffer.
    plural Wo sind die Schecks?—Hier sind **unsere** Schecks und da sind **euere** Schecks.

Übungen

A. Ersetzen Sie die Artikel!

1. **Der**-Wörter

    BEISPIEL: die Tasche *(this)*
    diese Tasche

    a. das Gepäck *(every, which, this)*
    b. der Ausweis *(this, every, which)*
    c. die Nummer *(which, every, this)*
    d. die Nächte *(some, such, these)*
    e. an dem Schalter *(this, which, each)*
    f. an der Kasse *(this, every, which)*
    g. mit den Schecks *(these, some, all)*

2. **Ein**-Wörter

    BEISPIEL: die Gäste *(your / 3 ×)*
    deine / euere / Ihre Gäste

    a. der Pass *(my, her, no, his)*
    b. das Bargeld *(our, her, their)*
    c. die Wohnung *(my, our, your / 3 ×)*
    d. neben den Koffer *(your / 3 ×, our, their)*
    e. in dem Doppelzimmer *(no, his, your / 3 ×)*
    f. mit den Schlüsseln *(your / 3 ×, my, her)*

3. **Der**- und **ein**-Wörter

    BEISPIEL: Das Bad ist klein. *(our)*
    Unser Bad ist klein.

    a. Das Zimmer hat einen Fernseher. *(each, my, his, our)*
    b. Bitte bringen Sie den Koffer zum Auto! *(this, her, our, my)*

c. Ich kann die Schlüssel nicht finden. *(your / 3 ×, our, some, my)*
d. Darf ich das Gepäck hier lassen? *(her, his, this, our)*
e. Der Ober kennt den Gast. *(each, our, this, your / 3 ×)*
f. Die Taschen sind schon vor dem Ausgang. *(our, all, some, my)*
g. Den Leuten gefällt das Hotel nicht. *(these, some, such)*
h. Du kannst den Scheck auf der Bank einlösen. *(this, my, every, such a, your / sg. fam.)*

B. Dias von einer Deutschlandreise *(Slideshow from a trip to Germany)*

1. Auf _____ Bild seht ihr _____ Freunde aus Holland.
       this   *my*
2. Das sind _____ Sohn Heiko und _____ Tochter Anke.
            their   *their*
3. In _____ Stadt ist _____ Kirche? 4. _____ Kirchen
      which   *this*   *Such*
gibt es in Norddeutschland. 5. _____ Haus ist sehr alt, aber
                                  This
nicht _____ Haus in Neubrandenburg ist so alt. 6. Ich
       every
finde _____ Häuser sehr schön; Müllers wohnen in _____
       such   *such a*
Haus. 7. Und hier sind _____ Onkel Thomas und _____ Tante
                         my   *my*
Hilde. 8. Ist das nicht _____ Auto da vor _____ Hotel?
                         your (pl. fam.)   *this*

II. Separable-prefix verbs

1. English has a number of two-part verbs that consist of a verb and a preposition or an adverb.

    Watch out! Hurry up! Come back!

In German such verbs are called SEPARABLE-PREFIX verbs. You are already familiar with two of them:

Passen Sie auf! Hören Sie zu!

Their infinitives are **aufpassen** and **zuhören**. The prefixes **auf** and **zu** carry the main stress: **auf'·passen, zu'·hören.** From now on we will identify such separable-prefix verbs by placing a raised dot (·) between the prefix and the verb in vocabulary lists: **auf·passen, zu·hören.**

- These verbs are separated from the prefixes when the inflected part of the verb is the first or second sentence element: in imperatives, questions, and statements.

Hören Sie bitte **zu!**
Hören Sie jetzt **zu?**
Warum **hören** Sie nicht **zu?**
Wir **hören** immer gut **zu.**
   V1   V2

- These verbs are NOT SEPARATED from the prefix when the verb stands at the end of a sentence or clause: with modals, in the present perfect, and in subordinate clauses.

Note, however, that in the present perfect the **-ge-** of the past participle is inserted between the stressed prefix and the participle.

> Ich soll immer gut **zuhören.**
>
> Ich habe immer gut **zugehört.**
>
> Ich weiß, dass ich immer gut **zuhöre.**
>
> Ich weiß, dass ich immer gut **zuhören** soll.
>
> Ich weiß, dass ich immer gut **zugehört** habe.

2. Knowing the basic meanings of some of the most frequent separable prefixes will help you derive the meanings of some of the separable-prefix verbs.

ab-	*away, off*	**mit-**	*together with, along with*
an-	*to, up to*	**nach-**	*after, behind*
auf-	*up, open*	**um-**	*around, over, from one to the other*
aus-	*out, out of*	**vor-**	*ahead, before*
ein-	*into*	**vorbei-**	*past, by*
her-	*toward (the speaker)*	**zu-**	*closed*
hin-	*away from (the speaker)*	**zurück-**	*back*

BEISPIEL:

an·kommen	*to arrive (come to)*
her·kommen	*to come (toward the speaker)*
herein·kommen	*to come in (toward the speaker)*
heraus·kommen	*to come out (toward the speaker)*
hin·kommen	*to get there (away from the point of reference)*
mit·kommen	*to come along*
nach·kommen	*to follow (come after)*
vorbei·kommen	*to come by*
zurück·kommen	*to come back*

You will need to learn these common separable-prefix verbs.

an·rufen, angerufen	*to call, phone*
auf·machen	*to open*
auf·passen	*to pay attention, watch (out)*
auf·schreiben, aufgeschrieben	*to write down*
auf·stehen, ist aufgestanden	*to get up*
aus·gehen, ist ausgegangen	*to go out*
ein·kaufen	*to shop*
ein·lösen	*to cash (in)*
mit·bringen, mitgebracht	*to bring along*
mit·gehen, ist mitgegangen	*to go along*
mit·kommen, ist mitgekommen	*to come along*
mit·nehmen, mitgenommen	*to take along*
um·tauschen	*to exchange*
vorbei·gehen, ist vorbeigegangen (an, bei)	*to pass (by)*
zu·hören (+ *dat.*)	*to listen*
zu·machen	*to close*
zurück·kommen, ist zurückgekommen	*to come back*

CAUTION: Not all verbs with prefixes are separable, e.g., **unterschreiben, wiederholen.** Here the main stress is on the verb, not on the prefix: **unterschrei'ben, wiederho'len.** Remember also the inseparable prefixes **be-, ent-, er-, ge-, ver-,** etc. (Chapter 4, Struktur I). They never stand alone.

Übungen

C. Was bedeuten diese Verben? *(Knowing the meanings of the basic verbs and the prefixes, can you tell what these separable-prefix verbs mean?)*
1. abgeben, abnehmen
2. ansprechen
3. aufbauen, aufgeben, aufstehen, aufstellen
4. ausarbeiten, aushelfen, aus(be)zahlen
5. heraufkommen, herauskommen, herüberkommen, herunterkommen
6. hinaufgehen, hinausgehen, hineingehen, hinuntergehen
7. mitgehen, mitfahren, mitfeiern, mitsingen, mitspielen
8. nachkommen, nachlaufen, nachmachen
9. vorbeibringen, vorbeifahren, vorbeikommen
10. zuhalten
11. zurückbekommen, zurückbleiben, zurückbringen, zurückgeben, zurücknehmen, zurücksehen

Mach's nach!

D. Noch einmal. Wiederholen Sie die Sätze ohne Modalverb!

BEISPIEL: Sie soll ihm zuhören.
Sie hört ihm zu.

1. Wir dürfen am Wochenende ausgehen. 2. Wann musst du morgens aufstehen? 3. Wollt ihr mit mir einkaufen gehen? 4. Ich soll Wein mitbringen. 5. Er will morgen zurückkommen. 6. Ich möchte dich gern mitnehmen. 7. Du kannst das Geld umtauschen. 8. Er will an der Universität vorbeigehen. 9. Können Sie bitte die Fenster aufmachen! 10. Ihr sollt gut aufpassen.

E. Am Telefon *(Report to a brother what your mother is telling or asking you about tomorrow's family reunion.)*

BEISPIEL: Sie möchte wissen, ob Rainer und Wolfgang die Kinder mitbringen.
Bringen Rainer und Wolfgang die Kinder mit?

Sie sagt, dass die Tante auch mitkommt.
Die Tante kommt auch mit.

1. Sie sagt, dass wir abends alle zusammen ausgehen.
2. Sie möchte wissen, ob du deine Kamera mitbringst.
3. Sie möchte wissen, wann die Bank aufmacht.
4. Sie sagt, dass sie noch etwas Geld umtauscht.
5. Sie sagt, dass sie dann hier vorbeikommt.

F. Das tut man. *(Say what things one needs to do before checking out of a hotel.)*

BEISPIEL: früh aufstehen
Man steht früh auf.

1. die Koffer zumachen 2. das Gepäck zur Rezeption mitnehmen 3. den Schlüssel zurückgeben 4. vielleicht ein Taxi anrufen 5. vielleicht einen Reisescheck einlösen

G. Hoppla, hier fehlt 'was! Fertig für die Reise? *(Work with a partner to find out whether various family members have finished their tasks. Take turns asking questions until you have both completed your lists. One list is below, the other in Section 11 of the Appendix.)*

S1:

Vater	bei der Bank vorbeigehen	
Vater	Geld umtauschen	
Mutter	Kamera mitbringen	Ja, ich glaube.
Mutter	die Nachbarn anrufen	Nein.
Thomas	die Telefonnummer aufschreiben	Ja, ich glaube.
Thomas	die Garagentür zumachen	
Carla	bei der Post vorbeigehen	
Carla	die Fenster zumachen	Nein, noch nicht.
Kinder	den Fernseher ausmachen *(turn off)*	Ja.
Kinder	die Lichter *(lights)* ausmachen	
ich	ein paar Bücher mitnehmen	Ja.

BEISPIEL: S1 Ist Vater bei der Bank vorbeigegangen?
S2 Ja, er ist gestern bei der Bank vorbeigegangen. Haben die Kinder den Fernseher ausgemacht?
S1 Ja, sie haben den Fernseher ausgemacht.

H. Auf Deutsch bitte!

1. You *(sg. fam.)* didn't close your book. 2. Listen! *(formal)* 3. They came back on the weekend. 4. Are you *(pl. fam.)* going out soon? 5. I don't know if he's coming along. 6. Do you *(sg. fam.)* know when she went out? 7. I exchanged our money. 8. Whom did you *(formal)* bring along?

I. Geben Sie alle vier Imperative!

BEISPIEL: Die Tür aufmachen
**Machen Sie die Tür auf!
Mach die Tür auf!
Macht die Tür auf!
Machen wir die Tür auf!**

1. jetzt aufstehen
2. in der Stadt einkaufen
3. den Scheck noch nicht einlösen
4. genug Bargeld mitbringen
5. das Gepäck mitnehmen
6. mit ihnen mitgehen
7. bei der Bank vorbeigehen
8. trotzdem zuhören
9. wieder zurückkommen

J. Interview. Fragen Sie einen Nachbarn / eine Nachbarin, . . . !
1. wann er / sie heute aufgestanden ist
2. wann er / sie gewöhnlich am Wochenende aufsteht
3. wohin er / sie gern geht, wenn er / sie ausgeht
4. wo er / sie einkauft
5. was er / sie heute mitgebracht hat (drei Beispiele bitte!)

III. Flavoring particles

In everyday speech, German uses many FLAVORING WORDS (or intensifiers) to convey what English often expresses through gestures or intonation, e.g., surprise, admiration, or curiosity. When used in these contexts, flavoring particles have no exact English equivalent. Here are some examples:

aber	*expresses admiration, or intensifies a statement*
denn	*expresses curiosity, interest (usually in a question)*
doch	*expresses concern, impatience, assurance*
ja	*adds emphasis*

Euer Haus gefällt mir **aber!**	*I do like your house.*
Die Möbel sind **aber** schön!	*Isn't this furniture beautiful!*
Was ist **denn** das?	*What (on earth) is that?*
Wie viel kostet **denn** so etwas?	*(Just) how much does something like that cost?*
Das weiß ich **doch** nicht.	*That I don't know.*
Frag **doch** Julia!	*Why don't you ask Julia!*
Du kennst **doch** Julia?	*You do know Julia, don't you?*
Euer Garten ist **ja** super!	*(Wow,) your garden is great!*
Ihr habt **ja** sogar einen Pool!	*(Hey,) you even have a pool!*

Übungen

K. Im Hotel. Auf Englisch bitte!

> **BEISPIEL:** Haben Sie denn kein Einzelzimmer mehr frei?
> *Don't you have any single room available?*

1. Hier ist ja der Schlüssel!
2. Das Zimmer ist aber schön!
3. Es hat ja sogar einen Balkon!
4. Hat es denn keine Dusche?
5. Wir gehen doch noch aus?
6. Hast du denn keinen Hunger?
7. Komm doch mit!
8. Ich komme ja schon!
9. Lass doch den Mantel hier!
10. Wohin gehen wir denn?

Hotel Names FOKUS

Germany, Austria, and Switzerland have many small hotels (**Gasthöfe** or **Gasthäuser**), a type of accommodation that first appeared around monasteries toward the end of the Middle Ages. Many of them still have names that refer to the Bible: *Gasthof Engel* (angel); *Gasthof Drei Könige* (the three kings were symbols of travel); *Gasthof Rose* or *Lilie* (both flowers represent the Virgin Mary); *Gasthof Lamm* (the Lamb of God). After a postal system began to develop in the 1400s, names such as *Gasthof Goldenes Posthorn, Alte Post, Neue Post,* and *Zur Post* became common.

Zusammenfassung

L. Bilden Sie Sätze! *(Use the verb form suggested.)*

BEISPIEL: Eva / gestern / ausgehen / mit Willi *(present perfect)*
Eva ist gestern mit Willi ausgegangen.

1. man / umtauschen / Geld / auf / eine Bank *(present tense)*
2. welch- / Koffer *(sg.)* / du / mitnehmen? *(present tense)*
3. einkaufen / ihr / gern / in / euer / Supermarkt? *(present tense)*
4. unser / Nachbarn *(pl.)* / zurückkommen / vor einer Woche *(present perfect)*
5. wann / ihr / aufstehen / am Sonntag? *(present perfect)*
6. ich / mitbringen / dir / mein / Stadtplan *(present perfect)*
7. vorbeigehen / noch / schnell / bei / Apotheke! *(imperative / sg. fam.)*
8. zumachen / Schalter / um 17.30 Uhr! *(imperative / formal)*
9. umtauschen / alles / in Dollar! *(imperative / pl. fam.)*

M. An der Rezeption. Auf Deutsch bitte!

1. All (the) hotels are full **(voll)**. 2. Look **(sehen,** *sg. fam.***)**, there's another hotel. 3. Let's ask once more. 4. Do you *(formal)* still have a room available? 5. Yes, one room without (a) bath on the first floor and one room with (a) shower **(Dusche)** on the second floor. 6. Excellent! Which room would you *(sg. fam.)* like? 7. Give *(formal)* us the room on the second floor. 8. Where can I leave these suitcases? 9. Over there. But don't go yet. 10. May I please see your ID? 11. Yes. Do you cash traveler's checks?—Of course. 12. Did you see our restaurant?—Which restaurant? 13. This restaurant. From each table you can see the sea. 14. You don't find a restaurant like this (such a restaurant) everywhere. 15. That's true.

EINBLICKE

Accommodations and Tourist Information

When looking for accommodations in a German city, you can choose from a wide range of prices and comfort, from campgrounds to luxury hotels. A **Pension** usually offers a simple room with a sink; toilets and showers are shared. Sometimes even medium-standard hotels have rooms without a bath. Homes offering inexpensive **Fremdenzimmer,** or rooms for tourists, are common in rural areas and can be spotted by a sign saying **Zimmer frei.** Breakfast is usually included in the price of accommodation, regardless of the price category. In the interest of public safety, hotel guests are required by law to fill out a form providing home address, date of birth, and other personal information.

To find accommodations, travelers can rely on a town's tourist information office **(Touristeninformation).** Usually located in train stations or city centers, the offices offer standard tourist information as well as the reservation of rooms in hotels or private homes **(Zimmervermittlung).**

Gasthof zur Post in Kochel am See

WORTSCHATZ 2

der Gasthof, ⸚e	*small hotel*
Wald, ⸚er	*forest, woods*
die Jugendherberge, -n	*youth hostel*
Pension, -en	*boarding house; hotel*
Reise, -n	*trip*

einfach	*simple, simply*
meistens	*mostly, usually*
an·kommen, ist angekommen[1]	*to arrive*
an·nehmen, angenommen	*to accept*
kennen lernen	*to get to know, meet*
packen	*to pack*
reisen, ist gereist	*to travel*
reservieren	*to reserve*
übernachten	*to spend the night*
Vorsicht!	*Careful!*
Das kommt darauf an.	*That depends.*

---

[1] Two-way prepositions take the dative with **an·kommen: Er ist am Bahnhof/in der Stadt angekommen.**

Vorm Lesen

A. Fragen

1. Wo kann man in den USA / in Kanada gut übernachten? 2. Wie heißen ein paar Hotels oder Motels? 3. Was gibt es in einem Hotelzimmer? 4. Was kostet ein Zimmer in einem Luxushotel in New York oder San Francisco? 5. Wo kann man frühstücken? Kostet das Frühstück extra? 6. Haben Sie schon einmal in einer Jugendherberge übernachtet? Wenn ja, wo? 7. Gehen Sie gern campen? Wenn ja, warum; wenn nein, warum nicht?

B. Was ist das?

der Campingplatz, Evangelist; das Formular, Symbol; die Adresse, Attraktion, Bibel, Möglichkeit, Übernachtung, Übernachtungsmöglichkeit; ausfüllen; international, luxuriös, modern, primitiv, privat

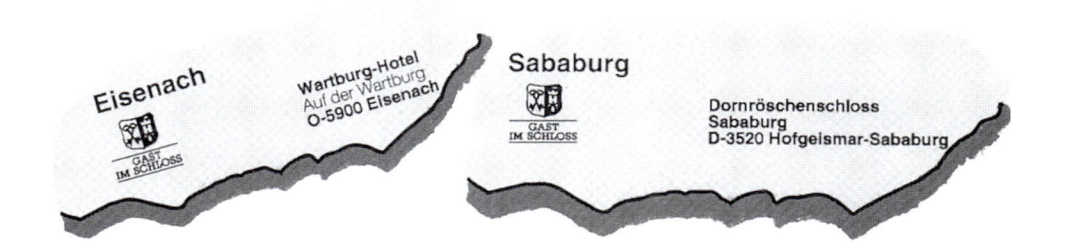

Übernachtungsmöglichkeiten

Wo kann man gut übernachten? Nun°, das kommt darauf an, ob das Hotel elegant oder einfach sein soll, ob es zentral liegen muss oder weiter draußen° sein darf. Wer will, kann auch Gast in einem Schloss oder auf einer Burg sein.

 In Amerika gibt es viele Hotels mit gleichen° Namen, weil sie zu einer Hotelkette° gehören, z.B. Holiday Inn oder Hilton. Bei diesen Hotels weiß man immer, was man hat, wenn man hineingeht. In Deutschland gibt es auch Hotels mit gleichen Namen, z.B. Hotel zur Sonne oder Gasthof Post. Aber das bedeutet nicht, dass solche Hotels innen gleich sind°. Im Gegenteil°! Sie sind meistens sehr verschieden°, weil sie zu keiner Kette gehören. Ihre Namen gehen oft bis ins Mittelalter zurück. Oft sagen sie etwas über° ihre Lage°, z.B. Berghotel, Pension Waldsee. Andere° Namen, wie z.B. Gasthof zum Löwen, zum Adler° oder zum Stier° sind aus der Bibel genommen. Sie sind Symbole für die Evangelisten Markus, Johannes und Lukas.

 Manche Hotels sind sehr luxuriös und teuer, andere sind einfach und billig. Sprechen wir von einem normalen Hotel, einem Gasthof oder Gasthaus! Wenn Sie ankommen, gehen Sie zur Rezeption. Dort müssen Sie meistens ein Formular ausfüllen und bekommen dann Ihr Zimmer: ein Einzelzimmer oder Doppelzimmer, ein Zimmer mit oder ohne Bad. Für Zimmer ohne Bad gibt es auf dem Flur eine Toilette und meistens auch eine Dusche. Das Frühstück ist gewöhnlich im Preis inbegriffen°. Übrigens hat jeder Gasthof seinen Ruhetag°. Dann ist das Restaurant geschlossen und man nimmt keine neuen Gäste an. Der Herr oder die Dame an der Rezeption kann Ihnen auch Geschäfte und Attraktionen in der Stadt empfehlen, manchmal auch Geld umtauschen. Aber Vorsicht! Auf der Bank ist der Wechselkurs° fast immer besser°.

 Wenn Sie nicht vorher° reservieren können, dann finden Sie auch Übernachtungsmöglichkeiten durch die Touristeninformation am Hauptbahnhof. Hier finden Sie nicht nur Adressen von Hotels, sondern auch von Privatfamilien und Pensionen. So eine Übernachtung ist gewöhnlich nicht sehr teuer, aber sauber und gut.

 Haben Sie schon einmal in einer Jugendherberge oder einem Jugendgästehaus übernachtet? Wenn nicht, tun Sie es einmal! Sie brauchen dafür° einen Jugendherbergsausweis. So einen Ausweis können Sie aber schon vorher in Amerika oder Kanada bekommen. Fast jede Stadt hat eine Jugendherberge, manchmal in einem modernen Haus, manchmal in einer Burg oder in einem Schloss. Jugendherbergen und Jugendgästehäuser sind in den Ferien meistens schnell voll, denn alle Gruppen reservieren schon vorher. Das Übernachten in einer Jugendherberge kann ein Erlebnis° sein, weil man oft interessante Leute kennen lernt. Jugendherbergen haben nur einen Nachteil°: Sie machen gewöhnlich abends um 23.00 Uhr zu. Wenn Sie später zurückkommen, haben Sie Pech gehabt. In fast allen Großstädten gibt es Jugendgästehäuser. Wenn Sie schon vorher wissen, dass Sie fast jeden Abend ausgehen und spät nach

well
farther out

same / ... franchise

are alike inside
on the contrary / different
about / location
other / eagle / bull

included / day off

exchange rate / better
in advance

for that

experience
disadvantage

rather / not until

in other ways
on the road / everybody

Hause kommen, dann übernachten Sie lieber° in einem Jugendgästehaus, denn diese machen erst° um 24.00 oder 1.00 Uhr zu, und in manchen Gästehäusern kann man sogar einen Hausschlüssel bekommen.

Man kann natürlich auch anders° übernachten, z.B. im Zelt auf einem Campingplatz. Das macht Spaß, wenn man mit dem Fahrrad unterwegs° ist; aber das ist nicht für jeden°. Ob im Hotel oder auf dem Campingplatz, in einer Pension oder Jugendherberge, überall wünschen wir Ihnen viel Spaß auf Ihrer Reise durch Europa.

Zum Text

A. Was passt? *(Choose the correct answer.)*

1. Deutsche Hotels mit gleichen Namen sind . . .
   a. immer alle gleich
   b. innen meistens nicht gleich
   c. alle aus dem Mittelalter
   d. Symbole
2. Wenn man in einem Gasthof ankommt, geht man erst . . .
   a. ins Bad
   b. ins Restaurant
   c. zur Rezeption
   d. ins Zimmer
3. Im Hotel kann man Geld umtauschen, aber . . .
   a. nur an der Rezeption
   b. nicht an der Rezeption
   c. der Wechselkurs ist meistens nicht sehr gut
   d. der Wechselkurs ist oft super
4. Das Übernachten in einer Jugendherberge kann sehr interessant sein, weil . . .
   a. Jugendherbergen in den Ferien schnell voll sind
   b. sie gewöhnlich abends um 22.00 Uhr zumachen
   c. man manchmal neue Leute kennen lernt
   d. sie immer auf einer Burg sind
5. Auf dem Campingplatz . . .
   a. gibt es eine Toilette auf dem Flur
   b. ist das Frühstück im Preis inbegriffen
   c. gibt es Zelte
   d. darf man nicht früh ankommen

B. Wo sollen wir übernachten? *(Match each lodging with the corresponding description.)*

Campingplatz, Gasthof, Jugendgästehaus, Jugendherberge, Luxushotel, Pension

1. Diese Übernachtungsmöglichkeit ist meistens nicht teuer, aber doch gut. Man kann sie z.B. durch die Touristeninformation am Bahnhof finden.
2. Hier ist es besonders billig, aber wenn es viel regnet, kann es sehr ungemütlich sein.
3. Wenn man viel Geld hat, ist es hier natürlich wunderbar.
4. Diese Möglichkeit ist für junge Leute. Sie ist nicht teuer und man kann abends spät zurückkommen oder einen Schlüssel bekommen.
5. Das Übernachten kann hier sehr bequem und gemütlich sein; das Frühstück kostet nichts extra. Am Ruhetag kann man dort nicht essen.
6. Hier können Leute mit Ausweis billig übernachten, aber man darf abends nicht nach elf zurückkommen.

C. Übernachtungsmöglichkeiten. Was fehlt?

1. In _____ Hotel kann man gut übernachten, aber das kann man nicht von _____ Hotel sagen. *(this, every)*
2. Bei _____ Hotel wissen Sie immer, wie es innen aussieht. *(such a)*
3. _____ Hotels sind sehr luxuriös und teuer, _____ Hotel zum Beispiel. *(some, this)*
4. _____ Hotel ist sehr schön gewesen. *(our)*
5. Hast du schon einmal von _____ Pension gehört? *(this)*
6. Wie gefällt es euch in _____ Jugendherberge? *(your)*
7. _____ Jugendherberge ist in einer Burg. *(our)*
8. In _____ Jugendherberge gibt es noch Platz. *(this)*
9. Wollen wir auf _____ Campingplatz übernachten? *(this)*
10. _____ Campingplatz meinst du *(do you mean)*? *(which)*

D. Kofferpacken. Was nehmen Sie mit, wenn Sie eine Reise . . . machen? Zusammen mit 3–4 Studenten / Studentinnen machen Sie für jede Reise eine Liste!

1. a) ans Meer b) in die Berge c) nach Europa
2. Und du, was hast du mitgenommen? *(Tell what you took along. One student starts, the next one repeats and adds to it, etc. When your memory fails, you're out.)*

   BEISPIEL: Ich habe eine Sonnenbrille mitgenommen. Und du?
   Ich habe eine Sonnenbrille und meine Kamera mitgenommen.

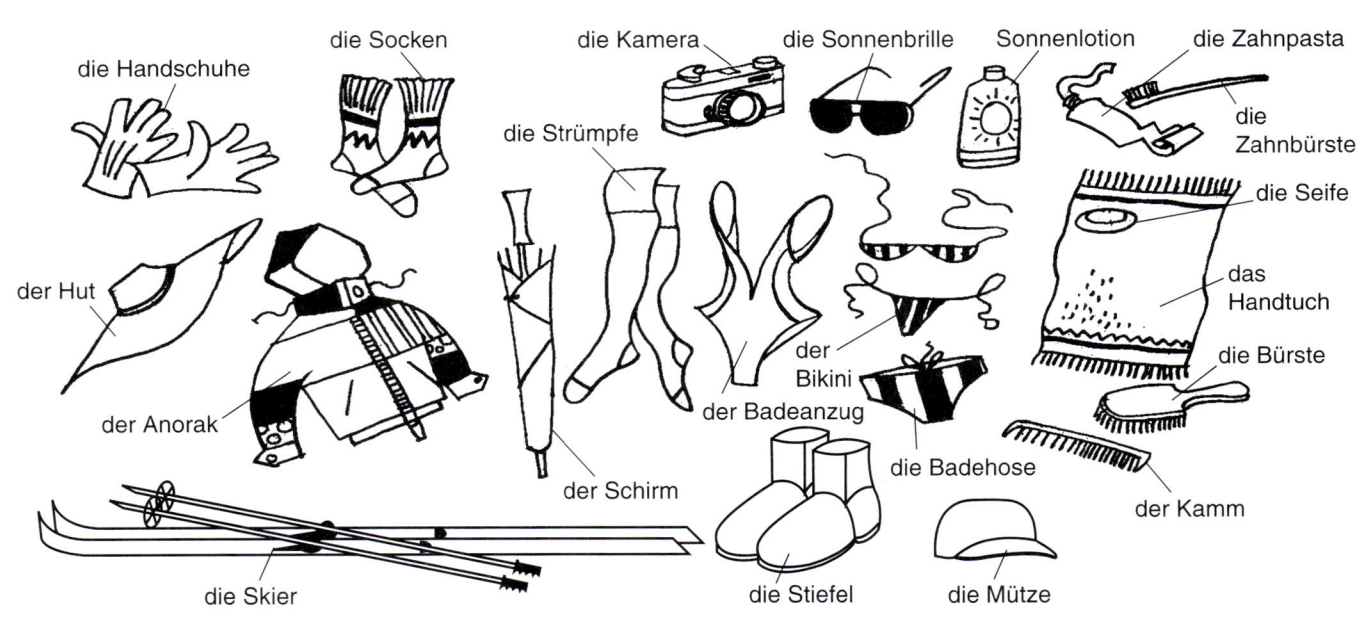

die Handschuhe, die Socken, die Kamera, die Sonnenbrille, Sonnenlotion, die Zahnpasta, die Zahnbürste, die Seife, das Handtuch, die Bürste, der Kamm, der Hut, der Anorak, die Strümpfe, der Schirm, der Bikini, der Badeanzug, die Badehose, die Skier, die Stiefel, die Mütze

E. In der Jugendherberge. Sagen Sie die Sätze noch einmal ohne Modalverb, (a) im Präsens und (b) im Perfekt!

BEISPIEL: Du kannst in den Ferien vorbeikommen.
Du kommst in den Ferien vorbei.
Du bist in den Ferien vorbeigekommen.

1. Wann möchtet ihr ankommen?
2. In der Jugendherberge könnt ihr Leute kennen lernen.
3. Du musst natürlich einen Jugendherbergsausweis mitbringen.
4. Wollt ihr abends spät ausgehen?
5. Die Jugendherberge soll um elf zumachen.
6. Wer spät zurückkommen möchte, kann Pech haben.

FOKUS Youth Hostels

Youth hostels (**Jugendherbergen**) are immensely popular among budget travelers in Germany, Switzerland, and Austria. They are open to individual travelers, groups, and families. There is no upper age limit. During peak season, however, members up to age 25 have priority. Accommodation is usually dormitory-style, with bunk beds and shared bathrooms. Many youth hostels offer laundry facilities, dining halls, and common rooms. Though they are not real hotels—many are closed during the day and have a curfew—youth hostels have reached a relatively high level of comfort for the price. Students and backpackers have come to value the hostels as places to meet other young people from around the world. If you plan on "hosteling," remember to purchase a membership card (**Jugendherbergsausweis**) before traveling overseas.

Jugendherberge in Nürnberg. Haben Sie noch Platz für zwei Leute?

F. Ruck, zuck! Wem gehört das? *(One person claims to own everything. Quickly correct him / her and tell whose property it is. You may mention the items suggested, or think of your own.)*

BEISPIEL: Das ist mein Buch. (Heft, Bleistift, Jacke, Tasche, Schlüssel usw.)
Quatsch *(nonsense)!* **Das ist nicht dein Buch; das ist mein (ihr, sein) Buch.**

G. Schreiben Sie! Meine Ferienreise *(Using the questions as a guideline, write a brief paragraph.)*
1. Wohin geht Ihre nächste *(next)* Reise? Wann? Wo übernachten Sie dann, und warum dort?
2. Wo sind Sie das letzte Mal *(the last time)* gewesen? Wann? Wo haben Sie übernachtet und wie hat es Ihnen gefallen?

HÖREN SIE ZU!

Hotel Lindenhof *(Mr. Baumann calls the reception of Hotel Lindenhof on Lake Constance. Listen to the conversation. Then complete the sentences below with the correct information from the dialogue.)*

Zum Erkennen: die Person, -en; das Frühstücksbüfett; schwimmen; das Schwimmbad; Minigolf; der Blick auf *(view of)*

1. Herr Baumann und seine Familie fahren im Sommer an den _____. 2. Sie wollen am _____ Juli ankommen und _____ bleiben. 3. Sie brauchen Zimmer für _____ Personen, also _____ Zimmer. 4. Die Zimmer kosten _____ pro Tag. 5. Das Frühstücksbüfett kostet _____ extra. 6. Herr Baumann findet das nicht _____. 7. Die Kinder können dort _____ und in der Nähe auch _____ und _____ spielen. 8. Zum See ist es auch nicht _____. 9. Vom Balkon hat man einen Blick auf den _____ und die _____. 10. Er _____ die Zimmer.

Luxembourg Fokus

The Grand Duchy of Luxembourg **(Luxemburg),** one of Europe's oldest and smallest independent countries, lies between Germany, France, and Belgium. Although it is one of the world's most industrialized nations, its heavy industry, mainly iron and steel production, has not spoiled the natural beauty of the country's rolling hills and dense forests. Almost all Luxembourgers speak Letzeburgish, a German dialect. French, German, and Letzeburgish are used in parliament. Despite close ties to their neighbors, the people of Luxembourg maintain an independent spirit, as expressed in the words of their national anthem: "Mir wölle bleiwe wat mir sin" **(Wir wollen bleiben, was wir sind).** Its capital by the same name (pop. 80,000) is a big financial and banking center and home to several European institutions, including the EURATOM (European Atomic Energy Community).

Blick auf Luxemburg, mit der Unterstadt an der Alzette

WEB-ECKE

For updates and online activities, visit the *Wie geht's?* homepage at http://www.hrwcollege.com/german/sevin/! You'll find out about various vacation options on an island in the North Sea, check the prices of a camping vacation in Germany, and learn more about Luxembourg.

SPRECHSITUATIONEN

Telling and asking about time

You have now learned both the formal and the informal (see *Schritt 5*) ways of telling time.

> Meine Vorlesung beginnt um Viertel nach eins.
> Meine Vorlesung beginnt um 13.15 Uhr.
>
> Sie dauert von Viertel nach eins bis um drei.
> Sie dauert von 13.15 Uhr bis 15.00 Uhr.
>
> Wie spät ist es?
> Wie viel Uhr ist es?
> Wann beginnt . . . ?
> Können Sie mir sagen, wie spät / wie viel Uhr es ist?

Es ist Viertel nach eins.

Es ist drei.

Expressing disbelief

What can you say when someone tells you something that is hard to believe?

Stimmt das?	Ach du liebes bisschen!
Wirklich?	*(My goodness!)*
Das glaube ich nicht.	Das ist ja Wahnsinn! *(That's crazy!)*
Das kann ich nicht glauben.	Du spinnst (wohl)! *(You're crazy!)*
Das ist doch nicht möglich!	Mach keine Witze! *(Stop joking!)*
Das kann doch nicht wahr *(true)* sein!	Quatsch! *(Nonsense!)*
Das gibt's doch nicht! *(That's not possible.)*	

Giving a warning

Here are a few ways to caution someone:

Vorsicht!	Warte! / Wartet! / Warten Sie! *(Wait!)*
Pass auf! / Passt auf! / Passen Sie auf!	Halt!

Übungen

A. **Was sagen Sie?** *(Use an appropriate expression for each of the following situations. Use each expression only once.)*
   1. Hier kostet ein Hotelzimmer 225 Mark.
   2. Ich habe ein Zimmer für 200 Mark im Monat gefunden.
   3. Du, die Vorlesung beginnt um 14.15 Uhr und es ist schon 14.05 Uhr!
   4. Sie bummeln mit einem Freund in der Stadt. Ihr Freund will bei Rot *(at a red light)* über die Straße laufen.
   5. Sie sind auf einer Party und es macht Ihnen viel Spaß. Aber morgen ist eine Prüfung und Sie hören, dass es schon zwei Uhr ist.
   6. Sie lernen auf einer Party einen Studenten kennen. Sie hören, dass sein Vater und Ihr Vater als Studenten Freunde gewesen sind.
   7. Sie stehen mit einer Tasse Kaffee an der Tür. Die Tür ist zu. Ein Freund möchte hereinkommen.
   8. Ein Freund aus Deutschland will die Kerzen auf seinem Weihnachtsbaum anzünden *(light)*. Sie sind sehr nervös.

B. **Öffnungszeiten.** Wann sind diese Restaurants und Kunstgalerien offen?

Gasthaus BAUER
1., Schottenbastei 4, Tel.:533 6128
Mo-Fr 9-24 Uhr, warme Küche bis 21 Uhr.
Café MUSEUM 1., Friedrichstraße 6,
Tel.: 56 52 02
tgl. 7-23 Uhr; Alt-Wiener Kaffeehaus

ZUR WEINPERLE
9., Alserbachstraße 2, Tel.: 34 32 52
Mo-Fr 9-21.30 Uhr, Sa 9-14.30 Uhr.
Café CENTRAL, 1., Herrengasse 14 (im inside Palais Ferstel), Tel.: 535 41 76
Mo-Sa 10-22 Uhr.

SCHNITZELWIRT
7., Neubaugasse 52, Tel.: 93 37 71
Mo-Sa 10-22 Uhr, warme Küche 11.30-14.30 Uhr und 17.30-22 Uhr.
SCHWEIZERHAUS 2., Prater, Straße des 1. Mai 116, Tel.: 218 01 52
tgl. 10-24 Uhr, mitten im Wurstelprater

GALERIE NÄCHST ST. STEPHAN
1., Grünangergasse 1, Tel.: 512 12 66
Mo-Fr 10-18 Uhr, Sa 11-14 Uhr.
GALERIE HUMMEL
1., Bäckerstraße 14, Tel.: 512 12 96
Di-Fr 15-18 Uhr, Sa 10-13 Uhr.

GALERIE PETER PAKESCH
1., Ballgasse 6, Tel.: 52 48 14 und
3., Ungargasse 27, Tel.: 713 74 56
Di-Fr 14-19 Uhr, So 11-14 Uhr.
GALERIE STEINEK
1., Himmelpfortgasse 22, Tel.: 512 87 59
Di-Fr 13-18 Uhr, Sa 10-12 Uhr.

C. **Kurzgespräche**
1. You are visiting your aunt in Heidelberg. As you tour the castle, you see a German student whom you got to know while you both stayed at a youth hostel in Aachen. Call out to the German student. Both of you express your disbelief that you have met again. Your friend is studying in Heidelberg; you explain why you are there. You ask whether your friend would like to go for a cola (drink), and he / she agrees.
2. You and a friend are in Stralsund and are looking for a hotel room. You have both inquired in several places. All the hotels you saw had no available rooms at all; in desperation your friend has taken a double room that will cost you 185 DM for one night. You both express your disbelief at your bad luck.

Rückblick: Kapitel 4–7

I. Verbs

p. 171 1. **Wissen**

Wissen, like the modals below, is irregular in the singular of the present tense. It means *to know a fact,* as opposed to **kennen,** which means *to be acquainted with a person or thing.*

singular	plural
ich weiß	wir wissen
du weißt	ihr wisst
er weiß	sie wissen

pp. 142–44 2. Modals

	dürfen	können	müssen	sollen	wollen	mögen	möchten
ich	darf	kann	muss	soll	will	mag	möchte
du	darfst	kannst	musst	sollst	willst	magst	möchtest
er	darf	kann	muss	soll	will	mag	möchte
wir	dürfen	können	müssen	sollen	wollen	mögen	möchten
ihr	dürft	könnt	müsst	sollt	wollt	mögt	möchtet
sie	dürfen	können	müssen	sollen	wollen	mögen	möchten

The modal is the second sentence element (V1); the infinitive of the main verb (V2) stands at the end of the sentence.

    Sie **sollen** ihr den Kaffee **bringen.**   *You're supposed to bring her the coffee.*
         V1   V2

pp. 170–71 3. Imperative

The forms of the familiar imperative have no pronouns; the singular familiar imperative has no **-st** ending.

formal sg. + pl.	fam. sg. (du)	fam. pl. (ihr)	1st pers. pl. (*let's . . .*)
Schreiben Sie!	Schreib!	Schreibt!	Schreiben wir!
Antworten Sie!	Antwort**e**!	Antwortet!	Antworten wir!
Fahren Sie!	**Fahr!**	Fahrt!	Fahren wir!
Nehmen Sie!	**Nimm!**	Nehmt!	Nehmen wir!

4. Present perfect

    a. Past participles

pp. 116–19

t-verbs (weak and mixed verbs)	n-verbs (strong verbs)
(ge) + stem(change) + (e)t	(ge) + stem(change) + en
gekauft	geschrieben
gearbeitet	
gebracht	
eingekauft	mitgeschrieben
verkauft	unterschrieben
reserviert	

Rückblick: Kapitel 4–7

b. Most verbs use **haben** as the auxiliary. Those that use **sein** are intransitive (take no object) and imply a change of place or condition; **bleiben** and **sein** are exceptions to the rule.

> Wir haben Wien gesehen.
> Wir sind viel gelaufen.
> Abends sind wir müde gewesen.

5. Verbs with inseparable and separable prefixes

   a. Inseparable-prefix verbs (verbs with the unstressed prefixes **be-, emp-, ent-, er-, ge-, ver-,** and **zer-**) are never separated. *pp. 117–18*

   > Was bedeutet das?
   > Das verstehe ich nicht.
   > Was empfehlen Sie?
   > Wer bezahlt das Mittagessen?

   über-, unter-, and **wieder-** can be used as separable or inseparable prefixes, depending on the particular verb and meaning.

   > Übernach'tet ihr in der Jugendherberge?
   > Unterschrei'ben Sie bitte hier!
   > Wiederho'len Sie bitte! BUT Hol das bitte wieder!

   b. Separable-prefix verbs (verbs where the prefix is stressed) are separated in statements, questions, and imperatives. *pp. 193–95*

   > Du **bringst** deine Schwester **mit**.
   > **Bringst** du deine Schwester **mit**?
   > **Bring** doch deine Schwester **mit**!

   They are not separated when used with modals, in the present perfect, or in dependent clauses.

   > Du **sollst** deine Schwester **mitbringen**.
   > **Hast** du deine Schwester **mitgebracht**?
   > Sie will wissen, ob du deine Schwester **mitbringst**.

II. Cases

1. Interrogative pronouns *pp. 43, 61, 86*

nom.	wer?	was?
acc.	wen?	was?
dat.	wem?	—

2. **Der**-words and **ein**-words *pp. 191–92*

   Der-words have the same endings as the definite article **der**; and **ein**-words (or possessive adjectives) have the same endings as **ein** and **kein**.

dieser	solcher (so ein)
jeder	welcher
mancher	alle

mein	unser
dein	euer
sein, sein, ihr	ihr, Ihr

209

Rückblick: Kapitel 4–7

pp. 165–67

3. Two-way prepositions: accusative or dative?

> an, auf, hinter, in, neben, über, unter, vor, zwischen

The nine two-way prepositions take either the dative or the accusative, depending on the verb.

> wo?   LOCATION, activity within a place → dative
> wohin?   DESTINATION, motion to a place → accusative

Remember the difference between these two sets of verbs:

to put (upright)	Er **stellt** den Koffer neben den Ausgang.
to stand	Der Koffer **steht** neben dem Ausgang.
to put (flat), lay	**Legen** Sie den Ausweis auf den Tisch!
to lie (flat)	Der Ausweis **liegt** auf dem Tisch.

4. Summary of the three cases

	use	follows . . .	masc.	neut.	fem.	pl.
nom.	Subject, Predicate noun	heißen, sein, werden	der dieser ein mein	das dieses ein mein	die diese eine meine	die diese keine meine
acc.	Direct object	durch, für, gegen, ohne, um	den diesen einen meinen			
		an, auf, hinter, in, neben, über, unter, vor, zwischen				
dat.	Indirect object	aus, außer, bei, mit, nach, seit, von, zu	dem diesem einem meinem	dem diesem einem meinem	der dieser einer meiner	den diesen keinen meinen
		antworten, danken, gefallen, gehören, helfen, zuhören				

p. 140   5. Personal pronouns

	singular				plural			sg. / pl.
nom.	ich	du	er	es	sie	wir	ihr	sie	Sie
acc.	mich	dich	ihn	es	sie	uns	euch	sie	Sie
dat.	mir	dir	ihm	ihm	ihr	uns	euch	ihnen	Ihnen

Don't confuse these pronouns with the **ein**-words (or possessive adjectives, see 2 above), which are always followed by a noun.

III. Sentence structure

Rückblick: Kapitel 4–7

1. Verb position
   a. V1—V2   pp. 28–29, 66

   In declarative sentences, yes / no questions, and imperatives, two-part verb phrases are split:
   - the inflected part (V1) is the first or second sentence element
   - the other part (V2) appears at the end of the clause.

   > Er **ist** hier an der Uni **Student.**
   > Er **ist** wirklich sehr **interessant.**
   > **Hast** du ihn schon **kennen gelernt?**
   > Ich **kann** jetzt nicht lange **sprechen.**
   > <u>**Komm**</u> doch später bei uns <u>**vorbei!**</u>
   > V1   V2

   b. Subordinate clauses   pp. 121–22
   - Subordinate clauses are introduced by subordinating conjunctions or interrogatives:

   > **bevor, dass, ob, obwohl, weil, wenn, etc.**

   > **wer? wen? wem? was? was für ein(e)? wohin? woher? wo? wann? warum? wie? wie lange? wie viel? wie viele? etc.**

   - In subordinate clauses the subject usually comes right after the conjunction, and the inflected verb (V1) is at the end of the clause.

     > Sie sagt, **dass** sie das Einzelzimmer **nimmt.**
     > Er sagt, **dass** er den Zimmerschlüssel **mitbringt.**

   - Two-part verb phrases appear in the order V2 V1.

     > Sie sagt, **dass** er den Koffer **mitbringen soll.**

   - If a subordinate clause is the first sentence element, then the inflected part of the verb in the main clause comes right after the comma, retaining second position in the overall sentence.

     > Ich **habe** den Schlüssel **mitgenommen,** weil das Hotel um 24.00 Uhr zumacht.
     > Weil das Hotel um 24.00 Uhr zumacht, **habe** ich den Schlüssel **mitgenommen.**

2. Sequence of objects

   The indirect object usually precedes the direct object, unless the direct object is a pronoun.   pp. 87, 140

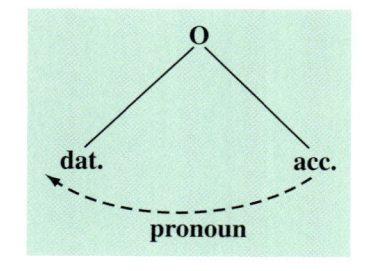

   Sie gibt **dem Herrn** den Reisescheck.
   Sie gibt **ihm** den Reisescheck.
   Sie gibt ihn **dem Herrn.**
   Sie gibt ihn **ihm.**

   (diagram: O — dat. / acc., with dashed arrow labeled **pronoun**)

211

Rückblick:
Kapitel 4–7

p. 147

3. **Sondern** vs. **aber**

   Sondern must be used when the first clause is negated AND the meaning *but on the contrary* is implied.

   Er wohnt hier, **aber** er ist gerade nicht zu Hause.
   Heinz ist nicht hier, **aber** er kommt in zehn Minuten zurück.
   Heinz ist nicht hier, **sondern** bei Freunden.

NOTE: Review exercises for both vocabulary and structures can be found in the Workbook.

Wer den Pfennig nicht ehrt, ist den Taler nicht wert.

(Take care of the pennies, and the pounds will look after themselves. Who doesn't value the penny, isn't worth the dollar.)

Rückblick: Kapitel 4–7

Eine Karte für drei Feste.

KAPITEL 8
POST UND REISEN

Das Reisen mit dem ICE ist schnell und bequem.

LERNZIELE

■ VORSCHAU
Spotlight on Switzerland

■ GESPRÄCHE AND WORTSCHATZ
Postal service and travel

■ STRUKTUR
Genitive case
Time expressions
Sentence structure: types and sequence of adverbs
The position of **nicht**

■ EINBLICKE
Switzerland and its languages
Tourists in Switzerland

■ FOKUS
Phoning and postal services
Train travel
Car travel
Switzerland's mountain world
William Tell
Hermann Hesse: "Im Nebel"

■ WEB-ECKE

■ SPRECHSITUATIONEN
Expressing sympathy and lack of sympathy
Expressing empathy
Expressing relief

VORSCHAU

Spotlight on Switzerland

Area. Approximately 16,000 square miles, about half the size of Indiana.
Population. About 7.1 million.
Religion. 46 percent Catholic, 40 percent Protestant, 14 percent other.
Geography. This landlocked country is clearly defined by three natural regions: the *Alpine ranges* that stretch from the French border south of Lake Geneva diagonally across the southern half of Switzerland and include the world-renowned resorts of the Bernese Oberland, Zermatt, and St. Moritz in the Inn River valley; the plateaus and valleys of the *midland* between Lake Geneva and Lake Constance; and the mountains of the *Jura* in the northernmost section of the Alps.
Currency. Schweizer Franken, 1 sfr = 100 Rappen or Centimes.
Principal cities. Capital Bern (pop. 141,000), Zurich (*Zürich,* pop. 370,000), Basel (pop. 180,000), Geneva (*Genf,* pop. 159,900), Lausanne (pop. 126,200).

Isolated and protected by its relative inaccessibility, Switzerland developed as a nation without major hindrance over a span of 700 years. It was founded in 1291, when the cantons of Uri, Schwyz, and Unterwalden formed an alliance against the ruling House of Habsburg. Over time, the original confederation grew into a nation of 26 cantons (states). These cantons maintain considerable autonomy, with their own constitutions and legislatures. The 1848 constitution merged the old confederation into a single state by eliminating all commercial barriers and establishing a common postal service, military, legislature, and judiciary.

Despite its small size, few natural resources, and ethnic diversity, Switzerland is one of the most stable nations in the world. Its stability can be attributed to its high standard of living, the conservative character of its people, and the country's neutrality in the two world wars. Switzerland has stubbornly adhered to the principle of neutrality—to the extent of staying out of NATO and the European Union. Although revelations during the 1990s about the role of Swiss banks in holding the Nazis' stolen gold during World War II have tarnished the image of these renowned financial institutions, Switzerland's stability and bank-secrecy law continue to attract capital from all over the world.

Switzerland is active in the Council of Europe and several specialized agencies of the United Nations. The seat of the League of Nations after World War I, Switzerland is now home to the UN's Economic and Social Council, the International Labor Organization, the World Health Organization, the World Council of Churches, and the International Red Cross. Founded in Geneva in 1864, the Red Cross derived its universally recognized symbol from the inverse of the Swiss flag, a white cross on a red background.

Museum für Völkerkunde.
Flügellöwe. Als Göttersänfte in Prozessionen mitgeführt. Bali, Indonesien.

Steigen Sie einfach aus!

BASEL -
die
Museumsstadt
mit den **30 Museen**
erwartet Sie!

GESPRÄCHE

Auf der Post am Bahnhof

UTA Ich möchte dieses Paket nach Amerika schicken.

HERR Normal oder per Luftpost?

UTA Per Luftpost. Wie lange dauert das denn?

HERR Ungefähr zehn Tage. Füllen Sie bitte diese Paketkarte aus! . . . Moment, hier fehlt noch Ihr Absender.

UTA Ach ja! . . . Noch etwas. Ich brauche eine Telefonkarte.

HERR Für sechs, zwölf oder fünfzig Mark?

UTA Für zwölf Mark. Vielen Dank!

Am Fahrkartenschalter in Zürich

ANNE Wann fährt der nächste Zug nach Interlaken?

FRAU In zehn Minuten. Abfahrt um 11.28 Uhr, Gleis 2.

ANNE Ach du meine Güte! Und wann kommt er dort an?

FRAU Ankunft in Interlaken um 14.16 Uhr.

ANNE Muss ich umsteigen?

FRAU Ja, in Bern, aber Sie haben Anschluss zum InterCity mit nur vierundzwanzig Minuten Aufenthalt.

ANNE Gut. Geben Sie mir bitte eine Hin- und Rückfahrkarte nach Interlaken!

FRAU Erster oder zweiter Klasse?

ANNE Zweiter Klasse.

Zug			118	518	1720		120	1520	1822	
Zürich HB			10 03	10 07	10 28		11 03	11 07	11 28	
Baden					10 45				11 45	
Brugg (Aargau)					10 53				11 53	
Aarau					11 07					
Olten	24016	○		10 35	11 15			11 35	12 07	
				10 44				11 44	12 15	
Olten	24000			10 47				11 47		
Biel/Bienne		○		11 33				12 33		
Lausanne		○						13 48		
Genève		○		13 05						
Zug			721	2521		73		1866		725
Basel SBB			10 00	10 11	10 29	11 00		11 29	12 00	
Liestal				10 21	10 46			11 46		
Olten		○	10 26	10 43	11 11	11 26		12 11	12 26	
Olten			10 28	10 48	11 17	11 28		12 17	12 28	
Langenthal				11 00	11 29			12 29		
Herzogenbuchsee				11 06	11 35			12 35		
Burgdorf				11 18	11 47			12 47		
Bern		○	11 10	11 14	11 35	12 04	12 10	12 14	13 04	13 10
Bern	24004		11 28			12 28	12 28		13 28	
Interlaken West		○	12 16			13 16	13 16		14 16	

Fragen

1. Wo ist die Post? 2. Wohin will Uta ihr Paket schicken? 3. Wie schickt sie es? 4. Wie lange soll das dauern? 5. Was muss man bei einem Paket ins Ausland *(abroad)* ausfüllen? 6. Was fehlt auf der Paketkarte? 7. Was braucht Uta noch? 8. Was kosten Tele-

fonkarten? 9. Wohin will Anne fahren? 10. Wann fährt der Zug ab und wann kommt er in Interlaken an? 11. Wo muss Anne umsteigen? 12. Was für eine Karte kauft sie?

Phoning and Postal Services

In spite of increasing competition, placing calls in the German-speaking countries is still relatively expensive. Even local calls are charged according to the time spent on the line. Most public phone booths **(Telefonzellen)** require a phone card **(Telefonkarte),** which can be bought at post offices and newspaper stands. Since hotels usually add a substantial surcharge for phoning, travelers often find it cheaper to use a long-distance calling card from home or to place calls from a post office. Post offices offer a far greater range of services than in the United States or Canada. For example, it is possible to open a bank account with the post office, wire money, buy travelers' checks, and send a telegram or fax. However, the post office no longer has a monopoly on mail delivery services; UPS and FedEx trucks have become a familiar sight in Europe.

WORTSCHATZ 1

Die Post (post office, mail)

der Absender, -	return address
Brief, -e	letter
Briefkasten, ⸚	mailbox
das Fax, -e	fax
Paket, -e	package, parcel
Postfach, ⸚er	P.O. box
die Adresse, -n	address
(Ansichts)karte, -n	(picture) postcard
Briefmarke, -n	stamp
E-Mail, -s	e-mail
Telefonkarte, -n	telephone card
Telefonnummer, -n	telephone number

Die Reise, -n (trip)

der Aufenthalt, -e	stopover, stay	das Flugzeug, -e	plane
Bahnsteig, -e	platform	Gleis, -e	track
Fahrplan, ⸚e	schedule	die Abfahrt, -en	departure

KAPITEL 8

der Flug, ⸚e	*flight*	die Ankunft, ⸚e	*arrival*
Flughafen, ⸚	*airport*	Bahn, -en	*railway, train*
Wagen, -	*car; railroad car*	Fahrkarte, -n	*ticket*
Zug, ⸚e	*train*	(Hin- und) Rück- fahrkarte, -n	*round-trip ticket*
		Fahrt, -en	*trip, drive*

Weiteres

Ach du meine Güte!	*My goodness!*
in einer Viertelstunde	*in a quarter of an hour*
in einer halben Stunde	*in half an hour*
in einer Dreiviertelstunde	*in three-quarters of an hour*
ab·fahren (fährt ab), ist abgefahren (von)	*to leave (from), depart*
ab·fliegen, ist abgeflogen (von)	*to take off, fly (from)*
aus·steigen, ist ausgestiegen	*to get off*
ein·steigen, ist eingestiegen	*to get on (in)*
um·steigen, ist umgestiegen	*to change (trains etc.)*
aus·füllen	*to fill out*
besuchen	*to visit*
fliegen, ist geflogen	*to fly, go by plane*
landen, ist gelandet	*to land*
schicken	*to send*
telefonieren	*to call up, phone*
mit dem Zug/der Bahn fahren	*to go by train*

Zum Erkennen: normal *(regular)*; per Luftpost *(by airmail)*; die Paketkarte, -n *(parcel form)*; noch etwas *(one more thing, something else)*; der nächste Zug nach *(the next train to)*; der Anschluss, ⸚e *(connection)*; die Klasse, -n

FOKUS Train Travel

Trains are a popular means of transportation in Europe, not only for commuting but also for long-distance travel. The rail network is extensive, and trains are generally clean, comfortable, and on time. Domestic InterCity **(IC)** and international EuroCity **(EC)** trains connect all major western European cities. In Germany, the high-speed InterCityExpress **(ICE),** which travels at speeds up to 280 km/h (175 mph), is an attractive alternative to congested highways. Business people can make or receive phone calls on board and even rent conference rooms equipped with fax machines. Non-European residents can benefit from a *Eurailpass,* which permits unlimited train—and some bus and boat—travel in most European countries, or from a *German Railpass,* which is less expensive but limited to Germany; both passes must be purchased outside of Europe. Larger train stations provide a wide range of services for the traveler, including coin-operated lockers **(Schließfächer)** or checked luggage rooms **(Gepäckaufgabe).**

POST UND REISEN 219

Zum Thema

A. Fragen. Diskutieren Sie!
1. Was kostet es, wenn man einen Brief innerhalb *(inside)* von Amerika oder Kanada schicken will? Wie lange braucht ein Brief innerhalb der Stadt? nach Europa?
2. Was muss man auf alle Briefe, Ansichtskarten und Pakete schreiben? Schreiben Sie oft Briefe? Wenn ja, wem? Schicken Sie Ihren Freunden manchmal E-Mails oder ein Fax?
3. In Deutschland sind die Briefkästen gelb. Welche Farbe haben die Briefkästen hier?
4. Wo kann man hier telefonieren? Gibt es Telefonkarten?
5. Wie kann man gut reisen? Wie reisen Sie gern? Warum?
6. Wo sind Sie zuletzt *(the last time)* gewesen? Sind Sie geflogen oder mit dem Wagen gefahren?
7. Wie heißt der Ort *(place)*, wo Züge abfahren und ankommen? wo Flugzeuge abfliegen und landen? wo Busse halten?
8. Was ist das Gegenteil von abfahren? abfliegen? einsteigen? Abfahrt? Abflug?

B. Am Flugschalter. Was sagen Sie?
S1 Wann gehen Flüge nach . . . ?
S2 Zu welcher Tageszeit möchten Sie denn fliegen?
S1 Ich muss um . . . in . . . sein.
S2 Es gibt einen Flug um . . .
S1 Hat er eine Zwischenlandung?
S2 Ja, in . . . Dort haben Sie . . . Aufenthalt.
S1 Muss ich umsteigen?
S2 . . .
S1 . . . Dann geben Sie mir eine Hin- und Rückflugkarte nach . . . !

C. Was sagt Ihnen der Fahrplan?

NOTE: 1 km = 0.62 miles. Here is an easy way to convert kilometers to miles: divide the km figure in half, and add a quarter of that to the half. Thus, 80 km ÷ 2 = 40 + 10 = 50 miles.

km	Stuttgart–Zürich	Zug	E 3504	D 83 R3)	D 381 R3)	D 383		D 85 R4)	D 389 R2)	D 87	D 385 R1) 1)	E 3309 R1) 1)	D 387 R1) 1)
0	Stuttgart Hbf	740		6 48	7 31	9 34		12 44	14 26	17 32	18 26	20 06	
26	Böblingen				7 53	9 56		13 06	14 48	17 55	18 48	20 29	
67	Horb			7 34	8 20	10 24		13 33	15 15	18 21	19 15	21 00	
110	Rottweil			8 05	8 59	10 54		14 02	15 52	18 51	19 45	21 36	
138	Tuttlingen			8 26	9 17	11 13		14 21	16 11	19 09	20 11	21 55	
172	Singen (Hohentwiel)			8 49	9 42	11 37		14 45	16 35	19 32	20 35	22 22	
		Zug					D 2162	×1)					
	Singen (Hohentwiel)	730		6 31	8 55	9 49	11 44	12 43	14 51	16 44	19 37	20 44	22 44
192	Schaffhausen			6 49	9 10	10 05	12 00	12 58	15 07	17 00	19 52	21 00	23 00
		Zug	1559	EC 83)			357	EC 85)		IC 87)			
	Schaffhausen	24032		7 02	9 12	10 09	12 09	13 09	15 09	17 09	19 55	21 09	23 09
238	Zürich HB		57 7 47	9 47	10 47	12 47	13 47	15 47	17 47	20 31	21 47	23 47	

1. Von Stuttgart nach Zürich sind es _____ Kilometer.
2. Der erste Zug morgens fährt um _____ Uhr und der letzte *(last)* Zug abends um _____ Uhr.
3. Die Reise von Stuttgart nach Zürich geht über _____.
4. Wenn man um 6.48 Uhr von Stuttgart abfährt, ist man um _____ Uhr in Zürich.
5. Die Fahrt dauert ungefähr _____ Stunden.

D. **Was bedeutet das und was ist der Artikel?**

Adressbuch, E-Mail-Adresse, Abfahrtszeit, Ankunftsfahrplan, Bahnhofseingang, Busbahnhof, Busfahrt, Faxnummer, Flugkarte, Flugschalter, Flugsteig, Gepäckkarte, Mietwagen, Nachtzug, Paketschalter, Postfachnummer, Speisewagen, Telefonrechnung

E. **Aussprache: e, er.** Sehen Sie auch II. 8–10 im Ausspracheteil des Arbeitsheftes!
1. [ə] Adress**e**, Eck**e**, Halt**e**stell**e**, b**e**komm**e**n, b**e**such**e**n, ein**e** halb**e** Stund**e**
2. [ʌ] ab**er**, saub**er**, schw**er**, eu**er**, uns**er**, Zimm**er**numm**er**, Uh**r**, vo**r**, nu**r**, unt**er**, üb**er**, auß**er**, wied**er**holen
3. Wortpaare
   a. Studenten / Studentin
   b. Touristen / Touristin
   c. diese / dieser
   d. arbeiten / Arbeitern
   e. lese / Leser
   f. mieten / Mietern

HÖREN SIE ZU!

Weg zur Post

Zum Erkennen: Na klar! *(Sure!)*; endlich mal *(finally)*; das Papierwarengeschäft, -e *(office supply store)*; Lass sie wiegen! *(Have them weighed!)*; Luftpostleichtbrief, -e *(aerogram)*

Richtig oder falsch?

_____ 1. Bill muss endlich mal an Claudias Eltern schreiben.
_____ 2. Claudia möchte wissen, wo man Papier, Ansichtskarten und Briefmarken bekommt.
_____ 3. Bei Schlegel in der Beethovenstraße gibt es Briefpapier.
_____ 4. Postkarten findet man nur in Drogerien.
_____ 5. Gegenüber vom Stadttheater ist die Post.
_____ 6. Bill kauft heute Briefmarken und geht morgen zum Bahnhof.
_____ 7. Er soll zur Post gehen und Claudia Briefmarken mitbringen.

FOKUS: Car Travel

A U.S. or Canadian driver's license **(der Führerschein)** can be used in the German-speaking countries. Most traffic signs are identical to those in the United States and Canada; others are self-explanatory. Unless otherwise indicated, the driver approaching from the right has the right-of-way. As a rule, right turns at a red light are prohibited, as is passing on the right. The speed limit **(Tempolimit** or **Geschwindigkeitsbegrenzung)** in cities and towns is generally 50 kph (31 mph), and on the open road 100 kph (62 mph). Except for certain stretches, there is no official speed limit on the freeway **(die Autobahn),** but drivers are recommended **(die Richtgeschwindigkeit)** not to exceed 130 kph (81 mph). The driving style is generally more aggressive than in North America.

Europcar Inter rent

RAIL ROAD

Raus aus dem Zug, rein ins Auto!

STRUKTUR

I. Genitive case

The genitive case has two major functions: it expresses possession or another close relationship between two nouns, and it follows certain prepositions.

1. The English phrases *the son's letter* and *the date of the letter* are expressed by the same genitive construction in German.

       Das ist **der Brief des Sohnes.**   *That's the son's letter.*

       Was ist **das Datum des Briefes?**   *What's the date of the letter?*

   a. The genitive form of the INTERROGATIVE PRONOUN **wer** is **wessen** (*whose*). The chart below shows all four cases of the interrogative pronouns.

	persons	things and ideas
nom.	wer?	was?
acc.	wen?	was?
dat.	wem?	—
gen.	wessen?	—

       Wessen Brief ist das?   *Whose letter is that?*

       Der Brief des Sohnes.   *The son's letter.*

   b. The genitive forms of the DEFINITE and INDEFINITE ARTICLES complete this chart of articles:

	SINGULAR masc.	neut.	fem.	PLURAL
nom.	der / ein / kein	das / ein / kein	die / eine / keine	die / — / keine
acc.	den / einen / keinen	das / ein / kein	die / eine / keine	die / — / keine
dat.	dem / einem / keinem	dem / einem / keinem	der / einer / keiner	den / — / keinen
gen.	**des / eines / keines**	**des / eines / keines**	**der / einer / keiner**	**der / — / keiner**

c. The genitive case is signaled not only by the forms of the articles, but also by a special ending for MASCULINE and NEUTER nouns in the singular.

- Most one-syllable nouns and nouns ending in **-s, -ss, -ß, -z, -tz,** or **-zt,** add **-es:**

der Zug	das Geld	der Ausweis	der Pass	der Platz
des Zug**es**	**des** Geld**es**	**des** Auswei**ses**	**des** Pas**ses**	**des** Plat**zes**

- Nouns with more than one syllable add only an **-s:**

  des Flughafen**s**   *of the airport, the airport's*
  des Wagen**s**   *of the car, the car's*

  NOTE: German uses NO apostrophe for the genitive!

- N-nouns have an **-n** or **-en** ending in ALL CASES except in the nominative singular. A very few n-nouns have a genitive **-s** as well.

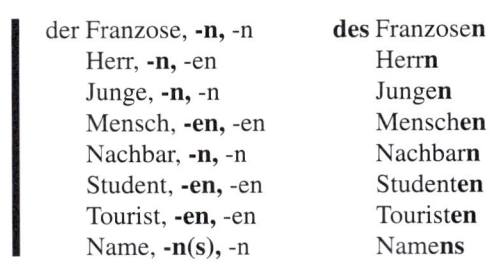

der Franzose, **-n,** -n	**des** Franzose**n**
Herr, **-n,** -en	Herr**n**
Junge, **-n,** -n	Junge**n**
Mensch, **-en,** -en	Mensche**n**
Nachbar, **-n,** -n	Nachbar**n**
Student, **-en,** -en	Studente**n**
Tourist, **-en,** -en	Touriste**n**
Name, **-n(s),** -n	Name**ns**

  Note how n-nouns are listed in vocabularies and dictionaries: the first ending usually refers to the accusative, dative, and genitive singular; the second one to the plural.

d. FEMININE NOUNS and PLURAL NOUNS have no special endings in the genitive.

die Reise	**der** Reise
die Reisen	**der** Reisen

e. Proper names usually add a final **-s:**

Annemarie**s** Flug	*Annemarie's flight*
Frau Strobel**s** Fahrt	*Ms. Strobel's trip*
Wien**s** Flughafen	*Vienna's airport*

  In colloquial speech, however, **von** is frequently used instead of the genitive of a name: **die Adresse von Hans.**

f. Nouns in the genitive NORMALLY FOLLOW the nouns they modify, whereas proper names precede them.

  Er liest den Brief **der Tante.**
  Er liest **Annemaries** Brief.
  Er liest **Herrn Müllers** Brief.

CAUTION: Even though the use of the possessive adjectives **mein, dein,** etc. inherently show possession, they still have the genitive case along with the noun.

Das ist **mein** Onkel.	*That's my uncle.*
Das ist der Koffer **meines Onkels.**	*That's my uncle's suitcase (the suitcase of my uncle).*
Er ist der Bruder **meiner Mutter.**	*He's my mother's brother (the brother of my mother).*

2. These prepositions are followed by the genitive case:

(an)statt	instead of	Ich nehme oft den Bus **(an)statt der Straßenbahn.**
trotz	in spite of	**Trotz des Wetters** bummele ich gern durch die Stadt.
während	during	**Während der Mittagspause** gehe ich in den Park.
wegen	because of	Heute bleibe ich **wegen des Regens** (rain) hier.

Übungen

A. Wissen Sie, wer das ist?

> BEISPIEL: Wer ist der Vater Ihrer Mutter?
> **Das ist mein Großvater.**

1. Wer ist der Sohn Ihres Vaters? 2. Wer ist die Mutter Ihrer Mutter? 3. Wer ist die Tochter Ihrer Mutter? 4. Wer sind die Söhne und Töchter Ihrer Eltern? 5. Wer ist der Sohn Ihres Urgroßvaters (great-grandfather)? 6. Wer ist der Großvater Ihrer Mutter? 7. Wer ist die Schwester Ihrer Mutter? 8. Wer ist der Mann Ihrer Tante? 9. Wer ist die Tochter Ihres Großvaters?

B. Im Reisebüro (At the travel agency. Make sure that your assistant followed all the necessary steps to organize the tour leaving for Bern tomorrow.)

> BEISPIEL: Wo ist die Liste der Touristen? (Hotel / pl.)
> **Wo ist die Liste der Hotels?**

1. Wie ist der Name des Reiseführers (tour guide)? (Schloss, Dom, Museum, Straße, Platz, Tourist, Touristin, Franzose, Französin)
2. Wo ist die Telefonnummer des Hotels? (Gästehaus, Pension, Gasthof, Jugendherberge)
3. Wo ist die Adresse dieser Dame? (Gast, Mädchen, Junge, Herr, Herren, Student, Studenten)
4. Wann ist die Ankunft unserer Gruppe? (Bus, Zug, Flugzeug, Reiseführerin, Gäste)
5. Haben Sie wegen der Reservierung (reservation) angerufen? (Zimmer, Schlüssel / sg., Gepäck, Adresse, Theaterkarten)
6. Wir fahren trotz des Gewitters (thunderstorm). (Wetter, Regen/m., Eis, Feiertag, Ferien)
7. Christiane Binder kommt statt ihrer Mutter mit. (Vater, Bruder, Onkel, Nachbar, Nachbarin, Geschwister)

C. Bilden Sie Sätze mit dem Genitiv! Benutzen Sie (use) Wörter von jeder Liste!

> BEISPIEL: Die Abfahrt des Zuges ist um 19.05 Uhr.

1	2	3	4	5
die Farbe	d-	Wagen	Gasthof	ist	_____
der Name	dies-	Bus	Ausweis	gefällt	
die Adresse	mein-	Zug	Pass		
die Nummer	unser-	Bahnsteig	Reisescheck		
das Zimmer		Koffer	Flug		
das Gepäck		Tasche	Frau		
die Abfahrt		Haus	Herr		
der Preis		Wohnung	Freund(in)		
die Lage (location)		Hotel	Tourist(in)		
. . .		Pension	Gäste		
		Berge	. . .		
		Postfach			

D. Wem gehört das?

BEISPIEL: Gehört die Jacke Ihrem Freund?
Nein, das ist nicht die Jacke meines Freundes. Das ist meine Jacke.

Gehört das Hemd Ihrem Bruder? die Uhr Ihrer Mutter? das Buch Ihrem Professor? die Tasche Ihrer Freundin? die Post Ihrem Nachbarn? der Kuli Frau . . . *(name a student)?* das Heft Herrn . . . *(name a student)?*

E. Bahnfahrt. Auf Deutsch bitte!

1. Is that Eva's train? 2. Do you know the number of the platform? 3. No. Where's the departure schedule (departure schedule of the trains)? 4. Her train leaves in a few minutes. 5. Take along Kurt's package. 6. Kurt is a student and a friend of a friend *(f.)*. 7. Eva, do you have the student's *(m.)* address? 8. No, but I know the name of the dorm. 9. I'll take (bring) it to him during the holidays. 10. Due to the exams I don't have time now. 11. I'll send you a postcard instead of a letter.

II. Time expressions

1. Adverbs of time

   a. To refer to SPECIFIC TIMES, such as *yesterday evening* or *tomorrow morning,* combine one word from group A with another from group B. The words in group A can be used alone, while those in group B must be used in combinations: **gestern Abend, morgen früh.**

   A

vorgestern	*the day before yesterday*
gestern	*yesterday*
heute	*today*
morgen	*tomorrow*
übermorgen	*the day after tomorrow*

   B

früh, Morgen[1]	*early, morning*
Vormittag[2]	*midmorning (9 to 12 A.M.)*[4]
Mittag	*noon (12 to 2 P.M.)*
Nachmittag	*afternoon (2 to 6 P.M.)*
Abend[3]	*evening (6 to 10 P.M.)*
Nacht[3]	*night (after 10 P.M.)*[4]

   ---

   [1] **heute früh** is used in southern Germany, **heute Morgen** in northern Germany; both mean *this morning.* BUT *Tomorrow morning* is always **morgen früh.**

   [2] The expressions in this column are commonly combined with the days of the week. In that combination—except for **früh**—they combine to make a compound noun: **Montagmorgen, Dienstagvormittag, Donnerstagabend** BUT **Montag früh.**

   [3] German distinguishes clearly between **Abend** and **Nacht**: Wir sind **gestern Abend** ins Kino gegangen. Ich habe **gestern Nacht** schlecht geschlafen. **Heute Nacht** can mean *last night* or *tonight* (whichever is closer), depending on context.

   [4] The times may vary somewhat, but these are reasonable guidelines.

   Heute fliege ich von New York ab.
   Morgen früh bin ich in Frankfurt.
   Übermorgen fahre ich nach Bonn.
   Montagabend besuche ich Krauses.
   Dienstagnachmittag fahre ich mit dem Zug zurück.

   b. Adverbs such as **montags** and **morgens** don't refer to a specific time (a specific *Monday* or *morning*), but rather imply that events USUALLY OCCUR (more or less regularly), for example, *on Mondays* or *in the morning, most mornings:*

> montags, dienstags, mittwochs, donnerstags, freitags, samstags, sonntags;
> morgens, vormittags, mittags, nachmittags, abends, nachts
> montagmorgens, dienstagabends[1]

---

[1] Note the difference in spelling: Kommst du **Dienstagabend?** Nein, **dienstagabends** kann ich nicht.

Sonntags tue ich nichts, aber **montags** arbeite ich schwer.

Morgens und **nachmittags** gehe ich zur Uni. **Mittags** spiele ich Tennis.

Freitagabends gehen wir gern aus und **samstagmorgens** stehen wir dann nicht so früh auf.

2. Other time expressions

   a. The accusative of time

   To refer to a DEFINITE point in time (**wann?**) or length of time (**wie lange?**), German often uses time phrases in the accusative, without any prepositions. Here are some of the most common expressions:

wann!		wie lange?	
jeden Tag	each day	zwei Wochen	for two weeks
diese Woche	this week	einen Monat	for one month

Haben Sie diese Woche Zeit?	Do you have time this week?
Die Fahrt dauert zwei Stunden.	The trip takes two hours.
Ich bleibe zwei Tage in Zürich.	I'll be in Zurich for two days.

   b. The genitive of time

   To refer to an INDEFINITE point in time (in the past or future), German uses the genitive:

eines Tages	one day, some day

Eines Tages ist ein Fax gekommen.	One day a fax came.
Eines Tages fahre ich in die Schweiz.	Some day I'll go to Switzerland.

   c. Prepositional time phrases

   You are already familiar with the following phrases:

an	am Abend, am Wochenende, am Montag, am 1. April
bis	bis morgen, bis 2.30 Uhr, bis (zum) Freitag, bis (zum) Januar
für	für morgen, für Freitag, für eine Nacht
in	im Juli, im Sommer, im Monat; in 10 Minuten, in einer Viertelstunde, in einer Woche, in einem Jahr
nach	nach dem Essen, nach einer Stunde
seit	seit einem Jahr, seit September
um	um fünf (Uhr)
von . . . bis	vom 1. Juni bis (zum) 25. August; von Juli bis August
vor	vor einem Monat, vor ein paar Tagen
während	während des Sommers, während des Tages

   - Two-way prepositions usually use the <u>dative</u> in time expressions: Wir fahren **in einer Woche** in die Berge. **Am Freitag** fahren wir ab.

- German uses **seit** plus the present tense to describe an action or condition that began in the past and is still continuing in the present. English uses the present perfect progressive to express the same thing: **Er wohnt seit zwei Jahren hier.** *(He has been living here for two years.)*

Übungen

F. Ein Besuch. Was fehlt?
1. Erich ist _____ angekommen. *(one week ago)*
2. Wir sind _____ abgefahren. *(Thursday evening at 7 o'clock)*
3. Er ist _____ geflogen. *(for nine hours)*
4. Ich habe ihn schon _____ nicht mehr gesehen. *(for one year)*
5. Er schläft _____ gewöhnlich nicht lange. *(in the morning)*
6. Aber er hat _____ geschlafen. *(Friday morning until 11 A.M.)*
7. Er bleibt noch ungefähr _____ bei uns. *(for one week)*
8. _____ sind wir bei meiner Tante gewesen. *(the day before yesterday)*
9. _____ gehen wir ins Kino. *(this evening)*
10. _____ kommen Erika und Uwe vorbei. *(tomorrow morning)*
11. _____ gehen wir alle essen. *(tomorrow at noon)*
12. _____ bummeln wir etwas durch die Stadt. *(in the afternoon)*
13. Was wir _____ tun, weiß ich noch nicht. *(the day after tomorrow)*
14. _____ machen wir etwas Besonderes. *(every day)*
15. _____ fahren wir ab. *(on Saturday morning)*
16. Schade, dass Erich _____ schon wieder zu Hause sein muss. *(in one week)*

G. Wie ist das bei Ihnen? *(How do you do things? Working in small groups, tell each other about your habits and routines. You may use the phrases from the columns below or add your own.)*

1	2	3	4	5	6
morgens	gewöhnlich	ausgehen	aber	letzte Woche	zu Hause bleiben
(nach)mittags	manchmal	in der Bibliothek arbeiten		diese Woche	meine Familie besuchen
(freitag)abends	meistens	die Wohnung putzen		vor ein paar Tagen	ins Konzert gehen
sonntags	oft	fernsehen *(watch TV)*		(vor)gestern	ein Buch lesen
in der Woche	immer	einkaufen gehen		gestern Abend	Tee trinken
am Wochenende	nie	E-Mails schreiben		heute Morgen	Musik hören
jeden Tag	. . .	im Internet surfen		(über)morgen	. . .
. . .		Kaffee trinken		. . .	
		. . .			

BEISPIEL: Morgens trinke ich gewöhnlich Kaffee, aber heute Morgen habe ich Tee getrunken.

III. Sentence structure

1. Types of adverbs

   You have already encountered various adverbs and adverbial phrases. They are usually divided into three major groups.

   a. ADVERBS OF TIME, answering the questions **wann? wie lange?**

   am Abend, am 1. April, eines Tages, heute, im Juni, immer, jetzt, manchmal, meistens, montags, morgens, nie, oft, um zwölf, vor einer Woche, während des Winters, bis Mai, eine Woche, stundenlang, ein paar Minuten usw.

b. ADVERBS OF MANNER, answering the question **wie?**

gemütlich, langsam, laut, mit der Bahn, ohne Geld, schnell, zu Fuß, zusammen usw.

c. ADVERBS OF PLACE, answering the questions **wo? wohin? woher?**

auf der Post, bei uns, da, dort, hier, im Norden, zu Hause, mitten in der Stadt, überall, nach Berlin, nach Hause, auf die Post, zur Uni, aus Kanada, von Amerika, aus dem Flugzeug usw.

2. Sequence of adverbs

If two or more adverbs or adverbial phrases occur in one sentence, they usually follow the sequence TIME, MANNER, PLACE.

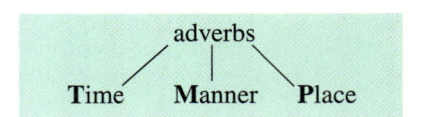

```
        adverbs
       /   |   \
    Time Manner Place
```

Er kann das Paket **morgen mit dem Auto zur Post** bringen.
                        T   M   P

- If there is more than one time expression, general time references precede specific time references:

    Er bringt das Paket **morgen um neun Uhr** zur Post.

- Like other sentence elements, adverbs and adverbial phrases may precede the verb.

    Morgen kann er das Paket mit dem Auto zur Post bringen.
    Mit dem Auto kann er das Paket morgen zur Post bringen.
    Zur Post kann er das Paket morgen mit dem Auto bringen.

3. Position of **nicht**

As you already know from Chapter 2, Section III, **nicht** usually comes <u>after adverbs of definite time</u> but <u>before other adverbs, such as adverbs of manner or place.</u>

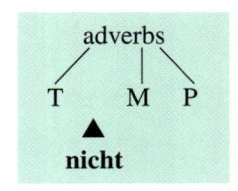

```
        adverbs
       /   |   \
      T    M    P
      ▲
    nicht
```

Er bringt das Paket ▲.
Er bringt das Paket ▲ mit.
Er kann das Paket ▲ mitbringen.
Er kann das Paket **morgen** ▲ mitbringen.
Er kann das Paket **morgen** ▲ **mit dem Auto** mitbringen.
Er kann das Paket **morgen** ▲ **mit dem Auto zur Post** bringen.

GELDWECHSEL - EXCHANGE - CHANGE - CAMBIO

AGW **Wechselstuben Berlin**
nur Joachimstaler Straße 1-3
und Joachimstaler Straße 39-41
Wir akzeptieren Kreditkarten von VISA und DINERS CLUB
SUPERKURSE - OHNE GEBÜHREN **882 10 86**

Übungen

H. Sagen Sie das noch einmal! *(Use the adverbial expressions in the proper order.)*

BEISPIEL: Ich kaufe die Briefmarken. (auf der Post, morgen)
Ich kaufe die Briefmarken morgen auf der Post.

1. Er kommt an. (heute Abend, in Wien, mit dem Bus)
2. Sie reist. (nach Deutschland, ohne ihre Familie)
3. Deine Jeans liegen auf dem Sofa. (da drüben, seit drei Tagen)
4. Wir fahren. (zu meiner Tante, am Sonntag, mit der Bahn)
5. Gehst du? (zu Fuß, in die Stadt, heute Nachmittag)
6. Ich kaufe die Eier. (samstags, auf dem Markt, billig)
7. Wir wollen ins Kino gehen. (zusammen, morgen Abend)
8. Ihr müsst umsteigen. (in einer Viertelstunde, in den Zug nach Nürnberg)
9. Sie lässt die Kinder in St. Gallen. (bei den Großeltern, ein paar Tage)

I. Ferienwünsche. Verneinen Sie die Sätze mit **nicht!**

GISELA Ich möchte diesen Winter in die Berge fahren.
OTTO Gefallen dir die Berge?
GISELA Das habe ich gesagt. Warum fliegen wir diesen Winter nach Spanien? 479 DM ist sehr teuer.
OTTO Ich weiß.
GISELA Im Flugzeug wird man so müde.
OTTO Ich fliege gern.
GISELA Ich möchte mit dem Auto fahren.
OTTO Mittags kannst du lange in der Sonne liegen.
GISELA Morgens und nachmittags ist die Sonne so heiß.
OTTO In den Bergen ist es so langweilig.
GISELA Gut. Wenn wir nach Spanien fliegen, komme ich mit.

J. So kann man's auch sagen. *(Start each sentence with the expression in boldface. How does this change affect the meaning?)*

BEISPIEL: Wir bleiben **während der Ferien** gewöhnlich zu Hause.
Während der Ferien bleiben wir gewöhnlich zu Hause.
During vacations we usually stay home.

1. Wir haben gewöhnlich keine Zeit **für Reisen.**
2. Manfred hat **gerade** mit seiner Schwester in Amerika gesprochen.
3. Sie ist **seit einer Woche** bei ihrem Bruder in Florida.
4. Wir wollen sie alle **am Wochenende** besuchen *(visit).*
5. Das finde ich **schön.**

Zusammenfassung

K. Hoppla, hier fehlt 'was! Schon lange nicht mehr gesehen. *(It's September, and you and your partner are catching up on what your friends did during the summer. Converse with him or her to compile your information. One of you looks at the chart below, the other at the one in the Appendix.)*

S1:

Wer	Wann / Wie lange	Wie / Obj. + Präposition	Wo und was
LUCIAN		gemütlich	durch Italien reisen
CHRISTL	ein- Monat		
STEFFI	dies- Sommer		zu Hause bleiben
NINA + KIM		mit dem Schiff	
BEN + MICHI	jed- Nachmittag	zusammen	in . . . arbeiten
GÜNTHER	im August		
JUTTA		als Au-Pair	in London arbeiten
NICOLE	vor einer Woche		
YVONNE		meistens	im Fitnessstudio trainieren
JOCHEN			im Restaurant jobben

BEISPIEL: S1 Ich weiß, dass Lucian gemütlich durch Italien gereist ist. Aber wann?
S2 Das weiß ich nicht genau. Ich weiß nur, dass er ein paar Wochen gereist ist. Und hast du gehört, was Christl gemacht hat? Sie ist . . .

L. Frau Köchli. Bilden Sie Sätze!

BEISPIEL: Hauptstadt / Schweiz / sein / Bern
Die Hauptstadt der Schweiz ist Bern.

1. Tante / unsere Freunde / leben / hier in Bern
2. leider / ich / nicht / wissen / die / Adresse / diese Tante
3. Name / Dame / sein / Köchli
4. wegen / dieser Name / ich / nicht / können / finden / Frau Köchli
5. statt / eine Köchli / da / sein / viele Köchlis
6. du / nicht / wissen / Telefonnummer / euere Freunde?
7. Nummer / stehen / in / Adressbuch / meine Frau
8. ich / nicht / können / finden / Inge / Adressbuch
9. ein Tag / Inge / es / hoffentlich / wieder / finden
10. können / ihr / mir / empfehlen / Name / ein Hotel?
11. trotz / Preise *(pl.)* / wir / brauchen / Hotelzimmer
12. während / Feiertage / du / haben / Probleme *(pl.)* / wegen / Touristen

M. Schreiben Sie! Mein Alltag *(My daily life. Write eight to ten sentences describing a typical week, i.e., when you get up; when you eat; when you leave for class; what classes you have when; what you do in the evening and on the weekend. Use as many time expressions as possible.)*

BEISPIEL: Ich bin fast jeden Tag an der Uni. Morgens stehe ich um sechs auf . . .

EINBLICKE

Switzerland and Its Languages

European cars usually carry a small sticker indicating the country of origin: *D* stands for Germany, *A* for Austria, and *CH* for Switzerland. The abbreviation *CH* stands for the Latin *Confoederatio Helvetica,* a reference to the Celtic tribe of the Helvetii who settled the territory of modern Switzerland when Julius Caesar prevented them from moving to Gaul (today's France). The neutral choice of *CH* is a good example of how the Swiss avoid giving preference to one of their four national languages.

Roughly 70 percent of the Swiss speak a dialect of Swiss-German **(Schwyzerdütsch)**; 20 percent speak French; and 9 percent Italian. A tiny minority (1 percent) speaks Romansh **(Rätoromanisch).** Most Swiss people understand two or three—some even all four—of these languages. This quadrilingualism goes back to the time when the Romans colonized the area. Over time, tribes from present-day Italy, France, and Germany migrated to the region. Romansh is a Romance language that has evolved little from Vulgar Latin and is spoken mainly in the remote valleys of the Grisons (canton Graubünden). Although it became one of the four official languages in 1938, Romansh has been under constant pressure from the other major languages in surrounding areas. The fact that Romansh is not one language but a group of dialects (including **Ladin**) makes it even harder to preserve.

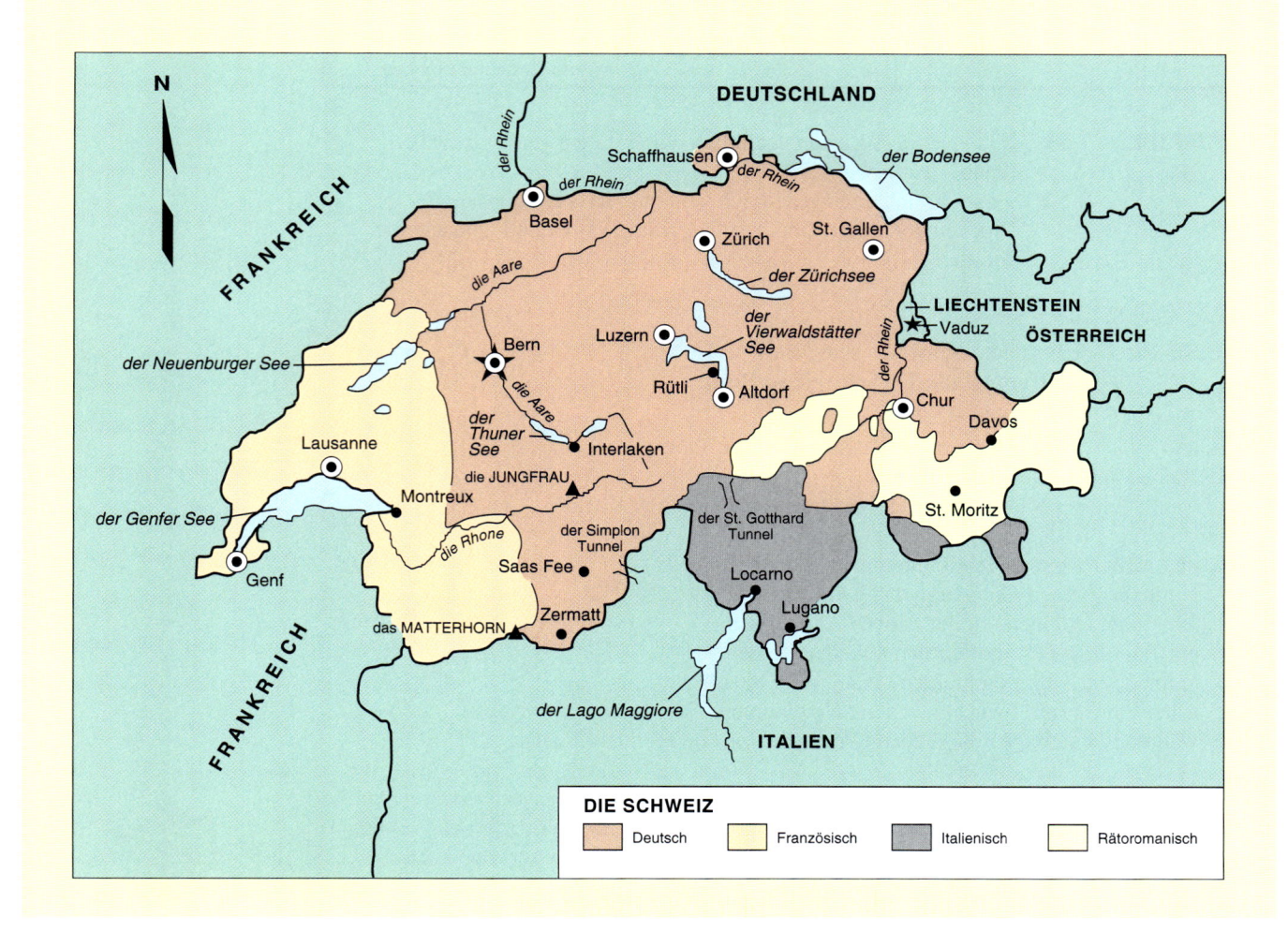

WORTSCHATZ 2

das Dorf, ¨er	*village*
die Gegend, -en	*area, region*
Geschichte, -n	*history; story*
herrlich	*wonderful, great*
hinauf·fahren (fährt hinauf), ist hinaufgefahren	*to go or drive up (to)*
weiter·fahren (fährt weiter), ist weitergefahren	*to drive on, keep on driving*

Vorm Lesen

A. Etwas Geographie. Sehen Sie auf die Landkarte der Schweiz und beantworten Sie die Fragen!
1. Wie heißen die Nachbarländer der Schweiz? Wo liegen sie?
2. Wie heißt die Hauptstadt der Schweiz?
3. Nennen Sie ein paar Schweizer Flüsse, Seen und Berge! Welcher Fluss fließt weiter *(flows on)* nach Deutschland / nach Frankreich? Welcher See liegt zwischen der Schweiz und Deutschland / Italien / Frankreich?
4. Wo liegt Bern? Basel? Zürich? Luzern? Genf? Lausanne? Zermatt? Lugano? St. Moritz? Davos? Saas Fee? Grindelwald?
5. Wo spricht man Deutsch? Französisch? Italienisch? Rätoromanisch?
6. Was assoziieren Sie mit der Schweiz?

B. Was ist das?

der Film, Besucher, Kanton, Wintersport; das Ende, Kurzinterview, Panorama; die Alpenblume, Arkade, Bergbahn, Konferenz, Nation, Rückreise, Schneeszene, Viersprachigkeit; Bergsteigen gehen, faszinieren, filmen; autofrei, elegant

Touristen in der Schweiz

In Kurzinterviews mit Touristen in Altdorf, Bern und Saas Fee hören wir, was Besuchern in der Schweiz besonders gefällt:

FELIX: Ich finde die Gegend um den Vierwaldstätter See besonders interessant wegen ihrer Geschichte. Gestern bin ich in Luzern gewesen und auch über die Holzbrücke° aus dem Jahr 1408 gelaufen. Heute früh bin ich mit dem Schiff von Luzern zum Rütli gefahren, wo 1291 die drei Kantone Uri, Schwyz und Unterwalden ihren Bund° gemacht haben und die Schweiz als eine Nation begonnen hat. Dann bin ich weitergefahren nach Altdorf zum Wilhelm-Tell-Denkmal und heute Abend gehe ich zu den Wilhelm-Tell-Freilichtspielen°. Dieses Wochenende ist hier auch Bundesfeier° mit Umzügen° und Feuerwerk. Dann geht's wieder zurück mit dem Zug. Die Fahrt durch die Berge ist einfach herrlich.

— wooden bridge
— confederation
— outdoor performances
— national holiday / parades

FRAU WEBER: Mir gefällt Bern wegen seiner Arkaden und Brunnen°. Mein Mann und ich fahren fast jedes Jahr zum Wintersport in die Schweiz. Auf unserer Fahrt kommen wir gewöhnlich durch Bern und bleiben hier einen Tag. Morgen fahren wir weiter nach Grindelwald, ins Berner Oberland. Wir wollen mit der Bergbahn zum Jungfraujoch hinauffahren und von dort oben den Blick auf die Berge genießen°. Trotz der vielen Touristen ist das Berner Oberland immer wieder schön. Haben Sie gewusst, dass man fast alle Schneeszenen der James-Bond-Filme im Berner Oberland gefilmt hat? Auf der Rückreise haben wir Aufenthalt in Zürich, wo mein Mann mit den Banken zu tun hat. Der See mit dem Panorama der Berge ist herrlich. Während der Konferenzen meines Mannes bummle ich gern durch die Stadt. Die Geschäfte in der Bahnhofsstraße sind elegant, aber teuer.

— fountains
— enjoy

Im Stadtzentrum von Bern

FRAU LORENZ: Die Viersprachigkeit der Schweiz fasziniert uns. Unsere Reise hat in Lausanne begonnen, wo wir Französisch gesprochen haben. Jetzt sind wir hier in Saas Fee bei Freunden. Mit uns sprechen sie Hochdeutsch, aber mit der Familie Schwyzerdütsch. Saas Fee ist nur ein Dorf, aber wunderschön. Es ist autofrei und in den Bergen kann man überall wandern und Bergsteigen gehen. Wegen der Höhenlage° gibt es viele Alpenblumen und Gämsen° und oben auf den Gletschern° kann man sogar während des Sommers immer noch Skilaufen gehen. Übermorgen fahren wir weiter nach St. Moritz, wo man viel Rätoromanisch hört. Am Ende der Reise wollen wir noch nach Lugano, wo das Wetter fast immer schön sein soll und die Leute Italienisch sprechen. Vier Sprachen in einem Land, das ist schon toll.

altitude / mountain goats
glaciers

Zum Text

A. Richtig oder falsch? Wenn falsch, sagen Sie warum!

_____ 1. Felix findet die Gegend um den Bodensee so interessant wegen ihrer Geschichte.
_____ 2. Die Schweiz hat 1691 als Nation begonnen.
_____ 3. Felix ist wegen des Wilhelm-Tell-Denkmals und der Freilichtspiele in Altdorf.
_____ 4. Frau Weber und ihr Mann fahren jeden Sommer zum Sport ins Berner Oberland.
_____ 5. Während ihrer Reise bleiben sie gewöhnlich einen Tag in Bern, weil ihnen die Stadt so gut gefällt.
_____ 6. Herr Weber hat in Zürich oft mit der Universität zu tun.
_____ 7. Zürich ist eine Stadt am Genfer See mit dem Panorama der Berge.
_____ 8. Familie Lorenz ist fasziniert von den Sprachen der Schweiz.
_____ 9. Mit ihren Freunden in Saas Fee sprechen sie Rätoromanisch.
_____ 10. Am Ende der Reise fahren sie noch nach Lausanne.

B. Etwas Geschichte. Lesen Sie laut!

1. 1291 machten Uri, Schwyz und Unterwalden am Rütli einen Bund. 2. Luzern ist 1332 dazu *(to it)* gekommen und Zürich 1351. 3. 1513 hat es 13 Kantone gegeben. 4. Heute, 20__ *(add current year),* sind es 26 Kantone. 5. 1848 ist die Schweiz ein Bundesstaat geworden. 6. Im 1. Weltkrieg (1914–1918) und im 2. Weltkrieg (1939–1945) ist die Schweiz neutral geblieben. 7. Trotz ihrer Tradition von Demokratie können die Frauen der

Schweiz erst seit 1971 in allen Kantonen wählen *(vote)*. 8. Seit 1981 gibt es offiziell auch keine Diskriminierung der Frau mehr.

C. Die Eidgenossenschaft *(The Swiss Confederacy. Restate these sentences, using the suggested expressions. There may be more than one appropriate place for the expressions.)*

BEISPIEL: Viele Touristen fahren in die Schweiz. (jedes Jahr)
**Viele Touristen fahren jedes Jahr in die Schweiz.
Jedes Jahr fahren viele Touristen in die Schweiz.**

1. Felix findet die Gegend um den Vierwaldstätter See interessant. (wegen ihrer Geschichte)
2. Felix ist mit einem Schiff zum Rütli gefahren. (von Luzern)
3. Die drei Kantone Uri, Schwyz und Unterwalden haben ihren Bund am Rütli gemacht. (1291)
4. Viele Touristen wollen Wilhelm Tells Denkmal sehen. (natürlich)
5. In der Schweiz feiert man die Bundesfeier. (jedes Jahr am 1. August)
6. Felix ist noch einen Tag geblieben. (wegen dieses Festes)

D. Welche Frage gehört zu welcher Antwort?

_____ 1. Hier hat die Schweiz als Nation begonnen.
_____ 2. In der Bahnhofsstraße.
_____ 3. Mein Mann hat dort mit Banken zu tun.
_____ 4. Mit der Bergbahn.
_____ 5. Nein, Hochdeutsch.
_____ 6. Nein, Schwyzerdütsch.
_____ 7. Gut, besonders wegen ihrer Arkaden und Brunnen.
_____ 8. Wegen der Bundesfeier.
_____ 9. Wegen des Wetters.
_____ 10. Wir haben hier Freunde.

a. Sprechen Ihre Freunde zu Hause Rätoromanisch?
b. Sprechen Sie mit Ihren Freunden Schwyzerdütsch?
c. Warum fahren Sie nach Zürich?
d. Warum fahren Sie nach Lugano?
e. Warum fasziniert die Gegend um den Vierwaldstätter See?
f. Warum gibt es in Altdorf ein Feuerwerk?
g. Was hat Sie nach Saas Fee gebracht?
h. Wie gefällt Ihnen die Stadt Bern?
i. Wie kommt man zum Jungfraujoch?
j. Wo gehen Sie in Zürich bummeln?

William Tell

William Tell (**Wilhelm Tell**) is a legendary Swiss folk hero and a universal symbol of resistance to oppression. In 1307, he purportedly refused to obey the commands of the tyrannical Austrian bailiff, Gessler, who then forced him to shoot an arrow through an apple on his son's head. Tell did so, but later took revenge by killing Bailiff Gessler. That event was the beginning of a general uprising of the Swiss against the Habsburgs, the ruling dynasty since 1273. In 1439, when the Habsburgs tried to bring Switzerland back under Austrian rule, the Confederation broke free of the Empire. The story of Tell's confrontation with Gessler inspired Friedrich Schiller's drama *Wilhelm Tell* (1804) and Rossini's opera *Guillaume Tell* (1829).

KAPITEL 8

HÖREN SIE ZU!

Im Reisebüro

Zum Erkennen: Skilift inbegriffen *(ski lift included)*; die Broschüre, -n *(brochure)*

Was stimmt?
1. Ulrike und Steffi möchten im _____ reisen.
   a. August   b. März   c. Januar

2. Sie wollen _____.
   a. wandern   b. Bergsteigen gehen   c. Skilaufen gehen

3. Ulrike reserviert ein Zimmer im Hotel _____.
   a. Alpenrose   b. Alpina   c. Eiger

4. Ulrike und Steffi fahren mit der Bahn bis _____.
   a. Bern   b. Interlaken   c. Grindelwald

5. Sie kommen um _____ Uhr an ihrem Ziel *(destination)* an.
   a. 12.16   b. 12.30   c. 1.00

6. Sie fahren am _____ um _____ nach Hause zurück.
   a. 15. / zwei   b. 14. / drei   c. 16. / sechs

> Wer nicht zum Bahnhof gehen mag, kann ja hinsurfen. Die Bahn online.

FOKUS: Switzerland's Mountain World

Not surprisingly, Switzerland has a number of popular and fashionable mountain resorts. The glacier village of **Grindelwald** in the Bernese Oberland is a favorite base for mountain climbers and skiers. **St. Moritz**, south of Davos, is nestled in the Upper Inn Valley next to a lake. Twice host to the Winter Olympics (1928 and 1948), the resort has become a jet-set sports mecca. Another fashionable area is **Saas Fee,** northeast of Zermatt. The village allows no motor vehicles to spoil its magnificent setting facing the great Fee glacier.

Besides the **Matterhorn** (14,692 ft.), the most famous Swiss peaks are the **Jungfrau, Mönch,** and **Eiger** (all around 13,000 ft.). A tunnel, almost 4.5 miles long, leads steeply up to the **Jungfraujoch** terminus (11,333 ft.). Its observation deck offers a superb view of the surrounding mountains and the lakes of central Switzerland. From there, on a very clear day, even the Black Forest in southern Germany can be spotted.

Blick aufs Matterhorn

Hermann Hesse

Hermann Hesse (1899–1962) was awarded the Nobel Prize for literature in 1946. Although born in Germany, he became a Swiss citizen at the outbreak of World War I. The first stage of his writing began with his romantic rendering of the artist as a social outcast. At the beginning of the war, the strain of his pacifist beliefs and domestic crises led him to undergo psychoanalysis, which gave a new dimension to his work. The novels *Demian, Siddharta,* and *Steppenwolf* were influenced by his readings of Nietzsche, Dostoyevsky, Spengler, and Buddhist mysticism, and are based on his conviction that people must discover their own nature. A third phase began in 1930, balancing the artist's rebellion against the constraints of social behavior. After 1943, when his name was put on the Nazi blacklist, he quit writing novels and concentrated on poems, stories, and essays that articulated a humanistic spirit reminiscent of Goethe's *Weltbürgertum (world citizenship)*. They also reflect Hesse's faith in the spirituality of all mankind, for which he coined the term *Weltglaube*.

Im Nebel

Seltsam°, im Nebel° zu wandern!   strange / fog
Einsam° ist jeder Busch und Stein,   lonely
Kein Baum sieht den andern,
Jeder ist allein.

Voll von Freunden war° mir die Welt°,   was / world
Als° noch mein Leben licht° war;   when / light
Nun, da der Nebel fällt,
Ist keiner mehr sichtbar°.   visible

Wahrlich°, keiner ist weise°,   truly / wise
Der nicht das Dunkel kennt,
Das unentrinnbar° und leise°   inescapably / quietly
Von allen ihn trennt°.   separates

Seltsam, im Nebel zu wandern!
Leben ist Einsamkeit.
Kein Mensch kennt den andern,
Jeder ist allein.

Hermann Hesse

WEB-ECKE For updates and online activities, visit the Wie geht's? home page at: http://www.hrwcollege.com/german/sevin/! You'll see some statistics about Switzerland, take a trip to Saas-Fee, and find out about some of Switzerland's popular export items.

SPRECHSITUATIONEN

There are times when you want to sympathize or empathize with a friend, and times when you feel less sympathetic. You may also feel the need to express relief when something has turned out better than expected. Here are appropriate expressions.

Expressing sympathy

(Ach, das ist aber) schade!
Das ist ja furchtbar!
So ein Pech!
Das tut mir (furchtbar) Leid.
Ach du liebes bisschen!
Ach du meine Güte!
Um Gottes willen! — *For heaven's sake.*
Das ist wirklich zu dumm! — *That's really too bad.*

Expressing a lack of sympathy

Das ist doch nicht wichtig.
Das macht doch nichts. ⎱
Das ist doch egal. ⎰ — *That doesn't matter. It's all the same to me.*
Na und! — *So what?*
Pech (gehabt)! — *Tough luck!*
Das geschieht dir recht. — *That serves you right.*
Das sieht dir ähnlich. — *That's typical of you.*

Expressing empathy

Das ist ja prima / wunderbar / toll!
Das freut mich (für dich). — *I'm happy (for you).*
Du Glückspilz! — *You lucky thing (literally: mushroom)!*

Expressing relief

Gut / Prima / Toll / Super!
(Na,) endlich! — *(Well,) finally!*
Gott sei Dank! — *Thank God!*
Ich bin wirklich froh. — *I'm really glad.*
(Da haben wir aber) Glück gehabt! ⎱
(Da haben wir aber) Schwein gehabt! ⎰ — *(We were really) lucky!*
Das ist noch mal gut gegangen. — *Things just worked out all right.*

Übungen

A. Momentan geht alles schief *(goes wrong)*. Was sagen Sie zu Daniels Pech?
1. Daniel hat von seinen Eltern zum Geburtstag ein Auto bekommen.
2. Das Auto ist nicht ganz neu.
3. Aber es fährt so schön ruhig und schnell, dass er gleich am ersten Tag einen Strafzettel *(ticket)* bekommen hat.
4. Am Wochenende ist er in die Berge gefahren, aber es hat immer nur geregnet.
5. Es hat ihm trotzdem viel Spaß gemacht, weil er dort eine Studentin kennen gelernt hat.
6. Auf dem Weg zurück ist ihm jemand in sein Auto gefahren. Totalschaden *(total wreck)*!

7. Daniel hat aber nur ein paar Kratzer *(scratches)* bekommen.
8. Er hat übrigens seit ein paar Tagen eine Wohnung mitten in der Stadt. Sie ist gar nicht teuer.
9. Er möchte das Mädchen aus den Bergen wiedersehen, aber er kann sein Adressbuch mit ihrer Telefonnummer nicht finden.
10. Momentan geht alles falsch. Er kann sein Portemonnaie *(wallet)* auch nicht finden.
11. Noch etwas. Die Katze *(cat)* des Nachbarn hat seine Goldfische gefressen *(ate)*.
12. Sein Bruder hat übrigens eine Operation gehabt. Aber jetzt geht es ihm wieder gut und er ist wieder zu Hause.

B. Jeder hat Probleme. *(Form small groups, and have each person name at least one problem he or she has. Take turns expressing sympathy or lack of it.)*

C. Kurzgespräche *(Your classmate expresses his/her feelings after each statement you make.)*
1. Trip home: The weather was awful. Your plane arrived two hours late (**mit zwei Stunden Verspätung**) and departed five hours late. You arrived at two o'clock in the morning. Your suitcase wasn't there. There were no buses into town. You didn't have enough cash for a cab. You phoned your father. You got home at 4 A.M. You were very tired.
2. Staying overnight: You and your friend arrived in Schaffhausen on the Rhine. You inquired at three hotels but they had no rooms available. They sent you to the *Schwyzerhüsli*. There they had some rooms. Since you were very tired, you went to bed early (**ins Bett**). There was a party in the hotel until midnight. Then cars drove by. It was very loud. At 4 A.M. your neighbors got up, talked in the hallway (**im Gang**) and got into their car. You couldn't sleep any more, got up too, and left. What a night!

KAPITEL 9

HOBBYS

Fahrradtour am Wochenende

LERNZIELE

■ VORSCHAU
Sports and clubs in the German-speaking countries

■ GESPRÄCHE AND WORTSCHATZ
Physical fitness and leisure time

■ STRUKTUR
Endings of preceded adjectives
Reflexive verbs
Infinitive with **zu**

■ EINBLICKE
Vacationing
Leisure time—pleasure or frustration?

■ FOKUS
Telephone courtesies
Animal and food talk (some idiomatic expressions)
Schrebergärten
Rose Ausländer: "Noch bist du da"

■ WEB-ECKE

■ SPRECHSITUATIONEN
Speaking on the telephone
Extending, accepting, and declining an invitation

VORSCHAU

Sports and Clubs in the German-Speaking Countries

Sports are very popular in Germany, Austria, and Switzerland, not only with spectators, but with amateur athletes as well. Whereas professional sports are big business like anywhere else, one out of three people belongs to a sports club **(Sportverein)**. The German Sports Federation **(Deutscher Sportbund)** has more than 75,000 affiliated sports clubs. It sponsors such programs as **Trimm dich** and **Sport für alle** with competitions in running, swimming, cycling, and skiing. Millions of people participate in these events every year. Soccer **(Fußball)** is as important in Europe as football, baseball, and basketball are in North America. Other popular sports are **Handball** and winter sports such as skating and ice hockey. **Volksmärsche** are group-hiking events open to the public. The successes of Steffi Graf, Boris Becker, Michael Stich, and Martina Hingis has given tennis a tremendous boost; and, although not as popular as in the United States, golf is becoming more common.

High schools and universities are not involved in competitive sports; for that purpose, students usually join a sports club. Such organizations are basically autonomous, but the government provides some support for those with insufficient funds. This applies particularly to the former East Germany, where an effort has been made to set up independent clubs. In the 1970s and 1980s, these clubs did not exist; instead, the East German government spent a great deal of money on making sports accessible to every citizen, seeking out young talents early and training them in special boarding schools—a practice that led to considerable success in the Olympics.

In addition to sports clubs, there are associations promoting all kinds of leisure activities, ranging from dog breeding and pigeon racing to gardening, crafts, music, and dancing. Clubs devoted to regional traditions and costumes **(Trachtenvereine)** and centuries-old rifle associations **(Schützenvereine)**—with their own emblems, uniforms, and ceremonial meetings—keep old traditions alive and draw thousands to their annual festivals.

GESPRÄCHE

Am Telefon

FRAU SCHMIDT Hier Schmidt.
BÄRBEL Guten Tag, Frau Schmidt. Ich bin's, Bärbel.
FRAU SCHMIDT Tag, Bärbel!
BÄRBEL Ist Karl-Heinz da?
FRAU SCHMIDT Nein, tut mir Leid. Er ist gerade zur Post gegangen.
BÄRBEL Ach so. Können Sie ihm sagen, dass ich heute Abend nicht mit ihm ausgehen kann?
FRAU SCHMIDT Natürlich. Was ist denn los?
BÄRBEL Ich bin krank. Mir tut der Hals weh und ich habe Kopfschmerzen.
FRAU SCHMIDT Das tut mir Leid. Gute Besserung!
BÄRBEL Danke. Auf Wiederhören!
FRAU SCHMIDT Wiederhören!

Bis gleich!

YVONNE Bei Mayer.
DANIELA Hallo, Yvonne! Ich bin's, Daniela.
YVONNE Tag, Daniela! Was gibt's?
DANIELA Nichts Besonderes. Hast du Lust, Squash zu spielen oder schwimmen zu gehen?
YVONNE Squash? Nein, danke. Ich habe noch Muskelkater von vorgestern. Ich kann mich kaum rühren. Mir tut alles weh.
DANIELA Lahme Ente! Wie wär's mit Schach?
YVONNE O.K., das klingt gut. Kommst du zu mir?
DANIELA Ja, bis gleich!

Wie geht's weiter?

1. Bärbels Freund heißt . . . 2. Bärbel spricht mit . . . 3. Karl-Heinz ist nicht zu Hause, weil . . . 4. Bärbel kann nicht mit ihm . . . 5. Bärbels Hals . . . 6. Sie hat auch . . . 7. Am Ende eines Telefongesprächs sagt man . . . 8. Danielas Freundin heißt . . . 9. Yvonne will nicht Squash spielen, weil . . . 10. Sie hat aber Lust, . . .

FOKUS Telephone Courtesies

When answering the phone, German-speakers usually identify themselves with their last names. If you were answering your own phone, you would say **Hier . . .** (plus your own name). If you were answering someone else's phone, say Ms. Schmidt's, you would say **(Hier) bei Schmidt.** Only afterwards do you say **Guten Tag!** or **Hallo!** If you are the one making the call, you usually give your own name before asking for the person you are trying to reach: **Guten Abend, hier spricht . . .** (or **Ich bin's, . . .**). **Ich möchte gern Frau Schmidt sprechen.** When ending a phone conversation formally, say **Auf Wiederhören!** (lit. *until we hear each other again*). Friends may simply say **Tschüss!**

WORTSCHATZ 1

Der Körper, - *(body)*
Das Hobby, -s *(hobby)*

der Fußball	soccer	die CD, -s	CD
Sport	sport(s), athletics	Freizeit	leisure time
das Klavier, -e	piano	Gitarre, -n	guitar
Spiel, -e	game	Idee, -n	idea
		Karte, -n	card
		Kassette, -n	cassette

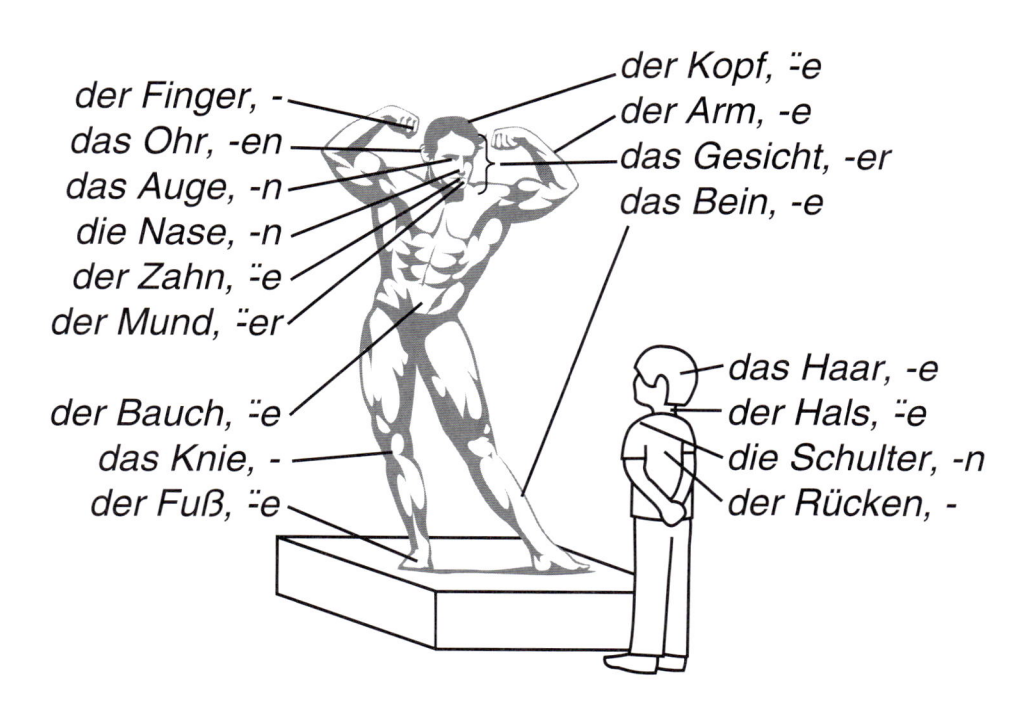

der Finger, -
das Ohr, -en
das Auge, -n
die Nase, -n
der Zahn, ̈e
der Mund, ̈er

der Bauch, ̈e
das Knie, -
der Fuß, ̈e

der Kopf, ̈e
der Arm, -e
das Gesicht, -er
das Bein, -e

das Haar, -e
der Hals, ̈e
die Schulter, -n
der Rücken, -

faulenzen	to be lazy
fern·sehen (sieht fern), ferngesehen	to watch TV
fotografieren	to take pictures
sammeln[1]	to collect
schwimmen, ist geschwommen	to swim
schwimmen gehen, ist schwimmen gegangen[2]	to go swimming
Ski laufen (läuft), ist gelaufen[3]	to ski
Skilaufen gehen, ist Skilaufen gegangen[3]	to go skiing
spazieren gehen, ist spazieren gegangen[2]	to go for a walk
(Dame, Schach) spielen[2]	to play (checkers, chess)
(Freunde) treffen (trifft), getroffen[2]	to meet, get together (with friends)
Sport treiben, getrieben[2]	to engage in sports
wandern, ist gewandert	to hike

Weiteres

gesund / krank	*healthy / sick, ill*
fantastisch	*fantastic, great, super*
Ich habe (Kopf)schmerzen.	*I have a (head)ache.*
Ich habe (keine) Lust, Tennis zu spielen.	*I (don't) feel like playing tennis.*
Mir tut der Hals weh.	*My throat hurts. I have a sore throat.*
Was gibt's (Neues)?	*What's up? What's new?*
Was ist los?	*What's the matter? What's going on?*
nichts Besonderes[4]	*nothing special*
zuerst	*first*
danach	*then*
Ach so.	*I see.*
Bis gleich!	*See you in a few minutes.*

---

[1] Like **bummeln**: ich samm(e)le, du sammelst, er sammelt, wir sammeln, ihr sammelt, sie sammeln.

[2] In each of these combinations, **gehen, spielen, treffen,** and **treiben** function as V1, while the other word, the verb complement, functions as V2: Ich **gehe** heute **schwimmen.** Du **spielst** manchmal **Schach.** Wir **treffen** dort **Freunde.** Sie **treiben** viel **Sport.**

[3] Note the difference between **Ski laufen** (two words) and **Skilaufen gehen**: Ich **laufe** gern **Ski** *(I like to ski).* BUT: Ich **gehe** gern **Skilaufen** *(I like skiing).*

[4] Similarly **nichts N**eues, **nichts S**chlechtes OR **etwas B**esonderes, **etwas S**chönes.

Zum Erkennen: Ich bin's. *(It's me.)*; Ich habe Muskelkater. *(My muscles are sore. I have a charley horse.)*; Ich kann mich kaum rühren. *(I can hardly move.)*; Lahme Ente! *(lit.: lame duck, someone with no pep)*; Wie wär's mit . . . ? *(How about . . . ?)*; zu mir *(to my place)*

Zum Thema

A. Mustersätze
 1. Hals: **Mir tut** der Hals **weh.**
    Kopf, Zahn, Bauch, Fuß, Knie, Hand
 2. Hände: **Mir tun die** Hände **weh.**
    Füße, Finger, Ohren, Beine, Augen
 3. Kopf: **Ich habe** Kopf**schmerzen.**
    Hals, Zahn, Bauch, Ohren
 4. Squash: **Hast du Lust,** Squash **zu spielen?**
    Tennis, Fußball, Klavier, CDs, Karten, Schach

B. Was tun Sie dann? Beenden Sie Sätze mit einer Antwort von der Liste oder mit Ihren eigenen *(own)* Worten!

_____ 1. Wenn ich Kopfschmerzen habe, . . .
_____ 2. Wenn mir die Füße wehtun, . . .
_____ 3. Wenn mir der Bauch wehtut, . . .
_____ 4. Wenn ich Halsschmerzen habe, . . .
_____ 5. Wenn ich Augenschmerzen habe, . . .
_____ 6. Wenn ich krank bin, . . .
_____ 7. Wenn ich gestresst bin, . . .
_____ 8. Wenn ich nicht schlafen kann, . . .

a. bleibe ich im Bett.
b. esse ich Hühnersuppe/nichts.
c. gehe ich ins Bett/in die Sauna.
d. gurgele *(gargle)* ich.
e. gehe ich nicht spazieren.
f. mache ich die Augen zu.
g. meditiere ich.
h. nehme ich Aspirin/Vitamin C.
i. sehe ich nicht fern.
j. rufe ich einen Arzt *(doctor)* an.
k. trinke ich Tee
l. trinke ich heiße Milch/Zitrone mit Honig *(honey).*

C. **Was tust du gern in deiner Freizeit?** *(Read through the list below and check things you like to do during your leisure time. Then tell classmates about your choices, and ask them about theirs. Poll the class to see which activities are the most popular.)*

    BEISPIEL: S1   Ich lese gern, und du?
                        S2   Ich auch. Ich spiele auch gern Videospiele, und du?
                        S1   Ich nicht, aber ich spiele gern Klavier . . .

Ich . . . gern	Ich gehe gern . . .	Ich spiele gern . . .
☐ backen	☐ angeln	☐ Basketball
☐ campen	☐ Bergsteigen	☐ Federball *(badminton)*
☐ essen	☐ bummeln	☐ Fußball
☐ faulenzen	☐ Radfahren	☐ Volleyball
☐ fernsehen	☐ Rollschuhlaufen	☐ Golf
☐ fotografieren	☐ Schlittschuhlaufen	☐ (Tisch)tennis
☐ joggen	☐ (Wasser)skilaufen	☐ Karten
☐ kochen *(cook)*	☐ Segeln *(sailing)*	☐ Schach
☐ lesen	☐ spazieren	☐ Videospiele
☐ reiten *(ride)*	☐ wandern	☐ Gitarre
☐ schwimmen	☐ zum Fitnessstudio	☐ Flöte *(flute)*
☐ tanzen	☐ ins Kino	☐ Klavier

D. **Interview.** Fragen Sie einen Nachbarn/eine Nachbarin, . . . !
1. ob er/sie als Kind ein Instrument gelernt hat; wenn ja, welches Instrument und ob er/sie es heute noch spielt
2. ob er/sie gern singt; wenn ja, was und wo (in der Dusche oder Badewanne, im Auto oder Chor)
3. was für Musik er/sie schön findet (klassische oder moderne Musik, Jazz, Rock-, Pop-, Country- oder Volksmusik)
4. ob er/sie viel fernsieht; wenn ja, wann gewöhnlich und was
5. ob er/sie oft lange am Telefon spricht; wenn ja, mit wem

E. **Am Telefon.** Was sagen Sie?

    S1   Hier . . .
    S2   Tag, . . . ! Ich bin's, . . . Sag mal, hast du Lust, . . . ?
    S1   Nein, ich kann nicht . . .
    S2   Warum nicht? Was ist los?
    S1   Ich bin krank. Mir tut/tun . . . weh.
    S2   . . . Wie lange hast du schon . . . schmerzen?
    S1   Seit . . .
    S2   Hoffentlich . . . Gute Besserung!
    S1   . . .

F. **Aussprache: l, z.** Sehen Sie auch III. 8–10 im Ausspracheteil des Arbeitsheftes!
1. [l]   **l**aut, **l**eicht, **l**ustig, **l**eider, Ha**l**s, Ge**l**d, ma**l**en, spie**l**en, f**l**iegen, ste**ll**en, schne**ll**, Ba**ll**, he**ll**
2. [ts]   **z**ählen, **z**eigen, **z**wischen, **z**urück, **z**uerst, **Z**ug, **Z**ahn, Schmer**z**en, Ker**z**en, Ein**z**elzimmer, Pi**zz**a, be**z**ahlen, tan**z**en, je**tz**t, schmu**tz**ig, tro**tz**, kur**z**, schwar**z**, Sal**z**, Schwei**z**, Sit**z**pla**tz**
3. Wortpaare
    a. *felt* / Feld   c. *plots* / Platz   e. seit / Zeit
    b. *hotel* / Hotel   d. Schweiß / Schweiz   f. so / Zoo

244   KAPITEL 9

FOKUS: Animal and Food Talk (Some Idiomatic Expressions)

As in the case of **Lahme Ente!** in the dialogue, names of animals are frequently used in everyday speech to characterize people—often in a derogatory way: **Ich Esel!** or **Du Affe!** *(donkey, monkey)* for someone who made a mistake or behaves in a silly manner; **Du hast einen Vogel!** or **Bei dir piept's!** *(You're cuckoo)*; **Fauler Hund!** *(dog)* for someone lazy; **Du Brummbär!** *(grumbling bear)* for someone grumpy; **(Das ist) alles für die Katz'!** if everything is useless or in vain; **Du Schwein!** *(pig)* for someone who is messy or a scoundrel. **Schwein haben,** however, has quite a different meaning: *to be lucky.* In addition, names of food are used in special expressions: **Das ist doch Käse!** *(That's nonsense)*; **Das ist mir Wurst!** *(I don't care!)*; or **Alles Banane?** *(Everything all right?)*

Hören Sie zu!

Beim Arzt

Zum Erkennen: passieren *(to happen);* war *(was);* der Ellbogen, - *(elbow);* hoch·legen *(to put up);* (Schmerz)tabletten *([pain] pills)*

Was fehlt?

1. Kim geht zum Arzt, weil ihr _____ wehtut. 2. Sie ist mit ihrer Freundin zum _____ im Harz gewesen. 3. Am letzten Tag ist sie _____. 4. Sie darf ein paar Tage nicht _____. 5. Sie soll das Bein _____. 6. Der Arzt gibt ihr ein paar _____ mit. 7. Kim kann bald wieder _____ oder _____. 8. Wenn Kim in einer Woche immer noch Schmerzen hat, soll sie _____.

STRUKTUR

I. Endings of adjectives preceded by *der*- and *ein*-words

1. PREDICATE ADJECTIVES and ADVERBS do not have endings.

Willi fährt schnell.	*Willi drives fast.*
Willi ist schnell.	*Willi is quick.*

2. However, ADJECTIVES PRECEDING A NOUN (attributive adjectives) do have an ending that varies with the preceding article and with the noun's case, gender, and number.

Der schnell**e** Fahrer *(m.)* ist mein Bruder.	*The fast driver is my brother.*
Mein Bruder ist ein schnell**er** Fahrer.	*My brother is a fast driver.*
Er hat ein schnell**es** Auto *(n.)*.	*He has a fast car.*

    If you compare the tables below, you will readily see that there are only FOUR DIFFERENT endings: **-e, -er, -es,** and **-en.**

    a. Adjectives preceded by a definite article, or **der**-word:

	masculine	neuter	feminine	plural
nom.	der neue Wagen	das neue Auto	die neue Farbe	die neuen Ideen
acc.	den neuen Wagen	das neue Auto	die neue Farbe	die neuen Ideen
dat.	dem neuen Wagen	dem neuen Auto	der neuen Farbe	den neuen Ideen
gen.	des neuen Wagens	des neuen Autos	der neuen Farbe	der neuen Ideen

    b. Adjectives preceded by an indefinite article, or **ein**-word:

	masculine	neuter	feminine	plural
nom.	ein neuer Wagen	ein neues Auto	eine neue Farbe	keine neuen Ideen
acc.	einen neuen Wagen	ein neues Auto	eine neue Farbe	keine neuen Ideen
dat.	einem neuen Wagen	einem neuen Auto	einer neuen Farbe	keinen neuen Ideen
gen.	eines neuen Wagens	eines neuen Autos	einer neuen Farbe	keiner neuen Ideen

    Comparing the two preceding tables, you can see:

    - Adjectives preceded by the definite article or any **der**-word have either an **-e** or **-en** ending.
    - Adjectives preceded by the indefinite article or any **ein**-word have two different adjective endings WHENEVER **ein** HAS NO ENDING: **-er** for masculine nouns and **-es** for neuter nouns. Otherwise the **-en** ending predominates and is used in the masculine accusative singular, all datives and genitives, and all plurals.

after der-words

	masc.	neut.	fem.	pl.
nom.		-e		
acc.				
dat.		-en		
gen.				

after ein-words

	masc.	neut.	fem.	pl.
nom.	-er	-es	-e	
acc.		-es	-e	
dat.		-en		
gen.				

Or, to put it in another way, the endings are:
- in the NOMINATIVE and ACCUSATIVE SINGULAR
  - after **der, das, die,** and **eine** → **-e**
  - after **ein**
    - with masc. nouns → **-er**
    - with neut. nouns → **-es**
- in ALL OTHER CASES → **-en**
  (incl. masc. accusative sg., all datives and genitives, and all plurals)

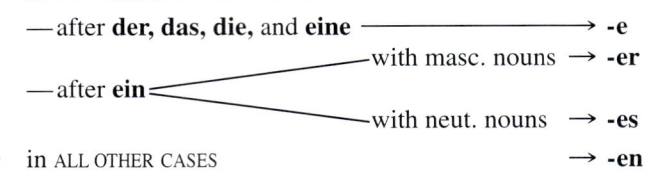

> Der groß**e** Ball, das schön**e** Spiel und die neu**e** CD sind gut.
>
> Das ist ein gut**er** Preis für so ein fantastisch**es** Geschenk.
>
> Das sind keine teur**en** Geschenke.

NOTE: Adjective endings are not hard to remember if you understand the following basic principle, which is this: in the nominative and the accusative, one of the words preceding the noun must convey information about its gender, number, and case. If an article does not do so, then the adjective must. For example, **der** is clearly masculine nominative; therefore the adjective can take the minimal ending **-e. Ein,** however, does not show gender or case; therefore the adjective must do so.

Mercedes-Benz
Ihr guter Stern auf allen Straßen.

3. If two or more adjectives precede a noun, all have the same ending.

> Das sind keine groß**en**, teur**en** Geschenke.

Übungen

A. Familienfotos. Sagen Sie, was man auf jedem Bild vom 50. Jubiläum *(anniversary)* Ihrer Großeltern sieht!

   BEISPIEL: Das ist mein Onkel Max mit seinen drei Kindern. (wild, klein)
   Das ist mein Onkel Max mit seinen drei wilden Kindern.
   Das ist mein Onkel Max mit seinen drei kleinen Kindern.

1. Das ist Tante Jutta mit ihrem Freund aus London. (verrückt, englisch)
2. Hier sitzen wir alle an einem Tisch und spielen Monopoly. (groß, rund)
3. Das ist Oma *(grandma)* mit ihrem Porsche *(m.)*. (teuer, rot)
4. Die Farbe dieses Autos gefällt mir. (toll, schnell)
5. Das ist wirklich ein Geschenk! (wunderbar, fantastisch)
6. Opa *(grandpa)* hat ein Fahrrad bekommen. (schön, neu)
7. Jetzt kann er mit seinen Freunden Fahrrad fahren. (viel, alt)

8. Das hier ist unser Hund *(dog, m.)*. (klein, braun)
9. Das ist wirklich ein Hündchen *(n.)*. (lieb, klein)
10. Wegen des Wetters haben wir nicht im Garten gefeiert. (schlecht, kalt)

B. **Die neue Wohnung.** Lesen Sie den Dialog mit den Adjektiven!
   BEISPIEL: Ist der Schrank neu? (groß)
               Ist der große Schrank neu?

   S1   Ist dieser Sessel bequem? (braun)
   S2   Ja, und das Sofa auch. (lang)
   S1   Die Lampe gefällt mir. (klein)
        Woher hast du diesen Teppich? (fantastisch)
        Und wo hast du dieses Bild gefunden? (supermodern)
   S2   In einem Geschäft. (alt)
        Wenn du willst, kann ich dir das Geschäft mal zeigen. (interessant)
   S1   Ist es in der Müllergasse *(f.)*? (klein)
   S2   Ja, auf der Seite. (link-)
   S1   Während der Woche habe ich keine Zeit. (nächst-)
        Sind diese Möbel teuer gewesen? (schön)
   S2   Natürlich nicht. Für solche Möbel gebe ich nicht viel Geld aus. (alt)

C. **Inge zeigt Jens ihr Zimmer.** Jens stellt Fragen und kommentiert *(comments)*. Bilden Sie aus zwei Sätzen einen Satz!
   BEISPIEL: Woher kommt dieses Schachspiel? Es ist interessant.
               Woher kommt dieses interessante Schachspiel?

   1. Weißt du, was so ein Schachspiel kostet? Es ist chinesisch.
   2. Bist du Schachspielerin? Spielst du gut? *(add ein!)*
   3. Ich bin kein Schachspieler. Ich spiele nicht gut.
   4. Woher hast du diese Briefmarkensammlung? Sie ist alt.
   5. Mein Vater hat auch eine Sammlung. Sie ist groß.
   6. Sammelst du solche Briefmarken auch? Sie sind normal.
   7. Was machst du mit so einer Briefmarke? Sie ist doppelt *(double)*.
   8. Darf ich diese Briefmarke haben? Sie ist ja doppelt!
   9. Hast du diese Bilder gemacht? Sie sind toll.
   10. Wer ist der Junge? Er ist klein.
   11. Was für ein Gesicht! Es ist fantastisch!
   12. Die Augen gefallen mir! Sie sind dunkelbraun.
   13. Mit meiner Kamera ist das nicht möglich. Sie ist billig.
   14. Und das hier ist ein Tennisspieler, nicht wahr? Er ist bekannt und kommt aus Deutschland.
   15. Weißt du, dass wir gestern trotz des Wetters Fußball gespielt haben? Das Wetter ist schlecht gewesen.
   16. Leider kann ich wegen meines Knies nicht mehr mitspielen. Das Knie ist kaputt.

D. **Ist das nicht schön?** *(Your classmate is very indecisive and continuously needs reassurance. Show agreement and ask a question according to the model.)*
   1. BEISPIEL: Ist der Pullover nicht warm?
                  Ja, das ist ein warmer Pullover.
                  Woher hast du den warmen Pullover?

      a. Ist das Hemd nicht elegant?
      b. Ist die Uhr nicht herrlich?
      c. Ist der Hut *(hat)* nicht verrückt?

2. **BEISPIEL:** Ist das Hotel nicht gut?
   Ja, das ist ein gutes Hotel.
   Wo hast du von diesem guten Hotel gehört?

   a. Ist die Pension nicht wunderbar?
   b. Ist der Gasthof nicht billig?
   c. Ist das Restaurant nicht gemütlich?

3. **BEISPIEL:** Ist das alte Schloss nicht herrlich?
   Ja, das ist ein altes, herrliches Schloss.
   Ich gehe gern in so alte, herrliche Schlösser.

   a. Ist der neue Supermarkt nicht modern?
   b. Ist das schöne Café nicht klein?
   c. Ist die alte Kirche nicht interessant?

E. Beschreibung *(description)* **einer Wohnung**

1. **Petras Wohnung.** Geben Sie die fehlenden *(missing)* Adjektivendungen!

   a. Petra wohnt in einem toll_____ Haus im neu_____ Teil unserer schön_____ Stadt. b. Ihre klein_____ Wohnung liegt im neunt_____ Stock eines modern_____ Hochhauses *(high-rise)*. c. Sie hat eine praktisch_____ Küche und ein gemütlich_____ Wohnzimmer. d. Von dem groß_____ Wohnzimmerfenster kann sie unsere ganz_____ Stadt und die viel_____ Brücken über dem breit_____ *(wide)* Fluss sehen. e. Petra liebt ihre Wohnung wegen des schön_____ Blickes *(view, m.)* und der billig_____ Miete. f. In ihrem hell_____ Schlafzimmer stehen ein einfach_____ Bett und ein klein_____ Nachttisch mit einer klein_____ Nachttischlampe. g. An der Wand steht ein braun_____ Schreibtisch und über dem braun_____ Schreibtisch hängt ein lang_____ Regal mit ihren viel_____ Büchern. Petra findet ihre Wohnung schön.

2. **Schreiben Sie!** Meine Wohnung (8–10 Sätze, mit 1–2 Adjektiven in jedem Satz)

FOKUS *Schrebergärten*

Many German city-dwellers are passionate gardeners, spending their summers in "garden colonies" or community gardens, assemblages of small garden plots in the middle or on the outskirts of large urban areas. The orthopedist Daniel Schreber (1808–1861) from Leipzig founded the garden movement in the nineteenth century as a means for workers to supplement their incomes and defuse urban angst. Today the gardens primarily provide an opportunity for recreation, as well as fresh flowers and home-grown vegetables and fruit.

Im Schrebergarten, für Stadtmenschen eine Oase im Grünen

II. Reflexive verbs

If the subject and one of the objects of a sentence are the same person or thing, a reflexive pronoun must be used for the object. In the English sentence, *I see myself in the picture,* the reflexive pronoun *myself* is the accusative object. *(Whom do I see?—Myself.)* In the sentence, *I am buying myself a CD,* the pronoun *myself* is the dative object. *(For whom am I buying the CD?—For myself.)*

In German only the third person singular and plural have a special reflexive pronoun: **sich.** The other persons use the accusative and dative forms of the personal pronouns, which you already know.

COMPARE: Ich sehe meinen Bruder auf dem Bild.
Ich sehe **mich** auf dem Bild.

Ich kaufe meinem Bruder eine CD.
Ich kaufe **mir** eine CD.

nom.	ich	du	er / es / sie	wir	ihr	sie	Sie
acc.	mich	dich	sich	uns	euch	sich	sich
dat.	mir	dir					

1. Many verbs you have already learned CAN BE USED REFLEXIVELY, although the English equivalent may not include a reflexive pronoun:

   • The reflexive pronoun USED AS THE DIRECT OBJECT (ACCUSATIVE):

sich fragen	*to wonder*	**sich treffen**	*to meet, gather*
sich legen	*to lie down*	usw.	
sich sehen	*to see oneself*		

   Ich frage **mich,** ob das richtig ist.   *I wonder (ask myself) whether that's right.*
   Ich lege **mich** aufs Sofa.   *I lie down on the sofa.*
   Ich sehe **mich** im Spiegel.   *I see myself in the mirror.*

   • The reflexive pronoun used AS THE INDIRECT OBJECT (DATIVE):

sich bestellen		**sich nehmen**	
sich kaufen		**sich wünschen**	*to wish*
sich kochen		usw.	

   Ich bestelle **mir** ein Eis.   *I am ordering ice cream (for myself).*
   Ich koche **mir** ein Ei.   *I'm cooking myself an egg.*
   Ich wünsche **mir** ein Auto.   *I'm wishing for a car (for myself).*

2. Some verbs are ALWAYS REFLEXIVE, or are reflexive when they express a certain meaning. Here are some important verbs that you need to know.

sich an·hören	*to listen to*
sich an·sehen, angesehen	*to look at*
sich an·ziehen, angezogen	*to put on (clothing), get dressed*
sich aus·ziehen, ausgezogen	*to take off (clothing), get undressed*
sich um·ziehen, umgezogen	*to change (clothing), get changed*
sich baden	*to take a bath*
sich beeilen	*to hurry*

sich duschen	*to take a shower*
sich erkälten	*to catch a cold*
sich (wohl) fühlen	*to feel (well)*
sich (hin·)legen	*to lie down*
sich kämmen	*to comb one's hair*
sich konzentrieren	*to concentrate*
sich (die Zähne / Nase) putzen	*to clean (brush one's teeth / blow one's nose)*
sich rasieren	*to shave*
sich (hin·)setzen	*to sit down*
sich waschen (wäscht), gewaschen	*to wash (oneself)*

Setz dich (hin)!	*Sit down.*
Warum müsst ihr euch beeilen?	*Why do you have to hurry?*
Ich fühle mich nicht wohl.	*I don't feel well.*
Letzte Woche hat sie sich erkältet.	*Last week she caught a cold.*
Wir treffen uns mit Freunden.	*We're meeting with friends.*

- With some of these verbs, the reflexive pronoun may be EITHER THE ACCUSATIVE OR THE DATIVE OBJECT. If there are two objects, then the person (the reflexive pronoun) is in the dative and the thing is in the accusative.

Ich wasche **mich.**	*I wash myself.*
Ich wasche **mir** die Haare.	*I wash my hair.*
Ich ziehe **mich** an.	*I'm getting dressed.*
Ich ziehe **mir** einen Pulli an.	*I'm putting on a sweater.*

3. In English, possessive adjectives are used to refer to parts of the body: *I'm washing my hands.* In German, however, the definite article is usually used together with the reflexive pronoun in the dative.

*I'm washing **my** hands.*	Ich wasche **mir die** Hände.
*She's combing **her** hair.*	Sie kämmt **sich die** Haare.
*Brush **your** teeth.*	Putz **dir die** Zähne!

REMEMBER: When there are two object pronouns, the accusative precedes the dative!

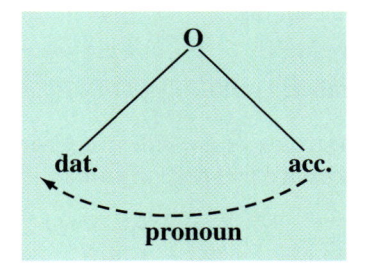

Ich wasche **mir die Hände.**   Ich wasche **sie mir.**
Du kämmst **dir die Haare.**   Du kämmst **sie dir.**
    dat.   acc.   acc. dat.

Übungen

F. Antworten Sie mit JA!
  1. **Singular**
     BEISPIEL: Soll ich mir die Hände waschen?
     Ja, waschen Sie sich die Hände!
     Ja, wasch dir die Hände!

     a. Soll ich mich noch umziehen?
     b. Soll ich mir die Haare kämmen?
     c. Soll ich mir ein Auto kaufen?
     d. Soll ich mich jetzt setzen?
     e. Soll ich mir die Bilder ansehen?

  2. **Plural**
     BEISPIEL: Sollen wir uns die Hände waschen?
     Ja, waschen Sie sich die Hände!
     Ja, wascht euch die Hände!

     a. Sollen wir uns ein Zimmer mieten?
     b. Sollen wir uns ein Haus bauen?
     c. Sollen wir uns in den Garten setzen?
     d. Sollen wir uns die Kassetten anhören?
     e. Sollen wir uns die Briefmarken ansehen?

Hör dir das an!

Du kannst dir auch mal wieder die Ohren waschen.

G. Was fehlt?
  1. Kinder, zieht _____ warm an!
  2. Einen Moment, ich muss _____ die Nase putzen.
  3. Gestern haben wir _____ ein Klavier gekauft.
  4. Setzen Sie _____ bitte!
  5. Peter, konzentrier _____!
  6. Kinder, erkältet _____ nicht!
  7. Ich habe _____ zum Geburtstag ein Schachspiel gewünscht.
  8. Willst du _____ etwas im Radio anhören?
  9. Junge, fühlst du _____ nicht wohl?
  10. Möchten Sie _____ die Hände waschen?
  11. Bestellst du _____ auch ein Stück Kuchen?
  12. Ich setze _____ gemütlich in den Garten.

Park Hotel Blub
blub, blub und sich wohl fühlen, wie ein Fisch im Wasser.
Park Hotel blub und blub Badeparadies.

H. Und du, was machst du den ganzen Tag? *(In pairs, ask each other what you do at certain hours of the day, using reflexive verbs whenever possible. Take notes and then report back to the class.)*

  S1   Was machst du abends um zehn?
  S2   Ich höre mir die Nachrichten an. Und du?
  S1   Um diese Zeit lege ich mich ins Bett. . . .

I. Auf Deutsch bitte! Frau Brockmann ist Gesundheitsfanatikerin *(a health nut)*, aber ihre Familie nicht.

1. Otto, get dressed! 2. Christian, hurry! 3. Lotte and Ulle, are you putting on a sweater? 4. We still have to brush our teeth. 5. Peter, comb your hair! 6. I don't feel well. 7. Today we're all going jogging. 8. Yes, but I've caught a cold. 9. Then lie down *(sg. fam.)*.

J. Hoppla, hier fehlt 'was! Jeder hat seine Morgenroutine. *(Use the information given in the following table to discuss the early-morning habits of four characters, Elke, Horst, Susi, and Ingo. Your partner will help you to fill in the missing information with details provided in the matching chart in Section 11 of the Appendix. What is your morning routine?)*

1. **BEISPIEL:** S1 Was macht Horst morgens?
   S2 Horst zieht sich schnell an und geht joggen. Dann . . .
2. **BEISPIEL:** S1 Ich bin wie *(like)* . . .
   S2 Wirklich? Ich bin wie . . .

S1:

	Zuerst	**Dann**	**Danach**
ELKE	s. duschen s. die Haare waschen	s. kämmen s. die Zähne putzen	s. in die Küche setzen s. ein Ei kochen gemütlich frühstücken s. Musik anhören
HORST			
SUSI	zu lang schlafen schnell aufstehen	s. schnell anziehen s. nicht kämmen	ihre Sachen nicht finden etwas zu essen mitnehmen
INGO			

III. Infinitive with *zu*

English and German use infinitives with **zu** *(to)* in much the same way.

Es ist interessant **zu reisen.**   *It's interesting to travel.*
Ich habe keine Zeit gehabt **zu essen.**   *I didn't have time to eat.*

1. In German, if the infinitive is combined with other sentence elements, such as a direct object or an adverbial phrase, a comma usually separates the infinitive phrase from the main clause.

   Haben Sie Zeit, eine Reise **zu** machen?   *Do you have time to take a trip?*

   Note that in German the infinitive comes at the end of the phrase.

2. If a separable-prefix verb is used, the **-zu-** is inserted between the prefix and the verb.

   prefix + **zu** + verb

   Es ist Zeit abzufahren.   *It's time to leave.*

CAUTION: No **zu** after modals! Wir **müssen** jetzt **abfahren.** See Caution on p. 143.

3. Infinitive phrases beginning with **um** explain the purpose of the action described in the main clause.

   Wir fahren nach Hessen, **um** unsere Oma **zu** besuchen.   *(in order to visit . . .)*
   Rudi geht ins Badezimmer, **um** sich **zu** duschen.   *(in order to take a shower)*

Übungen

K. Wie geht's weiter?

BEISPIEL: Hast du Lust . . . ? (sich Kassetten anhören)
Hast du Lust, dir Kassetten anzuhören?

1. Dort gibt es viel . . . (sehen, tun, fotografieren, zeigen, essen)
2. Habt ihr Zeit . . . ? (vorbeikommen, die Nachbarn kennen lernen, faulenzen, euch ein paar Bilder ansehen)
3. Es ist wichtig . . . (aufpassen, sich konzentrieren, Sprachen lernen, Freunde haben, Sport treiben)
4. Es ist interessant . . . (ihm zuhören, Bücher sammeln, mit der Bahn fahren, mit dem Flugzeug fliegen)
5. Es hat Spaß gemacht . . . (reisen, wandern, singen, spazieren gehen, aufs Land fahren, Freunde anrufen)

L. Bilden Sie Sätze!

1. heute / wir / haben / nicht viel / tun
2. es / machen / ihm / Spaß / / sich mit Freunden treffen
3. sie *(sg.)* / müssen / noch / einlösen / Scheck
4. ich / haben / keine Zeit / / Geschichten / sich anhören *(pres. perf.)*
5. du / haben / keine Lust / / mit uns / Skilaufen gehen? *(pres. perf.)*
6. möchten / du / fernsehen / bei uns?
7. wir / möchten / kaufen / neu / Auto
8. es / sein / sehr bequem / / hier / sitzen
9. ich / sein / zu müde / / Tennis spielen
10. du / sollen / anrufen / dein- / Kusine

M. So bin ich. Sprechen Sie mit den anderen über Ihre Hobbys und Ihre Freizeit!

1. Ich habe keine Lust . . .
2. Ich habe nie Zeit . . .
3. Mir macht es Spaß . . .
4. Ich finde es wichtig . . .
5. Ich finde es langweilig *(boring)* . . .
6. Als *(as)* Kind hat es mir Spaß gemacht . . .
7. Ich brauche das Wochenende gewöhnlich, um . . .
8. Ich lerne Deutsch, um . . .

MISEREOR

„Die Menschen haben gelernt, zu schwimmen wie die Fische und zu fliegen wie die Vögel, aber wie Brüder zusammenzuleben haben sie nicht gelernt"
M. L. King

Zusammenfassung

N. Rotkäppchen und der Wolf. Was fehlt?

1. Es hat einmal eine gut_____ Mutter mit ihrem klein_____ Mädchen in einem ruhig_____ Dorf gewohnt. 2. Sie hat zu ihrer klein_____ Tochter gesagt: „Geh zu deiner alt_____ Großmutter und bring ihr diese gut_____ Flasche Wein und diesen frisch_____ Kuchen! 3. Aber du musst im dunkl_____ Wald aufpassen, weil dort der groß_____ bös_____ *(bad)* Wolf wohnt." 4. Das klein_____ Mädchen ist mit seiner groß_____ Tasche in den grün_____ Wald gegangen. 5. Auf dem dunkl_____ Weg ist der bös_____ Wolf gekommen und hat das klein_____ Mädchen gefragt, wo seine alt_____ Großmutter lebt. 6. Er hat dem gut_____ Kind auch die wunderbar_____ Blumen am Weg gezeigt. 7. Dann hat der furchtbar_____ Wolf die arm_____ *(poor)* Großmutter gefressen *(devoured)* und hat sich in das bequem_____ Bett der alt_____ Frau gelegt. 8. Das müd_____ Rotkäppchen ist in das klein_____ Haus gekommen und hat gefragt: „Großmutter, warum hast du so groß_____ Ohren? Warum hast du so groß_____ Augen? Warum hast du so einen groß_____ Mund?" 9. Da hat der bös_____ Wolf geantwortet: „Dass ich dich besser fressen kann!" 10. Nun *(well)*, Sie kennen ja das Ende dieser bekannt_____ Geschichte *(story, f.)!* 11. Der Jäger *(hunter)* hat den dick_____ Wolf getötet *(killed)* und dem klein_____ Mädchen und seiner alt_____ Großmutter aus dem Bauch des tot_____ *(dead)* Wolfes geholfen.

O. Hallo, Max! Auf Deutsch bitte!

1. What have you been doing today? 2. Oh, nothing special. I listened to my old cassettes. 3. Do you feel like going swimming? 4. No, thanks. I don't feel well. I have a headache and my throat hurts. Call Stephan. 5. Hello, Stephan! Do you have time to go swimming? 6. No, I have to go to town **(in die Stadt)** in order to buy (myself) a new pair of slacks and a warm coat. Do you feel like coming along? 7. No, I already went shopping this morning. I bought (myself) a blue sweater and a white shirt. 8. Too bad. I've got to hurry. 9. OK, I'm going to put on my swim trunks **(die Badehose)** and go swimming. Bye!

Drachenflieger *(hang-gliders)* vor dem Abflug

EINBLICKE

Vacationing

In contrast to many North Americans who take their vacation days in short breaks combined with a holiday and one or two weekends, Germans are more likely to view their annual vacation as the year's major event. With relatively high incomes and a minimum of three weeks' paid vacation **(Urlaub)** each year, Germans are among the world's greatest travelers. Many head south to the beaches of Spain, Greece, Turkey, and North Africa. Others opt for educational trips, such as language courses abroad or cultural tours. Favorite destinations include Thailand, Kenya, and North America. Those who wish to stay closer to home may take bike tours or spend a week on a farm in the countryside.

Ferien auf dem Bauernhof

WORTSCHATZ 2

der Urlaub	*(paid) vacation*
das Leben[1]	*life*
die Musik	*music*
ander- *(adj.)*	*other, different*
anders *(adv.)*	*different(ly)*

beliebt	*popular*
ganz	*whole, entire(ly), all*
etwas (ganz) anderes	*something (totally) different*
(genauso) wie . . .	*(just) like . . .*
aus·geben (gibt aus), ausgegeben	*to spend (money)*
sich aus·ruhen	*to relax, rest*
sich fit halten (hält), gehalten	*to keep in shape*
sich langweilen	*to get (or be) bored*
vor·ziehen, vorgezogen	*to prefer*

---

[1] In German, **Leben** is used only in the singular: Sport ist wichtig **in ihrem Leben** *(in her life, in their lives)*.

Vorm Lesen

A. Allerlei Fragen

1. Wie viele Stunden die Woche *(per week)* arbeitet man in den USA / in Kanada? 2. Wie viele Wochen Urlaub hat man im Jahr? 3. Was tun die Amerikaner / Kanadier in ihrer Freizeit? 4. Was ist der Nationalsport hier? 5. Was sind andere populäre Sportarten? 6. Wohin gehen Sie gern in den Ferien? 7. Sind Ferien für Sie gewöhnlich Lust oder Frust? Warum?

B. Was ist das?

der Arbeiter, Freizeitboom, Freizeitfrust, Musikklub, Urlaubstag; das Fernsehen, Gartenhäuschen, Gartenstück, Industrieland, Musikfestspiel, Privileg, Problem, Schwimmbad, Windsurfen; die Aerobik, Aktivität, Autobahn, Disko, Kulturreise, Stadtwohnung; mit sich bringen, planen; aktiv, deutschsprachig, frustriert, täglich, überfüllt

Freizeit—Lust oder Frust?

Vor hundert Jahren war° es das Privileg der reichen° Leute, nicht arbeiten zu müssen. Die Arbeiter in den deutschsprachigen Ländern haben zu der Zeit aber oft noch 75 Stunden pro Woche gearbeitet. Urlaub für Arbeiter gibt es erst seit 1919: zuerst nur drei Tage im Jahr. Heute ist das anders. Die Deutschen arbeiten nur ungefähr 180 Tage im Jahr, weniger als° die Menschen in fast allen anderen Industrieländern. Außer den vielen Feiertagen haben sehr viele Leute fünf oder sechs Wochen Urlaub im Jahr. So ist die Freizeit ein sehr wichtiger Teil des Lebens und mehr als° nur Zeit, sich vom täglichen Stress auszuruhen.

    Was tut man mit der vielen Freizeit? Natürlich ist Fernsehen sehr wichtig. Viele sitzen mehr als zwei Stunden pro Tag vorm Fernseher. Auch Sport ist sehr populär, nicht nur das Zusehen°, sondern auch das aktive Mitmachen°, um sich fit zu halten. Heute sind Aerobik, Squash oder Windsurfen genauso „in" wie Tennis und Golf. Fußball ist bei den Deutschen und Österreichern, wie überall in Europa, der Nationalsport. Auch Handball und Volleyball sind in den deutschsprachigen Ländern sehr beliebt.

    Die Menschen sind gern draußen° in der Natur. An Wochenenden fahren sie oft mit dem Zug oder mit dem Auto aufs Land und gehen spazieren, fahren Rad oder wandern. Danach setzt man sich in ein schönes Gartenrestaurant und ruht sich aus. Im Sommer gehen sie oft ins öffentliche Schwimmbad oder fahren an einen schönen See. Sie sind auch viel im Garten. Wenn sie in einer Stadtwohnung leben, können sie sich ein kleines Gartenstück pachten° und dort Blumen und Gemüse ziehen°. Viele bauen sich dort ein Gartenhäuschen, wo sie sich duschen, umziehen oder ausruhen können.

    Die Deutschen sind reiselustig°. Immer wieder zieht es sie hinaus in die Ferne, z. B. nach Spanien, Griechenland oder Frankreich. Sie geben fast ein Sechstel° des Touristikumsatzes° der ganzen Welt aus. Manche machen Kulturreisen, um Land und Leute kennen zu lernen, in Museen zu gehen oder sich auf einem der vielen Festspiele Musik anzuhören. Andere° reisen, um Sprachen zu lernen oder einmal etwas ganz anderes zu tun. Viele fahren in den warmen Süden, um sich in die Sonne zu legen oder schön braun wieder nach Hause zu kommen.

Und die jungen Leute? Außer den oben genannten° Aktivitäten macht es ihnen besonders Spaß, sich mit Freunden zu treffen und in Kneipen°, Diskos, Cafés, Musikklubs oder ins Kino zu gehen. Auch gehen sie gern bummeln oder einkaufen.

Dieser ganze Freizeitboom bringt aber auch Probleme mit sich. Manche langweilen sich, weil sie nicht wissen, was sie mit ihrer Freizeit machen sollen. Andere sind frustriert, wenn sie auf der Autobahn in lange Staus° kommen oder die Züge überfüllt sind. Manchmal muss man eben° etwas planen. Man muss ja nicht am ersten oder letzten° Urlaubstag unterwegs° sein. Und wenn man seine Ruhe° haben will, darf man nicht in der Hauptsaison° zu den bekannten Ferienplätzen fahren. Sonst° wird Freizeitlust zum Freizeitfrust.

above-mentioned
pubs

traffic jams
just / last / on the road
peace and quiet / high season
otherwise

Windsurfen und Bergsteigen ist nicht für jeden.

Zum Text

A. Was passt?

a. im Garten
b. vorm Fernseher
c. Staus
d. den vielen Feiertagen
e. mit ihrer Freizeit
f. sich da richtig wohl fühlen
g. sich ein kleines Gartenstück zu pachten
h. auszuruhen
i. anzuhören
j. arbeiten zu müssen
k. schön braun zurückzukommen
l. in Diskos

_____ 1. Vor hundert Jahren war es das Privileg der reichen Leute, nicht . . .
_____ 2. Heute haben sehr viele Leute außer . . . auch noch fünf oder sechs Wochen Urlaub im Jahr.
_____ 3. Die Freizeit ist mehr als nur Zeit, sich von der Arbeit . . . und sich hinzulegen.
_____ 4. Viele Leute sitzen über zwei Stunden am Tag . . .
_____ 5. Man arbeitet auch gern . . .

_____ 6. Wer keinen Garten hat, hat die Möglichkeit, . . .
_____ 7. Wenn das Wetter schön ist, kann man . . .
_____ 8. Manche machen Kulturreisen, um sich zum Beispiel auf einem der vielen Musikfeste Musik . . .
_____ 9. Andere fahren in den warmen Süden, um . . .
_____ 10. Junge Leute gehen gern . . .
_____ 11. Weil zu viele Leute zur gleichen (same) Zeit in die Ferien fahren, ist auf den Autobahnen oft alles überfüllt (overcrowded) und es gibt . . .
_____ 12. Für manche Leute ist Freizeit ein Problem, weil sie nicht wissen, was sie . . . tun sollen.

B. Ich ziehe es vor . . . (You and your roommate can never agree on anything, especially when it comes to leisure activities. Follow the model.)

BEISPIEL: Ich habe Lust, . . . (baden gehen, hier bleiben)
Ich habe Lust, baden zu gehen. Und du?
Ich ziehe es vor, hier zu bleiben.

1. Nach der Vorlesung habe ich Zeit, . . . (Tennis spielen, mein Buch lesen)
2. Mir gefällt es, . . . (durch Geschäfte bummeln und einkaufen, nichts ausgeben)
3. Ich habe Lust, diesen Sommer . . . (in den Süden fahren, nach Norwegen reisen)
4. Ich finde es schön, abends . . . (in einen Musikklub gehen, sich Musik im Radio anhören)
5. Meine Freunde und ich haben immer Lust, . . . (Windsurfen gehen, in den Bergen wandern)
6. Mir ist es wichtig, . . . (viel reisen und Leute kennen lernen, sich mit Freunden gemütlich hinsetzen)

C. Mal etwas anderes in den Ferien!

1. Wo gibt es Sprachkurse in Französisch? Wie viele Stunden sind Sie da in der Klasse und wie viele Stunden Praxis *(practice)* bekommen sie in der Woche?
2. Was kann man in der Südschweiz in den Ferien machen?
3. Wohin kann man in den Osterferien fliegen? Wo fliegt man ab? Wie viele Tage braucht man für die Rundreise und was kann man nach der Rundreise tun?
4. Wo kann man Segelfliegen lernen? Wie lange braucht ein Anfänger *(beginner)*, bevor er/sie allein fliegen kann? Von wann bis wann gibt es Intensivkurse?
5. Was für eine Farm ist Hotel Tannenhof? Was kann man da wohl *(probably)* tun?
6. Welche Ferienidee finden Sie besonders interessant? Warum?
7. Kostet es immer Geld, Spaß in den Ferien zu haben?

HÖREN SIE ZU!

Eine tolle Radtour

Zum Erkennen: im Büro *(at the office)*; das Mietfahrrad, ¨er *(rent-a-bike)*; ab·holen *(to pick up)*; die Zahnradbahn *(cogwheel-railway)*; das Panorama; die Talfahrt *(descent)*; die Fähre, -n *(ferry)*

Richtig oder falsch?

_____ 1. Weil Sabrina bei der Post arbeitet, möchte sie in den Ferien etwas ganz anderes tun.
_____ 2. Im Frühling hat sie eine Radtour um den Bodensee gemacht.
_____ 3. Sie hat diese Tour mit ihrer Familie gemacht.
_____ 4. In Lindau haben sie ihre Fahrräder abgeholt.
_____ 5. Am ersten Tag sind sie bis nach Heiden gekommen.
_____ 6. Am zweiten Tag haben sie eine schnelle Talfahrt bis an den See gehabt.
_____ 7. Die zweite Nacht haben sie in Bregenz übernachtet.
_____ 8. Am dritten Tag hat sie eine Fähre zurück nach Friedrichshafen gebracht.
_____ 9. Sie sind in den paar Tagen in drei Ländern gewesen.
_____ 10. Die Tour hat mit Übernachtungen 233 Franken gekostet.
_____ 11. Zum Mittagessen haben sie meistens nichts gegessen.
_____ 12. Mit so einer Radtour hält man sich fit.

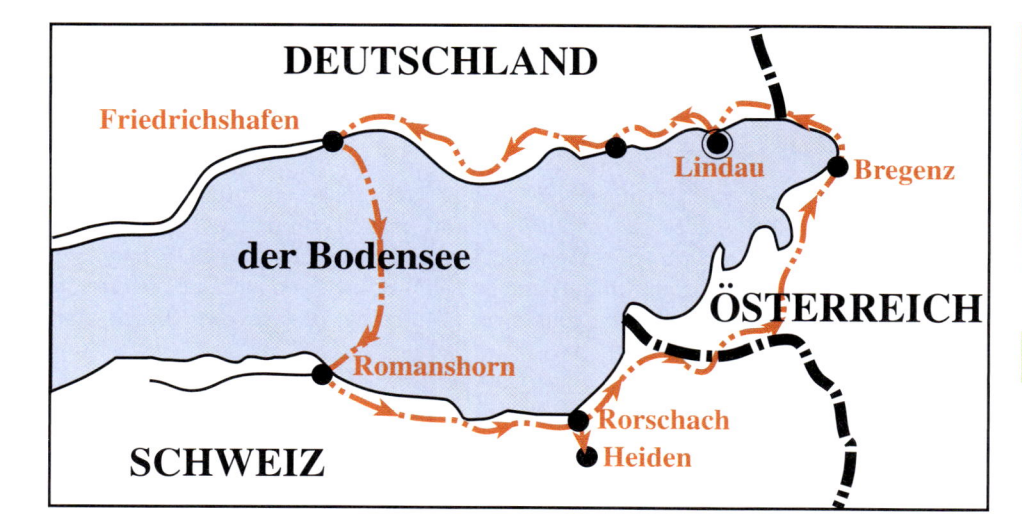

Fokus: Rose Ausländer

Rose Ausländer was one of Germany's most prominent writers of her time. Born into a Jewish family in 1907 in the German-speaking town of Czernowitz, Ukraine, she was transported to a Nazi-guarded ghetto in 1941 and emerged four years later to tell her story. After developing her writing talent during two decades of self-imposed exile in the United States, she returned to Europe in the mid-1960s to settle and publish in Düsseldorf. Themes of persecution, emigration, and loneliness marked her work, which appeared in collections of poetry: *Blinder Sommer* (1956), *Inventar* (1972), and *Ein Stück weiter* (1979), and in her outstanding volume of poetry and prose, *Ohne Visum* (1974). She died in Düsseldorf in 1988.

Noch bist du da

Wirf° deine Angst — throw
in die Luft° — air

Bald
ist deine Zeit um° — up
bald
wächst° der Himmel° — grows / sky
unter dem Gras
fallen deine Träume
ins Nirgends° — into nowhere

Noch
duftet° die Nelke° — is fragrant / carnation
singt die Drossel° — thrush (bird)
noch darfst du lieben
Worte verschenken
noch bist du da

Sei° was du bist — be
Gib was du hast

Rose Ausländer

Web-Ecke

For updates and online activities, visit the *Wie geht's?* home page at: http://www.hrwcollege.com/german/sevin/! You'll prepare a trip to Frankfurt, make hotel reservations, and plan some excursions. You can also learn about Germany's most successful soccer team, buy tickets for a game, and take a look at some online paraphernalia. Finally, you have the opportunity to do some guided Internet searching on your own, all relating, of course, to leisure-time activities.

SPRECHSITUATIONEN

Speaking on the telephone

Speaking on the telephone in a foreign language may seem scary, but with a little practice it is no more difficult than conversing in person.

When answering the phone, Germans identify themselves.

>Hier Schmidt. *(Mr./Ms. Schmidt speaking.)*
>(Hier) bei Schmidt. *(Schmidt residence.)*

When calling a business, you may hear:

>Guten Tag! Foto Albrecht, Margit *(Margit speaking)*. Wen möchten Sie sprechen?

To ask for your party, say:

>Kann ich bitte mit . . . sprechen?
>Ich möchte gern mit . . . sprechen.
>Ist . . . zu sprechen? *(May I speak to . . . ?)*

The answer might be:

>Einen Moment bitte!
>. . . ist nicht da. Kann ich ihm/ihr etwas ausrichten *(take a message)*?

At the end of a conversation you often hear:

>Auf Wiederhören! *(formal)*
>Tschüss! / Mach's gut! / Bis bald! / Bis gleich! *(informal)*

Extending an invitation[1]

>Wir möchten euch am . . . zu einer Party einladen.
>Darf ich Sie zum Essen einladen?
>Möchtest du mit uns . . . (ins Kino) gehen?
>Wir gehen . . . Willst / kannst du mitkommen?
>Wir gehen . . . Komm doch mit!
>Wir gehen . . . Wir nehmen Sie gern mit.
>Habt ihr Lust, mit uns . . . zu gehen?

Accepting an invitation

>Danke für die Einladung *(invitation)!*
>Das ist aber nett *(nice)*. Vielen Dank!
>Ja, gern.
>Prima! Wann denn?
>Sicher *(sure)!*
>Das klingt gut.

Declining an invitation

>Nein, danke. Heute kann ich nicht.
>Nein, das geht (heute) nicht. *(No, that won't work [today].)*
>Nein, ich kann leider nicht.
>Ach, es tut mir Leid . . .
>Schade, aber ich habe schon etwas vor *(planned)*.

Nein, ich habe keine Zeit / Lust.
Nein, ich bin zu müde.
Nein, ich fühle mich nicht wohl.
Nein, ich habe Kopfschmerzen.

---

[1] The forms of the pronouns and verbs depend, of course, on who the addressed person is.

Übungen

A. **Hast du Lust . . . ?** *(Working with a classmate, take turns extending invitations. Decline or accept them, depending on how they appeal to you. Use as many different expressions as you can.)*
   1. ins Kino gehen
   2. eine Vorlesung über Goethe anhören
   3. eine Oper ansehen
   4. in ein Kunstmuseum gehen
   5. am Wochenende mit dem Zug aufs Land fahren und wandern
   6. während der Semesterferien eine Reise in die Schweiz machen
   7. Skilaufen gehen
   8. sich ein Fußballspiel ansehen
   9. in ein Restaurant gehen
   10. eine Party für ein paar Freunde geben
   11. Tennis oder Golf spielen
   12. in den Park gehen und sich in die Sonne legen usw.

B. **Was tue ich gern?**

The class divides into two teams. One team thinks of a hobby, the other may ask ten (or more) questions to determine what the hobby might be. The teams alternate roles.

C. Kurzgespräche

1. Your aunt Elizabeth, who lives in Zurich, calls. You answer the phone, greet her, and ask how she and Uncle Hans are doing. She says how they are and asks about you. You tell her you've caught a cold and aren't feeling very well. She expresses her sympathy and asks whether you'd like to visit them during [spring break]. Do you want to accept? If so, your aunt says that she's glad, and she reminds you to tell her when you are going to arrive. You both say good-bye.

2. You call a travel agency, *Reisebüro Eckhardt*. An employee answers the phone and connects you with an agent. You ask the agent about trains to Zurich. He/she wants to know when you want to go. You tell him/her on [March 17]. He/she says that you need to reserve a seat (**einen Platz reservieren**). Since you will be departing for Zurich from Stuttgart, the travel agent will use the schedule on p. 219 to tell you about your options, depending on what time of day you would like to travel. You also ask him/her about the return schedule and the cost of a round-trip ticket. He/she says it costs [210 DM]; you tell him/her to reserve a seat. The agent asks when you want the tickets, and you reply that you'll come by on [Wednesday]. You both say good-bye.

Mit dem Schlitten den Berg hinunter. Das macht Spaß!

KAPITEL 10
UNTERHALTUNG

Szene aus Paul Hindemiths Oper *Cardillac*

LERNZIELE

VORSCHAU
The magic of the theater

GESPRÄCHE AND WORTSCHATZ
Entertainment

STRUKTUR
Verbs with prepositional objects
Da- and **wo-**compounds
Endings of unpreceded adjectives

EINBLICKE
German television
Choosing isn't easy.

FOKUS
German film
The world of music
The art scene
German cabaret
Wolf Biermann: "Ach, Freund, geht es nicht auch dir so?"

WEB-ECKE

SPRECHSITUATIONEN
Expressing satisfaction and dissatisfaction
Expressing anger

VORSCHAU

The Magic of the Theater

Theater plays a central role in the cultural life of Germany, Austria, and Switzerland. As in other European countries, the German government has traditionally subsidized the fine arts; but with recent budget cuts, many theater directors are beginning to rely more heavily on corporate sponsorship.

Germany has more than 400 stages, with the leading theaters in such metropolises as Berlin, Hamburg, and Munich. But even medium-sized and small cities have their own repertory theaters as well. Some date back to the 17th century, when—before Germany was united as a country—many local sovereigns founded their own court theaters. By the 19th century, a number of towns and cities had established theaters as public institutions. Theaters were, after all, a major source of entertainment.

Today theater continues to be popular. Works by William Shakespeare, Jean-Baptiste Molière, Johann Wolfgang von Goethe, Friedrich Schiller, Bertolt Brecht, Max Frisch, and Friedrich Dürrenmatt continue to draw large audiences, as do works by women authors such as Elfriede Jelinek and Gerlind Reinshagen. States and local governments subsidize tickets in public venues; and most houses offer reduced ticket prices for students, the elderly, and the unemployed. An active children's theater thrives across the country, with marionettes especially drawing delighted crowds.

Municipal theaters in medium-sized cities usually also offer ballet, musicals, and operas. Among the latter, works from the classical period still retain their popularity; opera enthusiasts flock to Mozart's *Don Giovanni, Die Zauberflöte,* and *Die Hochzeit des Figaro.* Broadway musicals have met with similar success. For example, special musical theaters are dedicated to performing British composer Andrew Lloyd Webber's *The Phantom of the Opera, Cats,* and *Starlight Express.* At the same time, German stages have supported experiments in the tradition of dance by artists such as Oskar Schlemmer, Gret Palucca, and Pina Bausch with her world-famous Wuppertal Dance Theater.

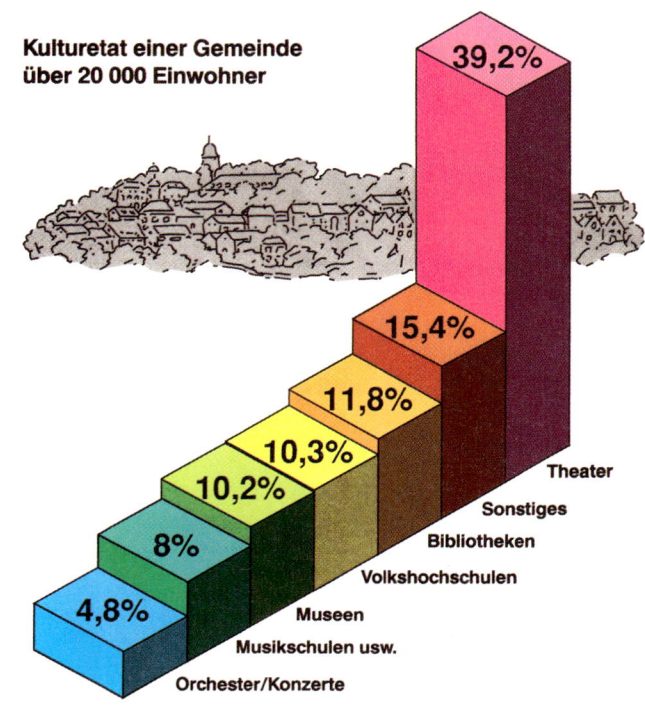

Kulturetat einer Gemeinde über 20 000 Einwohner

- 39,2% Theater
- 15,4% Sonstiges
- 11,8% Bibliotheken
- 10,3% Volkshochschulen
- 10,2% Museen
- 8% Musikschulen usw.
- 4,8% Orchester/Konzerte

Das PHANTOM der OPER — NEUE FLORA HAMBURG

GESPRÄCHE

Blick in die Zeitung

SONJA Du, was gibt's denn heute Abend im Fernsehen?
THEO Keine Ahnung. Sicher nichts Besonderes.
SONJA Mal sehen! *Die unendliche Geschichte,* einen Dokumentarfilm und einen Krimi.
THEO Dazu habe ich keine Lust.
SONJA Vielleicht gibt's 'was im Kino?
THEO Ja, *Männer, Titanic* und *Ein Herz im Winter.*
SONJA Hab' ich alle schon gesehen.
THEO Im Theater gibt's *Der kaukasische Kreidekreis,* von Brecht.
SONJA Nicht schlecht. Hast du Lust?
THEO Ja, das klingt gut. Gehen wir!

An der Theaterkasse

THEO Haben Sie noch Karten für heute Abend?
DAME Ja, erste Reihe erster Rang links und Parkett rechts.
THEO Zwei Plätze im Parkett! Hier sind unsere Studentenausweise.
DAME 20 Mark bitte!
SONJA Wann fängt die Vorstellung an?
DAME Um 20.15 Uhr.

Während der Pause

THEO Möchtest du eine Cola?
SONJA Ja, gern. Aber lass mich zahlen! Du hast schon die Programme gekauft.
THEO Na gut. Wie hat dir der erste Akt gefallen?
SONJA Prima. Ich habe das Stück schon mal in der Schule gelesen, aber noch nie auf der Bühne gesehen.
THEO Ich auch nicht.

Fragen

1. Was gibt's im Fernsehen? 2. Gefällt das Theo? 3. Hat Theo Lust, sich *Titanic* anzusehen? 4. Was gibt's im Theater? 5. Gibt es noch Karten für dieses Stück? 6. Wo sind Theos und Sonjas Plätze? 7. Wann fängt die Vorstellung an? 8. Was tun Theo und Sonja während der Pause? 9. Wer bezahlt dafür *(for it)?* 10. Woher kennt Sonja das Stück schon?

German Film

During the early days of film, the Ufa studios in Potsdam-Babelsberg were second only to Hollywood in churning out world-class productions, including such classics as *Nosferatu, Metropolis,* and *Der blaue Engel*. When the Nazis took power, film production continued, though many prominent directors and actors turned their backs on Germany, emigrating to the United States and elsewhere. After the war, those studios were taken over by Defa, whose films were subject to the approval of GDR authorities and have become a bridge to the past. Among Defa's best known films are Wolfgang Staudte's *Der Untertan* and Frank Beyer's *Jakob der Lügner*.

Beginning in the 1960s, a new wave of young West German filmmakers seized the world's attention. Directors such as Rainer Werner Fassbinder *(Die Ehe der Maria Braun)*, Werner Herzog *(Stroszek)*, Margarethe von Trotta *(Rosa Luxemburg)*, Doris Dörrie *(Männer)*, Volker Schlöndorff *(Die Blechtrommel,* based on a novel for which Günter Grass received the Nobel Prize in 1999), and Wolfgang Petersen *(Das Boot)* produced critically acclaimed movies. Many German directors continue to work closely with Hollywood. Examples are Roland Emmerich *(Independence Day),* and Wim Wenders *(Wings of Desire)*. Whereas many critics lament the domination of American blockbusters (most of which are dubbed), German film has been experiencing a renaissance. The share of domestic production has more than doubled during the 1990s. Large multiplex cinemas have sprung up in German cities to accommodate the crowds of film enthusiasts, often to the detriment of traditional art theaters *(Programmkinos)*.

Das Boot, von Wolfgang Petersen

WORTSCHATZ 1

Die Unterhaltung *(entertainment)*

der Anfang, ⸚e	*beginning, start*
Autor, -en	*author*
Chor, ⸚e	*choir*
Film, -e	*film, movie*
Komponist, -en, -en	*composer*
Krimi, -s	*detective story (book or film)*
Maler, -	*painter*
Roman, -e	*novel*
Schauspieler, -	*actor*
das Ballett, -s	*ballet*
Ende	*end*
Gemälde, -	*painting*
Konzert, -e	*concert*
Orchester, -	*orchestra*
Programm, -e	*(general) program; channel*
Stück, -e	*play, piece (of music or ballet)*
die Kunst, ⸚e	*art*
Oper, -n	*opera*
Pause, -n	*intermission, break*
Vorstellung, -en	*performance*
Werbung	*advertising*

die Zeitschrift, -en	*magazine*
Zeitung, -en	*newspaper*
dumm	*stupid, silly*
komisch	*funny (strange, comical)*
langweilig	*boring*
spannend	*exciting, suspenseful*
traurig	*sad*
an·fangen (fängt an), angefangen	*to start, begin*
an·machen / aus·machen	*to turn on / to turn off*
klatschen	*to clap, applaud*
lachen / weinen	*to laugh / to cry*
malen	*to paint*

Weiteres

am Anfang / am Ende	*in the beginning / at the end*
letzt-	*last*
Was gibt's im Fernsehen?	*What's (playing) on television?*
Keine Ahnung!	*No idea!*

Zum Erkennen: Dazu habe ich keine Lust. *(I don't feel like [doing] that.);* 'was = etwas; die Reihe, -n *(row);* im Rang *(in the balcony);* im Parkett *(in the orchestra);* der Akt, -e

Zum Thema

A. Hoppla, hier fehlt 'was! Was spielt wo und wann? *(Looking at the schedule of events listed below, find out what's playing where and when. Work with a partner. One of you looks at the chart below, the other at the corresponding one in the Appendix. First, exchange information to complete both charts. Then, decide what you'd like to see. You can also suggest a better idea at another place.)*

S1:

Wo?	Was?	Wann?
VOLKSBÜHNE		
URANIA-THEATER	**Eine Nacht in Venedig,** Operette von Johann Strauss	20.15
METROPOL-THEATER		
IM DOM	**Jedermann,** Schauspiel von Hugo von Hofmannsthal	15.00
PHILHARMONIE	**Original Wolga-Kosaken,** Lieder und Tänze	15.30
KONZERTHAUS		
KOMÖDIE	**Jahre später, gleiche Zeit,** Komödie von Bernhard Slade	16.00
KAMMERSPIELE	**Carmina Burana,** von Carl Orff	17.30
FILMBÜHNE 1		19.30
FILMBÜHNE 2		22.00

1. **BEISPIEL:** S2 Was gibt's heute in der Philharmonie?
   S1 Die Wolga-Kosaken.
   S2 Und wann?
   S1 Um halb vier . . . und im Dom gibt's . . .
   S2 O ja, wann denn?
   S1 . . .

2. **BEISPIEL:** S1 Hast du . . . schon gesehen/gehört? Das ist ein(e) . . . von . . .
   S2 Ja/Nein, . . . aber . . .
   S1 Dann hast du Lust . . . ?
   S2 . . .
   S2 Gut, . . .

B. **Wie geht's weiter?**
   1. Auf diesem Bild gehört die . . . zu einem guten Frühstück.
   2. Das ist natürlich Werbung für . . .
   3. Ich . . . *(know)* diese Zeitung (nicht).
   4. Auf dem Frühstückstisch sieht man . . .
   5. Ich esse morgens gern . . .
   6. Wenn ich Zeit habe, lese ich . . .
   7. Diese Woche liest man in den Zeitungen viel über *(about)* . . .
   8. Ich interessiere mich besonders für *(am interested in)* . . .
   9. Am . . . ist die Zeitung immer sehr dick.

C. **Allerlei Fragen**
   1. Lesen Sie gern? Sind Sie eine Leseratte *(bookworm)*? Wenn ja, was für Bücher interessieren Sie? Wie viele Bücher haben Sie in den letzten drei Monaten gelesen? Welche Autoren finden Sie besonders gut? Was für Zeitungen und Zeitschriften lesen Sie gern? Lesen Sie auch Comics?
   2. Wo kann man hier Theaterstücke, Opern oder Musicals sehen? Haben Sie dieses Jahr ein interessantes Stück oder ein gutes Musical/eine gute Oper gesehen? Wenn ja, wo und welche(s)? Wie hat es/sie Ihnen gefallen?
   3. Gehen Sie manchmal in ein Rock-, Jazz- oder Popkonzert? Mögen Sie klassische Musik? Welche Komponisten oder Musikgruppe hören Sie gern?
   4. Wer von Ihnen singt gern? Wer singt im Chor? Wer spielt im Orchester oder in einer Band? Wer von Ihnen spielt ein Instrument?
   5. Wer hat schon mal eine Rolle *(role, part)* in einem Theaterstück gespielt? Was für eine Rolle?
   6. Wie gefällt Ihnen abstrakte Kunst? Welche Maler finden Sie gut? Gehen Sie manchmal zu Kunstausstellungen *(art shows)*? Wenn ja, wo? Wessen Gemälde gefallen Ihnen (nicht)? Malen Sie auch? Wenn ja, was malen Sie gern?
   7. Was kann man hier noch zur *(for)* Unterhaltung tun?

D. **Einfach toll/furchtbar!** *(In small groups, talk about a movie, play, concert, or any kind of show that you have seen recently and discuss how you liked it.)*

E. **Mein Lieblingsplatz** *(My favorite place. Tell where you like best to relax and why. Choose from the options below or add your own.)*
   1. im Billardsalon
   2. unter einem Baum im Wald
   3. am Strand *(beach)* von . . .
   4. in meinem Zimmer
   5. bei uns im Keller
   6. im Fitnessstudio
   7. in der Bibliothek
   8. in unserer Garage
   9. vorm Computer
   10. im Café

F. **Aussprache: r, er.** Sehen Sie auch II. 9 und III. 11 in Ausspracheteil des Arbeitsheftes!
   1. [r] **r**ot, **r**osa, **r**uhig, **r**echts, **R**adio, **R**egal, **R**eihe, **R**oman, P**r**ogramm, Do**r**f, Konze**r**t, Fah**r**t, Gita**rr**e, t**r**au**r**ig, k**r**ank, He**rr**en
   2. [ʌ] Orchest**er**, Theat**er**, Mess**er**, Tell**er**, ab**er**, leid**er**, hint**er**, unt**er**, üb**er**, wied**er**, weit**er**

3. [ʌ / r] Uhr / Uhren; Ohr / Ohren; Tür / Türen; Chor / Chöre; Autor / Autoren; Klavier / Klaviere
4. Wortpaare
   a. *ring* / Ring   c. *fry* / frei   e. *tear* / Tier
   b. *Rhine* / Rhein d. *brown* / braun f. *tour* / Tour

HÖREN SIE ZU!

Biedermann und die Brandstifter

Zum Erkennen: mal eben *(just for a minute);* die Inszenierung *(production);* die Hauptrolle, -n *(leading role);* die Einladung, -en *(invitation)*

Richtig oder falsch?

_____ 1. Christians Vater hat ihm zwei Theaterkarten gegeben.
_____ 2. Christian fragt seinen Freund Daniel, ob er mitkommen möchte.
_____ 3. Die Plätze sind in der 2. Reihe vom 1. Rang.
_____ 4. Die Vorstellung beginnt um halb sieben.
_____ 5. Christian muss sich noch die Haare waschen.
_____ 6. Wenn Daniel sich beeilt, können sie noch schnell zusammen essen.
_____ 7. Sie treffen sich an der Straßenbahnhaltestelle in der Breslauerstraße.

FOKUS The World of Music

Composers from the German-speaking countries have played no small role in shaping the world of music. Johann Sebastian Bach remains the preeminent German composer. His rich work, including passions and secular concertos, is universally praised for its beauty and perfection. Other important composers of the baroque period are George Frideric Handel and Georg Philipp Telemann.

Wolfgang Amadeus Mozart, another musical genius, dominated the classical period, and Ludwig van Beethoven laid the foundations for the Romantic Movement. The final choral movement of Beethoven's Ninth Symphony, "Ode to Joy," was chosen as the European anthem. Composers Franz Schubert, Felix Mendelssohn-Bartholdy, Robert Schumann, Carl Maria von Weber, Richard Wagner, and Johannes Brahms all regarded their works as following in the tradition of Beethoven. Through the interpretation of their music, pianists like Clara Wieck (wife of Robert Schumann) and Elly Ney, violinist Anne-Sophie Mutter, and clarinetist Sabine Meyer have gained international acclaim in a previously male-dominated field.

Great innovators have also influenced the modern era. Gustav Mahler is a link between the lyrical impulse of the Romantic Movement and the more ironic attitudes of the arts in the 20th century. Richard Strauss pioneered musical drama; Paul Hindemith and Carl Orff established new standards in choral music; and Arnold Schönberg introduced the twelve-tone system of composition. Contemporary composers Bernd-Alois Zimmermann, Hans Werner Henze, and Karlheinz Stockhausen have all stretched the horizons of the avant-garde.

In der Dresdner Staatsoper

STRUKTUR

I. Verbs with prepositional objects

In both English and German a number of verbs are used together with certain prepositions. These combinations often have special idiomatic meanings.

I'm thinking of my vacation. I'm waiting for my flight.

Since the German combinations differ from English, they must be memorized.

denken an (+ *acc.*)	to think of / about
schreiben an (+ *acc.*)	to write to
warten auf (+ *acc.*)	to wait for
sich freuen auf (+ *acc.*)	to look forward to
sich ärgern über (+ *acc.*)	to get annoyed / upset about
sich informieren über (+ *acc.*)	to inform oneself / find out about
sich interessieren für (+ *acc.*)	to be interested in
erzählen von (+ *dat.*)	to tell about
halten von (+ *dat.*)	to think of, be of an opinion
sprechen von (+ *dat.*) / **über** (+ *acc.*)	to talk of / about

NOTE: In these idiomatic combinations, two-way prepositions most frequently take the accusative.

Er denkt an seine Reise.	*He's thinking about his trip.*
Sie schreibt an ihre Eltern.	*She's writing to her parents.*
Ich warte auf ein Telefongespräch.	*I'm waiting for a phone call.*
Freut ihr euch aufs Wochenende?	*Are you looking forward to the weekend?*
Ich ärgere mich über den Brief.	*I'm upset about the letter.*
Informier dich über das Programm!	*Find out about the program.*
Interessierst du dich für Sport?	*Are you interested in sports?*
Erzählt von euerem Flug!	*Tell about your flight.*
Was hältst du denn von dem Film?	*What do you think of the movie?*
Sprecht ihr von *Stadt der Engel*?	*Are you talking about* City of Angels?

CAUTION: In these idiomatic combinations, **an, auf, über,** etc., are not separable prefixes, but prepositions followed by nouns or pronouns in the appropriate cases:

Ich **rufe** dich morgen **an.**	BUT	Ich **denke an** dich.
I'll call you tomorrow.		*I'm thinking of you.*

Note also these two different uses of **auf**:

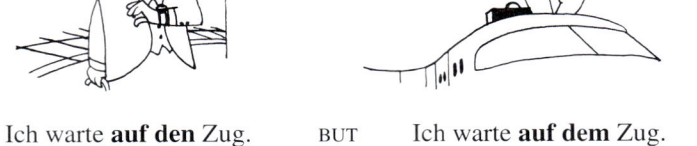

Ich warte **auf den** Zug.   BUT   Ich warte **auf dem** Zug.
For what? For the train.   *Where? On (top of) the train.*

Übungen

A. Sagen Sie es noch einmal! Ersetzen Sie *(replace)* die Hauptwörter!

BEISPIEL: Sie warten auf den Zug. (Telefongespräch)
Sie warten auf das Telefongespräch.

1. Wir interessieren uns für Kunst. (Sport, Musik)
2. Er spricht von seinem Urlaub. (Bruder, Hobbys)
3. Sie erzählt von ihrem Flug. (Familie, Geburtstag)
4. Ich denke an seinen Brief. (Ansichtskarte, Name)
5. Wartest du auf deine Familie? (Gäste, Freund)
6. Freut ihr euch auf das Ballett? (Vorstellung, Konzert)
7. Ich habe mich über das Wetter geärgert. (Junge, Leute)
8. Was haltet ihr von der Idee? (Gemälde, Maler)

B. Die Afrikareise. Was fehlt?

1. Meine Tante hat _____ mein_____ Vater geschrieben. 2. Sie will uns _____ ihr_____ Reise durch Afrika erzählen. 3. Wir freuen uns _____ ihr_____ Besuch *(m.)*. 4. Meine Tante interessiert sich sehr _____ Afrika. 5. Sie spricht hier im Museum _____ ihr_____ Fahrten. 6. Sie malt auch gern und ist _____ Kunst gut informiert. 7. Ich denke gern _____ sie. 8. Mein Vater ärgert sich _____ sie, wenn sie nicht schreibt. 9. Sie hält einfach nicht viel _____ Briefen und sie hat keinen Computer, aber sie ruft uns manchmal an.

C. Was tun Sie? *(Working in groups of two or three, complete each sentence. Then ask your partners "Und du?" until everyone has had a chance to answer each question.)*

1. Ich denke oft . . .
2. Ich warte . . .
3. Ich schreibe gern . . .
4. Ich interessiere mich . . .
5.
6. Ich freue mich . . .
7. Ich ärgere mich manchmal . . .
8. Ich spreche gern . . .
9. Ich halte nicht viel . . .

D. Die Kunstausstellung *(art show).* Auf Deutsch bitte!

1. I am looking forward to the art show. 2. Have you found out about the tickets? 3. We have talked about the show, but then I didn't think of the date. 4. Please don't wait for me *(pl. fam.)*, but go without me. 5. You *(pl. fam.)* know I'm not interested in arts. 6. Why do you get so upset about this painter? 7. I'm not upset, but I know this painter and don't think much of his paintings. 8. The whole town is talking about him. 9. You *(pl. fam.)* can tell me about him afterwards.

The Art Scene

As in other parts of Europe, early painting in the German-speaking countries was devoted to religious works, especially altar pieces. In the 16th century, Albrecht Dürer became the first important portrait painter; he also developed landscape painting and is regarded as the inventor of etching. His contemporaries include Lucas Cranach and Hans Holbein. Although painting followed the trends of western European art, it did not reach another high point until the 19th century. Caspar David Friedrich's landscapes are representative of the romantic era. Following the Congress of Vienna came the Biedermeier period with its idyllic settings, and towards the turn of the century the Viennese Secession (or **Jugendstil**), with Gustav Klimt.

Early 20th-century artists conveyed the fears and dangers of the times through expressionism. Two examples are Oskar Kokoschka, who reflected the anxious, decadent atmosphere of prewar Vienna, and Paul Klee, who ventured into abstract art. Others, including Käthe Kollwitz, Max Beckmann, and Otto Dix, exercised sharp social criticism through their sculptures and canvasses. The rise of the Nazis, who denounced most modern art as "degenerate," put an abrupt end to this creative period. In the second half of the century, Germany's art scene again came alive, with representatives like Joseph Beuys, who turned visual art into action, Rebecca Horn, who presents sculptures as performances, and Markus Lüpertz, whose representational painting wants to convey a "drunken, rapturous" feeling of life.

Maske, von Paul Klee

II. *Da-* and *wo-*compounds

1. **Da-**Compounds

    In English, pronouns following prepositions can refer to people, things, or ideas:

    > *I'm coming with him.*   *I'm coming with it.*

    In German, this is not the case; pronouns following prepositions refer only to people:

    > Ich komme **mit ihm (mit meinem Freund).**

    If you wish to refer to a thing or an idea, you must use a **da**-COMPOUND.

    > Ich komme **damit (mit unserem Auto).**

    Most accusative and dative prepositions (except **außer, ohne,** and **seit**) can be made into **da-**compounds. If the preposition begins with a vowel (**an, in,** etc.), it is used with **dar-:**

dafür	*for it (them)*	**darauf**	*on it (them)*
dagegen	*against it (them)*	**darin**	*in it (them)*
damit	*with it (them)*	**darüber**	*above/about it (them)*
danach	*after it (them)*	usw.	

    Können Sie mir sagen, wo ein Briefkasten ist?—Ja, sehen Sie die Kirche dort? **Daneben** ist eine Apotheke, **dahinter** ist die Post und **davor** ist ein Briefkasten mit einem Posthorn **darauf.**

2. **Wo**-compounds

The interrogative pronouns **wer, wen,** and **wem** refer to people.

| **Von wem** sprichst du? | About whom are you talking? (Who are you talking about?) |
| **Auf wen** wartet ihr? | For whom are you waiting? (Who are you waiting for?) |

In questions about things or ideas, **was** is used. If a preposition is involved, however, a **wo**-compound is required. Again, if the preposition begins with a vowel, it is combined with **wor-**.

wofür?	for what?	worauf?	on what?
wogegen?	against what?	worüber?	above, about what?
womit?	with what?	usw.	

| **Wovon** sprichst du? | About what are you talking? (What are you talking about?) |
| **Worauf** wartet ihr? | For what are you waiting? (What are you waiting for?) |

REMEMBER: To ask where something is located, use the question word **wo,** regardless of the answer expected: **Wo ist Peter?** To ask where someone is going, use **wohin** (NOT wo combined with nach or zu!): **Wohin ist Peter gegangen?** To ask where a person is coming from, use **woher** (NOT wo combined with aus or von!): **Woher kommt Peter?**

Übungen

E. Wo ist die Brille? *(Remind your roommate, who is very careless, where he/she can find his/her glasses. Use a **da**-compound.)*

BEISPIEL: auf dem Sofa
            Sie liegt darauf.

neben dem Bett, vor dem Telefon, hinter der Lampe, auf dem Kassettenrecorder, in der Tasche, unter den Photos, zwischen den Zeitungen und Zeitschriften, . . .

F. Noch einmal bitte! *(Replace the phrases in boldface with a preposition and a pronoun or with a **da**-compound. Always consider whether the sentence deals with a person or with an object or idea.)*

BEISPIEL: Hans steht **neben Christa.**
            Hans steht neben ihr.

            Die Lampe steht **neben dem Klavier.**
            Die Lampe steht daneben.

1. Was machst du **nach den Ferien?**
2. Bist du auch **mit dem Bus** gefahren?
3. Er hat das Gemälde **für seine Frau** gekauft.
4. Was hast du **gegen Skilaufen?**
5. Das Paket ist **von meinen Eltern** gewesen.
6. Die Karten liegen **auf dem Tisch.**
7. Die Kinder haben **hinter der Garage** gespielt.
8. Anja hat **zwischen Herrn Fiedler und seiner Frau** gesessen.
9. Was halten Sie **von dem Haus?**
10. Ist die Faxnummer **im Adressbuch?**
11. Wir denken oft **an unseren kranken Freund.**
12. Freust du dich auch so **auf unsere Fahrt?**

G. **Das Klassentreffen** (The class reunion. You are reporting to your grandma/grandpa about a recent reunion. As she/he is a little hard of hearing, she/he will ask you to repeat each statement. Use the chart to report about Horst, Max, and Eva; then switch roles, and respond as your partner tells you about Claire, Gerd, and Elke.)

S1:

	Horst	**Claire**	**Max + Eva**	**Gerd + Elke**
sprechen über	Sport	Arbeit	Familie	Schulzeit
denken an	Golfspielen	Mittagspause	Urlaub	Vergangenheit (*f., past*)
schreiben an	Golftrainer	Freunde	Reisebüro	Schulfreunde
warten auf	Freundin	Post	Antwort	Klassentreffen (*n.*)
s. freuen auf	jedes Spiel	Besuch	Seereise	Wiedersehen
s. interessieren für	nichts anderes	Kunst	Sprachen	alles
s. informieren über	Wetter	Ausstellungen	Städte in Amerika	Lehrer
s. ärgern über	jeden Fehler	Boss	Kinder	Essen

BEISPIEL:
S1 Claire spricht über die Arbeit.
S2 Worüber spricht Claire?
S1 Über die Arbeit.
S1 Claire ärgert sich über ihren Boss.
S2 Über wen ärgert sie sich?
S1 Über ihren Boss.

H. **Nur neugierig** (*just curious*). Auf Deutsch bitte!
1. a. She's sitting next to them (i.e., their friends). b. They have two presents, one (**eins**) for her and one for him. c. Do you (*sg. fam.*) see the chair? The presents are lying on it. d. What's in them? e. Is that for me? f. What does one do with it? g. What do you (*sg. fam.*) think of it? h. Don't (*sg. fam.*) sit down on it.
2. a. Who is he coming with (With whom . . .)? b. What are they talking about? c. What are you (*sg. fam.*) thinking of? d. Who is he waiting for (For whom . . .)? e. What are you (*pl. fam.*) annoyed about? f. What is she interested in? g. Who are you (*sg. fam.*) writing to (to whom . . .)? h. Who is this present for (For whom . . .)?

> **Wer weiß schon genau, woraus ein Hamburger besteht?**

III. Endings of unpreceded adjectives

You already know how to deal with adjectives preceded by either **der-** or **ein-**words. Occasionally, however, adjectives are preceded by neither; they are then called UNPRECEDED ADJECTIVES. The equivalent in English would be adjectives preceded by neither *the* nor *a(n)*:

We bought fresh fish and fresh eggs.

1. Unpreceded adjectives take the endings that the definite article would have, if it were used.

| der frische Fisch | das frische Obst | die frische Wurst | die frischen Eier |
| frischer Fisch | frisches Obst | frische Wurst | frische Eier |

	masculine	**neuter**	**feminine**	**plural**
nom.	frischer Fisch	frisches Obst	frische Wurst	frische Eier
acc.	frischen Fisch	frisches Obst	frische Wurst	frische Eier
dat.	frischem Fisch	frischem Obst	frischer Wurst	frischen Eiern
gen.[1]	(frischen Fisches)	(frischen Obstes)	(frischer Wurst)	frischer Eier

---

[1] The genitive singular forms are relatively rare, and the masculine and neuter forms of the genitive are irregular.

Heute Abend gibt es heiße Suppe, holländischen Käse, frische Brötchen und frisches Obst.

- If there are several unpreceded adjectives, all have the same ending.

Ich wünsche dir schöne, interessante Ferien.

2. Several important words are often used as unpreceded adjectives in the plural:

andere	*other*
einige	*some, a few (pl. only)*
mehrere	*several (pl. only)*
viele	*many*
wenige	*few*

Wir haben uns mehrere moderne Gemälde angesehen.

Sie haben einigen jungen Leuten gefallen, aber mir nicht.

- Usually neither **viel** *(much)* nor **wenig** *(little, not much)* has an ending in the singular, but these words are often used as unpreceded adjectives in the plural.

Viele Studenten haben **wenig** Geld, aber nur **wenige** Studenten haben **viel** Zeit.

- Numerals, **mehr,** and **ein paar** have no endings. The same holds true for a few colors, such as *purple* and *pink* (**lila, rosa**), and adjectives like **Frankfurter, Berliner, Schweizer,** etc.

Da sind **drei** junge **Wiener** Studenten mit **ein paar** kurzen Fragen.

Haben Sie noch **mehr** graues oder blaues Papier?

Was mache ich mit diesem alten **rosa** Pullover?

Übungen

I. Ersetzen Sie die Adjektive!

BEISPIEL: Das sind nette Leute. (verrückt)
Das sind verrückte Leute.

1. Ich trinke gern schwarzen Kaffee. (heiß, frisch)
2. Sie braucht dünnes Papier. (billig, weiß)

3. Er schreibt tolle Bücher. (spannend, lustig)
4. Heute haben wir wunderbares Wetter. (ausgezeichnet, furchtbar)
5. Dort gibt es gutes Essen. (einfach, gesund)
6. Hier bekommen wir frischen Fisch. (wunderbar, gebacken)
7. Er hat oft verrückte Ideen. (dumm, fantastisch)

J. Sagen Sie es noch einmal! *(Omit the **der-** or **ein-**word preceding the adjective.)*

BEISPIEL: Der holländische Käse ist ausgezeichnet.
Holländischer Käse ist ausgezeichnet.

1. Die deutschen Zeitungen haben auch viel Werbung.
2. Der Mann will mit dem falschen Geld bezahlen.
3. Sie hat das frische Brot gekauft.
4. Er hat den schwarzen Kaffee getrunken.
5. Wir haben die braunen Eier genommen.
6. Er ist mit seinen alten Tennisschuhen auf die Party gegangen.
7. Sie trinken gern das dunkle Bier.
8. Auf der Party haben sie diese laute Musik gespielt.
9. Er erzählt gern solche traurigen Geschichten.
10. Sie hat Bilder der bekannten Schauspieler.

K. Ein Brief an Freunde: Was fehlt?

Lieb_____ Gudrun, lieb_____ Bill! 1. Seit gestern bin ich mit ein paar ander_____ Studenten in Dresden. 2. Eine wunderbar_____ Stadt mit alt_____ Tradition *(f.)*! 3. Im Zentrum gibt es viel_____ schön_____ Gebäude mit barock_____ Fassaden *(pl.)*. 4. Die Ruine der Frauenkirche erinnert an *(reminds of)* furchtbar_____ Zeiten. 5. Bis zum Jahr 2006 will man sie mit alt_____ und neu_____ Steinen wieder aufgebaut haben *(rebuilt)*. 6. Gestern haben wir zwei alt_____ Dresdener kennen gelernt. 7. Sie haben uns einige interessant_____ Geschichten aus alt_____ und neu_____ Zeit erzählt. 8. Mit ihnen sind wir abends an der Elbe entlang gelaufen, mit herrlich_____ Blick auf *(m.)* die Stadt. 9. Danach haben wir bei „Watzke's" gegessen, einer alt_____ Brauerei *(brewery)* mit gut_____ Atmosphäre *(f.)* und gut_____ Bier. 10. Für heute Abend haben wir billig_____ Karten für die Oper bekommen. Wie ihr seht, es geht mir gut. Viele Grüße! Eure Anne

L. Was ich gern mache. *(Working in small groups, complete the sentences. Be sure to include an unpreceded adjective. Then ask "**Und du?**")*

BEISPIEL: Ich singe gern . . .
Ich singe gern alte Lieder.

1. Ich esse gern . . .
2. Ich trinke gern . . .
3. Ich sammle gern . . .
4. Ich lese gern . . .
5. Ich trage gern . . .
6. Ich sehe gern . . .
7. Ich finde . . . prima.
8. Ich möchte . . .

Zusammenfassung

M. Bilden Sie ganze Sätze!
1. wie lange / du / warten / — / ich? *(pres. perf.)*
2. ich / sich freuen / — / Reise nach Spanien *(pres.)*
3. er / sich ärgern / — / Film *(pres. perf.)*
4. wo- / ihr / sich interessieren? *(pres.)*
5. wollen / sich kaufen / du / einig- / deutsch / Zeitschriften? *(pres.)*
6. in London / wir / sehen / mehrer- / interessant / Stücke *(pres. perf.)*
7. während / Pause / wir / trinken / billig / Sekt *(pres. perf.)*
8. Renate / schon / lesen / ein paar / spannend / Krimi *(pres. perf.)*
9. am Ende / viel / modern / Stücke / Leute / nicht / klatschen / lange *(pres.)*

N. Interessanter Besuch. Auf Deutsch bitte!

1. Two weeks ago an old friend of my father visited us. 2. He is the author of several plays. 3. I'm very interested in the theater. 4. He knows many important people, also some well-known actresses. 5. Our friend knows many other authors. 6. He spoke about them. 7. He told us some exciting stories. 8. He has just been to **(in)** Vienna. 9. He saw several performances of his new play and bought a few expensive books. 10. He's coming back in the summer. 11. We are looking forward to that. 12. We have also bought him some new novels.

EINBLICKE

German Television

German public television and radio are run by independent public corporations. The main channels are ARD (or **1. Programm**) and ZDF (or **2. Programm**). Together they produce a third regional channel that concentrates on regional affairs and educational programming. Since 1985 these public corporations have been participating in additional ventures, for example, in 3-SAT, a ZDF joint venture with the Swiss and Austrian broadcasting corporations. Public broadcasting gets most of its funding from fees that owners of radios and television sets are required to pay. Revenues from advertising are becoming increasingly important.

The two major private German television networks are RTL and SAT-1, which show mainly sports, entertainment, and feature films. Other private broadcasters include TELE-5, PRO-7, DSF, FAB, ARTE, VOX, the KABELKANAL, and the all-news channel N-TV. Their programs are transmitted by satellite and cable but can also be received over regular frequencies. These broadcasters are operated by consortia—mostly publishing companies—and advertising is their sole source of revenue. Recently the future of digital television has become a point of contention among German broadcasters.

WORTSCHATZ 2

der Ausländer, -	*foreigner*
Bürger, -	*citizen*
Zuschauer, -	*viewer, spectator*
das Fernsehen	*television (the medium)*
die Auswahl (an + *acc.*)	*selection, choice (of)*
Nachricht, -en	*news (usually pl. on radio and television)*
Sendung, -en[1]	*(particular) program*
also	*in other words*
etwa	*about, approximately*
monatlich (täglich, wöchentlich)	*monthly (daily, weekly)*
öffentlich / privat	*public / private*
verschieden	*different (kinds of), various*
vor allem	*mainly, especially, above all*
weder . . . noch	*neither . . . nor*

Auf jeder Reise ist man Ausländer

---

[1] Note the difference between **das Programm** and **die Sendung** as they refer to television: **das Programm** refers to a *general program* or *channel* (Was gibt's **im Abendprogramm? im 1. Programm?**). **Die Sendung** refers to a *particular program* (Ich sehe mir gern diese **Kultursendung** an).

Vorm Lesen

A. Statistiken über junge Deutsche (Read what young Germans have to say about the influence of the mass media in their lives. Where do you and your compatriots fit in? Note: for %, read **Prozent**.)

Wie viele Stunden sehen Sie jeden Tag fern?	Kein TV 1–2 Stunden 2–4 Stunden 4–6 Stunden	3% 42% 28% 5%
Wie viele Videos sehen Sie pro Woche?	Kein Video 1–2 Videos 3–5 Videos	46% 42% 10%
Wie oft sehen Sie die Nachrichten im Fernsehen?	Täglich Manchmal Nie	39% 23% 4%
Wie oft lesen Sie eine Tageszeitung?	Täglich Manchmal Nie	42% 26% 7%

Gibt es zu viel Sex im Fernsehen und im Kino oder zu wenig?	Zu viel Zu wenig Genau richtig	38% 13% 48%
Gibt es zu viel Gewalt (crime) im Fernsehen und im Kino?	Zu viel Zu wenig Genau richtig	71% 4% 25%
Wie viele Bücher haben Sie in den letzten drei Monaten gelesen?	kein Buch 1–2 Bücher 3+ Bücher	41% 33% 25%

1. Wie vergleicht sich das (does that compare) zu Ihnen persönlich, zu Ihren Freunden und Ihren Mitbürgern? Kommentieren Sie!
2. Haben Sie einen Computer? Was tun Sie vor allem damit? Haben Sie E-Mail? Wie viele E-Mails pro Tag müssen Sie beantworten? Finden Sie das gut?
3. Können Sie ans Internet? Wenn ja, welche Rolle spielt das Internet in Ihrem Leben? Wie viele Stunden pro Tag sitzen Sie am Computer und surfen Sie im Internet? Was interessiert Sie darin besonders und was nicht?

B. Was ist das?

der Haushalt, Kritiker, Medienmarkt; das Kabarett, Kabelprogramm, Satellitenprogramm; die Buchproduktion, Interessengruppe, Kreativität, Tagespresse; finanzieren, präsentieren, registrieren; experimentell, finanziell, informativ, kulturell, passiv, politisch, staatlich kontrolliert, unterhaltend

Wer die Wahl hat, hat die Qual°.

Choosing isn't easy (lit.: it's a pain).

Wie überall spielen die Massenmedien, vor allem das Fernsehen, auch in Deutschland eine wichtige Rolle. Fast jeder Haushalt hat heute einen oder zwei Fernseher und die Auswahl an Sendungen ist groß und wird jedes Jahr größer°. Zu den Hauptprogrammen kommen Programme aus Nachbarländern und auch privates Fernsehen und interessante Kabel- und Satellitenprogramme. Die privaten Sender° leben natürlich von der Werbung. Aber um das öffentliche Fernsehen zu finanzieren, müssen die Deutschen ihre Fernseher und Radios bei der Post registrieren und monatliche Gebühren° zahlen. Werbung gibt es auch, aber nicht nach acht Uhr abends und selten während Filmsendungen. Sie kommt vor allem vor dem Abendprogramm und dauert fünf bis zehn Minuten. Damit° die Leute den Fernseher dann nicht einfach ausmachen, muss die Werbung natürlich unterhaltend sein.

Das öffentliche Fernsehen ist weder staatlich noch privat kontrolliert, sondern finanziell und politisch unabhängig°. Darum kann es auch leicht Sendungen für kleine Interessengruppen bringen, z. B. Nachrichten in verschiedenen Sprachen, Sprachunterricht° für Ausländer, experimentelle Musik, politische Diskussionen und lokales Kabarett. Das deutsche Fernsehen präsentiert eigentlich eine gute Mischung von° aktuellem° Sport und leichter Unterhaltung,

bigger

stations

fees

so that

independent

. . . instruction

mixture of / current

von informativen Dokumentarfilmen, internationalen Filmen und kulturellen Sendungen, z. B. Theaterstücken, Opern und Konzerten.

Manche Kritiker halten nicht viel vom Fernsehen. Sie ärgern sich zum Beispiel darüber, dass so viele amerikanische Filme und Seifenopern° laufen, obwohl die Statistiken zeigen, dass sich die Zuschauer dafür interessieren. Neben guten und informativen Kultursendungen sind auch spannende Filme mit Sex und Gewalt gefragt°. Aber nicht nur darin sehen die Kritiker Probleme, sondern auch in der passiven Rolle der Zuschauer. Manche Menschen, vor allem Kinder, sitzen viel zu lang vorm Fernseher. Sie werden dadurch passiv und verlieren an° Kreativität.

Trotz der Auswahl an Programmen muss das Fernsehen mit vielen anderen Medien konkurrieren°. Das Radio ist weiterhin° wichtig, denn man hört im Durchschnitt täglich zwei Stunden Radio und liest gern dabei. Viele Deutsche sind Leseratten. Die Tagespresse verkauft täglich über 30 Millionen Exemplare°. Dazu kommen fast 9 000 Zeitschriften und die zwei großen Nachrichtenmagazine *Der Spiegel* und *Focus*. Man liest auch gern Bücher. Die Buchproduktion steht international nach den USA am zweiten Platz. Mehr als° 600 000 Titel sind auf dem Markt und jedes Jahr kommen etwa 70 000 Erst- und Neuauflagen° dazu.

Wie sich das Internet auf die Rolle des Medienmarktes auswirkt°, ist die große Frage. Denn auch diese moderne Technik konkurriert um° die Zeit der Bürger. Die Menschen haben heute eine enorme Auswahl, woher sie ihre Informationen bekommen und womit sie ihre Freizeit ausfüllen. Diese Wahl ist nicht immer leicht. Ja, wer die Wahl hat, hat die Qual.

soap operas

popular

lose in

compete / still

copies

more than
new editions
effects
competes for

Zum Text

A. Richtig oder falsch? Wenn falsch, sagen Sie warum!

_____ 1. In Deutschland spielt das Fernsehen keine wichtige Rolle.
_____ 2. Nur wenige Haushalte haben einen Fernseher.
_____ 3. Die Auswahl an Sendungen ist groß.
_____ 4. Weil die Deutschen monatliche Gebühren zahlen, gibt es im privaten Fernsehen keine Werbung.
_____ 5. Werbung läuft im öffentlichen Fernsehen nie nach sechs Uhr abends.
_____ 6. Das öffentliche Fernsehen ist staatlich kontrolliert.
_____ 7. Es hat eine gute Mischung von verschiedenen Sendungen.
_____ 8. Manche Kritiker ärgern sich über zu viele deutsche Filme.
_____ 9. Sie denken auch, dass zu viel Fernsehen die Leute passiv macht.
_____ 10. Wie überall muss das Fernsehen mit anderen Medien konkurrieren.
_____ 11. Dazu gehören das Radio, Zeitungen, Zeitschriften und Bücher.
_____ 12. Wegen des Internets haben die Deutschen keine Zeit mehr fürs Fernsehen.

B. Was fehlt? Geben Sie die fehlenden Präpositionen!

1. Der Lesetext spricht _____ Deutschlands Massenmedien. 2. Wenn wir in Nordamerika fernsehen, denken wir nur _____ mögliche Kabelgebühren, aber nicht _____ Fernsehgebühren. Die Deutschen müssen _____ denken. 3. Sie ärgern sich oft _____ diese Gebühren, aber sie können nichts _____ *(against it)* tun. Sie haben keine Wahl. 4. Viele interessieren sich nicht nur _____ leichte Unterhaltung, sondern auch _____ informative Dokumentarfilme. 5. Andere warten jeden Abend _____ Nachrichten. 6. Sie freuen sich auch hier und da _____ ein Theaterstück oder ein Konzert. 7. Die großen Nachrichtenmagazine sprechen nicht nur _____ Politik, sondern auch _____ Kultur und Sport. 8. Manche Leute sitzen täglich am Computer, um sich _____ alles gut zu informieren. 9. Sie stellen Fragen _____ andere Leute im Internet und warten dann _____ ihre Antwort. 10. Ich halte nicht viel _____ Fernsehen. 11. Ich bin eine Leseratte und freue mich _____ mein nächstes *(next)* Buch. 12. _____ interessieren Sie sich, für Fernsehen, Zeitungen oder Bücher?

> Nur wer
> kritische Leser hat,
> macht eine
> gute Zeitung.
>
> Süddeutsche Zeitung

Der erste Shopping Guide fürs virtuelle Kaufhaus.
http://www.stern.de

C. Womit? Damit! Stellen Sie Fragen mit einem **wo**-Wort und antworten Sie mit einem **da**-Wort oder einer Präposition mit Pronomen!

BEISPIEL: Das deutsche Fernsehen ist unabhängig **von der Werbung.**
Wovon ist es unabhängig? — **Davon!**
Die Werbung ist abhängig **von den Käufern.**
Von wem ist sie abhängig? — **Von ihnen!**

1. Einige Kritiker halten nicht viel **vom Fernsehen.** 2. Vor allem ärgern sie sich **über die vielen amerikanischen Serien.** 3. Sie sprechen **über die Zuschauer.** 4. Sie warten jede Woche **auf die Fortsetzung** *(continuation).* 5. Diese Kritiker denken auch **an die Kinder.** 6. **Durch zu viel Fernsehen und zu viel Musik** verlieren sie an Kreativität. 7. **Fürs Hobby** haben sie oft keine Zeit.

D. Deutsches Fernsehen. Geben Sie die Adjektivendungen, wo nötig *(necessary)*!

1. Das deutsch____ Fernsehen ist eine gut____ Mischung von kulturell____ Sendungen und leicht____ Unterhaltung. 2. Man bekommt auch viel____ interessant____ Sendungen aus verschieden____ Nachbarländern. 3. Das öffentlich____ Fernsehen finanziert man durch monatlich____ Gebühren. 4. Öffentlich____ Sender *(pl.)* haben natürlich auch öffentlich____ Aufgaben. 5. Sie können leicht verschieden____ Sendungen für klein____ Interessengruppen bringen, z. B. international____ Nachrichten in verschieden____ Sprachen oder auch lokal____ Kabarett *(n.).* 6. Privat____ Fernsehen gibt es auch. 7. Diese klein____ Sender sind natürlich abhängig von viel____ Werbung. 8. Beim privat____ Fernsehen kann man auch viel____ amerikanisch____ Filme sehen. 9. Kritiker sprechen von schlecht____ Qualität beim privat____ Fernsehen. 10. Viele Deutsche sind groß____ Leseratten. 11. Sie lesen alles, was ihnen in die Hände fällt, von lokal____ Nachrichten und lokal____ Werbung bis zu intellektuell____ *(intellectual)* Nachrichtenmagazinen. 12. Sie hören aber auch gern Radio, von leicht____ bis zu klassisch____ Musik.

E. Was gibt's im Fernsehen? Sehen Sie aufs Programm auf Seite 283 und beantworten Sie die Fragen darüber!
1. Von wann bis wann ist (morgens) das gemeinsame *(joint)* Programm von ARD und ZDF?
2. Wann gibt es Nachrichten im 1. Programm **(die Tagesschau)?** im 2. Programm **(Heute)?** auf Englisch? auf Französisch?
3. Wo und wann gibt es eine Sendung über Sport und Gesundheit? über Hobbys, Freizeit und Reisen? Geschichte?
4. Worüber diskutieren Frauen in der Sendung um halb acht im 2. Programm? **(der Beruf** *profession, work)*
5. Worüber sind die Sendungen um elf Uhr und halb zwölf im 3. Programm? Um Viertel vor sechs im RTL und um Mitternacht im 2. Programm?
6. Was für amerikanische Filme finden Sie auf dem Programm? Was für deutsche Filme?
7. Was halten Sie von diesen Sendungen im deutschen Fernsehen?

UNTERHALTUNG

1. PROGRAMM ARD | 2. PROGRAMM ZDF
10. April DI

1. PROGRAMM

tagsüber

Das gemeinsame Programm von ARD und ZDF bis 13.45 Uhr:
- **9.00** Tagesschau
- **9.03** Unter der Sonne Kaliforniens
  Eine neue Familie (Wh. v. 1989)
- **9.45** Sport treiben – fit bleiben
- **10.00** Tagesschau
- **10.03** Gesundheitsmagazin Praxis
  Zum Weltgesundheitstag: "Handeln Sie jetzt!" Wo denn, wie denn, was denn? / Der unnötige Schmerz. Von Marlene Linke (Wh. vom 5. April)
- **10.50** Mosaik-Ratschläge
  Ostereier aus aller Welt – Färbemittel / Hasentreffen in Stuttgart
- **11.00** Tagesschau
- **11.03** Fantomas
  2. Teil: Tödliche Umarmung (Wh.) Ist Doktor Chaleck der geheimnisumwitterte Serienmörder Fantomas? Inspektor Juve findet im Haus des Arztes die Leiche einer Frau.
  3. Teil: nächsten Dienstag
- **12.30** Umschau
- **12.55** Presseschau
- **13.00** Tagesschau
- **13.05** ARD-Mittagsmagazin

3. PROGRAMM

- **9.50** Tele-Gymnastik (27)
- **10.00** News of the week
- **10.15** Actualités
- **10.30** Avanti! Avanti!
  Italienisch-Kurs (16)
- **11.00** Wer hat Angst vorm kleinen Chip?
  Mikroelektronik: Verwandelt
- **11.30** Computerclub (5)
- **12.15** Reiseführer Die Borinage: Auf den Spuren des niederländischen Malers Vincent van Gogh
- **13.00** Telekolleg II
  Deutsch (31): Das Buch des Lebens – Der Roman
- **13.30** Telekolleg II
  Mathematik, Trigonometrie
- **17.00** Ferntourismus am Beispiel Kenias
  Bericht. Letzter Teil: Hakuna Matata: Schönes Kenia – Keine Probleme?
- **17.30** Schüler machen Filme

RTL

- **16.25** Snoopy Zeichentrickfilm
- **17.45** Kunst und Botschaft Rembrandt »Josephs Traum im Stall« (1645)
- **17.50** Dirty Dancing Serie
  Gefährliche Gefühle
- **18.15** Dr. Who Serie
  Delta und die Bannermänner
- **18.45** RTL aktuell Nachrichten, Sport
- **19.00** Airwolf Serie
  Dem Wolf eine Falle stellen
- **19.50** Der Hammer Serie

SAT 1

- **21.00** Der junge Löwe
  Die Lebensgeschichte des Politikers Winston Churchill (1874–1965)
- **23.15** SAT 1-blick Berichte vom Tage
- **23.25** Grimms Märchen von [90] lüsternen Pärchen
  Spielfilm, Bundesrepublik 1969

2. PROGRAMM

- **13.00** Tennis:
  Grand-Prix-Turniere
  Grand-Prix der Damen in Hamburg. Reporter: Hans-Jürgen Pohmann
- **18.00** Sesamstraße
  Für Kinder im Vorschulalter
- **18.30** flicflac
  Magazin für Freizeit

abends

- **19.00** heute
- **19.30** Doppelpunkt
  "Baby oder Beruf?"
  Junge Frauen diskutieren über ihre Entscheidungen und Erfahrungen
  Moderation: Barbara Stöckl
  ▶ Siehe auch rechts
- **20.15** Der Club der toten Dichter
  US-Spielfilm von 1988
  deutsch / englisch
  John Keating .... Robin Williams
  Neil Perry . Robert Sean Leonard
  Todd Anderson ....Ethan Hawke
  Knox Overstreet ...Josh Charles
  Charlie Dalton ......Gale Hansen
  Richard Cameron . Dylan Kussman
  Steven Meeks . Allelon Ruggiero
  Gerard Pitts ...James Waterston
  Mr. Nolan .... Norman Lloyd
  Mr. Perry ....Kurtwood Smith
  Regie: Peter Weir
  Deutsche Fernsehpremiere
  "Ein Film, in dem sich Humor, Abenteuerlust, Tragik und revolutionärer Geist die Waage halten." (Lexikon des Internationalen Films)
  Siehe auch rechts
  Lesen Sie dazu bitte S. 37 und 116
- **21.45** 5 Zimmer, Küche, Bad
  Fernsehfilm von Thomas Kirdorf
  Pia Janzen ....Anica Dobra
  Hartwig ....Christoph Waltz
  Dr. Castellotti . Karl Michael Vogler
  Regine ....Marita Marschall
  Friedmann . Hans Jürgen Diedrich
  Schnieker ......Michael Greiling
  Schneider ......Andreas Wellano
  Roberto ....Camillo D'Ancona
  Boxmanager. Heinz-H. Kraehkamp
  Charlotte ..... Claudia Matschula
  Klara ....Raphaela Dell
  Maklerin ....Christina Gattys
  Makler ....Rudolf Kowalski
  Regie: Rolf Silber
  Siehe auch rechts
- **22.40** Gottes eigenes Land
  US-Dokumentarfilm von 1979/85
  Kamera, Buch, Regie: Louis Malle
  Der zweite Dokumentarfilm "... und das Streben nach Glück" folgt am 24. Mai.
  ▶ Siehe auch rechts
- **0.05** Europas Jugend musiziert
  Auszüge aus dem fünften internationalen Konzert junger Solisten Ha Young Soul (Schweden), Klavier; Emer McDonough (Irland), Flöte; Koh Gabriel Kameda (Deutschland), Violine; Velgko Klenkovski (Jugoslawien), Klarinette
  Werke von Haydn, Pergolesi und Weber. Das Orchester des belgischen Rundfunks und Fernsehens
  Leitung: Aleksander Rahbari
- **0.50** heute

17.45 Hotel Paradies
Lisa bekommt ihr Traumhaus

Vor dem Glück der Lindemanns gibt's erst mal Streß: Max hat Magenbeschwerden und ohrfeigt seinen Sohn Michael. Lisa bekommt einen Schwächeanfall. Das ist zuviel für Max: Er will das Hotel aufgeben! Zwischen Renate und ihrem Freund, dem Schiffsmakler Rowalt, gibt es Spannungen.

Max (Klaus Wildbolz) macht seine Frau (Grit Boettcher) überglücklich: Er hat ihr heimlich das Traumhaus gekauft

19.30 Doppelpunkt
Junge Frauen diskutieren: Baby oder Beruf?

Wie sie es macht, ist's verkehrt: Entscheidet sich eine junge Frau für die Familie, gilt sie als "naives Dummchen", räumt sie dem Beruf Vorrang ein, muß sie mit dem Vorwurf "Karrierefrau" leben. Beides unter einen Hut bringen kann nur eine "Rabenmutter". Gibt es Auswege aus dem Dilemma? Barbara Stöckl diskutiert heute live mit Betroffenen.

20.15 Der Club der toten Dichter
Robin Williams als vielbewunderter Internatslehrer

Tradition, Disziplin, Ehre, Leistung — Eckpfeiler einer US-Eliteschule Ende der 50er. Bis Lehrer John Keating auftaucht: Mit Geist und Witz ermutigt er die Jungen zu eigenem Denken, begeistert sie für Literatur. Sieben von ihnen gründen daraufhin einen Dichterclub. Als Neil, dessen Liebe fürs Theater vom Vater unterdrückt wird, Selbstmord begeht, wird John zum Sündenbock. **124 Min.**

Von den Schülern geliebt: Lehrer John Keating (Robin Williams)

21.45 5 Zimmer, Küche, Bad
Erlebnisse bei der Wohnungssuche

Die flippige Varieté-Tänzerin Pia sucht in Frankfurt eine Wohnung. Dabei lernt sie Hartwig Klemmnitz kennen, Sachbearbeiter bei einer Krankenkasse. Pia schlägt dem biederen Burschen zwecks Wohnungssuche ein Bündnis mit Amtsanmaßung vor. Ein weiterer Mann läßt auf Hilfe hoffen: Bankdirektor Dr. Castellotti. Mit ihm beginnt sie einen heißen Flirt. Doch er steckt mit dem Wohnungsmakler unter einer Decke... **89 Min.**

Bei einer Karambolage lernt die hübsche Pia (Anica Dobra) den Bankier Dr. Castellotti (Karl Michael Vogler) kennen

F. Schreiben Sie! Fernsehen in Deutschland und Amerika/Kanada (2–4 Sätze zu jedem der folgenden Punkte).
1. Popularität
2. Auswahl an Programmen
3. Art *(type)* der Programme
4. Werbung und Fernsehgebühren
5. Qualität
6. Rolle von Radio und Fernsehen

G. Wofür interessieren Sie sich im Fernsehen? *(Together as a class, create a ratings chart on various types of television programs. Use: 1 = sehr interessant; 2 = manchmal interessant; 3 = uninteressant.)*

❏ Nachrichten	❏ Konzerte	❏ Seifenopern
❏ Politik	❏ Opern	❏ Horrorfilme
❏ Reisen	❏ Krimis	❏ Dokumentarfilme
❏ Hobbys	❏ Western	❏ Geschichtsfilme
❏ Sport	❏ Theaterstücke	❏ Liebesfilme *(love...)*
❏ Sprachen	❏ Fernsehspiele	❏ Science-Fiction-Filme
❏ Ballett	❏ Fernsehquizze	❏ Zeichentrickfilme *(cartoons)*

FOKUS: German Cabaret

The term *cabaret* **(Kabarett)** describes both a form of theatrical entertainment and the dance halls where the genre emerged in the late 19th century. Performers satirized contemporary culture and politics through skits, pantomimes, poems, and songs. During the Weimar Republic (1919–1933), this type of variety show flourished in Germany but was then banned by the Nazis for its political nature. After World War II, the cabaret reemerged as a popular form of entertainment. Some of Germany's most popular cabarets are the *Lach- und Schießgesellschaft* in Munich, the *Floh de Cologne* in Cologne, the *Mausefalle* in Hamburg, and the *Herkules* in Dresden. Berlin, home to many cabarets during the roaring twenties, now has *Die Stachelschweine,* the *Distel* and *Die Wühlmäuse.*

Hören Sie zu!

Pläne für den Abend

Zum Erkennen: Hätten Sie noch . . . ? *(Would you still have . . . ?);* ausverkauft *(sold out);* die Anzeige, -n *(advertisement)*

Was ist richtig?
1. Monika möchte gern _____ gehen.
   a. ins Kino   b. in die Bibliothek   c. ins Theater
2. Felix und Stefan finden das ist _____.
   a. eine gute Idee   b. furchtbar langweilig   c. komisch
3. Monika ruft an, um _____.
   a. Karten zu bestellen   b. zu fragen, ob es noch Karten gibt
   c. zu fragen, wie man zum Theater kommt
4. Sie wollen zum KARTOON gehen, weil _____.
   a. das Programm sehr interessant ist   b. sie dort auch essen können
   c. Monika Gutes darüber gehört hat
5. Sie wollen um _____ Uhr essen.
   a. 18.30   b. 19.30   c. 21.00
6. Zum KARTOON kommt man _____.
   a. zu Fuß   b. mit der U-Bahn   c. das wissen wir nicht

Wolf Biermann FOKUS

Wolf Biermann, songwriter and poet, was one of East Germany's most famous dissident artists. Born in the port city of Hamburg in 1936, Biermann emigrated to East Germany in 1953 because of his socialist political convictions, but he soon became disillusioned. What he had imagined as a workers' paradise soon revealed a large gap between theory and practice, and Biermann turned a venomous pen to what he saw. Armed with a worn guitar and a gravelly voice, he attacked the ruling SED party with a blend of humor and indignant rage, until it expelled him in 1976 during a tour of West Germany. Since reunification in 1990, Biermann has urged eastern Germans in particular to critically rethink the political system they have inherited.

Ach, Freund, geht es nicht auch dir so?

Ich kann nur lieben
   was ich die Freiheit° habe   freedom
      auch zu verlassen°:   leave
dieses Land
diese Stadt
diese Frau
dieses Leben
Eben darum° lieben ja   that's why
wenige ein Land
manche eine Stadt
viele eine Frau
   aber das Leben alle
      Wolf Biermann

WEB-ECKE For updates and online activities, visit the *Wie geht's?* homepage at http://www.hrwcollege.com/german/sevin/! You'll discover what's playing in movie theaters in and around Düsseldorf, find out about Karl May and his books about a German cowboy in America, and be exposed to some of the rising stars of the German music scene.

SPRECHSITUATIONEN

There are times when you want or need to express satisfaction or dissatisfaction with something. You may even be pushed to the point of anger. Here are phrases to deal with such situations.

Expressing satisfaction

Das ist gut (prima, toll, wunderbar, fantastisch, super, herrlich, ausgezeichnet).
Das ist praktisch (bequem, interessant, spannend, nicht schlecht).
Das ist genau das Richtige *(exactly the right thing)*.
Das gefällt mir (gut).
Das schmeckt (gut).
Das finde ich . . .

Expressing dissatisfaction

Das ist schlecht (furchtbar, unpraktisch, unbequem, langweilig).
Das finde ich (nicht) . . .
Das ist zu . . .
Das ist nicht . . . genug.
Das gefällt mir nicht.
Das schmeckt mir nicht.

Expressing anger

Das ist doch unglaublich!	*That's hard to believe.*
Das ist doch ärgerlich!	*That's annoying.*
Das ärgert mich wirklich.	*That really makes me mad.*
Jetzt habe ich aber genug.	*That's enough. I've had it.*
Ich habe die Nase voll.	*I'm fed up (with it).*
Das hängt mir zum Hals heraus.	*I'm fed up (with it).*
(So eine) Frechheit!	*Such impertinence!*

Übungen

A. Weißt du . . . *(Working with a classmate, describe three situations that caused you satisfaction, dissatisfaction, or anger. Mention very briefly the cause, and then state your reaction.)*

BEISPIEL: Weißt du, das Autohaus hat mein Auto schon dreimal repariert. Ich habe über 400 Dollar dafür bezahlt und es läuft immer noch nicht richtig. Jetzt habe ich aber die Nase voll!

B. Was, wo und wann? *(You and some friends feel like going to the movies, but you don't know quite what you want to see. You check the movie section of the newspaper and find the following notices. Discuss with your friends what films are showing in which theaters, and when the shows begin. Talk over the choices, and decide what you want to see and why.)*

C. Kurzgespräche

1. You are in a department store. As the clerk approaches you, tell him/her you need a new coat. He/she shows you one that he/she says is very nice. You try it on but you soon realize that it is too big and the color is not practical. The next one doesn't fit either (**passt auch nicht**) and it's too expensive. The third one is just right: it fits, you like it, it's practical and comfortable, and the price is right. You take it.

2. You've lent your notebook with class notes (**Notizen**) to a classmate [give him/her a name] who has failed to return it when promised—again. Not only that, but this classmate has passed the notebook on to a third person who is supposed to return it to you. You have called there and didn't get an answer. You are trying to prepare for a test. Tell your roommate your tale of woe and vent your anger about the situation.

KAPITEL 11
BEZIEHUNGEN

Junges Paar (couple) auf der Straße

LERNZIELE

■ VORSCHAU
Women and society

■ GESPRÄCHE AND WORTSCHATZ
Relationships and character traits

■ STRUKTUR
Simple past
Conjunctions **als, wann,** and **wenn**
Past perfect

■ EINBLICKE
The Brothers Grimm and their fairy tales
Rumpelstilzchen

■ FOKUS
Love and marriage
Liechtenstein
Eva Strittmatter: "Werte"

■ WEB-ECKE

■ SPRECHSITUATIONEN
Expressing admiration
Telling a story
Encouraging a speaker

VORSCHAU

Women and Society

The role of women in German society has changed significantly in the past thirty years. Gone is the stereotype of the woman whose life revolves around children, the kitchen, and the church **(Kinder, Küche, Kirche)**; but old attitudes change very slowly. Until reunification, West German women, especially those older than 30, were far less likely to have full-time jobs than their counterparts in East Germany. Only half of West German women worked outside the home, compared to more than 90 percent in East Germany. Women in the GDR were able to combine motherhood with full-time employment because state-run day care and other services were readily available. Staying home with a sick child was taken for granted in East Germany, and mothers were able to take as much as a year of maternity leave with full pay. The loss of these facilities and benefits, coupled with record-high unemployment, caused a drastic decline in the number of births. This trend is gradually being reversed.

German laws regarding pregnancy and childbirth reflect the conviction that women who bear and raise children are performing a task vital to society. Working women are entitled to maternity leave with pay **(Mutterschaftsurlaub)** six weeks before and eight weeks after childbirth. After that, those parents who do not return to work or do not work full time receive a monthly child-raising benefit **(Erziehungsgeld)** for the first two years after the birth of each child. During this period, the parent who chooses to take the child-raising leave cannot be fired. Another advantage is that the child-raising period, like the time spent caring for sick family members, counts towards the parent's pension claim. This practice aims to assess fairly work within the home as equal to gainful employment.

Women have only had equal rights **(Gleichberechtigung)** since 1976. At that time, the constitutional clause stipulating that women could work outside the home only if the job was compatible with their family obligations was dropped. Since then, women have used equal access to schools, universities, and other training facilities to take advantage of new opportunities. Yet, while they have had the right to vote since 1918, women occupy only a small role in the upper levels of business and government. It is interesting that women in former East Germany have maintained some of their earlier independence: one-third of east German businesses are owned by women, compared to less than one-fourth in the west. And although women's incomes are generally lower than men's, in eastern Germany women earn about 90 percent as much as men, compared to only 75 percent in the west. In all of Germany, however, the unemployment rate for women is higher than for men.

Wir freuen uns über die Geburt unseres Sohnes

Jan

* 12. 9. 98 · 3740 g · 54 cm

Die glücklichen Eltern

Claudia und Dirk Haesloop

GESPRÄCH

Partnersuche per Zeitungsanzeige

♀

Gesucht wird: charmanter, unternehmungslustiger, zärtlicher ADAM. Belohnung: hübsche, temperamentvolle EVA, Mitte 20, mag Antiquitäten, alte Häuser, schnelle Wagen, Tiere, Kinder.

Es gibt, was ich suche. Aber wie finden? Akademikerin, Ende 20 / 153, schlank, musikalisch, sucht sympathischen, gebildeten, ehrlichen Mann mit Humor.

Welcher Mann mit Herz, bis 45 Jahre jung, mag reisen, tanzen, schwimmen, Ski laufen und mich? Ich: Attraktiv, dunkelhaarig, unternehmungslustig und schick. Geschieden, Anfang 30, zwei nette Jungen.

♂

Millionär bin ich nicht! Will mir ja auch kein Glück kaufen, sondern verdienen. Ich, 28 / 170, suche keine Modepuppe oder Disco-Queen, sondern ein nettes, natürliches Mädchen, das auch hübsch sein darf.

Tanzen, Segeln und Reisen sind meine drei großen Leidenschaften. Welche sympathische Frau mit Phantasie will mitmachen? Ich bin Journalist (Wassermann), optimistisch und unkonventionell.

Liebe gemeinsam erleben...zu Hause, im Konzert, beim Tanzen, in den Bergen, auf dem Tennis- oder Golfplatz, im und auf dem Wasser, wo auch immer, dazu wünsche ich mir eine gutaussehende, berufstätige Dreißigerin mit viel Charme und Esprit, die auch gern liest und schreibt.

FRANK Du, hör mal! „Gesucht wird: charmanter, unternehmungslustiger, zärtlicher ADAM. Belohnung: hübsche, temperamentvolle EVA, Mitte 20, mag Antiquitäten, alte Häuser, schnelle Wagen, Tiere, Kinder."

STEFAN Hmm, nicht schlecht, aber nicht für mich. Ich mag keine Kinder und gegen Tiere bin ich allergisch.

FRANK Dann sieh mal hier! „Es gibt, was ich suche. Aber wie finden? Akademikerin, Ende 20, schlank, musikalisch, sucht sympathischen, gebildeten, ehrlichen Mann mit Humor."

STEFAN Ja, das ist vielleicht 'was. Sie sucht jemand mit Humor. Das gefällt mir, und Musik mag ich auch. Aber ob sie Jazz mag? Vielleicht können wir beide kennen lernen?

FRANK Ich weiß nicht. Irgendwie ist mir das zu dumm, Leute durch Anzeigen in der Zeitung kennen zu lernen.

STEFAN Ach, Quatsch! Versuchen wir's doch! Was haben wir zu verlieren?

FRANK Wenn du meinst.

Fragen

1. Was sehen sich Frank und Stefan an? 2. Was sucht die erste Frau? 3. Wofür interessiert sie sich? 4. Wie reagiert *(react)* Stefan darauf? 5. Was sucht die zweite Frau? 6. Wie reagiert Stefan auf die zweite Anzeige? 7. Was meint Frank dazu? 8. Wie endet das Gespräch? Meinen Sie, daß die beiden auf die Anzeigen antworten?

Love and Marriage — FOKUS

Advertising for partners in newspapers and magazines is not at all unusual in the German-speaking countries. Dating shows on television are common, and Internet chat rooms are gaining in popularity.

Changing traditions and laws reflect the increasing equality of German women. For example, women no longer automatically take the name of their husband when marrying; more and more are using hyphenated last names—a practice that was written into law only recently. Married women are not addressed with their husband's first name, but with their own—for example, Ms. Christiane Binder, not Ms. Rudolf Binder. Widowed women keep their married name, whereas divorced women are free to use their maiden name again.

For a marriage to be legally recognized, it must be performed at the office of records **(Standesamt),** usually located in the city hall. A church ceremony afterwards is still popular. Traditionally, Germans wore the engagement ring on the left hand, and then switched it to the right hand as a wedding ring. Today the American custom of a separate engagement ring is becoming more common, but the wedding ring is still worn on the right hand.

Computer Magazin Partnersuche per Internet

Liebe auf den 1. Klick

Partnersuche im Datennetz: Finden Singles dort den Mann/die Frau fürs Leben?

WORTSCHATZ 1

Die Beziehung, -en (relationship)

der Partner, -	partner	ledig	single
Wunsch, ⸚e	wish	verliebt (in + acc.)	in love (with)
die Anzeige, -n	ad	verlobt (mit)	engaged (to)
Liebe	love	(un)verheiratet	(un)married
Hochzeit, -en	wedding	geschieden	divorced
Ehe, -n	marriage	sich verlieben (in + acc.)	to fall in love (with)
Scheidung, -en	divorce	sich verloben (mit)	to get engaged (to)
		heiraten	to marry, get married (to)

Die Eigenschaft, -en *(attribute, characteristic)*

ambitiös	*ambitious*	(un)ehrlich	*(dis)honest*
attraktiv	*attractive*	(un)freundlich	*(un)friendly*
charmant	*charming*	(un)gebildet	*(un)educated*
fleißig / faul	*industrious / lazy*	(un)geduldig	*(im)patient*
gut aussehend	*good-looking*	(un)glücklich	*(un)happy*
hübsch / hässlich	*pretty / ugly*	(un)kompliziert	*(un)complicated*
intelligent / dumm	*intelligent / stupid*	(un)musikalisch	*(un)musical*
jung	*young*	(un)selbstständig	*(dependent) independent*
nett	*nice*	(un)sportlich	*(un)athletic*
reich / arm	*rich, wealthy / poor*	(un)sympathisch	*(un)congenial, (un)likable*
schick	*chic, neat*		
schlank	*slim*	(un)talentiert	*(un)talented*
selbstbewusst	*self-confident*	(un)zuverlässig	*(un)reliable*
temperamentvoll	*dynamic*		
unternehmungslustig	*enterprising*		
verständnisvoll	*understanding*		
vielseitig	*versatile*		
zärtlich	*affectionate*		

Schick sein, reich sein, cool sein – und sonst nichts?

Weiteres

auf diese Weise	*in this way*
beid-	*both*
beide	*both (of them)*
bestimmt	*surely, for sure; certain(ly)*
damals	*then, in those days*
irgendwie	*somehow*
jemand	*someone, somebody*
ein·laden (lädt ein), lud ein, eingeladen	*to invite*
meinen	*to think, be of an opinion*
Wenn du meinst.	*If you think so.*
passieren (ist)	*to happen*
reagieren (auf + *acc.*)	*to react (to)*
Recht / Unrecht haben (hat), gehabt	*to be right / wrong*
träumen (von)	*to dream (of)*
vergessen (vergisst), vergessen	*to forget*
verlieren, verloren	*to lose*
versuchen	*to try*

Zum Erkennen: gesucht wird *(wanted);* die Belohnung *(reward);* Mitte . . . *(mid . . .);* die Antiquitäten *(pl., antiques);* das Tier, -e *(animal);* allergisch gegen *(allergic to);* die Akademikerin, -nen *(woman with university degree);* mit Humor *(with a sense of humor)*

Zum Thema

A. Was ist das Adjektiv dazu?

der Charme, Freund, Reichtum, Sport, Verstand; das Glück, Temperament, Unternehmen
die Allergie, Ambition, Attraktion, Bildung, Dummheit, Ehrlichkeit, Faulheit, Gemütlichkeit, Intelligenz, Komplikation, Natur, Musik, Scheidung, Selbstständigkeit, Sympathie, Zärtlichkeit, Zuverlässigkeit
sich verlieben, sich verloben, heiraten

B. Fragen
1. Was machen Sie und Ihre Freunde in der Freizeit? Worüber sprechen Sie?
2. Was für Eigenschaften finden Sie bei Freunden wichtig? Wie dürfen sie nicht sein?
3. Waren Sie schon einmal in einen Schauspieler/eine Schauspielerin oder einen Sänger/eine Sängerin verliebt? Wenn ja, in wen?
4. Was halten Sie vom Zusammenleben vor dem Heiraten? Was halten Sie vom Heiraten? Wie alt sollen Leute wenigstens *(at least)* sein, wenn sie heiraten? Finden Sie eine lange Verlobung wichtig? Warum (nicht)?
5. Sind Sie gegen etwas allergisch? Wenn ja, wogegen?

C. Anzeigen ohne Adjektivendungen. Geben Sie die fehlenden Endungen!

Millionär bin ich nicht. Will mein Glück auch nicht kaufen. Ich, 28/170, suche keine extravagant____ Modepuppe oder exotisch____ Diskoqueen, sondern ein nett____, natürlich____ Mädchen, darf auch hübsch____ sein.

Tanzen, Segeln und Reisen sind meine groß____ Liebe. Welche sympathisch____ Frau mit Fantasie will mitmachen? Ich bin Journalist, nicht hässlich____, verständnisvoll____ und mit unkonventionell____ Ideen.

Man(n) denkt, man(n) arbeitet, man(n) schläft, man(n) lebt? Ist das alles? Temperamentvoll____ Endzwanziger, 180, sucht charmant____, lustig____ EVA mit vielseitig____ Interessen.

Welcher nett____, intelligent____ Mann, bis 45 Jahre jung, mag reisen, tanzen, schwimmen, Skilaufen und mich? Ich: attraktiv____, dunkelhaarig____, unternehmungslustig____ Naturkind. Geschieden, Anfang 30, zwei sportlich____ Jungen.

Liebe gemeinsam erleben . . . zu Hause, im Konzert, beim Tanzen, in den Bergen, auf dem Tennis- oder Golfplatz, im und auf dem Wasser, irgendwo, dazu wünsche ich mir einen gut aussehend____, selbstständig____ Dreißiger mit viel Herz und Humor.

Ich, 32/160, zärtlich____ und gemütlich____, keine Rubensfigur, träume von glücklich____ Stunden mit unkompliziert____, lustig____ ADAM. Wo bist du nett____ Typ?

NOTE: In Europe the metric system is standard. Is someone who has a height of 180 cm short or tall? Figure it out yourself. Since one inch equals 2.54 cm, divide the height by 2.54 to get the number of inches. How tall are you in metric terms? Multiply your height in inches by 2.54.

Zum Erkennen: der Millionär; extravagant; die Modepuppe *(fashion doll);* exotisch; mit Fantasie *(with imagination);* unkonventionell; der Endzwanziger *(man in his late twenties);* das Naturkind *(natural type);* gemeinsam erleben *(to experience together);* mit Herz *(with feelings)*

294 KAPITEL 11

D. Wie Sie jetzt Ihren Partner finden können! *(Take this test. Which situation is most appealing to you? Label the picture you like best with a "1" and the one you like the least with a "0." Compare your evaluation to those of your classmates.)*

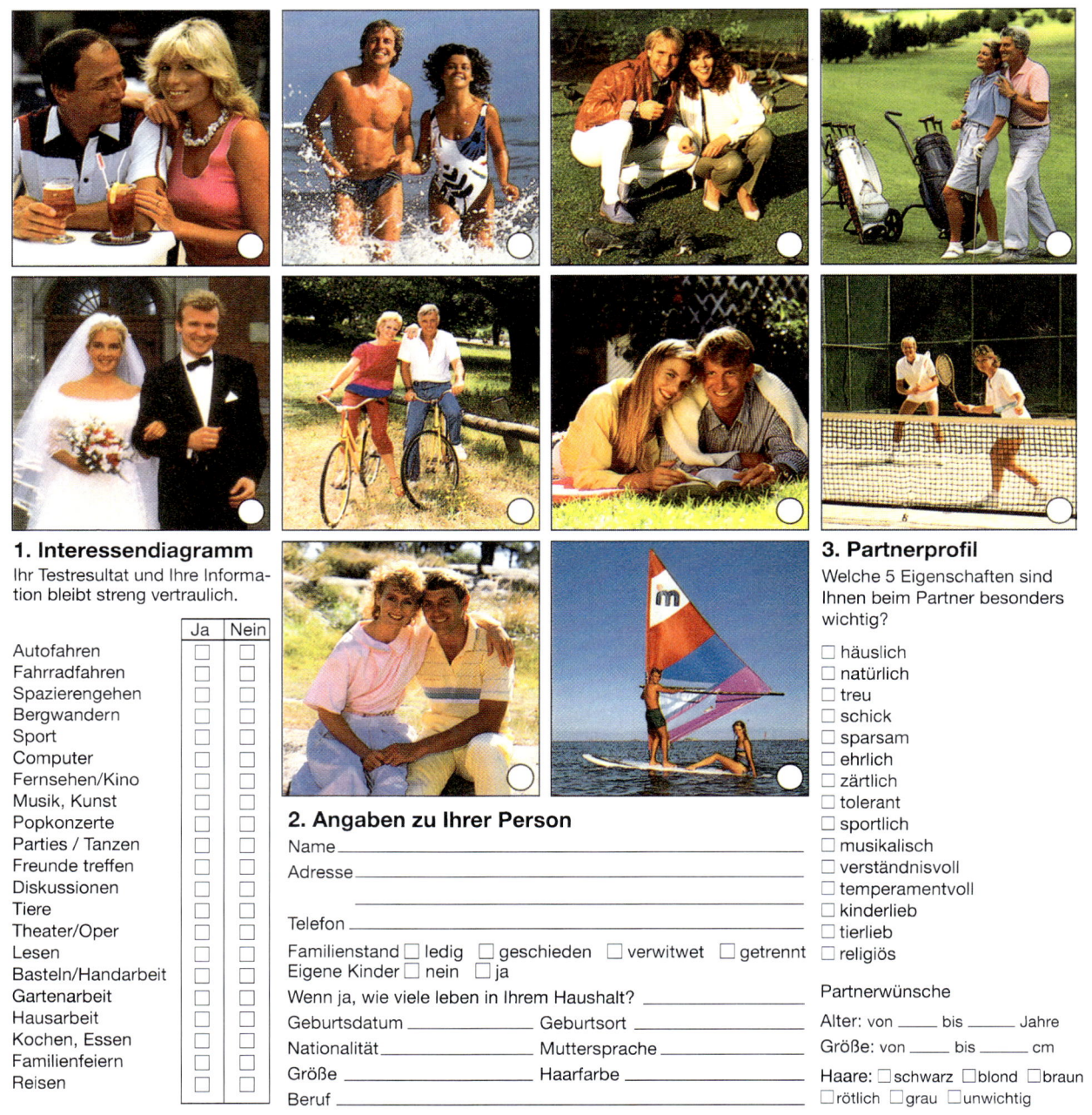

1. Interessendiagramm

Ihr Testresultat und Ihre Information bleibt streng vertraulich.

	Ja	Nein
Autofahren	☐	☐
Fahrradfahren	☐	☐
Spazierengehen	☐	☐
Bergwandern	☐	☐
Sport	☐	☐
Computer	☐	☐
Fernsehen/Kino	☐	☐
Musik, Kunst	☐	☐
Popkonzerte	☐	☐
Parties / Tanzen	☐	☐
Freunde treffen	☐	☐
Diskussionen	☐	☐
Tiere	☐	☐
Theater/Oper	☐	☐
Lesen	☐	☐
Basteln/Handarbeit	☐	☐
Gartenarbeit	☐	☐
Hausarbeit	☐	☐
Kochen, Essen	☐	☐
Familienfeiern	☐	☐
Reisen	☐	☐

2. Angaben zu Ihrer Person

Name _____
Adresse _____
_____
Telefon _____
Familienstand ☐ ledig ☐ geschieden ☐ verwitwet ☐ getrennt
Eigene Kinder ☐ nein ☐ ja
Wenn ja, wie viele leben in Ihrem Haushalt? _____
Geburtsdatum _____ Geburtsort _____
Nationalität _____ Muttersprache _____
Größe _____ Haarfarbe _____
Beruf _____

3. Partnerprofil

Welche 5 Eigenschaften sind Ihnen beim Partner besonders wichtig?

☐ häuslich
☐ natürlich
☐ treu
☐ schick
☐ sparsam
☐ ehrlich
☐ zärtlich
☐ tolerant
☐ sportlich
☐ musikalisch
☐ verständnisvoll
☐ temperamentvoll
☐ kinderlieb
☐ tierlieb
☐ religiös

Partnerwünsche

Alter: von ____ bis ____ Jahre
Größe: von ____ bis ____ cm
Haare: ☐ schwarz ☐ blond ☐ braun
☐ rötlich ☐ grau ☐ unwichtig

Zum Erkennen: bleibt streng vertraulich *(remains strictly confidential)*; Basteln *(crafts)*; Handarbeit *(needlework)*; die Angaben *(pl., information)*; verwitwet *(widowed)*; getrennt *(separated)*; eigen- *(own)*; die Größe *(size)*; der Beruf *(profession)*; häuslich *(home-loving, domestic)*; treu *(loyal, faithful)*; sparsam *(thrifty)*; kinderlieb *(loves children)*, tierlieb *(loves animals)*

E. **Partnerwünsche**
   1. **Was ist Ihre Reaktion?** Lesen Sie die Anzeigen in Übung C noch einmal und besprechen Sie *(discuss)* dann die Fragen unten!
      a. Wie soll der Partner/die Partnerin sein? Machen Sie eine Liste der gesuchten Qualitäten!
      b. Wie sehen die Leute sich selbst *(themselves)*? Was sagen sie und was sagen sie nicht? Machen Sie eine Liste!
   2. **Gesucht wird.** Schreiben Sie Ihre eigene Anzeige!

F. **Schreiben Sie!** Eine Charakterisierung (8–10 Sätze).
   1. So bin ich.
   2. Ein interessanter (langweiliger, furchtbarer . . .) Typ.

G. **Aussprache: f, v, ph, w.** Sehen Sie auch III. 1, 4 and 5 im Ausspracheteil des Arbeitsheftes!
   1. [f]   **f**ast, **f**ertig, **f**reundlich, ö**ff**nen, Brie**f**
   2. [f]   **v**erliebt, **v**erlobt, **v**erheiratet, **v**ersucht, **v**ergessen, **v**erloren, Philoso**ph**ie
   3. [v]   **V**ideo, Kla**v**ier, Sil**v**ester, Pullo**v**er, Uni**v**ersität
   4. [v]   **w**er, **w**en, **w**em, **w**essen, **w**arum, sch**w**arz, sch**w**er, **zw**ischen
   5. Wortpaare
      a. *wine* / Wein   c. *oven* / Ofen   e. Vetter / Wetter
      b. *when* / wenn   d. *veal* / viel   f. vier / wir

HÖREN SIE ZU!

Leute sind verschieden. (Select at least two adjectives that best describe each of the four people you hear discussed. Put their initials in front of the adjectives that apply to them: K for Kirsten, M for Martin, O for Oliver, S for Sabine. Not all adjectives will be used.)

Zum Erkennen: das Krankenhaus, ¨-er *(hospital)*; während *(while)*; die Katastrophe, -n; nicht einmal *(not even)*

Wie sind sie?

- ☐ arm
- ☐ reich
- ☐ ruhig
- ☐ fleißig
- ☐ faul
- ☐ intelligent
- ☐ attraktiv
- ☐ freundlich
- ☐ musikalisch
- ☐ sportlich
- ☐ unsportlich
- ☐ nett
- ☐ lustig
- ☐ selbstbewusst
- ☐ populär
- ☐ verständnisvoll
- ☐ temperamentvoll
- ☐ unternehmungslustig

Der Moderator kocht, wäscht, bügelt – und kann sogar Babys wickeln

Johannes B. Kerner: »**Ich bin ein perfekter Hausmann**«

STRUKTUR

I. Simple past *(imperfect, narrative past)*

The past tense is often referred to as the SIMPLE PAST because it is a single verb form in contrast to the perfect tenses (or "compound past tenses"), which consist of two parts, an auxiliary and a past participle.

We spoke German.   Wir **sprachen** Deutsch.

In spoken German, the present perfect is the preferred tense—especially in southern Germany, Austria, and Switzerland. Only the simple past of **haben, sein,** and the modals is common everywhere. The simple past is used primarily in continuous narratives such as novels, short stories, newspaper reports, and letters relating a sequence of events. Therefore it is often also called the "narrative past."

Again, one German verb form corresponds to several in English.

Sie **sprachen** Deutsch.
{ *They **spoke** German.*
*They **were speaking** German.*
*They **did speak** German.*
*They **used to speak** German.* }

1. T-verbs *(weak verbs)*

    T-verbs can be compared to such regular English verbs as *love / loved* and *work / worked*, which form the past tense by adding *-d* or *-ed* to the stem. To form the simple past of t-verbs, add **-te, -test, -te, -ten, -tet, -ten** to the STEM of the verb.

ich lern**te**	wir lern**ten**
du lern**test**	ihr lern**tet**
er lern**te**	sie lern**ten**

    Verbs that follow this pattern include: faulenzen, fragen, freuen, glauben, gratulieren, hören, interessieren, lachen, legen, machen, malen, meinen, passieren, reagieren, reisen, sagen, sammeln, setzen, spielen, suchen, stellen, stimmen, träumen, wandern, weinen, wohnen, wünschen.

    a. Verbs with stems ending in **-d, -t,** or certain consonant combinations add an **-e-** before the simple past ending.

ich arbeit**ete**	wir arbeit**eten**
du arbeit**etest**	ihr arbeit**etet**
er arbeit**ete**	sie arbeit**eten**

    Verbs that follow this pattern include: antworten, baden, bedeuten, heiraten, kosten, landen, mieten, öffnen, übernachten, warten.

    b. Irregular t-verbs (sometimes called *mixed verbs*) usually have a stem change. Compare the English *bring/brought* and the German **bringen/brachte.**

ich br**ach**te	wir br**ach**ten
du br**ach**test	ihr br**ach**tet
er br**ach**te	sie br**ach**ten

Here is a list of the PRINCIPAL PARTS of all the irregular t-verbs that you have used thus far. Irregular present-tense forms are also noted. You already know all the forms of these verbs except their simple past. Verbs with prefixes have the same forms as the corresponding simple verbs (**brachte mit**). If you know the principal parts of a verb, you can derive all the verb forms you need!

Infinitive	Present	Simple Past	Past Participle
bringen		**brachte**	gebracht
denken		**dachte**	gedacht
haben	hat	**hatte**	gehabt
kennen		**kannte**	gekannt
wissen	weiß	**wusste**	gewusst

Modals also belong to this group. (The past participles of these verbs are rarely used.)

Infinitive	Present	Simple Past	Past Participle
dürfen	darf	**durfte**	(gedurft)
können	kann	**konnte**	(gekonnt)
müssen	muss	**musste**	(gemusst)
sollen	soll	**sollte**	(gesollt)
wollen	will	**wollte**	(gewollt)

NOTE: The simple past of irregular t-verbs has the same stem change as the past participle.

2. N-verbs *(strong verbs)*

N-verbs correspond to such English verbs as *write / wrote* and *speak / spoke*. They usually have a stem change in the simple past that is difficult to predict and must therefore be memorized. (Overall they fall into a number of groups with the same changes. For a listing by group, see the Appendix.) To form the simple past, add **-, -st, -, -en, -t, -en** to the IRREGULAR STEM of the verb.

ich sprach	wir sprach**en**
du sprach**st**	ihr sprach**t**
er sprach	sie sprach**en**

Below is a list of the PRINCIPAL PARTS of n-verbs that you have used up to now. You already know all the forms except the simple past. Irregular present-tense forms and the auxiliary **sein** are also noted.

Infinitive	Present	Simple Past	Past Participle
an·fangen	fängt an	**fing an**	angefangen
an·ziehen		**zog an**	angezogen
beginnen		**begann**	begonnen
bleiben		**blieb**	ist geblieben
ein·laden	lädt ein	**lud ein**	eingeladen
empfehlen	empfiehlt	**empfahl**	empfohlen
essen	isst	**aß**	gegessen
fahren	fährt	**fuhr**	ist gefahren
fallen	fällt	**fiel**	ist gefallen
finden		**fand**	gefunden
fliegen		**flog**	ist geflogen
geben	gibt	**gab**	gegeben
gefallen	gefällt	**gefiel**	gefallen
gehen		**ging**	ist gegangen
halten	hält	**hielt**	gehalten
hängen		**hing**	gehangen
heißen		**hieß**	geheißen

helfen	hilft	**half**	geholfen
kommen		**kam**	ist gekommen
lassen	lässt	**ließ**	gelassen
laufen	läuft	**lief**	ist gelaufen
lesen	liest	**las**	gelesen
liegen		**lag**	gelegen
nehmen	nimmt	**nahm**	genommen
rufen		**rief**	gerufen
schlafen	schläft	**schlief**	geschlafen
schreiben		**schrieb**	geschrieben
schwimmen		**schwamm**	ist geschwommen
sehen	sieht	**sah**	gesehen
sein	ist	**war**	ist gewesen
singen		**sang**	gesungen
sitzen		**saß**	gesessen
sprechen	spricht	**sprach**	gesprochen
stehen		**stand**	gestanden
steigen		**stieg**	ist gestiegen
tragen	trägt	**trug**	getragen
treffen	trifft	**traf**	getroffen
treiben		**trieb**	getrieben
trinken		**trank**	getrunken
tun	tut	**tat**	getan
vergessen	vergisst	**vergaß**	vergessen
verlieren		**verlor**	verloren
waschen	wäscht	**wusch**	gewaschen
werden	wird	**wurde**	ist geworden

3. Sentences in the simple past follow familiar word-order patterns.

Der Zug **kam** um acht.
Der Zug **kam** um acht **an**.
Der Zug **sollte** um acht **ankommen**.
         V1   V2

Er wusste, dass der Zug um acht **kam.**
Er wusste, dass der Zug um acht **ankam.**
Er wusste, dass der Zug um acht **ankommen sollte.**
                                  V2   V1

Übungen

A. Geben Sie das Imperfekt (simple past)!

    BEISPIEL: feiern **feierte**

1. fragen, fehlen, erzählen, klatschen, lachen, legen, bummeln, wechseln, fotografieren, passieren, reagieren, schicken, putzen, sich kämmen, sich rasieren, sich setzen, versuchen
2. arbeiten, baden, bedeuten, kosten, antworten, übernachten, öffnen
3. haben, müssen, denken, wissen, können, kennen
4. nehmen, essen, sehen, lesen, ausgeben, finden, singen, sitzen, liegen, kommen, tun, sein, hängen, schreiben, treiben, heißen, einsteigen, schlafen, fallen, lassen, fahren, tragen, waschen, werden, einladen

B. Ersetzen Sie die Verben!

    BEISPIEL: Sie schickte das Paket. (mitbringen)
                      Sie brachte das Paket mit.

1. Sie schickten ein Taxi. (suchen, bestellen, mieten, warten auf)
2. Das hatte ich damals nicht. (wissen, kennen, denken, mitbringen)
3. Wann solltet ihr zurückkommen? (müssen, wollen, dürfen, können)
4. Wir fanden es dort. (sehen, lassen, verlieren, vergessen)
5. Er dankte seiner Mutter. (antworten, zuhören, helfen, schreiben)
6. Du empfiehlst den Sauerbraten. (bestellen, nehmen, wollen, bringen)

C. Wiederholen Sie die Texte im Imperfekt!

1. **Weißt du noch?** Ein Brüder und eine Schwester erinnern sich.

   BEISPIEL: Großvater erzählt stundenlang von seiner Kindheit *(childhood)*.
   Großvater erzählte stundenlang von seiner Kindheit.

   a. Ich setze mich aufs Sofa und höre ihm zu. Seine Geschichten interessieren mich.
   b. Vater arbeitet viel im Garten. Du telefonierst oder besuchst gern die Nachbarn.
   c. Karin und Jörg spielen stundenlang Karten. Mutter kauft ein oder bezahlt Rechnungen.
   d. Großmutter legt sich nachmittags ein Stündchen hin und freut sich danach auf ihre Tasse Kaffee. Richtig?

2. **Haben Sie das nicht gewusst?** Ein paar Nachbarn klatschen *(gossip)* über Lothar und Ute.

   BEISPIEL: Hat Ute ihren Mann schon lange gekannt?
   Kannte Ute ihren Mann schon lange?

   a. Wie hat sie ihn kennen gelernt?
   b. Hast du nichts von ihrer Anzeige gewusst? Sie hat Lothar durch die Zeitung kennen gelernt.
   c. Der Briefträger *(mail carrier)* hat ihr einen Brief von dem jungen Herrn gebracht.
   d. Gestern haben sie Hochzeit gehabt. Sie hat Glück gehabt.
   e. Das habe ich mir auch gedacht.

3. **Schade!** Bärbel erzählt ihrer Freundin, warum sie traurig ist.

   BEISPIEL: Was willst du denn machen?
   Was wolltest du denn machen?

   a. Ich will mit Karl-Heinz ins Kino gehen, aber ich kann nicht.
   b. Warum, darfst du nicht?
   c. Doch, aber meine Kopfschmerzen wollen einfach nicht weggehen.
   d. Musst du im Bett bleiben?
   e. Nein, aber ich darf nicht schon wieder krank werden. Leider kann ich nicht mit Karl-Heinz sprechen. Aber seine Mutter will es ihm sagen. Er soll mich anrufen.

4. **Wo wart ihr?** Caroline erzählt von ihrer kurzen Reise in die Schweiz.

   BEISPIEL: Wir sind eine Woche in Saas Fee gewesen.
   Wir waren eine Woche in Saas Fee.

   a. Von unserem Zimmer haben wir einen Blick auf die Alpen gehabt. b. Die Pension hat natürlich Alpenblick geheißen. c. Morgens haben wir lange geschlafen, dann haben wir gemütlich gefrühstückt. d. Später bin ich mit dem Sessellift auf einen Berg gefahren und bin den ganzen Nachmittag Skilaufen gegangen. e. Wolfgang ist unten geblieben, hat Bücher gelesen und Briefe geschrieben.

D. Eine vielseitige Persönlichkeit. Geben Sie die fehlenden Verbformen im Imperfekt!

1. Else Lasker-Schüler ist eine vielseitige Persönlichkeit aus der deutschen Kunstszene.
2. Geboren 1868 in Wuppertal, _____ (gehören) sie zu einer jüdischen Familie, wo man ihr damals viel Freiheit _____ (lassen). 3. 1894 _____ (heiraten) sie einen Berliner Arzt, _____ (beginnen) zu zeichnen *(draw)* und ihre ersten Gedichte *(poems)* zu schreiben. 4. In Berlin

_____ (bringen) sie 1899 ihren Sohn Paul zur Welt. 5. Bald danach _____ sie aus dem bürgerlichen *(bourgeois)* Leben _____ (aus·steigen), _____ (lassen) sich scheiden und _____ (heiraten) 1903 Herwarth Walden, den Herausgeber *(editor)* der Zeitschrift *Sturm*, mit Kontakt zu allen Künstlern Berlins. 6. Zwischen 1910 und 1930 _____ (werden) sie selbst sehr bekannt. 7. Sie _____ (leben) nicht nur von ihren Gedichten und ihrer Prosa, sondern auch als Grafikerin. 8. 1933 _____ die Nazis ihre Zeichnungen *(drawings)* _____ (weg·nehmen) und sie _____ (gehen) ins Exil in die Schweiz, später nach Palästina. 9. Als sie 1939 in Palästina _____ (an·kommen), _____ (sein) sie schockiert. 10. Ihr ganzes Leben lang _____ (träumen) sie von einem Land, wo verschiedene Kulturen und Religionen harmonisch _____ (zusammenleben). 11. Dieses Palästina _____ (haben) nichts mit dem Land ihrer Träume zu tun. 12. Sie _____ (fühlen) sich dort wie im Exil. 13. So _____ (schreiben) sie 1942: „Ich bin keine Zionistin, keine Jüdin, keine Christin, ich glaube aber ein tief trauriger Mensch." 14. Lasker-Schüler starb *(died)* 1945 im Alter von 77 Jahren in Jerusalem.

Lasker-Schülers Porträts einiger bekannter Freunde:

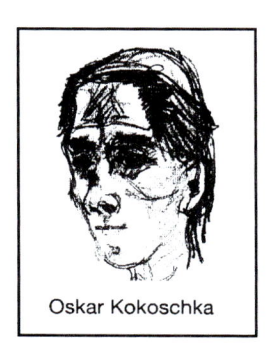

Georg Trakl   George Grosz   Oskar Kokoschka

II. Conjunctions *als, wann, wenn*

Care must be taken to distinguish among **als, wann,** and **wenn,** all of which correspond to the English *when.*

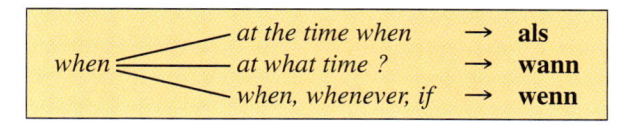

when		
at the time when	→	**als**
at what time ?	→	**wann**
when, whenever, if	→	**wenn**

- **Als** refers to a SINGLE (OR PARTICULAR) EVENT IN THE PAST.

    Als ich gestern Abend nach Hause kam, war er noch nicht zurück.
    When I came home last night, he wasn't back yet.

- **Wann** introduces direct or indirect questions REFERRING TO TIME.

    Ich frage mich, **wann** er nach Hause kommt.
    I wonder when (or at what time) he'll come home.

- **Wenn** covers all other situations.

    Wenn du ankommst, ruf mich an!
    When you arrive, call me! (referring to a present or future event)

Wenn er kam, brachte er immer Blumen.

Whenever he came, he brought flowers. (repeated event in the past)

Remember that **wenn** *(if)* can also introduce a conditional clause:

Wenn es nicht regnet, gehen wir spazieren.

If it doesn't rain, we'll take a walk.

Übungen

E. **Was fehlt:** *als,* **wann** *oder* **wenn***?*
   1. _____ ihr kommt, zeigen wir euch die Bilder von unserer Reise.
   2. Können Sie mir sagen, _____ der Zug aus Köln ankommt?
   3. _____ wir letzte Woche im Theater waren, sahen wir Stefan und Sonja.
   4. Sie freute sich immer sehr, _____ wir sie besuchten.
   5. Sie bekommen diese Möbel, _____ sie heiraten; aber wer weiß, _____ sie heiraten.
   6. _____ ich klein war, habe ich nur Deutsch gesprochen.

F. **Verbinden Sie die Sätze mit** *als,* **wann** *oder* **wenn***!* (*If* when *stands at the beginning, make the first sentence the dependent clause. Watch the position of the verb.*)

   BEISPIEL: Sie riefen an. Ich duschte mich. *(when)*
   Sie riefen an, als ich mich duschte.

   (when) Ich duschte mich. Sie riefen an.
   Als ich mich duschte, riefen sie an.

   1. Wir sahen Frau Loth heute früh. Wir gingen einkaufen. *(when)*
   2. *(when)* Sie spricht von Liebe. Er hört nicht zu.
   3. Sie möchte (es) wissen. Die Weihnachtsferien fangen an. *(when)*
   4. *(when)* Ich stand gestern auf. Es regnete.
   5. *(when)* Das Wetter war schön. Die Kinder spielten immer im Park.
   6. Er hat mir nicht geschrieben. Er kommt. *(when)*

G. **Schreiben Sie!** Blick zurück. (*Write eight to ten sentences on one of the topics below. Write in the simple past without using any verb more than once. Try to use the conjunctions* **als, wann,** *and* **wenn** *where possible.*)
   1. Eine schöne Reise (*Tell where you went, whom you traveled with, what you saw, etc.*)
   2. Als ich klein war . . . (*Tell where you grew up, why you liked or didn't like it, what you were like at that time, etc. You may pick any age.*)
   3. Das war mein (Großvater). (*Describe a person of your choice, what he/she was like, what he/she used to do, etc.*)
   4. Frauen früher (*Describe what life was like for women in earlier times*)

III. Past perfect

1. Like the present perfect, the PAST PERFECT in both English and German is a compound form consisting of an auxiliary and a past participle, with the AUXILIARY IN THE SIMPLE PAST.

   Ich **hatte** das gut **gelernt.**   *I had learned that well.*

   Er **war** um zehn Uhr nach Hause **gekommen.**   *He had come home at ten o'clock.*

ich	**hatte** . . . gelernt	**war**	. . . gekommen
du	**hattest** . . . gelernt	**warst**	. . . gekommen
er	**hatte** . . . gelernt	**war**	. . . gekommen
wir	**hatten** . . . gelernt	**waren**	. . . gekommen
ihr	**hattet** . . . gelernt	**wart**	. . . gekommen
sie	**hatten** . . . gelernt	**waren**	. . . gekommen

2. The past perfect is used to refer to EVENTS PRECEDING OTHER EVENTS IN THE PAST.

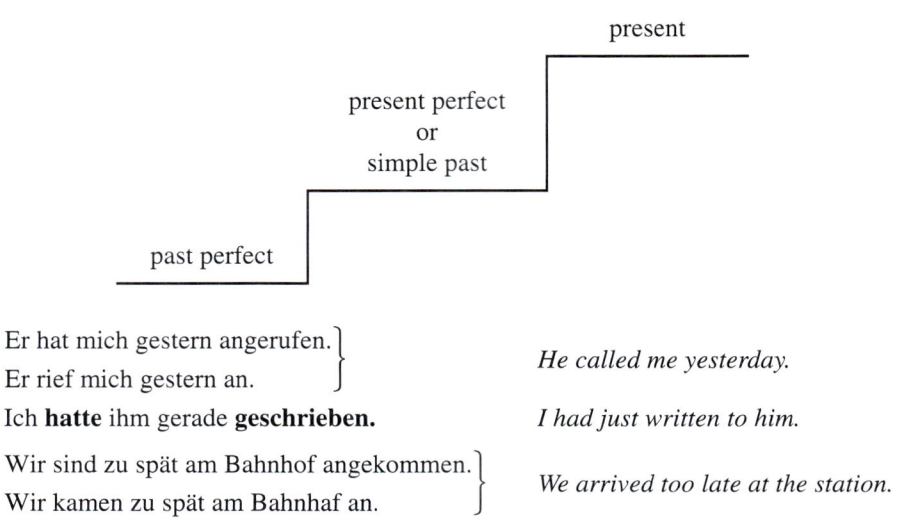

```
                                    present
                   present perfect
                        or
                   simple past

past perfect
```

Er hat mich gestern angerufen. ⎱ *He called me yesterday.*
Er rief mich gestern an. ⎰

Ich **hatte** ihm gerade **geschrieben.**   *I had just written to him.*

Wir sind zu spät am Bahnhof angekommen. ⎱ *We arrived too late at the station.*
Wir kamen zu spät am Bahnhaf an. ⎰

Der Zug **war** schon **abgefahren.**   *The train had already left.*

3. The conjunction **nachdem** *(after)* is usually followed by the past perfect in the subordinate clause, whereas the main clause is in the simple past or present perfect.

nachdem	*after*

Nachdem er mich **angerufen hatte,** schickte ich den Brief nicht mehr ab.

Nachdem der Zug **abgefahren war,** gingen wir ins Bahnhofsrestaurant.

Übungen

H. Ersetzen Sie das Subjekt!

BEISPIEL: Sie hatten uns besucht. (du)
   Du hattest uns besucht.

1. Du hattest den Schlüssel gesucht. (ihr, Sie, sie / *sg.*)
2. Sie hatten das nicht gewusst. (wir, du, ich)
3. Ich war nach Dresden gereist. (sie / *pl.,* ihr, er)
4. Sie waren auch in der Dresdener Oper gewesen. (du, ich, wir)

I. Nicht schon wieder! Auf Englisch bitte!

1. Meine Schwester wollte den Film sehen. 2. Er war ein großer Erfolg. 3. Ich hatte ihn schon zweimal gesehen. 4. Ich hatte schon lange nicht mehr so gelacht. 5. Aber meine

Schwester war nicht mit mir gegangen. 6. Sie hatte nicht genug Geld gehabt. So sind wir noch einmal zusammen/gemeinsam gegangen.

J. **Am Flughafen.** Auf Deutsch bitte! Benutzen Sie das Imperfekt und das Plusquamperfekt *(past perfect)!*

1. We got (**kommen**) to the airport after the plane had landed. 2. When I arrived, they had already picked up (**holen**) their luggage. 3. After I had found them, we drove home. 4. My mother had been looking forward to this day. 5. After she had shown them the house, we sat down in the living room and talked about the family.

K. **Und dann?**
 1. **Zu Hause** *(Ms. Schneider recounts a typical day at home. Find out what happened next by asking* **Und dann?** *After you have asked about a few activities, switch roles with your partner. Note how Ms. Schneider switches from the present perfect to the past perfect.)*

    BEISPIEL: S1 Ich bin aufgestanden.
                    S2 Und dann?
                    S1 Nachdem ich aufgestanden war, habe ich mir die Zähne geputzt.

    a. Ich bin aufgestanden.
    b. Ich habe mir die Zähne geputzt.
    c. Ich habe mich angezogen.
    d. Ich habe Frühstück gemacht.
    e. Alle haben sich an den Tisch gesetzt.
    f. Das Telefon hat geklingelt *(rang)*.
    g. Ich habe mit Helmut gesprochen.
    h. Er hat die Zeitung gelesen.
    i. Er ist zur Arbeit gegangen.
    j. Ich habe mich an den Computer gesetzt . . .

 2. **Was haben Sie am Wochenende gemacht?** *(Write five sentences in the simple past, then follow the pattern in part 1 [***Nachdem ich . . .***].)*

Zusammenfassung

L. **Wiederholen Sie die Sätze im Imperfekt!**

1. Lothar denkt an Sabine. 2. Er will ein paar Wochen segeln gehen. 3. Aber sie hat keine Lust dazu. 4. Er spricht mit Holger. 5. Die beiden setzen eine Anzeige in die Zeitung. 6. Ute liest die Anzeige und antwortet darauf. 7. Durch die Anzeige finden sie sich. 8. Danach hat Lothar für Sabine keine Zeit mehr. 9. Er träumt nur noch von Ute. 10. Am 24. Mai heiraten die beiden. 11. Sie laden Holger zur Hochzeit ein. 12. Die Trauung *(ceremony)* ist in der lutherischen Kirche. 13. Ute heißt vorher *(before)* Kaiser. 14. Jetzt wird sie Ute Müller. 15. Die Hochzeitsreise verbringen *(spend)* sie auf einem Segelboot.

Verliebt...
...Verlobt...
...Verheiratet

Lothar Müller
Ute Müller
geb. Kaiser

Vahrenwalder Str. 93
Hannover 1

Kirchliche Trauung am 24. Mai 1996, 15⁰⁰ Uhr in der Ev.-luth. Vahrenwalder Kirche

M. Hoppla, hier fehlt 'was! Ein Herz für Tiere. *(A heart for animals. Thomas and his roommate Ingo adopted a free cat through the paper, but all did not go as planned. With a partner, take turns piecing together the picture of what happened. One of you looks at the chart below, the other at the chart in the Appendix. Use the simple past and the past perfect tenses.)*

S1:

	Nachdem . . .	**Dann . . .**
THOMAS	die Anzeige lesen	
BESITZER	über die Katze erzählen	Thomas seine Adresse geben
THOMAS	dorthin fahren und s. die Katze ansehen	
THOMAS	die Katze mit nach Hause nehmen	sie Ingo zeigen
DIE BEIDEN	ihr etwas Milch geben	
DIE KATZE	s. einleben *(get used to the place)*	oft auf Ingos Bett schlafen
DIE BEIDEN	die Katze eine Woche haben	
INGO	die Katze zwei Wochen auf seinem Bett haben	richtig krank davon werden
DIE BEIDEN	eine lange Diskussion haben	
BESITZER	zwei Wochen ohne die Katze sein	sie sehr vermissen *(miss)*
BESITZER	auf die Anzeige antworten	

BEISPIEL: S1 Was passierte, nachdem Thomas die Anzeige gelesen hatte?
S2 Nachdem Thomas die Anzeige gelesen hatte, rief er den Besitzer *(owner)* an. Der Besitzer erzählte über die Katze — und dann?
S1 Nachdem der Besitzer über die Katze erzählt hatte, . . .

N. Die Hochzeit. Auf Deutsch bitte! *(Use the simple past unless another tense is clearly required.)*

1. Arthur had been thinking of his daughter's wedding. 2. When we saw her in December, she was in love with a charming, wealthy man. 3. They were supposed to get married in April. 4. I had already bought a beautiful present. 5. Two weeks ago she got engaged to another man. 6. Michael is a poor student at (**an**) her university. 7. They didn't say when they wanted to get married. 8. On the weekend she called her parents. 9. She and Michael had just gotten married. 10. They hadn't invited their parents to (**zu**) the wedding. 11. Arthur gets annoyed when he thinks about it.

EINBLICKE

The Brothers Grimm and Their Fairy Tales

The brothers Grimm, Jacob (1785–1863) and Wilhelm (1786–1859), are well remembered for their collection of fairy tales *(Märchen),* including **Hänsel und Gretel, Schneewittchen** *(Snow White),* **Rotkäppchen** *(Little Red Riding Hood),* **Aschenputtel** *(Cinderella),* **Dornröschen** *(Sleeping Beauty),* **Rumpelstilzchen, Rapunzel, König Drosselbart** *(King Thrushbeard),* **Die Bremer Stadtmusikanten,** and many others. Such stories had been transmitted orally from generation to generation and were long considered typically German. Modern research has shown, however, that some of these tales originated in other countries. The story of Rapunzel, for example, had already appeared in an Italian collection in 1634; there the heroine is called "Petrosinella." The next traceable reference is from France, where the girl's name is "Persinette." Researchers assume that the story travelled to Germany and Switzerland with the Huguenots who left France after Louis XIV lifted the edict that granted them religious freedom. Jacob and Wilhelm Grimm heard many of the stories from women living in and around Kassel in northern Hesse, among them the sixteen-year-old Dorothea Wild, who later became Wilhelm's wife.

Jacob Grimm also wrote the first historical German grammar, in which he compared fifteen different Germanic languages and analyzed their stages of development. The brothers' work on the *Deutsches Wörterbuch* was a pioneering effort that served as a model for later lexicographers. In 1840 the brothers became members of the German Academy of Sciences in Berlin.

KAPITEL 11

WORTSCHATZ 2

der König, -e	king
das Gold	gold
die Königin, -nen	queen
Welt	world

das erste (zweite . . .) Mal	the first (second . . .) time
zum ersten (dritten . . .) Mal	for the first (third . . .) time
allein	alone
froh	glad, happy
nächst-	next
niemand	nobody, no one
nun	now
plötzlich	sudden(ly)
sofort	right away, immediately
voll	full
geschehen (geschieht), geschah, ist geschehen	to happen
herein·kommen, kam herein, ist hereingekommen	to enter, come in
nennen, nannte, genannt	to name
spinnen, spann, gesponnen	to spin
springen, sprang, ist gesprungen	to jump
sterben (stirbt), starb, ist gestorben	to die
versprechen (verspricht), versprach, versprochen	to promise

Vorm Lesen

A. Allerlei Fragen

1. Was ist ein Märchen? 2. Wie beginnen viele Märchen auf Englisch? 3. Wo spielen sie? 4. Was für Personen sind typisch in einem Märchen? 5. Was für Märchen kennen Sie? 6. Haben Sie als Kind gern Märchen gelesen? Warum (nicht)?

B. Was ist das?

der Müller, Ring, Rückweg, Sonnenaufgang; das Feuer, Männchen, Spinnrad; die Nachbarschaft; testen; golden

Rumpelstilzchen

once upon a time — Es war einmal° ein Müller. Er war arm, aber er hatte eine schöne Tochter. Eines Tages geschah es, dass er mit dem König sprach. Weil er dem König gefallen wollte, sagte er ihm:
straw — „Ich habe eine hübsche und intelligente Tochter. Sie kann Stroh° zu Gold spinnen." Da sprach der König zum Müller: „Das gefällt mir. Wenn deine Tochter so gut ist, wie du sagst, bring sie morgen in mein Schloss! Ich will sie testen." Am nächsten Tag brachte der Müller seine
chamber — Tochter aufs Schloss. Der König brachte sie in eine Kammer° mit viel Stroh und sagte: „Jetzt fang an zu arbeiten! Wenn du bis morgen früh nicht das ganze Stroh zu Gold gesponnen hast,
locked — musst du sterben." Dann schloss er die Kammer zu° und die Müllerstochter blieb allein darin.

Da saß nun das arme Mädchen und weinte, denn sie wusste nicht, wie man Stroh zu Gold spinnt. Da öffnete sich plötzlich die Tür. Ein kleines Männchen kam herein und sagte: „Guten Abend, schöne Müllerstochter! Warum weinst du denn?" „Ach", antwortete das Mädchen,

„weil ich Stroh zu Gold spinnen soll, und ich weiß nicht wie." „Was gibst du mir, wenn ich dir helfe?", fragte das Männchen. „Meine goldene Kette°", antwortete das Mädchen. Das Männchen nahm die Goldkette, setzte sich an das Spinnrad und spann bis zum Morgen das ganze Stroh zu Gold. Bei Sonnenaufgang kam der König. Er freute sich, als er das viele Gold sah, denn das hatte er nicht erwartet°. Dann brachte er sie sofort in eine andere Kammer, wo noch viel mehr° Stroh lag. Er befahl° ihr, auch das Stroh in einer Nacht zu Gold zu spinnen, wenn ihr das Leben lieb war.

    Wieder weinte das Mädchen; und wieder öffnete sich die Tür und das Männchen kam herein. „Was gibst du mir, wenn ich dir das Stroh zu Gold spinne?", fragte es. „Meinen Ring vom Finger", antwortete das Mädchen. Wieder setzte sich das Männchen ans Spinnrad und spann das Stroh zu Gold. Der König freute sich sehr, aber er hatte immer noch nicht genug. Nun brachte er die Müllerstochter in eine dritte Kammer, wo noch sehr viel mehr Stroh lag und sprach: „Wenn du mir dieses Stroh auch noch zu Gold spinnst, heirate ich dich morgen." Dabei dachte er sich: Wenn es auch nur eine Müllerstochter ist, so eine reiche Frau finde ich in der ganzen Welt nicht. Als das Mädchen allein war, kam das Männchen zum dritten Mal. Es sagte wieder: „Was gibst du mir, wenn ich dir noch einmal das Stroh spinne?" Die Müllerstochter aber hatte nichts mehr, was sie ihm geben konnte. „Dann versprich mir dein erstes Kind, wenn du Königin bist", sagte das Männchen. Die Müllerstochter wusste nicht, was sie tun sollte und sagte ja. Am nächsten Morgen heiratete sie den König und wurde Königin.

    Nach einem Jahr brachte sie ein schönes Kind zur Welt. Sie hatte aber das Männchen schon lange vergessen. Da stand es aber plötzlich in ihrer Kammer und sagte: „Gib mir das Kind, wie du es mir versprochen hast!" Die Königin bekam Angst° und versprach dem Männchen das ganze Gold im Königreich°, wenn es ihr das Kind lassen wollte. Aber das Männchen sagte: „Nein, etwas Lebendes° ist mir wichtiger als° alles Gold in der Welt." Da fing die Königin an zu weinen, dass das Männchen Mitleid° bekam. „Na gut", sagte es, „du hast drei Tage Zeit. Wenn du bis dann meinen Namen weißt, darfst du das Kind behalten°."

    Nun dachte die Königin die ganze Nacht an Namen und sie schickte einen Boten° über Land. Er sollte fragen, was es sonst noch für Namen gab. Am ersten Abend, als das Männchen kam, fing die Königin an mit „Kaspar, Melchior, Balthasar . . . ", aber bei jedem Namen lachte das Männchen und sagte: „Nein, so heiß' ich nicht." Am nächsten Tag fragte man die Leute in der Nachbarschaft nach Namen. Am Abend sagte die Königin dem Männchen viele komische Namen wie „Rippenbiest" und „Hammelbein", aber es antwortete immer: „Nein, so heiß' ich nicht." Am dritten Tag kam der Bote zurück und erzählte: „Ich bin bis an die Grenzen° des Königreichs gegangen, und niemand konnte mir neue Namen nennen. Aber auf dem Rückweg kam ich in einen Wald. Da sah ich ein kleines Häuschen mit einem Feuer davor. Um das Feuer sprang ein komisches Männchen. Es hüpfte° auf einem Bein und schrie°:

> Heute back ich, morgen brau° ich,
> übermorgen hol ich der Königin ihr Kind;
> ach, wie gut, dass niemand weiß,
> dass ich Rumpelstilzchen heiß!

Die Königin war natürlich sehr froh, als sie das hörte. Am Abend fragte sie das Männchen zuerst: „Heißt du vielleicht Kunz?" „Nein." „Heißt du vielleicht Heinz?" „Nein." „Heißt du vielleicht Rumpelstilzchen?" „Das hat dir der Teufel° gesagt, das hat dir der Teufel gesagt!", schrie das Männchen und stampfte° mit dem rechten Fuß so auf den Boden°, dass es bis zum Körper darin versank°. Dann packte° es den linken Fuß mit beiden Händen und riss° sich selbst in Stücke°.

Märchen der Brüder Grimm (nacherzählt°)

Schloss Neuschwanstein von Ludwig II. stammt aus *(dates back to)* dem 19. Jahrhundert.

Zum Text

A. Rumpelstilzchen. Erzählen Sie die Geschichte noch einmal in Ihren eigenen Worten! Benutzen Sie das Imperfekt und die Stichwörter *(key words)* unten!

Müller, Tochter, König, Stroh zu Gold spinnen, Kammer, sterben, weinen, Männchen, Goldkette, Spinnrad, noch mehr, heiraten, Ring, Kind, Königin, nach einem Jahr, Angst, Mitleid, behalten, einen Boten schicken, Häuschen, Feuer, springen, Teufel, auf den Boden stampfen, im Boden versinken (versank), sich selbst in Stücke reißen (riss)

B. Wusstest du das? Lesen Sie, was die Königin ihrem Sohn nach dem Tod *(death)* des Vaters erzählt! Unterstreichen Sie *(underline)* das Plusquamperfekt!

Jetzt, wo dein Vater gestorben ist, kann ich dir erzählen, wie es dazu kam, dass dein Vater und ich heirateten. Er wollte nie, dass du weißt, dass dein Großvater nur Müller war. Mein Vater brachte mich eines Tages hier aufs Schloss, weil er am Tag davor dem König gesagt hatte, dass ich Stroh zu Gold spinnen kann. Der König brachte mich damals in eine Kammer voll Stroh und ich sollte es zu Gold spinnen. Ich wusste natürlich nicht, wie man das macht. Weil der König gesagt hatte, dass ich sterben sollte, wenn das Stroh nicht am nächsten Morgen Gold geworden war, hatte ich große Angst und fing an zu weinen. Da kam plötzlich ein Männchen in die Kammer. Für meine Halskette wollte es mir helfen. Bevor es Morgen war, hatte es das ganze Stroh zu Gold gesponnen. Aber dein Vater brachte mich in eine andere Kammer voll Stroh. Wieder kam das Männchen und half mir, nachdem ich ihm meinen Ring gegeben hatte. Aber in der dritten Nacht hatte ich nichts mehr, was ich ihm schenken konnte. Da musste ich ihm mein erstes Kind versprechen. Am nächsten Tag heirateten wir und ich wurde Königin. Nach einem Jahr kamst du auf die Welt und plötzlich stand das Männchen vor mir und wollte dich mitnehmen. Ich hatte es aber schon lange vergessen. Als ich weinte, sagte es, dass ich dich behalten dürfte, wenn ich in drei Tagen seinen Namen wüsste. Am letzten Tag kam mein Bote zurück und sagte mir, dass er ein Männchen gesehen hatte, wie es um ein Feuer tanzte und schrie: „Ach, wie gut, dass niemand weiß, dass ich Rumpelstilzchen heiß'." Nachdem ich dem Männchen seinen Namen gesagte hatte, riss es sich selbst in Stücke und du durftest bei mir bleiben.

C. *Als, wenn* oder *wann?*
1. _____ die Müllerstochter das hörte, fing sie an zu weinen.
2. Immer, _____ die Königin nicht wusste, was sie tun sollte, weinte sie.
3. _____ du mir das Stroh zu Gold spinnst, heirate ich dich morgen.
4. Das Männchen lachte nur, _____ die Königin fragte, ob es Melchior hieß.
5. _____ die Königin den Namen Rumpelstilzchen nannte, ärgerte sich das Männchen furchtbar.
6. Wir wissen nicht genau, _____ sie geheiratet haben, aber _____ sie nicht gestorben sind, dann leben sie noch heute.

D. Fragen
1. Aus welcher Zeit kommen solche Märchen wie *Rumpelstilzchen?*
2. Warum ist *Rumpelstilzchen* ein typisches Märchen? Was ist charakteristisch für Märchen?
3. Was ist die Rolle der Frau in diesem Märchen? Sieht man die Frau auch heute noch so?
4. Was für Frauen findet man oft in Märchen? In welchen Märchen findet man starke *(strong)* Frauen? Welche Rollen spielen sie meistens?
5. Warum heiratet der König die Müllerstochter? Gibt es das heute auch noch?
6. Wie endet die Geschichte in der englischen Version? Warum? Was für Geschichten hören (oder sehen) Kinder heute? Sind sie anders? Wenn ja, wie?

E. Mischmasch *(Following are three famous fairy tales all mixed together. In each numbered item, select one of the three phrases. Then connect them to one of these stories in its familiar form or, if you prefer, with a different twist. Alternatively, you can create an original fairy tale by supplying your own phrases.)*
1. Es war einmal _____.
   a. ein Müller b. ein kleines Mädchen
   c. ein kleiner Junge mit einer Schwester d. . . .
2. Der/Das/Die hatte _____.
   a. eine alte Großmutter b. eine hübsche Tochter
   c. immer Hunger d. . . .
3. Eines Tages _____.
   a. rief der König ihn/sie aufs Schloss b. wurde die Großmutter krank
   c. war wieder nichts im Kühlschrank d. . . .

4. Da ging er/es/sie ____ . . .
   a. in den dunklen Wald
   b. mit Kuchen und Wein hin
   c. natürlich hin
   d. . . .
5. . . . , um ____ .
   a. ihr zu helfen
   b. die Tochter zu zeigen
   c. etwas Essen zu bringen
   d. . . .
6. Aber er/es/sie ____ .
   a. wollte nur Gold
   b. verlor den Weg
   c. dachte nicht an den bösen *(bad)* Wolf
   d. . . .
7. Plötzlich ____ :
   a. sah er/sie ein paar Blumen und sagte
   b. kam ein Männchen und fragte
   c. war da ein Häuschen aus Plätzchen und jemand sagte
   d. . . .
8. ____
   a. „Wer knuspert *(nibbles)* an meinem Häuschen?"
   b. „Sie freut sich bestimmt über ein paar Blumen."
   c. „Warum weinst du?"
   d. „. . ."
9. Da ____ :
   a. ging er/es/sie zum Spinnrad und sagte
   b. kam eine alte Frau und sagte
   c. kam der böse Wolf und fragte
   d. . . .
10. ____ .
    a. „Bleib bei mir!"
    b. „Versprich mir dein erstes Kind!"
    c. „Wohin gehst du?"
    d. „. . ."
11. Später sagte (fragte) er/es/sie: ____
    a. „Gib mir das Kind, wenn du meinen Namen nicht weißt!"
    b. „Warum hast du so einen großen Mund?"
    c. „Ich habe genug und möchte nach Hause."
    d. „. . ."
12. Als er/es/sie das hörte, ____ .
    a. fraß er sie/ihn auf *(devoured)*
    b. wurde er/es/sie sehr böse
    c. freute er/es/sie sich und nannte ihn bei Namen
    d. . . .
13. Da ____ .
    a. schubste *(shoved)* er sie in den Backofen
    b. riss er sich in Stücke
    c. kam ein Jäger *(hunter)* zur Hilfe
    d. . . .
14. Und die Moral von der Geschicht': ____
    a. Geh zu fremden Leuten *(strangers)* nicht!
    b. Trau *(trust)* keinem Wolf!
    c. Man muss sich nur zu helfen wissen.
    d. . . .

F KUS Liechtenstein

Liechtenstein, a small principality about the size of Washington, D.C., lies between Austria and Switzerland. The country maintains close relations with Switzerland, sharing customs, currency, postal service, and management of foreign affairs. Liechtensteiners speak Alemannish, a German dialect. Thanks to favorable tax policies, more than 250,000 foreign business and banks have established nominal headquarters in Liechtenstein.

The castle in the capital Vaduz serves as the residence of Liechtenstein's royal family. According to the 1921 constitution, the country is a constitutional monarchy, hereditary in the male line. In 1989 Prince Hans Adam II succeeded to the throne. When his son Prince Alois married Princess Sophie in 1993, the royal family invited all 29,000 subjects to the wedding celebrations.

BEZIEHUNGEN 311

HERZLICHEN GLÜCKWUNSCH ZUR VOLLJÄHRIGKEIT!

UM SICH IN DIESER WELT DURCHZUSETZEN, MUSS MAN:

...SCHLAU sein wie ein FUCHS...

$E=Mc^2$

...TAPFER wie ein LÖWE...

...GEDULDIG wie ein LAMM...

UND ARBEITSAM wie ein PFERD!

HÖREN SIE ZU!

Vier berühmte Märchen

Zum Erkennen: brachen ab *(broke off)*; schütteten *(dumped)*; die Linsen *(lentils)*; die Asche; auslesen *(to pick out)*; der Turm *(tower)*; das Spinnrad *(spinning wheel)*; die Spindel *(spindle);* kaum *(hardly);* erfüllte sich *(was fulfilled);* der Zauberspruch *(magic spell);* stach *(pricked);* schlief ein *(fell asleep)*

Welcher Text gehört zu welchem Märchen? Schreiben Sie die Nummer daneben!

_____ Aschenputtel   _____ Hänsel und Gretel   _____ Rotkäppchen
_____ Dornröschen   _____ Rapunzel   _____ Schneewittchen

FOKUS: Eva Strittmatter

Eva Strittmatter (born in 1930) is hailed as one of the more "democratic" of her generation of poets for speaking in clear language about the feelings and issues that concern her. Popular across social classes and education levels, Strittmatter is prolific in her production of essays, published letters, poems, and children's books; but she is perhaps best known for her verse. Strittmatter often uses images from nature to illustrate a host of topics: the joys of love, the fear of loneliness, depression, aging, and motherhood. Her works, including the three volumes *Briefe aus Schulzenhof*, *Zwiegespräche*, and *Heliotrop*, have been translated into 17 languages.

Werte

Die guten Dinge° des Lebens — things
Sind alle kostenlos°: — free
Die Luft, das Wasser, die Liebe.
Wie machen wir das bloß°, — how on earth
Das Leben für teuer zu halten,
Wenn die Hauptsachen° kostenlos sind? — main things
Das kommt vom zu frühen Erkalten°. — becoming insensitive (lit. cold)

Wir genossen° nur damals als Kind — enjoyed
Die Luft nach ihrem Werte° — value
Und Wasser als Lebensgewinn°, — ... benefit
Und Liebe, die unbegehrte°, — undesired
Nahmen wir herzleicht hin°. — accepted easily
Nur selten noch atmen° wir richtig — breathe
Und atmen Zeit mit ein,
Wir leben eilig° und wichtig — in a hurry
Und trinken statt Wasser Wein.
Und aus der Liebe machen
Wir eine Pflicht° und Last°. — obligation / burden

Und das Leben kommt dem zu teuer,
Der es zu billig auffasst°. — considers it to be

Eva Strittmatter

WEB-ECKE

For updates and online activities, visit the *Wie geht's?* home page at http://www.hrwcollege.com/german/sevin/. You'll have fun reading various personal ads, look behind the scenes of one couple's wedding preparations, and go sightseeing in Liechtenstein.

SPRECHSITUATIONEN

Expressing admiration

You have now learned enough adjectives to express admiration for people as well as for objects. Remember that the flavoring particle (or intensifier) **aber** can also express admiration (see p. 197).

Was für eine sympathische Frau!	Wie nett! / Wie schön!
So ein interessantes Buch!	Das gefällt mir aber!
Das ist aber nett!	Das finde ich sehr schön!

Telling a story

As you have seen in the reading text, many fairy tales start with the phrase **Es war einmal . . .** Here are some common expressions to catch a listener's attention when beginning to relate a story:

Weißt du, was mir passiert ist?	Ich vergesse nie . . .
Du, mir ist heute / gestern 'was passiert!	Hast du gewusst, dass . . . ?
Mensch, du glaubst nicht, was . . .	Hast du schon gehört, dass . . . ?
Ich muss dir 'was erzählen.	

Encouraging a speaker

Wirklich?	Was hast du dann gemacht?
Natürlich! Klar!	Und wo warst du, als . . . ?
Und (dann)?	Und wie geht's weiter?

Übungen

A. **Was sagen Sie?** (Express your admiration.)
 1. Sie haben einen besonders guten Film (Stück, Konzert, Kunstausstellung) gesehen.
 2. Sie haben einen sehr netten Mann / eine sehr nette Frau kennen gelernt.
 3. Sie sind auf den Turm *(tower)* eines großen Domes gestiegen und haben einen wunderbaren Blick.
 4. Ein Freund hat ein sehr schönes, neues Auto.
 5. Freunde haben Sie zum Essen eingeladen. Sie haben nicht gewusst, dass Ihre Freunde so gut kochen können.
 6. Ihre Freunde haben ihre neue Wohnung sehr schick möbliert.
 7. Eine junge Frau mit einem süßen *(sweet)* Baby sitzt neben Ihnen im Flugzeug.
 8. Sie sehen sich zusammen ein Photoalbum an. Dabei sehen Sie einige interessante Bilder. (Fantasieren Sie etwas!)

B. **Ich muss dir 'was erzählen.** (Briefly tell a classmate something interesting that happened to you on your last vacation, during a plane trip, at work, or on a visit to your family. Your partner comments as you tell your story.)

C. **Kurzgespräche**
 1. Review the adjectives in *Wortschatz 1* and in Exercise A of the *Zum Thema* section. Then discuss with a classmate what kind of person your ideal partner should be.
    BEISPIEL: Er / sie muss zuverlässig sein, gern lesen und viel Fantasie haben . . .

 2. Describe yourself at an earlier age to a classmate. In some of your sentences use modals in the simple past to tell what you had to do or wanted to do.
    BEISPIEL: Als ich klein war, musste / wollte ich zu Fuß zur Schule gehen . . .

Rückblick: Kapitel 8–11

I. Verbs

pp. 249–50

1. **Reflexive verbs**

   If the subject and object of a sentence are the same person or thing, the object is a reflexive pronoun. The reflexive pronouns are as follows:

	ich	du	er / es / sie	wir	ihr	sie	Sie
acc.	mich	dich	sich	uns	euch	sich	sich
dat.	mir	dir	sich	uns	euch	sich	sich

   a. Many verbs <u>can</u> be used reflexively.

       Ich habe (**mir**) ein Auto gekauft.   *I bought (myself) a car.*

   b. Other verbs <u>must</u> be used reflexively, even though their English counterparts are often not reflexive.

       Ich habe **mich** erkältet.   *I caught a cold.*

   c. With parts of the body, German normally uses the definite article together with a reflexive pronoun in the dative.

       Ich habe **mir die Haare** gewaschen.   *I washed my hair.*

   You are familiar with the following:

   s. anhören, s. ansehen, s. anziehen, s. ausziehen, s. umziehen, s. ausruhen, s. baden, s. beeilen, s. duschen, s. erkälten, s. fit halten, s. (wohl) fühlen, s. (hin)legen, s. kämmen, s. konzentrieren, s. langweilen, s. (die Nase / Zähne) putzen, s. rasieren, s. (hin)setzen, s. verlieben, s. verloben, s. waschen, s. wünschen (see also 2 below).

pp. 271–72

2. **Verbs with prepositional objects**

   Combinations of verbs and prepositions often have a special idiomatic meaning. These patterns cannot be translated literally but must be learned.

       Er **denkt an** seine Reise.   *He's **thinking** of his trip.*

   You are familiar with the following:

   denken an, erzählen von, halten von, reagieren auf, schreiben an, sprechen von, träumen von, warten auf; s. ärgern über, s. freuen auf, s. informieren über, s. interessieren für.

p. 252

3. **Infinitive with zu**

   The use of the infinitive is similar in German and in English.

       Ich habe viel **zu** tun.

       Ich habe keine Zeit, eine Reise **zu** machen.

       Vergiss nicht, uns **zu** schreiben!

   If the infinitive is combined with other sentence elements, a COMMA separates the infinitive phrase from the main clause. If a separable prefix is used, **zu** is inserted between the prefix and the verb.

       Hast du Lust, heute Nachmittag mit**zu**kommen?

   REMEMBER: Don't use **zu** with modals! (Möchtest du heute Nachmittag **mitkommen**?)

Rückblick: Kapitel 8–11

4. Summary of past tenses

   Be sure to learn the principal parts of verbs (infinitive, simple past, past participle). If you know that a verb is a regular t-verb, all its forms can be predicted; but the principal parts of irregular t-verbs and n-verbs must be memorized. You must also remember which verbs take **sein** as the auxiliary verb in the perfect tenses.

   a. The perfect tenses

   - Past participles

     pp. 116–19

t-verbs (weak verbs)	n-verbs (strong verbs)
(ge) + stem (change) + (e)t	(ge) + stem (change) + en
gekauft	gestanden
geheiratet	
gedacht	
eingekauft	aufgestanden
verkauft	verstanden
informiert	

   - When used as auxiliaries in the present perfect, **haben** and **sein** are in the present tense. In the past perfect, **haben** and **sein** are in the simple past.

     Er **hat** eine Flugkarte gekauft.   Er **ist** nach Kanada geflogen.
     Er **hatte** eine Flugkarte gekauft.   Er **war** nach Kanada geflogen.

   - In conversation, past events are usually reported in the present perfect. (The modals, **haben,** and **sein** may be used in the simple past.) The past perfect is used to refer to events happening BEFORE other past events.

     Nachdem wir den Film **gesehen hatten,** haben wir eine Tasse Kaffee getrunken.

   b. The simple past

   - Forms

     pp. 296–98

	t-verbs (weak verbs)		n-verbs (strong verbs)
ich		(e)te	—
du		(e)test	st
er	stem (change) +	(e)te	stem (change) + —
wir		(e)ten	en
ihr		(e)tet	t
sie		(e)ten	en
	kaufte		stand
	heiratete		
	dachte		
	kaufte ein		stand auf
	verkaufte		verstand
	informierte		

   - In writing, the simple past is used to describe past events. In dialogues within narration, however, the present perfect is correct.

Rückblick: Kapitel 8–11

5. Sentence structure in the past tenses

Er **brachte** einen Freund.	. . . , weil er einen Freund **brachte**.
Er **brachte** einen Freund **mit**.	. . . , weil er einen Freund **mitbrachte**.
Er **wollte** einen Freund **mitbringen**.	. . . , weil er einen Freund **mitbringen wollte**.
Er **hat** einen Freund **mitgebracht**.	. . . , weil er einen Freund **mitgebracht hat**.
Er <u>hatte</u> einen Freund <u>**mitgebracht**</u>.	. . . , weil er einen Freund **<u>mitgebracht hatte</u>**.
V1 V2	V2 V1

pp. 300–01

II. The conjunctions *als, wann, wenn*

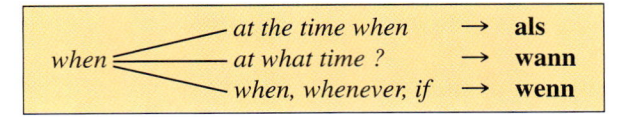

```
              at the time when     →  als
when  ────── at what time ?       →  wann
              when, whenever, if   →  wenn
```

pp. 273–74

III. *Da-* and *wo-*compounds

Pronouns following prepositions refer to people; **da-** and **wo-**compounds refer to objects and ideas. Most accusative and dative prepositions, and all two-way prepositions, can be part of such compounds. Prepositions beginning with a vowel are preceded by **dar-** and **wor-**.

        Er wartet **auf einen Brief.**

        Worauf wartet er? Er wartet **dar**auf.

IV. Cases

pp. 221–23

1. Genitive

   a. Masculine and neuter nouns have endings in the genitive singular.

      -es: for one-syllable nouns and nouns ending in **-s, -ss, -ß, -z, -tz, -zt** (des Kopf**es**, Hals**es**, Fluss**es**, Fuß**es**, Salz**es**, Platz**es**, Arzt**es** [*physician's*]).

      -s: for nouns of more than one syllable and proper nouns (des Bahnhof**s**, Lothar**s**, Lothar Müller**s**).

   b. N-nouns usually end in **(-e)n**; **der Name** is an exception (des Herr**n**, des Student**en**; BUT des Name**ns**).

2. Summary of the four cases

   a. Interrogative pronouns

nom.	wer?	was?
acc.	wen?	was?
dat.	wem?	—
gen.	wessen?	—

b. Use of the four cases and forms of **der-** and **ein-**words

Rückblick: Kapitel 8–11

	use	follows . . .	masc.	neut.	fem.	pl.
nom.	Subject, Predicate noun	heißen, sein, werden	der dieser ein mein	das dieses ein mein	die diese eine meine	die diese keine meine
acc.	Direct object	durch, für, gegen, ohne, um	den diesen einen meinen			
		an, auf, hinter, in, neben, über, unter, vor, zwischen				
dat.	Indirect object	aus, außer, bei, mit, nach, seit, von, zu	dem diesem einem meinem	dem diesem einem meinem	der dieser einer meiner	den diesen keinen meinen
		antworten, danken, gefallen, gehören, helfen, zuhören				
gen.	Possessive	(an)statt, trotz, während, wegen	des dieses eines meines	des dieses eines meines	der dieser einer meiner	der dieser keiner meiner

V. Adjective endings

1. Preceded adjectives

    pp. 245–46

    Predicate adjectives and adverbs have no endings. Adjectives followed by nouns do have endings.

	masculine	neuter	feminine	plural
nom.	der neue Krimi	das neue Stück	die neue Oper	die neuen Filme
acc.	den neuen Krimi	das neue Stück	die neue Oper	die neuen Filme
dat.	dem neuen Krimi	dem neuen Stück	der neuen Oper	den neuen Filmen
gen.	des neuen Krimis	des neuen Stückes	der neuen Oper	der neuen Filme

	masculine	neuter	feminine	plural
nom.	ein neuer Krimi	ein neues Stück	eine neue Oper	keine neuen Filme
acc.	einen neuen Krimi	ein neues Stück	eine neue Oper	keine neuen Filme
dat.	einem neuen Krimi	einem neuen Stück	einer neuen Oper	keinen neuen Filmen
gen.	eines neuen Krimis	eines neuen Stückes	einer neuen Oper	keiner neuen Filme

Rückblick: Kapitel 8–11

Comparing the two tables above, you can see:

- Adjectives preceded by the definite article or any **der-**word have either an **-e** or **-en** ending.
- Adjectives preceded by the indefinite article or any **ein-**word have two different adjective endings WHENEVER **ein** HAS NO ENDING: **-er** for masculine nouns and **-es** for neuter nouns. Otherwise the **-en** ending predominates and is used in the masculine accusative singular, all datives and genitives, and in all plurals.

after **der-**words

	masc.	neut.	fem.	pl.
nom.		-e		
acc.				
dat.		-en		
gen.				

after **ein-**words

	masc.	neut.	fem.	pl.
nom.	-er	-es	-e	
acc.		-es	-e	
dat.		-en		
gen.				

Or, to put it in another way, the endings are:

- in the NOMINATIVE and ACCUSATIVE SINGULAR
    - after **der, das, die,** and **eine** → **-e**
    - after **ein**
        - with masc. nouns → **-er**
        - with neut. nouns → **-es**
- in ALL OTHER CASES → **-en**

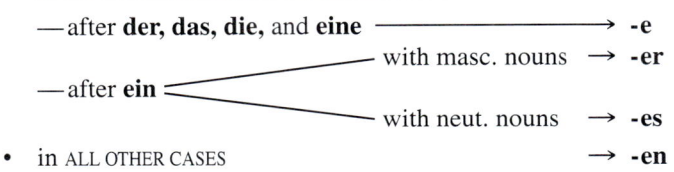

Der alt**e** Fernseher und das alt**e** Radio sind kaputt *(broken)*.

Mein alt**er** Fernseher und mein alt**es** Radio sind kaputt.

pp. 275–76

2. Unpreceded adjectives

    a. Unpreceded adjectives have the endings that the definite article would have, if it were used.

    Heiß**e** Suppe und heiß**er** Tee schmecken bei kalt**em** Wetter prima.

    b. The following words are often used as unpreceded adjectives: **andere, einige, mehrere, viele,** and **wenige.**

    Er hat mehrer**e** interessant**e** Theaterstücke geschrieben.

    c. **Viel** and **wenig** in the singular, **mehr** and **ein paar,** numerals, some names of colors (**rosa, lila, beige**), and place names used as adjectives (**Frankfurter, Wiener, Schweizer**) have no endings.

    Ich habe wenig Geld, aber viel Zeit.

    Sie hat zwei Romane und ein paar kurze Fernsehfilme geschrieben.

Gedichte • Romane • Märchen • Love-Story • Krimi
Und was lesen *Sie*?

VI. Sentence structure

Rückblick:
Kapitel 8–11

1. Sequence of adverbs

   If two or more adverbs or adverbial phrases occur in one sentence, they usually follow the sequence time, manner, place. The negative **nicht** usually comes after the adverbs of time but before adverbs of manner or place.

   p. 227

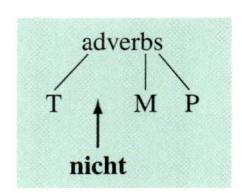

   ```
       adverbs
       |
    T   M   P
    ↑
   nicht
   ```

   Er fährt morgens gern mit dem Wagen zur Arbeit.
   Er fährt morgens **nicht** gern mit dem Wagen zur Arbeit.

2. Summary chart

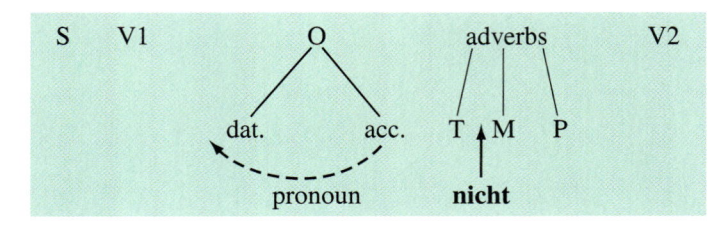

   ```
   S   V1        O              adverbs        V2
              dat.   acc.      T   M   P
                ⤺              ↑
              pronoun        nicht
   ```

   Er kann es ihm heute **nicht** mit Sicherheit *(for sure)* versprechen.

3. Time expressions

   pp. 224–26

   a. Specific time

   To refer to specific time, a definite point in time, or length of time, German uses the ACCUSATIVE: **jeden Tag, nächstes Jahr, eine Woche, einen Monat.**

   Other familiar phrases referring to specific time are:

   - gerade, sofort, am Abend, am 1. Mai, im Mai, in einer Viertelstunde, um zwei Uhr, von Juni bis September, vor einer Woche
   - vorgestern, gestern, heute, morgen, übermorgen, Montag, Dienstag, Mittwoch usw.
   - früh (Morgen), Vormittag, Mittag, Nachmittag, Abend, Nacht; gestern früh, heute Morgen, morgen Vormittag, Montagnachmittag, Samstagabend usw.

   b. Indefinite and nonspecific time

   - To refer to an indefinite point in time, the GENITIVE is used: **eines Tages.**
   - Familiar time expressions referring to nonspecific times are: montags, dienstags, mittwochs usw.; morgens, mittags, abends, mittwochmorgens, donnerstagabends usw.; bald, damals, danach, manchmal, meistens, monatlich, oft, sofort, stundenlang, täglich, zuerst usw.

NOTE: Review exercises for both vocabulary and structures can be found in the Workbook.

Morgen, morgen, nur nicht heute, sagen alle faulen Leute.

(Tomorrow, tomorrow, not today, all the lazy people say.)

319

KAPITEL 12
WEGE ZUM BERUF

Die Wissenschaftlerin Christiane Nüsslein-Vollhard vom Max-Planck-Institut in Tübingen erhielt 1995 für ihre Forschung *(research)* in Embryologie den Nobel Preis für Medizin.

LERNZIELE

■ VORSCHAU
German schools and vocational training

■ GESPRÄCHE AND WORTSCHATZ
Professions and education

■ STRUKTUR
Comparison of adjectives and adverbs
Future tense
Nouns with special features: predicate and adjectival nouns

■ EINBLICKE
Hard times and social policy
Choosing a profession

■ FOKUS
Women in business and industry
Gender bias and language
Foreign workers in Germany
Writing a résumé
Suna Gollwitzer: "Totales Versagen"

■ WEB-ECKE

■ SPRECHSITUATIONEN
Expressing agreement and disagreement
Expressing hesitation

VORSCHAU

German Schools and Vocational Training

In Germany, education is the responsibility of the individual states. Every child attends the **Grundschule** for the first four years. After that, teachers, parents, and children choose the educational track that best suits a child's interests and abilities. About one-third of German students go to a college preparatory school called **Gymnasium,** which in most of the **Länder** runs from grades 5 through 13. During their final two years, students must pass a series of rigorous exams to earn their diploma **(das Abitur),** a prerequisite for university admission. All other students attend either a **Hauptschule** or **Realschule.** The **Hauptschule** runs through grade 9 and leads to some form of vocational training. The **Realschule,** a four-year intermediate school covering grades 7 through 10, offers business subjects in addition to a regular academic curriculum, but one less demanding than that of a **Gymnasium.** Its diploma **(die Mittlere Reife)** qualifies students to enter a business or technical college (**Fachschule** or **Fachoberschule**).

This three-tiered school system has often been criticized for forcing decisions about a child's future too early. Therefore a so-called orientation phase **(Orientierungsstufe)** has been introduced for grades 5 and 6 that gives parents more time to decide what school their child should attend. In another effort to increase flexibility, comprehensive schools **(Gesamtschulen)** have been established that combine the three different types of schools into one and offer a wide range of courses at various degrees of difficulty.

Since school attendance is compulsory from ages six to eighteen, most of those who end their general schooling at age fifteen or sixteen must continue in a three-year program of practical, on-the-job training that combines apprenticeships **(Lehrstellen)** with eight to ten hours per week of theoretical instruction in a vocational school **(Berufsschule).** Apprentices are called **Lehrlinge** or **Auszubildende** (shortened to **der/die Azubi, -s**); they are considered invaluable by German business and industry. Apprenticeships date back to the Middle Ages, when apprentices served for approximately three years under one or several masters **(Meister)** in order to learn a trade. This principle extends today to all non-academic job training. Only few young Germans enter the work force without such preparation for the job market. Apprenticeship training is carefully regulated in order to ensure a highly skilled work force.

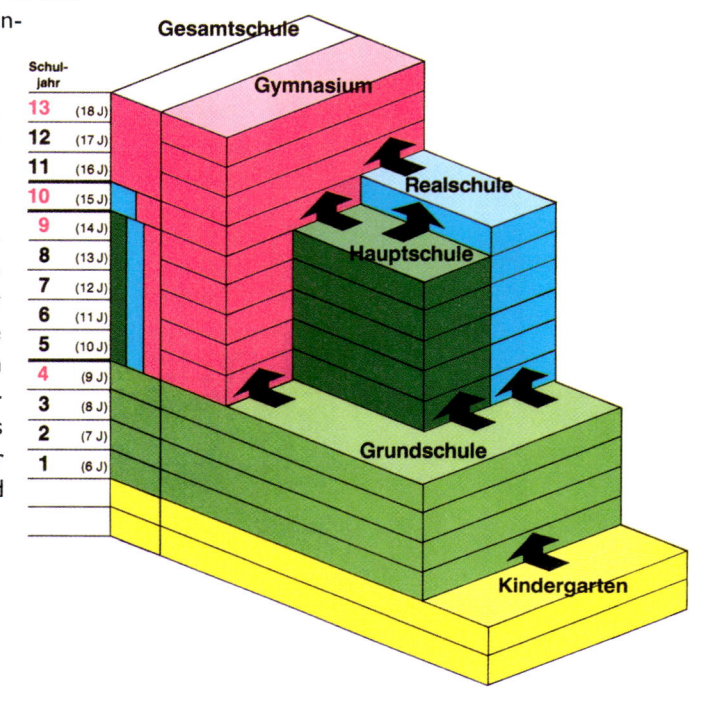

GESPRÄCHE

Weißt du, was du werden willst?

TRUDI Sag mal Elke, weißt du schon, was du werden willst?

ELKE Ja, ich will Tischlerin werden.

TRUDI Ist das nicht viel Schwerarbeit?

ELKE Ach, daran gewöhnt man sich. Ich möchte mich vielleicht mal selbstständig machen.

TRUDI Das sind aber große Pläne!

ELKE Warum nicht? Ich habe keine Lust, immer nur im Büro zu sitzen und für andere Leute zu arbeiten.

TRUDI Und wo willst du dich um eine Lehrstelle bewerben?

ELKE Überhaupt kein Problem. Meine Tante hat ihre eigene Firma und hat mir schon einen Platz angeboten.

TRUDI Da hast du aber Glück.

ELKE Und wie ist es denn mit dir? Weißt du, was du machen willst?

TRUDI Vielleicht werde ich Zahnärztin. Gute Zahnärzte braucht man immer, und außerdem verdient man sehr gut.

ELKE Das stimmt, aber das dauert doch so lange.

TRUDI Ich weiß, aber ich freue mich trotzdem schon darauf.

Was stimmt?
1. Elke will _____ werden.
   a. Lehrerin   b. Sekretärin   c. Tischlerin
2. Sie möchte später gern _____.
   a. selbstständig sein   b. im Büro sitzen   c. für andere Leute arbeiten
3. Elkes Tante hat _____ für sie.
   a. eine Lehrerstelle   b. eine Lehrstelle   c. ein Möbelgeschäft
4. Trudi will _____ werden.
   a. Augenärztin   b. Fußärztin   c. Zahnärztin
5. Zahnärzte sollen gut _____.
   a. dienen   b. verdienen   c. bedienen

WIE WERDE ICH MILLIONÄR?

SKL Süddeutsche Klassenlotterie

Women in Business and Industry

In Germany as in North America, in the past many jobs were considered exclusively "men's work." There has been a considerable shift in attitude, and more professions are now open to both sexes. In 1972, 37 percent of all apprentices were women; in 1998, this figure rose to nearly 50 percent. Likewise, the proportion of professionally trained working women increased from 38 percent in 1970 to 47 percent in 1998. In technical and scientific professions, however, women still make a rather low showing in the statistics.

At the university level, women account for only 20 percent of those studying technical and engineering subjects—courses leading to fast-growth professions. Instead, they are well represented in the arts and humanities, where career potential is more limited. More recently, an increasing number of female students is pursuing degrees in economics, law, and business administration. As this trend is relatively new, it is not yet reflected by the composition of leadership positions at the top of the professional ladder. Only 8 percent of senior consultants and around 7 percent of all full professors are women; in business and industry, 20 percent of the top positions are occupied by women. However, this situation should improve as more highly trained women enter the workforce.

Der Meister zeigt, wie's geht.

WORTSCHATZ 1

Der Beruf, -e *(profession, career)*

der Architekt, -en, -en[1]	*architect*	der Rechtsanwalt, ¨e[1]	*lawyer*
Arzt, ¨e[1]	*physician, doctor*	Reiseleiter, -	*travel agent*
Betriebswirt, -e	*graduate in business management*	Sekretär, -e	*secretary*
		Wissenschaftler, -	*scientist*
Geschäftsmann, ¨er[2]	*businessman*	Zahnarzt, ¨e	*dentist*
Hausmann, ¨er[2]	*househusband*	die Geschäftsfrau, -en[2]	*businesswoman*
Ingenieur, -e	*engineer*	Hausfrau, -en[2]	*housewife*
Journalist, -en, -en	*journalist*	Krankenschwester, -n	*nurse*
Krankenpfleger, -	*(male) nurse*		
Künstler, -	*artist*		
Lehrer, -	*teacher*		
Polizist, -en, -en	*policeman*		

Die Ausbildung (training, education)

der Plan, ⸚e	plan	
das Büro, -s	office	
Einkommen, -	income	
Geschäft, -e	business; store	
Problem, -e	problem	
die Erfahrung, -en	experience	
Firma, Firmen	company, business	
Sicherheit	safety, security	
Stelle, -n	position, job	
Verantwortung	responsibility	
Zukunft	future	

anstrengend	strenuous
eigen-	own
gleich	equal, same
hoch (hoh-)[3]	high
(un)sicher	(un)safe, (in)secure

Weiteres

überhaupt nicht	not at all
überhaupt kein Problem	no problem at all
an·bieten, bot an, angeboten	to offer
sich bewerben (bewirbt), bewarb, beworben (um)	to apply (for)
benutzen	to use
erklären	to explain
sich gewöhnen an (+ *acc.*)	to get used to
glauben (an + *acc.*)	to believe (in)
verdienen	to earn, make money
Ich will . . . werden.	I want to be a(n) . . .
Was willst du werden?	What do you want to be?

---

[1] In most cases the feminine forms can be derived by adding **-in** (der Architekt/die Architekt**in**; der Ingenieur/die Ingenieur**in**). Some require an umlaut in the feminine form (der Arzt/die **Ä**rztin; der Rechtsanwalt/die Rechtsanw**ä**ltin) and/or other small change (der Franzose/die Franz**ö**sin). For convenience, we are listing only the masculine forms, unless irregular changes are required for the feminine forms. In ads, both forms are usually listed as: **Journalist/in** or **Journalist(in)**.

[2] Note: der Geschäfts**mann**/die Geschäfts**frau** (likewise, der Hausmann/die Hausfrau); when referring to *business people*, the plural **Geschäftsleute** is common.

[3] **hoh-** is the attributive adjective; **hoch** is the predicate adjective and adverb: die **hohen** Berge BUT Die Berge sind **hoch**.

Zum Erkennen: der Tischler, - *(cabinet maker);* die Schwerarbeit *(hard /menial work)*

FOKUS Gender Bias and Language

The collective German plural, in the same way as English, has been reinforcing outmoded notions that certain professions are only for men, for example, **Ärzte, Wissenschaftler,** and so on. Women have been left out of the picture and out of speech. Today, however, many official communications use both masculine and feminine forms to break out of this pattern, e.g., **Ärzte und Ärztinnen, Wissenschaftler und Wissenschaftlerinnen.** Some publications have opted for a more equal new formation, e.g., **ÄrztInnen, WissenschaftlerInnen.**

Zum Thema

A. Kurze Fragen
1. Was ist die weibliche *(fem.)* Form von Ingenieur? Betriebswirt? Reiseleiter? Künstler? Arzt? Rechtsanwalt?
2. Was ist die männliche *(masc.)* Form von Architektin? Lehrerin? Krankenschwester? Geschäftsfrau? Hausfrau?
3. Wo arbeitet die Apothekerin? der Bäcker? der Fleischer? die Sekretärin? die Hausfrau? der Pfarrer *(pastor)*? der Lehrer? die Professorin? der Verkäufer?

B. Was sind das für Berufe? Sagen Sie's auf Englisch und erklären Sie dann auf Deutsch, was die Leute tun!

Zahntechniker/in Uhrmacher (Meister)
Gebrauchtwagenverkäufer Putzfrau
Fernfahrer Koch
Bankangestellter Chemie-Laboranten(innen)
Damen- und Herrenfriseur Telefonistin Sozialpädagogin
Phonotypistinnen Arztsekretärin
Industriekaufmann
Diplom-Ingenieur Rechtsanwaltsgehilfin
Krankengymnast(in)
REISELEITER/-INNEN Systemberater(in) Repräsentanten Bäcker
Haushälterin Zahnarzthelferin
Kassiererin Buchhalter/in PSYCHOLOGE/IN
Fremdsprachenkorrespondentin Hausmeister

Zum Erkennen: Bäcker, -; Bankier, -s; Briefträger, - *(mailman)*; Buchhalter, - *bookkeeper*; Dirigent, -en, -en *(conductor)*; Fernfahrer, - *(truck driver)*; Fleischer, - / Metzger, -; Friseur, -e / Friseuse, -n *(hairdresser)*; Kassierer, - *(cashier)*; Kindergärtner, -; Koch, ⸚e *(cook)*; Krankengymnast, -en, -en *(physical therapist)*; Makler, - *(real estate agent)*; Pilot, -en, -en; Psychiater, - *(psychiatrist)*; Psychologe, -n, -n; Steuerberater, - *(tax consultant)*; Wirtschaftsprüfer, - *(accountant)*

C. Zu welchem Arzt/welcher Ärztin geht man?
1. Wenn man Zahnschmerzen hat, geht man zu . . .
2. Wenn man schlechte Augen hat, geht man zu . . .
3. Mit einem kranken Kind geht man zu . . .
4. Wenn man Hals-, Nasen- oder Ohrenprobleme hat, geht man zu . . .
5. Frauen gehen zu . . .

D. Männerberufe, Frauenberufe? *(Working in groups, make a list of professions that in the past had gender preferences. Then decide how the picture looks today. You might like to include some of the vocabulary listed with exercise B.)*

E. Berufspläne. Was sagen Sie?

S1 Weißt du schon, was du werden willst?
S2 Ich werde . . .
S1 Und warum?
S2 . . . Und wie ist es denn mit dir? Weißt du, was du machen willst?
S1 . . .
S2 Ist das nicht sehr . . . ?
S1 . . .

F. Ein interessanter Beruf

1. **Was ist Ihnen am Beruf wichtig?** *(Poll each other as to the sequence of importance of the points below; then report to the class.)*

   - ☐ Reisen
   - ☐ freies Wochenende
   - ☐ lange Sommerferien
   - ☐ saubere Arbeit
   - ☐ interessante Arbeit
   - ☐ Kreativität
   - ☐ elegante Kleidung
   - ☐ flexible Arbeitszeit
   - ☐ Prestige
   - ☐ Sicherheit
   - ☐ Erfahrung
   - ☐ wenig Stress
   - ☐ wenig Papierkrieg *(paper work)*
   - ☐ Arbeit in der freien Natur
   - ☐ Abenteuer *(adventure)*
   - ☐ Abwechslung *(variety)*
   - ☐ Aussichten *(prospects)* für die Zukunft
   - ☐ eigener Firmenwagen
   - ☐ Verantwortung
   - ☐ Kontakt zu Menschen
   - ☐ Selbstständigkeit
   - ☐ hohes Einkommen

2. **In welchen Berufen findet man das?** *(Tell which professions best meet the criteria mentioned above.)*

G. Aussprache: b, d, g. Sehen Sie auch III. 3 im Ausspracheteil des Arbeitsheftes!

1. [p] O**b**st, Her**b**st, Er**b**se, hü**b**sch, o**b**, hal**b**, gel**b**
   BUT [p / b] verlie**b**t / verlie**b**en; blei**b**t / blei**b**en; ha**b**t / ha**b**en
2. [t] un**d**, gesun**d**, anstrengen**d**, Gel**d**, Han**d**, sin**d**
   BUT [t / d] Freun**d** / Freun**d**e; Ba**d** / Bä**d**er; Kin**d** / Kin**d**er; wir**d** / wer**d**en
3. [k] Ta**g**, Zu**g**, We**g**, Bahnstei**g**, Flu**g**zeug, Ber**g**
   BUT [k / g] fra**g**st / fra**g**en; flie**g**st / flie**g**en; trä**g**st / tra**g**en; le**g**st / le**g**en

Hören Sie zu!

Was bin ich?

Zum Erkennen: die Putzfrau *(cleaning lady)*; die Beraterin *(counselor)*; korrigieren *(to correct)*; unterwegs *(on the go)*; die Katastrophe; Politiker *(politicians)*; hoffen *(to hope)*; weg *(gone)*; Klienten *(clients)*; ein Testament machen *(to set up a will)*

Welcher Sprecher ist was auf dieser Liste?

_____ Architekt/in	_____ Journalist/in	_____ Rechtsanwalt/-anwältin
_____ Reiseleiter/in	_____ Künstler/in	_____ Sekretär/in
_____ Hausmann/-frau	_____ Lehrer/in	_____ Zahnarzt/-ärztin
_____ Ingenieur/in	_____ Polizist/in	_____ Zeitungsverkäufer/in

STRUKTUR

I. Comparison of adjectives and adverbs

In English and German, adjectives have three degrees:

POSITIVE	COMPARATIVE	SUPERLATIVE
cheap	*cheaper*	*cheapest*
expensive	*more expensive*	*most expensive*

Whereas there are two ways to form the comparative and the superlative in English, there is only ONE WAY in German; it corresponds to the forms of *cheap* above.

NOTE: In German there is no equivalent to such forms as *more expensive* and *most expensive*.

1. In the COMPARATIVE adjectives add **-er;** in the SUPERLATIVE they add **-(e)st.**

    billig   billig**er**   billig**st-**

    a. Many one-syllable adjectives with the stem vowel **a, o,** or **u** have an umlaut in the comparative and superlative, which is shown in the end vocabulary as follows: warm (**ä**), groß (**ö**), jung (**ü**).

    | warm | wärmer | wärmst- |
    | groß | größer | größt- |
    | jung | jünger | jüngst- |

    Other adjectives that take an umlaut include: alt, arm, dumm, gesund, kalt, krank, kurz, lang, nah, rot, schwarz.

    b. Most adjectives ending in **-d** or **-t,** in an **s**-sound, or in vowels add **-est** in the superlative.

    | gesund | gesünder | gesündest- |
    | kalt | kälter | kältest- |
    | heiß | heißer | heißest- |
    | kurz | kürzer | kürzest- |
    | neu | neuer | neuest- |

    Adjectives and adverbs that follow this pattern include: alt (ä), bekannt, beliebt, charmant, intelligent, interessant, kompliziert, laut, leicht, nett, oft (ö), rot (ö), schlecht, talentiert, verrückt; hübsch, weiß, schwarz (ä), stolz; frei.

    c. A few adjectives and adverbs have irregular forms in the comparative and/or superlative.

    | gern | **lieber** | **liebst-** |
    | groß | **größer** | **größt-** |
    | gut | **besser** | **best-** |
    | hoch (hoh-) | **höher** | **höchst-** |
    | nah | **näher** | **nächst-** |
    | viel | **mehr** | **meist-** |

2. The comparative of PREDICATE ADJECTIVES (after **sein, werden,** and **bleiben**) and of ADVERBS is formed as described above. The superlative, however, is preceded by **am** and ends in **-sten.**

    billig   billig**er**   **am** billig**sten**

Die Wurst ist billig.	The sausage is cheap.
Der Käse ist billig**er**.	The cheese is cheaper.
Das Brot ist **am** billig**sten**.	The bread is cheapest.
Ich fahre **gern** mit dem Bus.	I like to go by bus.
Ich fahre **lieber** mit dem Fahrrad.	I prefer to (I'd rather) go by bike.
Ich gehe **am liebsten** zu Fuß.	Best of all I like (I like best) to walk.
Ich laufe **viel**.	I walk a lot.
Theo läuft **mehr**.	Theo walks more.
Katrin läuft **am meisten**.	Katrin walks the most (i.e., more than Theo and I).

CAUTION: Meisten in **die meisten Leute** is an adjective; **am meisten** is an adverb of manner; and **meistens** an adverb of time.

Die **meisten** Leute gehen gern spazieren.	Most people love to walk.
Mein Vater geht **am meisten** spazieren.	My father walks the most.
Mein Vater geht **meistens** in den Park.	My father goes mostly to the park.

3. As you know, adjectives preceding nouns are called ATTRIBUTIVE ADJECTIVES. In the comparative and superlative they have not only the appropriate comparative or superlative markers, but also the adjective endings they would have in the positive forms (see Chapters 9 and 10).

der gut**e** Käse	der besser**e** Käse	der best**e** Käse
Ihr gut**er** Käse	Ihr besser**er** Käse	Ihr best**er** Käse
gut**er** Käse	besser**er** Käse	best**er** Käse

Haben Sie keinen besser**en** Käse? Doch, aber besser**er** Käse ist teu(e)r**er**.

4. There are four special phrases frequently used in comparisons:

   a. When you want to say that one thing is like another or not quite like another, use

   (genau)so . . . wie   or   **nicht so . . . wie**

Ich bin **(genau)so alt wie** er.	I'm (just) as old as he is.
Sie ist **nicht so fit wie** ich.	She is not as fit as I am.

   b. If you want to bring out a difference, use the

   comparative + als

Ich bin **älter als** Helga.	I'm older than Helga.
Sie ist **jünger als** er.	She is younger than he (is).

Lieber 🚂 **als** 🛣

c. If you want to express that something is getting continually more so, use

immer + comparative

Die Tage werden **immer länger.**	*The days are getting longer and longer.*
Ich gehe **immer später** ins Bett.	*I'm getting to bed later and later.*
Autos werden **immer teuerer.**	*Cars are getting more and more expensive.*

d. If you are dealing with a pair of comparatives, use

je + comparative . . . **desto** + comparative

Je länger, **desto** besser.	*The longer, the better.*
Je länger ich arbeite, **desto** müder bin ich.	*The longer I work, the more tired I am.*
Je früher ich ins Bett gehe, **desto** früher stehe ich morgens auf.	*The earlier I go to bed, the earlier I get up in the morning.*

Note that **je** introduces a dependent clause. The **desto + comparative** phrase is followed by a main clause in inverted word order.

> **Je exakter die Diagnose,
> desto größer die Chance für eine
> erfolgreiche Therapie**

Übungen

A. **Komparativ und Superlativ.** Geben Sie den Komparativ und den Superlativ, und dann die Formen des Gegenteils!

   BEISPIEL: schnell **schneller, am schnellsten**
              langsam **langsamer, am langsamsten**

   billig, sauber, schwer, gesund, groß, gut, hübsch, intelligent, jung, kalt, kurz, laut, nah, viel

B. **Ersetzen Sie die Adjektive!**

   BEISPIEL: Diese Zeitung ist so langweilig wie die andere Zeitung. (interessant)
              Diese Zeitung ist so interessant wie die andere Zeitung.

   1. Axel ist so groß wie Horst. (alt, nett)
   2. Hier ist es kühler als bei euch. (kalt, heiß)
   3. Fernsehsendungen werden immer langweiliger. (verrückt, dumm)
   4. Je länger das Buch ist, desto besser. (spannend / interessant; komisch / populär)

C. Antworten Sie mit NEIN! Benutzen Sie das Adjektiv oder Adverb in Klammern *(parentheses)*!

BEISPIEL: Ist dein Großvater auch so alt? (jung)
Nein, er ist jünger.

1. Waren eure Schuhe auch so schmutzig? (sauber)
2. Verdient Jutta auch so wenig? (viel)
3. Ist seine Wohnung auch so toll? (einfach)
4. Sind die Verkäufer dort auch so unfreundlich? (freundlich)
5. Ist es bei Ihnen auch so laut? (ruhig)
6. Ist die Schule auch so weit weg? (nah)
7. Ist Ihre Arbeit auch so anstrengend? (leicht)

D. Wie geht's weiter? Beenden Sie die Sätze zuerst mit einem Komparativ und dann mit einem Superlativ!

BEISPIEL: Inge spricht schnell, aber . . .
Maria spricht schneller. Peter spricht am schnellsten.

1. Willi hat lange geschlafen, aber . . .
2. Brot zum Frühstück schmeckt gut, aber . . .
3. Ich trinke morgens gern Tee, aber . . .
4. Die Montagszeitung ist dick, aber . . .
5. Ich spreche viel am Telefon, aber . . .
6. Deutsch ist schwer, aber . . .
7. Hier ist es schön, aber . . .

E. Ersetzen Sie die Adjektive!

BEISPIEL: Peter ist der sportlichste Junge. (talentiert)
Peter ist der talentierteste Junge.

1. Da drüben ist ein moderneres Geschäft. (gut)
2. Mein jüngster Bruder ist nicht verheiratet. (alt)
3. Das ist die interessanteste Nachricht. (neu)
4. Zieh dir einen wärmeren Pullover an! (dick)
5. Die besten Autos sind sehr teuer. (viel)

American Express Travelers Cheques

Das sicherste Geld der Welt für die schönsten Wochen des Jahres.

F. Eine bessere Stelle. Was fehlt?

1. Möchtest du nicht _____ Beamtin *(civil servant)* werden? *(rather)*
2. Der Staat *(state)* bezahlt _____ deine Firma. *(better than)*
3. Da hast du _____ Sicherheit. *(the greatest)*
4. Beim Staat hast du _____ Freizeit _____ bei deiner Firma. *(just as much . . . as)*
5. Vielleicht hast du _____ Zeit _____ jetzt. *(more . . . than)*
6. Es ist auch nicht _____ anstrengend _____ jetzt. *(as . . . as)*
7. _____ Leute arbeiten für den Staat. *(more and more)*
8. Den _____ Leuten gefällt es. *(most)*
9. Ich finde es beim Staat _____ und _____. *(the most interesting, the most secure)*
10. Eine _____ Stelle gibt es nicht. *(nicer)*
11. _____ du wirst, _____ ist es zu wechseln. *(the older . . . the harder)*
12. Vielleicht verdienst du etwas _____, aber dafür hast du _____ keine Probleme. *(less, mostly)*

G. Was ist für die jungen Deutschen das Wichtigste im Leben? *(Look at the following chart and, as a group, make as many comparisons about it as possible. Then take a class poll, and compare your priorities to those in the chart.)*

Gesundheit	54%	Geld	22%
Liebe	52%	Spaß	16%
Freundschaft	45%	Freizeit	12%
Familie	43%	Sex	10%
Gerechtigkeit *(justice)*	25%	Karriere	9%

BEISPIEL: Gesundheit ist am wichtigsten. Sie ist wichtiger als . . . Aber Liebe ist fast genauso wichtig wie . . .

H. Interview. Fragen Sie einen Nachbarn/eine Nachbarin, . . . !
1. ob er/sie jüngere Geschwister hat, und wer am jüngsten und wer am ältesten ist
2. was er/sie am liebsten isst und trinkt, und ob er/sie abends meistens warm oder kalt isst
3. wo er/sie am liebsten essen geht, und wo es am billigsten und am teuersten ist
4. welche Fernsehsendung ihm/ihr am besten gefällt, und was er/sie am meisten sieht
5. was er/sie am liebsten in der Freizeit macht, und was er/sie am nächsten Wochenende tut
6. welche amerikanische/kanadische Stadt er/sie am schönsten und am hässlichsten findet und warum
7. wo er/sie jetzt am liebsten sein möchte und warum

> **Die größten Ereignisse, das sind nicht unsere lautesten, sondern unsere stillsten Stunden.**
> *Friedrich Wilhelm Nietzsche*

II. Future tense

As you know, future events are often referred to in the present tense in both English and German, particularly when a time expression points to the future.

Wir **gehen** heute Abend ins Kino.
We're going to the movies tonight.
We will go to the movies tonight
We shall go to the movies tonight.

In German conversation this construction is the preferred form. German does have a future tense, however. It is used when there is no time expression and the circumstances are somewhat more formal.

werden . . . + infinitive	
ich **werde** . . . gehen	wir **werden** . . . gehen
du **wirst** . . . gehen	ihr **werdet** . . . gehen
er **wird** . . . gehen	sie **werden** . . . gehen

1. The FUTURE consists of **werden** as the auxiliary plus the infinitive of the main verb.

Ich **werde** ins Büro **gehen.** *I'll go to the office.*
Wirst du mich **anrufen?** *Will you call me?*

2. If the future sentence also contains a modal, the modal appears as an infinitive at the very end.

> **werden** . . . + verb infinitive + modal infinitive

    Ich **werde** ins Büro **gehen müssen.**   *I'll have to go to the office.*
    Wirst du mich **anrufen können?**   *Will you be able to call me?*

3. Sentences in the future follow familiar word order rules.

    Er **wird** auch **kommen.**
    Er **wird** auch **mitkommen.**
    Er **wird** auch **mitkommen wollen.**
      V1   V2

    Ich weiß, dass er auch **kommen wird.**
    Ich weiß, dass er auch **mitkommen wird.**
              V2   V1

4. The future form can also express PRESENT PROBABILITY, especially when used with the word **wohl.**

    Er wird wohl auf dem Weg sein.   *He is probably on the way (now).*
    Sie wird wohl krank sein.   *She is probably sick (now).*

5. Don't confuse the modal **wollen** with the future auxiliary **werden!**

    Er **will** auch mitkommen.   *He wants to (intends to) come along, too.*
    Er **wird** auch mitkommen.   *He will come along, too.*

Remember that **werden** is also a full verb in itself, meaning *to get, to become*.

    Es **wird** kalt.   *It's getting cold.*

Übungen

I. Sagen Sie die Sätze in der Zukunft!

    BEISPIEL: Gute Zahnärzte braucht man immer.
                     Gute Zahnärzte wird man immer brauchen.

1. Dabei verdiene ich auch gut. 2. Aber du studierst einige Jahre auf der Universität. 3. Ich gehe nicht zur Uni. 4. Meine Tischlerarbeit ist anstrengend. 5. Aber daran gewöhnst du dich. 6. Dieser Beruf hat bestimmt Zukunft. 7. Ihr seht das schon. 8. Eines Tages mache ich mich selbstständig. 9. Als Chefin *(boss)* in einem Männerberuf muss ich besonders gut sein. 10. Das darfst du nicht vergessen.

J. Beginnen Sie jeden Satz mit „Wissen Sie, ob . . . ?"!

    BEISPIEL: Er wird bald zurückkommen.
                     Wissen Sie, ob er bald zurückkommen wird?

1. Wir werden in Frankfurt umsteigen.
2. Sie wird sich die Sendung ansehen.
3. Zimmermanns werden die Wohnung mieten.
4. Willi und Eva werden bald heiraten.
5. Müllers werden in Zürich bleiben.
6. Er wird fahren oder fliegen.

K. Was bedeutet das auf Englisch?

BEISPIEL: Martina wird Journalistin.
Martina is going to be a journalist.

1. Walter will Polizist werden. 2. Die Kinder werden zu laut. 3. Ich werde am Bahnhof auf Sie warten. 4. Petra wird wohl nicht kommen. 5. Wir werden Sie gern mitnehmen. 6. Sie wird Informatik *(computer science)* studieren wollen. 7. Oskar wird wohl noch im Büro sein. 8. Wirst du wirklich Lehrer?

L. Eine moderne Familie. Auf Deutsch bitte!

1. Children, I want to tell you something. 2. Your mother is going to be a lawyer. 3. I'll have to stay home. 4. I'll (do the) cook(ing). 5. Helga, you will do the laundry (**die Wäsche waschen**). 6. Karl and Maria, you will (do the) clean(ing). 7. We'll (do the) shop(ping) together. 8. We'll have to work hard. 9. But we'll get used to it. 10. When we get tired, we'll take a break (**eine Pause machen**). 11. Your mother will make a lot of money (earn well). 12. And we will help her.

III. Nouns with special features

1. Certain predicate nouns

   As you already know, German—unlike English—does NOT use the indefinite article before predicate nouns denoting professions, nationalities, religious preference, or political adherence (see Chapter 1, *Zum Thema*).

Er ist **Amerikaner.**	*He is an American.*
Sie ist **Ingenieurin.**	*She's an engineer.*

   When an adjective precedes that noun, however, **ein** is used.

Er ist **ein** typischer Amerikaner.	*He's a typical American.*
Sie ist **eine** gute Ingenieurin.	*She's a good engineer.*

2. Adjectival nouns

   ADJECTIVAL NOUNS are nouns derived from adjectives, that is, the original noun is dropped and the adjective itself becomes the noun. Adjectival nouns are used in English, but not very often. Plural forms usually refer to people, singular nouns to abstract concepts.

   *Give me your **tired** (people), your **poor.***

   The movie: The **Good,** the **Bad,** and **the Ugly.**

   *The **best** is yet to come.*

   German uses adjectival nouns quite frequently. They are capitalized to show that they are nouns, and they have the endings they would have had as attributive adjectives, depending on the preceding article, case, number, and gender. Use the same system you have already learned to put the correct endings on adjectival nouns (see below and Chapters 9 and 10). Masculine forms refer to males, feminine forms to females, and neuter forms to abstract concepts.

der Alte	*the old man*	mein Alter	*my old man, my husband*
die Alte	*the old woman*	meine Alte	*my old woman, my wife*
die Alten	*the old people*	meine Alten	*my old people, my parents*
das Alte		*the old, that which is old, old things*	
das Beste		*the best thing(s)*	
das Wichtigste		*the most important thing*	

Examples of common adjectival nouns are:

der/die Angestellte	*employee*
der/die Bekannte[1]	*acquaintance*
der/die Deutsche	*German person*
der/die Kranke	*sick person*
der/die Verlobte	*fiancé/fiancée*
Also: **der Beamte**[2]	*civil servant*

---

[1] These adjectival nouns are commonly listed as **der Bekannte (ein Bekannter)/der Deutsche (ein Deutscher)**, assuming that the rest of the forms can be deduced.

[2] der Beamte BUT die Beam**tin**!

	SINGULAR masc.	SINGULAR fem.	PLURAL
nom.	der Deutsche ein Deutscher	die Deutsche eine Deutsche	die Deutschen keine Deutschen
acc.	den Deutschen einen Deutschen	die Deutsche eine Deutsche	die Deutschen keine Deutschen
dat.	dem Deutschen einem Deutschen	der Deutschen einer Deutschen	den Deutschen keinen Deutschen
gen.	des Deutschen eines Deutschen	der Deutschen einer Deutschen	der Deutschen keiner Deutschen

Karl ist Beam**ter** und seine Frau Beam**tin**.

Ein Beam**ter** hat das gesagt. Wie heißt der Beam**te**?

Hast du den Beam**ten** da drüben gefragt? Ich sehe keinen Beam**ten**.

Übungen

M. Was sind sie? Auf Deutsch bitte!
1. He's a composer.
2. Is she a housewife?
3. She's a very good scientist.
4. He's going to be a policeman.
5. He was a bad teacher but a good car salesman.
6. She is Austrian.

N. Adjektive als Hauptwörter. Finden Sie die substantivierten Adjektive *(adjectival nouns)* und sagen Sie's auf Englisch!
1. Dem Kranken geht es heute wieder besser.
2. Die Selbstständigen werden es leichter haben.
3. Das Dumme ist, dass Thomas morgen nicht kommen kann.
4. Ein Bekannter von uns will uns am Wochenende besuchen.
5. Er ist Angestellter bei der Bank.
6. Verheirateten ist so etwas nicht wichtig.
7. Gute Gesundheit ist das Wichtigste.
8. Du Glückliche!

Foreign Workers in Germany

Sixty years ago, the German and Turkish governments signed a contract that allowed Turkish workers to be recruited to work in Germany as guest workers **(Gastarbeiter)**. In 1961, 2,500 Turks were living in Germany; today there are 2.3 million, many of them second- and third-generation residents. In the 1960s and 1970s, Turks were mainly employed in mining and in the steel and auto industries; today more and more are working in the service sector. Turks are by far the biggest ethnic group in Germany, and they are becoming more involved in domestic politics and service organizations. In addition to foreign guest workers from around the Mediterranean and asylum-seekers from all over the world, Germany also has received many ethnic immigrants **(Aussiedler)**, most of them from the successor states to the Soviet Union. Although discrimination against immigrants still exists, education and fluency in the language help to facilitate integration into German society.

O. Was fehlt?
1. Ein Bekannt_____ hat mir das erzählt.
2. Hast du den nett_____ Deutsch_____ wiedergesehen?
3. Geben Sie dem Angestellt_____ die Papiere!
4. Viele Deutsch_____ suchen heute Arbeit.
5. Der Verlobt_____ ist Journalist.
6. Zeigen Sie dem Bekannt_____ das Büro!
7. Was hat der Krank_____ Ihnen gesagt?
8. In Deutschland verdient ein Beamt_____ sehr gut.

Zusammenfassung

P. Zukunftspläne. Auf Deutsch bitte!
1. Did you *(pl. fam.)* know that Volker wants to become a journalist? 2. He doesn't want to be a teacher. 3. There are only a few positions. 4. I've gotten used to it. 5. Trudi is as enterprising as he is. 6. She was my most talented student **(Schülerin)**. 7. If she wants to become a dentist, she will become a dentist. 8. She's smarter, more independent, and nicer than her brother. 9. She says that she will work hard. 10. I know that she'll be self-employed one day. 11. I'll go to her rather than to another dentist (I'll go rather to her than . . .). 12. The more I think of it, the better I like the idea.

Q. Hoppla, hier fehlt 'was! Jedem Tierchen sein Pläsierchen. *(To each his own. The following chart shows certain characteristics of various people; the corresponding chart is in section 11 of the Appendix. Work with a partner to complete both charts. Then, based on the information you have compiled, discuss who might be suited to which careers.)*

S1:

	−		+
INTELLIGENT	Peter		Martin
REIST GERN		Nina	Ninas Schwester Pia
KANN GUT MALEN	Wolfgang		
SCHREIBT VIEL	Petra	Petras Schwester	
FREUNDLICH		Thomas und Reinhard	
RUHIG	Hannelore		
ARBEITET SCHWER			Claudia

BEISPIEL: S1 Nina und ihre Schwester reisen gern, aber Pia reist lieber als Nina.
S2 Wirklich? Ninas Kusine reist überhaupt nicht gern.
S1 Pia wird bestimmt eine gute Reiseleiterin sein.
S2 Das glaube ich auch.

R. Schreiben Sie! Was ich einmal werden möchte/wollte und warum. (8–10 Sätze)

ALTES SCHAUSPIELHAUS
Stuttgart · Kleine Königstraße
Telefon 2 26 55 05

KOMÖDIE IM MARQUARDT
Stuttgart · Am Schloßplatz
Telefon 2 27 70 22

Altes Schauspielhaus
Dienstag 17.06.97 20:00 Uhr
EIN BESSERER HERR
von Walter Hasenclever

Parkett links   02
Reihe **11** Platz **207**   DM 22,00

0201 10207010

Dem Abonnenten ist sein guter Platz sicher.

EINBLICKE

Hard Times and Social Policy

The worldwide trend toward industrial efficiency, high productivity, and low labor costs, coupled with the enormous expenses of unification, has led to high unemployment **(Arbeitslosigkeit),** uncommon in Germany before 1990. Rebuilding and privatizing the uncompetitive, formerly state-run industries in the new federal states during an era of increased international competition and recession turned out to be much more difficult than anticipated; the extensive modernization necessitated costly federally-financed training and retraining programs, as well as large-scale early retirements **(Pensionierungen).**

The increased unemployment is mitigated by generous unemployment benefits. Indeed, despite some cutbacks in social benefits, the fundamental principles of a social policy aimed at achieving a high degree of social justice have not changed. All sorts of assistance is provided to those in need, including social security **(Rentenversicherung),** public welfare **(Sozialhilfe),** and health insurance **(Krankenversicherung).** With people living ever longer, the newest addition to this tightly knit social net is long-term care insurance **(Pflegeversicherung).**

Labor unions **(Gewerkschaften)** have always been very important in Germany. However, with harder times since unification, they have been forced to compromise on their long-standing goals of job security with ever higher pay and more fringe benefits. Nevertheless, they remain strong and were recently instrumental in reducing the 40-hour work week to 36 hours, and even fewer in some large industrial companies, in order to save jobs. Their relationship with management has, with few exceptions, been a flexible, cooperative, nonconfrontational partnership—which has contributed to industrial peace and to one of the highest standards of living in the world.

WORTSCHATZ 2

der Arbeiter, -	(blue-collar) worker
Handel	trade
das Ding, -e	thing
Praktikum, Praktika	internship
Unternehmen, -	large company
die Arbeitslosigkeit	unemployment
Berufswahl	choice of a profession
Entscheidung, -en	decision
Kenntnis, -se	knowledge, skill
ebenfalls	also, likewise
ins / im Ausland	abroad
sobald	as soon as
unbedingt	definitely

„Der Kontakt zu den Menschen gefällt mir."

unter (+ *dat.*)	*among*
wenigstens	*at least*
aus·sehen (sieht aus), sah aus, ausgesehen	*to look (like), appear*
bitten, bat, gebeten	*to ask, request*
erwarten	*to expect*
hoffen	*to hope*
sich Sorgen machen (um)	*to be concerned, worry (about)*
sich *(dat.)* vor·stellen	*to imagine*
ich stelle mir vor, dass . . .	*I imagine that . . .*

Vorm Lesen

A. Was denken Sie?

1. Ist es schwer, in den USA, in Kanada oder in Ihrem Land Arbeit zu finden? 2. Was für Stellen findet man leicht? 3. Was für Jobs sind schwerer zu finden? 4. Wie ist es für Leute mit einer Universitätsausbildung, für sogenannte Akademiker? 5. Was für Berufe haben eine gute Zukunft? 6. Was ist ein großes Problem mit vielen Stellen?

B. Was ist das?

der Arbeitgeber, Auslandsaufenthalt, Bauingenieur, Biochemiker, Biologe, Briefsortierer, Computerkünstler, Physiker, Telekommunikationsspezialist; das Industrieunternehmen, Studium; die Betriebswirtschaft, Flexibilität, Hälfte, Mobilität; Handelsbeziehungen, Handelsnationen, Informatikkenntnisse; in der Zwischenzeit; beruflich, chemisch, geschäftlich, kreativ, praktisch, problematisch, qualifiziert; eröffnen, organisieren, reduzieren, übernehmen, sich umsehen

Die Berufswahl

(Eine öffentliche Diskussion an der Universität Göttingen)

Wie viele andere Studenten und Studentinnen, macht Lore Weber sich Sorgen um ihre berufliche Zukunft. Sie hat darum eine Diskussionsgruppe organisiert und eine Professorin und andere Studenten gebeten, Ideen beizutragen°. [to contribute]

LORE WEBER: Eine der wichtigsten Entscheidungen heute ist die Frage der Berufswahl. Die Arbeitslosigkeit ist hoch, nicht nur unter den Arbeitern, sondern auch unter uns Akademikern. In der Zeitung lesen wir zum Beispiel, dass die chemische Industrie immer mehr Stellen reduzieren und ganze Forschungszweige° ins Ausland verlegen° will, wo gut ausgebildete° Physiker, Chemiker oder Biologen billiger zu haben sind. Nur in der Automobilbranche°, eine der wichtigsten Arbeitgeber für Ingenieure, ist es wenigstens wieder etwas besser geworden. Mehr als die Hälfte der Industrieunternehmen werden in den nächsten Jahren jedoch° Arbeitsplätze abbauen°; und im öffentlichen Dienst°, an Schulen und Universitäten wird es nicht besser aussehen. Viele meiner Freunde mit guter Ausbildung suchen Arbeit und jobben in der Zwischenzeit als Bedienung oder als Verkäufer, Taxifahrer oder Briefsortierer bei der Post. Wir fragen uns alle, wie unsere Zukunft aussehen wird, und hoffen, dass wir durch unsere Diskussion eine bessere Vorstellung° davon bekommen. Ich möchte jetzt Frau Professor Weigel bitten, ihre Ansichten° über das Problem zusammenzufassen°. Frau Professor Weigel! [research branches / transfer / trained / . . . industry / however / cut back / civil service / idea / opinions / to summarize]

PROFESSOR WEIGEL: Vielen Dank, Frau Weber! Auf die Frage nach sicheren Berufen kann man nur schwer eine Antwort geben. Ich stelle mir vor, dass die Berufswahl immer problematischer wird. Zu den Berufen mit Zukunft zählen aber bestimmt Umweltexperten°, Biochemiker, Telekommunikations- und Computerspezialisten oder Rechtsanwälte. Auch Architekten und Bauingenieure haben gute Chancen. Selbstständige in den verschiedenen Branchen werden ebenfalls genug Arbeit finden. Den Geisteswissenschaftlern° unter Ihnen empfehle ich, flexibel zu bleiben und auch außerhalb° Ihres Studiums praktische Erfahrungen [environmental experts / humanities scholars / outside of] zu sammeln, zum Beispiel bei Verlagen° und anderen Firmen oder durch Auslandsaufenthalte. Was Sie unbedingt brauchen, sind Informatikkenntnisse. Eins ist klar, eine gute und breite° Ausbildung ist und bleibt die beste Sicherheit. Neben guten Sprach- und Fachkenntnissen° wird man Zusatzqualifikationen° suchen, wie zum Beispiel Flexibilität, Mobilität und die Fähigkeit°, immer wieder Neues zu lernen und kreativ zu denken. Denken Sie daran, Deutschland ist und bleibt eine der größten Handelsnationen; und qualifizierte Angestellte mit Fachkenntnissen braucht man immer!

°publishing houses
°broad
°special skills
°additional . . .
°ability

JÜRGEN PETZOLD: Ich studiere Betriebswirtschaft. Nach dem Studium möchte ich mich selbstständig machen. Mein Bruder und ich haben schon ein kleines Geschäft für Kücheneinrichtungen° eröffnet. Zwei andere Studenten machen mit° und wir haben sogar eine Angestellte. Mein Bruder kümmert sich um° solche Dinge wie den Einbau° von Küchenschränken und ich übernehme den geschäftlichen Teil. Sobald ich meine Prüfungen hinter mir habe, werde ich mich in Dresden oder Leipzig umsehen, um dort vielleicht ein Geschäft zu eröffnen. Ich glaube, das ist eine gute Entscheidung. Unser Geschäft hier läuft ausgezeichnet und ich erwarte, dass die Nachfrage° dort noch größer sein wird.

°. . . furnishings and appliances
°participate
°takes care of / installation

°demand

BRIGITTE SCHINDLER: Ich studiere Kunst und Informatik. Ich hoffe, dass ich eines Tages als Computerkünstlerin für ein Filmstudio oder beim Fernsehen arbeiten werde. Ich finde es wichtig, dass die Arbeit Spaß macht. Nur wenn man etwas gern tut, wird man wirklich gut sein. Und weil die Arbeitslosigkeit unter uns Frauen größer ist als unter Männern, müssen wir einfach besser sein. Ich versuche gerade, einen Platz für ein Praktikum in Amerika zu finden. Je mehr man gemacht hat, desto besser die Chancen. Auslandserfahrung ist wichtig. Mit dem neuen Europa und Deutschlands Handelsbeziehungen mit der ganzen Welt werden unsere Berufsmöglichkeiten immer interessanter. Die Konkurrenz° wird natürlich auch größer. Ich stelle mir vor, dass jedes bisschen Erfahrung hilft. Die besten Jobs werden nur die Besten bekommen.

°competition

Es ist nicht gut genug, klug zu sein. Es ist besser, gut zu sein

Zum Text

A. **Was stimmt?** Aussagen *(statements)* zum Text.
1. Viele deutsche Firmen werden in den nächsten Jahren _____.
   a. die meisten Physiker, Chemiker und Biologen ins Ausland schicken
   b. Arbeitsplätze reduzieren
   c. die billigsten Arbeiter haben
2. Frau Professor Weigel glaubt, dass Studenten vor allem _____ brauchen.
   a. Auslandsaufenthalte
   b. Rechtsanwälte
   c. Flexibilität, Mobilität und Kreativität
3. Jürgen Petzold hofft, _____.
   a. ein Geschäft in Dresden oder Erfurt zu eröffnen
   b. dass die Nachfrage für Küchenmöbel in Leipzig besonders gut sein wird
   c. Betriebswirtschaft zu studieren
4. Brigitte Schindler stellt sich vor, dass _____.
   a. Informatik für sie sehr schwer sein wird
   b. Frauen beruflich besser sein müssen als Männer
   c. praktische Erfahrungen in der Berufswelt nicht immer helfen

B. **Wunschprofil von Arbeitgebern** (What employers are looking for. Working in groups, see how many statements you can make about this chart, using comparatives and superlatives.)

BEISPIEL: Flexibilität ist den Arbeitgebern am wichtigsten.

Zum Erkennen: der Abschluss (diploma); die Hochschule (university)

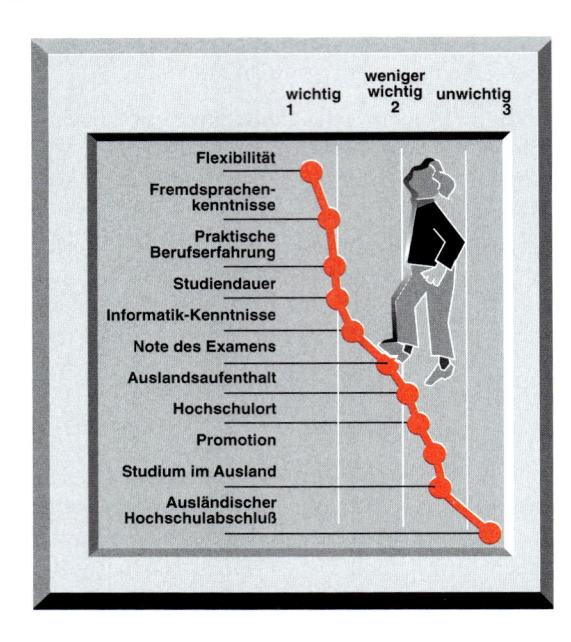

	wichtig 1	weniger wichtig 2	unwichtig 3
Flexibilität			
Fremdsprachenkenntnisse			
Praktische Berufserfahrung			
Studiendauer			
Informatik-Kenntnisse			
Note des Examens			
Auslandsaufenthalt			
Hochschulort			
Promotion			
Studium im Ausland			
Ausländischer Hochschulabschluß			

C. **Blick auf den Arbeitsmarkt.** Wiederholen Sie die Sätze in der Zukunft!

1. Die Berufswahl bleibt eine der wichtigsten Entscheidungen. 2. Gut ausgebildete Chemiker, Physiker und Biologen sind im Ausland billiger. 3. Darum verlegen immer mehr Unternehmen ganze Forschungszweige ins Ausland. 4. Das macht den Arbeitsmarkt (job market) für deutsche Wissenschaftler nicht leichter. 5. Ich stelle mir vor, dass wirklich gute Leute immer Arbeit finden. 6. Die besten Stellen bekommen aber nur die Besten.

D. **So wird's werden.** Was fehlt?
   1. _____ Leute müssen in der Zukunft wenigstens einmal ihren Beruf wechseln. (most)
   2. Gute theoretische Kenntnisse werden _____ wichtig sein _____ praktische Erfahrungen. (just as . . . as)
   3. _____ praktische Erfahrung man hat, _____ sind die Berufschancen. (the more . . . the better)
   4. Man wird auch _____ Zusatzqualifikationen suchen. (more and more)
   5. _____ man seine Prüfungen hinter sich hat, muss man bereit sein (willing), dorthin zu ziehen, wo es Arbeit gibt. (as soon as)
   6. Wer nicht flexibel ist, wird _____ Chancen auf dem Arbeitsmarkt haben und vielleicht auch _____ verdienen. (fewer; less)

E. **Schreiben Sie!** Was bin ich? Nehmen Sie die *Hören-Sie-zu*-Übung auf Seite 326 als Muster (model), und schreiben Sie en paar Sätze! Lesen Sie laut, was Sie geschrieben haben! Die anderen sagen dann, was Sie sind.

F. **Schreiben Sie!** Wie ich mir mein Leben in zehn, zwanzig oder dreißig Jahren vorstelle. (8–10 Sätze)

BEISPIEL: In zehn Jahren werde ich dreißig sein. Dann werde ich . . .
In zehn Jahren wird nichts mehr ohne den Computer gehen . . .

Writing a Résumé

A résumé gives general information about your life and describes the development of your professional career. While the traditional **Lebenslauf** was handwritten and in narrative form, the modern version is typed, brief, and to the point. The following sample shows you one way of preparing it.

```
Lebenslauf
Name:                    Andrea Fischer
Geburtsdatum:            21. November 1976
Geburtsort:              60439 Frankfurt/Main
Nationalität:            Deutsch
Familienstand:           ledig
Eltern:                  Wolf Fischer, Rechtsanwalt
                         und Notar
                         Elke Fischer, geb. Baumann,
                         Lehrerin
Geschwister:             Sabine Fischer, 24, Medizin-
                         studentin
Schulbildung:            1982-1986 Grundschule
                         Frankenstein
                         1986-1995 Schillergymnasium
                         Abschluss: 04.05.1995 Abitur
                         Note: 2
Berufsausbildung:        01.08.1995-28.01.1998
                         Bankkauffrau, Sparkasse-Süd
                         Abschluss: 28.01.1998
                         Bankkauffrau
                         Note: 1
Berufserfahrung:         29.01.1998-30.06.1999
                         Bankkauffrau, Sparkasse-Süd
Ferienbeschäftigungen:   bei der Sparkasse-Süd
Studium:                 ab  01.10.1999
                         Universität Freiburg
                         Fachrichtung: Psychologie und Betriebswirtschaft
Besondere Kenntnisse:    Englisch, Spanisch, Informatik
Hobbys:                  Schwimmen, Wandern, Musik, Lesen

Freiburg, den 1.1.2000   Andrea Fischer
```

Zum Erkennen: der Geburtsort *(birthplace)*; Beschäftigungen *(jobs)*; ab *(starting in)*; die Fachrichtung *(field of study)*

G. Schreiben Sie! Mein Lebenslauf.

Hören Sie zu!

Drei Lebensläufe *(Listen to the brief summaries of three young Germans' lives. It might be helpful to reread the* Vorschau *to this chapter before beginning the true/false activity.)*

Zum Erkennen: halbtags *(part-time)*; verlassen *(to leave)*; Schwerpunktfächer *(majors)*; der Vorarbeiter *(foreman)*; zum Militär *(to the army)*; der Autounfall *(accident)*

Richtig oder falsch?

_____ 1. Die Schmidts haben zwei Kinder, eine Tochter und einen Sohn.
_____ 2. Claudias Vater ist Ingenieur, ihre Mutter Sekretärin.
_____ 3. Claudias Schwerpunktfächer sind Deutsch und Französisch.
_____ 4. Wolf Wicke ist am 23. 11. 1977 geboren.
_____ 5. Wolf macht eine Lehre und geht zur Hauptschule.
_____ 6. Wolf war schon beim Militär.
_____ 7. Christinas Mutter lebt nicht mehr.
_____ 8. Christinas Bruder ist fünf Jahre älter als sie.
_____ 9. Nach dem Abitur hat sie zuerst ein Jahr gearbeitet.
_____ 10. Jetzt ist sie Medizinstudentin in Heidelberg.

FOKUS: Suna Gollwitzer

Suna Gollwitzer, a Turkish Cypriot, was born in 1954. After starting a career as an actress, she went to West Germany in 1971 to work as a nurse. The mother of two daughters, Gollwitzer has moved to Augsburg and is now married to a German.

Totales Versagen

Bin arbeitslos,
das Arbeitsamt° — *employment office*
schickt mich zum Sozialamt,
die letzte Hilfe in der Not°. — *help in distress*
Dann droht° das Ausländeramt — *threatens*
auch noch.
Da stempeln sie nach Laune°. — *They stamp however they please.*
Wenn ich von hier heil° wegkomme, — *unscathed*
werde ich in meiner Heimat° — *home country*
als Fremde empfangen°, — *received as a foreigner*
und die Diagnose lautet° — *is*
»Totales Versagen°«. — *failure*

Suna Gollwitzer

WEB-ECKE

For updates and online activities, visit the *Wie geht's?* home page at: http://www.hrwcollege.com/german/sevin/. You'll visit a *Realschule* in Langeoog and meet some of its students. In addition, you'll compare statistics dealing with national income and (un)employment figures and have a glance at the life of Turkish people in Germany.

SPRECHSITUATIONEN

When you participate in a discussion of a controversial topic, you need to be able to express agreement or disagreement.

Expressing agreement

(Das ist) richtig.
Genau. *(Exactly.)*
Das stimmt (genau).
Das ist (leider) wahr.
Natürlich. / (Na) klar. / Sicher.
Sie haben Recht. / Da hast du Recht.
Das finde / glaube ich auch.
Das hoffe ich auch.

Expressing disagreement

Das stimmt nicht.
(Das ist) gar nicht wahr.
Das finde ich (gar) nicht.
Das glaube ich (aber) nicht.
Das kann nicht sein.
Ach was! *(Oh, come on!)*
Unsinn! Quatsch! Blödsinn! *(Nonsense!)*
Im Gegenteil. *(On the contrary.)*
Das ist doch lächerlich *(ridiculous)*.
einerseits / andererseits *(on the one hand / on the other hand)*

Expressing hesitation

If you don't know how you feel about a topic or what to say—which might happen when conversing in a foreign language—you can use one of these phrases to bridge the gap or stall for time.

Ach so.
Nun / also / na ja / tja *(well)* . . .
Das kommt darauf an.
Gute Frage.
Ich weiß nicht.
(Ich habe) keine Ahnung.

Wir suchen lebensfrohe, selbstbewußte Frauen als Pflegemütter im SOS-Kinderdorf. Viele Kinder kennen kein intaktes Elternhaus. Im SOS-Kinderdorf finden sie eine neue Familie – ihre SOS-Kinderdorf-Familie.

SOS-Kinderdorf e.V.

Frau K. Wilhelms
Renatastr. 77
80639 München 19

Übungen

A. Was hältst du davon? Reagieren Sie auf die Aussagen! Wechseln Sie sich ab *(take turns)*!
1. Die Schweiz ist keine Reise wert.
2. Wir haben heute viel zu viel Freizeit.
3. Wir leben heute gesünder als unsere Eltern und Großeltern.
4. Es ist heute noch wichtiger als früher, Fremdsprachen zu lernen.
5. Wir sitzen alle zu viel vor dem Fernseher.
6. Fernsehen macht dumm.
7. Kinder interessieren sich heute nicht mehr für Märchen.
8. Die meisten Menschen verdienen lieber weniger Geld und haben mehr Freizeit.
9. Wenn mehr Menschen weniger arbeiten, können mehr Menschen arbeiten.
10. Je länger man im Ausland arbeitet, desto besser sind die Berufschancen.
11. Weil Deutschland eines der größten Industrie- und Handelsländer der Welt ist, wird es für Amerikaner und Kanadier immer interessanter, Deutsch zu lernen.
12. Ich stelle mir vor, dass es in den nächsten Jahren in der Wirtschaft viel besser aussehen wird.
13. Kriminalität in den Schulen hat mit Langeweile *(boredom)* zu tun.
14. Eltern sind verantwortlich für die Taten *(actions)* ihrer Kinder.

B. Was denkst du? *(Express hesitation before answering your partner's questions.)*
1. Was willst du einmal werden? Warum?
2. Wohin möchtest du am liebsten reisen? Warum?
3. Möchtest du gern für den Staat arbeiten? Warum (nicht)?
4. Was für Sendungen siehst du am liebsten im Fernsehen? Warum?
5. Wie hältst du dich am liebsten fit? Warum?
6. Welche Eigenschaft ist dir am wichtigsten bei einem Freund/einer Freundin oder einem Partner/einer Partnerin?
7. Was ist dir in deinem Leben am wichtigsten?

C. An wen denke ich? *(Work in groups of four to five students. One thinks of a famous person; the others may ask up to twenty questions to figure out who it is.)*

D. Kurzgespräche
1. With a partner, discuss what <u>you</u> see as the advantages and disadvantages of the German school and job-training system in comparison with the American or Canadian system. Express your agreement or disagreement with your partner's opinion.

2. You are discussing your job choice (**Autoverkäufer, Beamter, Krankenpfleger/in,** etc.) with your parents. They are not happy with your decision and express their disagreement. You agree or disagree with their objections.

Sie wissen, wie man gute Kuchen bäckt. Worauf haben Sie Appetit, eine Himbeertorte *(raspberry . . .)*, Blaubeerborte oder Zitronenrolle?

KAPITEL 13

DAS STUDIUM

Im Hörsaal an der Universität

LERNZIELE

VORSCHAU
German universities

GESPRÄCHE AND WORTSCHATZ
University study and student life

STRUKTUR
Subjunctive mood
Present-time general subjunctive (Subjunctive II)
Past-time general subjunctive

EINBLICKE
Studying in Germany
A year abroad

FOKUS
Red tape
Writing letters
Bertolt Brecht: "1940"

WEB-ECKE

SPRECHSITUATIONEN
Giving advice
Asking for permission
Granting or denying permission

VORSCHAU

German Universities

The first German universities were founded in the Middle Ages: Heidelberg in 1386, Cologne in 1388, Erfurt in 1392, Leipzig in 1409, and Rostock in 1419. In the beginning of the 19th century, Wilhelm von Humboldt redefined the purpose and mission of universities, viewing them as institutions for pure research and independent studies by the nation's preeminent minds. In time, however, it became obvious that this ideal conflicted with the requirements of modern industrial society. In an effort to open opportunities to more students, many new universities and technical colleges **(Fachhochschulen)** have been founded, especially in the last thirty-five years.

There is no tradition of private universities in Germany. Practically all universities are state supported and require no tuition **(Studiengebühren)**; students pay only certain activity fees and mandatory health insurance. Under the Federal Education Promotion Act **(Bundesausbildungsförderungsgesetz = BAföG),** students can obtain financial assistance, part of the amount as a grant and the other part as an interest-free loan to be repaid over several years after the student has entered a profession. Openings **(Studienplätze)** are filled on the basis of academic merit and allocated by a central office in Dortmund, with a certain percentage of places reserved for foreign applicants.

In the past, Germans took it for granted that they could study at minimal cost for as long as they wanted. But in recent years, as record numbers of young people have chosen the academic track, universities have come under extreme pressure to keep up with the influx of students. Admissions restrictions for certain subjects **(Numerus clausus)** are the norm at German universities, and discussions are underway to limit the number of semesters students may study. At the same time, federally funded support for students has decreased.

Educational reformers are looking at a number of issues. In addition to restricting length of study, many would like to issue more marketable degrees—the Bachelor's, for example, which is already widely recognized abroad. Overall, there is a push for greater competition among universities and their faculties that would make German universities more attractive internationally. Many students, however, fear that a sweeping reform could mean the introduction of the tuition payments that characterize American universities.

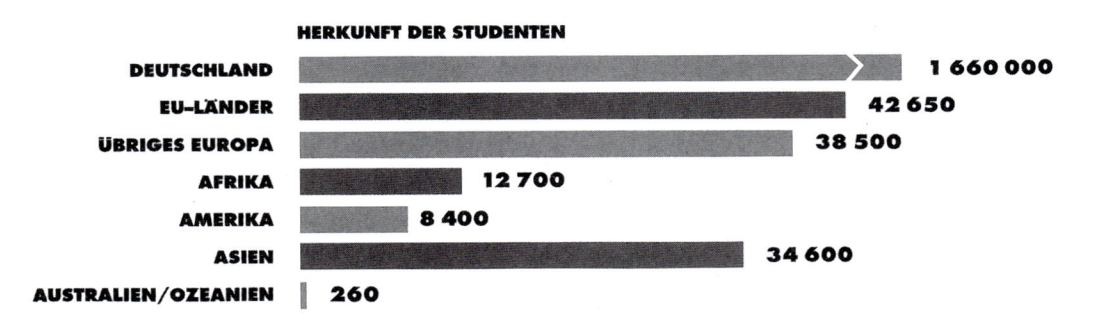

HERKUNFT DER STUDENTEN

DEUTSCHLAND	1 660 000
EU-LÄNDER	42 650
ÜBRIGES EUROPA	38 500
AFRIKA	12 700
AMERIKA	8 400
ASIEN	34 600
AUSTRALIEN/OZEANIEN	260

GESPRÄCHE

Bei der Immatrikulation

Petra Hallo, John! Wie geht's?
John Ganz gut. Und dir?
Petra Ach, ich kann nicht klagen. Was machst du denn da?
John Ich muss noch Immatrikulationsformulare ausfüllen.
Petra Soll ich dir helfen?
John Wenn du Zeit hast. Ich kämpfe immer mit der Bürokratie.
Petra Hast du deinen Pass dabei?
John Nein, wieso?
Petra Darin ist deine Aufenthaltserlaubnis; die brauchst du unbedingt.
John Ich kann ihn ja schnell holen.
Petra Tu das! Ich warte hier so lange auf dich.

Etwas später

John Hier ist mein Pass. Ich muss mich jetzt auch bald entscheiden, welche Seminare ich belegen will. Kannst du mir da auch helfen?
Petra Na klar. Was studierst du denn?
John Mein Hauptfach ist moderne Geschichte. Ich möchte Seminare über deutsche Geschichte und Literatur belegen.
Petra Hier ist mein Vorlesungsverzeichnis. Mal sehen, was sie dieses Semester anbieten.

Was fehlt?

1. John füllt gerade ein . . . aus. 2. Leider hat er seinen . . . nicht dabei. 3. Er muss ihn erst . . . 4. Im Pass ist seine . . . 5. John weiß noch nicht, was er . . . soll. 6. Petra fragt ihn, wofür er . . . 7. Sein Hauptfach ist . . . 8. Petra kann ihm helfen, weil sie ihr . . . dabei hat.

FOKUS Red Tape

All residents of Germany must register with the local registration office (**Einwohnermeldeamt**) within three to seven days of changing address. Standard registration forms can be bought at a stationer's and must be signed by the landlord. Likewise, when moving, residents give notice with an **Abmeldung**. Non-Germans who wish to stay in Germany longer than three months must have a residence permit (**Aufenthaltserlaubnis**). Because of the relatively high unemployment rate, a work permit (**Arbeitserlaubnis**) for non-EU citizens is difficult to obtain and usually is available only if a German or other EU-citizen cannot fill the job. Exceptions are made for students and participants in training programs.

WORTSCHATZ 1

Das Studium *([course of] study)*

der Hörsaal, -säle	lecture hall	das Seminar, -e	seminar
Mitbewohner, -	housemate	Stipendium, Stipendien	scholarship
Zimmerkollege, -n, -n[1]	roommate	System, -e	system
Professor, -en	professor	die Arbeit, -en	here: term paper
Schein, -e	certificate		
das Fach, ̈er	subject	Fachrichtung, -en	field of study
Hauptfach, ̈er	major (field)	Note, -n	grade
Nebenfach, ̈er	minor (field)	(Natur)wissenschaft, -en	(natural) science
Labor, -s	lab		
Referat, -e	oral presentation		
Quartal, -e	quarter		
Semester, -	semester		

belegen	to sign up for, take (a course)
sich entscheiden, entschied, entschieden	to decide
holen	to get (fetch)
lehren	to teach
eine Prüfung machen	to take an exam
(eine Prüfung) bestehen, bestand, bestanden	to pass (a test)
(bei einer Prüfung) durch·fallen (fällt durch), fiel durch, ist durchgefallen	to flunk, fail (a test)
ein Referat halten (hält), hielt, gehalten	to give an oral presentation

Weiteres

Mal sehen.	Let's see.
Na klar.	Of course.
schwierig	difficult
wieso?	why? how come?

---

[1] BUT: die Zimmerkollegin, -nen

Zum Erkennen: klagen *(to complain);* das Immatrikulationsformular, -e *(application for university registration);* kämpfen *(to struggle, fight);* die Bürokratie *(here: red tape);* dabei haben *(to have with you);* das Vorlesungsverzeichnis, -se *(course catalog)*

Zum Thema

A. Fragen übers Studium. Fragen Sie einen Nachbarn/eine Nachbarin, . . . !
1. wie viele Kurse er/sie dieses Semester/Quartal belegt hat und welche
2. welche Kurse er/sie besonders gut findet, und worin er/sie die besten Noten hat
3. ob er/sie viele Arbeiten schreiben muss; wenn ja, in welchen Fächern
4. ob er/sie schon Referate gehalten hat; wenn ja, worin und worüber
5. ob er/sie außer Deutsch noch andere Sprachen spricht oder lernt
6. wie lange er/sie noch studieren muss
7. was er/sie danach macht
8. wie die Chancen sind, in seinem/ihrem Beruf eine gute Stelle zu bekommen
9. in welchen Berufen es momentan schwierig ist, Arbeit zu finden
10. wo es noch bessere Möglichkeiten gibt

B. Deutsch als Fremdsprache. Sagen Sie in etwa fünf Sätzen, was Sie in diesem Schein über John und sein Studium erfahren *(find out)!*

Universität Regensburg
Lehrgebiet
Deutsch als Fremdsprache

~~Frau~~/Herrn   John Smith

aus   USA

wird hiermit bescheinigt, daß

~~sie~~/er an dem DEUTSCHKURS
Konversation - studienbegleitende Oberstufe II (2 SWS)
mit Referat zum Thema:

Amerikanische Einflüsse in Deutschland

im Winter-Semester 1996/97 regelmäßig teilgenommen hat.

~~Sie~~/Er hat den Kurs mit   sehr gut
bestanden/~~nicht bestanden~~.

Regensburg, den 28.02.1997   (Dr. Armin Wolff)

Bewertung:
Bestanden: Sehr gut (1); gut (2); befriedigend (3); ausreichend (4); *Nicht bestanden:* mangelhaft (5); ungenügend (6)

C. Sag mal, was studierst du? Finden Sie Ihr Hauptfach in der Liste; wenn es nicht dabei ist, addieren Sie es dazu! Fragen Sie dann herum, wer das auch noch studiert!

BEISPIEL: S1   Sag mal, was studierst du?
                S2   Ich studiere Psychologie. Und du?
                S1   Ich studiere Volkswirtschaft.

Anglistik° *(English)*	Gesundheitswissenschaft	Pädagogik
Archäologie	Hauswirtschaft° *(home economics)*	Pharmazie
Architektur	Informatik° *(computer science)*	Philosophie
Astronomie	Jura° *(law)*	Physik
Bergbau° *(mining)*	Krankenpflege	Politologie° *(political science)*
Betriebswirtschaft	Kunst	Psychologie
Biochemie	Landwirtschaft° *(agriculture)*	Romanistik° *(Romance lang.)*
Biologie	Lebensmittelchemie	Sport
Chemie	Linguistik	Theologie
Elektrotechnik	Maschinenbau° *(mechanical engineering)*	Tiefbau° *(civil...)*
Forstwirtschaft° *(forestry)*	Mathematik	Volkswirtschaft° *(economics)*
Geographie	Medizin	Tiermedizin° *(veterinary science)*
Geologie	Mineralogie	Zahnmedizin
Germanistik	Musik	
Geschichte	Naturwissenschaft	

D. Aussprache: s, ß, st, sp. Sehen Sie auch III. 6 und 12 im Ausspracheteil des Arbeitsheftes!
1. [z]   **s**auber, **s**icher, Seme**s**ter, **S**eminar, Pau**s**e
2. [s]   Auswei**s**, Kur**s**, Profe**ss**or, wi**ss**en, la**ss**en, flei**ß**ig, Fu**ß**, Grü**ß**e
3. [š]   **St**udium, **St**ipendium, **St**elle, **st**udieren, be**st**ehen, an**st**rengend
4. [st] zuer**st**, mei**st**ens, de**st**o, Kompoi**st**, Kün**st**ler
5. [šp] **Sp**iel, **Sp**ort, **Sp**aß, **Sp**rache, Bei**sp**iel, **sp**ät

Hören Sie zu!

Ein guter Start

Zum Erkennen: das Privileg; wissenschaftlich *(scientific)*; wirtschaftswissenschaftlich *(economic)*; verbessern *(to improve)*; die Wirtschaft *(economics)*; Vollzeitstudenten; die Abschlussarbeit *(thesis)*; Karriere *(career)*

Was stimmt?
1. Den MBA _____.
    a. gibt es nur in Amerika   b. wird es bald auch in Deutschland geben
    c. gibt es jetzt auch in Deutschland
2. Die Studenten am Europa-Institut kommen vor allem aus _____.
    a. Deutschland   b. dem Ausland   c. Amerika
3. Dieses Europa-Institut ist in _____.
    a. Saarbrücken   b. Heidelberg   c. Worms
4. Terry Furman war in Deutschland auf dem Gymnasium und hat dann in _____ Jura studiert.
    a. Frankreich   b. Spanien   c. England
5. Der Franzose Dominique Laurent ist _____ und verspricht sich vom MBA bessere Berufschancen.
    a. Rechtsanwalt   b. Ingenieur   c. Geschäftsmann
6. Am Ende des MBAs ist _____ mit einer Abschlussarbeit.
    a. ein Praktikum   b. eine Lehre   c. eine Auslandsreise
7. Die Wissenschaftliche Hochschule in Koblenz ist _____.
    a. schon alt   b. privat   c. öffentlich
8. Dort kostet der MBA _____.
    a. nichts   b. nicht sehr viel   c. viel Geld

Im Studentenheim

STRUKTUR

I. Subjunctive mood

Until now, almost all sentences in this book have been in the INDICATIVE MOOD. Sentences in the indicative mood are assumed to be based on reality. Sometimes, however, we want to speculate on matters that are unreal, uncertain, or unlikely; or we wish for something that cannot be; or we want to approach other people less directly, more discretely and politely. For that purpose we use the SUBJUNCTIVE MOOD.

1. Polite requests or questions

    Would you like a cup of coffee?
    Would you pass me the butter?
    Could you help me for a moment?

2. Hypothetical statements and questions

    He should be here any moment.
    What would you do?
    You should have been there.

3. Wishes

    If only I had more time.
    I wish you would hurry up.
    I wish I had known that.

4. Unreal conditions

    If I had time, I'd go to the movies. (But since I don't have time, I'm not going.)
    If the weather were good, we'd go for a walk. (But since it's raining, we won't go.)
    If you had told me, I could have helped you. (But since you didn't tell me, I couldn't help you.)

    Contrast the sentences above with real conditions:

    > *If I have time, I'll go to the movies.*
    > *If the weather is good, we'll go for a walk.*

    In real conditions the possibility exists that the events will take place. In unreal conditions this possibility does not exist or is highly unlikely.

    NOTE:

    - The forms of the PRESENT-TIME SUBJUNCTIVE are derived from the simple past: *If I told you (now) . . .*
    - Those of the PAST-TIME SUBJUNCTIVE are derived from the past perfect: *If you had told me (yesterday) . . .*
    - Another very common way to express the subjunctive mood is with the form *would*: *I'd go; I would not stay home.*

Übungen

A. Indikativ oder Konjunktiv (*subjunctive*)? *(Analyze whether these sentences are in the indicative or subjunctive mood, and whether they refer to the present, the future, or the past.)*

> **BEISPIEL:** If you don't ask, you won't know. = **indicative: present / future**
> How would you know? = **subjunctive: present-time**
> What would you have done? = **subjunctive: past-time**

1. If she can, she'll write.
2. If only I had known that.
3. They could be here any minute.
4. Will you take the bike along?
5. Would you please hold this?
6. I had known that for a long time.
7. We should really be going.
8. I wish you had told me that.
9. If you could stay over a Saturday, you could fly for a lower fare.
10. What would they have done if you hadn't come along?
11. If we had had the money, we'd have bought it.
12. If she has the money, she'll give it to us.

II. Present-time general subjunctive

German has two subjunctives. The one most commonly used is often referred to in grammar books as the GENERAL SUBJUNCTIVE or SUBJUNCTIVE II. (the SPECIAL SUBJUNCTIVE or SUBJUNCTIVE I, primarily found in written German, is explained in Chapter 15.)

1. Forms

    The PRESENT-TIME SUBJUNCTIVE refers to the present *(now)* or the future *(later)*. As in English, its forms are derived from the forms of the <u>simple past</u>. You already know the verb endings from having used the **möchte-**forms of **mögen,** which are actually subjunctive forms. All verbs in the subjunctive have these endings:

Infinitive	Simple Past, Indicative	Present-time Subjunctive
mögen	mochte	möchte
	mochtest	möchtest
	mochte	möchte
	mochten	möchten
	mochtet	möchtet
	mochten	möchten

    a. T-verbs *(weak verbs)*

    The present-time subjunctive forms of regular t-verbs are identical to those of the simple past. Their use usually becomes clear from context.

Infinitive	Simple Past, Indicative	Present-time Subjunctive
glauben	glaubte	**glaubte**
antworten	antwortete	**antwortete**

    Wenn Sie mir nur **glaubten!** — *If only you believed me!*
    Wenn er mir nur **antwortete!** — *If only he would answer me!*

    b. Irregular t-verbs *(mixed verbs)*

    Most of the irregular t-verbs, which include the modals, have an umlaut in the present-time subjunctive. Exceptions are **sollen** and **wollen.**

Infinitive	Simple Past, Indicative	Present-time Subjunctive
haben	hatte	**hätte**
bringen	brachte	**brächte**
denken	dachte	**dächte**
wissen	wusste	**wüsste**
dürfen	durfte	**dürfte**
müssen	musste	**müsste**
können	konnte	**könnte**
mögen	mochte	**möchte**
sollen	sollte	**sollte**
wollen	wollte	**wollte**

haben	
ich hätt**e**	wir hätt**en**
du hätt**est**	ihr hätt**et**
er hätt**e**	sie hätt**en**

wissen	
ich wüsst**e**	wir wüsst**en**
du wüsst**est**	ihr wüsst**et**
er wüsst**e**	sie wüsst**en**

Hättest du Zeit? — *Would you have time?*
Könntest du kommen? — *Could you come?*

c. N-verbs *(strong verbs)*

The present-time subjunctive forms of n-verbs add the subjunctive endings to the past stem. If the past stem vowel is an **a, o,** or **u,** the subjunctive forms have an umlaut.

Infinitive	Simple Past, Indicative	Present-time Subjunctive
sein	war	**wäre**
werden	wurde	**würde**
bleiben	blieb	**bliebe**
fahren	fuhr	**führe**
finden	fand	**fände**
fliegen	flog	**flöge**
geben	gab	**gäbe**
gehen	ging	**ginge**
laufen	lief	**liefe**
sehen	sah	**sähe**
tun	tat	**täte**

sein	
ich wär**e**	wir wär**en**
du wär**est**	ihr wär**et**
er wär**e**	sie wär**en**

gehen	
ich ging**e**	wir ging**en**
du ging**est**	ihr ging**et**
er ging**e**	sie ging**en**

Wenn ich du **wäre, ginge** ich nicht. — *If I were you, I wouldn't go.*
Wenn er **flöge, könnte** er morgen hier sein. — *If he were to fly, he could be here tomorrow.*

d. **Würde-**form

In conversation, speakers of German commonly use the subjunctive forms of **haben, sein, werden, wissen,** and the modals.

Hättest du Zeit?	*Would you have time?*
Das **wäre** schön.	*That would be nice.*
Was **möchtest** du tun?	*What would you like to do?*
Wenn ich das nur **wüsste!**	*If only I knew that!*

For the subjunctive forms of other verbs, however, German speakers frequently substitute a simpler verb phrase that closely corresponds to the English *would + infinitive*. It is <u>preferred</u> when the subjunctive form is identical to the indicative form, as is the case with t-verbs and with the plural forms of n-verbs whose subjunctive forms don't have an umlaut (e.g., **gingen**). It is also frequently used in the conclusion clause of contrary-to-fact conditions (see Section d. on p. 356).

Das täte ich nicht. Das **würde** ich nicht **tun.**	*I wouldn't do that.*
Wenn er mir nur glaubte! Wenn er mir nur **glauben würde!**	*If only he would believe me!*
Wir gingen lieber ins Kino. Wir **würden** lieber ins Kino **gehen.**	*We would rather go to the movies.*
Wenn sie Zeit hätte, käme sie mit. Wenn sie Zeit hätte, **würde** sie **mitkommen.**	*If she had time, she would come along.*

2. Uses

    You are already familiar with the most common uses of the subjunctive in English. Here are examples of these uses in German.

    a. Polite requests or questions

Möchtest du eine Tasse Kaffee?	*Would you like a cup of coffee?*
Würdest du mir die Butter geben?	*Would you pass me the butter?*
Könntest du mir einen Moment helfen?	*Could you help me for a minute?*

    b. Hypothetical statements and questions

Er sollte jeden Moment hier sein.	*He should be here any minute.*
Das wäre schön.	*That would be nice.*
Was würdest du tun?	*What would you do?*
Ich würde spazieren gehen.	*I'd go for a walk.*

    c. Wishes

    - Wishes starting with **Wenn . . .** usually add **nur** after the subject or any pronoun object.

Wenn ich nur mehr Zeit hätte!	*If only I had more time!*
Wenn er mir nur glauben würde!	*If only he'd believe me!*

    - Wishes starting with **Ich wünschte, . . .** have BOTH CLAUSES in the subjunctive.

Ich wünschte, ich hätte mehr Zeit.	*I wish I had more time.*
Ich wünschte, du würdest dich beeilen.	*I wish you'd hurry.*

d. Unreal conditions

Wenn ich morgen Zeit hätte, würde ich mit dir ins Kino gehen.	If I had time tomorrow, I'd go to the movies with you.
Wenn das Wetter schöner wäre, würden wir draußen essen.	If the weather were nicer, we'd eat outside.
Wenn wir euch helfen könnten, würden wir das tun.	If we could help you, we would do it.

Contrast the preceding sentences with real conditions.

Wenn ich morgen Zeit habe, gehe ich mit dir ins Kino.	If I have time tomorrow, I'll go to the movies with you.
Wenn das Wetter schön ist, essen wir draußen.	If the weather is nice, we'll eat outside.
Wenn wir euch helfen können, tun wir es.	If we can help you, we'll do it.

little bird/hat
wings

Wenn ich ein Vöglein° wär'
und auch zwei Flügel° hätt',
flög' ich zu dir.
Weil's aber nicht kann sein,
weil's aber nicht kann sein,
bleib' ich allhier°.

right here

Mein Hut°, der hat drei Ecken.
Drei Ecken hat mein Hut.
Und hätt' er nicht drei Ecken,
dann wär' es nicht mein Hut.

Übungen

B. Was tun? Auf Englisch bitte!
1. Wohin möchtest du gehen?
2. Wir könnten uns einen Film ansehen.
3. Wir sollten in die Zeitung sehen.
4. Ich würde lieber zu Hause bleiben.
5. Ich wünschte, ich wäre nicht so müde.
6. Hättest du morgen Abend Zeit?
7. Ich ginge heute lieber früh ins Bett.
8. Morgen könnte ich länger schlafen.

Wenn ich meinen Eltern alles erzählen würde, na dann gute Nacht!

C. Geben Sie das Imperfekt und die Konjunktivform!

BEISPIEL: ich hole   **ich holte**   **ich holte**
           du bringst   **du brachtest**   **du brächtest**
           er kommt   **er kam**   **er käme**

1. ich frage, mache, hoffe, belege, studiere, versuche
2. du arbeitest, antwortest, erwartest, öffnest, heiratest
3. er muss, kann, darf, soll, mag
4. wir bringen, denken, wissen, haben
5. ihr bleibt, schlaft, fliegt, seid, gebt, esst, singt, sitzt, tut, seht, versprecht, werdet, fahrt

D. Reisepläne. Was fehlt?
1. BEISPIEL: **Bauers *würden* nach Wien *fahren.***
   a. Dort _____ wir erst eine Stadtrundfahrt machen.
   b. Dann _____ Dieter sicher den Stephansdom ansehen. Und du _____ dann durch die Kärtner Straße bummeln. Natürlich _____ ihr auch in die Hofburg gehen.

c. Ja, und einen Abend _____ wir in Grinzing feiern.
d. Das _____ euch bestimmt gefallen.

2. **BEISPIEL: Ute *führe* in die Schweiz.**
   a. Ich _____ mit ein paar Freunden in die Schweiz fahren. (können)
   b. Erst _____ wir an den Bodensee. (fahren)
   c. Von dort _____ es weiter nach Zürich und Bern. (gehen)
   d. In Zürich _____ ich mir gern das Thomas-Mann-Archiv *(archives)* _____. (ansehen)
   e. Ihr _____ auch nach Genf fahren. (sollen)
   f. Dort _____ du Französisch sprechen. (müssen)
   g. Das _____ keine schlechte Idee! (sein)

E. **Sagen Sie's höflicher** *(more politely)*!
   1. **BEISPIEL:** Können Sie uns die Mensa zeigen?
      Könnten Sie uns die Mensa zeigen?

   a. Darf ich kurz mit Ihnen sprechen? b. Haben Sie Lust mitzukommen? c. Können wir uns an einen Tisch setzen? d. Haben Sie etwas Zeit?

   2. **BEISPIEL:** Rufen Sie mich morgen an!
      Würden/Könnten Sie mich morgen anrufen?

   a. Erzählen Sie uns von der Reise! b. Bringen Sie die Fotos mit! c. Machen Sie mir eine Tasse Kaffee! d. Geben Sie mir die Milch!

F. **Wünsche**
   1. **Beginnen Sie mit „Ich wünschte, . . .“!**
      BEISPIEL: Das Seminar ist schwer.
      Ich wünschte, das Seminar wäre nicht so schwer.

   a. Ich muss viel lesen. b. Das nimmt viel Zeit. c. Ich bin müde. d. Ihr seid faul.

   2. **Beginnen Sie mit „Wenn . . . nur . . .“!**
      BEISPIEL: Ich wünschte, ich könnte schlafen.
      Wenn ich nur schlafen könnte!

   a. Ich wünschte, wir hätten keine Referate.
   b. Ich wünschte, ich wüsste mehr über das Thema Wirtschaft.
   c. Ich wünschte, du könntest mir helfen.
   d. Ich wünschte, diese Woche wäre schon vorbei.

G. **Wiederholen Sie die Sätze im Konjunktiv!**
   BEISPIEL: Wenn das Wetter schön ist, kann man die Berge sehen.
   Wenn das Wetter schön wäre, könnte man die Berge sehen.

   1. Wenn es möglich ist, zeige ich euch das Schloss.
   2. Wenn du das Schloss sehen willst, musst du dich beeilen.
   3. Wenn ihr zu spät kommt, ärgert ihr euch.
   4. Wenn das Schloss zu ist, können wir wenigstens in den Schlosspark gehen.
   5. Wenn ihr mehr sehen wollt, müsst ihr länger hier bleiben.

H. Zwei wichtige Fragen für junge Deutsche: Was wäre, wenn . . . ? *(In small groups, look at the following chart. Discuss the ratings, then poll each other. You could also add other possible choices.)*

. . . Sie so leben könnten, wie Sie wollten?	
als Globetrotter um die Welt ziehen	25%
als Single in einer Penthouse-Wohnung wohnen	16%
als Handwerker/in in einer Kleinstadt leben	14%
als Chirurg/in mit Familie in einer Villa wohnen	13%
als Künstler in einem altem Haus leben	12%
als Playboy/Model immer da sein, wo etwas los ist	8%
Aktivist/in für Greenpeace sein	4%
als Bundespräsident/in im Schloss Bellevue wohnen	4%

. . . Ihre Oma Ihnen 10 000 DM hinterlassen würde?	
Ich bringe das Geld zur Bank.	43%
Ich verreise.	25%
Ich kaufe mir Kleidung.	20%
Ich kaufe etwas Größeres.	19%
Ich frage mich, wo die restlichen 90 000 Mark sind.	10%
Ich feiere mit Freunden und zahle alles.	6%
Ich kaufe Aktien *(stocks)*.	5%
Ich gebe den Armen etwas.	3%

I. Wie geht's weiter?

BEISPIEL: Ich wäre glücklich, wenn . . .
Ich wäre glücklich, wenn ich gut Deutsch sprechen könnte.

1. Ich wäre froh, wenn . . .
2. Ich fände es prima, wenn . . .
3. Es wäre furchtbar, wenn . . .
4. Ich würde mich ärgern, wenn . . .
5. Ich würde sparen, wenn . . .
6. Ich wüsste, was ich täte, wenn . . .

J. Wochenendpläne. Auf Deutsch bitte!

1. Can you *(pl. fam.)* stay? 2. We could go for a walk. 3. I was supposed to visit my grandfather last week. 4. Now we have to do it on Saturday. 5. I wish I knew why he has not called. 6. I know he would call me if he needed anything. 7. Would you *(pl. fam.)* feel like going to a restaurant? 8. That would be nice. 9. We wish we had time. 10. If Walter didn't have to work we could stay.

HÄTTE ICH DIE KRAFT NICHTS ZU TUN TÄTE ICH NICHTS.

III. Past-time general subjunctive

You already know that a simple-past form in English can express the present-time subjunctive (referring to *now* or *later*). The past-perfect form, or *would have* + participle, expresses the same thought in the PAST-TIME SUBJUNCTIVE (referring to *earlier*).

NOW OR LATER: If I *had* time, I *would* go with you.
EARLIER: If I *had had* time, I *would have* gone with you.

1. Forms

    a. In German, the forms of the past-time subjunctive are based on the forms of the past perfect. The past-time subjunctive is very easy to learn because it simply consists of a form of **hätte** or **wäre** plus the past participle:

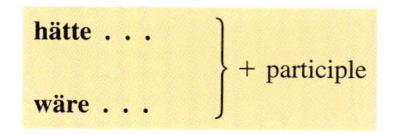

    hätte . . .
    wäre . . . } + participle

Das **hätte** ich nicht **getan.**	*I wouldn't have done that.*
Hättest du das **getan?**	*Would you have done that?*
Ich **wäre** lieber ins Kino **gegangen.**	*I would have rather gone to the movies.*
Wärest du nicht lieber ins Kino **gegangen?**	*Wouldn't you have rather gone to the movies?*
Ich wünschte, du **hättest** mir das **gesagt!**	*I wish you had told me that!*
Wenn ich das **gewusst hätte, wären** wir ins Kino **gegangen.**	*If I had known that, we would have gone to the movies.*

    b. All modals follow this pattern in the past-time subjunctive:

    hätte . . . + verb infinitive + modal infinitive

Du **hättest** mir das **sagen sollen.**	*You should have told me that.*
Wir **hätten** noch ins Kino **gehen können.**	*We still could have gone to the movies.*

    For now, avoid using these forms in dependent clauses.

2. Uses

The past-time subjunctive is used for the same purposes as the present-time subjunctive. Note that there are no polite requests in the past.

a. Hypothetical statements and questions

Ich wäre zu Hause geblieben.	*I would have stayed home.*
Was hättet ihr gemacht?	*What would you have done?*
Hättet ihr mitkommen wollen?	*Would you have wanted to come along?*

b. Wishes

Wenn ich das nur gewusst hätte!	*If only I had known that!*
Ich wünschte, du wärest da gewesen.	*I wish you had been there.*

c. Unreal conditions

Wenn du mich gefragt hättest, hätte ich es dir gesagt.	*If you had asked me, I would have told you.*
Wenn du da gewesen wärest, hättest du alles gehört.	*If you had been there, you would have heard everything.*

Übungen

K. Sagen Sie die Sätze in der Vergangenheit *(referring to earlier)!*

1. **BEISPIEL:** Sie würde das tun.
   Sie hätte das getan.

   a. Sie würde euch anrufen. b. Ihr würdet ihr helfen. c. Ihr würdet schnell kommen. d. Du würdest alles für sie tun.

2. **BEISPIEL:** Hannes sollte nicht so viel Schokolade essen.
   Hannes hätte nicht so viel Schokolade essen sollen.

   a. Wir dürften ihm keine Schokolade geben. b. Das sollten wir wissen. c. Er könnte auch Obst essen. d. Wir müssten besser aufpassen.

L. Was wäre gewesen, wenn . . . ?

1. **Wiederholen Sie die Sätze in der Vergangenheit!**

   BEISPIEL: Wenn ich es wüsste, würde ich nicht fragen.
   Wenn ich es gewusst hätte, hätte ich nicht gefragt.

   a. Wenn wir eine Theatergruppe hätten, würde ich mitmachen.
   b. Wenn der Computer billiger wäre, würden wir ihn kaufen.
   c. Wenn ich Hunger hätte, würde ich mir etwas kochen.
   d. Wenn sie fleißiger arbeitete, würde es ihr besser gehen.

2. **Und dann?** Was würden Sie tun oder hätten Sie getan? Wechseln Sie sich ab *(take turns)!*

   BEISPIEL: S1 Ich hatte keinen Hunger. Wenn ich Hunger gehabt hätte, . . .
   . . . wäre ich in die Küche gegangen.
   S2 Und dann?
   S1 **Dann hätte ich mir ein Wurstbrot gemacht.**

   a. Gestern hat es geregnet. Wenn das Wetter schön gewesen wäre, . . .
   b. Ich bin nicht lange auf der Party gewesen. Wenn ich zu lange gefeiert hätte, . . .
   c. Natürlich hatten wir letzte Woche Vorlesungen. Wenn wir keine Vorlesungen gehabt hätten, . . .

M. Hoppla, hier fehlt 'was! Oma und Opa. *(You and a friend are talking about your grandparents' lives. First, your partner will tell you about his or her grandfather, using the information in the Appendix; as you listen, check JA or NEIN, depending on whether the grandfather did or did not do the activity mentioned. Then reverse roles. Use the text below to tell your partner about your grandmother; your partner will check JA or NEIN, as appropriate.)*

S1:
Erzählen Sie Ihrem Partner/Ihrer Partnerin:

Meine Oma ist gern zur Schule gegangen. Sie war besonders gut in Mathe. Wenn ihre Familie Geld gehabt hätte, hätte sie gern studiert. Sie wäre furchtbar gern Lehrerin geworden. Aber sie musste als Kindermädchen *(nanny)* bei einer reichen Familie arbeiten. Dann hat sie meinen Großvater kennen gelernt und geheiratet. Meine Oma liebt Kinder und sie hätte gern eine große Familie gehabt. Sie hatten aber nur ein Kind. Sie ist immer gern gereist. Wenn mein Großvater länger gelebt hätte, hätten sie zusammen eine große Weltreise gemacht.

Und was sagt Ihnen Ihr Partner/Ihre Partnerin?

	Ja	Nein
Sein / Ihr Opa ist aus Deutschland gekommen.	x	
Seine Familie ist mit dem Schiff gefahren.		
Der Opa ist gern nach Amerika gekommen.		
Seine Familie hat in New York gewohnt.		
Er ist Polizist geworden.		
Er konnte gut singen.		
Er hat gelernt, Klavier zu spielen.		
Er ist dieses Jahr nach Deutschland gefahren.		

N. Schade! Auf Deutsch bitte!

1. Too bad, we should have stayed at home. 2. If the weather had been better, we could have gone swimming in the lake. 3. But it rained all day. 4. I wish they hadn't invited us. 5. If we had stayed home, we could have watched/seen the detective story. 6. You *(sg. fam.)* should have gone out with her. 7. If I had had time, I would have called her. 8. If I have time, I will call her tomorrow. 9. I had no time to call her yesterday. 10. I should have called the day before yesterday, but I forgot (it).

Zusammenfassung

O. Indikativ oder Konjunktiv? Was bedeutet das auf Englisch?
1. Wenn er uns besuchte, brachte er immer Blumen mit.
2. Können Sie mir Horsts Telefonnummer geben?
3. Wenn du früher ins Bett gegangen wärest, wärest du jetzt nicht so müde.
4. Gestern konnten sie nicht kommen, aber sie könnten uns morgen besuchen.
5. Er sollte gestern anrufen.
6. Ich möchte Architektur studieren.
7. Sie waren schon um 6 Uhr aufgestanden.
8. Ich wünschte, er ließe nicht immer alles auf dem Sofa liegen.

P. Guter Rat *(good advice)*

1. **Was soll ich tun?** *(In small groups, give each other advice. One person mentions a problem, real or invented—e.g., having no money or energy, being hungry or thirsty, missing something—and the others advise him or her what to do.)*

   BEISPIEL: Ich bin immer so müde.
   Wenn ich du wäre, würde ich früher ins Bett gehen.

2. **Was hätte ich tun sollen?** *(This time give advice as to what one should have done or not done.)*

   BEISPIEL: Ich habe meine Schlüssel verloren.
   Du hättest besser aufpassen sollen.

Q. Kommst du mit? Auf Deutsch bitte!

1. Would you *(sg. fam.)* like to go (**fahren**) with us to Salzburg? 2. We could go by train. 3. It ought to be quieter now than in the summer. 4. That would be nice. 5. I'd come along, if I could find my passport. 6. I wish you *(pl. fam.)* had thought of it earlier. 7. Then I could have looked for it. 8. If I only knew where it is. 9. I'd like to see the Mirabell Garden, the Mozart house, and the castle (**die Burg**). 10. The city is supposed to be wonderful. 11. Without my passport I'd have to stay home.—Here it is! 12. If you *(sg. fam.)* hadn't talked (**reden**) so much, you'd have found it more quickly.

Heidelberg am Neckar. Blick auf die Altstadt und das Schloss

EINBLICKE

Studying in Germany

Studying in Germany is considerably different from studying in the United States. Students enter the university with a broad general education and can therefore immediately focus on a major **(Hauptfach)**. They are responsible for their own progress and are able to select courses and seminars suited to their needs and interests, with only a few required courses. Lecture courses usually have no exams; seminars, however, require research papers, and students receive a certificate **(Schein)**. Ultimately, students are responsible for acquiring the necessary knowledge to pass an intermediate qualifying exam **(Zwischenprüfung)** and eventually a rigorous final exam **(Abschlussprüfung)**. The basic degree—the equivalent of an M.A. in the arts and humanities—is the **Magister**; in the natural or social sciences and in engineering, it is the **Diplom**. Some students choose to continue their studies to obtain a doctorate. Those who wish to become teachers, doctors, or lawyers must pass a board exam in their field **(1. Staatsexamen)**, followed by a second exam **(2. Staatsexamen)** after an internship.

The academic calendar is officially divided into a winter semester (from about October to March) and a summer semester (from about April to August), varying somewhat from state to state. The **Vorlesungfreie Zeit,** a two-month period of time to catch up on work, to take a job, or to go on a vacation, occurs in late winter and late summer between semesters.

German universities are academically self-governing and are headed by a president **(Rektor)** elected for several years. Purely administrative matters are handled by a permanent staff of civil servants under the direction of a chancellor **(Kanzler)**.

WORTSCHATZ 2

Ach was!	*Oh, come on.*
an deiner / seiner Stelle	*in your / his shoes; if I were you / he*
ausländisch	*foreign*
Das geht (nicht).	*That's (not) O.K.*
deshalb	*therefore*
gar nicht	*not at all*
jedenfalls	*in any case*
so dass	*so that*
sowieso	*anyhow*
wahrscheinlich	*probably*
Angst haben (vor + *dat.*)	*to fear, be afraid (of)*
an·nehmen (nimmt an), nahm an, angenommen	*to suppose; to accept*
auf·hören	*to end; to stop doing something*
teilen	*to share*
teil·nehmen (nimmt teil), nahm teil, teilgenommen (an + *dat.*)	*to participate, take part (in)*
sich vor·bereiten (auf + *acc.*)	*to prepare (for)*

Vorm Lesen

A. Allerlei Fragen
1. Würden Sie gern in Europa studieren? Wo, wann und wie lange?
2. Worauf würden Sie sich freuen?
3. Denken Sie, es würde mehr oder weniger kosten, drüben zu studieren?
4. Was würden Sie in den Ferien tun?
5. Hat Ihre Uni ein Austauschprogramm? Wenn ja, mit welcher Universität?
6. Haben Sie Freunde, die *(who)* drüben studiert haben? Wenn ja, wo; und wie hat es Ihnen gefallen?

B. Was ist das?

der Grammatikkurs, Intensivkurs, Lesesaal, Semesteranfang; das Archiv, Auslandsprogramm, Sommersemester; die Seminararbeit; Sprachprüfung; teilmöbliert

Ein Jahr drüben wäre super!

(Gespräch an einer amerikanischen Universität)

	TINA	Hallo, Margaret!
	MARGARET	Tag, Tina! Kennst du Bernd? Er ist aus Heidelberg und studiert ein Jahr bei uns.
well	TINA	Guten Tag! Na°, wie gefällt's dir hier?
	BERND	Sehr gut. Meine Vorlesungen und die Professoren sind ausgezeichnet. Ich wünschte nur, es gäbe nicht so viele Prüfungen!
	TINA	Habt ihr keine Prüfungen?
instead	BERND	Doch, aber weniger. Dafür° haben wir nach ungefähr vier Semestern eine große Zwischenprüfung und dann am Ende des Studiums das Examen.
	TINA	Ich würde gern einmal in Europa studieren.
	MARGARET	Ja, das solltest du unbedingt.
	TINA	Es ist bestimmt sehr teuer.
	MARGARET	Ach was, so teuer ist es gar nicht. Mein Jahr in München hat auch nicht mehr gekostet als ein Jahr hier.
	TINA	Wirklich?
tuition	BERND	Ja, unsre Studentenheime und die Mensa sind billiger als bei euch und wir haben praktisch keine Studiengebühren°. Ohne mein Stipendium könnte ich nicht in Amerika studieren.
	TINA	Ist es schwer, dort drüben einen Studienplatz zu bekommen?
depending on	BERND	Wenn du Deutsche wärst, wäre es wahrscheinlich nicht so einfach—je nachdem°, was du studieren willst. Aber als Ausländerin in einem Auslandsprogramm hättest du gar kein Problem.
	TINA	Ich muss noch mal mit meinen Eltern sprechen. Sie haben Angst, dass ich ein Jahr verlieren würde.
	MARGARET	Wieso denn? Wenn du mit einem Auslandsprogramm nach Deutschland gingest, würde das doch wie ein Jahr hier zählen.
	TINA	Ich weiß nicht, ob ich genug Deutsch kann.
	MARGARET	Keine Angst! Viele Studenten können weniger Deutsch als du. Du lernst es ja

schon seit vier Jahren. Außerdem bieten die meisten Programme vor Semesteranfang einen Intensivkurs für ausländische Studenten an. Damit würdest du dich auch auf die Sprachprüfung am Anfang des Semesters vorbereiten. Wenn du die Prüfung wirklich nicht bestehen solltest—was ich mir nicht vorstellen kann, denn dein Deutsch ist gut—, dann müsstest du eben° einen Grammatikkurs in „Deutsch als Fremdsprache" belegen und sie am Ende des Semesters wiederholen. *just*

TINA Das geht. Vielleicht kann ich doch im Herbst ein Semester nach Deutschland.

MARGARET Im Herbst ginge ich nicht, weil das Wintersemester in Deutschland erst Ende Februar aufhört.

TINA Ende Februar? Und wann ist das Frühjahrssemester°? *spring . . .*

BERND Bei uns gibt es ein Wintersemester und ein Sommersemester. Das Wintersemester geht von Oktober bis März, das Sommersemester von April bis August. Du müsstest deshalb ein ganzes Jahr bleiben oder nur für das Sommersemester kommen. Ein ganzes Jahr wäre sowieso besser, denn dann hättest du zwischen den Semestern Zeit zu reisen.

MARGARET Stimmt. In der Zeit bin ich auch viel gereist. Ich war in Frankreich, Spanien, Italien, Griechenland und danach noch in Ungarn.

TINA Super! Was für Vorlesungen sollte ich belegen?

BERND Im ersten Semester würde ich nur Vorlesungen belegen, keine Seminare. Da hört man nur zu und schreibt mit°. Im zweiten Semester solltest du dann aber auch ein Seminar belegen. Bis dann ist dein Deutsch jedenfalls gut genug, so dass du auch eine längere Seminararbeit schreiben oder ein Referat halten könntest. *takes notes*

TINA Seminararbeiten und Referate auf Deutsch?

MARGARET Am Anfang geht's langsam, aber man lernt's.

BERND Ich mach's ja auch auf Englisch. Übrigens, bei euch ist das Bibliothekssystem viel besser. Wir müssen Bücher immer zuerst bestellen, was oft Tage dauert. Man kann nicht einfach in die Archive wie hier. Und die Fachbibliotheken° leihen keine Bücher aus°, außer am Wochenende. *departmental libraries for a major / lend out*

TINA Ich kann mir ja die Bücher kaufen.

BERND Das wäre viel zu teuer! Dann würde ich schon lieber im Lesesaal sitzen.

TINA Und wie ist das mit Studentenheimen?

MARGARET Wenn du an einem Auslandsprogramm teilnimmst, hast du keine Probleme.

BERND An deiner Stelle würde ich versuchen, ein Zimmer im Studentenheim zu bekommen. Auf diese Weise lernst du leichter andere Studenten kennen. Die Zimmer sind nicht schlecht, teilmöbliert und mit Bad. Die Küche auf einem Flur müsstest du aber mit fünf oder sechs anderen Studenten teilen.

TINA Da habe ich nichts dagegen. Findet ihr, Heidelberg wäre besser als Berlin oder München?

BERND Ach, das ist schwer zu sagen.

MARGARET Ich glaube, wenn ich Berlin gekannt hätte, hätte ich dort studiert. Mir hat es da sehr gut gefallen. Aber erst musst du wissen, ob du wirklich nach Deutschland willst. Wenn du das weißt, dann kann ich dir weiterhelfen.

TINA Danke! Macht's gut! Ich muss zur Vorlesung.

Zum Text

A. Ein Jahr im Ausland. Was fehlt?

a. Angst haben b. Europa c. ein Jahr d. die Küche e. München f. Prüfungen g. Sommersemester h. Sprachprüfung i. andere Studenten j. Vorlesungen k. Heidelberg l. Wintersemester

1. Bernd ist aus _____ und studiert _____ in Amerika.
2. Ihm gefallen nur die vielen _____ nicht.
3. Tina möchte gern in _____ studieren.
4. Margarets Jahr in _____ hat nicht viel mehr gekostet als ein Jahr zu Hause.
5. Tinas Eltern _____, dass ihre Tochter drüben ein Jahr verliert.
6. Ausländische Studenten müssen vor Semesteranfang eine _____ machen.
7. Das _____ geht von November bis Ende Februar, das _____ von April bis Ende Juli.
8. Im ersten Semester sollte Tina nur _____ belegen.
9. In einem Studentenheim kann man leichter _____ kennen lernen.
10. In einem deutschen Studentenheim muss man _____ mit anderen Studenten teilen.

B. Das Studium hier und dort. Vergleichen Sie die beiden Systeme!

1. Prüfungen 2. Studiengebühren 3. Semesterkalender 4. Kurse 5. Bibliotheken

C. An der Uni. Was fehlt?

1. Bernd _____, es _____ nicht so viele Prüfungen. *(wishes, there were)*
2. Wenn Bernd kein Stipendium _____, _____ er hier nicht studieren können. *(had gotten, could have)*
3. Wenn Tina mit einem Austauschprogramm nach Deutschland _____, _____ das wie ein Jahr hier zählen. *(would go, would)*
4. Tina _____ ein ganzes Jahr bleiben, oder sie _____ nur für das Sommersemester gehen. *(would have to, could)*
5. Ein ganzes Jahr drüben _____ besser. *(would be)*
6. Dann _____ Tina Zeit, zwischen den Semestern zu reisen. *(would have)*
7. In einem Studentenheim _____ Tina leichter deutsche Studenten kennen lernen. *(would)*
8. Wenn Margaret Berlin _____, _____ sie dort studiert. *(had known, would have)*
9. Wenn sie nicht an einer deutschen Uni _____, _____ sie nicht so gut Deutsch sprechen. *(had studied, could)*
10. Tina _____, dass ihr Deutsch nicht gut genug _____. Aber das _____ kein Problem _____. *(is afraid, would be, shouldn't be)*

D. Das Vorlesungsverzeichnis. Lesen Sie das Verzeichnis und beenden Sie die Sätze!

1. Die Vorlesungen sind alle über . . . 2. Mich würde besonders die Vorlesung über . . . interessieren. Sie wäre . . . von . . . bis . . . 3. Außerdem dürfte Professor . . . s Vorlesung über . . . interessant sein. 4. . . . würde mich nicht/weniger interessieren, weil . . .

Geschichte der Stadt Rom in der Zeit der römischen Republik 3st., Mo 11 - 13, Mi 12 - 13	Lippold
Die sozialen und wirtschaftlichen Verhältnisse in der griechischen Welt von der Archaischen Zeit bis zum Beginn des Hellenismus 2st., Mo 14 - 15.30	Hennig
Kirche und Gesellschaft im früheren Mittelalter (5.-12. Jahrhundert) 3st., Do 12-13, Fr 11 - 13	Hartmann
Deutschland und Frankreich im 15. und 16. Jahrhundert. Der Beginn eines europäischen Gegensatzes 2st., Di, Mi 9 - 10	Schmid
Politik und Geschichte in Deutschland nach 1945 2st., Do 13 - 15	Haan
Demokratie oder Volksherrschaft? Zur Geschichte der Demokratie seit dem späten 18. Jahrhundert II 2st., Do 16 - 18	Lottes
Deutschland in der Industrialisierung 2st., Di 10 - 11, Mi 11 - 12	Bauer
Bayerische Geschichte zwischen 1800 und 1866 2st., Mi, Do 11 - 12	Volkert
Wirtschaft und Gesellschaft Bayerns im Industriezeitalter 2st., Mo, Di 11 - 12	Götschmann
Das Ostjudentum (19./20. Jahrhundert) 2st., Mi, Fr 8 - 9	Völkl
Europa zwischen den Weltkriegen (1919-1939) 2st., Mo 10 -12	Möller

E. Am liebsten würde ich . . .
1. Wenn ich könnte, würde ich einmal in . . . studieren.
2. Am liebsten würde ich in . . . wohnen, weil . . .
3. Am Anfang des Semesters . . .
4. Am Ende des Semesters . . .
5. Während der Semesterferien . . .

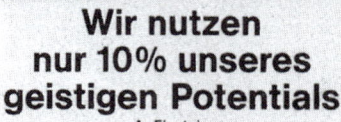

F. Schreiben Sie! Das wäre schön. (6–8 Sätze im Konjunktiv über eines der Themen)
1. Ein Jahr drüben wäre super!
2. Mein Traumhaus
3. Meine Traumfamilie
4. Das würde mir gefallen.
5. Das hätte mir gefallen.

Wir nutzen nur 10% unseres geistigen Potentials
A. Einstein

Writing Letters

You are familiar with writing letters to friends and relatives, which usually start with **Liebe(r) . . .** and end with **Viele liebe Grüße, Dein(e)/Euer(e) . . .** No special format is necessary. However, when writing a more formal letter, certain rules apply. The following letter is just one example of the appropriate style. After giving the date, your address, and the recipient's address, you might refer to a particular matter or previous letter by writing **Betr(eff):** When addressing one or more people, use **Sehr geehrter Herr/Sehr geehrte Frau,** or **Sehr geehrte Damen und Herren,** followed by a comma. After the comma, continue writing in lower case. Common phrases to end a letter are **Mit freundlichen Grüßen** or **Mit freundlichem Gruß! Ihr(e) . . .**

368 KAPITEL 13

Ina Bachmann
Mainstraße 15
64625 Bensheim
Tel. (06251) 67 123

Bensheim, den 15.03.2000

Herrn
Dr. Alfred Kleese
Grethenweg 40
60598 Frankfurt/Main

Betr.: Berufsinformation

Sehr geehrter Herr Dr. Kleese,

successful — von meinen Eltern höre ich, dass Sie ein sehr erfolgreicher° Rechtsanwalt sind. Diesen Beruf fand ich schon immer faszinierend, aber ich weiß eigentlich wenig über die tägliche Arbeit und die näheren Details. Ich würde mich freuen, wenn ich *office* Sie einmal in Ihrer Praxis° besuchen dürfte, um Ihnen ein paar *early* Fragen zu stellen? Um eine baldige° Antwort wäre ich Ihnen sehr *grateful* dankbar°.

Mit freundlichen Grüßen
Ihre *Ina Bachmann*

G. Schreiben Sie! Bitte um Information (Thema 1 oder 2).

1. **Karrierefragen** (As Ina Bachmann did in the Fokus section, write a short letter to someone in a particular profession, asking for specific information about that field.)
2. **Bitte um Informationsmaterial** (Write a short letter in German to one of the addresses listed below, requesting informational material and/or an application form.)

Adresse	Wofür?
Carl-Duisburg-Gesellschaft e. V. Hohenstaufenring 30–32 Postfach 26 01 20 50514 Köln	– Work-Study Programm – Career-Training-Programm – Praktikantenprogramm
Goethe-Institut Helene-Weber-Allee 1 Postfach 19 04 19 80604 München	– Deutsche Sprachkurse – Credit-Programm mit der University of Connecticut
DAAD Kennedyallee 50 53175 Bonn	– Information über Studienmöglichkeiten im Ausland – Stipendien

HÖREN SIE ZU!

Zwei Briefe

Zum Erkennen: das Stellenangebot *(job opening);* erfüllen *(to fulfill);* ADAC *(AAA);* beigelegt *(enclosed);* sich vorstellen *(to introduce or present oneself);* absolvieren *(to complete);* vermitteln *(to help find);* das Formular *([application] form)*

Richtig oder falsch?

_____ 1. Dagmar Schröder hat Touristik studiert.
_____ 2. Sie würde gern als Reiseleiterin arbeiten.
_____ 3. Sie spricht gut Italienisch.
_____ 4. Das Reisebüro hätte aber gern jemand mit Russischkenntnissen.
_____ 5. Frau Schröder hofft, dass ihre Auslandsaufenthalte für sie sprechen.
_____ 6. Dem Brief ist ein Lebenslauf beigelegt.
_____ 7. Joe Jackson studiert Betriebswirtschaft in Seattle, Washington.
_____ 8. Er würde gern ein Praktikum in Österreich absolvieren.
_____ 9. Davor würde er aber gern noch etwas mehr Geschäftsdeutsch lernen.
_____ 10. Er würde sich freuen, wenn ihm die Carl-Duisburg-Gesellschaft in Köln Informationen und Formulare dazu schicken könnte.

Bertolt Brecht FOKUS

Bertolt Brecht (1898–1956) is one of Germany's most celebrated 20th-century playwrights. His theory of the "epic theater" has had a considerable influence on modern theories of drama. By using various visual techniques and artificial acting styles—such as having the actors deliver their lines in a deliberately expressionless way—he tried to minimize the audience's rapport with the action, while increasing its awareness of the play's moral and political message. Brecht fled Berlin in 1933, seeking refuge in Switzerland, Denmark, Finland, and finally the United States (1941–1947). He returned to East Berlin in 1949 and founded the Berlin Ensemble. Brecht's works include *Die Dreigroschenoper* (1928; first film adaptation in 1931), *Mutter Courage und ihre Kinder* (1939), *Der gute Mensch von Sezuan* (1942), *Das Leben des Galilei* (1938/39), and *Der kaukasische Kreidekreis* (1945). Some of his works have been set to music; he worked extensively with composers Kurt Weill, Hanns Eisler, and Paul Dessau.

1940

Mein junger Sohn fragt mich: Soll ich Mathematik lernen?
Wozu, möchte ich sagen. Daß zwei Stück Brot mehr ist
    als eines
Das wirst du auch so merken°.   find out
Mein junger Sohn fragt mich: Soll ich Französisch lernen?
Wozu, möchte ich sagen. Dieses Reich geht unter. Und
Reibe° du nur mit der Hand den Bauch und stöhne°   rub / moan
Und man wird dich schon verstehn.
Mein junger Sohn fragt mich: Soll ich Geschichte lernen?
Wozu, möchte ich sagen. Lerne du deinen Kopf in die
    Erde stecken°   stick
Da wirst du vielleicht übrigbleiben°.   survive

Ja, lerne Mathematik, sage ich
Lerne Französisch, lerne Geschichte!

Bertolt Brecht

WEB-ECKE

For updates and online activities, visit the *Wie geht's?* home page at: http://www.hrwcollege.com/german/sevin/. You'll check out various universities and learn more about Bertolt Brecht.

SPRECHSITUATIONEN

As you know, the subjunctive can express politeness. It is therefore used quite frequently when giving advice or asking for permission.

Giving advice

Sie sollten / könnten . . .
Es wäre besser, wenn . . .
Wie wär's, wenn . . .?
Ich würde . . .
An deiner / Ihrer Stelle, würde ich . . .
Wenn ich du / Sie wäre, würde ich . . .
Ich empfehle dir / Ihnen . . .
Du musst unbedingt . . .
Du kannst / darfst nicht . . .
Ich rate dir / Ihnen . . . *(I advise you . . .)*

Asking for permission

Darf / dürfte ich . . .?
Kann / könnte ich . . .?
Haben / hätten Sie etwas dagegen, wenn . . .? *(Do / would you mind, if . . .?)*
Ist es erlaubt, . . . (zu + *infinitive*)? *(Is it permitted, to . . .?)*

Granting or denying permission

Ja, natürlich. Gern.
Es ist mir recht.
Ich habe nichts dagegen.
Es tut mir Leid, aber . . .
Hier darf man nicht . . . *(It is not permitted . . .)*
Es ist nicht erlaubt . . . (zu + *infinitive*). *(You are not allowed to . . .)*
Es ist verboten . . . (zu + *infinitive*). *(It is forbidden to . . .)*
Es wäre mir lieber, wenn . . . *(I would prefer it if . . .)*

Übungen

A. Was tun? Geben Sie Rat *(advice)* oder fragen Sie um Rat! Wechseln Sie sich ab!
1. Sie wissen nicht, was Sie werden wollen (oder welche Arbeitsmöglichkeiten es gibt).
2. Sie wissen nicht, was Sie als Hauptfach studieren wollen (oder was Sie tun müssen), um einen besseren Arbeitsplatz zu finden).
3. Sie möchten eigentlich gern Lehrer(in) werden, aber wenn Sie . . . studierten, könnten Sie bei Ihrem (Schwieger)vater arbeiten und mehr verdienen.
4. Sie möchten in Deutschland studieren/arbeiten, aber Ihre Familie ist dagegen.
5. Sie sollen heute Abend mit einem Freund in ein Konzert gehen; er hat auch schon Karten. Aber Sie haben keine Lust dazu.

B. Dürfte ich . . .? *(Working with a classmate, take turns asking for permission and granting or denying it.)*
1. mal kurz dein Buch haben
2. deine Hausaufgaben sehen / abschreiben *(copy)*
3. mein Radio anmachen / eine neue Kassette spielen

4. deinen Kuli / deinen Pullover . . . borgen *(borrow)*
5. für dich zahlen / dir die Rechnung geben
6. deine Kreditkarte / dein Handy / dein Auto . . . borgen

C. Kurzgespräch

You call Margaret, who has been to Germany. Introduce yourself and inquire whether you might ask her some questions. She says to go ahead, and you ask whether you should study in Germany. She replies that she would do so if she were you. You ask for how long you should go. She suggests that you go (for) a year. You would learn more German and see more of Europe. You ask whether you could have lunch together the next day. She says she would prefer it if you could have supper. You agree and say good-bye.

Studenten vor der Johann Wolfgang von Goethe Universität in Frankfurt am Main

KAPITEL 14
EINST UND JETZT

Der Kurfürstendamm mit Blick auf die Gedächtniskirche

LERNZIELE

■ VORSCHAU
Chronicle of German history since World War II

■ GESPRÄCHE AND WORTSCHATZ
A visit to Berlin

■ STRUKTUR
Relative clauses
Indirect speech

■ EINBLICKE
Berlin's past
Berlin, a gate to the world

■ FOKUS
Berliners
Berlin today
Berlin, a multicultural melting pot
Erich Kästner: "Fantasie von übermorgen"

■ WEB-ECKE

■ SPRECHSITUATIONEN
Expressing doubt and uncertainty
Expressing probability and possibility
Expressing concern
Drawing conclusions

VORSCHAU

Chronicle of German History since World War II

EXTRABLATT
Berliner Zeitung
MITTWOCH, 3. OKTOBER 1990 ● EXTRABLATT ● 46. JAHRGANG ● KOSTENLOS ● 90 020 ● ISSN 0323–5793

Adé DDR — Willkommen Deutschland! Nach 45 Jahren sind wir wieder ein Volk in einem geeinten Land
Festakt im Schauspielhaus / Schwarzrotgoldene Fahne vor dem Reichstag / Berlin seit heute wieder deutsche Hauptstadt

Letzte Nachrichten aus der DDR

1945	Unconditional surrender of Germany (May 9). The Allies assume supreme power, dividing Germany into four zones and Berlin (in the middle of the Russian zone) into four sectors. Potsdam Conference determines Germany's new borders.
1947	American Marshall Plan provides comprehensive aid for the rebuilding of Europe, including West Germany. Plan is rejected by the Soviet Union and its Eastern European satellites.
1948	Introduction of D-Mark in the Western Zone leads to the Soviet blockade of West Berlin. Allies respond with Berlin Airlift (June 1948–May 1949).
1949	Founding of Federal Republic of Germany in the West (May 23) and German Democratic Republic (October 7) in the East.
1952	East Germany begins to seal the border with West Germany (May 27).
1953	Workers' uprising in East Berlin (June 17) is crushed by Soviet tanks.
1954	West Germany becomes a NATO member.
1955	East Germany joins the Warsaw Pact. West Germany becomes a sovereign country; the occupation is ended.
1961	East Germany constructs the Berlin Wall and extensive fortifications along the border to West Germany to prevent East Germans from fleeing to the West.
1970	As an important step in his new *Ostpolitik,* West German Chancellor Willy Brandt meets with East German Premier Willi Stoph in Erfurt, East Germany.
1971	Four-Power Agreement on Berlin guarantees unhindered traffic between West Berlin and West Germany. De facto recognition of East Germany.
1973	Bundestag approves treaty of mutual recognition with East Germany. Brandt's opponents accuse him of forsaking the goal of unification.
1989	Opening of Hungarian border to Austria (September 10) brings streams of refugees from East to West Germany, protest rallies take place all across East Germany. Berlin Wall opens on November 9.
1990	Economic union of both German states (July 2) is followed by German unification (October 3). First all-German elections are held (December 2).
1994	Last Allied troops withdraw from Berlin.
1999	Reopening of the renovated Reichstag building.
2000	Relocation of the federal government to Berlin complete.

GESPRÄCHE

Hier ist immer etwas los.

HEIKE Und das hier ist die Gedächtniskirche mit ihren drei Gebäuden. Wir nennen sie den „Hohlen Zahn," den „Lippenstift" und die „Puderdose".

MARTIN Berliner haben doch für alles einen Spitznamen.

HEIKE Der alte Turm der Gedächtniskirche soll als Mahnmal so bleiben, wie er ist. Die neue Gedächtniskirche mit dem neuen Turm ist aber modern.

MARTIN Und sie sehen wirklich ein bisschen aus wie ein Lippenstift und eine Puderdose. Sag mal, wohnst du gern hier in Berlin?

HEIKE Na klar! Berlin ist unheimlich lebendig und hat so viel zu bieten, nicht nur historisch, sondern auch kulturell. Hier ist immer 'was los. Außerdem ist die Umgebung wunderschön.

MARTIN Ich hab' irgendwo gelesen, dass 24 Prozent der Stadtfläche Wälder und Seen sind, mit 800 Kilometer Fahrradwegen.

HEIKE Ist doch toll, oder?

MARTIN Wahnsinn! Sag mal, warst du dabei, als sie die Mauer durchbrochen haben?

HEIKE Und ob! Das werde ich nie vergessen.

MARTIN Ich auch nicht, obwohl ich's nur im Fernsehen gesehen habe.

HEIKE Wir haben die ganze Nacht gewartet, obwohl es ganz schön kalt war. Als das erste Stück Mauer kippte, haben wir alle laut gesungen: „So ein Tag, so wunderschön wie heute, so ein Tag, der dürfte nie vergeh'n."

MARTIN Ich sehe immer noch die Leute oben auf der Mauer tanzen und feiern.

HEIKE Ja, Mensch, das war schon einmalig. Wer hätte gedacht, dass das alles so schnell gehen würde.

MARTIN Und so friedlich.

Richtig oder falsch?

_____ 1. Martin ist Berliner.
_____ 2. Der „Hohle Zahn" ist ein Teil der Gedächtniskirche.
_____ 3. Er soll die Berliner an den Zahnarzt erinnern.
_____ 4. Martin hat verschiedene Spitznamen für die Berliner.
_____ 5. Heike gefällt's unheimlich gut in Berlin.
_____ 6. Heike war dabei, als sie die Mauer durchbrochen haben.
_____ 7. Martin hat dort auch mitgefeiert.
_____ 8. Das Ganze geschah an einem schönen, warmen Nachmittag.
_____ 9. Als das erste Stück Mauer kippte, haben die Leute die Polizei gerufen.
_____ 10. Manche haben auf der Mauer getanzt.

WORTSCHATZ 1

Einst und jetzt

der Frieden	*peace*	die Grenze, -n	*border*
Krieg, -e	*war*	Mauer, -n	*wall*
Spitzname, -ns, -n	*nickname*	Umgebung	*surrounding(s)*
Turm, ⸚e	*tower*		
das Gebäude, -	*building*		
Volk, ⸚er	*people (as a whole or nation)*		

Weiteres

einmalig	*unique, incredible*
historisch	*historical(ly)*
wunderschön	*very beautiful*
aus·sehen (sieht aus), sah aus, ausgesehen wie (+ *nom.*)	*to look like (something or someone)*
berichten	*to report*
erinnern (an + *acc.*)[1]	*to remind (of)*
sich erinnern (an + *acc.*)[1]	*to remember*
eine Frage stellen	*to ask a question*
teilen	*to divide*
führen	*to lead*
vorbei·führen (an + *dat.*)	*to pass by*
einst	*once*
kaum	*barely, scarcely*
oder?	*isn't it? don't you think so?*
Und ob!	*You bet. You better believe it.*
unheimlich[2]	*tremendously, extremely*
Wahnsinn!	*Awesome! lit.: Crazy!*

---

[1] **Ich werde *dich* an die Karten erinnern.** *(I'll remind you of the tickets.)* BUT **Ich kann *mich* nicht daran erinnern.** *(I can't remember it.)*

[2] A very common phrase: **unheimlich schön, unheimlich interessant,** etc.

Zum Erkennen: hohl *(hollow);* der Lippenstift *(lipstick);* die Puderdose, -n *(compact);* als Mahnmal *(as a memorial);* lebendig *(lively);* bieten *(to offer);* die Stadtfläche *(. . . area);* durchbrochen *(broken through);* (um)kippen *(to tip over);* vergehen *(to pass);* friedlich *(peacefully)*

FOKUS: Berliners

Berliners are known for their self-assured manner, their humor, and their "big mouth" **(Berliner Schnauze).** They always manage to find the right words at the right time, especially when it comes to choosing amusing names for places around their city. Besides the nicknames mentioned in the dialogue, there are the **Schwangere Auster** *(pregnant oyster),* a cultural center; the **Hungerkralle** *(hunger claw),* the monument to the Berlin Airlift; the **Telespargel** *(television-asparagus)* the television tower; the old **Palazzo Prozzo** *(Braggarts' Palace)* or **Honeckers Lampenladen** *([East German leader Erich] Honecker's lampstore),* the former parliament building of East Germany; and the **Mauerspechte** *(wall woodpeckers),* the souvenir hunters who chipped away at the Berlin Wall after it was opened.

Zum Thema

A. Wie geht's weiter? Benutzen Sie Ihre Fantasie!

BEISPIEL: . . . sieht gut aus.
Mein Bruder sieht gut aus.

1. . . . sieht aus wie ein(e) . . .
2. . . . hat viel zu bieten.
3. . . . ist immer etwas los.
4. Ich erinnere mich gern an . . .
5. Ich kann mich noch gut erinnern an die Zeit, als . . .
6. Bitte erinnere mich nicht an . . . !
7. Der Spitzname von . . . ist . . .

B. Stadtführung. Was würden Sie einem ausländischen Besucher sagen, dem *(to whom)* Sie Ihre Stadt zeigen? Machen Sie es so interessant, wie möglich!

S1 Und das ist . . .
S2 . . .
S1 Ja, wir finden das auch . . .
S2 Wie ist das Leben . . . ?
S1 . . .
S2 Ist hier kulturell viel los?
S1 . . .
S2 Die Umgebung ist . . .
S1 Wie findest du / finden Sie . . . ?
S2 . . .

Mauerdurchbruch am 9. 11. 1989

C. Stadtplan von Berlin. Sehen Sie auf den Stadtplan und beenden Sie dann die Sätze mit einem Wort von der Liste!

a. Brandenburger
b. Dom
c. Fernsehturm
d. Gedächtniskirche
e. Juni
f. Kulturen der Welt
g. Philharmonie
h. Reichstagsgebäude
i. Spree
j. Stadtplan
k. Unter den Linden
l. Zoo(logische Garten)

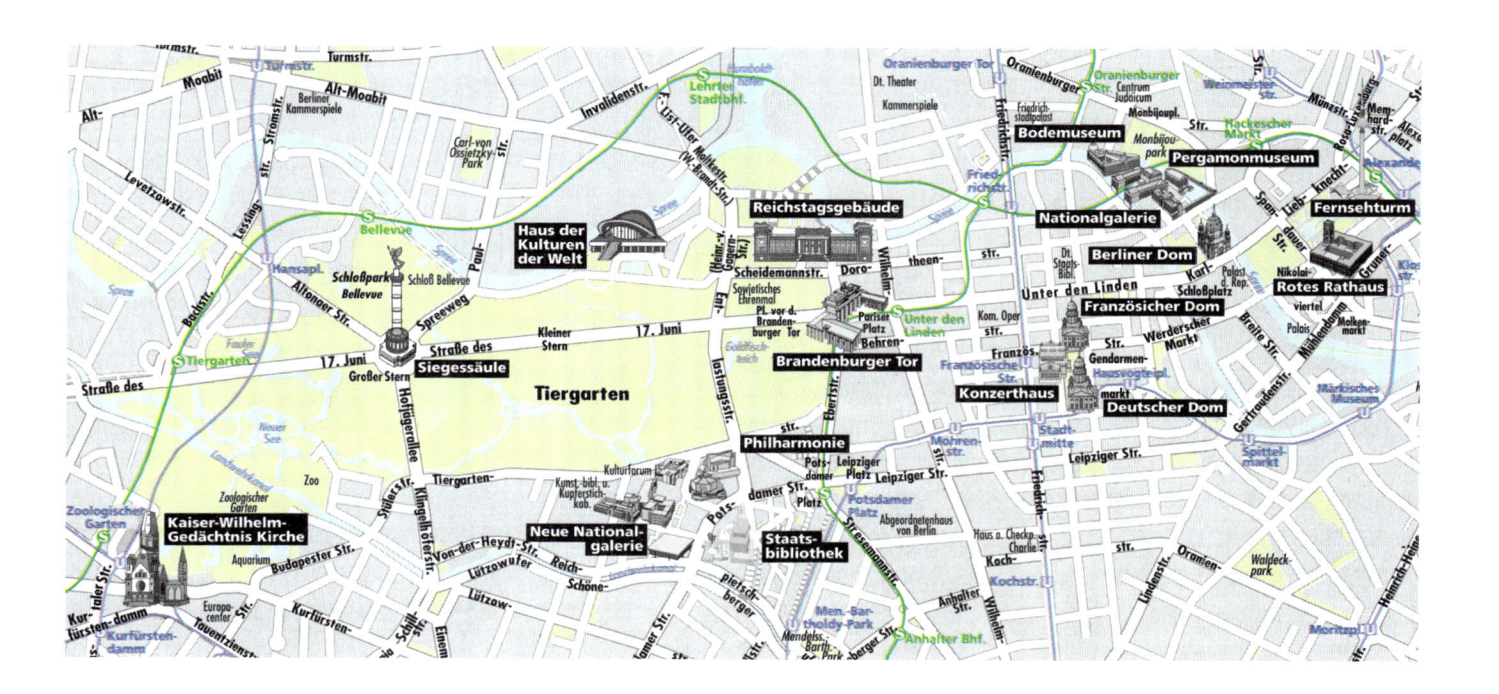

1. Dieser _____ von Berlin zeigt Ihnen, wo die verschiedenen Straßen und wichtigsten Gebäude sind. 2. Im Südwesten ist der Kurfürstendamm oder Ku'damm. Er führt zur _____ 3. In der Nähe ist auch der _____. 4. Quer durch den großen Park läuft eine lange Straße. Sie erinnert an den 17. _____ 1953, als die Ostberliner und die Deutschen in Ostdeutschland gegen die Sowjetunion rebellierten. 5. Sie führt vorbei am Großen Stern mit der Siegessäule *(Victory Column)* und weiter bis zum _____ Tor *(gate)*. 6. Die Straße hat verschiedene Namen. Östlich vom Brandenburger Tor heißt sie _____. 7. Südlich vom Brandenburger Tor ist der Potsdamer Platz und an der Potsdamer Straße die Staatsbibliothek und die _____. 8. Ganz in der Nähe vom Brandenburger Tor ist auch das für den Bundestag *(federal parliament)* renovierte _____. 9. Nicht weit davon ist das Haus der _____, die frühere Kongresshalle mit dem Spitznamen „Schwangere Auster". 10. Unter den Linden führt ins alte Zentrum von Berlin und auf eine Insel mit dem Pergamonmuseum und dem Berliner _____. 11. Auf beiden Seiten der Insel fließt *(flows)* die _____. 12. Beim Dom bekommt die Straße wieder einen neuen Namen und geht weiter bis zum Alexanderplatz mit dem modernen _____, „dem Telespargel".

D. Aussprache: pf, ps, qu. Sehen Sie auch III. 19, 21 und 22 im Ausspracheteil des Arbeitsheftes!
1. [pf] **Pf**arrer, **Pf**effer, **Pf**ennig, **Pf**und, A**pf**el, Ko**pf**, em**pf**ehlen
2. [ps] **Ps**ychologe, **Ps**ychologie, **ps**ychologisch, **Ps**alm, **Ps**eudonym, Ka**ps**el
3. [kv] **Qu**atsch, **Qu**alität, **Qu**antität, **Qu**artal, be**qu**em

FOKUS: Berlin Today

Since becoming the capital of reunified Germany, Berlin has seen tremendous changes, especially as a new government and business district is built up where the wall once stood. The historic Reichstag building has been transformed by the British architect Sir Norman Foster into a modern seat of parliament, with a glass dome atop the roof to represent a link between past and present. Numerous embassies and organizations are located in Berlin, and numerous prominent German and foreign firms have chosen Berlin as their headquarters.

Berlin now boasts some thirty art museums, two important symphony orchestras, three opera houses, numerous theaters and cabarets, and three major universities. Young people from all over Europe have come to appreciate Berlin's ground-breaking music scene, the highlight of which, the annual "Love Parade," draws up to a million ravers.

More than any other city in Europe, Berlin has embodied both the confrontation of the Cold War and the growing together of the continent ever since. Its proximity to Poland, only 65 miles away, symbolizes Germany's reaching out toward the countries of the former Soviet Union and its role as mediator between East and West.

Der Sitz des Bundestages in Berlin

HÖREN SIE ZU!

Die Info-Box

Zum Erkennen: das Niemandsland *(no-man's-land)*; schwärmen von *(to rave about)*; die Baustelle *(construction site)*; Kräne *(cranes)*; das Projekt; mitten drin *(right in the middle)*; Ausstellungen *(exhibits)*; Tiefbauingenieur *(civil engineer)*

Was fehlt?

1. Martin und Heike bummeln durch Geschäfte, wo in den achtziger Jahren *(in the 1980s)* noch ein _____ war. 2. Von der _____ ist kaum noch 'was zu sehen. 3. Martins Freunde schwärmten von der Info-Box am _____ Platz, damals eine ganz große Baustelle. 4. Von dort konnte man _____ übersehen. 5. Die Computeranimationen _____ der Info-Box hätten Martin besonders interessiert. 6. Sie hätten ihm einen _____ in den Städtebau der Zukunft gegeben. 7. Martin möchte _____ werden.

STRUKTUR

I. Relative clauses

RELATIVE CLAUSES supply additional information about a noun in a sentence.

*There's the professor **who** teaches the course.*

*He taught the course **(that)** I enjoyed so much.*

*He teaches a subject **in which** I'm very interested (I'm very interested in).*

*He's the professor **whose** course I took last semester.*

English relative clauses may be introduced by the relative pronouns *who, whom, whose, which,* or *that.* The noun to which the relative pronoun "relates" is called the ANTECEDENT. The choice of the relative pronoun depends on the antecedent (is it a person or a thing?) and on its function in the relative clause. The relative pronoun may be the subject *(who, which, that),* an object or an object of a preposition *(whom, which, that),* or it may indicate possession *(whose).* German relative clauses work essentially the same way. However, whereas in English the relative pronouns are frequently omitted (especially in conversation), IN GERMAN THEY MUST ALWAYS BE USED.

   Ist das der Roman, **den** ihr gelesen habt?   *Is that the novel you read?*

1. Forms and use

   The German relative pronouns have the same forms as the definite article, EXCEPT FOR THE GENITIVE FORMS AND THE DATIVE PLURAL.

	masc.	neut.	fem.	pl.
nom.	der	das	die	die
acc.	den	das	die	die
dat.	dem	dem	der	denen
gen.	dessen	dessen	deren	deren

The form of the relative pronoun is determined by two factors:

- Its ANTECEDENT: is the antecedent masculine, neuter, feminine, or in the plural?

   Das ist **der Fluss, der** auf der Karte ist.

   Das ist **das Gebäude, das** auf der Karte ist.

   Das ist **die Kirche, die** auf der Karte ist.

   Das sind **die Plätze, die** auf der Karte sind.

- Its FUNCTION in the relative clause: is the relative pronoun the subject, an accusative or dative object, an object of a preposition, or does it indicate possession?

   Ist das der Mann, **der** in Berlin wohnt?   = SUBJECT
   Ist das der Mann, **den** du meinst?   = ACCUSATIVE OBJECT
   Ist das der Mann, **dem** du geschrieben hast?   = DATIVE OBJECT
   Ist das der Mann, **mit dem** du gesprochen hast?   = OBJECT OF A PREPOSITION
   Ist das der Mann, **dessen** Tochter hier studiert?   = GENITIVE

The following examples indicate the antecedent and state the function of the relative pronoun (RP) in each relative clause.

> . . . ANTECEDENT, (preposition +) RP _____ V1.
> gender? number?   function?

Da ist der Professor. Er lehrt an meiner Universität.
Da ist **der Professor, der** an meiner Universität lehrt.
*That's **the professor who** teaches at my university.*
ANTECEDENT: der Professor = sg. / masc.
PRONOUN FUNCTION: subject > nom.

Wie heißt der Kurs? Du findest ihn so interessant.
Wie heißt **der Kurs, den** du so interessant findest?
*What's the name of **the course (that)** you find so interesting?*
ANTECEDENT: der Kurs = sg. / masc.
PRONOUN FUNCTION: object of **finden** > acc.

Da ist der Student. Ich habe ihm mein Buch gegeben.
Da ist **der Student, dem** ich mein Buch gegeben habe.
*There's **the student to whom** I gave my book (I gave my book to).*
ANTECEDENT: der Student = sg. / masc.
PRONOUN FUNCTION: object of **geben** > dat.

Kennst du die Professorin? Erik hat ihr Seminar belegt.
Kennst du **die Professorin, deren Seminar** Erik belegt hat?
*Do you know **the professor whose seminar** Erik took?*
ANTECEDENT: die Professorin = sg. / fem.
PRONOUN FUNCTION: related possessively to **Seminar** > gen.

Das Buch ist von einem Autor. Ich interessiere mich sehr für ihn.
Das Buch ist von **einem Autor, für den** ich mich sehr interessiere.
*The book is by **an author in whom** I'm very interested.*
ANTECEDENT: der Autor = sg. / masc.
PRONOUN FUNCTION: object of **für** > acc.

Die Autoren sind aus Leipzig. Der Professor hat von ihnen gesprochen.
Die Autoren, von denen der Professor gesprochen hat, sind aus Leipzig.
*The authors **of whom** the professor spoke are from Leipzig.*
ANTECEDENT: die Autoren = pl.
PRONOUN FUNCTION: object of **von** > dat.

erdgas

**ENERGIE, MIT DER WIR
LEBEN KÖNNEN**

CAUTION: Don't use the interrogative pronoun in place of the relative pronoun!

Wer hat das Seminar gegeben?
Das ist der Professor, **der** das Seminar gegeben hat.
Who *gave the seminar?*
*That's the professor **who** gave the seminar.*

2. Word order

   a. Relative pronouns can be the objects of prepositions. If that is the case, the preposition will always precede the relative pronoun.

   Das Buch ist von einem Autor, **für den** ich mich sehr interessiere.
   *The book is by an author **in whom** I'm very interested.*

   b. The word order in THE RELATIVE CLAUSE is like that of all subordinate clauses: the inflected part of the verb (V1) comes last. Always separate the relative clause from the main clause by a comma.

   $$\ldots, \text{RP} \underline{\hspace{3cm}} \text{V1}, \ldots$$

   Der Professor, **der** den Prosakurs **lehrt,** ist sehr nett.
                  RP   V1

   c. Relative clauses immediately follow the antecedent unless the antecedent is followed by a prepositional phrase that modifies it, by a genitive, or by a verb complement (V2).

   Das Buch von Dürrenmatt, **das wir lesen sollen,** ist leider ausverkauft.
   Das Buch des Autors, **das wir lesen sollen,** ist teuer.
   Ich kann **das Buch** nicht bekommen, **das wir lesen sollen.**

Übungen

A. Analysieren Sie die Sätze! Finden Sie das vorhergehende Wort *(antecedent)*, beschreiben Sie es und nennen Sie die Funktion des Relativpronomens im Relativsatz!

BEISPIEL: Renate Berger ist eine Frau, die für gleiche Arbeit gleiches Einkommen möchte.
                ANTECEDENT: **eine Frau** = sg. / fem.
                PRONOUN FUNCTION: **subject** > nom.

1. Der Mann, der neben ihr arbeitet, verdient pro Stunde 1,80 DM mehr.
2. Es gibt leider noch viele Frauen, deren Kollegen ein höheres Einkommen bekommen.
3. Und es gibt Frauen, denen schlecht bezahlte Arbeit lieber ist als keine Arbeit.
4. Was denken die Männer, deren Frauen weniger Geld bekommen als ihre Kollegen?
5. Der Mann, mit dem Renate Berger verheiratet ist, findet das nicht so schlecht.
6. Aber die Frauen, die bei der gleichen Firma arbeiten, ärgern sich sehr darüber.
7. Es ist ein Problem, das die meisten Firmen haben.
8. Es gibt Berufe, in denen Männer für gleiche Arbeit mehr verdienen.
9. Und die Berufe, in denen fast nur Frauen arbeiten, sind am schlechtesten bezahlt.
10. Wir leben in einer Welt, in der Gleichberechtigung noch nicht überall Realität ist.

B. **Rundfahrt durch Berlin.** Während Sepp ein paar Bilder von seinem Besuch in Berlin zeigt, stellen seine österreichischen Freunde Fragen darüber. Antworten Sie wie im Beispiel und benutzen Sie dabei Relativpronomen!

1. BEISPIEL: Ist das der Alexanderplatz?
Ja, das ist der Alexanderplatz, der so bekannt ist.

a. Ist das der Fernsehturm? b. Ist das das Rote Rathaus? c. Ist das der Berliner Dom? d. Ist das die Staatsbibliothek? e. Sind das die Museen?

2. BEISPIEL: Ist das der Potsdamer Platz?
Ja, das ist der Potsdamer Platz, den du da siehst.

a. Ist das die Leipziger Straße? b. Ist das das Konzerthaus? c. Ist das der Französische Dom? d. Ist das die Spree? e. Ist das das Nikolaiviertel?

3. BEISPIEL: Ist das die Hochschule für Musik?
Ja, das ist die Hochschule für Musik, zu der wir jetzt kommen.

a. Ist das der Zoo? b. Ist das die Siegessäule? c. Ist das die alte Kongresshalle? d. Ist das das Reichstagsgebäude? e. Sind das die Universitätsgebäude?

4. BEISPIEL: Wo ist der Student? Sein Vater lehrt an der Universität.
Da ist der Student, dessen Vater an der Universität lehrt.

a. Wo ist die Studentin? Ihre Eltern wohnten früher *(formerly)* in Berlin. b. Wo ist das Mädchen? Ihr Bruder war so lustig. c. Wo ist der Herr? Seine Frau sprach so gut Englisch. d. Wo sind die alten Leute? Ihr Sohn ist jetzt in Amerika.

C. **Was gefällt Ihnen?** Geben Sie Beispiele!
BEISPIEL: Stück
Ein Stück, das mir gefällt, ist Goethes *Faust*.

1. Buch 2. Film 3. Fernsehsendung 4. Zeitschrift 5. Schlagersänger(in) *(pop singer)* 6. Komponist(in) 7. Restaurant 8. Auto 9. Stadt

EUROCARD. Für Leute, die auch sonst gute Karten haben.

D. **Kein Wiedersehen.** Ergänzen Sie *(add)* die fehlenden Relativpronomen!
1. Der junge Mann, _____ da steht, heißt David.
2. Das Mädchen, mit _____ er spricht, heißt Tina.
3. Das andere Mädchen, _____ daneben steht, heißt Margaret.
4. Sie sprechen über einen Film, _____ früher einmal im Kino gelaufen ist.
5. Der Film, über _____ sie sprechen, spielte in Berlin.
6. Die Geschichte spielte kurz vor dem Bau der Mauer, _____ Berlin von 1961 bis 1989 geteilt hat.
7. In den fünfziger Jahren sind viele mit der S-Bahn, _____ ja quer durch *(right through)* die Stadt fuhr, geflohen.
8. Ein junger Mann, _____ Freundin auch weg wollte, fuhr mit der S-Bahn nach West-Berlin und blieb dort.

9. Die Freundin, _____ Familie in Weimar wohnte, wollte noch einmal ihre Eltern sehen.
10. Das war aber gerade an dem Tag, an _____ man die Mauer baute.
11. Das bedeutete, dass sie den Freund, _____ sie in West-Berlin zurückgelassen hatte und _____ dort auf sie wartete, nie wiedersehen würde.
12. Am Ende des Filmes, _____ sehr spannend gewesen sein soll, blieb nur die Erinnerung an den Freund.

E. **Verbinden Sie die Sätze!** Verbinden Sie die Sätze mit Hilfe von Relativpronomen! Wenn nötig, übersetzen Sie den Satz zuerst!

BEISPIEL: Der Ku'damm ist eine bekannte Berliner Straße. Jeder kennt sie.
(The Ku'damm is a famous Berlin street [that] everyone knows.)
Der Ku'damm ist eine bekannte Berliner Straße, die jeder kennt.

1. Die Gedächtniskirche gefällt mir. Ihr habt schon von der Gedächtniskirche gehört.
2. Der alte Turm soll kaputt bleiben. Die Berliner nennen ihn „Hohlen Zahn".
3. Der Ku'damm beginnt bei der Gedächtniskirche. Am Ku'damm gibt es viele schöne Geschäfte.
4. Mittags gingen wir ins Nikolaiviertel. Es hat schöne alte Gebäude und die älteste Kirche Berlins.
5. Da gibt's auch kleine Restaurants. Man kann in den Restaurants gemütlich sitzen.
6. Wir waren ins „Wirtshaus *(n.)* zum Nußbaum" gegangen. Seine Alt-Berliner Küche ist bekannt.
7. Mein Freund hat mir wirklich alles gezeigt. Seine Familie wohnt in Berlin.
8. Seine Schwester war auch sehr nett. Ich bin mit ihr am Abend in eine Disko in den Hackeschen Höfen gegangen.
9. Diese Disko war in der Nähe der Neuen Synagoge. Die Atmosphäre der Disko war einmalig.
10. Die Synagoge ist im maurischen Stil *(Moorish style)* gebaut. In dieser Synagoge hatte Albert Einstein am 29. 1. 1930 ein Violinenkonzert gegeben.

F. **An der Uni.** Auf Deutsch bitte!

1. Where's the lecture hall in which Professor Kunert is lecturing (reading)? 2. The course he teaches is modern German history. 3. The students who take his courses must work hard. 4. History is a subject that I find very interesting. 5. But I have a roommate *(m.)* who finds nothing interesting. 6. He's a person (**Mensch**) I don't understand. 7. He studies subjects he doesn't like. 8. The friends he goes out with (with whom he goes out) are boring. 9. He laughs at his father, whose money he gets every month. 10. But the woman he's engaged to (to whom he is engaged) is very nice.

Fokus: Berlin, a Multicultural Melting Pot

Berlin is one of Europe's most cosmopolitan urban centers, with 400,000 foreign nationals of more than 180 countries living within the city limits. In addition to an influx of Jews from the former Soviet Union since the fall of the Berlin Wall in 1989, the country's liberal asylum laws, and the need for manual laborers have drawn people to Berlin from around the globe. Relations with the German majority, however, have shown signs of strain. Because some residents claim their neighborhoods are being "taken over" by foreigners, local politicians have discussed placing limits on the number of foreign residents in some areas to avoid "ghettoization." Although many leaders of ethnic communities in Berlin agree that more integration is needed, they have dismissed such calls for "quotas on foreigners" as outrageous. Despite such problems, the presence and continuing influx of foreigners adds to the cosmopolitan flair of Berlin, and the traditional homogeneous German society is thus changing rapidly in the capital of the united Germany.

Diese Synagoge ist heute ein Jüdisches Museum.

II. Indirect speech

When reporting what someone else has said, you can use DIRECT SPEECH with quotation marks, or INDIRECT SPEECH without quotation marks.

Heike said, "Berlin has a lot to offer."

Heike said (that) Berlin has a lot to offer.

Often, corresponding direct and indirect speech will require different personal pronouns and possessive adjectives, depending on who reports the conversation.

- If Heike says to Martin "I'll bring my map," and she reports the conversation, she will say: *I told him I would bring my map.*
- If Martin reported the conversation, he would say: *She told me she would bring her map.*
- If a third person reported, he or she would say: *She told him she would bring her map.*

In spoken German, such indirect reports are generally in THE INDICATIVE when the opening verb is in the present (**Sie sagt, . . .**). However, when the opening verb is in the past (**Sie sagte, . . .**), the subjunctive usually follows. This section focuses on the latter.

Direct speech:	„Ich **bringe** meinen Stadtplan mit."
Indirect speech:	
Indicative	Sie sagt, sie **bringt** ihren Stadtplan mit.
Subjunctive	Sie sagte, sie **würde** ihren Stadtplan **mitbringen**.

NOTE: In German, opening quotation marks are placed at the bottom of the line, especially in handwriting. Many publishers now use an alternative form of quotation marks: »Ich bringe meinen Stadtplan mit.«

1. Statements

   The tense of the indirect statement is determined by the tense of the direct statement.

   a. Direct statements in the present or future are reported indirectly in the present-time subjunctive or the **würde-**form.

   > present tense
   > future tense } → present-time subjunctive or **würde**-form

   „Ich komme später."   Sie sagte, sie käme später.
   „Ich werde später kommen."   Sie sagte, sie würde später kommen.

   b. Direct statements IN ANY PAST TENSE are reported indirectly in the past-time subjunctive.

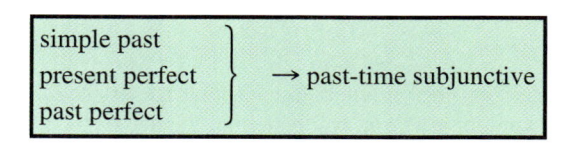

   > simple past
   > present perfect } → past-time subjunctive
   > past perfect

   „Sie hatte keine Zeit."
   „Sie hat keine Zeit gehabt." } Sie sagte, sie hätte keine Zeit gehabt.
   „Sie hatte keine Zeit gehabt."

   c. The conjunction **dass** may or may not be used. If it is not used, the clause retains the original word order. If **dass** is used, the inflected part of the verb comes last.

   Sie sagte, sie käme morgen.
   Sie sagte, **dass** sie morgen **käme.**
   Sie sagte, sie hätte andere Pläne gehabt.
   Sie sagte, **dass** sie andere Pläne gehabt **hätte.**

2. Questions

   The tense of the indirect question is also determined by the tense of the direct question. Indirect YES/NO QUESTIONS are introduced by **ob,** and indirect INFORMATION QUESTIONS by the question word.

   Er fragte: „Hast du jetzt Zeit?"   *He asked, "Do you have time now?"*
   Er fragte, **ob** sie jetzt Zeit hätte.   *He asked whether she had time now.*
   Er fragte: „Wo warst du?"   *He asked, "Where were you?"*
   Er fragte, **wo** sie gewesen wäre.   *He asked where she had been.*

3. Imperatives

   Direct requests in the imperative are expressed indirectly with the auxiliary **sollen.**

   Sie sagte: „Frag(e) nicht so viel!"   *She said, "Don't ask so many questions."*
   Sie sagte, er **sollte** nicht so viel **fragen.**   *She said he shouldn't ask so many questions.*

Übungen

G. Von Bonn nach Berlin. Bestätigen Sie *(confirm)*, dass die Leute in Phillips Familie das wirklich gesagt haben! Beginnen Sie die indirekte Rede mit **dass**!

BEISPIEL: Hat Phillip Sanders gesagt, er hätte vorher in Bonn gewohnt?
Ja, er hat gesagt, dass er vorher in Bonn gewohnt hätte.

1. Hat Phillip gesagt, seine Familie wäre nicht gern nach Berlin gezogen *(moved)*?
2. Hat seine Mutter gesagt, sie wäre lieber in Bonn geblieben?
3. Hat seine Mutter gesagt, sie hätten dort ein wunderschönes Haus mit Garten gehabt?
4. Hat sein Bruder gesagt, er wollte nicht die Schule wechseln?
5. Hat sein Bruder gesagt, er würde lieber in Bonn sein Abitur machen?
6. Hat Phillip gesagt, er könnte auch hier Freunde finden?
7. Hat Phillip gesagt, er würde Berlin eine Chance geben?

H. Verschiedene Leute im Gespräch. Auf Englisch bitte!

1. **Elke erzählt über Trudi**

   Trudi sagte, . . .

   a. Sie wollte Zahnärztin werden. b. Gute Zahnärzte würde man immer brauchen. c. Sie könnte leicht weniger arbeiten, wenn sie mal Kinder hätte. d. Als Zahnarzt würde man gut verdienen. e. Man müsste natürlich lange studieren, aber darauf würde sie sich schon freuen.

2. **Bernd erzählt über Carolyn**

   Carolyn sagte, . . .

   a. Sie hätte letztes Jahr in Deutschland studiert. b. Es hätte ihr unheimlich gut gefallen. c. Sie hätte die Sprachprüfung leicht bestanden. d. Während der Semesterferien wäre sie in die Schweiz gefahren. e. Sie wäre erst vor drei Wochen zurückgekommen.

3. **Martin und Heike**

   Er hat sie gefragt, . . .

   a. ob ihr Berlin jetzt besser gefallen würde. b. ob sie beim Mauerdurchbruch *(opening of the Wall)* dabei gewesen wäre. c. wie lange sie schon in Berlin wäre. d. wo das Brandenburger Tor wäre. e. wie man dorthin käme. f. was es hier noch zu sehen gäbe.

   Sie hat ihm gesagt, . . .

   g. er sollte sich die Museen ansehen. h. er sollte in ein Konzert gehen. i. er sollte die Filmfestspiele besuchen.

4. **Leonie und Simone**

   a. Leonie erzählte, dass sie letzten Sommer in Berlin gewesen wäre. b. Sie hätte dort ein Praktikum an einem Krankenhaus gemacht. c. Sie hätte viel gearbeitet aber auch unheimlich viel gesehen. d. Sie hätte viele nette Leute kennen gelernt. e. Natürlich wäre sie auch in Potsdam gewesen. f. Das hätte ihr besonders gut gefallen. g. Auch hätte sie die Filmstudios in Babelsberg besucht, wo Marlene Dietrich die Hauptrolle in dem Film *Der blaue Engel* gespielt hatte. h. Als Leonie sagte, dass sie diesen Sommer wahrscheinlich wieder nach Berlin gehen würde, wollte ihre Schwester Simone wissen, ob sie mitkommen könnte. i. Leonie meinte, dass das keine schlechte Idee wäre. j. Die Wohnung wäre groß genug für beide.

I. Was hat er/sie gesagt? Stellen Sie Ihrem Nachbarn/Ihrer Nachbarin ein paar persönliche Fragen. Berichten Sie dann den anderen in indirekter Rede!

BEISPIEL: Er/sie hat mir erzählt, er/sie wäre aus Chicago, er/sie hätte zwei Brüder . . .

Zusammenfassung

J. Ein toller Tag. Ergänzen Sie das fehlende Relativpronomen!

1. Christa Grauer ist eine junge Frau, _____ mit einem Computer die Anzeigetafeln *(scoreboards)* in einem Kölner Fußballstadion bedient *(operates)*. 2. Sie erzählt von einem Tag, _____ sie nie vergessen wird. 3. Eine Woche nach dem 9. November 1989, einem Tag, _____ Geschichte gemacht hat, spielte die deutsche Fußballnationalmannschaft *(. . . team)* gegen Wales. 4. Vor dem Spiel, zu _____ 60 000 Menschen gekommen waren, schrieb Christa wie immer die dritte Strophe *(stanza)* des Deutschlandliedes auf die Anzeigetafeln. 5. Das hatte sie schon 14 Jahre lang getan. Aber es gab wenige Spiele, bei _____ die Leute wirklich mitsangen. 6. Aber diesmal sangen Tausende mit, denn die Strophe, _____ Text ihnen bisher nicht viel bedeutet hatte, bedeutete ihnen plötzlich sehr viel.

> „Einigkeit und Recht und Freiheit
> für das deutsche Vaterland.
> Danach lasst uns alle streben,
> brüderlich mit Herz und Hand.
> Einigkeit und Recht und Freiheit sind des Glückes Unterpfand.
> Blüh im Glanze dieses Glückes, blühe
> deutsches Vaterland!"

K. Stimmen der Zeit. Berichten Sie in indirekter Rede, was die zwei Sprecher gesagt haben!

1. **Hiroko Hashimoto, Journalistin**

   a. Hiroko sagte, sie wäre Journalistin und arbeitete freiberuflich *(freelance)* für eine japanische Firma. b. Ihr Mann wäre Deutscher und Wissenschaftler an der Technischen Universität. c. Ihr hätte Berlin schon immer gefallen, aber jetzt wäre es noch viel interessanter geworden. d. Hier gäbe es alles und auch Leute aus der ganzen Welt. e. Am Wochenende nähmen sie oft ihre Fahrräder und führen in die Umgebung. f. Kaum eine andere Stadt hätte so viel zu bieten. g. Sie hätte nie gedacht, dass sie so lange hier bleiben würde. h. Aber sie fühlten sich hier unheimlich wohl.

2. **Moha Rezaian, Schüler**

   a. Moha sagte, er wäre Schüler an einem Gymnasium. b. Seine Eltern wären vor Jahren aus dem Iran gekommen, weil sein Onkel in Kreuzberg einen Teppichladen gehabt hätte. c. Seine Schwester und er wären aber in Berlin geboren und hier groß geworden. d. Sie wären noch nie im Iran gewesen und würden den Rest der Familie nur von Besuchen kennen. e. Sein Vater hätte jetzt ein Autogeschäft und verdiente gut. f. Das würde ihn aber nicht interessieren. g. Er wollte Arzt werden. h. So könnte er vielen Menschen helfen.

L. Hoppla, hier fehlt 'was! Wer hat was zum Mauerdurchbruch im November 1989 gesagt? *(Below are ten statements that various people made about the opening of the Berlin Wall. Some statements show who made them; others do not. Below the chart is a list of people. Who do you think made which statement? Make a guess, then ask your partner, whose corresponding lists are in the Appendix. Take turns.)*

S1:

Wer?	Was?
	„Es ist eine verrückte Zeit."
NBC-Korrespondent:	„Vor meinen Augen tanzte die Freiheit."
	„So viel Fernsehen haben wir noch nie gesehen."
Westberliner Polizist über seinen Kollegen in Ost-Berlin:	„Wir haben uns jeden Tag gesehen. Jetzt will ich ihm mal die Hand schütteln *(shake)*."
	„Ich dachte, die Deutschen können nur Fußball spielen oder im Stechschritt *(goose-step)* marschieren, aber jetzt können sie sogar Revolutionen machen."
Ronald Reagan:	„Auf beiden Seiten sind Deutsche. Der Kommunismus hat seine Chance gehabt. Er funktioniert nicht."
	„Die einzige Chance, die wir haben, den Sozialismus zu retten *(save)*, ist richtiger Sozialismus."
Ex-Bundeskanzler Willy Brandt:	„Ich bin Gott dankbar, dass ich das noch erleben *(experience)* darf."
	„Mauern sind nicht für ewig *(forever)* gebaut . . . In Berlin habe ich für mein Herz gespielt."
Tschechischer Reformpräsident Alexander Dubček:	„Wir haben zu lange im Dunkeln gelebt. Treten wir *(let's step)* ins Licht!"

War das . . .?

ein Major der DDR-Grenztruppe   eine Schullehrerin
Richard Nixon   Luciano Pavarotti
ein Ostberliner Taxifahrer   der Autor Stephan Heym
ein afrikanischer Diplomat   der Cellist Mstislaw Rostropowitsch
ein kanadischer Fußballspieler   Michail Gorbatschow
die Autorin Christa Wolf   Sophia Loren

BEISPIEL: S1 Wer hat gesagt, es wäre eine verrückte Zeit? War das Richard Nixon?
S2 Nein, das war nicht Richard Nixon, sondern ein Major der DDR-Grenztruppe. Wer hat gesagt, vor seinen Augen hätte die Freiheit getanzt? War das . . .?

Der Cellist Mstislaw Rostropowitsch am 11. 11. 1989 an der Berliner Mauer

M. Eine bekannte Berlinerin: Käthe Kollwitz. Auf Deutsch bitte!

1. Käthe Kollwitz was an artist who was at home in Berlin. 2. Her pictures and sculptures **(Skulpturen)** were full of compassion **(voller Mitgefühl)** for poor people, whose suffering **(Leid)** she wanted to show. 3. They remind us of hunger and war, which make the life of people terrible. 4. Kaiser Wilhelm II was no friend of her art, which for him was "gutter art" **(Kunst der Gosse)**. 5. In 1918 she became professor at the Art Academy **(Akademie)** in Berlin, at which she taught until 1933. 6. Then came the Nazis, who also didn't like/care for her art, and she lost her position. 7. She died **(starb)** in 1945, shortly before the end of the war.

Skulptur von Käthe Kollwitz: „Mutter mit totem Sohn"

EINBLICKE

Berlin's Past

Today it is nearly impossible to pass through Berlin without uncovering reminders of the city's long history. Founded more than 750 years ago, Berlin became the seat of the Prussian kings in 1701. The Brandenburg Gate, constructed at the end of the 18th century, was intended as a "Gate of Peace." Instead, it would witness two centuries of war and revolution.

Unter den Linden, the city's most prominent boulevard, led up to the famous gate. Here Napoleon's victorious army paraded through Berlin; revolutionaries erected barricades in 1848 and 1918; and the Nazis staged their book burnings in 1933. After World War II, the devastated capital was divided into Allied and Soviet sectors. At first it was relatively easy to cross from one zone to the other. But Berlin soon became the first battlefield in the Cold War. The Soviet blockade of the Allied zones in 1948–1949 triggered the Berlin airlift, a humanitarian effort that won over the hearts of West Berliners. Later, as increasing numbers of East Berliners fled to the West, the East German regime constructed the Berlin Wall in 1961. The wall, which cut through the heart of the city, was reinforced with minefields, self-firing machine guns, and steel fences to prevent East Germans from escaping. The Brandenburg Gate stood right next to the wall, just inside East Berlin.

For almost thirty years, West Berlin remained an island of capitalism in Communist East Germany—until Mikhail Gorbachev's spirit of reform in the Soviet Union swept across Eastern Europe. Again, thousands of East Germans tried to flee to West Germany, and in the confusion that ensued, a Communist Party official mistakenly announced an easing of travel restrictions. Almost by accident, the wall was opened on November 9, 1989. Reunification followed a year later, and the Brandenburg Gate once more took its central location in the city.

Blick aufs Brandenburger Tor

WORTSCHATZ 2

der Gedanke, -ns, -n	*thought*
das Tor, -e	*gate*
die Heimat	*homeland, home*
Insel, -n	*island*
Jugend	*youth*
Luft	*air*
Macht, ⸚e	*power*
Mitte	*middle*
(Wieder)vereinigung	*(re)unification*
berühmt	*famous*
leer	*empty*
aus·tauschen	*to exchange*
erkennen, erkannte, erkannt	*to recognize*
erleben	*to experience*
verlassen (verlässt), verließ, verlassen	*to leave (a place)*

Vorm Lesen

A. Allerlei Fragen

1. Wo liegt Berlin? 2. An welchem Fluss liegt es? 3. Was sind die Daten des 2. Weltkrieges? 4. In wie viele Teile war Berlin geteilt? 5. Wann endete die Teilung *(division)* von Berlin? 6. Was war Ost-Berlin bis dann? 7. Seit wann ist Berlin wieder die Hauptstadt/der Regierungssitz *(seat or parliament)* von Deutschland? 8. Was wissen Sie noch über Berlin?

B. Was ist das?

der Bomber, Einmarsch, Ökologe, Sonderstatus, Städteplaner; das Angebot, Turmcafé; die Blockade, Luftbrücke, Metropole, Olympiade, Orientierung, Passkontrolle, Reaktion, Rote Armee; *(pl.)* die Medikamente, Westmächte, zwanziger Jahre; grenzenlos, kapitalistisch, sowjetisch, sozialistisch, teils, total blockiert, ummauert, (un)freiwillig

Berlin, ein Tor zur Welt

Besuch in Berlin, 1985

Da saßen wir nun, Vater und Tochter, im Flugzeug auf dem Weg zu der Stadt, die er eigentlich nie vergessen konnte: Berlin. „Ich bin schon lange in Amerika, aber Berlin . . . Nun, Berlin ist eben meine Heimat." Und dann wanderten seine Gedanken zurück zu den zwanziger bis vierziger Jahren, zu der Zeit, als er dort gelebt hatte. Die Viereinhalbmillionenstadt, von deren Charme und Esprit er heute noch schwärmt°, hatte seine Jugend geprägt°. Und er erzählte mir von dem, was er dort so geliebt hatte: von den Wäldern und Seen in der Umgebung und von der berühmten Berliner Luft; von den Museen, der Oper und den Theatern, deren Angebot damals einmalig gewesen wäre; vom Kabarett mit seiner typischen „Berliner Schnauze" und den Kaffeehäusern, in denen immer etwas los war. „In Berlin liefen eben alle Fäden° zusammen, nicht nur kulturell, sondern auch politisch und wirtschaftlich. Es war einst die größte Industriestadt Europas. Die Zentralverwaltung° fast aller wichtigen Industriefirmen war in Berlin. Und man kannte sich, tauschte Gedanken aus, auch mit Wissenschaftlern an der Universität. Einfach fantastisch!"

„Und dann kam 1933. Viele verließen Berlin, teils freiwillig, teils unfreiwillig. Die Nazis beherrschten° das Straßenbild°. Bei der Olympiade 1936 sah die ganze Welt nicht nur Berlins

raves/shaped

threads

. . . headquarters

dominated / . . . scene

Ein „Rosinenbomber" während der Blockade

moderne S-Bahn und schöne Straßen, sondern auch Hitler. Und drei Jahre später war Krieg!" Nun sprach er von den schweren Luftangriffen° und den Trümmern°, die diese hinterlassen hätten, vom Einmarsch der Roten Armee, der Teilung Deutschlands unter den vier Siegermächten° (1945) und auch von der Luftbrücke, mit der die Westmächte auf die sowjetische Blockade reagiert hätten. „Plötzlich waren wir total blockiert, eine Insel. Es gab nichts zu essen, keine Kleidung, kein Heizmaterial°, keine Medikamente, kaum Wasser und Strom°. An guten Tagen landeten in den nächsten zehn Monaten alle paar Minuten britische und amerikanische Transportflugzeuge — wir nannten sie die Rosinenbomber° — und brachten uns, was wir brauchten. Ohne die Westmächte hätten wir es nie geschafft°!" . . .

air raids / rubble / left behind

victorious Allies

fuel/electricity

raisin . . .
accomplished

Dann kamen wir in West-Berlin an. Erst machten wir eine Stadtrundfahrt. „Es ist wieder schön hier; und doch, die Weite° ist weg. Berlin schien früher grenzenlos, und jetzt . . . überall diese Grenze." Immer wieder stand man vor der Mauer, die seit 1961 mitten durch Berlin lief. Besonders traurig machte ihn der Blick auf das Brandenburger Tor, das auf der anderen Seite der Mauer stand. Und doch gefiel mir diese ummauerte Insel. West-Berlin war wieder eine lebendige Metropole, die unheimlich viel zu bieten hatte.

wide-open space

Der Besuch in Ost-Berlin, der Hauptstadt Ostdeutschlands, war wie eine Reise in eine andere Welt. Allein schon die Gesichter der Vopos° am Checkpoint Charlie und das komische Gefühl, das man bei der Passkontrolle hatte! Berlin-Mitte war für meinen Vater schwer wieder zu erkennen. Der Potsdamer Platz, der früher voller Leben gewesen war, war leer. Leichter zu erkennen waren die historischen Gebäude entlang Unter den Linden: die Staatsbibliothek, die Humboldt-Universität und die Staatsoper. Interessant waren auch das Pergamonmuseum, der Dom und gegenüber der Palast der Republik, den die Berliner „Palazzo Prozzo" nannten und in dem die Volkskammer° saß. Dann über allem der Fernsehturm, dessen Turmcafé sich dreht°. Wir sahen auch einen britischen Jeep, der Unter den Linden Streife fuhr°, was uns an den Sonderstatus Berlins erinnerte. Hier trafen die kapitalistische und die sozialistische Welt aufeinander°; und für beide Welten waren Ost- und West-Berlin Schaufenster° zweier gegensätzlicher° Systeme.

GDR police (Volkspolizei)

GDR house of representatives
turns / patrolled

came together / display window
opposing

Heute

Heute ist das alles Geschichte. Die Berliner können wieder reisen, wohin sie wollen. Berlin ist keine Insel mehr. Ich erinnere mich noch gut an die Reaktion meines Vaters, als wir den Mauerdurchbruch im amerikanischen Fernsehen sahen. Immer wieder sagte er, „Dass ich das noch erleben durfte!" Und unsere Gedanken gingen damals zurück zu Präsident Kennedys Worten 1963 an der Mauer: „Alle freien Menschen sind Bürger Berlins . . . Ich bin ein Berliner!"

John F. Kennedy in Berlin am 26. 6. 1963

Seit der Wiedervereinigung hat sich in Berlin viel getan°. Es ist auf dem Weg, wieder eine Vier- bis Fünfmillionenstadt zu werden. Politiker, Städteplaner, Architekten und Ökologen haben enorme Arbeit geleistet°. Da, wo einst die Mauer stand, stehen jetzt moderne Gebäude und die Alte Mitte Berlins ist wieder Stadtmitte geworden. Als Hauptstadt des vereinten Deutschlands in einem neuen Europa hat Berlin neue Aufgaben bekommen; und durch seine Lage—nur rund 100 km zur polnischen Grenze—erlebt es jetzt auch eine größere Orientierung nach Osten. Berlin ist wieder ein Tor zur Welt.

° has happened
° achieved

Zum Text

A. Richtig oder falsch?
_____ 1. Der Vater und die Tochter fliegen nach Amerika.
_____ 2. Der Vater hatte lange in Berlin gelebt.
_____ 3. Er hatte Berlin sehr geliebt.
_____ 4. In Berlin war aber damals nicht viel los.
_____ 5. 1939 hatte der Krieg begonnen.
_____ 6. 1945 teilten die Siegermächte Deutschland und Berlin.
_____ 7. Die Luftbrücke brachte den Berlinern nur Rosinen.
_____ 8. Von 1961 bis 1989 teilte die Mauer Berlin.
_____ 9. Ein Vopo war ein ostdeutsches Auto.
_____ 10. Der Potsdamer Platz war der „Palazzo Prozzo" Ost-Berlins.
_____ 11. Unter den Linden ist eine berühmte alte Straße in Berlin.
_____ 12. Ost-Berlin war ein Schaufenster des Kapitalismus.
_____ 13. Der Vater ist beim Öffnen der Mauer in Berlin gewesen.
_____ 14. Präsident Nixon sagte 1963: „Ich bin ein Berliner."
_____ 15. Seit der Wiedervereinigung ist Berlin wieder die Hauptstadt Deutschlands.
_____ 16. Politiker und Städteplaner können sich nicht entscheiden, was sie mit Berlin tun sollen.
_____ 17. Wo einst die Mauer stand, ist jetzt ein langer Park.
_____ 18. Von Berlin sind es nur 10 km bis zur polnischen Grenze.

B. Suchen Sie die Relativpronomen im Text! Unterstreichen Sie *(underline)* zusammen mit zwei oder drei anderen Studenten alle Relativpronomen und vorhergehenden Wörter *(antecedents)* im Lesetext! Welche Gruppe findet die meisten?

C. Wie geht's weiter? Beenden Sie die Sätze als Relativsätze. Vergleichen Sie Ihre Sätze mit denen *(those)* der anderen!
1. Berlin ist eine Stadt, die . . .
2. Berlin ist eine Stadt, in der . . .
3. Berlin ist eine Stadt, deren . . .
4. Berlin ist eine Stadt, von der . . .
5. Berlin ist eine Stadt, um die . . .

D. Was fehlt?
1. Mir gefällt diese Stadt, in _____ mehr als drei Millionen Menschen wohnen.
2. Es ist ein Kulturzentrum *(n.)*, _____ unheimlich viel zu bieten hat. 3. Die Filmfestspiele, _____ Filme meistens sehr gut sind, muss man mal gesehen haben. 4. Der letzte Film, _____ ich mir angesehen habe, war herrlich. 5. Ein anderer Film, an _____ Titel *(m.)* ich mich nicht erinnern kann, war etwas traurig. 6. Es war ein Film, in _____ mehrere berühmte Schauspieler mitspielten. 7. Der Hauptdarsteller *(main actor)* _____ am Ende seine Heimat verlässt, hieß Humphrey Bogart.

8. Morgen Abend gehe ich mit Heike, _____ Vater Extrakarten hat, ins Kabarett. 9. Das Kabarett, _____ Name nicht nur in Berlin bekannt ist, heißt „Die Stachelschweine" *(The Porcupines)*. 10. Die Leute, über _____ man lacht, sind meistens Politiker oder andere berühmte Persönlichkeiten *(pl.)*, _____ jeder kennt.

E. Gespräch zwischen Vater und Tochter. Lesen Sie das Gespräch und berichten Sie indirekt zusammen mit einem Partner/einer Partnerin, was die beiden gesagt haben!

BEISPIEL: S1 Die Tochter fragte, wie lange er dort gewohnt hätte.
S2 Er sagte, dass er ungefähr 25 Jahre dort gewohnt hätte.

TOCHTER Wie lange hast du dort gewohnt?
VATER Ungefähr 25 Jahre.
TOCHTER Wohnten deine Eltern damals auch in Berlin?
VATER Nein, aber sie sind 1938 nachgekommen.
TOCHTER Hast du dort studiert?
VATER Ja, an der Humboldt-Universität.
TOCHTER Hast du dort Mutti kennen gelernt?
VATER Ja, das waren schöne Jahre.
TOCHTER Und wann seid ihr von dort weggegangen?
VATER 1949.
TOCHTER Erzähl mir davon!
VATER Ach, das ist eine lange Geschichte. Setzen wir uns in ein Café! Dann werde ich dir davon erzählen.

F. Schreiben Sie! Wenn Sie die Wahl *(choice)* hätten, würden Sie in Berlin leben oder dort studieren wollen? Warum oder warum nicht? (8–10 Sätze)

HÖREN SIE ZU!

Nach der Wiedervereinigung

Zum Erkennen: das Textilgeschäft, -e *(clothing store)*; viel geschafft *(accomplished a lot)*; profitieren; garantieren; das Gefängnis, -se *(prison)*; existieren; die Direktorin, -nen *(principal)*; klagen *(to complain)*

Richtig oder falsch?
_____ 1. Die Wiedervereinigung Deutschlands war nicht so leicht, wie man sich das vorgestellt hatte.
_____ 2. Nach drei Jahren waren die Menschen im Westen nicht so optimistisch über die Zukunft wie die Menschen im Osten.
_____ 3. Nach drei Jahren hatten mehr als 75 Prozent der Westdeutschen ein Auto und fast alle hatten Farbfernseher.
_____ 4. Ein Arbeiter in Ostdeutschland verdiente damals so viel wie dreißig Arbeiter in Russland.
_____ 5. In Altdöbeln hatte man in drei Jahren 164 neue Geschäfte und Firmen eröffnet.
_____ 6. Jutta Laubach ist eine Altdöbelner Geschäftsfrau, die ein Textilgeschäft aufgemacht hat.
_____ 7. Sie fand das alte System besser, weil früher alles garantiert war.
_____ 8. Helga Müller weinte, als sie hörte, dass die Berliner Mauer plötzlich offen war.
_____ 9. Sie glaubte, dass der Kommunismus ein gutes System war.
_____ 10. Monika Bernhart findet ihr neues Leben schwerer, aber schöner.

Erich Kästner

Erich Kästner (1899–1974) was a German writer known for his sarcastic poems—often directed against narrow-mindedness and militarism—and his witty novels and children's books. In 1933 Kästner's disrespectful books were banned and burned by the Nazis. His works include the poem collection *Bei Durchsicht meiner Bücher* (1946), the stories *Emil und die Detektive* (1929), *Das fliegende Klassenzimmer* (1933), *Konferenz der Tiere* (1949), *Das doppelte Lottchen* (1949), and the comedy *Die Schule der Diktatoren* (1956).

Fantasie von übermorgen

Und als der nächste Krieg begann,
da sagten die Frauen: Nein!

und schlossen Bruder, Sohn und Mann
fest in der Wohnung ein°.   locked up

Dann zogen sie, in jedem Land,
wohl vor des Hauptmanns° Haus   captain
und hielten Stöcke° in der Hand   sticks
und holten die Kerls° heraus.   guys

Sie legten jeden übers Knie,
der diesen Krieg befahl°:   ordered
die Herren der Bank und Industrie,
den Minister und General.

Da brach so mancher Stock entzwei°.   broke apart
Und manches Großmaul° schwieg°.   big mouth / shut up
In allen Ländern gab's Geschrei°,   screaming
und nirgends gab es Krieg.

Die Frauen gingen dann wieder nach Haus,
zum Bruder und Sohn und Mann,
und sagten ihnen, der Krieg sei aus°!   was over
Die Männer starrten° zum Fenster hinaus   stared
und sahn die Frauen nicht an . . .

Erich Kästner

WEB-ECKE For updates and online activities, visit the *Wie geht's?* home page at: http://www.hrwcollege.com/german/sevin/. You'll go sightseeing in Berlin and Potsdam, check out what's going on in Berlin right now and during the Love Parade, and be introduced to several famous Berliners.

SPRECHSITUATIONEN

Expressing doubt and uncertainty

If you are unsure of your response, you can use any of the following expressions:

> Vielleicht . . .
> Ich bin mir nicht sicher, aber . . .
> Es ist möglich, dass . . .
> Ich glaube (nicht), dass . . .
> Soviel ich weiß *(as far as I know, . . .)*

If you don't know at all, use:

> Ich weiß (es) nicht.
> (Ich habe) keine Ahnung.

Expressing probability and possibility

You know that the future can be used to express probability. There are also other ways to express this.

> Bestimmt.
> Sicher.
> Vielleicht.
> Wahrscheinlich.
> Es ist möglich, dass . . .
> Ich bin sicher, dass . . .
> Ich glaube, . . .
> Ich nehme an, . . .

Expressing concern

Here are several ways to say you are worried:

> Ich mache mir Sorgen, dass . . .
> Ich habe Angst, dass . . .
> Ich (be)fürchte, dass . . . *(I fear that . . .)*
> Ich mache mir Sorgen um . . .
> Ich habe Angst vor (+ *dat.*) . . .

Drawing conclusions

> Darum / deshalb / . . .   *Therefore / That's why* . . .
> Aus dem / diesem Grund . . .   *For that / this reason* . . .
> Das (End)resultat ist . . .   *The (end) result is* . . .
> Im Großen und Ganzen . . .   *On the whole* . . .

Übungen

A. **Was nun?** *(Work in small groups of two to four students. Take turns asking a classmate many questions about his/her future plans. He/she is not at all certain about details and expresses this uncertainty in the responses. Choose one of the following situations, or invent your own.)*
  1. He/she is going to study in one of the German-speaking countries.
  2. He/she is about to graduate and has no definite plans for the future.

3. He/she has just applied to join the Peace Corps **(Entwicklungshilfedienst)**.

B. **Warum? Darum!** *(Work in pairs. Your partner asks you questions about your future plans. This time you have a pretty good idea of what you are planning to do. Express the probability in your responses.)*
   1. You are taking time off from your studies.
   2. You are traveling in Europe for two and a half months.
   3. During the summer you will be working as an intern for an American bank in Frankfurt.

C. **Kurzgespräch**

You tell a fellow student, Gunther, that two mutual friends, Karin and Thomas, didn't return from a car trip to Italy yesterday, as they had said they would. You are worried that they might have had an accident **(einen Autounfall haben)** or bad weather as they crossed the mountains **(schlechtes Wetter / Schnee in den Bergen),** or that their car broke down **(eine Panne haben).** Gunther tries to reassure you. He comes up with various ideas as to why they might have been delayed: they wanted to stay a little longer, stopped to see another museum or town, are probably arriving any minute, etc.

KAPITEL 15
DEUTSCHLAND, EUROPA UND DIE ZUKUNFT

Das Goethe-Schiller-Denkmal vor dem Nationaltheater in Weimar

LERNZIELE

■ VORSCHAU
The path to a united Europe

■ GESPRÄCHE AND WORTSCHATZ
Nature and environmental protection

■ STRUKTUR
Passive voice
Review of the uses of **werden**
Special subjunctive (Subjunctive I)

■ EINBLICKE
In search of an identity
The wind knows no borders

■ FOKUS
Cultural capital Weimar
The German spelling reform
Goethe: "Erinnerung"
Schiller: "Ode an die Freude"

■ WEB-ECKE

■ SPRECHSITUATIONEN
Describing objects

VORSCHAU

The Path to a United Europe

1945   World War II leaves Europe devastated and hungry.
1949   The North Atlantic Treaty Organization (NATO) and the Council of Europe are established.
1950   France launches Schuman Plan, which proposes putting French and West German coal and steel production under a single authority.
1951   Italy, Belgium, the Netherlands, and Luxembourg found the European Coal and Steel Community (ECSC), known as Montanunion.
1957   France, Germany, Italy, Belgium, the Netherlands, and Luxembourg establish the European Economic Community (EEC) and the European Atomic Energy Commission (EURATOM), known collectively as the Treaties of Rome. The EEC, EURATOM, and ECSC are called the "European Communities," or EC.
1960   Great Britain, Austria, Switzerland, Portugal, and the Scandinavian countries form the European Free Trade Association (EFTA), an alternative to the EEC.
1973   Denmark, Ireland, and Great Britain join the EC.
1979   First direct elections to the European Parliament are held.
1981   Greece joins the EC.
1986   Spain and Portugal become members of the EC.
1989   With the fall of the Berlin Wall, Europe's division is ended.
1990   German unification extends EC membership to the former East Germany.
1993   Signed in 1991, the Maastricht Treaty now goes into effect, paving the way to economic and monetary union and increasing political unity. The "European Communities" are now called the European Union (EU).
1995   The entry of Austria, Finland, and Sweden into the EU brings the number of member states to fifteen. The Schengen Agreement, an EU treaty that makes passport-free travel possible between signatory states, goes into effect.
1997   The heads of the member states draw up the Amsterdam Treaty, which lays out internal reform and expansion eastward.
1999   The euro is introduced as common currency for financial transactions in eleven member states, marking the beginning of the end of the D-Mark and the various national EU currencies.
2002   The euro replaces national currencies such as the D-Mark and Schilling in all daily transactions.

Das neue Geld

GESPRÄCHE

Besuch in Weimar

Tom Komisch, dieses Denkmal von Goethe und Schiller kenne ich doch! Ich glaube, ich habe es schon irgendwo gesehen.

Daniela Warst du eigentlich schon mal in San Francisco?

Tom Na klar!

Daniela Warst du auch im Golden Gate Park?

Tom Ach ja, da steht genau das gleiche Denkmal! Das haben, glaub' ich, die Deutsch-Amerikaner in Kalifornien einmal bauen lassen.

Daniela Richtig! Übrigens, weißt du, dass Weimar 1999 Kulturhauptstadt Europas war?

Tom Nein, das ist mir neu. Wieso denn?

Daniela Im 18. Jahrhundert haben hier doch viele berühmte Leute gelebt und die Weimarer Republik ist auch danach benannt.

Tom Ja ja. Aber heute früh, als ich am Mahnmal vom Konzentrationslager Buchenwald auf die Stadt herabblickte, hatte ich sehr gemischte Gefühle.

Daniela Ja, da hast du natürlich Recht.

In der Altstadt

Daniela Schau mal, die alten Häuser hier sind doch echt schön.

Tom Ja, sie sind gut restauriert worden. Ich finde es vor allem schön, dass hier keine Autos fahren dürfen.

Daniela Gott sei Dank! Die Fassaden hätten die Abgase der Trabbis[1] nicht lange überlebt.

Tom Bei uns gibt es jetzt auch eine Bürgerinitiative, alle Autos in der Altstadt zu verbieten, um die alten Gebäude zu retten.

Daniela Das finde ich gut.

Tom Sind die Container da drüben für die Mülltrennung?

Daniela Ja, habt ihr das auch?

Tom Das schon, aber da könnte man sicherlich noch viel mehr tun.

---

[1] The **Trabant,** or **Trabbi,** was an East German car with a 2-stroke engine that emitted roughly nine times more hydrocarbons and five times more carbon dioxide than cars with 4-stroke engines. Nicknamed **Plastikbomber, Asphaltblase** *(Asphalt Bubble),* or **Rennpappe** *(Racing Cardboard),* it was nevertheless expensive by GDR standards. People had to save the equivalent of 10–27 months' salary; credit did not exist. Delivery of the 26 HP car normally took at least 10 years; and its spare parts were one of the underground currencies of the former GDR.

Richtig oder falsch?

_____ 1. Tom und Daniela sind in Weimar.
_____ 2. Sie sehen ein Denkmal von Goethe und Nietzsche.
_____ 3. Eine Kopie dieses Denkmals steht in New York.
_____ 4. Die Gebäude in der Innenstadt sind schön restauriert.
_____ 5. Im Zentrum gibt es auch eine Fußgängerzone.
_____ 6. Tom kommt aus einer Stadt, in deren Altstadt bis jetzt noch Autos fahren dürfen.
_____ 7. Für die Mülltrennung gibt es in Weimar besondere Container.
_____ 8. Tom meint, dass es das bei ihm zu Hause nicht gibt.

Cultural Capital Weimar

In 1985, the European Community selected for the first time a cultural capital of Europe: Athens. Luxembourg, Thessaloniki, Stockholm, and other cities followed. Weimar had this honor for the year 1999. It is not only the smallest of the European cultural capitals to date; it is also the first city from one of the former communist countries to bear this title.

Weimar boasts a proud cultural history. Johann Sebastian Bach was court organist there in the early eighteenth century. Goethe, who lived and worked in Weimar from 1775 until his death, drew Schiller, Gottfried Herder, and many others to the town, which, nourished by genius, gave birth to "Weimar Classicism." Franz Liszt was musical director in Weimar in the mid-nineteenth century, and the philosopher and author Friedrich Nietzsche lived there for a time as well. In 1919, following World War I, the National Assembly met in Weimar to draft a constitution for the new republic—henceforth known as the Weimar Republic. The assembly chose this site because of its popular associations with Germany's classical tradition. The new republic lasted only fourteen years, dissolved by Hitler soon after he was appointed chancellor in 1933. During the Nazi period, Weimar and its traditions were used selectively to promote Nazi ideology and some of Goethe's works were even banned from schools. On the Ettersberg, a hill above the town, a memorial recalls the nearby Nazi concentration camp of Buchenwald. Since the fall of East Germany, tourists from across Europe are again flocking to Weimar's historical and cultural landmarks.

Auf dem Marktplatz in Weimar

WORTSCHATZ I

Die Landschaft *(landscape, scenery)*

das Denkmal, ¨er	*monument*	die Küste, -n	*coast*
Gebiet, -e	*area, region*	Natur	*nature*

Die Umwelt *(environment)*

der Abfall, ¨e	*trash*	die Erhaltung	*preservation*
Giftstoff, -e	*toxic waste*	Mülltrennung	*waste separation*
Müll	*garbage; waste*	Sammelstelle, -n	*collection site*
Schutz	*protection*	Verschmutzung	*pollution*

gemeinsam	*together; common*
umweltbewusst	*environmentally aware*

ab·reißen, riss ab, abgerissen	*to tear down*
(wieder) auf·bauen	*to (re)build*
finanzieren	*to finance*
garantieren	*to guarantee*
planen	*to plan*
reden (mit, über)	*to talk (to, about)*
renovieren	*to renovate*

restaurieren	to restore
retten	to save, rescue
schützen	to protect
trennen	to separate
(sich) verändern	to change
verbieten, verbot, verboten	to forbid
weg·werfen (wirft weg), warf weg, weggeworfen	to throw away, discard
verwenden	to use, utilize
zerstören	to destroy

Weiteres

allerdings	however
Gott sei Dank!	Thank God!
Schau mal!	Look!
sicherlich	surely; certainly, undoubtedly
übrigens	by the way

Wirf Altglas nicht fort, Container stehn an jedem Ort!

Zum Erkennen: bauen lassen *(to have built)*; benennen nach *(to name after)*; das Mahnmal, -e *(memorial)*; das Konzentrationslager, -; herab·blicken auf *(to look down on)*; gemischte Gefühle *(mixed feelings)*; echt *(really)*; die Fassade, -n; die Abgase *(pl., exhaust fumes)*; überleben *(to survive)*; die Bürgerinitiative, -n *(citizens' initiative)*; der Container, -; das schon *(here: sure)*

Zum Thema

A. Reporter im Rathaus *(You are a radio reporter attending a meeting of the city-planning commission. Read what one man says, then report to your listeners.)*

> **BEISPIEL:** Er hat gesagt, wir sollten nicht auf die Bürger hören, die immer . . .

„Hören Sie nicht auf die Bürger, die immer wieder alles, ja die ganze Altstadt, retten wollen. Viele alte Innenhöfe *(inner courts)* sind dunkel und hässlich. Abreißen ist viel billiger und einfacher als renovieren. Wenn man die alten Gebäude abreißt und die Innenstadt schön modern aufbaut, dann kommt bestimmt wieder Leben in unser Zentrum. Auf diese Weise kann man auch die Straßen verbreitern *(widen)* und alles besser planen. Fußgängerzonen sind sicherlich schön und gut, aber nicht im Zentrum, denn alle wollen ihr Auto in der Nähe haben. Das ist doch klar, weil's viel bequemer und sicherer ist! Ich kann Ihnen garantieren, wenn Sie aus dem Zentrum eine Einkaufszone machen, zu deren Geschäften man nur zu Fuß hinkommt *(gets to)*, dann verlieren Sie alle, meine Damen und Herren, viel Geld!"

B. Altbau oder Neubau? Wo würden Sie lieber wohnen? Was spricht dafür und was dagegen? Stellen Sie eine Liste auf! Machen Sie eine Meinungsumfrage *(opinion poll)*!

C. Schützt unsere Umwelt! Interview. Fragen Sie einen Nachbarn/eine Nachbarin, . . . !
1. was er/sie mit Altglas, Altpapier, Altbatterien, Altöl, alten Dosen *(cans)*, alter Kleidung, Plastikflaschen und Plastiktüten *(. . . bags)* macht
2. ob er/sie eine Waschmaschine oder Spülmaschine *(dishwasher)* benutzt; wenn ja, wie viel Waschmittel oder Spülmittel er/sie dafür benutzt
3. wofür er/sie Chemikalien *(chemicals)* benutzt und wie oft
4. ob er/sie manchmal ein Umweltverschmutzer ist; wieso (nicht)
5. ob er/sie gern Musik hört; wenn ja, ob er/sie sie auf laut oder leise *(quiet)* stellt und ob andere darüber hier und da auch böse sind
6. ob er/sie einen Hund hat; wenn ja, was für einen und ob er/sie beim „Gassi gehen" seine „Geschäfte" aufsammelt
7. was er/sie und seine/ihre Freunde für die Umwelt tun

Zum Erkennen: sich erbauen an *(to enjoy)*; schaden *(to hurt)*; der Abfall-Wurf *(littering)*; das Waschmittel, *(laundry detergent)*; in kleinen Gaben *(in small amounts)*; Salbe, -n *(ointment)*; üblich *(usual)*; entgegen·nehmen *(to receive)*; der Verstand *(common sense)*; der Ölwechsel *(oil change)*; sei helle *(be smart)*; Gassi gehen *(to walk the doggie)*

D. **Aussprache:** Glottal Stops. Sehen Sie auch II. 42 im Ausspracheteil des Arbeitsheftes!
  1. + Erich + arbeitet + am + alten Schloss.
  2. Die + Abgase der + Autos machen + einfach + überall + alles kaputt.
  3. + Ulf + erinnert sich + an + ein + einmaliges + Abendkonzert + im + Ulmer Dom.
  4. + Otto sieht + aus wie + ein + alter + Opa.
  5. + Anneliese + ist + attraktiv + und + elegant.

HÖREN SIE ZU!

Habitat Wattenmeer

Zum Erkennen: das flache Vorland *(tidal flats)*; grenzen an *(to border)*; die Ebbe *(low tide)*; die Flut *(high tide)*; die Muschel, -n *(clam)*; das Paradies; die Krabbe, -n *(crab)*; knabbern *(to nibble)*; der Pferdewagen, - *(horse-drawn carriage)*; der Seehund, -e *(seal)*; das empfindliche Ökosystem *(delicate ecosystem)*; das Düngemittel, - *(fertilizer)*; die Landwirtschaft *(agriculture)*; der Kompromiss, -e; das Reservat, -e *(reservation)*; der Fischfang *(fishing)*; begrenzt *(limited)*

Richtig oder falsch?
  _____ 1. Das Wattenmeer liegt vor der Ostseeküste.
  _____ 2. Alle zwölf Stunden ist Ebbe und Flut.
  _____ 3. Bei Ebbe kann man weit ins Watt hinaus laufen.
  _____ 4. Dabei kann man alle möglichen *(all sorts of)* Tiere beobachten.
  _____ 5. Gehfaule können auch mit dem Pferdewagen ins Watt fahren.

_____ 6. Wegen seines empfindlichen Ökosystems haben die Deutschen dieses Gebiet zum Naturschutzgebiet erklärt.
_____ 7. Auch die Dänen und Niederländer sind am Schutz dieser Landschaft interessiert.
_____ 8. Die Dänen dürfen noch im Wattenmeer fischen, aber nicht die Deutschen.

Mit dem Pferdewagen durchs Wattenmeer

STRUKTUR

I. Passive voice

English and German sentences are in one of two voices: the active or the passive. In the ACTIVE VOICE the subject of the sentence is doing something; it's "active."

The students ask the professor.

In the PASSIVE VOICE, the subject is not doing anything, rather, something is being done to it; it's "passive."

The professor is asked by the students.

Note what happens when a sentence in the active voice is changed into the passive voice: The direct object of the active becomes the subject of the passive.

        subj.   obj.
*The students ask **the professor**.*

***The professor** is asked by the students.*
    subj.   obj. of prep.

In both languages the active voice is used much more frequently than the passive voice, especially in everyday speech. The passive voice is used when the focus is on the person or thing at whom the action is directed, rather than on the agent who is acting.

| Active Voice | **Die Studenten** fragen den Professor. |
| Passive Voice | **Der Professor** wird von den Studenten gefragt. |

1. Forms
   a. In English the passive voice is formed with the auxiliary *to be* and the past participle of the verb. In German it is formed with the auxiliary **werden** and the past participle of the verb.

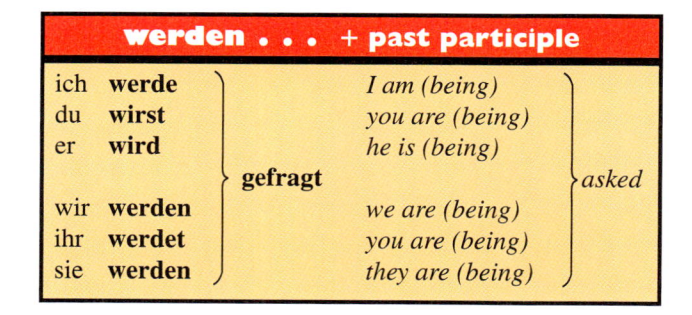

werden . . . + past participle

ich	werde		I am (being)	
du	wirst		you are (being)	
er	wird	gefragt	he is (being)	asked
wir	werden		we are (being)	
ihr	werdet		you are (being)	
sie	werden		they are (being)	

Der Professor **wird** von den Studenten **gefragt**.
Die Professoren **werden** von den Studenten **gefragt**.

b. The passive voice has the <u>same tenses</u> as the active voice. They are formed with the various tenses of **werden + the past participle of the verb.** Note, however, that in the perfect tenses of the passive voice, the past participle of **werden** is **worden!** When you see or hear **worden,** you know immediately that you are dealing with a sentence in the passive voice.

PRESENT	Er **wird** . . . gefragt.	*He is being asked . . .*
SIMPLE PAST	Er **wurde** . . . gefragt.	*He was asked . . .*
FUTURE	Er **wird** . . . gefragt **werden.**	*He will be asked . . .*
PRES. PERF.	Er **ist** . . . gefragt **worden.**	*He has been asked . . .*
PAST PERF.	Er **war** . . . gefragt **worden.**	*He had been asked . . .*

Die Altstadt wird renoviert.	*The old part of town is being renovated.*
Die Pläne wurden letztes Jahr gemacht.	*The plans were made last year.*
Alles wird finanziert werden.	*Everything will be financed.*
Das ist entschieden worden.	*That has been decided.*
Manche Gebäude waren im Krieg zerstört worden.	*Some buildings had been destroyed during the war.*

In subordinate clauses, the pattern is:

Ich weiß, dass die Altstadt renoviert wird.

, dass die Pläne letztes Jahr gemacht wurden.

, dass alles finanziert werden wird.

, dass alles schon entschieden worden ist.

, dass manche Gebäude im Krieg zerstört worden waren.

c. Modals themselves are not put into the passive voice. Rather, they follow this pattern:

modal . . . + past participle + **werden**

In this book only the present and simple past tense of the modals will be used.

PRESENT	Er **muss** . . . gefragt **werden.**	*He must (has to) be asked.*
SIMPLE PAST	Er **musste** . . . gefragt **werden.**	*He had to be asked*

Das Gebäude muss renoviert werden.	*The building must be renovated.*
Das Gebäude sollte letztes Jahr renoviert werden.	*The building was supposed to be renovated last year.*

In subordinate clauses the inflected verb stands at the end.

Ich weiß, dass das Gebäude renoviert werden **muss.**

, dass das Gebäude letztes Jahr renoviert werden **sollte.**

2. Expression of the agent

If the agent who performs the act is expressed, the preposition **von** is used.

Der Professor wird **von den Studenten** gefragt.	*The professor is asked by the students.*
Alles ist **vom Staat** finanziert worden.	*Everything was financed by the state.*

3. Impersonal use

   In German the passive voice is frequently used without a subject or with **es** functioning as the subject.

   > Hier darf nicht gebaut werden. *You can't build here.*
   > **Es** darf hier nicht gebaut werden. *Building is not permitted here.*

4. Alternative to the passive voice

   One common substitute for the passive voice is a sentence in the active voice with **man** as the subject.

   > Hier darf nicht gebaut werden.
   > Es darf hier nicht gebaut werden.
   > **Man darf hier nicht bauen.**

> Besser informiert ist,
> wer besser informiert wird.
>
> **Süddeutsche Zeitung**
> Deutschlands große Tageszeitung

Übungen

A. Trier. Aktiv oder Passiv?
1. Trier was founded by the Romans in 15 B.C.
2. Its original name was *Augusta Treverorum*.
3. Under Roman occupation, Germania along the Rhine and Danube had been transformed into a series of Roman provinces.
4. The names of many towns are derived from Latin.
5. Remnants from Roman times can still be seen today.
6. New discoveries are made from time to time.
7. Beautiful Roman museums have been built.
8. One of them is located in the former *Colonia Agrippina* (Köln).

> „Je weniger die Leute darüber wissen,
> wie Würste und Gesetze gemacht werden,
> desto besser schlafen sie nachts."
>
> Otto von Bismarck

B. Köln. Was bedeutet das auf Englisch?
1. a. Köln wurde während des Krieges schwer zerbombt.
   b. Achtzig Prozent der Häuser in der Innenstadt waren zerbombt *(destroyed by bombs)* worden.
   c. Inzwischen *(in the meantime)* ist Köln wieder schön aufgebaut und restauriert worden.
   d. Zur Karnevalszeit wird hier schwer gefeiert.
   e. Es ist eine Stadt, in der jedes Jahr verschiedene Messen *(fairs)* gehalten werden.

f. DIE POPKOMM, Kölns Messe für Popmusik und Unterhaltung, wird von einem großen Musikfestival begleitet *(accompanied)*, das in der ganzen Stadt gefeiert wird.

2. a. Erst mussten natürlich neue Wohnungen gebaut werden.
   b. Manche alten Gebäude konnten gerettet werden.
   c. Der Dom musste restauriert werden.
   d. Aber die alten Kirchen aus dem 12. Jahrhundert dürfen auch nicht vergessen werden.
   e. Das kann natürlich nicht ohne Geld gemacht werden.
   f. Durch Bürgerinitiativen sollte genug Geld für die Restaurierung gesammelt werden.

3. a. In der Altstadt wird in Parkgaragen geparkt.
   b. Es wird viel mit dem Bus gefahren.
   c. In der „Hohen Straße" wird nicht Auto gefahren.
   d. Dort wird zu Fuß gegangen.
   e. Dort wird gern eingekauft.
   f. In der Vorweihnachtszeit wird die Fußgängerzone mit vielen Lichtern dekoriert.

C. **Ein schönes Haus.** Sagen Sie die Sätze im Aktiv!

1. **BEISPIEL:** Nicht alle Gebäude waren vom Krieg zerstört worden.
   Der Krieg hatte nicht alle Gebäude zerstört.

   a. Viele Gebäude sind von Planierraupen *(bulldozers)* zerstört worden.
   b. Dieses Haus wurde von den Bürgern gerettet.
   c. Viele Unterschriften *(signatures)* wurden von Studenten gesammelt.
   d. Das Haus ist von der Uni gekauft worden.
   e. Die Fassade wird von Spezialisten renoviert werden.
   f. Die Hauspläne werden von Architekten gemacht.

2. **BEISPIEL:** Der Hausplan darf von den Architekten nicht sehr verändert werden.
   Die Architekten dürfen den Hausplan nicht sehr verändern.

   a. Ein Teil soll von der Stadt finanziert werden.
   b. Der Rest muss von der Uni bezahlt werden.
   c. Das Haus konnte von der Universität als Gästehaus ausgebaut werden.
   d. Der große Raum im Parterre darf von den Studenten als Treffpunkt *(meeting place)* benutzt werden.

3. **BEISPIEL:** Das Gästehaus wird viel besucht.
   Man besucht das Gästehaus viel.

   a. Dort werden Gedanken ausgetauscht.
   b. Es wird auch Englisch und Italienisch gesprochen.
   c. Heute Abend wird ein Jazzkonzert gegeben.
   d. Letzte Woche wurde ein Film gezeigt.
   e. Hier werden auch Seminare gehalten werden.

D. **Ein alter Film.** Wiederholen Sie die Sätze im Passiv, aber in einer anderen Zeitform *(tense)!*

BEISPIEL: Ein alter Film wird gespielt. *(simple past)*
Ein alter Film wurde gespielt.

1. Er wird von den Studenten sehr empfohlen. *(present perfect)*
2. Zu DDR-Zeiten wird er nicht gezeigt. *(simple past)*
3. Er wird verboten. *(past perfect)*
4. Es wird viel darüber geredet. *(future)*
5. Daraus kann viel gelernt werden. *(simple past)*
6. Er soll übrigens wiederholt werden. *(simple past)*

E. **Post und Geld.** Wiederholen Sie die Sätze im Passiv, aber mit einem Modalverb! Wie heißt das auf Englisch?

BEISPIEL: Das Paket wird zur Post gebracht. (sollen)
Das Paket soll zur Post gebracht werden.
The package is supposed to be taken to the post office.

1. Ein Formular *(form)* wird noch ausgefüllt. (müssen)
2. Dann wird es am ersten Schalter abgegeben. (können)
3. Auf der Post werden auch Telefongespräche gemacht. (dürfen)
4. Dollar werden auf der Bank umgetauscht. (sollen)
5. Nicht überall wird mit Reiseschecks bezahlt. (können)
6. Taxifahrer werden mit Bargeld bezahlt. (wollen)

F. **Im Restaurant.** Sagen Sie die Sätze im Passiv!

BEISPIEL: Hier spricht man Deutsch.
Hier wird Deutsch gesprochen.

1. Am anderen Tisch spricht man Französisch.
2. Mittags isst man warm.
3. Dabei redet man gemütlich.
4. Natürlich redet man nicht mit vollem Mund.
5. Übrigens hält man die Gabel in der linken Hand.
6. Und vor dem Essen sagt man „Guten Appetit!"

G. **Schont** *(protect)* **die Parkanlagen!** Sie und ein Freund sind in einem deutschen Park und sehen dieses Schild. Ihr Freund liest es, aber versteht es nicht. Erklären Sie ihm, was es bedeutet!

BEISPIEL: S1 Es wird gebeten, auf den Wegen zu bleiben.
S2 Man soll auf den Wegen bleiben.

SCHONT DIE PARKANLAGEN!
Es wird gebeten°:
Auf den Wegen zu bleiben
Blumen nicht abzupflücken°
Hunde an der Leine zu führen°
Denkmäler° sauber zu halten
Im Park nicht Fußball zu spielen
Fahrräder nicht in den Park mitzunehmen

please; lit. it is requested

pick
lead on a leash
monuments

H. Die Party: Was muss noch gemacht werden? Sagen Sie im Passiv, dass alles schon gemacht ist!

BEISPIEL: Fritz und Lisa müssen noch angerufen werden.
Fritz und Lisa sind schon angerufen worden.

1. Die Wohnung muss noch geputzt werden. 2. Der Tisch muss noch in die Ecke gestellt werden. 3. Die Gläser müssen noch gewaschen werden. 4. Das Bier muss noch kalt gestellt werden. 5. Die Kartoffelchips müssen noch in die Schüssel (*bowl*) getan werden.

II. Review of the uses of *werden*

Distinguish carefully among the various uses of **werden**.

1. **werden** + predicate noun / adjective = a FULL VERB

    Er wird Arzt.   *He's going to be a doctor.*
    Es wird dunkel.   *It's getting dark.*

2. **werden** + infinitive = auxiliary of the FUTURE TENSE

    Ich werde ihn fragen.   *I'll ask him.*

3. **würde** + infinitive = auxiliary in the PRESENT-TIME SUBJUNCTIVE

    Ich würde ihn fragen.   *I would ask him.*

4. **werden** + past participle = auxiliary in the PASSIVE VOICE

    Er wird von uns gefragt.   *He's (being) asked by us.*
    Goethe wurde 1749 geboren. *Goethe was born in 1749.*

Übungen

I. Analysieren Sie, wie *werden* benutzt wird! Was bedeutet das auf Englisch?

BEISPIEL: Leonie ist nach Amerika eingeladen worden.
werden + past participle = PASSIVE VOICE
Leonie was invited (to go) to America.

1. Leonie möchte Englischlehrerin werden.
2. Das Studium dort musste von ihr bezahlt werden.
3. Es ist allerdings teurer geworden, als sie dachte.
4. Das wurde ihr nie erklärt.
5. Was würdest du an ihrer Stelle tun?
6. Ich würde ein Semester arbeiten.
7. Das wird nicht erlaubt werden.
8. Übrigens wird ihr Englisch schon viel besser.
9. Der Amerikaaufenthalt wird ihr später helfen.

> Unser Telefonnetz wird digital. Jetzt wird alles möglich.

III. Special subjunctive

German has another subjunctive, often called the SPECIAL SUBJUNCTIVE or SUBJUNCTIVE I. English only has a few remnants of this subjunctive.

Thanks be to God! Long live Freedom! Be that as it may.

In German, the special subjunctive is used in similar expressions.

Gott sei Dank!
Es lebe die Freiheit!
Wie dem auch sei.

Other than in such phrases, Subjunctive I is rarely heard in conversation. It is primarily used in formal writing and indirect speech, often to summarize another person's findings or opinion. It is most frequently encountered in critical literary or scientific essays, in literature, and in news articles, where it distances the author from his or her report and preserves a sense of objectivity.

In general, the forms of the third person singular are the ones used most often because they clearly differ from those of the indicative. When the forms of the special subjunctive are identical with those of the indicative, the general subjunctive is used. At this point, you need only to be able to recognize the forms of the special subjunctive and know why they are used.

1. PRESENT-TIME forms

    The PRESENT-TIME forms of the special subjunctive have the same endings as the general subjunctive and are added to the stem of the infinitive:

glauben	
ich glaube	wir glauben
du glaubest	ihr glaubet
er glaube	sie glauben

Verbs that have a vowel change in the second and third person singular of the indicative don't have that vowel change in the special subjunctive. Note that the first and third person singular forms of **sein** are irregular in that they do not have an **-e** ending.

Infinitive	Special Subj. er/es/sie	Indicative er/es/sie
haben	**habe**	hat
sein	**sei**	ist
tun	**tue**	tut
denken	**denke**	denkt
fahren	**fahre**	fährt
sehen	**sehe**	sieht
werden	**werde**	wird
wissen	**wisse**	weiß
dürfen	**dürfe**	darf
können	**könne**	kann
mögen	**möge**	mag
müssen	**müsse**	muss
wollen	**wolle**	will

ich habe	wir haben
du habest	ihr habet
er habe	sie haben

ich müsse	wir müssen
du müssest	ihr müsset
er müsse	sie müssen

ich sei	wir seien
du seiest	ihr seiet
er sei	sie seien

Er sagte, er **habe** keine Zeit. *He said he had no time.*
Er sagte, sie **sei** nicht zu Hause. *He said she wasn't home.*

„Möge diese Welt mit Gottes Hilfe eine Wiedergeburt der Freiheit erleben."
(Text der Freiheitsglocke in Berlins Schöneberger Rathaus, ein Geschenk der Amerikaner nach der Berliner Blockade)

2. To refer to the FUTURE *(to later)*, combine the special subjunctive of **werden** with an infinitive.

$$\boxed{\textbf{werde} \ldots \; + \text{infinitive}}$$

    Er sagte, er **werde** bald fertig **sein**.   *He said he'd be finished soon.*

3. To form the PAST-TIME special subjunctive, use the special subjunctive of **haben** or **sein** with a past participle.

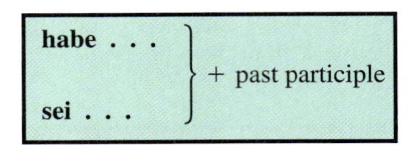

$$\boxed{\left.\begin{array}{l}\textbf{habe} \ldots \\ \textbf{sei} \ldots\end{array}\right\} + \text{past participle}}$$

    Er sagt, er **habe** keine Zeit **gehabt**.   *He says he didn't have time.*
    Er sagte, **sie sei** nicht zu Hause **gewesen**.   *He said she hadn't been home.*

Übungen

J. Finden Sie den Konjunktiv und unterstreichen *(underline)* **Sie ihn!**

1. **Dresdens Frauenkirche**

   Der Reporter erklärte, die Stadt Dresden und ihre Frauenkirche seien 1945 durch Bomben zerstört worden. Einer Bürgerinitiative sei es zu verdanken, dass die Ruine der Kirche nicht einfach weggeräumt *(removed)* worden sei, wie ein Großteil der Stadt. Seit 1993 arbeite man an ihrem Wiederaufbau. Das werde rund 250 Millionen Mark kosten; wobei die eine Hälfte des Geldes aus Politik und Wirtschaft komme und die andere Hälfte der Kosten durch private Gelder getragen werden solle. Es gebe viele verschiedene Wege, Geld zu sammeln. Dazu gehöre der Verkauf einer Uhr mit Originalsteinstücken der Kirche. Man könne auch einen Stein der Kirche adoptieren. Alles, was aus dem großen Trümmerhaufen *(pile of rubble)* wieder verwendet werden könne, werde verwendet. Das bedeute, dass die Steine gesammelt, sortiert und ausgewertet *(evaluated)* werden müssen. Das aber gehe nicht ohne Computer. Wenn alles nach Plan verlaufe, dann werde die Frauenkirche im Jahr 2006 wieder auf dem Platz stehen, wo sie seit 1726 gestanden hat.

2. **Städte deutscher Kultur**

   Mein Onkel schrieb, dass Weimar, Leipzig, Halle, Wittenberg und Eisenach wichtige deutsche Kulturstädte seien. In Weimar sei Goethe Theaterdirektor und Staatsminister gewesen und dort habe Schiller seine wichtigsten Dramen geschrieben. In Leipzig habe Bach 27 Jahre lang Kantaten und Oratorien für den Thomanerchor komponiert. Dieser Knabenchor *(boys choir)* sei heute noch sehr berühmt. Nicht weit von Leipzig liege Halle, wo Händel geboren worden sei. In Wittenberg, das man heute die Lutherstadt nenne, habe Luther mit seinen 95 Thesen die Reformation begonnen. Sein Zimmer auf der Wartburg bei Eisenach, wo er die Bibel ins Deutsche übersetzt hat, sei heute noch zu besichtigen. Man könne auch heute noch sehen, wo er dem Teufel ein Tintenfass nachgeworfen habe *(had thrown an inkwell at the devil)*. Er wisse allerdings nicht, woher diese Geschichte komme. Er glaube sie nicht.

Die Wartburg bei Eisenach

Zusammenfassung

K. Wo ist mein Pass? Auf Deutsch bitte!

1. Yesterday was a bad day. 2. First I lost my passport. 3. Then my handbag and my money were stolen (**gestohlen**). 4. I tried to pay with traveler's checks. 5. But without my passport, my checks weren't accepted. 6. It was good that Anne was there. 7. The bill was paid by Anne. 8. This morning I was called by the police (**die Polizei**). 9. They had found my handbag. 10. But my passport hasn't been found yet. 11. I wish I knew what I did with it. 12. I hope it will be found soon.

Im Leipziger Hauptbahnhof

EINBLICKE

In Search of an Identity

The unification of Germany and the progressive rise of an ever more integrated Europe have been contributing toward a new assessment of what it means to be German. This search for a national identity goes back to a time well before Bismarck united the country in 1871. For centuries, Germany had been divided into numerous small, autocratically ruled principalities. This fragmentation contributed to the significant diversity among various parts of Germany, yet also inhibited the development of a broadly based democratic consciousness. While most Germans continue to reject nationalism and embrace the idea of a united Europe enthusiastically, a new pride in their own localities is noticeable at the same time. A new interest in local dialects, history, and the restoration and rebuilding of destroyed historical sites is symptomatic of this trend.

Dresdens Frauenkirche, ein Neubeginn

WORTSCHATZ 2

der (Geld)schein, -e	*banknote*
Staat, -en	*state*
das Jahrtausend, -e	*millennium*
die Bevölkerung	*population*
Münze, -n	*coin*
einzeln	*individual(ly)*
endlich	*finally*
gefährlich	*dangerous*
stolz (auf + *acc.*)	*proud (of)*
typisch	*typical(ly)*
vereint	*united*
verbinden, verband, verbunden	*to connect, tie together, link*
wachsen (wächst), wuchs, ist gewachsen	*to grow*

Vorm Lesen

A. Fragen über das eigene Land
1. Wie lange ist dieses Land schon ein Bundesstaat?
2. Wird Ihre Ausbildung im ganzen Land anerkannt *(recognized)* oder müssen Prüfungen wiederholt werden? Können Sie überall arbeiten?
3. Was finden Sie typisch für Ihr Land (Amerika, Kanada usw.)?
4. Gibt es etwas, was typisch ist für die Bewohner *(residents)* mancher Staaten? Gibt es Spitznamen für sie?
5. Gibt es regionale Dialekte? Wenn ja, wo?
6. Glauben Sie, dass Amerikaner (Kanadier usw.) einen besonders hohen Lebensstandard haben? Wieso (nicht)?

B. Was ist das?

die Europäisierung, Identität, Kooperation, Luftverschmutzung, Schwierigkeit, Souveränität; aufwachsen, zusammenwachsen, formulieren; arrogant, europaweit, kritisch, offiziell, regional, weltoffen; im Prinzip, teilweise, zu Beginn

Der Wind kennt keine Grenzen

Zu Beginn des neuen Jahrtausends verbindet Europa eine neue, gemeinsame Währung°: der Euro. Ab 2002 werden Touristen, die nach Deutschland kommen, dann nicht mehr mit der Deutschen Mark sondern mit Euroscheinen und Euromünzen zahlen. Europa soll enger zusammenwachsen. Jeder Europäer soll zum Beispiel in jedem europäischen Land arbeiten dürfen; und auch seine Ausbildung soll europaweit anerkannt° werden. Das heißt aber nicht, dass Europa ein einziger Bundesstaat wird, sondern es soll ein loser Staatenbund° sein, in dem die einzelnen Staaten ihre Souveränität, ihre eigene Sprache und Kultur behalten wollen. Auf eine europäische Hauptsprache hat man sich nicht einigen° können.

    Natürlich fühlen sich die Deutschen als Europäer, aber sie wollen auch Deutsche bleiben. Vor allem aber muss Deutschland selbst erst einmal° zusammenwachsen, denn es war ja bis 1990 offiziell ein geteiltes Land. Als die Mauer dann endlich fiel, existierte sie weiter in den Köpfen: Plötzlich gab es „Ossis" und „Wessis"°. Viele Westdeutsche meinten, dass die „Ossis" unselbstständige und ehrgeizlose arme Teufel° seien. Auf der anderen Seite meinten viele Ostdeutsche, dass die „Wessis" arrogant seien und dächten, ihnen gehöre die Welt. Sie würden immer alles besser wissen—daher° der Spitzname „Besserwessis".

    Was verbindet nun eigentlich alle Deutschen? Natürlich die Sprache, Kultur und Geschichte, aber im Prinzip gibt es eigentlich wenig, was typisch für alle Deutschen wäre. Vielleicht sind es die kleineren Dinge im Leben. So könnte man zum Beispiel sagen, dass die meisten gesellig° sind und gern in Straßencafés oder Gartenrestaurants sitzen, dass sie Fußball lieben und sich in Vereinen organisieren. Die Familie und die Freizeit bedeutet ihnen oft mehr als der Staat. Sicherlich sind sie ein reiselustiges° Volk, aber sie lieben auch ihre Heimat: die Landschaft, in der sie aufgewachsen sind, die Stadt oder das Dorf. Viele sind wieder stolz auf ihre Herkunft°; regionale Dialekte werden wieder mehr gesprochen und auch im Radio und im Theater gepflegt°. Das mag teilweise historische Gründe° haben, denn die Bevölkerung bestand schon immer aus° verschiedenen Volksstämmen° und sie waren nur kurze Zeit EIN Staat, nämlich von Bismarcks Reichsgründung° 1871 bis zum Ende des 2. Weltkrieges 1945. Mit der zunehmenden° Europäisierung möchten viele gerade heute ihre regionale Identität nicht verlieren.

    Wenn es schon schwer zu sagen ist, wie die Deutschen sind, so kann man doch sehen, dass sie europäischer geworden sind, das heißt, weltoffener und informierter. Auch sind sie heute kritischer und nicht mehr so autoritätsgläubig° wie zu Beginn des 20. Jahrhunderts. Das sogenannte typisch Deutsche ist nicht mehr so wichtig; das Ausländische ist interessanter geworden. Es werden Jeans statt Lederhosen° getragen. Ihre Musik ist international. Man isst besonders gern italienisch, und französischer Wein wird genauso gern getrunken wie

416 KAPITEL 15

gets involved / struggle for deutsches Bier. Ja, und man engagiert sich° wieder. Der Kampf um° Umweltschutz und um eine bessere Lebensqualität ist auch sehr wichtig geworden und man weiß, wie wichtig die Kooperation der Nachbarländer dabei ist. Natürlich wollen die Deutschen ihren hohen Lebensstandard erhalten, aber sie glauben, das dürfte auch mit weniger Energieverbrauch° und weniger Chemie möglich sein. Mülltrennung wird zum Beispiel in weiten Kreisen der Bevölkerung sehr ernst genommen°. Auch wissen sie, dass zum Beispiel die Luftverschmutzung nur europaweit bewältigt° werden kann, denn der Wind kennt keine Grenzen.

. . . consumption

taken seriously

overcome

Zum Erkennen: der Identitätsschwund *(loss of identity)*

Zum Text

A. Was passt?
1. Die Ausbildung der verschiedenen europäischen Staaten soll in Zukunft in ganz _____ anerkannt werden.
    a. Amerika   b. Deutschland   c. Europa
2. Damit können die Deutschen _____ überall in Europa studieren oder arbeiten.
    a. fast   b. kaum   c. vielleicht
3. Als die Mauer 1989 fiel, existierte sie weiter in manchen _____.
    a. Bächen   b. Gesichtern   c. Köpfen
4. Manche Westdeutschen dachten, dass „Ossis" _____ seien.
    a. unselbstständig   b. arrogant   c. gefährlich
5. Manche Ostdeutschen dachten, dass „Wessis" _____.
    a. arme Teufel seien   b. alle arm wären   c. immer alles besser wüssten
6. Vielleicht kann man allgemein *(in general)* von den Deutschen sagen, dass sie _____.
    a. keine Fragen stellen   b. reiselustig sind   c. alle Dialekt sprechen
7. Sie lieben ihre _____.
    a. Heimat   b. Spitznamen   c. Ausländer
8. Die Deutschen sollen _____ geworden sein.
    a. autoritätsgläubiger   b. weltfremder   c. weltoffener
9. Auch sind sie umweltbewusster geworden und nehmen _____ ernst.
    a. alle Schwierigkeiten   b. alles Ausländische   c. den Umweltschutz
10. Sie wissen, dass zum Beispiel die Luftverschmutzung nur _____ mit den Nachbarn bewältigt werden kann.
    a. allein   b. einzeln   c. gemeinsam

B. **Noch einmal in indirekter Rede!** Wiederholen Sie den Lesetext (Paragraphen 3–4) in indirekter Rede. Benutzen Sie den Konjunktiv I!

BEISPIEL: Der Autor fragte sich, was alle Deutschen **verbinde**. Natürlich die Sprache, Kultur und Geschichte, aber im Prinzip **gebe** es eigentlich wenig, was typisch für alle Deutschen **sei**.

C. **Typisch Deutsch!** Machen Sie eine Liste mit all den Eigenschaften, die der Autor im Text über die Deutschen erwähnt *(mentions)*! Wie vergleichen sich diese mit dem Bild, das Sie von den Deutschen haben?

D. **Meinungsumfrage unter Deutschen.** Was erfahren Sie *(learn)* durch die Meinungsumfrage unter deutschen Jugendlichen im Alter von 18–25 Jahren? Wie hätten Sie darauf reagiert? Machen Sie eine Meinungsumfrage in Ihrer Klasse!

Wovor haben Sie am meisten Angst?	
Umweltkatastrophen	28%
Arbeitslosigkeit	25%
Einsamkeit *(loneliness)*	21%
Kriminalität	15%
Scheidung *(divorce)* der Eltern	5%
Prüfungen	3%
Ausländer	2%

Beim Wort „Europa" denke ich an . . .	
Kultur	29%
Zukunft	28%
Frieden	26%
Bürokratie	23%
Zahlmeister *(paymaster)* Deutschland	22%
Heimat	16%
Nichts Besonderes	16%

Ich fühle mich vor allem als . . .	
Deutscher	31%
Kölner, Leipziger, Münchner . . .	16%
Europäer	14%
Weltbürger	13%
Hesse, Sachse, Thüringer . . .	10%
Ostdeutscher oder Westdeutscher	6%

The German Spelling Reform

As you are completing your first year of German, you should be aware of the German spelling reform that was adopted in 1998. The spelling that you were introduced to in *Wie geht's?* follows the new guidelines, but older texts, especially literary ones, might not. So don't be concerned when words are occasionally spelled differently than you have learned.

The most visible change was the partial abolition of the ß, which the Swiss dropped long ago. Under the new rules, the ß is now used only after a long vowel, e.g., **heiß, Größe**; after a short vowel it is replaced with an *ss*, e.g., **daß > dass** and **er/sie ißt > isst**. The guidelines also allow now the triplication of consonants (if followed by a vowel) in compound nouns, e.g., **Schiffahrt > Schifffahrt; Balletheater > Balletttheater.** Many of the changes dealt with imported words. For instance, the diphthong *ai* in foreign words became *eingedeutscht* with an umlauted *ä* (e.g., **Affaire > Affäre**); *ph* and *ch* can be replaced with *f* and *sch* (e.g., **Asphalt > Asfalt; Sketch > Sketsch**). Also affected were the capitalization of certain phrases (e.g., **auf deutsch > auf Deutsch; gestern abend > gestern Abend**), certain word combinations (e.g., **wieviel > wie viel; kennenlernen > kennen lernen; radfahren > Rad fahren**), some hyphenation (e.g., **bak-ken > ba-cken; mei-stens > meis-tens**), and punctuation (usually no more COMMA before the conjunctions **und** or **oder**). Since German is a living language and still evolving, do not be surprised by certain variations.

E. Hoppla, hier fehlt 'was! Hallo, Herr Nachbar! *(Look at the following collage of national characteristics; a second set is in the Appendix. Work with a partner to find out the traits of all twelve nationalities. You don't need to write the entire description; just jot down a phrase or two.)*

Versorgte Belgier
Belgien ist mit Medikamenten super versorgt, hat die meisten Apotheken je Einwohner.

Patente Deutsche
Die Deutschen sind in Europa die größten Erfinder – sie melden jährlich über 260 000 Patente an.

Gesunde Griechen
Die Griechen essen die meisten Vitamine. Je Einwohner und Jahr 195 Kilo Gemüse und 76 Kilo Obst.

Gesellige Dänen
Die Dänen sind die geselligsten Europäer. 83 Prozent der Bevölkerung sind Mitglieder in Vereinen.

Lebensfrohe Franzosen
In Frankreich leben die Europäer am längsten. Besonders Frauen. Sie werden im Schnitt älter als 80.

Belesene Briten
Die Briten sind zeitungsgierig. Auf jeden kommen 3 Zeitungen – Europa-Rekord im Zeitungslesen.

S1:

BEISPIEL: S1 Wie sind die Iren?
S2 Die Iren lieben den Sport. Jeder zweite . . . Und wie sind die Belgier?
S1 Sie haben . . .

Die Iren: <u>sehr sportlich</u> . . . Die Italiener: . . .
Die Luxemburger: . . . Die Holländer: . . .
Die Portugiesen: . . . Die Spanier: . . .

F. Schreiben Sie: Was wäre, wenn . . . ? Stellen Sie sich vor, Sie hätten in ein anderes Land geheiratet. Was würde Ihnen als typisch amerikanisch (kanadisch usw.) dort fehlen? Oder meinen Sie, dass Sie überall gleich *(equally)* zu Hause sein könnten? (8–10 Sätze)

HÖREN SIE ZU!

Europa-Schulen

Zum Erkennen: erziehen *(to educate, raise)*; die Klassenkameradin *(classmate)*; das Lehrbuch, ¨er *(textbook)*; chauvinistisch; die Flotte *(fleet)*; sich konzentrieren auf *(to concentrate on)*; der Rektor, -en *(vice chancellor)*

Was stimmt?
1. Europa-Schulen gibt es in _____.
   a. jedem Land der EU
   b. mehreren europäischen Ländern
   c. auf der ganzen Welt
2. Die Schüler lernen _____.
   a. keine Fächer in ihrer Muttersprache
   b. manche Fächer in ihrer Muttersprache
   c. nicht mehr als drei Sprachen
3. Sie lernen Geschichte _____.
   a. immer in ihrer Muttersprache
   b. aus internationalen Lehrbüchern
   c. nie in ihrer Muttersprache

4. In französischen Lehrbüchern liest man _____.
   a. nicht viel über solche Länder wie Belgien oder Luxemburg
   b. interessante Information über englische Kultur
   c. wie Nelson die spanische Flotte bei Trafalgar zerstört hat
5. Die Schüler lernen im Geschichtsunterricht, _____
   a. chauvinistischer zu werden
   b. die Geschichte ihres eigenen Landes objektiver zu sehen
   c. gutes Deutsch

Goethe and Schiller — FOKUS

- Johann Wolfgang von Goethe (1749–1832) was one of Germany's greatest poets, novelists, and playwrights. He was also a leading thinker and scientist. His works include *Faust, Wilhelm Meister,* and *Die Leiden des jungen Werther,* a sensationally successful novel about a sensitive young man alienated from the world around him, which Napoleon is said to have read seven times. Because of his vast scope of knowledge and his comprehensive interest in the world of human experience, Goethe is often referred to as "the last universal man."
- Friedrich von Schiller (1759–1805) ranks second only to Goethe among the leading figures of classical German literature. His dramas, often pleas for human freedom and dignity, inspired liberals in their fight for liberty during the early 1800s and during the Revolution of 1848. His works include *Don Carlos, Die Jungfrau von Orleans, Maria Stuart,* and *Wilhelm Tell.* The last stanza of his well-known poem "Ode an die Freude," set to music by Beethoven, has been selected as anthem for a unified Europe—to be played instrumentally rather than sung at special occasions, thus avoiding the use of any particular language.

Erinnerung

Willst du immer weiter schweifen°? — continue wandering
Sieh, das Gute liegt so nah.
Lerne nur das Glück ergreifen°, — grab
Denn das Glück ist immer da.

Johann Wolfgang von Goethe

Ode „An die Freude"

Freude, schöner Götterfunken°, — bright spark of divinity
Tochter aus Elysium,
Wir betreten feuertrunken°, — fire-inspired we tread
Himmlische°, dein Heiligtum°! — Heavenly one / sanctuary
Deine Zauber° binden wieder°, — magic power / reunites
was die Mode° streng geteilt; — custom
Alle Menschen werden Brüder,
wo dein sanfter Flügel weilt°. — under the sway of thy gentle wing(s)

Friedrich von Schiller

WEB-ECKE For updates and web activities, visit the *Wie geht's?* home page at http://www.hrwcollege.com/german/sevin/! You'll learn more about the EU and the euro, visit Weimar and other cities in the new *Länder,* and become acquainted with environmental concerns of people in the German-speaking countries.

SPRECHSITUATIONEN

Describing objects

When you are abroad, you may have to describe something you need or want to buy for which you don't know the appropriate German word. Here are some useful descriptive adjectives or phrases.

Wie ist es?

so groß wie
größer als
dick / dünn
groß / klein
kurz / lang
leicht / schwer
hell(blau) / dunkel(blau)

breit / eng *(wide / narrow)*
bunt / einfarbig *(colorful / all one color)*
gepunktet / gestreift / kariert *(dotted / striped / plaid)*
hoch / niedrig *(high / low)*
rund / viereckig *(round / square)*
süß / sauer / salzig *(sweet / sour / salty)*
weich / hart *(soft / hard)*

Woraus ist es?

das Glas	*glass*	die Baumwolle	*cotton*
Holz	*wood*	Pappe	*cardboard*
Leder	*leather*	Synthetik	*synthetics*
Metall	*metal*	Wolle	*wool*
Papier	*paper*		
Plastik	*plastic*		
Porzellan	*porcelain*		

Was macht man damit? — Man schreibt damit.
Wozu benutzt man es? — Man benutzt es, um besser zu sehen.

Often a sentence with a relative pronoun will be helpful in describing people or things.

Kennst du die Leute, die in dem neuen Gebäude an der Ecke wohnen?
Ist das nicht das Gebäude, in dem Alfred arbeitet?

Übungen

A. Woran denke ich? *(Work in small groups. One person thinks of an object, the others have twenty questions to figure out what it is. The German word for the object should be one that has been used in the course.)*

B. Beschreiben Sie! *(Working with a partner, describe at least two of the following.)*
 1. an item of clothing you can't part with
 2. a favorite dish or snack
 3. a painting or other piece of art you really like
 4. a building (church, public building, museum, residence) you think is particularly interesting

C. Wie bitte? *(Pretend you are in a store and need to purchase something, but you don't know the German word for it. Describe it as best as you can, using gestures if necessary.[1])*

1. towel
2. soap
3. deodorant stick
4. shampoo
5. suntan lotion
6. scissors
7. bandaids
8. needle
9. hair dryer
10. iron
11. umbrella
12. clothes hanger
13. checkered shirt
14. round tablecloth

D. Kurzgespräch

You have lost your new book bag (billfold, key chain, designer sunglasses, etc.) and have gone to the university's lost-and-found office **(das Fundbüro).** Describe the items as best you can. The person on duty writes down the information and asks you for additional details (color, material, contents, value, special features, etc.)

---

[1] 1. ein Handtuch 2. Seife 3. einen Deo-Stift 4. Shampoo 5. Sonnencreme 6. eine Schere 7. Pflaster 8. eine Nadel 9. einen Fön 10. ein Bügeleisen 11. einen Regenschirm 12. einen Kleiderbügel 13. ein kariertes Hemd 14. eine runde Tischdecke

Rückblick: KAPITEL 12–15

pp. 327–29 **I. Comparison**

1. The comparative is formed by adding **-er** to an adjective, the superlative by adding **-(e)st.** Many one-syllable adjectives and adverbs with the stem vowel **a, o,** or **u** have an umlaut.

POSITIVE	COMPARATIVE	SUPERLATIVE
schnell	schneller	schnellst-
lang	länger	längst-
kurz	kürzer	kürzest-

   A few adjectives and adverbs have irregular forms in the comparative and superlative.

POSITIVE	COMPARATIVE	SUPERLATIVE
gern	lieber	liebst-
groß	größer	größt-
gut	besser	best-
hoch	höher	höchst-
nah	näher	nächst-
viel	mehr	meist-

2. The comparative of predicate adjectives and of adverbs ends in **-er;** the superlative is preceded by **am** and ends in **-sten.**

   > Ich esse schnell.
   > Du isst schneller.
   > Er isst am schnellsten.

3. In the comparative and superlative, adjectives preceding nouns have the same endings under the same conditions as adjectives in the positive form.

der gut**e** Wein	der besser**e** Wein	der best**e** Wein
Ihr gut**er** Wein	Ihr besser**er** Wein	Ihr best**er** Wein
gut**er** Wein	besser**er** Wein	best**er** Wein

4. Here are four important phrases used in comparisons:

Gestern war es nicht **so heiß wie** heute.	. . . as hot as . . .
Heute ist es **heißer als** gestern.	. . . hotter than . . .
Es wird **immer heißer.**	. . . hotter and hotter.
Je länger du wartest, **desto heißer** wird es.	The longer, the hotter . . .
Je heißer, desto besser.	The hotter, the better.

422

II. Relative clauses

1. Relative clauses are introduced by relative pronouns.

	masc.	neut.	fem.	plural
nom.	der	das	die	die
acc.	den	das	die	die
dat.	dem	dem	der	denen
gen.	dessen	dessen	deren	deren

The form of the relative pronoun depends ON THE NUMBER AND GENDER OF THE ANTECEDENT and on the FUNCTION of the relative pronoun WITHIN THE RELATIVE CLAUSE.

```
. . . ANTECEDENT, (preposition) RP _____ V1, . . .
      gender? number?            function?
```

2. The word order in the relative clause is like that of all subordinate clauses: the inflected part of the verb (V1) comes last.

```
. . . , RP _____ V1, . . .
```

Der junge Mann, **der** gerade hier **wa**r, studiert Theologie.

Die Universität, **an der** er **studiert**, ist schon sehr alt.

III. Future tense

1. The future consists of a present tense form of **werden** plus an infinitive.

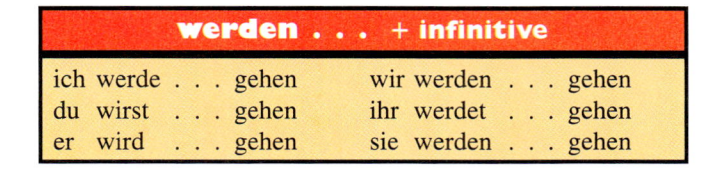

werden . . . + infinitive	
ich werde . . . gehen	wir werden . . . gehen
du wirst . . . gehen	ihr werdet . . . gehen
er wird . . . gehen	sie werden . . . gehen

Er **wird** es dir **erklären.**

2. The future of a sentence with a modal follows this pattern:

```
werden . . . + verb infinitive + modal infinitive
```

Er **wird** es dir **erklären können.**

IV. Subjunctive

English and German follow very similar patterns in the subjunctive:

If he came . . .   Wenn er käme, . . .

If he had come . . .   Wenn er gekommen wäre, . . .

Rückblick: Kapitel 12–15

German, however, has two subjunctives, the GENERAL SUBJUNCTIVE (SUBJUNCTIVE II) and the SPECIAL SUBJUNCTIVE (SUBJUNCTIVE I); the latter is primarily used in writing. The endings of both subjunctives are the same.

pp. 353–56, 359–60

ich	-e	wir	-en
du	-est	ihr	-et
er	-e	sie	-en

1. Forms

   a. GENERAL SUBJUNCTIVE (II)

present time or future time		past time
Based on the forms of the simple past; refers to *now/later*	Based on the forms of **werden** + infinitive; refers to *now/later*	Based on the forms of the past perfect; refers to *earlier*
er **lernte**	er **würde lernen**	er **hätte gelernt**
brächte	würde bringen	hätte gebracht
hätte	(würde haben)	hätte gehabt
wäre	(würde sein)	wäre gewesen
nähme	würde nehmen	hätte genommen
käme	würde kommen	wäre gekommen

- In conversation, the **würde**-form is commonly used when referring to <u>present time</u>. However, avoid using the **würde**-form with **haben, sein, wissen,** and the modals.

   Er **würde** es dir **erklären.**

   Du **wärest** stolz darauf.

- Modals in the past-time subjunctive follow this pattern:

   hätte . . . + verb infinitive + modal infinitive

   Er **hätte** es dir **erklären können.**

pp. 410–12

   b. SPECIAL SUBJUNCTIVE (I)

present time	future time	past time
Based on the forms of the infinitive; refers to *now/later*	Based on the forms of the future; refers to *later*	Based on the forms of the present perfect; refers to *earlier*
er **lerne**	er **werde lernen**	er **habe gelernt**
bringe	werde bringen	habe gebracht
habe	werde haben	habe gehabt
sei	werde sein	sei gewesen
nehme	werde nehmen	habe genommen
komme	werde kommen	sei gekommen

Rückblick: Kapitel 12–15

2. Use
   a. The GENERAL SUBJUNCTIVE is quite common in everyday speech and is used in:
   - Polite requests or questions

     Könnten Sie mir sagen, wo die Uni ist?   *Could you tell me where the university is?*

   - Hypothetical statements or questions

     | Er sollte bald hier sein. | *He should be here soon.* |
     | Was würdest du tun? | *What would you do?* |
     | Was hättest du getan? | *What would you have done?* |

   - Wishes

     | Wenn ich das nur wüsste! | *If only I knew that!* |
     | Wenn ich das nur gewusst hätte! | *If only I had known that!* |
     | Ich wünschte, ich hätte das gewusst! | *I wish I had known that!* |

   - Unreal conditions

     | Wenn wir Geld hätten, würden wir fliegen. | *If we had the money, we'd fly.* |
     | Wenn wir Geld gehabt hätten, wären wir geflogen. | *If we had had the money, we would have flown.* |

   - Indirect speech (see Section V)

   b. The SPECIAL SUBJUNCTIVE is used primarily for indirect speech in news reports and in formal writing, unless the form of the indicative is the same as the subjunctive, in which case the general subjunctive is used.

   ich komme = ich **komme** → ich **käme**
   ich frage = ich **frage** → ich **würde fragen**

V. Indirect speech

pp. 384–85

The tense of the indirect statement is determined by the tense of the direct statement.

direct statement	indirect statement
present tense	→ present-time subjunctive or **würde**-form
future tense	→ **würde**-form or **werde**-form
simple past present perfect past perfect	→ past-time subjunctive

„Ich komme nicht."   Sie sagte, sie käme (komme) nicht.
                              Sie sagte, sie würde nicht kommen.

„Ich werde nicht kommen."   Sie sagte, sie würde (werde) nicht kommen.

„Ich hatte keine Lust."   Sie sagte, sie hätte (habe) keine Lust gehabt.
„Ich bin nicht gegangen."   Sie sagte, sie wäre (sei) nicht gegangen.
„Ich hatte nichts davon gewusst."   Sie sagte, sie hätte (habe) nichts davon gewusst.

Rückblick: Kapitel 12–15

This is also true of questions. Remember to use **ob** when the question begins with the verb.

„Kommt sie mit?" Er fragte, ob sie mitkäme (mitkomme).
  Er fragte, ob sie mitkommen würde.

„Wird sie mitkommen?" Er fragte, ob sie mitkommen würde (werde).

„Wo war sie?" Er fragte, wo sie gewesen wäre (sei).

„Warum hat sie mir nichts davon gesagt?" Er fragte, warum sie ihm nichts davon gesagt hätte (habe).

Indirect requests require the use of sollen.

„Frag nicht so viel!" Er sagte, sie sollte (solle) nicht so viel fragen.

VI. Passive voice

pp. 405–07

In the active voice the subject of the sentence is doing something. In the passive voice the subject is not doing anything; rather, something is being done to it.

1. Forms

werden . . . + past participle	
ich werde . . . gefragt	wir werden . . . gefragt
du wirst . . . gefragt	ihr werdet . . . gefragt
er wird . . . gefragt	sie werden . . . gefragt

2. The tenses in the passive are formed with the various tenses of **werden** + past participle.

er **wird** . . . gefragt	er **ist** . . . gefragt **worden**
er **wurde** . . . gefragt	er **war** . . . gefragt **worden**
er **wird** . . . gefragt **werden**	

Das ist uns nicht erklärt worden.

3. Modals follow this pattern:

modal . . . + past participle + infinitive of **werden**

Das muss noch einmal erklärt werden.

4. In German the passive is often used without a subject or with **es** functioning as the subject.

Hier wird viel renoviert.
Es wird hier viel renoviert.

5. Instead of using the passive voice, the same idea may be expressed in the active voice with the subject **man.**

Man hat alles noch einmal erklärt.

VII. Review of the uses of *werden*

1. FULL VERB: Er **wird** Arzt.   *He's going to be a doctor.*
2. FUTURE: Ich **werde** danach **fragen.**   *I'll ask about it.*
3. SUBJUNCTIVE: Ich **würde** danach **fragen.**   *I'd ask about it.*
4. PASSIVE: Er **wird** danach **gefragt.**   *He's (being) asked about it.*

REMEMBER: Review exercises for vocabulary and structures can be found in the Workbook.

Rückblick:
Kapitel 12–15

p. 410

Ohne Fleiß kein Preis
No pain, no gain.

APPENDIX

1. Predicting the gender of certain nouns

As a rule, nouns must be learned with their articles, because their genders are not readily predictable. However, here are a few hints to help you determine the gender of some nouns in order to eliminate unnecessary memorizing.

a. Most nouns referring to males are MASCULINE.

   der Vater, der Bruder, der Junge

   - Days, months, and seasons are masculine.

     der Montag, der Juni, der Winter

b. Most nouns referring to females are FEMININE; BUT **das Mädchen, das Fräulein** (see c. below).

   die Mutter, die Schwester, die Frau

   - Many feminine nouns can be derived from masculine nouns. Their plurals always end in **-nen.**

     sg.: der Schweizer / die Schweizerin; der Österreicher / die Österreicherin

     pl.: die Schweizerinnen, Österreicherinnen

   - All nouns ending in **-heit, -keit, -ie, -ik, -ion, -schaft, -tät,** and **-ung** are feminine. Their plurals end in **-en.**

     sg.: die Schönheit, Richtigkeit, Geographie, Musik, Religion, Nachbarschaft, Qualität, Rechnung

     pl.: die Qualitäten, Rechnungen usw.

   - Most nouns ending in **-e** are feminine. Their plurals end in **-n.**

     sg.: die Sprache, Woche, Hose, Kreide, Farbe, Seite

     pl.: die Sprachen, Wochen usw.

c. All nouns ending in **-chen** or **-lein** are NEUTER. These two suffixes make diminutives of nouns, i.e., they denote them as being small. In the case of people, the diminutive may indicate affection, or also belittling. Such nouns often have an umlaut, but there is no plural ending.

   sg.: der Bruder / das Brüderchen; die Schwester / das Schwesterlein

   pl.: die Brüderchen, Schwesterlein

   - Because of these suffixes, two nouns referring to females are neuter.

     das Mädchen, das Fräulein (seldom used today)

   - Most cities and countries are neuter.

     (das) Berlin, (das) Deutschland BUT die Schweiz, die Türkei

2. Summary chart of the four cases

	use	follows...	masc.	neut.	fem.	pl.
nom.	Subject, Predicate noun wer? was?	heißen, sein, werden	der dieser[1] ein mein[2]	das dieses ein	die diese eine	die diese keine
acc.	Direct object wen? was?	durch, für, gegen, ohne, um	den diesen einen meinen	mein	meine	meine
		an, auf, hinter, in, neben, über, unter, vor, zwischen				
dat.	Indirect object wem?	aus, außer, bei, mit, nach, seit, von, zu	dem diesem einem meinem	dem diesem einem meinem	der dieser einer meiner	den diesen keinen meinen
		antworten, danken, gefallen, gehören, glauben,[3] helfen, zuhören usw.				
gen.	Possessive wessen?	(an)statt, trotz, während, wegen	des dieses eines meines	des dieses eines meines	der dieser keiner meiner	der dieser keiner meiner

NOTE: 1. The **der**-words are **dieser, jeder, welcher, alle, manche, solche**.
  2. The **ein**-words are **kein, mein, dein, sein, ihr, unser, euer, ihr, Ihr**.
  3. Ich glaube **ihm**. BUT Ich glaube **es**.

3. Adjective endings

a. **Preceded adjectives**

	masculine	neuter	feminine	plural
nom.	der neue Krimi	das neue Stück	die neue Oper	die neuen Filme
acc.	den neuen Krimi	das neue Stück	die neue Oper	die neuen Filme
dat.	dem neuen Krimi	dem neuen Stück	der neuen Oper	den neuen Filmen
gen.	des neuen Krimis	des neuen Stückes	der neuen Oper	der neuen Filme

Appendix

	masculine	neuter	feminine	plural
nom.	ein neuer Krimi	ein neues Stück	eine neue Oper	keine neuen Filme
acc.	einen neuen Krimi	ein neues Stück	eine neue Oper	keine neuen Filme
dat.	einem neuen Krimi	einem neuen Stück	einer neuen Oper	keinen neuen Filmen
gen.	eines neuen Krimis	eines neuen Stückes	einer neuen Oper	keiner neuen Filme

Comparing the two tables above, you can see:

- Adjectives preceded by the definite article or any **der**-word have either an **-e** or **-en** ending.
- Adjectives preceded by the indefinite article or any **ein**-word have two different adjective endings WHENEVER **ein** HAS NO ENDING: **-er** for masculine nouns and **-es** for neuter nouns. Otherwise the **-en** ending predominates and is used in the masculine accusative singular, all datives and genitives, and in all plurals.

after **der**-words

	masc.	neut.	fem.	pl.
nom.	-e	-e	-e	
acc.		-e	-e	-en
dat.				-en
gen.				-en

after **ein**-words

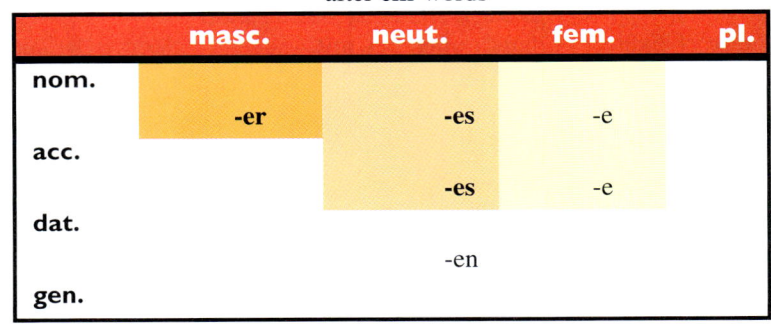

	masc.	neut.	fem.	pl.
nom.	-er	-es	-e	
acc.		-es	-e	-en
dat.				-en
gen.				-en

Or, to put it in another way, the endings are:

- in the NOMINATIVE AND ACCUSATIVE SINGULAR
  – after **der, das, die,** and **eine** → **-e**
  – after **ein**
     with masc. nouns → **-er**
     with neut. nouns → **-es**
- in ALL OTHER CASES → **-en**

b. **Unpreceded adjectives**

Unpreceded adjectives take the endings that the definite article would have, if it were used.

der frische Fisch	das frische Obst	die frische Wurst	die frischen Eier
frischer Fisch	frisches Obst	frische Wurst	frische Eier

	masculine	neuter	feminine	plural
nom.	frischer Fisch	frisches Obst	frische Wurst	frische Eier
acc.	frischen Fisch	frisches Obst	frische Wurst	frische Eier
dat.	frischem Fisch	frischem Obst	frischer Wurst	frischen Eiern
gen.	(frischen Fisches)	(frischen Obstes)	(frischer Wurst)	frischer Eier

Several important words are often used as unpreceded adjectives in the plural: **andere, einige, mehrere, viele, wenige.**

4. Endings of nouns

a. **N-nouns**

	singular	plural
nom.	der Student	die Studenten
acc.	den Student**en**	die Studenten
dat.	dem Student**en**	den Studenten
gen.	des Student**en**	der Studenten

Other n-nouns are: **Herr (-n, -en), Franzose, Gedanke (-ns, -n), Journalist, Junge, Komponist, Mensch, Nachbar, Name (-ns, -n), Polizist, Tourist, Zimmerkollege.**

b. **Adjectival nouns**

	SINGULAR masc.	SINGULAR fem.	PLURAL
nom.	der Deutsche / ein Deutscher	die Deutsche / eine Deutsche	die Deutschen / keine Deutschen
acc.	den Deutschen / einen Deutschen	die Deutsche / eine Deutsche	die Deutschen / keine Deutschen
dat.	dem Deutschen / einem Deutschen	der Deutschen / einer Deutschen	den Deutschen / keinen Deutschen
gen.	des Deutschen / eines Deutschen	der Deutschen / einer Deutschen	der Deutschen / keiner Deutschen

Other adjectival nouns are: **der/die Angestellte, Bekannte, Kranke, Verlobte, der Beamte** (BUT **die Beamtin**).

5. Pronouns

a. **Personal pronouns**

nom.	ich	du	er	es	sie	wir	ihr	sie	Sie
acc.	mich	dich	ihn	es	sie	uns	euch	sie	Sie
dat.	mir	dir	ihm	ihm	ihr	uns	euch	ihnen	Ihnen

b. **Reflexive pronouns**

nom.	ich	du	er/es/sie	wir	ihr	sie	Sie
acc.	mich	dich	sich	uns	euch	sich	sich
dat.	mir	dir	sich	uns	euch	sich	sich

c. **Relative pronouns**

	masc.	neut.	fem.	pl.
nom.	der	das	die	die
acc.	den	das	die	die
dat.	dem	dem	der	denen
gen.	dessen	dessen	deren	deren

6. Comparison of irregular adjectives and adverbs

	gern	groß	gut	hoch	nah	viel
comparative	lieber	größer	besser	höher	näher	mehr
superlative	liebst-	größt-	best-	höchst-	nächst-	meist-

7. N-verbs ("strong verbs") and irregular t-verbs ("weak verbs")

a. **Principal parts listed alphabetically**

This list is limited to the active n-verbs and irregular t-verbs used in this text. Compound verbs like **ankommen** or **abfliegen** are not included, since their principal parts are the same as those of the basic verbs **kommen** and **fliegen.**

infinitive	present	simple past	past participle	meaning
anfangen	fängt an	fing an	angefangen	to begin
backen	bäckt	buk (backte)	gebacken	to bake
beginnen		begann	begonnen	to begin
bekommen		bekam	bekommen	to receive, get
bewerben	bewirbt	bewarb	beworben	to apply
bieten		bot	geboten	to offer
bitten		bat	gebeten	to ask, request
bleiben		blieb	ist geblieben	to remain
bringen		brachte	gebracht	to bring
denken		dachte	gedacht	to think
einladen	lädt ein	lud ein	eingeladen	to invite
empfehlen	empfiehlt	empfahl	empfohlen	to recommend
entscheiden		entschied	entschieden	to decide
essen	isst	aß	gegessen	to eat
fahren	fährt	fuhr	ist gefahren	to drive, go
fallen	fällt	fiel	gefallen	to fall
finden		fand	gefunden	to find
fliegen		flog	ist geflogen	to fly
geben	gibt	gab	gegeben	to give
gefallen	gefällt	gefiel	gefallen	to please
gehen		ging	ist gegangen	to go
geschehen	geschieht	geschah	ist geschehen	to happen

infinitive	present	simple past	past participle	meaning
haben	hat	hatte	gehabt	to have
halten	hält	hielt	gehalten	to hold; stop
hängen		hing	gehangen	to be hanging
heißen		hieß	geheißen	to be called/named
helfen	hilft	half	geholfen	to help
kennen		kannte	gekannt	to know
klingen		klang	geklungen	to sound
kommen		kam	ist gekommen	to come
lassen	lässt	ließ	gelassen	to let; leave (behind)
laufen	läuft	lief	ist gelaufen	to run; walk
lesen	liest	las	gelesen	to read
liegen		lag	gelegen	to lie
nehmen	nimmt	nahm	genommen	to take
nennen		nannte	genannt	to name, call
rufen		rief	gerufen	to call
scheinen		schien	geschienen	to shine; seem
schlafen	schläft	schlief	geschlafen	to sleep
schreiben		schrieb	geschrieben	to write
schwimmen		schwamm	ist geschwommen	to swim
sehen	sieht	sah	gesehen	to see
sein	ist	war	ist gewesen	to be
singen		sang	gesungen	to sing
sitzen		saß	gesessen	to sit
spinnen		spann	gesponnen	to spin
sprechen	spricht	sprach	gesprochen	to speak
springen		sprang	ist gesprungen	to jump
stehen		stand	gestanden	to stand
steigen		stieg	ist gestiegen	to climb
tragen	trägt	trug	getragen	to carry; wear
treiben		trieb	getrieben	to engage in (sports)
trinken		trank	getrunken	to drink
tun	tut	tat	getan	to do
verlieren		verlor	verloren	to lose
wachsen	wächst	wuchs	ist gewachsen	to grow
waschen	wäscht	wusch	gewaschen	to wash
werden	wird	wurde	ist geworden	to become; get
wissen	weiß	wusste	gewusst	to know
ziehen		zog	(ist) gezogen	to pull; (move)

b. **Principal parts listed by stem-changing groups**

This is the same list as the previous one, but this time it is divided into groups with the same stem changes.

I.	essen	(isst)	aß	gegessen
	geben	(gibt)	gab	gegeben
	geschehen	(geschieht)	geschah	ist geschehen
	sehen	(sieht)	sah	gesehen
	lesen	(liest)	las	gelesen
	bitten		bat	gebeten
	liegen		lag	gelegen
	sitzen		saß	gesessen
II.	bewerben	(bewirbt)	bewarb	beworben
	empfehlen	(empfiehlt)	empfahl	empfohlen
	helfen	(hilft)	half	geholfen
	nehmen	(nimmt)	nahm	genommen
	sprechen	(spricht)	sprach	gesprochen
	beginnen		begann	begonnen
	schwimmen		schwamm	ist geschwommen
	spinnen		spann	gesponnen
	bekommen		bekam	bekommen
	kommen		kam	ist gekommen
III.	finden		fand	gefunden
	klingen		klang	geklungen
	singen		sang	gesungen
	springen		sprang	ist gesprungen
	trinken		trank	getrunken
IV.	bleiben		blieb	ist geblieben
	entscheiden		entschied	entschieden
	scheinen		schien	geschienen
	schreiben		schrieb	geschrieben
	steigen		stieg	ist gestiegen
	treiben		trieb	getrieben
V.	bieten		bot	geboten
	fliegen		flog	ist geflogen
	verlieren		verlor	verloren
	ziehen		zog	ist gezogen
VI.	einladen	(lädt ein)	lud ein	eingeladen
	fahren	(fährt)	fuhr	ist gefahren
	tragen	(trägt)	trug	getragen
	wachsen	(wächst)	wuchs	ist gewachsen
	waschen	(wäscht)	wusch	gewaschen

VII.	fallen	(fällt)	fiel	ist gefallen
	gefallen	(gefällt)	gefiel	gefallen
	halten	(hält)	hielt	gehalten
	lassen	(lässt)	ließ	gelassen
	schlafen	(schläft)	schlief	geschlafen
	laufen	(läuft)	lief	ist gelaufen
	heißen		hieß	geheißen
	rufen		rief	gerufen

VIII. N-verbs that do not belong to any of the groups above:

	anfangen	(fängt an)	fing an	angefangen
	backen	(bäckt)	buk (backte)	gebacken
	gehen		ging	ist gegangen
	hängen		hing	gehangen
	sein	(ist)	war	ist gewesen
	stehen		stand	gestanden
	tun	(tut)	tat	getan
	werden	(wird)	wurde	ist geworden

IX. Irregular t-verbs:

	bringen		brachte	gebracht
	denken		dachte	gedacht
	haben		hatte	gehabt
	kennen		kannte	gekannt
	nennen		nannte	genannt
	wissen	(weiß)	wusste	gewusst

8. Sample forms of the subjunctive

a. **General subjunctive (Subjunctive II)**

	können	haben	sein	werden	lernen	bringen	gehen
ich	könnte	hätte	wäre	würde	lernte	brächte	ginge
du	könntest	hättest	wärest	würdest	lerntest	brächtest	gingest
er	könnte	hätte	wäre	würde	lernte	brächte	ginge
wir	könnten	hätten	wären	würden	lernten	brächten	gingen
ihr	könntet	hättet	wäret	würdet	lerntet	brächtet	ginget
sie	könnten	hätten	wären	würden	lernten	brächten	gingen

b. **Special subjunctive (Subjunctive I)**

	können	haben	sein	werden	lernen	bringen	gehen
ich	könne	habe	sei	werde	lerne	bringe	gehe
du	könnest	habest	seiest	werdest	lernest	bringest	gehest
er	könne	habe	seie	werde	lerne	bringe	gehe
wir	können	haben	seien	werden	lernen	bringen	gehen
ihr	könnet	habet	seiet	werdet	lernet	bringet	gehet
sie	können	haben	seien	werden	lernen	bringen	gehen

9. Table of verb forms in different tenses

a. **Indicative**

	present		simple past		future	
ich	frage	fahre	fragte	fuhr	werde	
du	fragst	fährst	fragtest	fuhrst	wirst	
er	fragt	fährt	fragte	fuhr	wird	fragen / fahren
wir	fragen	fahren	fragten	fuhren	werden	
ihr	fragt	fahrt	fragtet	fuhrt	werdet	
sie	fragen	fahren	fragten	fuhren	werden	

	pres. perf.				past perf.			
ich	habe			bin		hatte		war	
du	hast			bist		hattest		warst	
er	hat	gefragt	ist	gefahren	hatte	gefragt	war	gefahren
wir	haben			sind		hatten		waren	
ihr	habt			seid		hattet		wart	
sie	haben			sind		hatten		waren	

b. **Subjunctive**

PRESENT-TIME

	general subj.				special subj.	
ich	fragte	führe	würde		frage	fahre
du	fragtest	führest	würdest		fragest	fahrest
er	fragte	führe	würde	fragen / fahren	frage	fahre
wir	fragten	führen	würden		fragen	fahren
ihr	fragtet	führet	würdet		fraget	fahret
sie	fragten	führen	würden		fragen	fahren

PAST-TIME

	general subj.				special subj.		
ich	hätte		wäre		habe		sei	
du	hättest		wärest		habest		seiest	
er	hätte	gefragt	wäre	gefahren	habe	gefragt	sei	gefahren
wir	hätten		wären		haben		seien	
ihr	hättet		wäret		habet		seiet	
sie	hätten		wären		haben		seien	

c. **Passive voice**

	present		simple past		future	
ich	werde		wurde		werde	
du	wirst		wurdest		wirst	
er	wird	gefragt	wurde	gefragt	wird	gefragt werden
wir	werden		wurden		werden	
ihr	werdet		wurdet		werdet	
sie	werden		wurden		werden	

	pres. perf.		past perf.	
ich	bin		war	
du	bist		warst	
er	ist	gefragt worden	war	gefragt worden
wir	sind		waren	
ihr	seid		wart	
sie	sind		waren	

10. Translation of the *Gespräche*

Schritt 1 p. 2

How are you? MR. SANDERS: Hello. MS. LEHMANN: Hello. MR. SANDERS: My name is Sanders, Willi Sanders. And what's your name? MS. LEHMANN: My name is Erika Lehmann. MR. SANDERS: Pleased to meet you.

MR. MEIER: Good morning, Mrs. Fiedler. How are you? MRS. FIEDLER: Fine, thank you. And you? MR. MEIER: I'm fine too, thank you.

HEIDI: Hi, Ute! How are you? UTE: Hi, Heidi! Oh, I'm tired. HEIDI: Me too. Too much stress. See you later! UTE: Bye!

Schritt 2 p. 5

What's that? GERMAN PROFESSOR: Listen carefully and answer in German. What is that? JIM MILLER: That's the pencil. GERMAN PROFESSOR: What color is the pencil? SUSAN SMITH: Yellow. GERMAN PROFESSOR: Make a sentence, please. SUSAN SMITH: The pencil is yellow. GERMAN PROFESSOR: Is the notebook yellow too? DAVID JENKINS: No, the notebook isn't yellow. The notebook is light blue. GERMAN PROFESSOR: Good. SUSAN SMITH: What does *hellblau* mean? GERMAN PROFESSOR: *Hellblau* means *light blue* in English. SUSAN SMITH: And how does one say *dark blue?* GERMAN PROFESSOR: *Dunkelblau.* SUSAN SMITH: Oh, the pen is dark blue. GERMAN PROFESSOR: Correct. That's all for today. For tomorrow please read the dialogue again and learn the vocabulary, too.

Schritt 3 p. 10

In the department store SALESCLERK: Well, how are the pants? CHRISTIAN: Too big and too long. SALESCLERK: And the sweater? MAIKE: Too expensive. CHRISTIAN: But the colors are great. Too bad!

SALESCLERK: Hello. May I help you? SILVIA: I need some pencils and paper. How much are the pencils? SALESCLERK: 95 pfennig. SILVIA: And the paper? SALESCLERK: 4 marks 80. SILVIA: Fine. I'll take six pencils and the paper. SALESCLERK: Is that all? SILVIA: Yes, thank you. SALESCLERK: 10 marks 50, please.

Schritt 4 p. 15

The weather in April NORBERT: It's nice today, isn't it? JULIA: Yes, that's for sure. The sun is shining again. RUDI: Only the wind is cool. JULIA: Oh, that doesn't matter. NORBERT: I think it's great.

HANNES: Man, what lousy weather! It's already snowing again. MARTIN: So what? HANNES: In Mallorca it's nice and beautiful. MARTIN: But we're here, and not in Mallorca. HANNES: Too bad.

DOROTHEA: The weather is awful, isn't it? MATTHIAS: I think so, too. It's raining and raining. SONJA: And it's so cold again. Only 7 degrees! MATTHIAS: Yes, typical April.

Schritt 5 p. 19

What time is it? RITA: Hi, Axel! What time is it? AXEL: Hi, Rita! It's ten to eight. RITA: Oh no, in ten minutes I have philosophy. AXEL: Take care, then. Bye! RITA: Yes, bye!

PHILLIP: Hi, Steffi! What time is it? STEFFI: Hi, Phillip! It's eleven thirty. PHILLIP: Shall we eat now? STEFFI: OK, the lecture doesn't start till a quarter past one.

MR. RICHTER: When are you finished today? MR. HEROLD: At two o'clock. Why? MR. RICHTER: Are we going to play tennis today? MR. HEROLD: Yes, great! It's now twelve thirty. How about a quarter to three? MR. RICHTER: Fine! See you later!

Kapitel 1 p. 34

At the Goethe Institute SHARON: Roberto, where are you from? ROBERTO: I'm from Rome. And you? SHARON: I'm from Sacramento, but now my family lives in Seattle. ROBERTO: Do you have (any) brothers or sisters? SHARON: Yes, I have two sisters and two brothers. How about you? ROBERTO: I have only one sister. She lives in Montreal, in Canada. SHARON: Really? What a coincidence! My uncle lives there, too.

Later ROBERTO: Sharon, when is the test? SHARON: In ten minutes. Say, what are the names of some rivers in Germany? ROBERTO: In the north is the Elbe, in the east the Oder, in the south . . . SHARON: The Danube? ROBERTO: Right! And in the west the Rhine. Where is Düsseldorf? SHARON: Düsseldorf? Hm. Where's a map? ROBERTO: Oh, here. In the west of Germany, north of Bonn, on the Rhine. SHARON: Oh yes, right! Well, good luck!

Kapitel 2 p. 56

At the grocery store CLERK: Hello. May I help you? OLIVER: I'd like some fruit. Don't you have any bananas? CLERK: Yes, over there. OLIVER: How much are they? CLERK: 1 mark 80 a pound. OLIVER: And the oranges? CLERK: 90 pfennig each. OLIVER: Fine, two pounds of bananas and six oranges, please. CLERK: Anything else? OLIVER: Yes, 2 kilos of apples, please. CLERK: 16 marks 20, please. Thank you. Good-bye.

In the bakery CLERK: Good morning. May I help you? SIMONE: Good morning. One rye bread and six rolls, please. CLERK: Anything else? SIMONE: Yes, I need some cake. Is the apple strudel fresh? CLERK: Of course, very fresh. SIMONE: Fine, then I'll take four pieces. CLERK: Is that all? SIMONE: I'd also like some cookies. What kind of cookies do you have today? CLERK: Lemon cookies, chocolate cookies, butter cookies . . . SIMONE: Hm . . . I'll take 300 grams of chocolate cookies. CLERK: Anything else? SIMONE: No, thank you. That's all. CLERK: Then that comes to 18 marks 90, please.

Kapitel 3 p. 80

In the restaurant AXEL: Waiter, the menu, please. WAITER: Here you are. AXEL: What do you recommend today? WAITER: All of today's specials are very good. AXEL: Gabi, what are you having? GABI: I don't know. What are you going to have? AXEL: I think I'll take menu number one: veal cutlet and potato salad. GABI: And I'll take menu number two: stuffed beef rolls with potato dumplings. WAITER: Would you like something to drink? GABI: A glass of apple juice. And what about you? AXEL: Mineral water. *(The waiter comes with the food.)* Enjoy your meal! GABI: Thanks, you too . . . Mm, that tastes good. AXEL: The veal cutlet, too.

Later GABI: We'd like to pay, please. WAITER: All right. All together? GABI: Yes. Please give me the bill. AXEL: No, no, no. GABI: Yes, Axel. Today I'm paying. WAITER: Well, one menu number one, one menu number two, one apple juice, one mineral water, two cups of coffee. Anything else? AXEL: Yes, one roll. WAITER: That comes to 60 marks 60, please. GABI: *(She gives the waiter 70 marks.)* Make it 62 marks, please. WAITER: And eight marks change (back). Thank you very much.

Kapitel 4 p. 110

On the telephone CHRISTA: Hi, Michael! MICHAEL: Hi, Christa! How are you? CHRISTA: Not bad, thanks. What are you doing on the weekend? MICHAEL: Nothing special. Why? CHRISTA: It's Klaus's birthday the day after tomorrow, and we're giving a party. MICHAEL: Great! But are you sure that Klaus's birthday is the day after tomorrow? I think his birthday is on May 7. CHRISTA: Nonsense. Klaus's birthday is on May 3. And Saturday is the third. MICHAEL: OK. When and where is the party? CHRISTA: Saturday at seven at my place. But don't say anything. It's a surprise. MICHAEL: OK. Well, see you then. CHRISTA: Bye. Take care!

Klaus rings Christa's doorbell CHRISTA: Hi, Klaus! Happy birthday! KLAUS: What? MICHAEL: All the best on your birthday! KLAUS: Hi, Michael! . . . Hello, Gerda! Kurt and Sabine, you too? ALL: We're wishing you a happy birthday! KLAUS: Thanks! What a surprise! But my birthday isn't today. My birthday is on the seventh. CHRISTA: Really?—Well, it doesn't matter. We're celebrating today.

Kapitel 5 p. 136

Excuse me! Where is . . . ? TOURIST: Excuse me! Can you tell me where the Hotel Sacher is? VIENNESE PASSERBY: First street on the left behind the opera. TOURIST: And how do I get from there to St. Stephen's Cathedral? VIENNESE PASSERBY: Straight ahead along Kärtner Straße. TOURIST: How far is it to the cathedral? VIENNESE PASSERBY: Not far. You can walk (there). TOURIST: Thank you. VIENNESE PASSERBY: You're welcome.

Over there TOURIST: Excuse me. Where is the Burgtheater? GENTLEMAN: I'm sorry. I'm not from Vienna. TOURIST: Pardon me. Is that the Burgtheater? LADY: No, that's not the Burgtheater, but the opera house. Take the streetcar to city hall. The Burgtheater is across from city hall. TOURIST: And where does the streetcar stop? LADY: Over there on your left. TOURIST: Thank you very much. LADY: You're most welcome.

Kapitel 6 p. 160

Apartment for rent INGE: Hello, my name is Inge Moser. I've heard that you have a two-room apartment for rent. Is that right? LANDLORD: Yes, near the cathedral. INGE: How old is the apartment? LANDLORD: Fairly old, but it's been renovated and is quite big and light. It even has a balcony. INGE: What floor is it on? LANDLORD: On the fourth floor. INGE: Is it furnished or unfurnished? LANDLORD: Unfurnished. INGE: And how much is the rent? LANDLORD: 1,100 marks. INGE: Is that with or without heat? LANDLORD: Without heat. INGE: Oh, that's a little too expensive. Thank you very much. Good-bye! LANDLORD: Good-bye!

Living in a co-op INGE: I like your house. HORST: We still have room for you. Come, I'll show you everything . . . Here on the left is our kitchen. It's small but practical. INGE: Who does the cooking? HORST: We all (do): Jens, Gisela, Renate, and I. INGE: And that's the living room? HORST: Yes. It's a bit dark, but that's all right. INGE: I like your chairs. HORST: They're old, but really comfortable. Upstairs there are four bedrooms and the bathroom. INGE: Only one bathroom? HORST: Yes, unfortunately. But down here there is another toilet. INGE: How much do you pay per month? HORST: 400 marks each. INGE: Not bad. And how do you get to the university? HORST: I walk, of course. It's not far. INGE: (That) sounds good!

Kapitel 7 p. 186

At the bank TOURIST: Hello. Can you tell me where I can exchange money? TELLER: At counter 1. TOURIST: Thank you very much. *(She goes to counter 1.)* Hello. I'd like to change (some) dollars into schilling. Here are my traveler's checks. TELLER: May I please see your passport? TOURIST: Here you are. TELLER: Sign here, please, then go to the cashier over there. There you'll get your money. TOURIST: Thank you. *(She goes to the cashier.)* CASHIER: 324 schilling 63: one hundred, two hundred, three hundred, ten, twenty, twenty-four schilling and sixty-three groschen. TOURIST: Thank you. Good-bye.

At the hotel reception desk RECEPTIONIST: Good evening. GUEST: Good evening. Do you have a single room available? RECEPTIONIST: For how long? GUEST: For two or three nights; if possible, quiet and with a bath. RECEPTIONIST: Unfortunately today we have only one double room, and that for only one night. But tomorrow there'll be a single room available. Would you like to see the double room? GUEST: Yes, I would. RECEPTIONIST: Room number 12, on the second floor to the right. Here's the key. GUEST: Say, can I leave my suitcase here for a minute? RECEPTIONIST: Yes, of course. Put it over there in the corner. GUEST: Thank you. One more thing, when do you close at night? RECEPTIONIST: At midnight. If you come later, you'll have to ring the bell.

Kapitel 8 p. 216

At the post office in the train station UTA: I'd like to send this package to the United States. CLERK: By surface mail or by airmail? UTA: By airmail. How long will it take? CLERK: About ten days. Please fill out this parcel form! . . . Just a minute. Your return address is missing. UTA: Oh yes . . . One more thing. I need a telephone card. CLERK: For 6, 12, or 50 marks? UTA: For 12 marks. Thank you very much.

At the ticket counter ANNE: When does the next train for Interlaken leave? CLERK: In ten minutes. Departure at 11:28 A.M., track 2. ANNE: Good grief! And when will it arrive there? CLERK: Arrival in Interlaken at 2:16 P.M. ANNE: Do I have to change trains? CLERK: Yes, in Bern, but you have a connection to the InterCity Express with only a 24-minute stopover. ANNE: Fine. Give me a round-trip ticket to Interlaken, please. CLERK: First or second class? ANNE: Second class.

Kapitel 9 p. 240

On the telephone MRS. SCHMIDT: Mrs. Schmidt (speaking). BÄRBEL: Hello, Mrs. Schmidt. It's me, Bärbel. MRS. SCHMIDT: Hi, Bärbel! BÄRBEL: Is Karl-Heinz there? MRS. SCHMIDT: No, I'm sorry. He just went to the post office. BÄRBEL: I see. Can you tell him that I can't go out with him tonight? MRS. SCHMIDT: Of course. What's the matter? BÄRBEL: I'm sick. My throat hurts and I have a headache. MRS. SCHMIDT: I'm sorry. I hope you get better soon. BÄRBEL: Thank you. Good-bye. MRS. SCHMIDT: Good-bye.

See you in a few minutes YVONNE: Mayer residence. DANIELA: Hi, Yvonne! It's me, Daniela. YVONNE: Hi, Daniela! What's up? DANIELA: Nothing special. Do you feel like playing squash or going swimming? YVONNE: Squash? No thanks. I'm still sore from the day before yesterday. I can hardly move. I am hurting all over. DANIELA: Poor baby (*lit.:* lame duck)! How about chess? YVONNE: OK, that sounds fine. Are you coming to my place? DANIELA: Yes, see you in a few minutes.

Kapitel 10 p. 266

A glance at the newspaper SONJA: Say, what's on TV tonight? THEO: I have no idea. Nothing special for sure. SONJA: Let me see. *The Neverending Story,* a documentary, and a detective story. THEO: I don't feel like (watching) that. SONJA: Maybe there's something at the movies? THEO: Yes, *Men, Titanic,* and *A Heart in Winter.* SONJA: I've already seen them all. THEO: *The Caucasian Chalk Circle,* by Brecht, is playing at the theater. SONJA: Not bad. Do you feel like going? THEO: Yes, that sounds good. Let's go.

At the ticket window THEO: Do you still have tickets for tonight? LADY: Yes, in the first row of the first balcony on the left, and on the right in the orchestra. THEO: Two seats in the orchestra. Here are our student ID's. LADY: 20 marks, please. SONJA: When does the performance start? LADY: At 8:15 P.M.

During the intermission THEO: Would you like a cola (drink)? SONJA: Yes, I'd love one. But let me pay. You've already bought the programs. THEO: OK. How did you like the first act? SONJA: Great. I once read the piece in school, but I've never seen it on stage. THEO: I haven't either.

Kapitel 11 p. 290

Searching for a partner through personal ads FRANK: Hey, listen! "Wanted: charming, adventurous, affectionate ADAM. Reward: pretty, dynamic EVE, mid 20s, likes antiques, old houses, fast cars, animals, (and) children." STEFAN: Hmm, not bad, but not for me. I don't like children and I'm allergic to animals. FRANK: Then have a look here! "What I'm looking for exists. But how to find it? Woman with university degree, late 20s, slim, musical, is looking for congenial, well-educated, honest man with a sense of humor." STEFAN: Yes, that might be something. She's looking for someone with a sense of humor. I like that, and I also like music. But (I wonder) whether she likes jazz? Perhaps we could meet both of them? FRANK: I don't know. I think it's sort of stupid to meet people through ads in the newspaper. STEFAN: Oh, nonsense! Let's try it! What do we have to lose? FRANK: If you think so.

Kapitel 12 p. 322

Do you know what you want to be? TRUDI: Say, Elke, do you already know what you want to be? ELKE: Yes, I'd like to become a cabinet-maker. TRUDI: Isn't that very strenuous? ELKE: Oh, you get used to it. Perhaps someday I'll open my own business. TRUDI: Those are big plans. ELKE: Why not? I don't feel like always sitting in an office and working for other people. TRUDI: And where do you want to apply for an apprenticeship? ELKE: No problem at all. My aunt has her own business and has already offered me a position. TRUDI: You're lucky. ELKE: And how about you? Do you know what you want to do? TRUDI: Perhaps I'll be a dentist. Good dentists are always needed and besides, it pays very well. ELKE: That's true, but that takes so long. TRUDI: I know, but I'm looking forward to it anyway.

Kapitel 13 p. 348

During registration PETRA: Hi, John. How are you? JOHN: Pretty good, and you? PETRA: Well, I can't complain. What are you doing there? JOHN: I've still got to fill out these registration forms. PETRA: Shall I help you? JOHN: If you have time. I'm always struggling with red tape. PETRA: Do you have your passport with you? JOHN: No, why? PETRA: Your residence permit is in it; you really need it. JOHN: I can get it quickly. PETRA: Do that. I'll wait for you here.

A little later JOHN: Here's my passport. I'll also have to decide soon what seminars I want to take. Can you help me with that, too? PETRA: Sure. What's your major? JOHN: My major is modern history. I'd like to take some seminars in German history and literature. PETRA: Here's my course catalog. Let's see what they're offering this semester.

Kapitel 14 p. 374

There's always something going on here HEIKE: And that's the Memorial Church with its three buildings. We call them the "Hollow Tooth," the "Lipstick," and the "Compact." MARTIN: Berliners have nicknames for everything, you know. HEIKE: The old tower of the Memorial Church is to stay the way it is, as a memorial (to the war). The new Memorial Church with the new tower is modern. MARTIN: And they really look a little like a lipstick and a compact. Tell me, do you like living here in Berlin? HEIKE: Of course! Berlin is really lively and has so much to offer, not only historically but also culturally. There's always something going on here. Besides, the surroundings are beautiful. MARTIN: Somewhere I read that 24 percent of Berlin's total area consists of forests and lakes, with 800 kilometers of biking trails. HEIKE: That's great, isn't it? MARTIN: Awesome! Say, were you there when they broke through the Wall? HEIKE: You bet! I'll never forget that. MARTIN: I won't either, although I only saw it on TV. HEIKE: We waited all night, even though it was really cold. When the first piece of wall tipped over, we all sang loudly: "A beautiful day like today, a day like this should never end." MARTIN: I (can) still see the people dancing and celebrating on top of the Wall. HEIKE: Yes, that was really incredible (*lit.*: unique). Who would have thought that it all would happen so fast. MARTIN: And so peacefully.

Kapitel 15 p. 400

A visit to Weimar TOM: It's funny, but this monument of Goethe and Schiller seems so familiar to me. I think I've seen it somewhere before. DANIELA: Have you (ever) been to San Francisco? TOM: Of course! DANIELA: Were you in Golden Gate Park, too? TOM: I see, there's exactly the same monument! I think the German-Americans in California had it built. DANIELA: Right! By the way, did you know that Weimar was the cultural capital of Europe for the year 1999? TOM: No, that's new to me. How come? DANIELA: In the 18th century a lot of famous people lived here, and the Weimar Republic is also named for it. TOM: Yes, that's true. But this morning, when I looked down at the town from the memorial of the Buchenwald concentration camp, I had very mixed feelings. DANIELA: Yes, there you have a point (*lit.*: you're right).

In the old part of town DANIELA: Look, the old houses here are really pretty, aren't they? TOM: Yes, they've been wonderfully restored. I find it especially nice that no cars are allowed here. DANIELA: Thank God. The façades wouldn't have survived the exhaust fumes of the Trabbis for long. TOM: In our city there's now also a citizens' initiative to ban all cars from the old part of town in order to save the old buildings. DANIELA: I think that's good. TOM: Are the containers over there for recycling (*lit.*: waste separation)? DANIELA: Yes, do you have that too? TOM: We do, but certainly much more could be done in that respect.

11. Supplementary charts for *Hoppla, hier fehlt 'was!*

Kapitel 1 p. 48

S2:

Name	Nationalität	Wohnort	Alter
Toni	Schweizer		32
Katja	Deutsche	Ulm	
	Österreicherin		61
Nicole	Französin	Lyon	
Pierre	Franzose		
	Italiener		25
Maria	Spanierin	Madrid	
Tom	Kanadier		28
Amy	Amerikanerin	Miami	

Kapitel 2 p. 70

S2:

	Gibt es hier . . . ?	**Gibt es da . . . ?**
Eier	ja	ja
Brot		
Milch		
Joghurt		
Erdbeeren		
Gurken		
Wein	ja	nein
. . .		

Kapitel 3   p. 90

S2:

	Bruder	**Schwester**	**Mutter**	**Vater**	**Großeltern**
Bild					
Bücher					x
Tennishose					
Hausschuhe				x	
Pulli					
Ringe *(pl.)*					
T-Shirts		x			
Mantel			x		
Messer *(sg.)*	x				
Gläser					

Kapitel 4   p. 120

S2:

	Max	**Stefan**	**Petra**	**Ute**	**ich**	**wir**	**dein(e) Freund(in) + du**
die Party gegeben			x				
mit dem Essen geholfen				x			
Getränke gebracht							
viel getanzt							
laut gesungen		x					
viel getrunken							
sehr müde gewesen					x		
bis um zehn geschlafen							
zu lange geblieben							x
nicht da gewesen							
nach Hause gelaufen						x	
mit Max gefahren							

Kapitel 5

p. 145

S2:

	ich	Thomas	Kevin und du	Mareike	Frank und Margit
den Stadtplan nicht finden (können)	x				
zum Burgtheater gehen (sollen)					
die Hofburg besichtigen (mögen)					
die Uni sehen (wollen)		x			
durch die Kärntner Straße laufen (können)					
noch Bilder machen (müssen)				x	
keinen Wein trinken (dürfen)					x
Sachertorte essen (mögen)					

Kapitel 6

p. 173

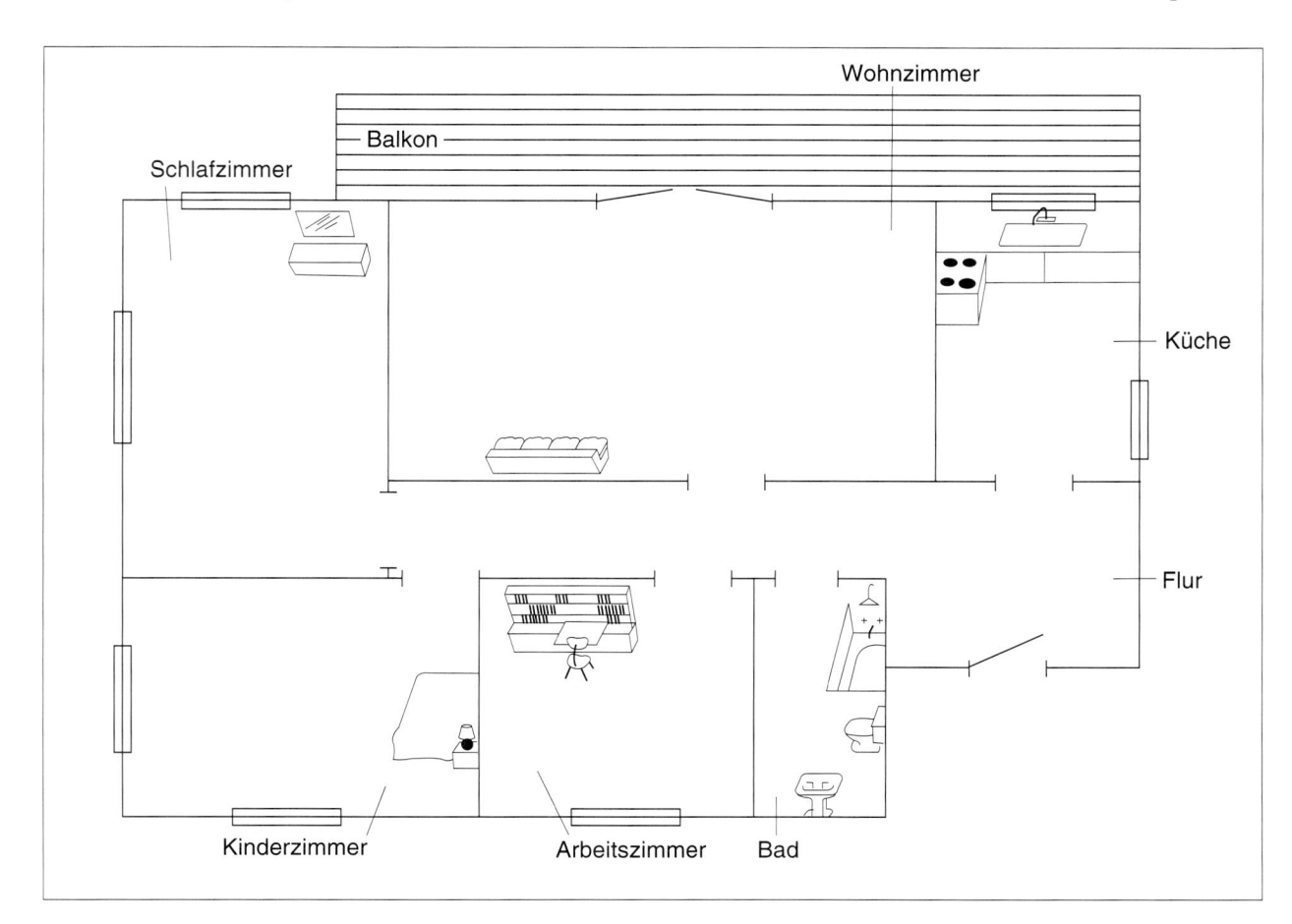

Kapitel 7
p. 196

S2:

Vater	bei der Bank vorbeigehen	Ja, gestern.
Vater	Geld umtauschen	Ja.
Mutter	Kamera mitnehmen	
Mutter	die Nachbarn anrufen	
Thomas	die Telefonnummer aufschreiben	
Thomas	die Garagentür zumachen	Nein, noch nicht.
Carla	bei der Post vorbeigehen	Ja, gestern.
Carla	die Fenster zumachen	
Kinder	den Fernseher ausmachen *(turn off)*	
Kinder	die Lichter *(lights)* ausmachen	Nein, noch nicht.
Du	ein paar Bücher mitnehmen	

Kapitel 8
p. 229

S2:

Wer	Wann/Wie lange	Wie/Obj. + Präposition	Wo und was
LUCIAN	ein paar Wochen		
CHRISTL		bei ein- Gastfamilie	in Amerika sein
STEFFI		wegen ihr- Prüfung	
NINA + KIM	während d- Ferien		von Passau bis Wien fahren
BEN + MICHI			in ein- Pizzeria arbeiten
GÜNTHER		trotz d- Wetter	auf der Insel Rügen campen
JUTTA	vom 1.–31. Juli		
NICOLE		wieder	von Griechenland zurückkommen
YVONNE	morgens		
JOCHEN	mittags	gewöhnlich	

Kapitel 9
p. 252

S2:

	Zuerst	Dann	Danach
ELKE			
HORST	s. schnell anziehen joggen gehen	s. duschen s. umziehen s. vor den Spiegel stellen	s. die Haare kämmen s. rasieren Joghurt und Müsli essen
SUSI			
INGO	s. das Gesicht waschen s. eine Tasse Kaffee machen s. anziehen	s. an den Computer setzen s. die E-Mails ansehen	s. wieder hinlegen s. nicht beeilen

Kapitel 10
p. 268

S2:

Wo?	Was?	Wann?
VOLKSBÜHNE	**Macbeth,** Schauspiel von William Shakespeare	19.30
URANIA-THEATER		
METROPOL-THEATER	**West Side Story,** Musical von Leonard Bernstein	19.00
IM DOM		
PHILHARMONIE		
KONZERTHAUS	**Flamenco-Festival,** mit Montse Salazar	20.00
KOMÖDIE		
KAMMERSPIELE		
FILMBÜHNE 1	**Das Versprechen,** von Margarethe von Trotta	
FILMBÜHNE 2	**Das Boot,** von Wolfgang Petersen	

Kapitel 11
p. 304

S2:

	Nachdem . . .	**Dann . . .**
THOMAS	die Anzeige lesen	den Besitzer (owner) anrufen
BESITZER	über die Katze erzählen	
THOMAS	dorthin fahren und s. die Katze ansehen	s. in die Katze verlieben
THOMAS	die Katze mit nach Hause nehmen	
DIE BEIDEN	ihr etwas Milch geben	mit ihr spielen wollen
DIE KATZE	s. einleben *(get used to the place)*	
DIE BEIDEN	die Katze eine Woche haben	wässrige *(watery)* Augen und eine verstopfte *(stuffed-up)* Nase bekommen
INGO	die Katze zwei Wochen auf seinem Bett haben	
DIE BEIDEN	eine lange Diskussion haben	eine Anzeige in die Zeitung setzen
BESITZER	zwei Wochen ohne die Katze sein	
BESITZER	auf die Anzeige antworten	die Katze zurücknehmen

Kapitel 12
p. 336

S2:

	−		+
INTELLIGENT		Jörg	
REIST GERN	Ninas Kusine		
KANN GUT MALEN		Wolfgangs Freund	Wolfgangs Freundin
SCHREIBT VIEL			Petras Bruder
FREUNDLICH	Uwe		Regine
RUHIG		Inge und Heidi	Uta
ARBEITET SCHWER	Petra	Petras Nichte *(niece)*	

Kapitel 13

p. 361

S2:

Erzählen Sie Ihrem Partner/Ihrer Partnerin:

Mein Opa ist aus Deutschland gekommen. Seine Familie ist mit dem Schiff nach Amerika gefahren. Opa konnte kein Englisch, und er wäre lieber in Deutschland geblieben. Seine Familie hat in New York gewohnt. Er ist Polizist geworden. Er hat sich immer für Musik interessiert. Er konnte gut singen, und ich habe viele deutsche Lieder von ihm gelernt. Wenn er Zeit gehabt hätte, hätte er gelernt, Klavier zu spielen. Er hat seine Verwandten in Deutschland oft besucht. Dieses Jahr wäre er auch nach Deutschland gefahren, wenn er nicht krank geworden wäre.

Und was sagt Ihnen Ihr Partner/Ihre Partnerin?

	Ja	Nein
Seine/Ihre Oma ist gern zur Schule gegangen.	x	
Sie war gut in Mathe.		
Sie hat an der Uni studiert.		
Sie ist Lehrerin geworden.		
Sie hat bei einer reichen Familie gearbeitet.		
Sie hat geheiratet.		
Sie hatte viele Kinder.		
Sie hat mit ihrem Mann eine große Weltreise gemacht.		

Kapitel 14

p. 388

S2:

Wer?	Was?
MAJOR DER DDR-GRENZTRUPPE:	„Es ist eine verrückte Zeit."
	„Vor meinen Augen tanzte die Freiheit."
OSTBERLINER TAXIFAHRER:	„So viel Fernsehen haben wir noch nie gesehen."
	„Wir haben uns jeden Tag gesehen. Jetzt will ich ihm mal die Hand schütteln *(shake)*."
AFRIKANISCHER DIPLOMAT:	„Ich dachte, die Deutschen können nur Fußball spielen oder im Stechschritt marschieren *(goose-step)*, aber jetzt können sie sogar Revolutionen machen."
	„Auf beiden Seiten sind Deutsche. Der Kommunismus hat seine Chance gehabt. Er funktioniert nicht."
AUTOR STEPHAN HEYM:	„Die einzige Chance, die wir haben, den Sozialismus zu retten *(save)*, ist richtiger Sozialismus."
	„Ich bin Gott dankbar, dass ich das noch erleben *(experience)* darf."
CELLIST MSTISLAW ROSTROPOWITSCH:	„Mauern sind nicht für ewig *(forever)* gebaut ... In Berlin habe ich für mein Herz gespielt."
	„Wir haben zu lange im Dunkeln gelebt. Treten wir *(let's step)* ins Licht!"

War das . . . ?

ein NBC-Korrespondent
Lyndon Johnson
ein West-Berliner Polizist
Ronald Reagan
ein 16-Jähriger aus Ost-Berlin
eine amerikanische Studentin

eine Ärztin aus München
die Cellistin Sophie-Marie Mutter
Ex-Bundeskanzler Willy Brandt
Paul Newman
Tschechischer Reformpräsident Alexander Dubcek
Leonard Bernstein

Kapitel 15

p. 418

S2:

Sportliche Iren
Die Iren lieben den Sport mehr als alle anderen Europäer. Jeder zweite ist verrückt danach.

Offene Luxemburger
Luxemburg hat europaweit die meisten Ausländer—29%. Die meisten Beamte der EU.

Fleißige Portugiesen
Die Portugiesen sind das fleißigste Völkchen Europas, höchste Jahresarbeitszeit—2025 Stunden.

Schnelle Italiener
Jedes Jahr kommen die Hälfte aller europäischen Telegramme allein aus ihrem Land.

Maritime Holländer
Die Holländer sind die größten Seefahrer Europas. Das Land besitzt fast 4000 Schiffe.

Sehfreudige Spanier
Die Spanier sitzen am häufigsten unter den Europäern vor dem Fernseher—vier Stunden am Tag.

Die Belgier: . . .
Die Deutschen: . . .
Die Griechen: . . .
Die Dänen: . . .
Die Franzosen: . . .
Die Briten: . . .

VOCABULARIES

GERMAN-ENGLISH

The vocabulary includes all the ACTIVE AND PASSIVE vocabulary used in *Wie geht's?* The English definitions of the words are limited to their use in the text. Each active vocabulary item is followed by a number and a letter indicating the chapter and section where it first occurs.

NOUNS Nouns are followed by their plural endings unless the plural is rare or nonexistent. In the case of n-nouns the singular genitive ending is also given: **der Herr, -n, -en.** Nouns that require adjective endings appear with two endings: **der Angestellte (ein Angestellter).** Female forms of masculine nouns are not listed if only **-in** needs to be added: **der Apotheker.**

VERBS For regular t-verbs ("weak verbs"), only the infinitive is listed. All irregular t-verbs ("irregular weak verbs") and basic n-verbs ("strong verbs") are given with their principal parts: **bringen, brachte, gebracht; schreiben, schrieb, geschrieben.** Separable-prefix verbs are identified by a dot between the prefix and the verb: **mit·bringen.** Compound, mixed, and n-verbs are printed with an asterisk to indicate that the principal parts can be found under the listing of the basic verb: **mit·bringen*, beschreiben*.** When **sein** is used as the auxiliary of the perfect tenses, the form **ist** is given: **wandern (ist); kommen, kam, ist gekommen.**

ADJECTIVES and ADVERBS Adjectives and adverbs that have an umlaut in the comparative and superlative are identified by an umlauted vowel in parentheses: **arm (ä) = arm, ärmer, am ärmsten.**

ACCENTUATION Stress marks are provided for all words that do not follow the typical stress pattern. The accent follows the stressed syllable: **Balkon', Amerika'ner, wiederho'len.** The stress is not indicated when the word begins with an unstressed prefix, such as **be-, er-, ge-.**

ABBREVIATIONS

~	*repetition of the key word*	nom.	*nominative*
abbrev.	*abbreviation*	o.s.	*oneself*
acc.	*accusative*	pl.	*plural*
adj.	*adjective*	refl. pron.	*reflexive pronoun*
adv.	*adverb*	rel. pron.	*relative pronoun*
comp.	*comparative*	sg.	*singular*
conj.	*subordinate conjunction*	s.th.	*something*
dat.	*dative*	S	*Schritt*
fam.	*familiar*	SS	*Sprechsituation*
gen.	*genitive*	W	*Wortschatz 1*
inf.	*infinitive*	G	*Grammatik, Struktur*
lit.	*literally*	E	*Einblicke (Wortschatz 2)*

A

der **Aal, -e** eel
ab- away, off
ab starting, as of
ab·bauen to reduce
ab·brechen* to break off
ab·brennen* to burn down
der **Abend, -e** evening; **(Guten) ~!** (Good) evening. (S1); **am ~** in the evening (6E); **gestern ~** yesterday evening (8G); **heute ~** this evening (8G); **Donnerstagabend** Thursday evening (8G)
das **Abendessen, -** supper, evening meal (3W); **zum ~** for supper (3W)
abends in the evening, every evening (S5); **donnerstag~** Thursday evenings (8G)
das **Abenteuer, -** adventure
aber but, however (S3,2G,5G); flavoring particle expressing admiration (7G)
ab·fahren* (von) to depart, leave (from) (8W)
die **Abfahrt, -en** departure (8W); descent
der **Abfall, ̈e** waste, garbage (15W)
ab·fliegen* (von) to take off, fly (from) (8W)
die **Abgase** *(pl.)* exhaust fumes
ab·geben* to give away, hand in
abhängig (von) dependent (on)
die **Abhängigkeit** dependence
ab·holen to pick up
das **Abitur, -e** final comprehensive exam (at the end of the *Gymnasium*)
die **Abmeldung** report that one is leaving or moving
ab·nehmen* to take s.th. from sb., take off
abonnieren to subscribe
ab·pflücken to pick, break off
ab·reißen* to tear down (15W)

der **Abschluss, ̈e** diploma, degree
die **Abschlussparty, -s** graduation party
die **Abschlussprüfung, -en** final exam
der **Absender, -** return address (8W)
absolut' absolute(ly)
absolvieren to complete
sich **ab·wechseln** to take turns
die **Abwechslung, -en** distraction, variety
ach oh; **~ so!** Oh, I see! (9W); **~ was!** Oh, come on! (13E)
die **Achtung** respect; **~!** Watch out! Be careful!
der **ADAC = Allgemeiner Deutscher Automobil-Club** German version of AAA
ade (or **adé**) good-bye, farewell
addieren to add
das **Adjektiv, -e** adjective
der **Adler, -** eagle
die **Adresse, -n** address (8W)
der **Adventskranz, ̈e** Advent wreath
die **Adventszeit** Advent season
das **Adverb', -ien** adverb
die **Aerobik** arobics
der **Affe, -n, -n** monkey; **Du ~!** You nut!
(das) **Ägypten** Egypt
der **Ägypter, -** the Egyptian
ägyptisch Egyptian
Aha'! There, you see. Oh, I see.
ähnlich similar; **Das sieht dir ~.** That's typical of you.
die **Ahnung: Keine ~!** I've no idea. (10W)
die **Akademie', -n** academy
der **Akademiker, -** (university) graduate
akademisch academic
der **Akkusativ, -e** accusative
der **Akt, -e** act (play)
das **Aktiv** active voice
aktiv active

die **Aktivität', -en** activity
aktuell' up to date, current
der **Akzent', -e** accent
akzeptieren to accept
all- all (7G); **vor ~em** above all, mainly (10E); **~e drei Jahre** every three years
allein' alone (11E)
allerdings however (15W)
allergisch gegen allergic to
allerlei all sorts of
alles everything, all (2W); **Das ist ~.** That's all. (2W)
allgemein' (in) general; **im ~en** in general
der **Alltag** everyday life
die **Alpen** *(pl.)* Alps
die **Alpenblume, -n** Alpine flower
das **Alphabet'** alphabet
als as; *(conj.)* (at the time) when (11G); *(after comp.)* than (12G)
also therefore, thus, so; well; in other words (10E)
alt (ä) old (S3); **ur~** ancient
der **Alte (ein Alter)** old man (12G); **die ~** old lady (12G); **das ~** old things (12G)
das **Alter** age
die **Altstadt, ̈e** old part of town
der **Amateur', -e** amateur
ambitiös' ambitious (11W)
die **Ameise, -n** ant
(das) **Amerika** America (1W)
der **Amerikaner, -** the American (1W)
amerikanisch American (1W)
die **Ampel, -n** traffic light
an- to, up to
an (+ *acc. / dat.*) to, at (the side of), on (vertical surface) (6G)
analysieren to analyze
an·bieten to offer (12W)
ander- other (9E)
andererseits on the other hand
anders different(ly), in other ways (9E); **etwas (ganz) anderes** something (quite) different (9E)

anerkannt recognized, credited
an·erkennen* to recognize; acknowledge
die **Anerkennung, -en** recognition
der **Anfang, ⸚e** beginning, start (10W): **am ~** in the beginning (10W)
an·fangen* to begin, start (10W)
der **Anfänger, -** beginner
die **Angabe, -n** information
das **Angebot, -e** offering, offer
angeln to fish; **~ gehen*** to go fishing
angepasst geared to
angeschlagen posted
der **Angestellte (ein Angestellter)** employee, clerk (12G)
die **Angestellte (eine Angestellte)** employee, clerk (12G)
die **Angli'stik** study of English
der **Angriff, -e** attack; raid
die **Angst, ⸚e** fear, anxiety; **~ haben*** (**vor** + *dat.*) to fear, be afraid (of) (13E); **~ bekommen*** to become afraid, get scared
an·halten* to continue
sich **an·hören** to listen to (9G); **Hör dir das an!** Listen to that.
an·kommen* (**in** + *dat.*) to arrive (in) (7E); **Das kommt darauf an.** That depends. (7E)
die **Ankunft** arrival (8W)
an·machen to turn on (a radio, etc.) (10W)
die **Anmeldung** reception desk; registration
die **Annahme, -n** hypothetical statement or question
an·nehmen* to accept (7E, 13E)
der **Anorak, -s** parka
anpassungsfähig adaptable
an·reden to address
an·richten to do (damage)
der **Anruf, -e** (phone) call
der **Anrufbeantworter, -** answering machine

an·rufen* to call up, phone (7G)
an·schlagen* to post
der **Anschluss, ⸚e** connection
die **Anschrift, -en** address
(sich) **an·sehen*** to look at (9G)
die **Ansicht, -en** opinion, attitude; view
die **Ansichtskarte, -n** (picture) postcard (8W)
an·sprechen* to address, speak to
(an)statt (+ *gen.*) instead of (8G)
anstrengend strenuous (12W)
die **Antiquität', -en** antique
der **Antrag, ⸚e** application
die **Antwort, -en** answer
antworten to answer (S2)
an·wachsen* to increase
die **Anwaltsfirma, -firmen** law firm
die **Anzahl** number, amount
die **Anzeige, -n** ad (11W)
die **Anzeigetafel, -n** scoreboard
(sich) **an·ziehen*** to put on (clothing), get dressed (9G)
an·zünden to light
der **Apfel, ⸚** apple (2W)
der **Apfelstrudel, -** apple strudel
die **Apothe'ke, -n** pharmacy (2E)
der **Apothe'ker, -** pharmacist
der **Appetit'** appetite; **Guten ~!** Enjoy your meal. (3W)
der **April'** April (S4); **im ~** in April (S4)
der **Äqua'tor** equator
das **Äquivalent'** equivalent
die **Arbeit, -en** work (6E); **~** (term) paper (13W); **bei der ~** at work; **Tag der ~** Labor Day
arbeiten to work (1E)
der **Arbeiter, -** (blue-collar) worker (12W); **Vor~** foreman
der **Arbeitgeber, -** employer
der **Arbeitnehmer, -** employee
die **Arbeitserlaubnis** work permit
das **Arbeitsheft, -e** workbook
das **Arbeitsklima** work climate

der **Arbeitsplatz, ⸚e** job; job location
arbeitslos unemployed
der **Arbeitslose (ein Arbeitsloser)** unemployed person
die **Arbeitslosigkeit** unemployment (12E)
der **Arbeitsmarkt, ⸚e** job market
der **Arbeitsplatz, ⸚e** ob; place of employment
das **Arbeitszimmer, -** study (6W)
archa'isch archaic
die **Archäologie'** archaeology
der **Architekt', -en, -en** architect (12W)
die **Architektur'** architecture
das **Archiv', -e** archive
ärgerlich annoying
sich **ärgern über** (+ *acc.*) to get annoyed (upset) about (10G); **Das ärgert mich.** That makes me mad.
die **Arka'de, -n** arcade
arm (ä) poor (11W)
der **Arm, -e** arm (9W)
die **Armbanduhr, -en** wristwatch
die **Armee, -n** army
die **Armut** poverty
arrogant' arrogant
das **Arsenal', -e** arsenal
die **Art, -en** kind, type
der **Arti'kel, -** (**von**) article (of)
der **Arzt, ⸚e / die Ärztin, -nen** physician, doctor (12W)
die **Asche** ashes
ästhe'tisch aesthetic
atmen to breathe
die **Atmosphä're** atmosphere
die **Attraktion', -en** attraction
attraktiv' attractive (11W)
auch also, too (S1)
auf (+ *acc.* / *dat.*) on (top of) (6G); open (7W)
auf- up, open
auf·bauen to build up (15W); **wieder ~** to rebuild (15W)
aufeinan'der treffen* to come together
der **Aufenthalt, -e** stay, stopover (8W); **Auslands~** stay abroad
die **Aufenthaltserlaubnis** residence permit

VOCABULARIES

auf·essen* o eat up
auf·fassen to consider (to be)
die **Aufgabe, -n** assignment; task, challenge
auf·geben* to give up
auf·halten* to hold open
auf·hören (zu + *inf.*) to stop (doing s.th.) (13E)
der **Aufkleber, -** sticker
auf·machen to open (7G)
die **Aufnahme** acceptance, reception
auf·nehmen* to take (a picture)
auf·passen to pay attention, watch out (7G); **Passen Sie auf!** Pay attention. (SSS)
der **Aufsatz, ¨e** essay, composition, paper
der **Aufschnitt** (*sg.*) assorted meats/cheeses, cold cuts
auf·schreiben* to write down (7G)
auf·stehen* to get up (7G)
auf·stellen to put up, set up
auf·wachsen* to grow up
der **Aufzug, ¨e** elevator
das **Auge, -n** eye (9W)
der **Augenblick, -e** moment; **(Einen) ~!** Just a minute!
der **August'** August (S4); **im ~** in August (S4)
aus (+ *dat.*) out of, from (a place of origin) (3G); **Ich bin ~** . . . I'm from (a native of) . . . (1W)
aus- out, out of
aus sein* to be over
aus·arbeiten to work out
aus·(be)zahlen to pay out
aus·bilden to train, educate
die **Ausbildung** training, education (12W)
sich **auseinan'der entwickeln** to develop apart
die **Ausfuhr** export
aus·füllen to fill out (8W)
der **Ausgang, ¨e** exit (7W)
aus·geben* to spend (money) (9E)
aus·gehen* to go out (7G)
ausgezeichnet excellent (6E)

aus·helfen* to help out
das **Ausland** foreign country; **im / ins ~** abroad (12E)
der **Ausländer, -** foreigner (10E)
ausländisch foreign (13E)
der **Auslandsaufenthalt, -e** stay abroad
das **Auslandsprogramm, -e** foreign-study program
aus·leihen* to loan, lend out
aus·lesen* to pick out
aus·machen turn off (a radio etc.) (10W)
aus·packen to unpack
aus·richten to tell; **Kann ich etwas ~?** Can I take a message?
(sich) **aus·ruhen** to relax (9E)
die **Aussage, -n** statement
aus·sehen* to look, appear (12E); **~ (wie** + *nom.*) to look (like) (14W)
außer (+ *dat.*) besides, except for (3G)
äußer- outer
außerdem (*adv.*) besides (6E)
außerhalb (+ *gen.*) outside (of)
die **Aussicht, -en (auf** + *acc.*) prospect (for)
der **Aussiedler, -** emigrant; resettled person
die **Aussprache** pronunciation
aus·steigen* to get off (8W)
die **Ausstellung, -en** exhibition
aus·sterben* to become extinct
der **Austausch** exchange; **das ~programm, -e** exchange program
aus·tauschen to exchange (14E)
die **Auster, -n** oyster
ausverkauft sold out
die **Auswahl (an** + *dat.*) choice, selection (of) (10E)
der **Ausweis, -e** ID, identification (7W)
aus·werten to evaluate, assess
sich **aus·wirken auf** (+ *acc.*) to affect

aus·zahlen to pay out
(sich) **aus·ziehen*** to take off (clothing), get undressed (9G)
der **Auszubildende (ein -bildender)** = **Azubi, -s** trainee
authen'tisch authentic
das **Auto, -s** car (5W)
die **Autobahn, -en** freeway
autofrei free of cars
automatisiert' automated
die **Automobil'branche** car industry
der **Autor, -en** author (10W)
autoritäts'gläubig believing in authority

B

backen (bäckt), buk (backte), gebacken to bake
das **Backblech, -e** cookie sheet
der **Bäcker, -** baker
die **Bäckerei', -en** bakery (2W)
das **Bad, ¨er** bath(room) (6W)
der **Badeanzug, ¨e** swimsuit
die **Badehose, -n** swimming trunks
baden to bathe, swim (6W); **sich ~** to take a bath (9G)
die **Badewanne, -n** bathtub
das **Badezimmer, -** bathroom
die **Bahn, -en** railway, train (8W); **~übergang, ¨e** railroad crossing
der **Bahnhof, ¨e** train station (5W)
der **Bahnsteig, -e** platform (8W)
bald soon (7W); **so~'** as soon as (12E)
baldig soon-to-come
der **Balkon', -s/-e** balcony (6W)
der **Ball, ¨e** ball
das **Ballett'** ballet (10W)
die **Bana'ne, -n** banana (2W); **Alles ~?** Everything all right?
bange worried
die **Bank, -en** bank (7W)
die **Bank, ¨e** bench
der **Bankier', -s** banker
der **Bann** ban

die **Bar, -s** bar, pub
der **Bär, -en** bear; **Du bist ein Brumm~.** You're a grouch.
barfuß barefoot
das **Bargeld** cash (7W)
der **Bart, ⸚e** beard
basteln to do crafts
der **Bau, -ten** building, construction
der **Bauch, ⸚e** stomach, belly (9W)
bauen to build (6E); **~ lassen*** to have built
der **Bauer, -n, -n** farmer
der **Bauernhof, ⸚e** farm
das **Baugesetz, -e** building code
der **Bauingenieur, -e** tructural engineer
das **Bauland** building lots
der **Baum, ⸚e** tree (6W)
die **Baumwolle** cotton
die **Baustelle, -n** construction site
der **Baustoff, -e** building material
der **Bayer, -n, -n** the Bavarian
(das) **Bayern** Bavaria (in southeast Germany)
bay(e)risch Bavarian
der **Beamte (ein Beamter)** / die **Beamtin, -en** civil servant (12G)
beantworten to answer
bedeuten to mean, signify (S2)
die **Bedeutung, -en** meaning, significance
bedienen to take care of, serve
die **Bedienung** server, service (3W); service charge
sich **beeilen** to hurry (9G)
beeindrucken to impress
beeinflussen to influence
beenden to finish
der **Befehl, -e** order, request, command
befehlen (befiehlt), befahl, befohlen to order
befriedigend satisfactory
befürchten to fear
begehrt desired
der **Beginn** beginning; **zu ~** in the beginning

beginnen, begann, begonnen to begin (S5)
begleiten to accompany
begrenzt limited
die **Begrenzung, -en** limitation, limit
begrüßen to greet, welcome
die **Begrüßung, -en** greeting; **zur ~** as greeting
behalten* to keep
die **Behandlung, -en** treatment
beherrschen to dominate, rule
bei (+ *dat.*) at, near, at the home of (3G); **Hier ~.** This is __'s office/residence.
beide both (11W)
bei·legen to enclose
das **Bein, -e** leg (9W); **auf den ~en** on the go
das **Beispiel, -e** example; **zum ~ (z. B.)** for example (e.g.)
bei·tragen* (zu) to contribute (to)
bekannt well known (5E); **Das kommt mir ~ vor.** that seems familiar to me.
der **Bekannte (ein Bekannter)** / die **Bekannte, -n, -n** acquaintance (12G)
bekommen* (hat) to get, receive (4W)
belasten to burden; pollute
belegen to sign up for, take (a course) (13W)
belgisch Belgian
beliebt popular (9E)
die **Belohnung, -en** reward
benennen* nach to name after
benutzen to use (12W)
das **Benzin'** gas(oline)
beo'bachten to watch, observe
die **Beo'bachtung, -en** observation
bequem' comfortable, convenient (6W)
der **Berater, -** counselor, adviser, consultant
berauben to rob
der **Berg, -e** mountain (1W)

bergab' downhill
die **Bergbahn, -en** mountain train
der **Bergbau** mining
berghoch' uphill
Bergsteigen gehen* to go mountain climbing
der **Bericht, -e** report
berichten to report (14W)
berieseln *here:* to shower with
der **Beruf, -e** profession (12W)
beruflich professional(ly); **~ engagiert'** professionally active
die **Berufsschule, -n** vocational school
der **Berufstätige (ein Berufstätiger)** member of the workforce
die **Berufswahl** choice of profession (12E)
berühmt famous (14E)
die **Beschäftigung** activity; occupation
bescheinigen to verify, document
beschreiben* to describe
die **Beschreibung, -en** description
beschriftet labeled
besichtigen to visit (an attraction), tour (5W)
der **Besitz** property
besitzen* to own
der **Besitzer, -** owner
besonders especially (3E); **nichts Besonderes** nothing special (9W)
besser better (12G)
die **Besserung** improvement; **Gute ~!** Get well soon. I hope you get better.
best- best (12G); **am ~en** it's best (12G)
bestätigen to verify
bestehen* to pass (an exam) (13W); **~ aus** (+ *dat.*) to consist of; **es besteht** there is
bestellen to order (3W)
die **Bestellung, -en** order
bestimmt surely, for sure, certain(ly) (11W)

der **Besuch, -e** visit, visitor
besuchen to visit (8W); attend
der **Besucher, -** visitor
beten to pray
der **Beton′** concrete
betonen to stress, emphasize
Betr(eff) concerning
betreffen* to concern
betreten* to enter, step on
der **Betriebswirt, -e** graduate in business management (12W)
die **Betriebswirtschaft** business administration
das **Bett, -en** bed (6W); **ins ~** to bed
die **Bevölkerung** population (15E)
bevor (*conj.*) before (4G)
bewältigen to overcome, cope with; finish
sich bewerben (um) to apply (for) (12W)
die **Bewertung, -en** evaluation, grading
der **Bewohner, -** inhabitant; resident
bewusst conscious(ly)
bezahlen to pay (for) (3W)
die **Beziehung, -en** relationship (11W)
der **Bezirk, -e** district
die **Bibel, -n** Bible
die **Bibliothek′, -en** library (5W)
die **Biene, -n** bee
das **Bier, -e** beer (2W)
bieten, bot, geboten to offer
der **Biki′ni, -s** bikini
die **Bilanz′, -en: eine ~ auf·stellen** to make an evaluation
das **Bild, -er** picture (S2)
bilden to form; **~ Sie einen Satz!** Make a sentence.
die **Bildung** education
das **Billard** billiards
billig cheap, inexpensive (S3)
binden, band, gebunden to bind
die **Biochemie′** biochemistry
der **Bioche′miker, -** biochemist
der **Bio-Laden, ̈** health-food store
der **Biolo′ge, -n, -n / die Biolo′gin, -nen** biologist

die **Biologie′** biology
bis to, until; **~ später!** See you later! So long! (S5); **~ gleich!** See you in a few minutes (9W); **bisher′** until now
bisschen: ein ~ some, a little bit (4E); **Ach du liebes ~!** Good grief!, My goodness!, Oh dear! (2E)
bitte please (S1); **~! / ~ bitte!** You're welcome. (S5, 2E); **~ schön!** You're welcome.; **Hier ~ !** Here you are.; **~ schön?** May I help you?; **Wie ~?** What did you say? Could you say that again? (S3)
bitten, bat, gebeten to ask, request (12E); **um etwas ~** to request s.th.
das **Blatt, ̈-er** leaf; sheet
blau blue (S2)
das **Blei** lead
bleiben, blieb, ist geblieben to stay, remain (3W)
der **Bleistift, -e** pencil (S2)
der **Blick (auf** + *acc.*) view (of), glance at
der **Blickpunkt, -e** focus
blind blind
blitzen to sparkle
der **Block, ̈-e** block
die **Blocka′de, -n** blockade
die **Blockflöte, -n** recorder (musical instrument)
blockie′ren to block
der **Blödsinn** nonsense
blond blond
bloß only; **was . . . ~?** what on earth . . . ?; **wie . . . ~?** how on earth?
blühen to flourish
die **Blume, -n** flower (2E)
die **Bluse, -n** blouse (S3)
der **Boden** ground, floor
die **Bohne, -n** bean (2W)
der **Bomber, -** bomber
der **Bonus, -se** bonus
das **Boot, -e** boat
borgen to borrow
böse angry, mad, upset

der **Bote, -n, -n** messenger
die **Bouti′que, -n** boutique
die **Bowle, -n** alcoholic punch
boxen to box
die **Branche, -n** branch
der **Braten, -** roast
die **Bratwurst, ̈-e** fried sausage
der **Brauch, ̈-e** custom
brauchen to need (S3)
brauen to brew
die **Brauerei, -en** brewery
braun brown (S2); **~ gebrannt** tanned
die **Braut, ̈-e** bride
der **Bräutigam, -e** bridegroom
das **Brautkleid, -er** wedding dress
die **BRD (Bundesrepublik Deutschland)** FRG (Federal Republic of Germany)
brechen (bricht), brach, gebrochen to break
der **Brei, -e** porridge
breit broad, wide
das **Brett, -er** board; **Schwarze ~** bulletin board
die **Brezel, -n** pretzel
der **Brief, -e** letter (8W)
der **Briefkasten, ̈** mailbox (8W)
brieflich by letter
die **Briefmarke, -n** stamp (8W)
der **Briefsortierer, -** mail sorter
der **Briefträger, -** mailman
die **Brille, -n** glasses
bringen, brachte, gebracht to bring (3W); **mit sich ~** to bring with it
die **Broschü′re, -n** brochure
das **Brot, -e** bread (2W)
das **Brötchen, -** roll (2W); **belegte ~** sandwich
der **Brotwürfel, -** small piece of bread, cube
die **Brücke, -n** bridge (5W)
der **Bruder, ̈** brother (1W)
das **Brüderchen, -** little brother
brummig grouchy
der **Brunnen, -** fountain
das **Buch, ̈-er** book (S2)
der **Bücherwurm, ̈-er** bookworm
die **Buchführung** bookkeeping
der **Buchhalter, -** bookkeeper

die **Buchhandlung, -en** bookstore (2W)
das **Büchlein, -** booklet, little book
buchstabie′ren to spell
die **Bude, -n** booth, stand; **Schieß~** shooting gallery
das **Büfett′, -s** dining room cabinet; buffet
das **Bügeleisen, -** iron (for clothes)
die **Bühne, -n** stage; **auf der ~** on stage
bummeln (ist) to stroll (5E)
der **Bund, ⸚e** confederation; federal government
die **Bundesbank** central bank
der **Bundesbürger, -** citizen of the Federal Republic
die **Bundesfeier, -n** Swiss national holiday
das **Bundesland, ⸚er** state, province
die **Bundespost** federal postal service
die **Bundesrepublik (BRD)** Federal Republic of Germany (FRG)
der **Bundesstaat, -en** federal state
bunt colorful; multicolored
die **Burg, -en** castle
der **Bürger, -** citizen (10E)
bürgerlich bourgeois, middle-class
der **Bürgersteig, -e** sidewalk
das **Bürgertum** citizenry
das **Büro′, -s** office (12W)
die **Bürokratie′** bureaucracy, red tape
die **Bürste, -n** brush
der **Bus, -se** bus (5W); **mit dem ~ fahren*** to take the bus (5W)
der **Busbahnhof, ⸚e** bus depot
der **Busch, ⸚e** bush
die **Butter** butter (2W)

C

das **Café′, -s** café (3W)
campen to camp; **~ gehen*** to go camping

der **Campingplatz, ⸚e** campground
die **CD, -s** CD, compact disc (9W)
der **Cellist′, -en, -en** cello player
das **Cello, -s** cello
das **Chaos** chaos
die **Charakterisie′rung, -en** characterization
charakteri′stisch characteristic
charmant′ charming (11W)
der **Charme** charm
der **Chauffeur′, -e** chauffeur
chauvini′stisch chauvinist
der **Chef, -s** boss
die **Chemie′** chemistry
die **Chemika′lie, -n** chemical
chemisch chemical(ly)
der **Chor, ⸚e** choir (10W)
der **Christbaum, ⸚e** Christmas tree
der **Christkindlmarkt, ⸚e** Christmas fair
der **Clown, -s** clown
die **Cola** cola drink, soft drink (2W)
das **College, -s** college
die **Combo, -s** (musical) band
der **Compu′ter, -** computer; **~künstler, -** graphic designer
computerisiert′ computerized
der **Contai′ner, -** container
die **Cornflakes** (pl.) Cornflakes, cereal
cremig creamy, smooth

D

da there (S2); **~ drüben** over there (5W)
dabei′ along; there; yet; **~ haben*** to have with you
das **Dach, ⸚er** roof
der **Dachboden, ⸚** attic
der **Dachdecker, -** roofer
der **Dachshund, -e** = **Dackel, -** dachshund
dafür for it; instead

dagegen against it; **Hast du etwas ~, wenn . . . ?** Do you mind, if . . . ?
daher therefore; from there
dahin: bis ~ until then
die **Dahlie, -n** dahlia
damals then, in those days (11W)
die **Dame, -n** lady (5W); **~ spielen** to play checkers (9W); **Sehr geehrte ~n und Herren!** Ladies and gentlemen!
danach later, after that (9W)
der **Däne, -n, -n / die Dänin, -nen** the Dane
(das) **Dänemark** Denmark
dänisch Danish
der **Dank: Vielen ~!** Thank you very much. (5W); **Gott sei ~!** Thank God!
dankbar grateful, thankful
danke thank you (S1); **~ schön!** Thank you very much; **~ gleichfalls!** Thanks, the same to you. (3W)
danken (+ *dat.*) to thank (3G); **Nichts zu ~!** You're welcome. My pleasure.
dann then (2W)
dar·stellen to portray
darum therefore; **eben ~** that's why
das that (S2)
dass (*conj.*) that (4G); **so ~** (*conj.*) so that (13E)
der **Dativ, -e** dative
das **Datum, Daten** (calendar) date (4W); **Welches ~ ist heute?** What date is today? (4W)
die **Dauer** length, duration
dauern to last (duration) (4W); **Wie lange dauert das?** How long does that take? (4W)
die **DDR (Deutsche Demokratische Republik)** German Democratic Republic (GDR)
dein (*sg. fam.*) your (1W)
die **Dekoration′, -en** decoration
dekorie′ren to decorate

der **Demokrat'**, -en, -en democrat
die **Demokratie'** democracy
demokra'tisch democratic
der **Demonstrant'**, -en, -en demonstrator
die **Demonstration'**, -en demonstration
demonstrie'ren to demonstrate
denken, dachte, gedacht to think (4W); **~ an** (+ *acc.*) to think of/about (10G)
der **Denker**, - thinker
das **Denkmal, ̈er** monument (15W)
denn because, for (2G); flavoring particle expressing curiosity, interest (7G)
der **Deo-Stift**, -e deodorant stick
die **Depression'**, -en (mental) depression
deshalb therefore (13E)
deswegen therefore
deutsch German
(das) **Deutsch: auf ~** in German (S2); **Sprechen Sie ~?** Do you speak German? (1W); **Hoch~** (standard) High German; **Platt~** Low German (dialect)
der **Deutsche (ein Deutscher) / die Deutsche**, -n, -n the German (1W, 12G)
die **Deutsche Demokratische Republik (DDR)** German Democratic Republic (GDR)
(das) **Deutschland** Germany (1W)
deutschsprachig German-speaking
der **Dezem'ber** December (S4); **im ~** in December (S4)
sich **drehen** to turn
d. h. (das heißt) that is (i.e.)
das **Dia**, -s slide (photograph)
der **Dialekt'**, -e dialect
der **Dialog'**, -e dialogue
dick thick, fat (S3); **~ machen** to be fattening (3E)
dienen to serve
der **Dienst**, -e service; **öffentliche ~** civil service

der **Dienstag** Tuesday (S4); **am ~** on Tuesday (S4)
dienstags on Tuesdays (2E)
dies- this, these (7G)
das **Diktat'**, -e dictation
die **Dimension'**, -en dimension
das **Ding**, -e thing (12E)
der **Dinosau'rier**, - dinosaur
das **Diplom'**, -e diploma (e.g., in natural and social sciences, engineering), M.A.; **der ~ingenieur'**, -e academically trained engineer
der **Diplomat'**, -en, -en diplomat
direkt' direct(ly)
die **Direkto'rin**, -nen (school), principal, manager
der **Dirigent'**, -en, -en (music) conductor
die **Diskothek'**, -en = **Disko**, -s discotheque
die **Diskussion'**, -en discussion
diskutie'ren to discuss
sich **distanzie'ren** to keep apart
die **Disziplin'** discipline
die **DM (Deutsche Mark)** German mark
doch yes (I do), indeed, sure (2W); yet, however, but; on the contrary; flavoring particle expressing concern, impatience, assurance (7G)
der **Dokumentar'film**, -e documentary film
der **Dollar**, - dollar (7W)
der **Dolmetscher**, - interpreter
der **Dom**, -e cathedral (5W)
dominie're to dominate
der **Donnerstag** Thursday (S4); **am ~** on Thursday (S4)
donnerstags on Thursdays (2E)
doppelt double
das **Doppelzimmer**, - double room (7W)
das **Dorf, ̈er** village (8E)
dort (over) there (4E)
die **Dose**, -n can
draußen outside, outdoors; **hier ~** out here; **weit ~** far out
die **Dreißigerin**, -nen woman in her 30s

die **Droge**, -n drug
die **Drogerie'**, -n drugstore (2E)
drohen to threaten
die **Drossel**, -n thrush (bird)
duften to smell good
dumm (ü) stupid, silly (10W,11W); **Das ist zu ~.** That's too bad.
die **Dummheit**, -en stupidity
der **Dummkopf, ̈e** dummy
das **Düngemittel**, - fertilizer
dunkel dark (6W); **~haarig** dark-haired; **im Dunkeln** in the dark(ness)
dünn thin, skinny (S3)
durch (+ *acc.*) through (2G); **mitten ~** right through
durchbre'chen* to break through, penetrate
der **Durchbruch** breaching; breakthrough
durcheinander mixed up, confused
durch·fallen* to flunk (an exam) (13W)
der **Durchschnitt** average; **im ~** on the average
dürfen (darf), durfte, gedurft to be allowed to, may (5W); **Was darf's sein?** May I help you?
der **Durst** thirst (2E); **Ich habe ~.** I'm thirsty. (2E)
die **Dusche**, -n shower
der **Duschvorhang, ̈e** shower curtain
(sich) **duschen** to take a shower (6W;9G)
das **Dutzend**, -e dozen
sich **duzen** to call each other *du*

E

die **Ebbe** low tide
eben after all, just (*flavoring particle*)
die **Ebene**, -n plain
ebenfalls also, likewise (12E)
echt authentic; real(ly), genuine(ly) (15W)
die **Ecke**, -n corner (6W)

egal′ the same **Es ist mir ~.** It doesn't matter. It's all the same to me.; **~ wie/wo** no matter how/where
die **Ehe, -n** marriage (11W)
ehemalig former
das **Ehepaar, -e** married couple
eher rather
die **Ehre** honor
ehrgeizlos without ambition
ehrlich honest (11W)
die **Ehrlichkeit** honesty
das **Ei, -er** egg (2W); **ein gekochtes~** boiled egg; **Rührei~** scrambled eggs; **Spiegel~** fried egg
die **Eidgenossenschaft** Swiss Confederation
das **Eigelb** egg yolk
eigen- own (12W)
die **Eigenschaft, -en** characteristic (11W)
eigentlich actual(ly) (4E); **~ schon** actually, yes
die **Eigentumswohnung, -en** condo (6E)
eilig hurried; **es ~ haben*** to be in a hurry
ein a, an (16G,7G); **die einen** the ones; **einer** one
einan′der each other
die **Einbahnstraße, -n** one-way street
der **Einbau** installation
der **Einblick, -e** insight
der **Eindruck, ⸚e** impression
einfach simple, simply (7E)
die **Einfahrt, -en** driveway; **Keine ~!** Do not enter.
einfarbig all one color
der **Einfluss, ⸚e** influence
die **Einfuhr** import
ein·führen to introduce; to import
die **Einführung, -en** introduction
sich **engagie′ren** to engage, commit oneself
einerseits on the one hand
der **Eingang, ⸚e** entrance (7W)
einig- *(pl. only)* some, a few (10G); **so ~es** all sorts of things

sich **einigen** (+ *acc.*) to agree (on)
ein·kaufen to shop; **~ gehen*** to go shopping (2E,7G)
die **Einkaufsliste, -n** shopping list
die **Einkaufstasche, -n** shopping bag
das **Einkaufszentrum, -zentren** shopping center
das **Einkommen, -** income (12W)
ein·laden* (**zu**) to invite (to) (11W)
die **Einladung, -en** invitation
sich **ein·leben** to settle down
ein·lösen to cash (in) (7G); **einen Scheck ~** to cash a check (7W)
einmal once, (at) one time; **noch ~** once more, again (S3); **auch ~** for once; **erst ~** first of all; **nicht ~** not even; **es war ~** once upon a time
einmalig unique (14W)
der **Einmarsch, ⸚e** entry, invasion
ein·packen to pack (in a suitcase)
ein·richten to furnish
die **Einrichtung, -en** furnishings and appliances
einsam lonely
ein·schlafen* to fall asleep
ein·schließen* to lock up
sich **ein·schreiben*** to register
das **Einschreibungsformular′, -e** application for university registration
sich **ein·setzen (für)** to support actively
einst once (14W)
ein·steigen* to get on or in (8W)
der **Eintritt** entrance fee
der **Einwohner, -** inhabitant
das **Einwohnermeldeamt, ⸚er** resident registration office
einzeln individual(ly) (15E)
das **Einzelzimmer, -** single room (7W)
einzig- only
das **Eis** ice, ice cream (3W)
eisern (made of) iron
eisig icy

eiskalt ice-cold
eitel vain
der **Elefant′, -en, -en** elephant
elegant′ elegant
der **Elek′triker, -** electrician
elek′trisch electric
die **Elektrizität′** electricity
der **Elek′tromecha′niker, -** electrical technician/mechanic
elektro′nisch electronic
die **Elek′trotech′nik** electrical engineering
das **Element′, -e** element
der **Ellbogen, -** elbow
die **Eltern** *(pl.)* parents (1W); **Groß~** grandparents (1W); **Schwieger~** parents-in-law; **Stief~** step-parents; **Urgroß~** great-grandparents
die **E-Mail, -s** e-mail (8W)
die **Emanzipation′** emancipation
emanzipiert′ emancipated
emotional′ emotional(ly)
empfangen* to receive
die **Empfangsdame, -n** receptionist
empfehlen (empfiehlt), empfahl, empfohlen to recommend (3W)
die **Empfehlung, -en** recommendation
empfindlich delicate; sensitive
das **Ende** end (10W); **am ~** in the end (10W); **zu ~ sein*** to be finished
enden to end
endlich finally (15E)
die **Endung, -en** ending
die **Energie′** energy
eng narrow
sich **engagie′ren** (**in** + *dat.*) to get involved (in)
der **Engel, -** angel
(das) **England** England (1W)
der **Engländer, -** the Englishman (1W)
englisch English
(das) **Englisch: auf ~** in English (S2); **Sprechen Sie ~?** Do you speak English? (1W)

enorm′ enormous; ~ **viel** an awful lot
die **Ente, -n** duck; **Lahme ~!** Poor baby! Lame duck!
entfernt away
entgegen·nehmen* to accept
enthalten* to contain
der **Enthusias′mus** enthusiasm
entlang along; **die Straße ~** along the street
sich **entscheiden, entschied, entschieden** to decide (13W)
die **Entscheidung, -en** decision (12E); **eine ~ treffen*** to make a decision
entschuldigen to excuse; ~ **Sie bitte!** Excuse me, please. (5W)
die **Entschuldigung, -en** excuse; **~!** Excuse me! Pardon me! (5W)
entsprechen* to correspond to
entstehen* (ist) to develop, be built
entwerten to cancel (ticket); devalue (currency)
(sich) **entwickeln** to develop; **sich auseinander ~** to develop apart
die **Entwicklung, -en** development
entzwei·brechen* to break apart
(sich) **entzwei·reißen*** to tear (oneself) apart
sich **erbauen an** (+ *dat.*) to be delighted about, enjoy
die **Erbse, -n** pea (2W)
das **Erdbeben, -** earthquake
die **Erdbeere, -n** strawberry (2W)
die **Erde** earth (12E); **unter der ~** underground
das **Erdbeben** earthquake
erfahren* to find out, learn
die **Erfahrung, -en** experience (12W)
der **Erfolg, -e** success
erfolgreich successful
sich **erfüllen** to be fulfilled, come true

ergänzen to supply, complete
ergreifen, ergriff, ergriffen to grab
erhalten* to keep up, preserve, maintain
die **Erhaltung** preservation (15W)
die **Erholung** recuperation, relaxation
erinnern (an + *acc.*) to remind (of) (14W)
sich **erinnern (an** + *acc.*) to remember (14W)
die **Erinnerung, -en (an** + *acc.*) reminder, memory of
erkalten (ist) to grow cold; *(poetic)* to become insensitive
sich **erkälten** to catch a cold (9G)
die **Erkältung, -en** cold
erkennen* to recognize (14E); **Zum ~** for recognition (only)
erklären to explain (12W)
die **Erklärung, -en** explanation
erlauben to permit, allow
die **Erlaubnis** permit, permission
erleben to experience (14E)
das **Erlebnis, -se** experience
die **Ermäßigung, -en** discount
die **Ernährung** nutrition
ernst serious(ly)
die **Ernte, -n** harvest
das **Erntedankfest** (Harvest) Thanksgiving
eröffnen to open up, establish
erreichen to reach
erscheinen* (ist) to appear, seem (4G)
erschrecken (erschrickt), erschrak, ist erschrocken to be frightened
ersetzen to replace
erst- first
erst only, not until
erwähnen to mention
erwärmen to heat (up)
erwarten to expect (12E)
erzählen (von + *dat.*) to tell (about) (10G); **nach•~** to retell
erziehen* to educate

die **Erziehung** education
der **Esel, -** donkey; **Du ~!** You dummy!
der **Esprit′** esprit
essbar edible
essen (isst), aß, gegessen to eat (S5)
das **Essen, -** food, meal (2W); **beim ~** while eating
das **Esszimmer, -** dining room (5W)
die **Etage, -n** floor
ethnisch ethnic
etwa about, approximately (10E)
etwas some, a little (2W); something (3W); **so ~ wie** s.th. like; **noch ~** one more thing, s.th. else; **Sonst noch ~?** Anything else?
euer *(pl. fam.)* your (7G)
der **Euro, -s** euro
(das) **Euro′pa** Europe
der **Europä′er, -** the European
europä′isch European
die **Europäisie′rung** Europeanization
euro′paweit all over Europe
der **Evangelist′, -en, -en** evangelist
ewig eternal(ly); **für ~** forever
exakt′ exact(ly)
das **Exa′men, -** exam
das **Exemplar′, -e** sample, copy
das **Exil′, -e** exile
existie′ren to exist
experimentell′ experimental
der **Exper′te, -n, -n / die Expertin, -nen** expert
extra extra
das **Extrablatt, ¨er** special edition

F

das **Fach, ¨er** subject (13W); **Haupt~** major (field) (13W); **Neben~** minor (field) (13W); **Schwerpunkt~** major (field)
der **Fachbereich, -e** field (of study)
die **Fachkenntnis, -se** special skill

die **Fach(ober)schule, -n** business or technical school
die **Fachrichtung, -en** specialization (13W)
das **Fachwerkhaus, ⸚er** half-timbered house
der **Faden, ⸚** thread
die **Fähigkeit, -en** ability
die **Fähre, -n** ferry
fahren (fährt), fuhr, ist gefahren to drive, go (by car, etc.) (3G)
die **Fahrerei′** (incessant) driving
die **Fahrkarte, -n** ticket (8W)
der **Fahrplan, ⸚e** schedule (of trains, etc.) (8W)
das **(Fahr)rad, ⸚er** bicycle (5W); **mit dem ~ fahren*** to ride a bike
der **(Fahr)radweg, -e** bike path
die **Fahrt, -en** trip, drive (8W)
fair fair
der **Fall, ⸚e** case; **auf jeden ~** in any case
fallen (fällt), fiel, ist gefallen to fall (4E); **~ lassen*** to drop
falsch wrong, false (S2)
die **Fami′lie, -en** family (1W)
der **Familienstand** marital status
fangen (fängt), fing, gefangen to catch
die **Fantasie′, -n** fantasy, imagination
fantas′tisch fantastic (9W)
die **Farbe, -n** color (S2); **Welche ~ hat . . . ?** What color is . . . ? (S2)
der **Farbstoff, -e** dye, (artificial) color
der **Fasching** carnival; **zum ~** for carnival (Mardi Gras)
die **Fassa′de, -n** façade
fast almost (6E)
die **Fastenzeit** Lent
die **Faszination′** fascination
faszinie′ren to fascinate
faul lazy (11W)
faulenzen to be lazy (9W)
die **Faulheit** laziness
das **Fax, -e** fax (8W)
das **Faxgerät, -e** fax machine

der **Februar** February (S4); **im ~** in February (S4)
fechten (ficht), focht, gefochten to fence
der **Federball, ⸚e** badminton (ball)
fehlen to be missing, lacking
fehlend missing
der **Fehler, -** mistake
feierlich festive
feiern to celebrate (4W)
der **Feiertag, -e** holiday (4W)
die **Feind, -e** enemy
feindlich hostile
das **Feld, -er** field
das **Fenster, -** window (S2)
die **Ferien** (pl.) vacation (4W)
der **Ferienplatz, ⸚e** vacation spot
fern far, distant
die **Ferne** distance
der **Fernfahrer, -** truck driver
das **Ferngespräch, -e** long-distance call
fern·sehen* to watch TV (9W)
das **Fernsehen** TV (the medium) (10W); **im ~** on TV (10W)
der **Fernseher, -** TV set (6W)
fertig finished, done (S5); **~ machen** to finish
das **Fest, -e** celebration (4W)
festgesetzt fixed
festlich festive
das **Festspiel, -e** festival
das **Feuer, -** fire
feuertrunken (poetic) fire-inspired; **wir betreten ~** fire-inspired we tread
das **Feuerwerk, -e** firework(s)
die **Figur′, -en** figure
der **Film, -e** film (10W)
filmen to shoot a film
die **Finan′zen** (pl.) finances
finanziell′ financial(ly)
finanzie′ren to finance (15W)
die **Finanzie′rung** financing
finden, fand, gefunden to find (S4); **Ich finde es . . .** I think it's . . . (S4); **Das finde ich auch.** I think so, too. (S4)
der **Finger, -** finger (9W)

der **Finne, -n, -n / die Finnin, -nen** the Finn
finnisch Finnish
die **Firma, Firmen** company, business (12W)
der **Fisch, -e** fish (2W); **ein kalter ~** a cold-hearted person
der **Fischfang** (industrial) fishing
fit: sich ~ halten* to keep in shape (9E)
das **Fitnessstudio, -s** health club
das **flach** flat
die **Fläche, -n** area
der **Flachs** flax
die **Flamme, -n** flame
die **Flasche, -n** bottle (3E); **eine ~ Wein** a bottle of wine (3E)
das **Fleisch** (sg.) meat (2W)
der **Fleischer, -** butcher
die **Fleischerei′, -en** butcher shop
der **Fleiß** industriousness; **Ohne ~ kein Preis.** No pain, no gain.
fleißig industrious(ly), hard-working (11W)
flexi′bel flexible
die **Flexibilität′** flexibility
fliegen, flog, ist geflogen to fly (8W); **mit dem Flugzeug ~** to go by plane (8W)
fliehen, floh, ist geflohen to flee, escape
fließen, floss, ist geflossen to flow
fließend fluent(ly)
das **Floß, -e** raft
die **Flöte, -n** flute, recorder
die **Flotte, -n** fleet
die **Flucht** escape
der **Flüchtling, -e** refugee
der **Flug, ⸚e** flight (8W)
der **Flügel, -** wing
der **Flughafen, ⸚** airport (8W)
die **Flugkarte, -n** plane ticket
der **Flugsteig, -e** gate
das **Flugzeug, -e** airplane (8W)
der **Flur** hallway, entrance foyer (6W)
der **Fluss, ⸚e** river (1W)
die **Flut** high tide
folgen (ist) (+ dat.) to follow
folgend following

der **Fokus** focus
der **Fön, -e** hair dryer
das **Fondue′, -s** fondue
fördern to encourage
die **Forel′le, -n** trout
die **Form, -en** form, shape
das **Formular′, -e** form
formulie′ren to formulate
der **Forschungszweig, -e** field of research
der **Förster, -** forest ranger
die **Forstwirtschaft** forestry
fotografie′ren to take pictures (9W)
die **Frage, -n** question (1W); **Ich habe eine ~.** I have a question. (S5); **eine ~ stellen** to ask a question (14W);
fragen to ask (S2); **sich ~** to wonder (9G)
fraglich questionable
(der) **Frankfurter Kranz** rich cake ring with whipped cream and nuts
(das) **Frankreich** France (1W)
der **Franzo′se, -n, -n / die Franzö′sin, -nen** French person (1W, 2G)
franzö′sisch French (1W)
(das) **Franzö′sisch; auf ~** in French (1W); **Ich spreche ~.** I speak French. (1W)
die **Frau, -en** Mrs., Ms. (S1); woman; wife (1W)
die **Frauenbewegung** women's movement
das **Fräulein, -** Miss, Ms.; young lady
frech impudent, sassy, fresh
die **Frechheit** impertinence
frei free, available (7W)
freiberuf′lich self-employed, free-lance
freigiebig generous
die **Freiheit** freedom
das **Freilichtspiel, -e** outdoor performance
frei·nehmen* to take time off
der **Freitag** Friday (S4); **am ~ on** Friday (S4); **Kar~** Good Friday
freitags on Fridays (2E)

freiwillig voluntary; voluntarily
die **Freizeit** leisure time (9W)
fremd foreign
das **Fremdenzimmer, -** guestroom
die **Fremd′sprache, -n** foreign language
der **Fremd′sprachenkorrespondent′, -en, -en** bilingual secretary
fressen (frisst), fraß, gefressen to eat (like a glutton or an animal); **auf·~** to devour
die **Freude, -n** joy
sich **freuen auf** (+ *acc.*) to look forward to (10G); **Freut mich.** I'm pleased to meet you. (S1); **(Es) freut mich auch.** Likewise, pleased to meet you, too; **Das freut mich für dich.** I'm happy for you.
der **Freund, -e** (boy)friend (3E)
die **Freundin, -nen** (girl)friend (3E)
freundlich friendly (11W)
die **Freundlichkeit** friendliness
die **Freundschaft, -en** friendship
der **Frieden** peace (14W)
friedlich peaceful(ly)
frieren, fror, gefroren to freeze
frisch fresh (2W)
der **Friseur′, -e** barber, hairdresser
die **Friseu′se, -n** beautician, hairdresser
froh glad, happy (11E)
fröhlich cheerful, merry
der **Fronleich′nam(stag)** Corpus Christi (holiday)
der **Frosch, ⸚e** frog
früh early, morning (8G)
früher earlier, once, former(ly) (12E)
der **Frühling, -e** spring (S4)
das **Frühjahrssemester, -** spring semester
das **Frühstück** breakfast (3W); **Was gibt's zum ~?** (What's) for breakfast? (3W)

frühstücken to eat breakfast (3W)
frustriert′ frustrated
die **Frustrie′rung** frustration
der **Fuchs, ⸚e** fox; **ein alter ~** a sly person
sich **fühlen** to feel (a certain way) (9W)
führen to lead (14W)
der **Führerschein, -e** drivers' license
die **Führung, -en** guided tour
die **Fülle** abundance
füllen to fill
die **Funktion′, -en** function
für (+ *acc.*) for (S2,2G); **was ~ ein . . . ?** what kind of a . . . ? (2W)
die **Furcht** fear, awe
furchtbar terrible, awful (S4)
sich **fürchten (vor** + *dat.*) to be afraid (of)
der **Fürst, -en, -en** sovereign, prince
der **Fuß, ⸚e** foot (9W); **zu ~ gehen*** to walk (5W)
der **Fußball, ⸚e** soccer (ball) (9W)
der **Fußgänger, -** pedestrian; **~überweg, -e** pedestrian crossing; **~weg, -e** side-walk; **~zone, -n** pedestrian area

G

die **Gabe, -n** gift; **in kleinen ~n** in small amounts/doses
die **Gabel, -n** fork (3W)
die **Galerie′, -n** gallery
die **Gams, ⸚en** mountain goat
die **Gans, ⸚e** goose; **eine dumme ~** a silly person (*fem.*)
ganz whole, entire(ly) (9E); very; **~ meinerseits.** The pleasure is all mine; **~ schön** quite (nice); **~tags** full-time
das **Ganze** he whole thing; **im Großen und ~n** on the whole
die **Gara′ge, -n** garage (6W)
garantie′ren to guarantee (15W)
die **Gardi′ne, -n** curtain

gar nicht not at all (13E)
der **Garten, ⸚** garden (6W)
das **Gartenstück, -e** garden plot
die **Gasse, -n** narrow street
Gassi gehen* to take a dog on a walk
der **Gast, ⸚e** guest (7W)
der **Gastarbeiter, -** foreign (guest) worker
das **Gästezimmer, -** guest room
das **Gasthaus, ⸚er** restaurant, inn
der **Gasthof, ⸚e** small hotel (7E)
die **Gaststätte, -n** restaurant, inn
die **Gastwirtschaft, -en** restaurant, inn
das **Gebäck** pastry
das **Gebäude, -** building (14W)
geben (gibt), gab, gegeben to give (3G); **es gibt** there is, there are (2W); **Was gibt's?** What's up?; **Was gibt's Neues?** What's new? (9W); **Was gibt's im . . . ?** What's (playing) on . . . ? (10W); **Das gibt's doch nicht!** That's not possible!
das **Gebiet, -e** area, region (15W)
gebildet well educated (11W)
geboren: Ich bin . . . ~ I was born . . . (S4); **Wann sind Sie ~?** When were you born? (S4); **Wann wurde . . . geboren?** When was . . . born?
gebrauchen to use, utilize
der **Gebrauchtwagen, -** used car
die **Gebühr, -en** fee
der **Geburtstag, -e** birthday (4W); **Wann haben Sie ~?** When is your birthday? (4W); **Ich habe am . . . (s)ten ~.** My birthday is on the . . . (date) (4W); **Ich habe im . . . ~.** My birthday is in . . . (month). (4W); **Herzlichen Glückwunsch zum ~!** Happy birthday!; **zum ~** at the/for the birthday (4W)
der **Geburtsort, -e** place of birth
der **Gedanke, -ns, -n** thought (14E)

das **Gedeck, -e** complete dinner; *also:* table setting
geduldig patient (11W)
die **Gefahr, -en** danger (12E)
gefährlich dangerous (15E)
das **Gefälle, -** decline
gefallen (gefällt), gefiel, gefallen (+ *dat.*) to like, be pleasing to (3G); **Es gefällt mir.** I like it. (3G)
das **Gefängnis, -se** prison
gefettet greased
der **Gefrierschrank, ⸚e** freezer
das **Gefühl, -e** feeling; **Mit~** compassion
gegen (+ *acc.*) against (2G); toward (time), around
die **Gegend, -en** area, region (8E)
der **Gegensatz, ⸚e** contrast, opposite
gegensätzlich opposing
das **Gegenteil, -e** opposite (S3); **im ~** on the contrary
gegenüber (von + *dat.*) across (from) (5W)
die **Gegenwart** present (tense)
das **Gehalt, ⸚er** salary
gehen, ging, ist gegangen to go, walk (S5); **Es geht mir . . .** I am (feeling) . . . (S1); **Wie geht's? Wie geht es Ihnen?** How are you? (S1); **zu Fuß ~** to walk (5W); **Das geht.** That's OK (13E); **Das geht nicht.** That's not OK. That doesn't work. (13E); **So geht's.** That's the way it goes.
gehören (+ *dat.*) to belong to (3G)
die **Geige, -n** violin
der **Geisteswissenschaftler, -** humanities scholar
geistig mentally, intellectual(ly)
geizig stingy
das **Geländer, -** railing
gelb yellow (S2)
das **Geld** money (7W); **Bar~** cash (7W); **Klein~** change (7W); **das Erziehungs~** government stipend for child care;

~ aus·geben* to spend money (9E)
der **Geldschein, -e** banknote (15E)
die **Gelegenheit, -en** opportunity, chance
gelten (gilt), galt, gegolten to apply to, be valid for, be true
das **Gemälde, -** painting (10W)
die **Gemeinde, -n** community
gemeinsam together, shared, joint(ly); (in) common (15E)
die **Gemeinschaft, -en** community
gemischt mixed
das **Gemüse, -** vegetable(s) (2W)
gemütlich cozy, pleasant, comfortable, convivial (5E)
die **Gemütlichkeit** nice atmosphere, coziness
genau exact(ly); **~so** the same; **~ wie** just like (9E)
die **Generation', -en** generation
generös' generous
genießen, genoss, genossen to enjoy
der **Genitiv, -e** genitive
genug enough (5E); **Jetzt habe ich aber ~.** That's enough. I've had it.
geöffnet open (7W)
die **Geographie'** geography
die **Geologie'** geology
das **Gepäck** baggage, luggage (7W)
gepunktet dotted
gerade just, right now (4W); **~ als** just when; **(immer) geradeaus'** (keep) straight ahead (5W)
die **Gerechtigkeit** justice
germa'nisch Germanic
die **Germani'stik** study of German language and literature
gern (lieber, liebst-) gladly (2W); **furchtbar ~** very much; **~ geschehen!** Glad to . . . ; **Ich hätte ~ . . .** I'd like to have . . . (2W)
die **Gesamtschule, -n** comprehensive high school
das **Geschäft, -e** store (2W); business (12W)

geschäftlich concerning business
die Geschäftsfrau, -en businesswoman (12W)
der Geschäftsmann, ̈-er businessman (12W); **die Geschäftsleute** business people (12W)
geschehen (geschieht), geschah, ist geschehen to happen (11E); **das geschieht dir recht.** That serves you right.
das Geschenk, -e present (4W)
die Geschichte, -n story, history (8E)
geschickt talented, skillful
geschieden divorced (11W)
das Geschlecht, -er gender, sex
geschlossen closed (7W)
das Geschrei screaming
die Geschwindigkeit, -en speed; **~sbegrenzung** speed limit
die Geschwister (pl.) brothers and/or sisters, siblings (1W)
gesellig sociable
die Gesellschaft, -en society
das Gesetz, -e law
gesetzlich legal(ly)
gesichert secure
das Gesicht, -er face (9W)
das Gespräch, -e conversation, dialogue
gestern yesterday (4W,8G)
gestreift striped
gesucht wird wanted
gesund (ü) healthy (9W)
die Gesundheit health
das Gesundheitsamt health department
der Gesundheitsfana′tiker, - health nut
geteilt divided; shared
das Getränk, -e beverage
getrennt separated, separately
die Gewalt violence
die Gewerkschaft, -en trade union
der Gewinn, -e profit, benefit
gewinnen, gewann, gewonnen to win (12E)
das Gewitter, - thunderstorm

sich **gewöhnen an** (+ acc.) to get used to (12W)
gewöhnlich usual(ly) (3E)
gierig greedy
gießen, goss, gegossen to pour
das Gift, -e poison
der Giftstoff, -e toxic waste (15W)
die Giraf′fe, -n giraffe
die Gitar′re, -n guitar (9W)
die Gladio′le, -n gladiola
das Glas, ̈-er glass (2E); **ein ~** a glass of (2E)
glauben to believe, think (2W;3G); **Ich glaube es/ihr.** I believe it/her.; **~ an** (+ acc.) to believe (in) (12W)
gleich equal, same (12W); right away; **Bis ~!** See you in a few minutes! (9W)
gleichberechtigt with equal rights
die Gleichberechtigung equality, equal rights
gleichfalls: Danke ~! Thank you, the same to you. (3W)
das Gleis, -e track (8W)
der Gletscher, - glacier
die Glocke, -n bell
glorreich glorious
das Glück luck; **~ haben*** to be lucky (4E); **Viel ~!** Good luck!; **Du ~spilz!** You lucky thing!
glücklich happy (11W)
der Glückwunsch, ̈-e congratulation; **Herzliche Glückwünsche!** Congratulations! Best wishes! (4W)
der Glühwein mulled wine
der Gnom, -e gnome, goblin
das Gold gold (11E)
golden golden
der Goldfisch, -e gold fish
(das) **Golf** golf; **Mini~** miniature golf
der Gott God; **~ sei Dank!** Thank God!; **Um ~es willen!** For Heaven's sake! My goodness!
der Gott, ̈-er god; **schöner Götterfunken** beautiful bright spark of divinity
der Grad, -e degree

die Gramma′tik grammar
gramma′tisch grammatical(ly)
gratulie′ren (+ dat.) to congratulate (4W); **Wir ~!** Congratulations.
grau gray (S2)
die Grenze, -n border (14W)
grenzen (an + acc.) to border, share a border with
grenzenlos unlimited, endless
der Grieche, -n, -n / die Griechin, -nen the Greek
(das) **Griechenland** Greece
griechisch Greek
die Grippe flu
groß (größer, größt-) large, big, tall (S3); **im Großen und Ganzen** on the whole, by and large
die Größe, -n size, height
die Großeltern (pl.) grandparents (1W); **Ur~** great-grandparents
das Großmaul, ̈-er big mouth
die Großmutter, ̈ grandmother (1W); **Ur~** great-grandmother
der Großteil major part/portion
der Großvater, ̈ grandfather (1W); **Ur~** great-grandfather
Grüezi! Hi! (in Switzerland)
grün green (S2); **ins Grüne / im Grünen** out in(to) nature
der Grund, ̈-e reason; **aus diesem ~** for that reason
gründen to found
das Grundgesetz constitution, basic law
die Grundschule, -n elementary school, grades 1–4
die Gründung, -en founding
die Grünfläche, -n green area
das Grundstück, -e building lot
die Gruppe, -n group
der Gruß, ̈-e greeting; **Viele Grüße (an** + acc.). . . ! Greetings (to . . .)!
grüßen to greet; **Grüß dich!** Hi!; **Grüß Gott!** Hello! Hi! (in southern Germany)
der Gummi rubber
gurgeln to gargle

die **Gurke, -n** cucumber (2W); **saure ~** pickle
gut (besser, best-) good, fine (S1); **~ aussehend** good-looking (11W); **Das ist noch mal ~ gegangen.** Things worked out all right (again); **na ~** well, all right; **Mach's ~!** Take care. (4W)
das **Gute: Alles ~!** All the best.
die **Güte** goodness; **Ach du meine ~!** My goodness! (8W)
das **Gymna′sium, Gymna′sien** academic high school (grades 5-13)

H

das **Haar, -e** hair (9W)
haben (hat), hatte, gehabt to have (S5,2G); **Ich hätte gern . . .** I'd like (to have) . . . (2W)
das **Habitat, -e** habitat
der **Hafen, ¨** port
der **Haken, -** hook
halb half (to the next hour) (S5); **~tags** part-time; **in einer ~en Stunde** in half an hour (8W)
die **Hälfte, -n** half
die **Halle, -n** large room for work, recreation, or assembly
Hallo! Hello! Hi!
der **Hals, ¨e** neck, throat (9W); **Das hängt mir zum ~ heraus.** I'm fed up (with it).
halten (hält), hielt, gehalten to hold, stop (a vehicle) (5W); **~ von** to think of, be of an opinion (10G)
die **Haltestelle, -n** (bus, etc.) stop (5W)
das **Halteverbot, -e** no stopping or parking
der **Hamster, -** hamster
die **Hand, ¨e** hand (3E,9W)
die **Handarbeit, -en** needlework
der **Handball, ¨e** handball
der **Handel** trade (12E)
die **Handelsbeziehung, -en** trade relation(s)

die **Handelsnation′, -en** trading nation
der **Handschuh, -e** glove
das **Handtuch, ¨er** towel
der **Handwerker, -** craftsman
das **Handy, -s** cellular phone
hängen to hang (up) (6W)
hängen, hing, gehangen to hang (be hanging) (6W)
harmo′nisch harmonious
hart (ä) hard; tough
hassen to hate
hässlich ugly (11W)
die **Hässlichkeit** ugliness
das **Hauptfach, ¨er** major (field of study) (13W)
der **Hauptmann, ¨er** captain
die **Hauptrolle, -n** leading role
die **Hauptsache, -n** main thing
hauptsächlich mainly
die **Hauptsaison** (high) season
die **Hauptschule, -n** basic secondary school (grades 5–9)
die **Hauptstadt, ¨e** capital (1W)
die **Hauptstraße, -n** main street
das **Hauptwort, ¨er** noun
das **Haus, ¨er** house (6W); **nach ~e** (toward) home (3W); **zu ~e** at home (3W); **das Zuhause** home
das **Häuschen, -** little house
die **Hausfrau, -en** housewife (12W)
der **Haushalt, -e** household
die **Haushälterin, -nen** housekeeper
häuslich home-loving, domestic
die **Hauswirtschaft** home economics
das **Heft, -e** notebook (S2)
heilig holy; **Aller~en** All Saints' Day; **~e Drei Könige** Epiphany
der **Heiligabend** Christmas Eve; **am ~** on Christmas Eve
das **Heiligtum** shrine, sanctuary
die **Heimat** homeland, home (14E)
der **Heimcomputer, -** home computer
heiraten to marry, get married (11W)

heiratslustig eager to marry
heiß hot (S4)
heißen, hieß, geheißen to be called; **Ich heiße . . .** My name is . . . (S1); **Wie ~ Sie?** What's your name? (S1)
die **Heizung** heating (system)
das **Heiz′material′** heating material, fuel
helfen (hilft), half, geholfen (+ *dat.*) to help (3G)
hell light, bright (6W); **Sei ~e!** Be smart!
das **Hemd, -en** shirt (S3)
die **Henne, -n** hen
herab′·blicken (auf + acc.) to look down (on)
heran′- up to
der **Herbst, -e** fall, autumn (S4)
der **Herd, -e** (kitchen) range
herein′- in(to)
herein·kommen* to come in, enter (11E)
herein·lassen* to let in
die **Herkunft** origin
der **Herr, -n, -en** Mr., gentleman (S1,2G); Lord; **Sehr geehrte Damen und ~en!** Ladies and gentlemen!
herrlich wonderful, great (8E)
herum′- around
herum·laufen* to run around
herum·reisen (ist) to travel around
das **Herz, -ens, -en** heart; **mit ~** with feelings
der **Heurige, -n** (*sg.*) new wine
die **Heurigenschänke, -n** Viennese wine-tasting inn
heute today (S4); **für ~** for today (S2)
heutig- of today
hier here (S2)
die **Hilfe, -n** help (15E)
hilfsbereit helpful
der **Himmel** sky; heaven; **~fahrt(stag)** Ascension (Day)
himmlisch heavenly
der **Himmlische (ein Himmlischer) / die Himmlische, -n, -n** Heavenly one

hin und her back and forth
hinauf·fahren* to go or drive up (to) (8E)
hinein·gehen* to go in(to), enter
hin·legen to lay or put down; **sich ~** to lie down (9G)
hin·nehmen* to accept
sich **(hin·)setzen** to sit down (9G)
hinter (+ *acc./dat.*) behind (6G)
hinterlassen* to leave behind
die **(Hin- und) Rückfahrkarte, -n** round trip ticket (8W)
hinun'ter·fahren* to drive down
histo'risch historical(ly) (14W)
das **Hobby, -s** hobby (9W)
hoch (hoh-) (höher, höchst-) high(ly) (12W)
das **Hochhaus, ⸚er** high-rise building
hoch·legen to put up (high)
die **Hochschule, -n** university, college
die **Hochzeit, -en** wedding (11W)
(das) **Hockey** hockey
der **Hof, ⸚e** court, courtyard
hoffen to hope (12E)
hoffentlich hopefully, I hope (5E)
die **Hoffnung, -en** hope
höflich polite(ly)
die **Höhe, -n** height, altitude; **Das ist doch die ~!** That's the limit!
der **Höhepunkt, -e** climax
hohl hollow
die **Höhle, -n** cave
holen (go and) get, pick up, fetch (13W)
der **Holländer, -** the Dutchman
holländisch Dutch
die **Hölle** hell
das **Holz** wood
hoppla hoops, whoops
hörbar audible
hören to hear (S2)
der **Hörer, -** listener; receiver
der **Hörsaal, -säle** lecture hall (13W)

das **Hörspiel, -e** radio play
die **Hose, -n** slacks, pants (S3)
das **Hotel', -s** hotel (5W,7W)
hübsch pretty (11W)
der **Hügel, -** hill
das **Hühnchen, -** chicken
der **Humor'** (sense of) humor
der **Hund, -e** dog; **Fauler ~!** Lazy bum!
hundert hundred; **Hunderte von** hundreds of
der **Hunger** hunger (2E); **Ich habe ~.** I'm hungry. (2E)
hungrig hungry
hüpfen (ist) to hop
der **Hut, ⸚e** hat
die **Hütte, -n** hut, cottage

I

ideal' ideal
das **Ideal', -e** ideal
der **Idealis'mus** idealism
die **Idee', -n** idea (9W)
sich **identifizie'ren** to identify oneself
iden'tisch identical
die **Identität', -en** identity
idyl'lisch idyllic
ignorie'ren to ignore
ihr her, its, their (7G)
Ihr (*formal*) your (1W,7G)
die **Imbissbude, -n** snack bar, fast-food stand
die **Immatrikulation'** enrollment (at university)
immer always (4E); **~ geradeaus** always straight ahead (5W); **~ länge** longer and longer (12G); **~ noch** still; **~ wieder** again and again (12G)
der **Imperativ, -e** imperative
das **Imperfekt** imperfect, simple past
in (+ *acc./dat.*) in, into, inside of (6G)
inbegriffen in (+ *dat.*) included in
der **India'ner, -** the Native American
der **In'dikativ** indicative
in'direkt indirect(ly)

die **Individualität'** individuality
individuell' individual(ly)
die **Industrie', -n** industry
der **Industrie'kaufmann, -leute** industrial manager
industriell' industrial
das **Industrie'unternehmen, -** large industrial company
der **Infinitiv, -e** infinitive
die **Informa'tik** computer science
die **Information', -en** information
die **Informations'suche** search for information
informativ' informative
(sich) **informie'ren (über** + *acc.*) to inform, get informed (about) (10G)
der **Ingenieur', -e** engineer (12W)
die **Initiati've, -n** initiative
innen (*adv.*) inside
der **Innenhof, ⸚e** inner court
die **Innenstadt, ⸚e** center (of town), downtown
inner- inner
innerhalb within
die **Insel, -n** island (14E)
das **Institut', -e** institute
das **Instrument', -e** instrument; **Musik~** musical instrument
die **Inszenie'rung, -en** production
intellektuell' intellectual(ly)
intelligent' intelligent (11W)
die **Intelligenz'** intelligence
intensiv' intensive
interessant' interesting (5E); **etwas Interessantes** s.th. interesting
das **Interes'se, -n (an** + *dat.*) interest (in)
sich **interessie'ren für** to be interested in (10G)
international' international
interpretie'ren to interpret
das **Interview, -s** interview
interviewen to interview
in'tolerant intolerant
das **Inventar', -e** inventory
inzwi'schen in the meantime

irgendwie somehow (11W)
irgendwo somewhere
(das) **Ita′lien** Italy (1W)
der **Italie′ner, -** the Italian (1W)
italie′nisch Italian (1W)

J

ja yes (S1); flavoring particle expressing emphasis (7G)
die **Jacke, -n** jacket, cardigan (S3)
der **Jäger, -** hunter
das **Jahr, -e** year (S4)
jahrelang for years
die **Jahreszeit, -en** season
das **Jahrhun′dert, -e** century
-jährig years old; years long
das **Jahrtau′send, -e** millennium (15E)
jammern to complain, grieve
der **Januar** January (S4); **im ~ in** January (S4)
je (+ *comp.*) **. . . desto** (+ *comp.*) **. . . the . . . the . . .** (12G); **~ nachdem′** depending on
die **Jeans** (*pl.*) jeans (S3)
jed- (*sg.*) each, every (7G)
jedenfalls in any case (13E)
jeder everyone, everybody
jederzeit any time
der **Jeep, -s** jeep
jemand someone, somebody (11W)
jetzt now (S5)
der **Job, -s** job
jobben to have a job that is not one's career
joggen to jog; **~ gehen*** to go jogging
das **Joghurt, -s** yogurt
der **Journalist′, -en, -en** journalist (12W)
das **Jubilä′um, Jubilä′en** anniversary
der **Jude, -n, -n** Jew / die **Jüdin, -nen** Jew
das **Judentum** Jewry
jüdisch Jewish
(das) **Judo: ~ kämpfen** to do judo
die **Jugend** youth (14E)

die **Jugendherberge, -n** youth hostel (7E)
der **Juli** July (S4); **im ~** in July (S4)
jung (ü) young (11W)
der **Junge, -n, -n** boy (1W,2G)
der **Junggeselle, -n, -n** bachelor
der **Juni** June (S4 **im ~** in June (S4)
Jura: Er studiert ~. He's studying law.

K

das **Kabarett′, -e** (*or* **-s**) cabaret
das **Kabelfernsehen** cable TV
der **Kaffee, -s** coffee (2W); **~ mit Schlag** coffee with whipped cream
der **Kaffeeklatsch** coffeeklatsch, chatting over a cup of coffee (and cake)
der **Kaiser, -** emperor
der **Kaka′o** hot chocolate
das **Kalb, ¨er** calf; **die ~sleber** calves' liver
der **Kalen′der, -** calendar
kalt (ä) cold (S4); **~ oder warm?** with or without heat?
die **Kälte** cold(ness)
die **Kamera, -s** camera
der **Kamin′, -e** fireplace, chimney
der **Kamm, ¨e** comb
(sich) **kämmen** to comb (o.s.) (9G)
die **Kammer, -n** chamber
der **Kampf, ¨e (um)** fight, struggle (for)
kämpfen to fight, struggle
(das) **Kanada** Canada (1W)
der **Kana′dier, -** the Canadian (1W)
kana′disch Canadian (1W)
der **Kanal′, ¨e** channel
das **Känguru, -s** kangaroo
die **Kanti′ne, -n** cafeteria (at a workplace)
der **Kanton′, -e** canton
das **Kanu′, -s** canoe
der **Kanzler, -** chancellor
kapitali′stisch capitalist

das **Kapi′tel, -** chapter
kaputt′ broken
kaputt·gehen* to get broken, break
der **Karfreitag** Good Friday
kariert′ checkered
der **Karneval** carnival
die **Karot′te, -n** carrot (2W)
die **Karrie′re, -n** career
die **Karte, -n** ticket (8W); card (9W); **~n spielen** to play cards (9W)
die **Kartof′fel, -n** potato (3W); **der ~brei** (*sg.*) mashed potatoes; **die ~chips** (*pl.*) potato chips; **das ~mehl** potato flour, starch; **der ~salat** potato salad
der **Käse** cheese (2W); **Das ist (doch) ~!** That's nonsense.
die **Kasse, -n** cash register, cashier's window (7W)
das **Kasseler Rippchen, -** smoked loin of pork
die **Kasset′te, -n** cassette (9W)
die **Kassie′rer, -** cashier; clerk, teller
die **Katze, -n** cat; **(Das ist) alles für die Katz′!** (That's) all for nothing!
kaufen to buy (2W)
das **Kaufhaus, ¨er** department store (2W)
der **Kaufmann, -leute** merchant
kaum hardly (14W)
kein no, not a, not any (1G)
der **Keller, -** basement
der **Kellner, -** waiter (3W)
die **Kellnerin, -nen** waitress (3W)
kennen, kannte, gekannt to know, be acquainted with (6G)
kennen lernen to get to know, meet (7E)
der **Kenner, -** connoisseur
die **Kenntnis, -se** knowledge, skill (12E)
der **Kerl, -e** guy
der **Kern, -e** core
die **Kerze, -n** candle (4E)
die **Kette, -n** chain, necklace

die **Ket′tenreaktion′, -en** chain reaction
das **Kilo, -s (kg)** kilogram
der **Kilome′ter, - (km)** kilometer
das **Kind, -er** child (1W)
der **Kindergarten, ⸚** kindergarten
der **Kindergärtner, -** kindergarten teacher
kinderlieb loves children
das **Kinn, -e** chin
das **Kino, -s** movie theater (5W)
die **Kirche, -n** church (5W)
die **Kirsche, -n** cherry
klagen to complain
die **Klammer, -n** parenthesis
klappen to work out
klar clear; **(na)** ~! Sure! Of course! (13W)
die **Klasse, -n** class
die **Klas′senkamerad′, -en, -en** classmate
das **Klassentreffen, -** class reunion
das **Klassenzimmer, -** classroom
klassisch classical
klatschen to clap (10W); to gossip
das **Klavier′, -e** piano (9W)
das **Kleid, -er** dress (S3)
der **(Kleider)bügel, -** clothes hanger
der **Kleiderschrank, ⸚e** closet
die **Kleidung** clothing (S3)
der **Klei′dungsarti′kel, -** article of clothing
klein small, little, short (S3)
das **Kleingeld** change (7W)
der **Klient′, -en, -en [Kli:ent′]** client
das **Klima, -s** climate
die **Klimaanlage, -n** air conditioning
klingeln to ring a bell
klingen, klang, geklungen to sound; **(Das) klingt gut.** (That) sounds good. (6W)
das **Klo, -s** toilet
klopfen to knock
der **Kloß, ⸚e** dumpling
das **Kloster, ⸚** monastery; convent
der **Klub, -s** club
klug (ü) smart, clever

knabbern to nibble
der **Knabe, -n, -n** boy
die **Knappheit** shortage
die **Kneipe, -n** pub
das **Knie, -** knee (9W)
der **Knirps, -e** little fellow, dwarf
der **Knoblauch** garlic
der **Knöd(e)l, -** dumpling (in southern Germany)
der **Knopf, ⸚e** button
der **Knoten, -** knot
knuspern to nibble
der **Koch, ⸚e / die Köchin, -nen** cook
kochen to cook (6W)
der **Koffer, -** suitcase (7W)
der **Kolle′ge, -n, -n / die Kolle′gin, -nen** colleague; **Zimmer~** roommate (13W)
die **Kolonialisie′rung** colonization
kombinie′ren to combine
der **Komfort′** comfort
komisch funny (strange, comical) (10W)
das **Komitee, -s** committee
kommen, kam, ist gekommen to come (1W); **Komm rüber!** Come on over!
der **Kommentar′, -e** commentary
kommentie′ren to comment
kommerziell′ commercial
die **Kommo′de, -n** dresser (6W)
kommunis′tisch communist
der **Kom′parativ, -e** comparative
kompliziert′ complicated (11W)
komponie′ren to compose
der **Komponist′, -en, -en** composer (10W)
das **Kompott′, -e** stewed fruit
der **Kompromiss′, -e** compromise
die **Konditorei′, -en** pastry shop
die **Konferenz′, -en** conference
der **Konflikt′, -e** conflict
der **Kongress′, -sse** conference
der **König, -e** king (11E); **Heilige Drei ~e** Epiphany (Jan. 6)
die **Königin, -nen** queen (11E)
das **Königreich, -e** kingdom
die **Konjunktion′, -en** conjunction

der **Kon′junktiv** subjunctive
die **Konkurrenz′** competition
können (kann), konnte, gekonnt to be able to, can (5G)
die **Konsequenz′, -en** consequence
das **Konservie′rungsmittel, -** preservative
das **Konsulat′, -e** consulate
die **Kontakt′linse, -n** contact lense
das **Konto, -s (or Konten)** account
der **Kontrast′, -e** contrast
die **Kontrol′le, -n** control
kontrollie′ren to control, check
die **Konversation′, -en** conversation; **~sstunde, -n** conversation lesson
das **Konzentrations′lager, -** concentration camp
sich **konzentrie′ren (auf +** *acc.***)** to concentrate (on)
das **Konzert′, -e** concert (10W)
die **Kooperation′** cooperation
der **Kopf, ⸚e** head (9W)
kopf·stehen* to stand on one's head
die **Kopie′, -n** copy
der **Kopie′rer, -** copying machine
der **Korb, ⸚e** basket
der **Korbball, ⸚e** basketball
der **Körper, -** body (9W)
körperlich physical(ly)
der **Korrespondent′, -en, -en** correspondent
korrigie′ren to correct
kosten to cost; **Was ~ . . . ?** How much are . . . ? (S3); **Das kostet (zusammen) . . .** That comes to . . . (S3)
die **Kosten** (*pl.*) cost
kostenlos free (of charge)
das **Kostüm′, -e** costume; woman's suit
die **Krabbe, -n** crab
der **Kracher, -** firecracker
die **Kraft, ⸚e** strength, power

die **Kralle, -n** claw
der **Kran, ⸚e** crane
krank (ä) sick, ill (9W)
der **Kranke (ein Kranker) / die Kranke, -n, -n** sick person (12G)
die **Kran′kengymna′st, -en, -en** physical therapist
das **Krankenhaus, ⸚er** hospital
die **Krankenkasse, -n** health insurance
die **Krankenpflege** nursing
der **Krankenpfleger, -** male nurse (12W)
die **Krankenschwester, -n** nurse (12W)
die **Krankheit, -en** sickness
der **Kranz, ⸚e** wreath
der **Krapfen, -** doughnut
der **Kratzer, -** scratch
die **Krawatte, -n** tie
kreativ′ creative
die **Kreativität′** creativity
der **Krebs, -e** crab; cancer
die **Kredit′karte, -n** credit card
die **Kreide** chalk (S2)
der **Kreis, -e** circle; county
die **Kreuzung, -en** intersection
das **Kreuzworträtsel, -** crossword puzzle
der **Krieg, -e** war (14W)
der **Kri′tiker, -** critic
der **Krimi, -s** detective story (10W)
der **Krimskrams** old junk
der **Kritiker, -** critic
kritisch critical(ly)
kritisie′ren to criticize
die **Krone, -n** crown
krönen to crown
die **Küche, -n** kitchen (6W); cuisine
der **Kuchen, -** cake (2W)
die **Kugel, -n** ball, sphere
kühl cool (S4)
der **Kühlschrank, ⸚e** refrigerator (6W)
der **Kuli, -s** pen (S2)
die **Kultur′, -en** culture
kulturell′ cultural(ly) (14W)
sich **kümmern (um)** to take care (of)

die **Kunst, ⸚e** art (10W)
der **Künstler, -** artist (12W); **Computer~** graphic designer
der **Kurfürst, -en, -en** elector
der **Kurort, -e** health resort, spa
der **Kurs, -e** course (S5)
kurz (ü) short (S3); **~ vor** shortly before; **vor ~em** recently
die **Kürze** shortness, brevity
das **Kurzgespräch, -e** brief conversation
die **Kusi′ne, -n** (fem.) cousin (1W)
küssen to kiss
die **Küste, -n** coast (15W)

L

das **Labor′, -s** (or **-e**) lab (13W)
der **Laboran′t, -en, -en** lab assistant
lachen to laugh (10W)
lächerlich ridiculous
laden (lädt), lud, geladen to load
der **Laden, ⸚** store; **Bio-~ /grüne ~** environmental store; **Tante-Emma-~** small grocery store
die **Lage, -n** location
lahm lame
das **Lamm, ⸚er** lamb
die **Lampe, -n** lamp (6W); **Hänge~** hanging lamp; **Steh~** floor lamp
das **Land, ⸚er** country, state (1W); **auf dem ~(e)** in the country (6E); **aufs ~** in(to) the country(side) (6E)
landen (ist) to land (8W)
die **Landeskunde** cultural and geographical study of a country
die **Landkarte, -n** map (1W)
die **Landschaft, -en** landscape, scenery (15W)
die **Landung, -en** landing
der **Landwirt, -e** farmer
die **Landwirtschaft** agriculture
landwirtschaftlich agricultural

lang (ä) (adj.) long (S3)
lange (adv.) long, for a long time; **noch ~ nicht** not by far; **schon ~ (nicht mehr)** (not) for a long time; **wie ~?** how long? (4W)
langsam slow(ly) (S3)
sich **langweilen** to get/be bored (9E)
langweilig boring, dull (10W)
lassen (lässt), ließ, gelassen to leave (behind) (7W)
die **Last, -en** burden
(das) **Latein′** Latin
laufen (läuft), lief, ist gelaufen to run, walk (3G)
laut loud(ly), noisy (4E;7W); **Sprechen Sie ~er!** Speak up. (S3)
läuten to ring
der **Lautsprecher, -** loudspeaker
leben to live (6E)
das **Leben** life (9E)
lebend living; **etwas Lebendes** something living
lebendig alive
die **Lebensfreude** joy of living
lebensfroh cheerful, full of life
die **Lebensmittel** (pl.) groceries (2W)
der **Lebenslauf, ⸚e** resumé, curriculum vitae
der **Lebensstandard** standard of living
die **Leber, -n** liver
der **Leberkäse** (Bavarian) meat loaf made from minced pork
der **Lebkuchen, -** gingerbread
das **Leder** leather
die **Lederhose, -n** leather pants
ledig single (11W)
leer empty (14E)
legen to lay, put (flat) (6W); **sich (hin)•~** to lie down (9G)
das **Lehrbuch, ⸚er** textbook
die **Lehre, -n** apprenticeship
lehren to teach (13W)
der **Lehrer, -** teacher (12W)
der **Lehrling, -e** apprentice
die **Lehrstelle, -n** apprenticeship (position)

leicht light, easy, easily (6E)
das **Leid** misery; **Es tut mir ~.** I'm sorry. (5W)
die **Leidenschaft, -en** passion
leider unfortunately (5E)
leihen, lieh, geliehen to lend
die **Leine, -n** leash
leise quiet(ly), soft(ly)
leisten to achieve
leiten to direct
die **Leiter, -n** ladder
das **Leitungswasser** tap water
lernen to learn, study (S2)
der **Lerntipp, -s** study suggestion
das **Lernziel, -e** learning objective
lesbar legible
lesen (liest), las, gelesen to read (S2); **~ Sie laut!** Read aloud. (SSS)
der **Leser, -** reader
die **Leseratte, -n** bookworm
der **Lesesaal, -säle** reading room
letzt- last (10W)
(das) **Letzeburgisch** Luxembourg dialect
die **Leute** (*pl.*) people (1W)
licht (*poetic*) light
das **Licht, -er** light; **ins ~ treten*** to step out into the light
die **Lichterkette, -n** candlelight march
lieb- dear (5E)
die **Liebe** love (11W)
lieben to love (6E)
lieber rather (12G); **Es wäre mir ~, wenn . . .** I would prefer it, if . . .
der **Liebling, -e** darling, favorite; **~sdichter** favorite poet; **~sfach** favorite subject
liebst-: am ~en best of all (12G)
das **Lied, -er** song (4E); **Volks~** folk song
liegen, lag, gelegen to lie, be (located) (1W); be lying (flat) (6W)
der **Liegestuhl, -e** lounge chair
lila purple
die **Lilie, -n** lily, iris
die **Limona'de, -n** soft drink, lemonade (2W)

die **Lingui'stik** linguistics
die **Linie, -n** line
link- left; **auf der ~en Seite** on the left
links left (5W); **erste Straße ~** first street to the left (5W)
die **Linse, -n** lentil; lense
die **Lippe, -n** lip
der **Lippenstift, -e** lipstick
der **Liter, -** liter
das **Loch, -̈er** hole
locken to lure, attract
der **Löffel, -** spoon (3W); **ein Ess~** one tablespoon (of); **ein Tee~** teaspoon
logisch logical
lokal' local(ly)
los: ~·werden* to get rid of; **etwas ~ sein*** to be happening, going on; **Was ist ~?** What's the matter? (9W)
lose loose
lösen to solve
die **Lösung, -en** solution
der **Löwe, -n, -n/die Löwin, -nen** lion
die **Luft** air (14E)
die **Luftbrücke** airlift
der **Luftangriff** air raid
die **Luftpost** airmail; **der ~leichtbrief, -e** aerogram; **per ~** by airmail
die **Luftverschmutzung** air pollution
die **Lüge, -n** lie
die **Lust** inclination, desire, fun; **Ich habe (keine) ~ (zu) . . .** I (don't) feel like (doing s.th.) . . . (9W)
lustig funny (4E) **reise~** eager to travel
luxemburgisch Luxembourgish
luxuriös' luxurious
der **Luxus** luxury

M

machen to make, do (2W); **Spaß ~** to be fun (4E); **Mach's gut!** Take care! (4W); **Was machst du Schönes?** What are you doing?; **(Das) macht nichts.** (That) doesn't matter. That's OK. (5E); **das macht zusammen** that comes to
die **Macht, -̈e** power (14E); **die Westmächte** (*pl.*) western Allies
das **Mädchen, -** girl (1W)
das **Magazin', -e** magazine; feature (e.g., on TV)
die **Magd, -̈e** maid
der **Magi'ster, -** M.A.
die **Mahlzeit, -en** meal; **~!** Enjoy your meal (food)!
das **Mahnmal, -e** memorial (of admonishment)
der **Mai** May (S4); **im ~** in May (S4)
der **Mais** corn
der **Makler, -** (real-estate) agent, broker
mal times, multiplied by
das **Mal, -e: das erste ~** the first time (11E); **zum ersten ~** for the first time (11E); **~ sehen!** Let's see. (13W)
malen to paint (10W)
der **Maler, -** painter (10W)
man one (they, people, you) (3E)
das **Management** management
manch- many a, several, some (7G)
manchmal sometimes (3E)
manipuliert' manipulated
der **Mann, -̈er** man, husband (1W)
das **Männchen, -** midget, dwarf
männlich masculine, male
die **Mannschaft, -en** team
der **Mantel, -̈** coat (S3)
das **Manuskript', -e** manuscript
das **Märchen, -** fairy tale
die **Margari'ne, -n** margarine
die **Mari'ne, -n** navy
die **Mark (DM)** mark (S3); **zwei ~** two marks (S3)
der **Markt, -̈e** market (2W)
die **Marmela'de, -n** marmalade, jam (2W)
der **März** March (S4); **im ~** in March (S4)

die **Maschi′ne, -n** machine
der **Maschi′nenbau** mechanical engineering
die **Maske, -n** mask
die **Massa′ge, -n** massage
die **Masse, -n** mass
die **Massenmedien** *(pl.)* mass media
das **Material′** material
die **Mathematik′** mathematics
die **Mauer, -n** wall (14W)
das **Maul, ¨er** big mouth (of animal)
der **Maurer, -** bricklayer
maurisch Moorish
die **Maus, ¨e** mouse; **~efalle, -n** mousetrap
das **Mecha′niker, -** mechanic
die **Medien** *(pl.)* media
das **Medikament′, -e** medicine, prescription
die **Medizin′** (the field of) medicine
das **Mehl** flour
mehr more (12G); **immer ~** more and more (12G)
mehrer- *(pl.)* several (10G)
die **Mehrwertsteuer, -n** value-added tax
meiden, mied, gemieden to avoid
mein my (1W,7G)
meinen to mean, think (be of an opinion) (11W); **Wenn du meinst.** If you think so. (11W)
die **Meinung, -en** opinion; **meiner ~ nach** in my opinion
die **Meinungsumfrage, -n** opinion poll
meist-: am ~en most (12G)
meistens mostly, usually (7E)
der **Meister, -** master
die **Mensa** student cafeteria (3W)
der **Mensch, -en, -en** human being, person; people *(pl.)* (1E,2G); **~!** Man! Boy! Hey!; **Mit** fellow man
die **Menschheit** humankind
das **Menü′, -s** dinner, daily special
merken to notice, find out

die **Messe, -n** (trade) fair
das **Messegelände, -** fairgrounds
das **Messer, -** knife (3E); **Taschen~** pocket knife
das **Metall′, -e** metal
der **Meter, -** meter
die **Metropo′le, -n** metropolis
der **Metzger, -** butcher
die **Metzgerei′, -en** butcher shop
mies miserable
die **Miete, -n** rent
mieten to rent (6W)
der **Mieter, -** renter, tenant
die **Mietwohnung, -en** apartment
der **Mikrowellenherd, -e** microwave oven
die **Milch** milk (2W)
das **Militär′** military, army
militä′risch military
die **Million′, -en** million
der **Millionär′, -e** millionaire
mindestens at least
die **Mineralogie′** mineralogy
das **Mineral′wasser** mineral water
der **Minimumbestellwert** minimal order
minus minus
die **Minu′te, -n** minute (S5)
mischen to mix; **darunter ~** to blend in
der **Mischmasch** mishmash, hodgepodge
die **Mischung, -en** mixture
misera′bel miserable
die **Mission′, -en** mission
mit (+ *dat.*) with (3G); along
der **Mitbewoh′ner, -** housemate (13W)
mit·bringen* to bring along (7G)
mit·fahren* to drive along
mit·feiern to join in the celebration
das **Mitgefühl** compassion
mit·gehen* to go along (7G)
mit·kommen* to come along (7G)
das **Mitleid** pity
mit·machen to participate
mit·nehmen* to take along (7G)

mit·schicken to send along
mit·singen* to sing along
der **Mittag, -e** noon; **heute ~** today at noon (8G); **Dienstag-mittag** Tuesday at noon (8G)
das **Mittagessen, -** lunch, midday meal (3W); **beim ~** at lunch; **zum ~** for lunch (3W)
mittags at noon (S5); **dienstag~** Tuesday at noon (8G)
die **Mitte** middle, center (14E); mid
das **Mittel, -** means (of)
das **Mittelalter** Middle Ages; **im ~** in the Middle Ages (14W)
mittelalterlich medieval
(das) **Mitteleuropa** Central Europe
mittelgroß average size
mitten: ~ durch right through; **~ in** in the middle of (6E)
die **Mitternacht: um ~** at midnight
der **Mittwoch** Wednesday (S4); **am ~** on Wednesday (S4); **Ascher~** Ash Wednesday
mittwochs on Wednesdays (2E)
die **Möbel** *(pl.)* furniture (6W)
die **Mobilität′** mobility
möbliert′ furnished
möchten, mochte, gemocht to like (2W;5G); **Ich möchte . . .** I would like (to have) . . . (2W)
das **Modal′verb, -en** modal auxiliary
die **Mode** fashion; custom; **~puppe, -n** fashion doll
modern′ modern
mögen (mag), mochte, gemocht to like (5G)
möglich possible (7W); **alle ~en** all sorts of
die **Möglichkeit, -en** possibility
der **Mohnkuchen** poppy-seed cake
der **Moment′, -e** moment; **(Einen) ~!** One moment. Just a minute. (7W)

momentan′ at the moment, right now
der **Monat, -e** month (S4); **im ~** a month, per month (6W)
monatelang for months
monatlich monthly (10E)
der **Mond, -e** moon
der **Montag** Monday (S4); **am ~** on Monday (S4)
montags on Mondays (2E)
die **Moral′** moral
der **Mörder, -** murderer
morgen tomorrow (S4,4W); **Bis ~!** See you tomorrow; **für ~** for tomorrow (S2)
der **Morgen** morning: **Guten ~!** Good morning. (S1); **heute ~** this morning (8G); **Montag~** Monday morning (8G)
morgens in the morning (S5), every morning; **montag~** Monday mornings (8G)
das **Mosai′k, -e** mosaic
müde tired (S1); **tod~** dead tired
die **Müdigkeit** fatigue
der **Müll** garbage (15W)
der **Müller, -** miller
der **Müllschlucker, -** garbage disposal
die **Mülltrennung** waste separation (15W)
der **Mund, ⸚er** mouth (9W)
die **Mundharmonika, -s** harmonica
mündlich oral(ly)
die **Münze, -n** coin (15E)
die **Muschel, -n** clam; shell
das **Muse′um, Muse′en** museum (5W)
die **Musik′** music (9E)
musika′lisch musical (11W)
der **Musiker, -** musician
die **Musik′wissenschaft** musicology
(der) **Muskat′** nutmeg
der **Muskelkater** charley horse; **Ich habe ~.** My muscles are sore.
das **Müesli** whole-grain granola
müssen (muss), musste, gemusst to have to, must (5G)
das **Muster, -** example, model; pattern
der **Mustersatz, ⸚e** sample sentence
die **Mutter, ⸚** mother (1W); **Groß~** grandmother (1W); **Schwieger~** mother-in-law; **Urgroß~** great-grandmother
mütterlich motherly
die **Muttersprache** mother tongue
die **Mutti, -s** Mom

N

na well; **~ also** well; **~ gut** well, all right; **~ ja** well; **~ klar** of course (13W); **~ und!** So what?
nach (+ *dat.*) after (time), to (cities, countries, continents) (3G); **je ~** depending on
der **Nachbar, -n, -n** neighbor (1E,2G)
die **Nachbarschaft, -en** neighborhood; neighborly relations
nachdem′ (*conj.*) after (11G)
nacherzählt retold, adapted
die **Nachfrage** demand
nachher afterwards
nach·kommen* to follow
nach·laufen* to run after
nach·machen to imitate
der **Nachmittag, -e** afternoon; **am ~** in the afternoon; **heute ~** this afternoon (8G); **Freitagnachmittag** Friday afternoon (8G)
nachmittags in the afternoon (S5), every afternoon; **freitag~** Friday afternoons (8G)
der **Nachname, -ns, -n** last name
die **Nachricht, -en** news (10E)
nächst- next (11E)
die **Nacht, ⸚e** night (7W); **Gute ~!** Good night!; **heute ~** tonight (8G); **Sonntagnacht** Sunday night (8G)
der **Nachteil, -e** disadvantage

die **Nachteule, -n** night owl
der **Nachtisch** dessert (3W); **zum ~** for dessert (3W)
nachts during the night, every night (8G); **sonntag~** Sunday nights (8G)
der **Nachttisch, -e** nightstand
nach·werfen* to throw after
nackt naked
die **Nadel, -n** needle
nah (näher, nächst-) near (5W,12G)
die **Nähe** nearness, vicinity; **in der ~** nearby; **in der ~ von** (+ *dat.*) near (5W)
nähen to sew
der **Name, -ns, -n** name (8G); **Mein ~ ist . . .** My name is . . . (S1); **Mädchen~** maiden name; **Vor~** first name; **Nach~** last name; **Spitz~** nickname (14W)
nämlich namely, you know
die **Nase, -n** nose (9W); **Ich habe die ~ voll.** I'm fed up (with it).
die **Nation′, -en** nation, state
national′ national
der **Nationalis′mus** nationalism
die **Nationalität′, -en** nationality
die **Natur′** nature (15W)
das **Natur′kind** child of nature
natür′lich natural(ly), of course (2W)
die **Natur′wissenschaft, -en** natural science (13W)
natur′wissenschaftlich scientific
der **Nebel** fog
neben (+ *acc. / dat.*) beside, next to (6G)
nebeneinander next to each other
das **Nebenfach, ⸚er** minor (field of study) (14W)
der **Nebensatz, ⸚e** ubordinate clause
negativ negative(ly)
nehmen (nimmt), nahm, genommen to take (S3); to have (food) (3G)
nein no (S1)

die **Nelke, -n** carnation
nennen, nannte, genannt to name, call (11E); **ich nenne das** that's what I call
nett nice (11W)
neu new (S3); **Was gibt's Neues . . . ?** What's new? (9W)
die **Neuauflage, -n** new edition
neugierig curious
der **Neujahrstag** New Year's Day
nicht not (S1); **~ wahr?** isn't it? (S4); **gar ~** not at all (13E); **~ nur . . . sondern auch** not only . . . but also (3E)
nichts nothing (3W); **~ Besonderes** nothing special (9W)
nicken to nod
nie never (4E); **noch ~** never before, not ever (4E)
niedrig low
niemand nobody, no one (11E)
das **Niemandsland** no man's land
nimmermehr never again; no longer
nirgends nowwhere; **ins Nirgends** into nowhere
nobel noble
noch still (4W); **~ einmal** once more, again (S2); **~ ein** another (3W); **~ lange nicht** not by far; **~ nie** never (before), not ever (4E); **~ nicht** not yet (6E); **Sonst ~ etwas?** Anything else?; **weder . . . ~** neither . . . nor (10E)
der **Nominativ, -e** nominative
die **Nonne, -n** nun
der **Norden: im ~** in the north (1W)
nördlich (von) to the north, north (of) (1W)
normal normal; by regular (surface) mail
(das) **Norwegen** Norway
der **Norweger, -** the Norwegian
norwegisch Norwegian
die **Note, -n** grade, score (13W)
nötig necessary, needed

die **Notiz', -en** note; **~en machen** to take notes
der **November** November (S4); **im ~** in November (S4)
nüchtern sober
die **Nudel, -n** noodle (3W)
null zero (S3)
der **Numerus clausus** admissions restriction at a university
die **Nummer, -n** number (7W)
nun now (11E)
nur only (S4)
die **Nuss, ̈e** nut
der **Nussknacker, -** nutcracker
nutzen to use

O

ob *(conj.)* if, whether (4G); **Und ~!** You bet. You better believe it. (14W)
oben upstairs (6W); up; **~ genannt** above mentioned
der **Ober, -** waiter (3W); **Herr ~!** Waiter! (3W)
die **Oberin, -nen** mother superior
die **Oberstufe, -n** upper level
das **Objekt', -e** object
objektiv' objective(ly)
das **Obst** *(sg.)* fruit (2W)
obwohl *(conj.)* although (4G)
oder or (S3,2G); **~?** isn't it? don't you think so? (14W)
der **Ofen, ̈** oven
offen open (2E)
offiziell' official
öffnen to open; **~ Sie das Buch auf Seite . . . !** Open the book on page . . . (SSS)
öffentlich public (10E)
oft often (2E)
ohne (+ *acc.*) without (2G)
das **Ohr, -en** ear (9W)
Oje'! Oops! Oh no!
die **Ökologie'** ecology
ökologisch ecologic(ally)
das **Ökosystem', -e** ecological system
der **Oktober** October (S4); **im ~** in October (S4)
das **Öl, -e** oil; lotion

der **Ölwechsel** oil change
die **Olympiade, -n** Olympics
die **Oma, -s** grandma
das **Omelett', -s** omelet
der **Onkel, -** uncle (1W)
der **Opa, -s** grandpa
die **Oper, -n** opera (10W); **die Seifen~** soap opera
das **Opfer, -** victim
orange (color) orange (S2)
die **Orange, -n** orange (2W)
das **Orchester, -** orchestra (10W)
ordentlich orderly; regular
die **Ordinalzahl, -en** ordinal number (4W)
die **Ordnungszahl, -en** ordinal number
die **Organisation', -en** organization
(sich) **organisieren** to organize
die **Orientierung** orientation
das **Original', -e** original
der **Ort, -e** place, town; location
der **Ossi, -s** *(nickname)* = **Ostdeutsche** East German
der **Osten: im ~** in the east (1W)
(das) **Ostern: zu ~** at/for Easter (4W); **Frohe ~!** Happy Easter.
(das) **Österreich** Austria (1W)
der **Österreicher, -** the Austrian (1W)
österreichisch Austrian
östlich (von) east (of), to the east (of) (1W)
der **Ozean, -e** ocean

P

paar: ein ~ a couple of, some (2E)
das **Paar, -e** couple, pair
pachten to lease
packen to pack (7E); to grab
die **Pädagogik** education
das **Paddelboot, -e** canoe
paddeln to paddle
das **Paket', -e** package, parcel (8W)
die **Paketkarte, -n** parcel form
die **Palatschinken** *(pl.)* crêpes
das **Panorama** panorama

die **Panne, -n** mishap
der **Panzer, -** tank
das **Papier', -e** paper (S2)
der **Papier'krieg** paper work, red tape
das **Papier'warengeschäft, -e** office supply store
die **Pappe** cardboard
das **Paradies'** paradise
der **Paragraph', -en, -en** paragraph
das **Parfüm', -s** perfume
der **Park, -s** park (5W)
die **Parkanlage, -n** park
parken to park (15W)
das **Parkett':** **im ~** (seating) in the orchestra
der **Parkplatz, ⸚e** parking lot
parlamenta'risch parliamentary
die **Partei', -en** (political) party
das **Parter're: im ~** on the first floor (ground level) (6W)
das **Partizip', -ien** participle
der **Partner, -** partner (11W)
die **Party, Partys** party (4W)
der **Pass, ⸚e** passport (7W)
passen to fit; **Was passt?** What fits?; **Das passt mir nicht.** That doesn't suit me.
passend appropriate, suitable
passie'ren (ist) to happen (11W)
passiv passive
das **Passiv** passive voice
die **Pasta, -s** pasta
die **Pause, -n** intermission, break (10W); **eine ~ machen** to take a break
das **Pech** tough luck, misfortune; **~ haben*** to be unlucky (4W); **~ gehabt!** Tough luck!
pendeln (ist) to commute; **hin- und her~** to commute back and forth
die **Pension', -en** boarding house; hotel (7E)
die **Pensionierung** retirement
das **Perfekt** present perfect
permanent' permanent
die **Person', -en** person; **pro ~** per person

persön'lich personal(ly)
die **Persön'lichkeit, -en** personality
der **Pfannkuchen, -** pancake
der **Pfarrer, -** pastor; cleric
der **Pfeffer** pepper (3W)
die **Pfefferminze** peppermint
die **Pfeife, -n** pipe
der **Pfennig, -e** German penny (S3); **zwei ~** two pennies (S3)
das **Pferd, -e** horse; **~ewagen,** horse-drawn buggy
(das) **Pfingsten** Pentecost
die **Pflanze, -n** plant
das **Pflaster, -** bandaid
die **Pflegemutter, ⸚** foster mother
pflegen to take care of; **er pflegt zu tun** he usually does
die **Pflicht, -en** duty, obligation
das **Pflichtfach, ⸚er** required subject
das **Pfund, -e** pound (2W); **zwei ~** two pounds (of) (2W)
die **Pharmazie'** pharmaceutics, pharmacy
die **Philologie'** philology
der **Philosoph', -en, -en** philosopher
die **Philosophie'** philosophy
die **Phonotypi'st, -en, -en** dictaphone-typist
die **Photographie'** photography
die **Physik'** physics
der **Physiker, -** physicist
physisch physical(ly)
das **Picknick, -s** picnic
picknicken to (have a) picnic; **~ gehen*** to go picnicking
piepen to peep, chirp; **Bei dir piept's!** You're cuckoo. You must be kidding.
der **Pilot', -en, -en** pilot
die **Pizza, -s** pizza (3W)
der **Plan, ⸚e** plan (12W)
planen to plan (15W)
die **Planier'raupe, -n** bulldozer
das **Plastik** plastic
die **Plastiktüte, -n** plastic bag
die **Platte, -n** record; platter
der **Plattenspieler, -** record player

der **Platz, ⸚e** (town) square, place (5W); seat
die **Platzanweiser,** usher
das **Plätzchen, -** cookie (2W)
plötzlich suddenly (11E)
der **Plural, -e (von)** plural of (S2)
plus plus
das **Plusquamperfekt** past perfect
der **Pole, -n, -n / die Polin, -nen** native of Poland
(das) **Polen** Poland
polnisch Polish
die **Politik'** politics
die **Politik'(wissenschaft)** political science, politics
poli'tisch political(ly)
die **Polizei'** (sg.) police
der **Polizi'st, -en, -en** policeman (12W)
die **Pommes frites** (pl.) French fries (3W)
der **Pool, -s** swimming pool
populär' popular
die **Popularität'** popularity
das **Portemonnaie,-s** wallet
der **Portier', -s** desk clerk
das **Porto** postage
das **Porträt, -s** portrait
(das) **Portugal** Portugal
der **Portugie'se, -n, -n / die Portugiesin, -nen** the Portuguese
portugie'sisch Portuguese
das **Porzellan'** porcelain
die **Post** post office (5W); mail (8W)
der **Postdienst** postal service
das **Postfach, ⸚er** P.O. box (8W)
das **Posthorn, ⸚er** bugle
die **Postkarte, -n** postcard (8W)
die **Postleitzahl, -en** zip code
prägen to shape
das **Praktikum, Praktika** practical training (12E)
praktisch practical(ly) (6W)
die **Präposition', -en** preposition
präsentie'ren to present
der **Präsident', -en, -en** president
die **Praxis** practical experience; practice

der **Preis, -e** price; prize
die **Preiselbeere, -n** type of cranberry
die **Presse** press; **Tages~** daily press
das **Presti′ge** prestige
prima great, wonderful (S4)
primitiv′ primitive
der **Prinz, -en, -en** prince
die **Prinzes′sin, -nen** princess
das **Prinzip′, -ien** principle; **im ~** in principle
privat′ private (10E)
das **Privat′gefühl, -e** feeling for privacy
das **Privileg′, Privile′gien** privilege
pro per
die **Probe, -n** test; **auf die ~ stellen** to test
probie′ren to try
das **Problem′, -e** problem (12W)
problema′tisch problematic
das **Produkt′, -e** product
die **Produktion′** production; **Buch~** book publishing
der **Produzent′, -en, -en** producer
produzie′ren to produce
der **Profes′sor, -en** professor (13W)
das **Profil′, -e** profile
profitie′ren to profit
das **Programm′, -e** program, channel (10W)
der **Programmie′rer, -** programmer
das **Projekt′, -e** project
das **Prono′men, -** pronoun
proportional′ proportional(ly)
die **Prosa** prose
Prost! Cheers!; **~ Neujahr!** Happy New Year!
der **Protest′, -e** protest
protestie′ren to protest
protzen to brag
das **Proviso′rium** provisional state
das **Prozent′, -e** percent
die **Prüfung, -en** test, exam (1W); **eine ~ bestehen*** to pass an exam (13W); **bei einer ~ durch·fallen*** to flunk an exam (13W); **eine ~ machen** to take an exam (13W)
der **Psalm, -e** psalm
das **Pseudonym′, -e** pseudonym
der **Psychia′ter, -** psychiatrist
die **Psy′choanaly′se** psychoanalysis
der **Psycholo′ge, -n, -n / die Psycholo′gin, -nen** psychologist
die **Psychologie′** psychology
psycholo′gisch psychological(ly)
das **Publikum** audience
die **Puderdose, -n** compact
der **Pudding, -s** pudding (3W)
die **Pulle, -n** (colloquial) bottle; **volle ~** with the pedal to the metal
der **Pulli, -s** sweater (S3)
der **Pullo′ver, -** pullover, sweater (S3)
der **Punkt, -e** point
pünktlich on time
die **Puppe, -n** doll
das **Putenfleisch** turkey meat
putzen to clean; **sich die Zähne ~** to brush one's teeth (9G)
die **Putzfrau, -en** cleaning lady
die **Pyramide, -n** pyramid

Q

die **Qual, -en** torment, agony
die **Qualifikation′, -en** qualification; **Zusatz~** additional qualification
qualifiziert′ qualified
die **Qualität′, -en** quality
die **Quantität′** quantity
das **Quartal′, -e** quarter (university) (13W)
das **Quartett′, -e** quartet
das **Quartier′, -s** (or **-e**) lodging
der **Quatsch** nonsense
die **Quelle, -n** source
quer durch all across
die **Querflöte, -n** flute
das **Quintett′, -s** quintet
das **Quiz** quiz
die **Quote, -n** quota

R

das **Rad, ⸚er** bicycle, bike; **~ fahren*** to bicycle
das **Radio, -s** radio (6W)
der **Rand, ⸚er** edge
der **Rang, ⸚e** theater balcony; **im ersten ~** in the first balcony
der **Rasen, -** lawn
sich **rasie′ren** to shave o.s. (9G)
der **Rat** advice, counsel
raten (rät), riet, geraten to advise, guess
das **Rathaus, ⸚er** city hall (5W)
rätoromanisch Romansh
die **Ratte, -n** rat
rauchen to smoke
der **Raum** space
räumen to clear
das **Raumschiff, -e** spaceship
reagie′ren (auf + *acc.***)** to react (to) (11W)
die **Reaktion′, -en** reaction
die **Real′schule, -n** secondary school (grades 5–10)
rebellie′ren to rebel
rechnen to calculate
die **Rechnung, -en** check, bill (3W)
das **Recht, -e** right; **Du hast ~.** You're right. (11W)
recht: Das geschieht dir ~. That serves you right.
recht-: auf der ~en Seite on the right side
rechts right (5W); **erste Straße ~** first street to the right (5W)
der **Rechtsanwalt, ⸚e** lawyer (12W)
die **Rechtsanwältin, -nen** lawyer (12W)
der **Rechts′radikalis′mus** right-wing radicalism
die **Rechtswissenschaft** study of law
die **Rede, -n** speech; **indirekte ~** indirect speech

reden (mit / über) to talk (to/about), chat (15W)
die **Redewendung, -en** idiom, saying
reduzie′ren to reduce
das **Referat′, -e** oral presentation (13W); **ein ~ halten*** to give an oral presentation (13W)
reflexiv′ reflexive
das **Reform′haus, ¨er** health-food store
das **Regal′, -e** shelf (6E)
regeln to regulate
der **Regen** rain
der **Regenschirm, -e** umbrella
die **Regie′rung, -en** government
das **Regi′me, -** regime
die **Region′, -en** region
regional′ regional(ly)
der **Regisseur′, -e** director (film)
registrie′ren to register
regnen to rain; **Es regnet.** It's raining. (S4).
regulie′ren to regulate
reiben, rieb, gerieben to rub
reich rich (11W)
das **Reich, -e** empire, kingdom
reichen to suffice; **~ bis an** (+ *acc.*) to go up to
der **Reichtum, ¨er** wealth
reif ripe; mature
die **Reife** maturity; **Mittlere ~** diploma of a *Realschule*
die **Reihe, -n** row
das **Reihenhaus, ¨er** townhouse (6E)
der **Reis** rice (3W)
die **Reise, -n** trip (7E); **eine ~ machen** to take a trip, travel
das **Reisebüro, -s** travel agency
der **Reiseführer, -** (travel) guide; guide (book)
der **Reiseleiter, -** tour guide (12W)
reiselustig travel-hungry
reisen (ist) to travel (7E)
der **Reisescheck, -s** traveler's check
reißen, riss, ist gerissen to tear
reiten, ritt, ist geritten to ride (on horseback)

die **Reitschule, -n** riding academy
der **Rektor, -en** university president
relativ′ relative(ly)
das **Relativ′pronomen, -** relative pronoun
der **Relativ′satz, ¨e** relative clause
die **Religion′, -en** religion
das **Rendezvous, -** date
rennen, rannte, ist gerannt to run
renovie′ren to renovate (15W)
der **Repräsentant′, -en, -en** representative
repräsentativ′ representative
das **Reservat′, -e** reservation, preserve
reservie′ren to reserve (7E)
die **Reservie′rung, -en** reservation
die **Residenz′, -en** residence
resignie′ren to resign, give up
der **Rest, -e** rest
das **Restaurant′, -s** restaurant (3E)
restaurie′ren to restore (15W)
die **Restaurie′rung** restoration
das **Resultat′, -e** result
retten to save, rescue (15W)
das **Rezept′, -e** recipe
die **Rezeption′, -en** reception (desk)
das **R-Gespräch, -e** collect call
richtig right, correct (S2); **Das ist genau das Richtige.** That's exactly the right thing.
die **Richtigkeit** correctness
die **Richtung, -en** direction; **in ~** in the direction of
riechen, roch, gerochen to smell
das **Riesenrad, ¨er** ferris wheel
riesig huge, enormous
die **Rindsroulade, -n** stuffed beef roll
der **Ring, -e** ring

rings um (+ *acc.*) all around
das **Risiko, Risiken** risk
der **Ritter, -** knight
der **Rock, ¨e** skirt (S3)
der **Rollladen, ¨** (roller) shutter
die **Rolle, -n** role; **Haupt~** leading role
das **Rollo′, -s** blinds
der **Rollschuh, -e** roller skate; **~ laufen*** to rollerskate; **~laufen gehen*** to go roller skating
der **Roman′, -e** novel (10W)
die **Romani′stik** study of Romance languages
die **Roman′tik** romanticism
roman′tisch romantic
römisch Roman
rosa pink (S2)
die **Rose, -n** rose
die **Rosi′ne, -n** raisin
rot (ö) red (S2); **bei Rot** at a red light
die **rote Grütze** berry sauce thickened with cornstarch
das **Rotkäppchen** Little Red Riding Hood
das **Rotkraut** red cabbage
rötlich reddish
die **Roula′de, -n** stuffed beef roll
die **Routi′ne, -n** routine
der **Rückblick, -e** review
die **(Hin- und) Rückfahrkarte, -n** round-trip ticket (8W)
die **Rückreise, -n** return trip
der **Rückgang** decline
der **Rucksack, ¨e** backpack
der **Rückweg, -e** return trip, way back
ruck, zuck quickly, in a jiffy
das **Ruderboot, -e** rowboat
rudern to row
rufen, rief, gerufen to call
die **Ruhe** peace and quiet
der **Ruhetag, -e** holiday, day off
ruhig quiet (7W)
der **Ruhm** fame
rühren to stir; **sich ~ to** move; **Ich kann mich kaum ~.** I can hardly move.
der **Rum** rum
rund round

die **Rundfahrt, -en** sightseeing trip
der **Rundfunk** radio, broadcasting
der **Russe, -n, -n** / die **Russin, -nen** the Russian
russisch Russian
(das) **Russland** Russia

S

der **Saal, Säle** large room, hall
die **Sache, -n** thing, matter; **Haupt~** main thing
der **Saft, ¨e** juice (2W)
sagen to say, tell (S2); **Wie sagt man . . . ?** How does one say . . . ? (S2); **Sag mal!** Say. Tell me (us etc.); **wie gesagt** as I (you etc.) said
die **Saison', -s** season
der **Salat', -e** salad, lettuce (2W)
die **Salbe, -n** ointment
das **Salz** salt (3W)
salzig salty
die **Salzstange, -n** pretzel stick
sammeln to collect (9W)
die **Sammelstelle, -n** collection site (15W)
der **Sammler, -** collector
der **Samstag** Saturday (S4); **am ~** on Saturday (S4)
samstags on Saturdays (2E)
der **Samt** velvet
der **Sand** sand
sanft gentle
der **Sängerknabe, -n, -n** choir boy
der **Satellit', -en** satellite
der **Satz, ¨e** sentence (1W); **Bilden Sie einen ~!** Make a sentence.
die **Sau, ¨e** dirty pig, *lit.*sow; **Mensch, so ein ~wetter!** Man, what a lousy weather!
sauber clean, neat (S3)
die **Sauberkeit** cleanliness
sauber·machen to clean
sauer sour; acid
der **Sauerbraten** marinated pot roast

das **Sauerkraut** sauerkraut
die **Säule, -n** column
die **S-Bahn, -en** commuter train
das **Schach: ~ spielen** to play chess (9W)
schade too bad (S4)
schaden to hurt, damage
der **Schaden, ¨** damage; **Total~** total wreck
das **Schaf, -e** sheep
schaffen to work hard, accomplish
schaffen, schuf, geschaffen to create
der **Schaffner, -** conductor
die **Schale, -n** shell, peel
die **(Schall)platte, -n** record
der **Schalter, -** ticket window, counter (7W)
das **Schaschlik, -s** shish kebab
schätzen to appreciate; to appraise
schauen to look; **Schau mal!** Look! (15E)
das **Schaufenster, -** display window; **in die ~ sehen*** to go window-shopping
das **Schaumbad, ¨er** bubble bath
der **Schauspieler, -** actor (10W)
der **Scheck, -s** check (7W)
die **Scheidung, -en** divorce (11W)
der **Schein, -e** certificate (13W); **Geld~** banknote (15E)
scheinen, schien, geschienen to shine (S4); to seem (like), appear (to be) (14E)
schenken to give (as a present) (4W)
die **Schere, -n** scissors
die **Schicht, -en** level; **die obere ~** upper level of society
schick chic, neat (11W)
schicken to send (8W)
schief crooked, not straight; **~ gehen*** to go wrong
die **Schießbude, -n** shooting gallery
das **Schiff, -e** ship, boat; **mit dem ~ fahren*** to go by boat
das **Schild, -er** sign
der **Schinken, -** ham

der **Schirm, -e** umbrella
der **Schlachter, -** butcher
schlafen (schläft), schlief, geschlafen to sleep (3E)
schlaflos sleepless
der **Schlafsack, ¨e** sleeping bag
die **Schlafstadt, ¨e** bedroom community
das **Schlafzimmer, -** bedroom (6W)
schlagen (schlägt), schlug, geschlagen to hit
der **Schlager, -** popular song, hit
der **Schlagersänger, -** pop singer
die **Schlagsahne** whipped cream
die **Schlange, -n** snake
schlank slim, slender (11W)
schlecht bad(ly) (S1)
schließen, schloss, geschlossen to lock, close
das **Schließfach, ¨er** locker
schließlich after all, in the end
schlimm bad, awful
das **Schloss, ¨er** palace (5W)
der **Schlüssel, -** key (7W)
schmecken to taste (good); **Das schmeckt (gut).** That tastes good. (3W)
schmelzen (schmilzt), schmolz, ist geschmolzen to melt
der **Schmerz, -en** pain, ache; **Ich habe (Kopf)schmerzen.** I have a (head)ache. (9W)
der **Schmied, -e** blacksmith
der **Schmutz** dirt
der **Schmutzfink, -en** (dirty) pig
schmutzig dirty (S3)
der **Schnee** snow
schneiden, schnitt, geschnitten to cut
schneien to snow; **es schneit** it's snowing (S4)
schnell quick(ly), fast (S3)
der **Schnellweg, -e** express route
das **Schnitzel, -** veal cutlet
der **Schock, -s** shock
die **Schokola'de** chocolate
schon already (1E); **das ~** that's true
schön fine, nice, beautiful (S4)

schonen to protect
die **Schönheit** beauty
der **Schrank, ¨e** closet, cupboard (6W); **Gefrier~** freezer; **Kleider~** closet; **Küchen~** kitchen cabinet; **Kühl~** refrigerator
der **Schrebergarten, ¨** leased garden
der **Schreck** shock; **Ach du ~!** My goodness!
schrecklich terrible
schreiben, schrieb, geschrieben to write (S3); **~ Sie bitte!** Please, write! (SSS); **~ an** (+ *acc.*) to write to (10G)
die **Schreibmaschine, -n** typewriter
der **Schreibtisch, -e** desk (6W)
schreien, schrie, geschrien to scream
schriftlich written; in writing
die **Schrift, -en** script; (hand)writing
der **Schriftsteller, -** writer, author
der **Schritt, -e** step; pre-unit
schubsen to shove
der **Schuh, -e** shoe (S3); **Sport~** gym shoe, sneaker
die **Schule, -n** school (5W)
der **Schüler, -** pupil, student
die **Schüssel, -n** bowl
schütteln to shake
schütten (in + *acc.*) to dump, pour (into)
der **Schutz** protection (15W)
der **Schütze, -n, -n** rifleman, marksman; Sagittarius
schützen to protect (15E)
der **Schwabe, -n, -n / die Schwäbin, -nen** the Swabian
(das) **Schwaben(land)** Swabia
schwäbisch Swabian
die **Schwäche, -n** weakness
schwanger pregnant
schwärmen (von + *dat.*) to rave (about)
schwarz (ä) black (S2); **~·fahren*** to ride [on a bus or subway] without paying
das **Schwarzbrot, -e** rye bread

der **Schwede, -n, -n / die Schwedin, -nen** the Swede
(das) **Schweden** Sweden
schwedisch Swedish
schweifen (ist) to wander, roam; **immer weiter·~** to continue wandering
schweigen, schwieg, geschwiegen to remain silent, shut up
das **Schwein, -e** pig, pork; scoundrel; **~ haben*** to be lucky; **~ gehabt!** You were lucky!
die **Schweinshaxe, -n** pigs' knuckles
der **Schweiß** sweat
die **Schweiz** Switzerland (1W)
der **Schweizer, -** the Swiss (1W)
Schweizer/schweizerisch Swiss
schwer heavy, hard, difficult (6E)
die **Schwester, -n** sister (1W)
das **Schwesterchen, -** little sister
schwierig difficult (13W)
die **Schwierigkeit, -en** difficulty
schwimmen, schwamm, geschwommen to swim (9W); **~ gehen*** to go swimming (9W)
das **Schwimmbad, ¨er** swimming pool
der **Schwimmer, -** swimmer
ein Sechstel one sixth
der **See, -n** lake (1W)
die **See** sea, ocean
der **Seehund, -e** seal
das **Segelboot, -e** sailboat
Segelfliegen gehen* to go gliding
segeln to sail; **Segeln gehen*** to go sailing
sehen (sieht), sah, gesehen to see, look (3G); **Mal ~!** Let's see! (13W)
die **Sehenswürdigkeit, -en** sight (worth seeing), attraction
sehr very (S4)
die **Seide, -n** silk
die **Seife, -n** soap
die **Seifenoper, -n** soap opera

die **Seilbahn, -en** cable car
sein his, its (7G)
sein (ist), war, ist gewesen to be (S1, S2, 2G); **Ich bin's.** It's me; **So bin ich.** That's the way I am.
seit (+ *dat.*) since, for (time) (3G)
die **Seite, -n** page; **auf ~** on page, to page (SSS)
der **Sekretär, -e** secretary (12W)
der **Sekt** champagne (4W)
die **Sekunde, -n** second (S5)
selbst -self; **~ wenn** even if
selbstbewusst self-confident (11W)
das **Selbstbewusstsein** self-confidence
selbstständig self-employed, independent (11W)
die **Selbstständigkeit** independence
selten seldom
seltsam strange, odd
das **Semester, -** semester (13W)
das **Seminar, -e** seminar paper (13W)
die **Seminararbeit, -en** term paper
der **Sender, -** (radio or TV) station
die **Sendung, -en** (part of) TV or radio program (10E)
das **Sendungsbewusstsein** sense of mission
der **Senf** mustard
der **September** September (S4); **im ~** in September (S4)
die **Serie, -n** series
servieren to serve (food)
die **Serviette, -n** napkin (3W)
Servus! Hi! (Bavaria, Austria)
die **Sesamstraße** Sesame Street
der **Sessel, -** armchair (6W)
der **Sessellift, -e** chairlift
setzen to set (down), put (6W); **sich ~** to sit down (9G); **sich dazu ~** to join sb. at a table
das **Shampoo, -s** shampoo
die **Show, -s** show

VOCABULARIES

  sicher sure, certain (4W); safe, secure (12W)
die **Sicherheit** safety, security (12W)
  sicherlich surely, certainly, undoubtedly (15W)
  sichern to secure
  sichtbar visible
die **Siedlung, -en** settlement, subdivision
der **Sieg, -e** victory
der **Sieger, -** victor
die **Siegermächte** *(pl.)* Allies
  siezen to call each other "Sie"
das **Silber** silver
(das) **Silvester: zu ~** at/for New Year's Eve (4W)
  singen, sang, gesungen to sing (4W)
  sinken, sank, ist gesunken to sink
der **Sinn, -e** mind, sense, meaning; **in den ~ kommen*** to come to mind
die **Situation, -en** situation
  sitzen, saß, gesessen to sit (be sitting) (6W)
der **Ski, -er** ski; **~ laufen*** to ski; **~laufen gehen*** to go skiing (9W)
der **Skiläufer, -** skier
der **Skilift, -e** skilift
  skrupellos unscrupulous
die **Skulptur, -en** sculpture
die **Slawistik** study of Slavic language and literature
die **Slowakische Republik** Slovac Republic
  so so, like that; in this way; **~ dass** *(conj.)* so that (13E); **~ ein** such a (7G); **~ so** fair; **~ . . . wie** as . . . as (12G)
  sobald as soon as (12E)
die **Socke, -n** sock
das **Sofa, -s** sofa, couch (6W)
  sofort immediately, right away (11E)
  sogar even (6W)
  sogenannt so-called
der **Sohn, ⸚e** son (1W)
  solch- such (7G)

der **Soldat, -en, -en** soldier
  sollen (soll), sollte, gesollt to be supposed to (5G)
der **Sommer, -** summer (S4); **im ~** in the summer (S4)
das **Sonderangebot, -e: im ~** on sale, special
  sondern but (on the contrary) (5W,5G); **nicht nur . . . ~ auch** not only . . . but also (3E)
der **Sonderstatus** special status
die **Sonne** sun; **Die ~ scheint.** The sun is shining. (S4)
der **Sonnenaufgang, ⸚e** sunrise
die **Sonnenblume, -n** sunflower
die **Sonnenbrille, -n** sunglasses
die **Sonnencreme, -s** suntan lotion
das **Sonnenöl** suntan lotion
der **Sonnenuntergang, ⸚e** sunset
der **Sonntag** Sunday (S4); **am ~** on Sunday (S4); **Toten~** Memorial Day
  sonntags on Sundays (2E)
  sonst otherwise; **~ noch etwas?** Anything else?
die **Sorge, -n** worry, concern; **sich ~en machen (um)** to be concerned, worry (about) (12E)
  sortieren to sort
die **Soße, -n** sauce, gravy
  soviel as much as; **~ ich weiß** as much as I know
  sowieso anyway, anyhow (13E)
  sowjetisch Soviet
  sowohl . . . als auch as well as
der **Sozialismus** socialism
  sozialistisch socialist
die **Sozialkunde** social studies
der **Sozialpädagoge, -n,- n / die Sozialpädagogin, -nen** social worker
die **Souveränität** sovereignty
die **Soziologie** social studies, sociology
(das) **Spanien** Spain (1W)
der **Spanier, -** the Spaniard (1W)
  spanisch Spanish (1W)

  spannend exciting, suspenseful (10W)
  sparen to save (money or time) (6E)
der **Spargel** asparagus
die **Sparkasse, -n** savings bank
  sparsam thrifty
  spartanisch Spartan, frugal
der **Spaß, ⸚e** fun; **~ machen** to be fun (4E)
  spät late; **Wie ~ ist es?** How late is it? What time is it? (S5)
  später ater; **Bis ~!** See you later! (S5)
der **Spatz, -en** sparrow
  spazieren gehen* to go for a walk (9W)
der **Spaziergang, ⸚e** walk
der **Speck** bacon
die **Speise, -n** food, dish
die **Speisekarte, -n** menu (3W)
die **Spekulation, -en** speculation
das **Spezialgeschäft, -e** specialty shop
die **Spezialisierung** specialization
der **Spezialist, -en, -en** specialist
die **Spezialität, -en** specialty
der **Spiegel, -** mirror
das **Spiel, -e** game, play (9W)
  spielen to play; **Tennis ~** to play tennis (S5); **Dame ~** to play checkers (9W); **Schach ~** to play chess (9W)
der **Spielplan, ⸚e** program, performance schedule
der **Spielplatz, ⸚e** playground
das **Spielzeug** toys
der **Spieß, -e** spit; spear
die **Spindel, -n** spindle
  spinnen, spann, gesponnen to spin (yarn) (11E); **Du spinnst wohl!** You're crazy!
das **Spinnrad, ⸚er** spinning-wheel
der **Spitzname, -ns, -n** nickname (14W)
  spontan spontaneous
der **Sport** sport(s) (9W); **~ treiben*** to engage in sports (9W)
der **Sportler, -** athlete

sportlich athletic, sporty (11W)
die **Sprache, -n** language (1W)
-sprachig -speaking
sprechen (spricht), sprach, gesprochen to speak (S3); **~ sie langsam bitte!** Speak slowly, please. (SSS); **~ Sie lauter!** Speak louder (S3); **Man spricht . . .** They (people) speak. . . ; **~ von** (+ *dat.*) / **über** (+ *acc.*) to speak of/about (10G); **Ist . . . zu ~?** May I speak to . . . ?
der **Sprecher, -** speaker
die **Sprech'situation', -en** (situation for) communication
das **Sprichwort, ⁻er** saying, proverb
springen, sprang, ist gesprungen to jump (11E)
das **Spritzgebäck** cookies shaped with a cookie press
der **Spruch, ⁻e** saying
die **Spülmaschine, -n** dishwasher
das **Spülmittel, -** dishwashing detergent
der **Staat, -en** state (15E)
der **Staatenbund** confederation
staatlich public; **~ kontrolliert** state-controlled
die **Staatsangehörigkeit** citizenship
der **Staatsbürger, -** citizen
der **Staatssicherheitsdienst = die Stasi** GDR secret police
die **Stadt, ⁻e** city, town (1W)
das **Stadtbild, -er** overall appearance of a city
das **Städtchen, -** small town
der **Stadtplan, ⁻e** city map (5W)
der **Stadtrand** outskirts (of town)
der **Stamm, ⁻e** tribe
der **Stammbaum, ⁻e** family tree
stammen (aus + *dat.*) to stem (from), originate
stampfen to stomp
der **Standard, -s** standard
das **Standesamt, ⁻er** marriage registrar
stark (ä) strong

starren to stare
die **Station', -en** (bus) stop
die **Stati'stik, -en** statistic
statt (+ *gen.*) instead of (8G)
der **Stau, -s** traffic jam
der **Staub** dust
der **Staubsauger, -** vacuum cleaner
staunen to be amazed
stechen (sticht), stach, gestochen to prick
der **Stechschritt** goose-step
stecken to stick
stehen, stand, gestanden to stand (or be standing) (6W)
stehen bleiben* to come to a stop, remain standing
stehlen (stiehlt), stahl, gestohlen to steal
steif stiff
steigen, stieg, ist gestiegen to go up, rise, climb
steigern to increase
steil steep
der **Stein, -e** stone
die **Stelle, -n** job, position, place (12W); **an deiner ~** in your shoes, if I were you (13E)
stellen to stand (upright), put (6W); **eine Frage ~** to ask a question (15E)
sterben (stirbt), starb, ist gestorben to die (11E)
der **Stern, -e** star
die **Stereoanlage, -n** stereo set
die **Steuer, -n** tax
der **Steuerberater, -** tax preparer
Stief-: die ~eltern stepparents; **die ~mutter** stepmother; **der ~vater** stepfather
der **Stier, -e** bull
der **Stil, -e** style
still quiet
die **Stimme, -n** voice
stimmen: (Das) stimmt. (That's) true. (That's) right. (6W)
das **Stipen'dium, Stipen'dien** scholarship (13W)
der **Stock, ⁻e** stick
der **Stock, -werke: im ersten ~** on the second floor (6W)

stöhnen to complain, moan
der **Stollen, -** Christmas cake/bread with almonds, raisins, and candied peel
stolz (auf + *acc.*) proud (of) (15E)
der **Stopp, -s** stop
das **Stoppschild, -er** stop sign
der **Storch, ⁻e** stork
stören to bother, disturb
der **Strafzettel, -** (traffic violation) ticket
der **Strand, ⁻e** beach
die **Straße, -n** street (5W)
die **Straßenbahn, -en** streetcar (5W)
strate'gisch strategic
der **Strauch, ⁻er** bush
der **Streber, -** geek
die **Streife, -n** patrol; **~ fahren** to patrol
der **Streifen, -** strip of land
streng strict(ly)
der **Stress** stress; **zu viel ~** too much stress
das **Stroh** straw
der **Strom** electricity
die **Strophe, -n** stanza
die **Struktur', -en** structure; *here:* grammar
der **Strumpf, ⁻e** stocking
das **Stück, -e** piece; **ein ~** a piece of (2W); **zwei ~** two pieces of (2W); (theater) play (10W)
der **Student', -en, -en / die Studen'tin, -nen** student (S5)
das **Studentenheim, -e** dorm (6W)
die **Studiengebühr, -en** tuition
der **Studienplatz, ⁻e** opening to study at the university
studie'ren to study a particular field; **~ (an** + *dat.*) to be a student at a university (4E)
der **Studie'rende (ein Studierender)** student
das **Studio, -s** studio
das **Studium, Studien** course of study (13W)
der **Stuhl, ⁻e** chair (S2,5W)

die **Stunde, -n** hour, class, lesson (S5); **in einer halben ~** in half an hour (8W); **in einer Viertel~** in 15 minutes (8W); **in einer Dreiviertel~** in 45 minutes (8W)
stundenlang for hours (5E)
der **Stundenplan, ⁻e** schedule (of classes)
das **Subjekt', -e** subject
die **Suche** search
suchen to look for (2W); **gesucht wird** wanted
der **Süden: im ~** in the south (1W)
südlich (von) south (of), to the south (of) (1W)
super superb, terrific (S4)
der **Superlativ, -e** superlative
der **Supermarkt, ⁻e** supermarket (2W)
su'permodern' very modern
die **Suppe, -n** soup (3W)
süß sweet
das **Sweatshirt, -s** sweatshirt (S3)
das **Symbol', -e** symbol
die **Sympathie'** congeniality
sympa'thisch congenial, likable (11W)
die **Symphonie', -n** symphony
die **Synago'ge, -n** synagogue
synchronisiert' dubbed
die **Synthe'tik** synthetics
das **System', -e** system (13W)
die **Szene, -n** scene

T

die **Tablet'te, -n** pill
die **Tafel, -n** (black)board (S2); **Gehen Sie an die ~!** Go to the (black)board. (SSS)
der **Tag, -e** day (S4); **~!** Hi (informal)! **am ~** during the day (6E); **eines Tages** one day (8G); **Guten ~!** Hello. (S1); **jeden ~** every day (8G); **~ der Arbeit** Labor Day
tagelang for days
-tägig days long
täglich daily (10E)
das **Tal, ⁻er** valley

das **Talent', -e** talent
talentiert' talented (11W)
die **Tante, -n** aunt (1W)
der **Tanz, ⁻e** dance
tanzen to dance (4W)
die **Tasche, -n** bag, pocket (7W); handbag
die **Tasse, -n** cup (2E); **eine ~ a** cup of (2E)
die **Tatsache, -n** fact
die **Taube, -n** dove; pigeon
tauchen (in + *acc.*) to dip (into)
tauschen to trade
das **Taxi, -s** taxi (5W)
die **Technik** technology
der **Techniker, -** technician
technisch technical
der **Tee, -s** tea (2W)
der **Teenager, -** teenager
der **Teil, -e** part (1E)
teilen to share (13E); to divide (14W)
teilmöbliert partly furnished
die **Teilnahme** participation
teil·nehmen* (an + *dat.*) to participate (in), take part (in) (13E)
teils partly
die **Teilung, -en** division
teilweise partly
das **Telefon', -e** telephone (6W); **die ~karte, -n** telephone card (8W); **die ~nummer, -n** telephone number (8W); **die ~zelle, -n** telephone booth
telefonie'ren to call up, phone (8W)
die **Telekommunikation'** telecommunications
der **Teller, -** plate (3W)
das **Temperament', -e** temperament
temperament'voll dynamic (11W)
die **Temperatur', -en** temperature
das **Tennis: ~ spielen** to play tennis (S5)
der **Teppich, -e** carpet (6W)
die **Terras'se, -n** terrace
das **Testament', -e** last will and testament

testen to test
teuer expensive (S3)
der **Teufel, -** devil
der **Text, -e** text
das **Thea'ter, -** theater (5W)
das **Thema, Themen** topic
der **Theolo'ge, -n, -n** theologian
die **Theologie'** theology
die **Theorie', -n** theory
das **Thermome'ter, -** thermometer
der **Tiefbau** civil engineering
der **Tiefbauingenieur', -e** civil engineer
die **Tiefkühlkost** frozen foods
das **Tier, -e** animal; **die ~art, -en** animal species
tierlieb fond of animals
das **Tierkreiszeichen, -** sign of the zodiac
der **Tiger, -** tiger
die **Tinte** ink
das **Tintenfass, ⁻er** inkwell
der **Tipp, -s** hint
der **Tisch, -e** table (S2,5W); **Nacht~** nightstand
die **Tischdecke, -n** tablecloth
der **Tischler, -** cabinet-maker
das **Tischtennis: ~ spielen** to play Ping-Pong
der **Titel, -** title
tja well
der **Toast, -s** toast; **das ~brot** toast
die **Tochter, ⁻** daughter (1W)
der **Tod** death
todmüde dead-tired
Toi, toi, toi! Good luck!
die **Toilet'te, -n** toilet (6W)
tolerant' tolerant
toll great, terrific (S4)
die **Toma'te, -n** tomato (2W)
der **Ton, ⁻e** tone, note, pitch
der **Topf, ⁻e** pot
das **Tor, -e** gate (14E)
die **Torte, -n** (fancy) cake
tot dead
total' total(ly)
der **Total'schaden, ⁻** total wreck
töten to kill
die **Tour, -en** tour
der **Touris'mus** tourism

der **Tourist′, -en, -en** tourist (5W)
der **Touri′stikumsatz** spending on travel
das **Tournier, -e** tournament
die **Tracht, -en** (folk) costume
der **Trachtenzug, ⸚e** parade with people dressed in traditional costumes
traditionell′ traditional(ly)
tragen (trägt), trug, getragen to carry (3G); to wear (3G)
die **Tragetasche, -n** tote bag
der **Trainer, -** coach
das **Training** training
das **Transport′flugzeug, -e** transport plane
transportie′ren to transport
trauen to trust
der **Traum, ⸚e** dream
träumen (von) to dream (of) (11W)
der **Träumer, -** dreamer
traurig sad (10W)
die **Traurigkeit** sadness
die **Trauung, -en** wedding ceremony
(sich) **treffen (trifft), traf, getroffen** to meet (with) (9W); **Freunde ~** to meet with friends (9W)
das **Treffen, -** meeting, reunion
der **Treffpunkt, -e** meeting place
treiben, trieb, getrieben to push
trennen to separate (15W)
die **Treppe, -n** stairs, stairway
das **Treppenhaus, ⸚er** stairwell
treten (tritt), trat, ist getreten to step
treu faithful, true, loyal
sich **trimmen** to keep fit
trinken, trank, getrunken to drink (2W)
das **Trinkgeld, -er** tip
der **Trockner, -** dryer
die **Trommel, -n** drum
die **Trompe′te, -n** trumpet
trotz (+ *gen.*) in spite of (8G)
trotzdem nevertheless, in spite of that (6E)
die **Trümmer** (*pl.*) rubble; ruins

der **Trümmerhaufen, -** pile of rubble
der **Tscheche, -n, -n / die Tschechin, -nen** the Czech
tschechisch Czech
die **Tschechische Republik′ = (das) Tschechien** Czech Republic
die **Tschechoslowakei′** (former) Czechoslovakia
tschechisch Czech
Tschüss! So long; (Good-)bye! (S1)
das **T-Shirt, -s** T-shirt (S3)
tun (tut), tat, getan to do (4W)
die **Tür, -en** door (S2)
der **Türke, -n, -n / die Türkin, -nen** the Turk
die **Türkei′** Turkey
türkisch Turkish
der **Turm, ⸚e** tower (14W); steeple
turnen to do sports or gymnastics
typisch typical(ly) (15E)

U

die **U-Bahn, -en** subway (5W)
über (+ *acc.* / *dat.*) over, above (6G); about (10G)
überall everywhere (3E)
überein′·stimmen to agree
überfüllt′ (over)crowded
überhaupt′ at all; **~ nicht** not at all (12W); **~ kein Problem** no problem at all (12W)
das **Überhol′verbot, -** no-passing zone
überle′ben to survive
überneh′men* to take over
übermorgen the day after tomorrow (4W)
übernach′ten to spend the night (7E)
die **Übernach′tung, -en** (overnight) accommodations
überra′schen to surprise (4W)
die **Überra′schung, -en** surprise (4W)

überset′zen to translate
die **Überset′zung, -en** translation
üblich usual, customary
übrig bleiben* to be left, remain
die **Übrigen** the rest
übrigens by the way (15W)
die **Übung, -en** exercise, practice
das **Ufer, -** riverbank
die **Uhr, -en** watch, clock; o'clock (S5); **Wie viel ~ ist es?** What time is it? (S5); **~zeit** time of the day (7W)
der **Uhrmacher, -** watchmaker
um (+ *acc.*) around (the circumference) (2G); at . . . o'clock (S5); **~ . . . zu** in order to (9G); **fast ~** almost over
um sein* to be over/up; **deine Zeit ist ~** your time is up
die **Umgangsform, -en** manners
umge′ben (von) surrounded by
die **Umge′bung** (*sg.*) surroundings (14W)
umgekehrt vice versa
(um·)kippen (ist) to tip over
um·leiten to detour, redirect (traffic)
umliegend surrounding
ummau′ern to surround by a wall
der **Umsatz** sales, spending
sich **um·sehen*** to look around
der **Umstand, ⸚e** circumstance
um·steigen* (ist) to change (trains etc.) (8W)
der **Umtausch** exchange
um·tauschen to exchange
die **Umwelt** environment, surroundings (15W)
umweltbewusst environmentally aware (15W)
der **Umweltverschmutzer, -** polluter
sich **um·ziehen*** to change (clothing), get changed (9G)
der **Umzug, ⸚e** parade; move, moving
unabhängig (von) independent (of)

un'attraktiv' unattractive
unbebaut vacant, empty
unbedingt definitely (12E)
unbegehrt undesired
unbegrenzt unlimited
unbequem uncomfortable, inconvenient (6W)
und and (S1,2G)
und so weiter (usw.) and so on (etc.) (5E)
unehrlich dishonest (11W)
unentrinnbar inescapable
der Unfall, ⸚e accident
unfreiwillig involuntary
unfreundlich unfriendly (11W)
der Ungar, -n, -n the Hungarian
ungarisch Hungarian
(das) Ungarn Hungary
ungebildet uneducated (11W)
ungeduldig impatient (11W)
ungefähr about, approximately (1E)
ungemütlich unpleasant, uncomfortable
ungestört unhindered
unglaublich unbelievable, incredible
das Unglück bad luck
unglücklich unhappy (11W)
unheimlich tremendously, extremely (14W)
die Uni, -s (abbrev.) university (5W)
die Universität', -en university (5W)
unkompliziert' uncomplicated (11W)
unmöbliert unfurnished
unmög'lich impossible
unmusikalisch unmusical (11W)
Unrecht haben* to be wrong (11W)
uns us, to us (5G); bei ~ at our place (3G); in our city/country
unselbstständig dependent (11W)
unser our (7G)
unsicher insecure, unsafe (12W)

der Unsinn nonsense
unsportlich unathletic (11W)
unsympathisch uncongenial, unlikable (11W)
untalentiert untalented (11W)
unten downstairs (6W)
unter (+ acc. / dat.) under, below (6G); among (12E); ~einander among each other
der Untergang fall, downfall
unterhal'tend entertaining
die Unterhal'tung entertainment (10W)
das Unterneh'men, - large company (12E)
unterneh'mungslustig enterprising (11W)
der Unterricht instruction, lesson, class
der Unterschied, -e difference
unterschrei'ben* to sign (7W)
die Unterschrift, -en signature
unterstreichen, unterstrich, unterstrichen to underline
unterstüt'zen to support
unterwegs' on the go, on the road
untreu unfaithful
unverheiratet unmarried, single (11W)
die Unwahrscheinlichkeit here: unreal condition
unzerstört intact
unzufrieden discontent
unzuverlässig unreliable (11W)
Urgroß-: die ~eltern great-grandparents; die ~mutter great-grandmother; der ~vater great-grandfather
der Urlaub paid vacation (9E); der Mutterschafts~ maternity leave
ursprünglich original(ly)
der Urlaubstag, -e (paid) vacation day
die USA = Vereinigten Staaten von Amerika (pl.) United States of America
u.s.w. (und so weiter) etc. (and so on)

V

der Vampir', -e vampire
die Vanil'le vanilla
die Variation', -en variation
variie'ren to vary
die Vase, -n vase
der Vater, ⸚ father (1W); Groß~ grandfather (1W); Urgroß~ great-grandfather; Stief~ step-father
der Vati, -s Dad
verallgemei'nern to generalize
die Verallgemei'nerung, -en generalization
(sich) verändern to change (15W)
verantwortlich responsible
die Verantwortung, -en responsibility (12W)
verantwortungsvoll responsible
das Verb, -en verb
verbannen to ban
verbessern to improve
verbieten, verbot, verboten to forbid, prohibit (15W)
verbinden, verband, verbunden to connect, tie together, link (15E)
das Verbot, -e restriction
verboten forbidden (15W)
der Verbrauch consumption
der Verbraucher, - consumer
verbreiten to distribute, spread
die Verbreitung, -en distribution
verbrennen, verbrannte, verbrannt to burn
verbunden in touch, close
die Verbundenheit closeness
verdammen to curse
verderben (verdirbt), verdarb, verdorben to spoil
verdienen to deserve; earn; make money (12W)
der Verein, -e club, association; Turn~ athletic club
vereinigen to unite; wieder~ to reunite
die Vereinigten Staaten (U.S.A.) (pl.) United States (U.S.)

die **Vereinigung** unification (15E)
vereint united (15E)
das **Verfassungsgericht** Supreme/Constitutional Court
Verflixt! Darn it!
die **Vergangenheit** past (tense); simple past
vergehen* (ist) to pass (time), end
vergessen (vergisst), vergaß, vergessen to forget (11W)
der **Vergleich, -e** comparison
vergleichen, verglich, verglichen to compare
das **Verhältnis, -se** relationship, condition
verheiratet married (11W)
verhindern to prevent
die **Verkabelung** connecting by cable
verkaufen to sell (2W)
der **Verkäufer, -** salesman, sales clerk (2W)
der **Verkehr** traffic
das **Verkehrsmittel, -** means of transportation
der **Verlag, -e** publishing house
verlassen (verlässt), verließ, verlassen to leave (14E)
sich **verlaufen*** to get lost
verlegen to transfer, relocate
sich **verlieben (in** + *acc.*) to fall in love (with) (11W)
verliebt (in + *acc.*) in love (with) (11W)
verlieren, verlor, verloren (an + *dat.*) to lose (in) (11W)
sich **verloben (mit)** to get engaged (to)
verlobt (mit) engaged (to) (11W)
der **Verlobte (ein Verlobter)** fiancé (12G)
die **Verlobte (eine Verlobte)** fiancée (12G)
die **Verlobung, -en** engagement
verlockend tempting
vermieten to rent out (6W)
der **Vermieter, -** landlord
vermissen to miss

verneinen to negate
die **Vernichtung** destruction
verrückt crazy (4E)
verschenken to give away
verschieden various, different (kinds of) (10E)
verschlechtern to deteriorate
verschlingen, verschlang, verschlungen to gulp down, devour
die **Verschmutzung** pollution (15W)
verschönern to beautify
verschwiegen discreet
die **Versicherung, -en** insurance
versinken* to sink (in)
die **Version', -en** version
die **Verspätung** delay; **Der Zug hat ~.** The train is late.
versprechen* to promise (11E)
der **Verstand** reasoning, logic; common sense
verständlich understandable
verständnisvoll understanding (11W)
verstecken to hide
verstehen* (hat) to understand (S3); **Ich verstehe (das) nicht.** I don't understand (that). (SSS)
versuchen to try (11W)
die **Verteidigung** defense
der **Vertrag, ⁻e** contract
vertraulich confidential
die **Verwaltung, -en** administration
der **Verwandte (ein Verwandter)** relative
verwenden to use, utilize (15W)
verwitwet widowed
verwöhnen to indulge, spoil
das **Verzeichnis, -se** index, catalog
verzeihen, verzieh, verziehen to forgive; **~ Sie (mir)!** Forgive me. Pardon (me)!
die **Verzeihung** pardon; **~!** Excuse me! Pardon me! (5W)
der **Vetter, -n** cousin (1W)
der **Videorecorder, -** VCR
viel- (mehr, meist-) much, many (3W,10G,12G); **ganz schön ~** quite at lot; **so~ ich weiß** as much as I know
vielleicht' perhaps (3E)
vielseitig versatile (11W)
viereckig square
vielsprachig multilingual
die **Viersprachigkeit** speaking four languages
das **Viertel, -:** **(um) ~ nach** (at) a quarter past (S5); **(um) ~ vor** (at) a quarter to (S5); **in einer ~stunde** in a quarter of an hour (8W); **in einer Dreiviertelstunde** in three quarters of an hour (8W)
die **Vision', -en** vision
vital' vital
der **Vogel, ⁻** bird; **Du hast einen ~.** You're crazy.
die **Voka'bel, -n** (vocabulary) word
das **Vokabular'** vocabulary
das **Volk, ⁻er** folk; people, nation (14W)
die **Volkskammer** *(GDR)* the People's Chamber
die **Völkerkunde** ethnology
die **Volksherrschaft** *here:* domination by the people
das **Volkslied, -er** folk song
die **Volkspolizei** *(GDR)* People's Police
der **Volkspolizist, -en, -en =** **Vopo, -s** member of the GDR People's Police
der **Volksstamm, ⁻e** ethnic group
der **Volkswagen, -** VW
die **Volkswirtschaft** (macro)economics
voll full (11E)
der **Volleyball, ⁻e** volleyball
der **Vollzeitstudent, -en, -en** full-time student
von (+ *dat.*) of, from, by (3G); **~ . . . bis** from . . . until; **vom . . . bis zum** from the . . . to the (4W)
vor (+ *acc. / dat.*) in front of, before (6G); **~ einer Woche** a week ago (4W): **~ allem** above all, mainly (10E)

VOCABULARIES V-35

    voran·kommen* to advance
der **Vorarbeiter, -** foreman
    vorbei'·bringen* to bring over
    vorbei'·fahren* to drive by, pass
    vorbei'·führen (an + *dat.*) to pass (by) (14W)
    vorbei·'gehen* (*bei* + *dat.*) to pass by (7G)
    vorbei'·kommen* to come by, pass by
    vorbei' sein* to be over, finished
(sich) **vor·bereiten (auf** + *acc.*) to prepare (for) (13E)
die **Vorbereitung, -en** preparation
die **Vorbeugung, -en** prevention
die **Vorfahrt** right of way
    vor·gehen* to proceed; **der Reihe nach ~** to proceed one after the other
    vorgestern the day before yesterday (4W)
    vor·haben* to plan (to), intend (to)
der **Vorhang, ⸚e** curtain (6W)
    vorher ahead (of time), in advance; before, previously
    vorher'gehend preceding; **das ~e Wort** antecedent
    vor·kommen* (**in** + *dat.*) to appear (in); **Das kommt mir . . . vor.** That seems . . . to me.
das **(flache) Vorland** *here:* tidal flats
die **Vorlesung, -en** lecture, class (university) (S5); **~sverzeichnis, -se** course catalog
der **Vormittag, -e** (mid-)morning; **heute ~** this (mid-)morning (8G)
der **Vorname, -ns, -n** first name
die **Vorschau** preview
die **Vorsicht: ~!** Careful! (7E)
    vor·stellen to introduce; **Darf ich ~?** May I introduce?; **sich ~** to introduce oneself
sich **vor·stellen** to imagine (12E); **ich stelle mir vor, dass** I imagine that (12E)

die **Vorstellung, -en** performance (10W); idea
der **Vorteil, -e** advantage
der **Vortrag, ⸚e** talk, speech, lecture
    vorü'bergehend temporary
    vor·wärmen to preheat
    vor·ziehen* to prefer (9E)

W

das **Wachs** wax
    wachsen (wächst), wuchs, ist gewachsen to grow (15E)
die **Waffe, -n** weapon
die **Waffel, -n** waffle
    wagen to dare
der **Wagen, -** car (8W); railroad car (8W)
die **Wahl** choice, selection
    wählen to choose; elect; select
das **Wahlfach, ⸚er** elective (subject)
der **Wahnsinn** insanity; **(Das ist ja) ~!** (That's) awesome/crazy. (14E)
    wahnsinnig crazy
    während (+ *gen.*) during (8G); while *(conj.)*
    wahr true; **nicht ~?** isn't it? (S4)
    wahrlich *(poetic)* truly
    wahrschein'lich probably (13E)
die **Währung, -en** currency
der **Wald, ⸚er** forest, woods (7E)
der **Walzer, -** waltz
die **Wand, ⸚e** wall (S2)
der **Wanderer, -** hiker
    wandern (ist) to hike (9W)
der **Wanderweg, -e** (hiking) trail
    wann? when?, at what time? (S4,11G)
    wäre: Wie wär's mit. . . ? How about . . . ?
die **Ware, -n** goods, wares, merchandise
    warm (ä) warm (S4)
die **Wärme** warmth
    warnen (vor + *dat.*) to warn (against)

    warten to wait; (**~ auf** + *acc.*) to wait for (10G)
    warum? why? (2E)
    was? what? (S2,2G); **~ für (ein)?** what kind of (a)? (2W)
das **Waschbecken, -** sink
die **Wäsche** laundry; **~ waschen*** to do the laundry
die **Waschecke, -n** corner reserved for washing
(sich) **waschen (wäscht), wusch, gewaschen** to wash (o.s.) (6W;9G)
der **Waschlappen, -** washcloth (*fig.* wimp)
die **Waschmaschi'ne, -n** washing machine
das **Waschmittel, -** (washing) detergent
das **Wasser** water (2W)
der **Wassermann, ⸚er** Aquarius
der **Wasserski, -er** water ski; **~ laufen*** to water ski; **~laufen gehen*** to go waterskiing
die **Web-Ecke, -n** *here:* name of updates and online activities
die **Web-Seite, -n** webpage
der **Wechsel** change
der **Wechselkurs, -e** exchange rate
    wechseln to (ex)change (7W)
die **Wechselstube, -n** exchange office
    weder . . . noch neither . . . nor (10E)
    weg away, gone
der **Weg, -e** way, path, trail (5W); route; **nach dem ~ fragen** to ask for directions
    wegen (+ *gen.*) because of (8G)
    weg·werfen* to throw away (15W)
    weh·tun* to hurt; **Mir tut (der Hals) weh.** My (throat) hurts. I have a sore throat. (9W)
    weich soft
die **Weide, -n** willow
(das) **Weihnachten: zu ~** at/for Christmas (4W);

Frohe/Fröhliche ~! Merry Christmas!
der **Weihnachtsbaum, ⸚e** Christmas tree
das **Weihnachtsessen, -** Christmas dinner
das **Weihnachtslied, -er** Christmas carol
der **Weihnachstmann, ⸚er** Santa Claus
weil *(conj.)* because (4G)
die **Weile: eine ~** for a while
weilen *(poetic)* to stay, be
der **Wein, -e** wine (2W); **Tafel~** table wine; **Qualitäts~** quality wine; **Qualitäts~ mit Prädikat** superior wine
der **Weinberg, -e** vineyard
weinen to cry (10W)
die **Weinstube, -n** wine cellar, tavern
weise wise
die **Weise: auf diese ~** (in) this way (11W)
weiß white (S2)
weit far (5W)
die **Weite** distance; wide-open spaces
weiter: und so ~ (usw.) and so on (etc.): **~ draußen** farther out; **Wie geht's ~?** How does it go on? What's next?
Weiteres *here:* additional words and phrases
weiter·fahren* (ist) to drive on, keep on driving (8E); continue the trip
weiter·geben* to pass on
weiter·gehen* (ist) to continue, go on
weiterhin still
welch- which (7G); **Welche Farbe hat . . . ?** What color is . . . ? (S2)
die **Welle, -n** wave
die **Welt, -en** world (11E)
weltoffen cosmopolitan
wem? (to) whom? (3G)
wen? whom? (2G)
wenig- little (not much), few (10G)
wenigstens at least (12E)

wenn *(conj.)* if, (when)ever (4G,11G); **selbst ~** even if
wer? who? (1G); who(so)ever
die **Werbung** advertisement (10W)
werden (wird), wurde, ist geworden to become, get (3G); **Was willst du ~?** What do you want to be? (12W); **Ich will . . . ~.** I want to be a . . . (12W)
werfen, (wirft), warf, geworfen to throw (15W)
der **Wert, -e** value; worth
wertvoll valuable
wessen (+ *gen.*) whose? (8G)
der **Wessi, -s** *(nickname)* = **Westdeutsche** West German
der **Westen: im ~** in the west (1W)
westlich von west of
die **Westmächte** *(pl.)* Western Allies
der **Wettbewerb, -e** contest
das **Wetter** weather (S4)
wichtig important (1E)
wickeln to wrap
widersteh'en* (+ *dat.*) to withstand
wie? how? (S1); like, as; **~ sagt man . . . ?** How does one say . . . ? (S2); **~ bitte?** What did you say, please? (SSS); **so . . . ~ as . . . as** (1E); **~ lange?** how long? (4W); **~ gesagt** as I (you, etc.) said
wieder again (S4); **schon ~** already again (S4); **immer ~** again and again, time and again (12G); **Da sieht man's mal ~!** That just goes to show you. (15W)
der **Wiederaufbau** rebuilding, reconstruction
wieder auf·bauen to rebuild, reconstruct
wiederho'len to repeat (S2)
die **Wiederho'lung, -en** repetition, review
wiederhören to hear again;

Auf Wiederhören! Goodbye. (on the phone) (6W)
wiedersehen* to see again; **Auf Wiedersehen!** Goodbye (S1)
(wieder)vereinigen to (re)unite
die **(Wieder)vereinigung** (re)unification (14E)
wiegen, wog, gewogen to weigh; **Lass es ~!** Have it weighed.
der **Wiener, -** the Viennese
die **Wiese, -n** meadow
Wieso' (denn)? How come? Why? (13W)
wie viel? how much? (S3,3W)
wie viele? how many? (S3,3W)
wild wild
der **Wille, -ns, -n** will; **Wo ein ~ ist, ist auch ein Weg.** Where there's a will, there's a way.
der **Wind, -e** wind
windig windy (S4)
Windsurfen gehen* to go windsurfing
der **Winter, -** winter (S4); **im ~** in (the) winter (S4)
das **Winzerfest, -e** vintage festival
wirken to appear
wirklich really, indeed (S4)
die **Wirklichkeit** reality
die **Wirtschaft** economy
wirtschaftlich economical(ly)
der **Wirtschaftsprüfer, -** accountant
das **Wirtschaftswunder** economic boom (*lit.:* miracle)
wissen (weiß), wusste, gewusst to know (a fact) (6G); **Ich weiß (nicht).** I (don't) know. (SSS); **soviel ich weiß** as far as I know
die **Wissenschaft, -en** science, academic discipline (13W); **Natur~** natural science(s) (13W)
der **Wissenschaftler, -** scientist (12W)

wissenschaftlich scientific
der **Witz, -e** joke; **Mach (doch) keine ~e!** Stop joking!
witzig witty, funny
wo? where? (S2,6G)
die **Woche, -n** week (S4)
das **Wochenende, -n** weekend; **am ~** on the weekend (4W)
wochenlang for weeks
wöchentlich weekly (10E)
-wöchig weeks long
woher'? from where? (1W)
wohin'? where to? (6G)
wohl flavoring particle expressing probability
wohlriechend fragrant
die **Wohngemeinschaft, -en =** **WG, -s** group sharing a place to live, co-op
wohnen to live, reside (1E)
das **Wohnsilo, -s** (high-rise) apartment (cluster)
der **Wohnsitz, -e** residence
die **Wohnung, -en** apartment (6W)
der **Wohnwagen, -** camper
das **Wohnzimmer, -** living room (6W)
der **Wolf, ⸚e** wolf
die **Wolke, -n** cloud
die **Wolle** wool
wollen (will), wollte, gewollt to want to (5G)
das **Wort, -e** (connected) word; **mit anderen ~en** in other words
das **Wort, ⸚er** (individual) word
das **Wörtchen, -** little word
das **Wörterbuch, ⸚er** dictionary
der **Wortschatz** vocabulary
das **Wunder, -** wonder, miracle
wunderbar wonderful(ly) (S1)
sich **wundern: ~ Sie sich nicht!** Don't be surprised.
wunderschön beautiful (14W)
der **Wunsch, ⸚e** wish (11W) **~traum, ⸚e** ideal dream
(sich) **wünschen** to wish (4W)
die **Wunschwelt** ideal world
die **Wurst, ⸚e** sausage (2W); **Das ist doch ~!** It doesn't matter.

das **Würstchen, -** wiener, hot dog (2E)
würzen to season

Z

die **Zahl, -en** number (S3); **Ordinal** ordinal number (4W)
zählen to count (S3)
der **Zahn, ⸚e** tooth (9W); **sich die Zähne** to brush one's teeth (9G)
der **Zahnarzt, ⸚e / die Zahnärztin, -nen** dentist (12W)
die **Zahnbürste, -n** toothbrush
die **Zahn'medizin'** dentistry
die **Zahnpasta, -pasten** toothpaste
die **Zahnradbahn, -en** cogwheel railway
der **Zahntechniker , -** dental technician
zart tender
zärtlich affectionate (11W)
die **Zärtlichkeit** affection
der **Zauber** magic (power)
der **Zauberspruch, ⸚e** magic spell
z. B. (zum Beispiel) e.g. (for example)
das **Zeichen, -** signal, sign
der **Zeichentrickfilm, -e** cartoon, animated film
die **Zeichnung, -en** drawing
zeigen to show (5W); **Zeig mal** Show me (us, etc.)!
die **Zeit, -en** time (S5); tense; **die gute alte ~** the good old days
die **Zeitform, -en** tense
die **Zeitschrift, -en** magazine (10W)
die **Zeitung, -en** newspaper (10W); **Wochen~** weekly newspaper
die **Zelle, -n** cell, booth
das **Zelt, -e** tent
zentral' central(ly)
das **Zentrum, Zentren** center; **im ~** downtown
zerbomben to destroy by bombs

zerstören to destroy (15W)
die **Zerstörung** destruction
ziehen, zog, gezogen to pull (11E); to raise (vegetables, etc.)
ziehen, zog, ist gezogen to move (relocate)
das **Ziel, -e** goal, objective; destination
ziemlich quite, fairly (6W)
die **Zigeu'nerin, -nen** gypsy
das **Zimmer, -** room (S2)
der **Zim'merkolle'ge, -n, -n / die Zimmerkolle'gin, -nen** roommate (13W)
der **Zimmernachweis, -e** room-referral service
die **Zimmervermittlung** room-referral agency
das **Zitat', -e** quote
die **Zitro'ne, -n** lemon (2W)
der **Zoll customs;** toll
die **Zone, -n** zone, area
der **Zoo, -s** zoo
zu (+ *dat.*) to, in the direction of, at, for (purpose) (3G); too (S3); closed (2); (+ *inf.*) to (9G)
zu·bleiben* (ist) to stay closed
der **Zucker** sugar (3W)
zuerst' (at) first (9W)
der **Zufall, ⸚e** coincidence; **So ein ~!** What a coincidence!
zufrie'den satisfied, content
der **Zug, ⸚e** train (8W); **mit dem ~ fahren*** to go by train (8W)
zu·halten* to hold closed
zu·hören to listen (7G); **Hören Sie gut zu!** Listen well. (SSS)
die **Zukunft** future (12W)
zukunftsorientier't future-oriented
zuletzt last (of all); finally
zu·machen to close (7G)
zurück'- back
zurück·bleiben* (ist) to stay behind
zurück·bringen* to bring back

zurück·fliegen* (ist) to fly back
zurück·geben* to give back, return
zurück·halten* to hold back
zurück·kommen* to come back, return (7G)
zurück·nehmen* to take back
zurück´·sehen* to look back
sich **zurück´·ziehen*** to withdraw
zusam´men together (2W); **alle ~** all together; **~gewürfelt** thrown together
zusam´men·fassen to summarize
die **Zusam´menfassung, -en** summary
die **Zusam´mengehörigkeit** affiliation; solidarity
zusammen·wachsen* to grow together
der **Zusatz, ¨e** addition
der **Zuschauer, -** spectator (10E)
zu·schließen* to lock
zu·sehen* to watch; see to it
der **Zustand, ¨e** conditions
zu·stimmen to agree
zuverlässig reliable (11W)
zuvor´ previously; **wie nie ~** as never before
die **Zwiebel, -n** onion
zwischen (+ *acc. / dat.*) between (6G); **in~** in the meantime; **~durch** in between
die **Zwischenlandung, -en** stopover
die **Zwischenzeit** time in between; **in der ~** in the meantime, meanwhile

ENGLISH-GERMAN

Except for numbers, pronouns, and **da-** and **wo-**compounds, this vocabulary includes all active words used in this book. If you are looking for certain idioms, feminine equivalents, or other closely related words, look at the key word given and then refer to it in the German-English vocabulary. Irregular t-verbs ("irregular weak verbs" and n-verbs ("strong verbs" are indicated by an asterisk (*); for their forms and auxiliaries, go to the list of principal parts in the Appendix.

A

able: to be ~ können*
about (approximately) ungefähr, etwa
above über (+ *dat./ acc.*); **~all** vor allem
abroad im/ins Ausland
academic discipline die Wissenschaft, -en
to **accept** an·nehmen*
ache: I have a (head)~. Ich habe (Kopf)schmerzen.
acquaintance der Bekannte (ein Bekannter)
across (from) gegenüber (von + *dat.*)
actor der Schauspieler, -
actual(ly) eigentlich
ad die Anzeige, -n
address die Adresse, -n; **return ~** der Absender, -
advertising die Werbung
affectionate zärtlich
afraid: to be ~ (of) Angst haben* (vor + *dat.*)
after (time) nach (+ *dat.*); **~** (+ *past perf.*) nachdem
afternoon der Nachmittag, -e; **in the ~** nachmittags; **Monday ~** Montagnachmittag
afterwards danach
again wieder, noch einmal; **Could you say that ~?** Wie bitte?; **~ and ~** immer wieder
against gegen (+ *acc.*)
ago vor (+ *dat.*); **a week ~** vor einer Woche
ahead: straight ~ geradeaus
aid die Hilfe
air die Luft
airplane das Flugzeug, -e

airport der Flughafen, ⸚
all all-, alles (*sg.*); **That's ~.** Das ist alles.
to **allow** erlauben
allowed: to be ~ to dürfen*
almost fast
alone allein
already schon
also auch, ebenfalls
although (*conj.*) obwohl
always immer
ambitious ambitiös
America (das) Amerika
American (*adj.*) amerikanisch; (**person**) der Amerikaner, -
among unter (+ *acc./dat.*)
and und
angry: to get ~ about sich ärgern über (+ *acc.*)
another noch ein
to **answer** antworten
answer die Antwort, -en
anyhow sowieso
anyway sowieso
apart auseinander
apartment die Wohnung, -en
to **appear (to be)** scheinen*, aus·sehen*
to **applaud** klatschen
apple der Apfel, ⸚
to **apply** sich bewerben (um)
approximately ungefähr, etwa
April der April; **in ~** im April
area die Gegend, -en
arm der Arm, -e
armchair der Sessel, -
around um (+ *acc.*)
arrival die Ankunft
to **arrive (in)** an·kommen* (in + *dat.*)

art die Kunst, ⸚e
artist der Künstler, -
as wie; **~ . . . ~** so . . . wie
to **ask** fragen, bitten*; **to ~ a question** eine Frage stellen
at an (+ *dat.*); (**o'clock**) um . . . (Uhr); (**the place of**) bei (+ *dat.*)
athletic sportlich; **un~** unsportlich
at least wenigstens
attention: to pay ~ auf·passen
attractive attraktiv, hübsch
attribute die Eigenschaft, -en
August der August; **in ~** im August
aunt die Tante, -n
Austria (das) Österreich
Austrian (language) österreichisch; (**person**) der Österreicher, -
author der Autor, -en
available frei
awesome: ~! Wahnsinn!

B

bad(ly) schlecht; schlimm; **too ~** schade
bag die Tasche, -n
baggage das Gepäck
bakery die Bäckerei, -en
balcony der Balkon, -e (*or* -s)
banana die Banane, -n
bank die Bank, -en
banknote der (Geld)schein, -e
barely kaum
bath(room) das Bad, ⸚er; **to take a ~** sich baden

to **be** sein*; **(become)** werden*; **Be . . . !** Sei (Seid, Seien Sie) . . . !
bean die Bohne, -n
beautiful (wunder)schön
because *(conj.)* weil, denn; **~ of** wegen *(+ gen.)*
to **become** werden*
bed das Bett, -en; **~room** das Schlafzimmer, -
beer das Bier
before vor *(+ acc./dat.)*; *(conj.)* bevor; **not ~ (time)** erst; *(adv.)* vorher
to **begin** beginnen*, an·fangen*
beginning der Anfang, ⁻e; **in the ~** am Anfang
behind hinter *(+ acc./dat.)*
to **believe (in)** glauben (an + *acc.*); **(things)** Ich glaube es.; **(persons)** Ich glaube ihm/ihr.; **you better ~ it!** Und ob!
belly der Bauch, ⁻e
to **belong** to gehören *(+ dat.)*
below unter *(+ acc./dat.)*
beside neben *(+ acc./dat.)*
besides *(adv.)* außerdem
best best-, am besten
bet: you ~! Und ob!
better besser; **you ~ believe it** Und ob!
between zwischen *(+ acc./dat.)*
bicycle das Fahrrad, ⁻er
to **bicycle** mit dem Fahrrad fahren*
big groß (ö)
bill die Rechnung, -en
billion *(American)* die Milliarde, -n
birthday der Geburtstag, -e; **on/for the ~** zum Geburtstag
bit: a little ~ ein bisschen
black schwarz (ä)
blackboard die Tafel, -n
blouse die Bluse, -n
blue blau
boarding house die Pension, -en
body der Körper, -
book das Buch, ⁻er; **~ store** die Buchhandlung, -en
border die Grenze, -n
bored: to get (or be) ~ sich langweilen
boring langweilig
born geboren (ist); **I was ~ May 3, 1968, in Munich.** Ich bin am 3. 5. 68 in München geboren.
both **(things,** *sg.)* beides; *(pl.)* beide
bottle die Flasche, -n; **a ~ of . . .** eine Flasche . . .
boy der Junge, -n, -n
bread das Brot, -e
break (intermission) die Pause, -n
breakfast das Frühstück; **(What's) for ~?** (Was gibt's) zum Frühstück?; **to eat ~** frühstücken
bridge die Brücke, -n
bright **(light)** hell; intelligent
to **bring** bringen*; **to ~ along** mit·bringen*
brother der Bruder, ⁻
brown braun
to **brush (one's teeth)** sich (die) Zähne putzen
to **build** bauen; **to re~** wieder auf·bauen; **to be built** entstehen*
building das Gebäude, -
bus der Bus, -se
business das Geschäft, -e
businessman der Geschäftsmann, ⁻er
businesswoman die Geschäftsfrau, -en
businesspeople Geschäftsleute
business management Betriebswirtschaft; **graduate in ~** Betriebswirt, -e
but aber; doch; **not only . . . ~ also** nicht nur . . . sondern auch
butter die Butter
to **buy** kaufen
by *(passive voice)* von *(+ dat.)*

C

café das Café, -s
cafeteria (student) die Mensa
cake der Kuchen, -
to **call** rufen*; **to ~ (up)** an·rufen*, telefonieren; **to ~ (name)** nennen*; **to be ~ed** heißen*
campground der Campingplatz, ⁻e
can können*
Canada (das) Kanada
Canadian *(adj.)* kanadisch; **(person)** der Kanadier, -
candle die Kerze, -n
capital die Hauptstadt, ⁻e
car das Auto, -s, der Wagen, -; **(railroad ~)** der Wagen, -
card die Karte, -n; **post~** die Postkarte, -n; **telephone ~** die Telefonkarte, -n
cardigan die Jacke, -n
to **care: Take ~ !** Mach's gut! **Careful!** Vorsicht!
carpet der Teppich, -e
carrot die Karotte, -n
to **carry** tragen*
case: in any ~ jedenfalls
cash das Bargeld; **~ register** die Kasse, -n
to **cash (in) (a check)** (einen Scheck) ein·lösen
cassette die Kassette, -n
cathedral der Dom, -e
to **celebrate** feiern
celebration das Fest, -e
center die Mitte
certain(ly) bestimmt, sicherlich
certificate der Schein, -e
chair der Stuhl, ⁻e; **arm~** der Sessel, -
chalk die Kreide
champagne der Sekt
change das Kleingeld
to **change** (sich) ändern, (sich) verändern; **(clothing)** sich um·ziehen*; **(money, etc.)** wechseln, um·tauschen; **(trains)** um·steigen*

channel das Programm, -e
characteristic die Eigenschaft, -en
charming charmant
cheap billig
check der Scheck, -s; **traveler's ~** der Reisescheck, -s
cheese der Käse
chic schick
child das Kind, -er
choice (of) die Auswahl (an + *dat.*)
choir der Chor, ⸚e
Christmas (das) Weihnachten; **at/for ~** zu Weihnachten
church die Kirche, -n
citizen der Bürger, -
city die Stadt ⸚e; **~ hall** das Rathaus, ⸚er; **~ map** der Stadtplan, ⸚e
civil servant der Beamte (ein Beamter)
to **clap** klatschen
class (group) die Klasse, -n; **(time)** die Stunde, -n; **(instruction, school)** der Unterricht; **(instruction, university)** die Vorlesung, -en
clean sauber
to **clean** putzen
clerk: civil servant der Beamte (ein Beamter); **(salesman)** der Verkäufer, -
clock die Uhr, -en; **o'clock** Uhr
to **close** zu·machen
closed zu, geschlossen
closet der Schrank, ⸚e
clothing die Kleidung
coat der Mantel, ⸚
coast die Küste, -n
coffee der Kaffee, -s
coin die Münze, -n
cola (drink) die Cola
cold kalt (ä)
cold: to catch a ~ sich erkälten
to **collect** sammeln
color die Farbe, -n; **What ~ is . . . ?** Welche Farbe hat . . . ?

colorful bunt
to **comb** (sich) kämmen
to **come** kommen*; **to ~ along** mit·kommen*; **to ~ back** zurück·kommen*; **to ~ in** herein·kommen*; **That comes to . . . (altogether).** Das kostet (zusammen) . . . ; **Oh, ~ on!** Ach was!
comfortable bequem
comical komisch
common gemeinsam
compact disc, CD die CD, -s
company die Firma, Firmen; **large ~** das Unternehmen, -
composer der Komponist, -en, -en
concern die Sorge, -n
to **be concerned (about)** sich Sorgen machen (um)
concert das Konzert, -e
condo die Eigentumswohnung, -en
congenial sympathisch; **un~** unsympathisch
to **congratulate** gratulieren
to **connect** verbinden*
to **continue** weiter·gehen*, weiter·machen
convenient bequem
to **cook** kochen
cookie das Plätzchen, -
cool kühl
corner die Ecke, -n
correct richtig
to **cost** kosten
to **count** zählen
counter der Schalter, -
country das Land, ⸚er; **in(to) the ~(side)** auf dem/aufs Land
couple: a ~ of ein paar
course der Kurs, -e; **(~ of study)** das Studium; **of ~** natürlich; (na) klar
cousin der Vetter, -n/die Kusine, -n
cozy gemütlich
crazy verrückt; **~!** Wahnsinn!
to **cry** weinen
cucumber die Gurke, -n
cup die Tasse, -n; **a ~ of . . .** eine Tasse . . .

cupboard der Schrank, ⸚e
cultural(ly) kulturell
curtain der Vorhang, ⸚e

D

daily täglich
to **dance** tanzen
danger die Gefahr, -en
dangerous gefährlich
dark dunkel
date (calendar) das Datum, Daten; **What's the ~ today?** Welches Datum haben wir heute?
daughter die Tochter, ⸚
day der Tag, -e; **during the ~** am Tag **one ~** eines Tages; **all ~ long, the whole ~** den ganzen Tag; **each ~** jeden Tag; **in those days** damals
dear lieb-; **Oh ~!** Ach du liebes bisschen!
December der Dezember; **in ~** im Dezember
to **decide** sich entscheiden*
decision die Entscheidung, -en
definitely unbedingt
dentist der Zahnarzt, ⸚e / die Zahnärztin, -nen
departure die Abfahrt, -en
to **depend: That depends.** Das kommt darauf an.
dependent unselbstständig
desk der Schreibtisch, -e
dessert der Nachtisch
to **destroy** zerstören
to **develop** (sich) entwickeln; **~ apart** sich auseinander entwickeln
to **die** sterben (stirbt), starb, ist gestorben
difference der Unterschied, -e
different(ly) verschieden, anders; **something ~** etwas anderes
difficult schwer, schwierig
dining room das Esszimmer, -
dinner das Abendessen
dirty schmutzig

to **discard**   weg·werfen*
dishonest   unehrlich
to **divide**   teilen
divorce   die Scheidung, -en
divorced   geschieden
to **do**   tun*, machen
doctor   der Arzt, ⸚e / die Ärztin, -nen
dollar   der Dollar, -
door   die Tür, -en
dorm   das Studentenheim, -e
downstairs   unten
to **dream (of)**   träumen (von)
dress   das Kleid, -er
dressed: to get ~   (sich) an·ziehen*; **to get un~**   (sich) aus·ziehen*
dresser   die Kommode, -n
to **drink**   trinken*
to **drive**   fahren*; **to ~ on (keep on driving)**   weiterfahren*; **to ~ up**   hinauf·fahren*
drugstore   die Drogerie, -n
dull   langweilig
during   während (+ *gen.*)
dynamic   temperamentvoll

E

each   jed-
ear   das Ohr, -en
earlier   früher
early   früh
to **earn**   verdienen
earth   die Erde
east   der Osten; **~ of**   östlich von
Easter   Ostern; **at/for ~**   zu Ostern
easy   leicht
to **eat**   essen*; **to ~ breakfast**   frühstücken
economy   die Wirtschaft
educated   gebildet
education   die Ausbildung
egg   das Ei, -er
e-mail   die E-Mail, -s
employee   der Angestellte (ein Angestellter) / die Angestellte, -n, -n
empty   leer

end   das Ende; **in the ~**   am Ende
to **end**   auf·hören
engaged   verlobt; **to get ~ (to)**   sich verloben (mit)
engineer   der Ingenieur, -e
England   (das) England
English *(adj.)*   englisch; **in ~**   auf Englisch; **(language)**   Englisch; **Do you speak ~?**   Sprechen Sie Englisch?; **(person)**   der Engländer, -
enough   genug
to **enter**   herein·kommen*
enterprising   unternehmungslustig
entertainment   die Unterhaltung
entire(ly)   ganz
entrance   der Eingang, ⸚e
environment   die Umwelt
environmentally aware   umweltbewusst
equal   gleich
especially   besonders, vor allem
etc.   usw., und so weiter
euro   der Euro, -s
even   sogar
evening   der Abend, -e; **Good ~!**   Guten Abend! **in the ~**   abends, am Abend; **Monday ~**   Montagabend
every   jed-
everything   alles
everywhere   überall
exact(ly)   genau
exam   die Prüfung, -en; **to pass an ~**   eine Prüfung bestehen*; **to flunk an ~**   bei einer Prüfung durch·fallen*; **take an ~**   eine Prüfung machen
excellent   ausgezeichnet
exchange   der Umtausch
to **exchange**   um·tauschen, aus·tauschen, wechseln
exciting   spannend
to **excuse**   sich entschuldigen; **~ me!**   Entschuldigen Sie! Entschuldigung! Verzeihung!
exit   der Ausgang, ⸚e

to **expect**   erwarten
expensive   teuer
to **experience**   erleben
experience   die Erfahrung, -en
to **explain**   erklären
extremely (loud)   unheimlich (laut)
eye   das Auge, -n

F

face   das Gesicht, -er
fairly   ziemlich
to **fall**   fallen*; **to ~ in love (with)**   sich verlieben (in + *acc.*)
fall   der Herbst, -e; **in (the) ~**   im Herbst
false   falsch
family   die Familie, -n
famous   berühmt
fantastic   fantastisch, toll
far   weit
fast   schnell
fat   dick; **to be fattening**   dick machen
father   der Vater, ⸚
fear   die Angst, ⸚e
to **fear**   Angst haben* (vor + *dat.*)
February   der Februar; **in ~**   im Februar
to **feel (a certain way)**   sich fühlen; **How are you (feeling)?**   Wie geht es Ihnen? Wie geht's?; **I'm (feeling) . . .**   Es geht mir . . . ; **to ~ like (doing something)**   Lust haben* (zu + *inf.*)
few   wenig -; **ein paar**
field   das Feld, -er; **(~ of study)**   das Fach, ⸚er
to **fill out**   aus·füllen
film   der Film, -e
finally   endlich
to **finance**   finanzieren
to **fin**   finden*
fine   gut (besser, best-), schön
finger   der Finger, -
finished   fertig
firm   die Firma, Firmen

first erst-; **~ of all, at ~** (zu)erst
fish der Fisch, -e
flight (plane) der Flug, ⁻e
to **fly** fliegen*
floor: on the first ~ im Parterre; **on the second ~** im ersten Stock
flower die Blume, -n
to **follow** folgen (ist) (+ *dat.*)
food das Essen; **Enjoy your ~.** Guten Appetit!
foot der Fuß, ⁻e
for für (+ *acc.*); **(since)** seit (+ *dat.*)
to **forbid** verbieten*
forbidden verboten
foreign ausländisch
foreigner der Ausländer, -
forest der Wald, ⁻er
to **forget** vergessen*
fork die Gabel, -n
foyer der Flur
France (das) Frankreich
free rei
French *(adj.)* französisch; **in ~** auf Französisch; **(language)** Französisch; **Do you speak ~?** Sprechen Sie Französisch?; **(person)** der Franzose, -n, -n/die Französin, -nen
(French) fries die Pommes (frites)*(pl.)*
fresh frisch
Friday (der) Freitag; **on Fridays** freitags
friend der Freund, -e
friendly freundlich; **un~** unfreundlich
from von (+ *dat.*); **(a native of)** aus (+ *dat.*); **I'm ~ . . .** Ich bin aus . . . , Ich komme aus . . . ; **(numbers) ~ . . . to . . .** von . . . bis . . . ; **(place) ~ . . . to . . .** von . . . zu/nach . . .
front: in ~ of vor (+ *acc./dat.*)
fruit das Obst
full voll

fun der Spaß; **to be ~** Spaß machen
funny lustig, witzig; komisch
furniture die Möbel *(pl.)*
future die Zukunft

G

game das Spiel, -e
garage die Garage, -n
garantieren to guarantee
garbage der Müll
garden der Garten, ⁻
gate das Tor, -e
gentleman der Herr, -n, -en
genuine(ly) echt
German *(adj.)* deutsch; **in ~** auf Deutsch; **(language)** Deutsch; **Do you speak ~?** Sprechen Sie Deutsch?; **(person)** der Deutsche (ein Deutscher)/die Deutsche (eine Deutsche)
Germany (das) Deutschland
to **get (become)** werden*; **(fetch)** holen; **(receive)** bekommen*; **to ~ off** aus·steigen*; **to ~ on** *or* **in** ein·steigen*; **to ~ up** auf·stehen*; **to ~ to know** kennen lernen; **to ~ used to** sich gewöhnen an (+ *acc.*)
girl das Mädchen, -
to **give** geben*; **(as a present)** schenken
glad froh
gladly gern (lieber, liebst-)
Glad to meet you. Freut mich.
glass das Glas, ⁻er; **a ~ of . . .** ein Glas . . .
to **go** gehen*; **to ~ by (e.g., bus)** fahren* mit; **to ~ by plane** fliegen*; **to ~ out** aus·gehen*; **to ~ up** hinauf·fahren*
going: What's ~ on? Was ist los?
good gut (besser, best-); **~-looking** gut aussehend

Good-bye! Auf Wiedersehen! Tschüss!; **(on the phone)** Auf Wiederhören!
goodness: My ~! Ach du liebes bisschen!
grade die Note, -n
grandfather der Großvater, ⁻
grandmother die Großmutter, ⁻
grandparents die Großeltern *(pl.)*
gray grau
great (size) groß; **(terrific)** prima, toll, herrlich
green grün
greeting der Gruß, ⁻e
grief: Good ~! Ach du liebes bisschen!
groceries die Lebensmittel *(pl.)*
to **grow** wachsen*; **to ~ together** zusammen·wachsen*
to **guarantee** garantieren
guest der Gast, ⁻e
guitar die Gitarre, -n

H

hair das Haar, -e
half halb; **in ~ an hour** in einer halben Stunde
hallway der Flur
hand die Hand, ⁻e
to **hang (up)** hängen
to **hang (be hanging)** hängen*
to **happen** geschehen*, passieren (ist)
happy glücklich, froh
hard (difficult) schwer
hardly kaum
to **have** haben*; **to ~ to** müssen*
head der Kopf, ⁻e
healthy gesund (ü)
to **hear** hören
heavy schwer
Hello! Guten Tag!
help die Hilfe
to **help** helfen* (+ *dat.*)
her ihr
here hier
Hi! Guten Tag! Hallo!

high hoch (hoh-) (höher, höchst)
to **hike** wandern (ist)
his sein
historical(ly) historisch
history die Geschichte
hobby das Hobby, -s
to **hold** halten*
holiday der Feiertag, -e
home: at ~ zu Hause; **(toward) ~** nach Hause; **at the ~ of** bei (+ *dat.*); **(homeland)** die Heimat
honest ehrlich
to **hope** hoffen
hot heiß
hotel das Hotel, -s, der Gasthof, ⸚e, die Pension, -en
hour die Stunde, -n; **for hours** stundenlang
house das Haus, ⸚er
household der Haushalt
househusband der Hausmann, ⸚er
housemate der Mitbewohner, -
housewife die Hausfrau, -en
how wie **~ much?** wie viel?; **~ many?** wie viele?; **~ much is/are . . . ?** Was kostet/kosten . . . ?; **~ are you?** Wie geht's?, Wie geht es Ihnen?; **~ come?** wieso?
however aber, allerdings; doch
human being der Mensch, -en, -en
hunger der Hunger
hungry: I'm ~. Ich habe Hunger.
to **hurry** sich beeilen
to **hurt** weh·tun*; **My (throat) hurts.** Mir tut (der Hals) weh.
husband der Mann, ⸚er

I

ice, ice cream das Eis
ID der Ausweis, -e
idea die Idee, -n; **I've no ~!** Keine Ahnung!
identification der Ausweis, -e
if *(conj.)* wenn; ob
ill krank (ä)
to **imagine** sich vor·stellen; **I ~ that** ich stelle mir vor, dass
immediately sofort
impatient ungeduldig
important wichtig
in in (+ *dat./acc.*)
income das Einkommen, -
independent selbstständig, unabhängig
individual(ly) einzeln
inexpensive billig
indeed wirklich, doch
industrious(ly) fleißig
inn der Gasthof, ⸚e
insecure unsicher
inside in (+ *dat./acc.*)
in spite of trotz (+ *gen.*)
instead of (an)statt (+ *gen.*)
intelligent intelligent
interest (in) das Interesse (an + *dat.*)
interested: to be ~ in sich interessieren für
interesting interessant
intermission die Pause, -n
internship das Praktikum, Praktiken/Praktika
to **invite (to)** ein·laden* (zu)
island die Insel, -n
isn't it? nicht wahr?
Italian *(adj.)* italienisch; **in ~** auf Italienisch; **(language)** Italienisch; **Do you speak ~?** Sprechen Sie Italienisch?; **(person)** der Italiener, -
Italy (das) Italien
its sein, ihr

J

jacket die Jacke, -n
jam die Marmelade, -n
January der Januar; **in ~** im Januar
Jeans die Jeans *(pl.)*
job die Arbeit; **(position)** die Stelle, -n
joint(ly) gemeinsam
juice der Saft, ⸚e
July der Juli; **in ~** im Juli
to **jump** springen*
June der Juni; **in ~** im Juni
just gerade; **~ like** genau(so) wie; **~ when** gerade als

K

to **keep** behalten*; **to ~ in shape** sich fit halten*
key der Schlüssel, -
kind nett; **what ~ of (a)?** was für (ein)?
king der König, -e
kitchen die Küche, -n
knee das Knie, -
knife das Messer, -
to **know** **(be acquainted with)** kennen*; **(a fact)** wissen*; **(a skill)** können*
knowledge die Kenntnis, -se
known bekannt

L

lab das Labor, -s *(or -e)*
lady die Dame, -n
lake der See, -n
lamp die Lampe, -n
to **land** landen (ist)
landscape die Landschaft
language die Sprache, -n
large groß (ö)
last letzt-
late spät; **How ~ is it?** Wie spät ist es?, Wie viel Uhr ist es?
later später; **See you ~.** Bis später!
to **laugh** lachen
lawyer der Rechtsanwalt, ⸚e / die Rechtsanwältin, -nen
to **lay (down)** legen
lazy faul
to **lead** führen
to **learn** lernen
to **leave (behind)** lassen*; **~ from** ab·fahren* von, ab·fliegen* von; **(~ a place)** verlassen*
lecture die Vorlesung, -en; **~ hall** der Hörsaal, -säle

left links; link-
leg das Bein, -e
leisure time die Freizeit
lemonade die Limonade, -n
to **let** lassen*
letter der Brief, -e
lettuce der Salat
library die Bibliothek, -en
to **lie** (**to be located**) liegen*; **to ~ down** sich (hin·)legen
life das Leben
light (**weight**) leicht; (**bright**) hell
likable sympathisch; **un~** unsympathisch
like wie; **just ~** genau(so) wie; **s.th. ~** so etwas wie
to **like** gefallen*; **I would ~ (to have)** ich möchte, ich hätte gern
likewise ebenfalls
to **link** verbinden*
to **listen** zu·hören (+ *dat.*); **to ~ to** sich an·hören
little klein; (**amount**) wenig, ein bisschen; (**some**) etwas
to **live** leben; (**reside**) wohnen
living room das Wohnzimmer, -
long (*adj.*) lang (ä); (*adv.*) lange; **how ~?** wie lange?; **So ~!** Tschüss!
to **look** sehen*; **to ~ (like)** aus·sehen* (wie + *nom.*); **~ at** sich an·sehen*; **to ~ for** suchen; **to ~ forward to** sich freuen auf (+ *acc.*); **~!** Schau mal!
to **lose** verlieren*
loud(ly) laut
love die Liebe; **to be in ~ (with)** verliebt sein* (in + *acc.*); **to fall in ~ (with)** sich verlieben (in + *acc.*)
to **love** lieben
luck das Glück; **to be lucky** Glück haben*; **to be unlucky** Pech haben*
luggage das Gepäck
lunch das Mittagessen, -; **for ~** zum Mittagessen

M

magazine die Zeitschrift, -en
mail die Post; **~box** der Briefkasten, ⸚
mainly vor allem
major (**field of study**) das Hauptfach, ⸚er
to **make** machen
man der Mann, ⸚er; (**human being**) der Mensch, -en, -en; **gentle~** der Herr, -n, -en
many viele; **how ~?** wie viele?; **~ a** manch-
map die Landkarte, -n; (**city ~**) der Stadtplan, ⸚e
March der März; **in ~** im März
mark (*German*) die Mark (DM)
market der Markt, ⸚e
marmalade die Marmelade, -n
marriage die Ehe, -n
married verheiratet
to **marry, get married** heiraten
matter: (**That**) **doesn't ~.** (Das) macht nichts.; **What's the ~?** Was ist los?
may dürfen*
May der Mai; **in ~** im Mai
meal das Essen, -; **Enjoy your ~.** Guten Appetit!
to **mean** (**signify**) bedeuten; (**think**) meinen
meanwhile inzwischen
meat das Fleisch
to **meet** (**get to know**) kennen lernen; **Glad to ~ you.** Freut mich (sehr, Sie kennen zu lernen).
menu die Speisekarte, -n
middle die Mitte; **in the ~ of** mitten in/auf (+ *dat.*)
milk die Milch
millennium das Jahrtausend, -e
minor (**field of study**) das Nebenfach, ⸚er
minute die Minute, -n; **See you in a few ~s!** Bis gleich!
Monday (der) Montag; **on ~s** montags

money das Geld; **to earn ~** Geld verdienen; **to spend ~** Geld aus·geben*
month der Monat, -e; **per ~** im Monat, pro Monat; **for one ~** einen Monat
monthly monatlich
monument das Denkmal, ⸚er
more mehr; **once ~** noch einmal; **~ and ~** immer mehr
morning der Morgen; **Good ~!** Guten Morgen!; **in the ~** morgens; (**early**) **~** früh, (früh) morgen; **mid~** der Vormittag, -e; **Monday ~** Montagmorgen
most meist-; am meisten
mostly meistens
mother die Mutter, ⸚
mountain der Berg, -e
mouth der Mund, ⸚er
movie (**film**) der Film, -e; (**theater**) das Kino, -s
Mr Herr
Mrs. Frau
Ms. Frau
much viel (mehr, meist-); **how ~?** wie viel?
museum das Museum, Museen
music die Musik
musical musikalisch; **un~** unmusikalisch
must müssen*
my mein

N

name der Name, -ns; -n; **What's your ~?** Wie heißen Sie?; **My ~ is . . .** Ich heiße . . . , Mein Name ist . . .
to **name** nennen*
napkin die Serviette, -n
nation das Volk, ⸚er
nature die Natur
near (**distance**) nah (näher, nächst-); (**vicinity**) bei (+ *dat.*), in der Nähe von (+ *dat.*)
neat prima; schick

neck der Hals, ⸚e
to **need** brauchen
neighbor der Nachbar, -n, -n
neither . . . nor weder . . . noch
never nie
nevertheless trotzdem
new neu; **s.th. ~** etwas Neues; **nothing ~** nichts Neues; **What's ~?** Was gibt's Neues?
New Year's Eve Silvester; **at/for ~** zu Silvester
news die Nachricht, -en
newspaper die Zeitung, -en
next nächst-; **~ to** neben (+ *dat./acc.*)
nice schön, nett
nickname der Spitzname, -ns, -n
night die Nacht, ⸚e; **Good ~!** Gute Nacht!; **at ~** nachts; **to spend the ~** übernachten
no nein
nobody niemand
noisy laut
no one niemand
noodle die Nudel, -n
noon der Mittag, -e; **at ~** mittags; **after~** der Nachmittag, -e; **Monday (after)~** Montag(nach)mittag
north der Norden; **in the ~** im Norden; **~ of** nördlich von
nose die Nase, -n
not nicht; **~ any** kein; **~ only . . . but also** nicht nur . . . sondern auch; **~ yet** noch nicht; **~ at all** gar nicht, überhaupt nicht
notebook das Heft, -e
nothing (to) nichts (zu); **~ special** nichts Besonderes
novel der Roman, -e
November der November; **in ~** im November
now jetzt, nun; **just ~** gerade
number die Nummern -n, die Zahl, -en
nurse die Krankenschwester, -n; **(male)** der Krankenpfleger, -

O

o'clock Uhr
October der Oktober; **in ~** im Oktober
of course natürlich; doch
to **offer** an·bieten*
office das Büro, -s
often oft
OK: that's ~ das geht; **that's not ~** das geht nicht
old alt (ä)
on auf (+ *acc./dat.*); **~ the first of July** am ersten Juli
once einmal, einst; **~ more** noch einmal; **~ in a while** manchmal; **(formerly)** früher
one (people, they) man
only nur; **(not before)** erst; **not ~ . . . but also** nicht nur . . . sondern auch
open auf, offen, geöffnet
to **open** öffnen, auf·machen
opposite das Gegenteil, -e
or oder
oral presentation das Referat, -e; **to give an ~** ein Referat halten*
orange die Orange, -n; **(color)** orange
orchestra das Orchester, -
order: in ~ to um . . . zu (+ *inf.*)
to **order** bestellen
other ander-
our unser
out of aus (+ *dat.*)
over (location) über (+ *acc./dat.*); **(finished)** vorbei; **~ there** da drüben
own *(adj.)* eigen-

P

to **pack** packen
package das Paket, -e
page die Seite, -n; **on/to ~ . . .** auf Seite . . .
to **paint** malen
palace das Schloss, ⸚er
pants die Hose, -n

paper das Papier, -e; **(term ~)** die (Seminar)arbeit, -en
parcel das Paket, -e
parents die Eltern *(pl.)*
to **pardon: ~ me!** Entschuldigung! Entschuldigen Sie! Verzeihung!
park der Park, -s
to **park** parken
part der Teil, -e; **to take ~ (in)** teil·nehmen* (an + *dat.*)
to **participate (in)** teil·nehmen* (an + *dat.*)
partner der Partner, -
party die Party, -s
to **pass (an exam)** bestehen*; **to ~ by** vorbei·gehen*, vorbei·kommen*, vorbei·fahren*, vorbei·führen (an + *dat.*)
passport der Pass, ⸚e
past in the ~ früher
patient geduldig
to **pay** bezahlen
pea die Erbse, -n
peace der Frieden
pen der Kuli, -s
pencil der Bleistift, -e
penny der Pfennig, -e; **two pennies** zwei Pfennig
people die Leute *(pl.)*; **(human being)** der Mensch, -en, -en; **(as a whole or nation)** das Volk, ⸚er
pepper der Pfeffer
per pro
performance die Vorstellung, -en
perhaps vielleicht
person der Mensch, -en, -en
pharmacy die Apotheke, -n
to **phone** an·rufen*, telefonieren
physician der Arzt, ⸚e / die Ärztin, -nen
piano das Klavier, -e; **to play the ~** Klavier spielen
picture das Bild, -er; **to take ~s** fotografieren
piece das Stück, -e; **~ (of music or ballet)** das Stück, -e
pink rosa

pizza die Pizza, -s
place (**location**) der Platz, ⸚e; **at our ~** bei uns; **in your ~** an deiner Stelle
plan der Plan, ⸚e
to **plan** planen, vor·haben*
plane das Flugzeug, -e
plate der Teller, -
platform der Bahnsteig, -e
play das Stück, ⸚e
to **play** spielen; (**checkers**) Dame spielen; (**chess**) Schach spielen; (**tennis**) Tennis spielen
pleasant gemütlich; **un~** ungemütlich
to **please** gefallen*
please bitte
pocket die Tasche, -n
police (force) die Polizei; **~man** der Polizist, -en, -en; **~woman** die Polizistin, -nen
poor arm (ä)
population die Bevölkerung
position die Stelle, -n
possible möglich; **im~** unmöglich
postcard Ansichtskarte, -n
post office ie Post
P.O. box das Postfach, ⸚er
potato die Kartoffel, -n
pound das Pfund, -e; **a ~ of . . .** ein Pfund . . .
power die Macht, ⸚e
practical(ly) praktisch
to **prefer** lieber tun*; vor·ziehen*
to **prepare** vor·bereiten; **~ oneself (for)** sich vor·bereiten (auf + *acc.*)
present (gift) das Geschenk, -e
pretty hübsch
probably wahrscheinlich
problem das Problem, -e
profession der Beruf, -e; **choice of ~** die Berufswahl
professor der Professor, -en
program das Programm, -e; die Sendung, -en
to **promise** versprechen*
to **protect** schützen
protection der Schutz

proud (of) stolz (auf + *acc.*)
public öffentlich
pudding der Pudding, -s
to **pull** ziehen*
pullover der Pullover, -, Pulli, -s
purple lila
to **put** (**set down**) setzen; (**stand upright**) (hin·)stellen; (**lay down**) (hin·)legen; (**hang up**) (hin·)hängen; **to ~ on (clothing)** (sich) an·ziehen*

Q

quarter das Viertel; **a ~ to** Viertel vor; **a ~ past** Viertel nach; **in a ~ of an hour** in einer Viertelstunde; (**university quarter**) das Quartal, -e
queen die Königin, -nen
question die Frage, -n; **to ask a ~** eine Frage stellen
quick(ly) schnell
quiet(ly) ruhig, leise
quite ziemlich

R

radio das Radio, -s
railway die Bahn, -en
to **rain** regnen; **It's raining.** Es regnet.
rather lieber; ziemlich
to **react (to)** reagieren (auf + *acc.*)
to **read** lesen*
ready fertig
really wirklich; echt
to **rebuild** wieder auf·bauen
to **receive** bekommen*
to **recognize** erkennen*
to **recommend** empfehlen*
red rot (ö)
refrigerator der Kühlschrank, ⸚e
region die Gegend, -en; das Gebiet, -e
regular normal
relationship die Beziehung, -en

to **relax** sich aus·ruhen
to **remain** bleiben*
to **remember** sich erinnern (an + *acc.*)
to **remind (of)** erinnern (an + *acc.*)
to **renovate** renovieren
to **rent** mieten; **to ~ out** vermieten
to **repeat** wiederholen
to **report** berichten
reporter der Journalist, -en, -en
to **request** bitten*
to **rescue** retten
to **reserve** reservieren
to **reside** wohnen
responsibility die Verantwortung
responsible verantwortungsvoll
to **rest** sich aus·ruhen
restaurant das Restaurant, -s
to **restore** restaurieren
to **return** zurück·kommen*
return address der Absender, -
(re)unification die (Wieder)vereinigung
rice der Reis
rich reich
right rechts, recht-; (**correct**) richtig; **You're ~.** Du hast Recht.; **isn't it (~)?** nicht wahr?; (**That's**) **~.** (Das) stimmt.; **~ away** sofort
river der Fluss, ⸚sse
roll das Brötchen, -
room das Zimmer, -; **bed~** das Schlafzimmer, -; **bath~** das Bad, ⸚er (Badezimmer, -); **dining ~** das Esszimmer, -; **living ~** das Wohnzimmer, -; **guest ~** das Gästezimmer, -; **single ~** das Einzelzimmer, -; **double ~** das Doppelzimmer, -
roommate der Zimmerkollege, -n, -n / die Zimmerkollegin, -nen
round-trip ticket die Hin- und Rückfahrkarte, -n
to **run** laufen*

S

sad   traurig
safe   sicher
safety   die Sicherheit
salad   der Salat, -e
salt   das Salz
same   gleich; **the ~ to you** gleichfalls
Saturday   (der) Samstag; **on ~s** samstags
sausage   die Wurst; ¨e
to save   **(money or time)** sparen; **(rescue)** retten
to say   sagen; **Could you ~ that again? What did you ~?** Wie bitte?
scared: **to be ~ (of)** Angst haben* (vor + *dat.*)
scarcely   kaum
scenery   die Landschaft
schedule **(transportation)**   der Fahrplan, ¨e
scholarship   das Stipendium, Stipendien
school   die Schule, -n
science   die Wissenschaft, -en; **natural ~** die Naturwissenschaft, -en
scientist   der Wissenschaftler, -
second   die Sekunde, -n
secretary   die Sekretärin, -nen
secure   sicher
security   die Sicherheit
to see   sehen*; **Let's ~!** Mal sehen!; **Oh, I ~.** Ach so!
to seem   scheinen*
selection   die Auswahl
self-confident   selbstbewusst
self-employed   selbstständig
to sell   verkaufen
semester   das Semester, -
seminar   das Seminar, -e
to send   schicken
sentence   der Satz, ¨e
to separate   trennen
September   der September; **in ~** im September
server   die Bedienung
to set (down)   setzen
several   mehrer- *(pl.)*
to share   teilen
shared   gemeinsam
to shave   sich rasieren
shelf   das Regal, -e
to shine   scheinen*
shirt   das Hemd, -en
shoe   der Schuh, -e; **in your/his ~s** an deiner/seiner Stelle
shop   das Geschäft, -e
to shop   ein·kaufen; **to go ~ping** einkaufen gehen*
short   klein; kurz (ü)
to show   zeigen
shower   die Dusche, -n; **to take a ~** (sich) duschen
sick   krank (ä)
to sign   unterschreiben*
to sign up for   belegen
to signify   bedeuten
silly   dumm (ü)
simple, simply   einfach
since (time)   seit (+ *dat.*)
to sing   singen*
single **(unmarried)**   unverheiratet, ledig
sister   die Schwester, -n
to sit (be sitting)   sitzen*; **to ~ down** sich (hin·)setzen
to ski   Ski laufen*; **to go ~ing** Skilaufen gehen*
skill   die Kenntnis, -se
skinny   dünn
skirt   der Rock, ¨e
slacks   die Hose, -n
slender   schlank
to sleep   schlafen*
slim   schlank
slow(ly)   langsam
small   klein
to snow   schneien
soccer: **to play ~** Fußball spielen
sofa   das Sofa, -s
some   etwas *(sg.)*; einig- *(pl.)*; **(many a)** manch-; **(a couple of)** ein paar
somebody   jemand
someone   jemand
somehow   irgendwie
something (to)   etwas (zu)
sometimes   manchmal
son   der Sohn, ¨e
song   das Lied, -er
soon   bald; **See you ~!** Bis bald!; **as ~ as** sobald
sore: **I have a ~ throat.** Mir tut der Hals weh.
sorry: **I'm ~.** Es tut mir Leid.
so that   *(conj.)* so dass
soup   die Suppe, -n
south   der Süden; **in the ~** im Süden; **~ of** südlich von
Spain   (das) Spanien
Spanish   *(adj.)* spanisch; **in ~** auf Spanisch; **(language)** Spanisch; **Do you speak ~?** Sprechen Sie Spanisch?; **(person)** der Spanier, -
to speak   sprechen*; **~ up (louder)!** Sprechen Sie lauter!
special: **something ~** etwas Besonderes; **nothing ~** nichts Besonderes
spectator   der Zuschauer, -
to spend (money)   aus·geben*
to spin   spinnen, spann, gesponnen
spoon   der Löffel, -
sport(s)   der Sport; **to engage in ~** Sport treiben*
spring   der Frühling, -e; **in (the) ~** im Frühling
square   der Platz, ¨e
stamp   die Briefmarke, -n
to stand (upright), be standing   stehen*
start   der Anfang, ¨e
state   der Staat, -en
to stay   bleiben*
still   noch
stomach   der Bauch, ¨e
stop (for buses etc.)   die Haltestelle, -n
to stop (doing s.th.)   auf·hören (zu + *inf.*)
to stop (in a vehicle)   halten*
stopover   der Aufenthalt, -e
store   das Geschäft, -e; **department ~** das Kaufhaus, ¨er
story   die Geschichte, -n; **detective ~** der Krimi, -s

straight gerade; **~ ahead** geradeaus
strange komisch
strawberry die Erdbeere, -n
street die Straße, -n; **main ~** die Hauptstraße, -n
streetcar die Straßenbahn, -en
strenuous anstrengend
strict(ly) streng
to **stroll** bummeln (ist)
student der Student, -en, -en / die Studentin, -nen
study das Studium, Studien; **(course of ~)** das Studium; **(room)** das Arbeitszimmer, -
to **study** lernen; **(a particular field, be a student at a university)** studieren (an + dat.)
stupid dumm (ü)
subject das Fach, ̈er
subway die U-Bahn
such so ein (sg.); solch (pl.)
sudden(ly) plötzlich
sugar der Zucker
suitcase der Koffer, -
summer der Sommer, -; **in (the) ~** im Sommer
sun die Sonne; **The ~ is shining.** Die Sonne scheint.
Sunday (der) Sonntag; **on ~s** sonntags
superb super
supermarket der Supermarkt, ̈e
supper das Abendessen; **for ~** zum Abendessen
to **suppose** an·nehmen*
sure sicher; doch; (na) klar; **for ~** bestimmt
surely bestimmt, sicher(lich)
surprise die Überraschung, -en
to **surprise** überraschen
surroundings die Umgebung; **(ecology)** die Umwelt
suspenseful spannend
system das System, -e
sweater der Pullover, -, der Pulli, -s
sweatshirt das Sweatshirt, -s
to **swim** schwimmen*, baden

Swiss (person) der Schweizer, -; (adj.) Schweizer
Switzerland die Schweiz

T

table der Tisch, -e
to **take** nehmen*; **to ~ along** mit·nehmen*; **to ~ off (clothing)** (sich) aus·ziehen*; **to ~ off (plane)** ab·fliegen*; **(last)** dauern; **to ~ (a course)** belegen; **to ~ an exam** eine Prüfung machen; **~ care!** Mach's gut!
talented talentiert; **un~** untalentiert
to **talk** reden, sprechen*; **to ~ to/about/of** reden mit/über (+ acc.), sprechen* mit/über (+ acc.)/von (+ dat.)
to **taste** schmecken; **That tastes good.** Das schmeckt (gut).
taxi das Taxi, -s
tea der Tee, -s
to **teach** lehren
teacher der Lehrer, -
to **tear down** ab·reißen*
telephone das Telefon, -e
tell sagen, erzählen (von + dat.)
tennis Tennis
term paper die (Seminar)arbeit, -en
terrible, terribly furchtbar
terrific toll, super
test die Prüfung, -en; **to take a ~** eine Prüfung machen
than (after comp.) als
to **thank** danken (+ dat.); **~ you!** Danke!; **~ you very much.** Vielen Dank!; **~ God!** Gott sei Dank!;
that das; (conj.) dass; **so ~** (conj.) so dass
the . . . the je (+ comp.) . . . desto (+ comp.)
theater das Theater, **movie ~** das Kino, -s
their ihr
then dann; **(in those days)** damals

there da, dort; **over ~** da drüben; **~ is/are** es gibt
therefore deshalb
thick dick
thin dünn
thing das Ding, -e
things: all sorts of ~ so einiges
to **think (of)** denken* (an + acc.); **(be of an opinion)** glauben, meinen; **I ~ it's . . .** Ich finde es . . . ; **I ~ so, too.** Das finde ich auch.; **if you ~ so** wenn du meinst; **don't you ~ so?** oder?
thinker der Denker, -
thirst der Durst
thirsty: I'm ~. Ich habe Durst.
this dies-
thought der Gedanke, -ns, -n
throat der Hals, ̈e
through durch (+ acc.)
to **throw away** weg·werfen*
Thursday (der) Donnerstag; **on ~s** donnerstags
ticket die Karte, -n; **(bus, etc.)** die Fahrkarte, -n; **(round-trip ~)** die (Hin- und) Rückfahrkarte, -n; **~ window** der Schalter, -
to **tie together** verbinden*
time die Zeit, -en; **What ~ is it?** Wie spät ist es? Wie viel Uhr ist es?; **at what ~?** wann?; **in the mean~** inzwischen; **one ~** einmal; **the first ~** das erste Mal; **for the first ~** zum ersten Mal
tired müde
to zu (+ dat.); an (+ acc.); **(a country, etc.)** nach
today heute
together gemeinsam, zusammen; **~ with** mit (+ dat.)
toilet die Toilette, -n
tomato die Tomate, -n
tomorrow morgen; **the day after ~** übermorgen
too (also) auch; **~ much** zu viel
tooth der Zahn, ̈e

tour guide der Reiseleiter, -
tourist der Tourist, -en, -en
tower der Turm, ¨e
town die Stadt, ¨e
townhouse das Reihenhaus, ¨er
toxic waste der Giftstoff, -e
track das Gleis, -e
trade der Handel
traffic der Verkehr
trail der Weg, -e
train der Zug, ¨e, die Bahn, -en; **~ station** der Bahnhof, ¨e
training die Ausbildung
trash der Abfall, ¨e
to **travel** reisen (ist)
tree der Baum, ¨e
tremendously unheimlich
trillion *(American)* die Billion, -en
trip die Reise, -n, die Fahrt, -en; **to take a ~** eine Reise machen
true richtig, wahr; **(That's) ~.** (Das) stimmt.; **isn't that ~?** nicht wahr?
to **try** versuchen
T-shirt das T-Shirt, -s
Tuesday (der) Dienstag; **on ~s** dienstags
to **turn: to ~ off (radio, etc.)** aus·machen; **to ~ on (radio, etc.)** an·machen
TV (medium) das Fernsehen; **(set)** der Fernseher, -; **to watch ~** fern·sehen*
typical(ly) typisch

U

ugly hässlich
unathletic unsportlich
uncle der Onkel, -
under unter (+ *acc./dat.*)
to **understand** verstehen*
understanding verständnisvoll
undoubtedly sicherlich
uneducated ungebildet
unemployment die Arbeitslosigkeit
unfortunately leider
unfriendly unfreundlich
unification die Vereinigung
united vereint, vereinigt
United States (U.S.) die Vereinigten Staaten (U.S.A.) *(pl.)*
university die Universität, -en, die Uni, -s
unlucky: to be ~ Pech haben*
unmarried unverheiratet
unmusical unmusikalisch
unique einmalig
unsafe unsicher
untalented untalentiert
until bis; **not ~** erst
upset: to get ~ about sich ärgern über (+ *acc.*)
upstairs oben
usual(ly) gewöhnlich, meistens
to **use** gebrauchen, benutzen, verwenden
to **utilize** gebrauchen, verwenden

V

vacation die Ferien *(pl.)*
various verschieden-
vegetable(s) das Gemüse, -
versatile vielseitig
very sehr; ganz
viewer der Zuschauer, -
village das Dorf, ¨er
to **visit** besuchen; **(sightseeing)** besichtigen

W

to **wait (for)** warten (auf + *acc.*)
waiter der Kellner, -, der Ober, -; **~!** Herr Ober!
waitress die Kellnerin, -nen, die Bedienung
to **walk** zu Fuß gehen*, laufen*; **to go for a ~** spazieren gehen*
wall die Wand, ¨e; **(thick)** die Mauer, -n
to **want to** wollen*, möchten*
war der Krieg, -e
warm warm (ä)
to **wash (o.s.)** (sich) waschen*
waste der Müll
watch (clock) die Uhr, -en
to **watch: (TV)** fern·sehen*; **(pay attention)** auf·passen; **~ out!** Passen Sie auf! / Pass auf!
water das Wasser
way der Weg, -e; **by the ~** übrigens; **this ~** auf diese Weise
to **wear** tragen*
weather das Wetter
wedding die Hochzeit, -en
Wednesday (der) Mittwoch; **on ~s** mittwochs
week die Woche, -n; **all ~ long** die ganze Woche; **this ~** diese Woche
weekend das Wochenende, -n; **on the ~** am Wochenende
weekly wöchentlich
welcome: You're ~. Bitte (bitte)! Nichts zu danken!
well *(adv.)* gut
west der Westen; **in the ~** im Westen; **~ of** westlich von
what? was?; **~ did you say?** Wie bitte?; **~'s new?** Was gibt's (Neues)?; **~'s on . . . ?** Was gibt's im . . . ?; **So ~!** Na und!; **~ kind of (a)?** was für (ein)?
when (at what time) wann?; **(whenever)** *(conj.)* wenn; *(conj., single action in past)* als; **just ~** *(conj.)* gerade als
where? wo?; **from ~?** woher?; **~ to?** wohin?
whether *(conj.)* ob
which? welch-?
while *(conj.)* während
white weiß
who? wer?
whole ganz
whom? wen?, wem?
whose? wessen?
why? warum?, wieso?
wife die Frau, -en
wild wild

to **win** gewinnen*
window das Fenster, -; **ticket ~** der Schalter, -
wine der Wein, -e
winter der Winter; **in (the) ~** im Winter
to **wish** (sich) wünschen
wish der Wunsch, ¨e
with mit (+ *dat.*); **(at the home of)** bei (+ *dat.*); **~ me (us . . .)** bei mir (uns . . .)
without ohne (+ *acc.*)
woman (Mrs., Ms.) die Frau, -en
wonderful(ly) wunderbar, prima, herrlich

woods der Wald, ¨er
word das Wort, ¨er; **in other ~s** also
work die Arbeit
to **work** arbeiten
worker der Arbeiter, -
world die Welt, -en
worry die Sorge, -n
to **worry (about)** sich Sorgen machen (um)
to **write** schreiben* **to ~ to** schreiben* an (+ *acc.*); **to ~ about** schreiben* über (+ *acc.*); **to ~ down** auf·schreiben*
wrong falsch; **You are ~.** Du hast Unrecht.

Y

year das Jahr, -e; **all ~ long** das ganze Jahr; **next ~** nächstes Jahr
yellow gelb
yes ja; doch
yesterday gestern; **the day before ~** vorgestern
yet doch; **not ~** noch nicht
young jung (ü)
your dein, euer, Ihr
youth die Jugend
youth hostel die Jugendherberge, -n

Photo and Illustrations Credits

2	Progressive Information Technologies	151	Austrian National Tourist Office
5	Progressive Information Technologies	152	Andreas Friess/Gamma-Liaison
10	Progressive Information Technologies	158	Inter Nationes
15	Progressive Information Technologies	159	Inter Nationes
19	Progressive Information Technologies	169	Progressive Information Technologies
31	Inter Nationes	172	G. Hinterlaitner/The Liaison Agency
32	Ulrike Welsch	173	Progressive Information Technologies
33	Walter Hanel/Econ Verlag	177	Inter Nationes
38	Paul Gerda/Leo de Wys Inc.	177	Kevin Galvin
39	Inter Nationes	178	Inter Nationes
47	Inter Nationes	180	Progressive Information Technologies
49	DeRichemond/The Image Works	183	Dieter Sevin
54	Inter Nationes	184	Deutsche Bank
55	Inter Nationes	185	Jürgen Tomicek, in *Ratgeber Euro*
60	Palmer-Brilliant	190	Douglas Guy
69	Ulrike Welsch	199	Kevin Galvin
70	Progressive Information Technologies	204	DJH Archiv
71	Inter Nationes	205	B. Roland/The Image Works
74	Joan Schoellner	213	Citysights AG
78	Inter Nationes	214	German National Tourist Office
93	Inter Nationes	218	Inter Nationes
95	Ingrid Sevin	232	Wolfgang Kaehler
96	Hugh Rogers/Monkmeyer Press Photo	234	Keystone/The Image Works
98	Inter Nationes	238	Inter Nationes
101	Christian Teubner	241	Progressive Information Technologies
107	Progressive Information Technologies	248	Inter Nationes
108	Inter Nationes	254	R. Schwerzel/Stock Boston
109	David Simson/Stock Boston	255	Inter Nationes
114	Goethe Institut München	257	Michael Bry/Monkmeyer Press Photo
124	Presse und Informationsamt	257	Alain Revel/Agency Vandystadt
126	Inter Nationes	263	Inter Nationes
128	Larry Mulvehill/The Image Works	264	Inter Nationes
128	Inter Nationes	267	The Kobal Collection
129	Nobory Komine/Photo Researchers Inc.	270	Inter Nationes
134	Robert Bendick/Monkmeyer Press Photo	270	Erwin Döring
135	Keystone/The Image Works	273	Scala/Art Resource
137	FridmarDamm/Leo dy Wys Inc.	288	Palmer-Brilliant
139	Siegfried Purschke/Ullstein Bilderdienst	308	Keystone/The Image Works
148	Erich Lessing/Art Resource	319	Progressive Information Technologies
149	Inter Nationes	320	Max Planck/Gesellsch.Pressestelle
150	H. Lanks/Monkmeyer Press Photo	323	Inter Nationes

Photo and Illustrations Credits

335	David Simson/Stock Boston	389	Inter Nationes
337	Ulrike Welsch	389	Erich Lessing/Art Resource
341	Ingrid Sevin	390	Inter Nationes
345	Inter Nationes	391	German Information Center
346	David Ausserhofer	392	German Information Center
351	Ulrike Welsch	398	Margot Granitsas/The ImageWorks
358	Homemade Postcards	399	Christian Vioujard/The Liaison Agency
359	Little Monster Cards	401	Gerd Schnürer/Ullstein Bilderdienst
362	Masa Uemura/Leo de Wys Inc.	404	*Impressum*
363	David Ausserhofer	413	Inter Nationes
371	Ulrike Welsch	413	Jürgen Ritter/Ullstein Bilderdienst
372	Ulrike Welsch	414	Topham/The Image Works
376	Rene Burri/MAGNUM	414	Inter Nationes
377	StadtINFO Verlag	416	*Scala*
378	*Impressum*	418	*Journal für Deutschland*
384	Ulrike Welsch	427	Progressive Information Technologies

Poems Credits

235	Hermann Hesse, "Im Nebel," in *Gesammelte Dichtungen,* V (Frankfurt/Main: Suhrkamp, 1952).
260	Rose Ausländer, "Noch bist du da," in *Ich höre das Herz des Oleanders. Gedichte* 1977–1979, hrsg. H. Braun (Frankfurt/Main: S. Fischer, 1984).
285	Wolf Biermann, "Ach, Freund, geht es nicht auch dir so?", in *Wolfgang Biermann: Alle Gedichte* (Köln: Verlag Kiepenheuer & Witsch, 1995).
312	Eva Strittmatter, "Werte," in *Die eine Rose überwältigt alles* (Berlin: Aufbau, 1977).
342	Aysel Özakin, "Wie lernt man in Deutschland eine merkwürdige Türkin kennen?" in *Du bist willkommen. Gedichte* (Hamburg: Buntbuch-Verlag, 1985).
369	Bertolt Brecht, "1940," in *Gesammelte Werke,* IX, Gedichte 2 (Frankfurt/Main: Suhrkamp Verlag, 1967).
395	Erich Kästner, "Fantasie von übermorgen," in *Erich Kästner: Gesammelte Schriften, Band I-Gedichte,* hrsg. Hermann Kesten (Köln: Verlag Kiepenheuer & Witsch, 1959).
419	Johann Wolfgang von Goethe, "Erinnerung," in *Goethes Werke,* I (Hamburg: Christian Wegner Verlag).
419	Friedrich von Schiller, "An die Freude," in *Sämtliche Werke,* hrsg. G. Fricke und H. G. Göpfert, 3. Auflage (München: Carl Hanser, 1962).

INDEX

This index is limited to grammatical entries. Topical vocabulary and material from the *Sprechsituationen* can be found in the table of contents. Entries appearing in the *Rückblicke* are indicated by parentheses.

aber vs. **sondern** 147, (212)
accusative case 61–63, 87, (105–06), 140, (209–10), 249–50, (316–17), A-1
   time 225, (319)
   with prepositions 63, (105), 165–67, (210), 271, (317), A-1
adjectival nouns 333–34, A-3
adjectives
   after **nichts** 242
   attributive 245
   comparison 327–29, (422), A-4
   possessive 35, 43, 62, 86, (106), 191–92, (209–10), 222, A-1
   preceded 245–46, (317–18), 328, A-1/2
   predicate 45–46, 66, (106), (211), 245, 328, (422)
   unpreceded 275–76, (318), 328, A-2
adverbs
   comparison 327–29, (422), A-4
   sequence of 67, (107), 226–27, (319)
   time, manner, place 224–27 (319)
alphabet 4
als, wann, wenn 300–01, (316)
articles
   contractions with prepositions 63, 88, 165
   definite 6, 43, 61–62, 86, (106), 191–92, (210), 221, 245–46, 250, (314, 317), A-1
   indefinite 43, 62, 86, (106), 191, (210), 221, 245–46, (317), A-3
   omission with nationalities and professions 36, 46, 333
   with parts of body 250, (314)
auxiliaries
   haben 21, (28), 61, (104), 116, (209), 296–97, 301–02, (315), A-5/7/8

   modals 142–44, 194, (208), 252, 297, (314), 332, 353–54, 359–60, 385, 406, (423–24, 426)
   sein 7, (28), 61, (104), 119, (209), 298, 301–02, (315, 317), 359, A-5/7/8
   werden 84, (104), 119, (210), 298, (317), 331–32, 354, 385, 405–07, (423, 427), A-5/7

capitalization 2, (27)
cases
   nominative 43–44, 45, (105–06), 140, (210), (317), A-1
   accusative 61–63, 87, (105–06), 140, (209–10), 249–50, (316–17), A-1
   dative 86–89, (105), 140, (209–10), 249–50, (316–17), A-1
   genitive 221–23, (316–17), A-1
cardinal numbers 11, 276
clauses
   coordinate 67, (107)
   indirect questions 385, (426)
   infinitive + **zu** 252, (314)
   relative 379–81, (423)
   subordinate 121–22, 144, 194, (209, 211), 300, (316), 381, 385
commands
   direct (29), 170, 193, (208–09, 211)
   indirect 385, (426)
comparative. See comparison.
comparison of adjectives and adverbs 327–29, (422), A-4
complements, verb 66, (106), 241–42
compound nouns 46
conditions, unreal 352, 356, 360, (425)
conjunctions
   coordinating 67, (107), 147, (212)
   subordinating 121–22, 144, 194, (209, 211), 300, (316), 385

coordinate clauses 67, (107)
coordinating conjunctions 67, (107), 147, (212)

da-compounds 273–74, (316)
dative case 86–89, (105), 140, (209–10), 249–50, (316–17), A-1
   with prepositions 88, (105), 165–67, (209–10), 225, 271, (316–17), A-1
   with verbs 88, (105), 165–67, (210), 271, (317), A-1
definite article 6, 43, 61–62, 86, (106), 191–92, (209–10), 221, 245–46, 250, (314, 317), A-1
der-words 191–92, (209–10), 221, 245–46, (317), A-1
direct object 61–63, 87, (105–06), 140, (209–10), 249–50, (316–17), A-1

ein-words 191, (209–10), 245–46, (317–18), A-1
elements, sentence (28), 45–46, (106), 122, 143, 193, (211, 314)
es gibt 58, 63
Euro 10, 56, 75, 185–86, 399

flavoring particles 197
future tense 41, (105), 331–32, 410, (423), A-8

gender 6, (27), 35, A-0
genitive case 221–23, (316–17), A-1
   proper names 222, (316)
   time 225, (319)
   with prepositions 223, (317), A-1
gern 58, 143, 327–28, A-4
gesture words 197

haben 21, (28), 61, (104), 116, (209), 296–97, 301–02, (315), A-5/7/8

I-1

imperative (29), 170, 193, (208–09, 211), 385
indefinite article 43, 62, 86, (106), 191, (210), 221, 245–46, (317), A-1
indirect commands 385, (426)
indirect object case 86–89, (105), 140, (209–10), 249–50, (316–17), A-1
indirect questions 385, (426)
indirect speech 384–385, 411–12, (425)
indirect statements 385, (425)
infinitive 40
  with modals 143, (208), 252, (314), 332, 359, 406, (423–24, 426)
  with **zu** 252, (314)
inseparable prefixes 117–18, 195, (208–09), (315)
interrogative pronouns (28), 43, 61, 86, (106), (209), 221, 273–74, (316), 381, A-3
intransitive verbs 63, 119, 165–67, (209)
irregular t-verbs 116, (208–09), 296–97, (315–16), 354, A-4/5/6/7
irregular weak verbs. See irregular t-verbs.

kein 43, 62, 66–67, 86, (106), 192, (210), (317), A-1
kennen vs. **wissen** 171–72, (208)

linking verbs 45–46, (105), (210), (317), A-1

man 94, 407, (426)
metric system
  weights 57
  liquid measures 57
  distance 219
  temperature 19
modal auxiliaries 142–44, 194, (208), 252, 297, (314), 332, 353–54, 359–60, 385, 406, (423–24, 426)

names, proper
  genitive 222, (316)
negation 66–67, (107), 227, (319)

nicht, position of 66–67, (107), 227, (319)
n-nouns 62, 87, (105), (316), A-3
nominative case 43–44, 45, (105–06), 140, (210), (317), A-3
  predicate nouns 43–44, 45, 66, (105–06), (210), (317), A-1
nouns
  adjectival 333–34, A-3
  compound 46
  dative plural 87, (105)
  feminine equivalents 43, 333, 343, 434
  gender 6, (27), 35, A-0
  genitive singular 230–32, (323)
  n-nouns 62, 87, (105), (316), A-3
  plural 6, (27), 87, (105)
  predicate 43–44, 45, 66, (105–06), (210), (317), A-1
numbers
  cardinal 11, 276
  ordinal 111
n-verbs 116–17, 119, (208), 297–98, (315), A-4/5/6/7

objects. See direct / indirect object.
objects, sequence of 87, 140, (211), 250
ordinal numbers 111

participles. See past participles.
passive voice 405–07, 410, (426–27), A-9
  agent 405–06
  with modals 406–07, (426)
past participles
  -ieren-verbs 118, (208), (315)
  inseparable-prefix verbs 117–18, 195, (208–09), (315)
  irregular t-verbs 116, (208–09), 296–97, (315–16), 354, A-4/5/6/7
  n-verbs 116–17, 119, (208), 297–98, (315), A-4/5/6/7
  separable-prefix verbs 193–95, (208–09, 211), 298, (315–16), 332
  t-verbs 116, (208), 296, (315–16)
past perfect tense 301–02, (315), A-8
past tenses. See simple past, present / past perfect

personal pronouns (27–28), 40, 43–44, 140, (210–11), A-1
plural of nouns 6, (27), 87, (105)
possessive adjectives 35, 43, 62, 86, (106), 191–92, (209–10), 222, A-1
predicate adjectives 45–46, 66, (106), (211), 245, 328, (422)
predicate nouns 43–44, 45, 66, (105–06), (210), (317), A-1
prepositional objects 271–72, (314)
prepositions
  contractions with articles 63, 88, 165
  with accusative 63, (105), 165–67, (210), 271, (317), A-1
  with dative 88, (105), (210), 225–26, 271, (317), A-1
  with dative or accusative 165–67, (210), 225, 271–72, (317), A-1
  with genitive 223, (317), A-1
  with verbs 271, (314)
present perfect tense 116–18, 119, 193–94, (208–09), (315), A-8
  with **haben** 116–18, (208–09), (315), A-8
  with **sein** 119, (209), (315), A-8
present tense 40–41, 84, (104–05), 226, 331, A-8
  to express future time 41, (105), 331
  to express past actions continuing into present 88, 226
principal parts 297–98, (315), A-4/5/6/7
pronouns
  interrogative (28), 43, 61, 86, (106), (209), 221, 273–74, (316), 381, A-1
  personal (27–28), 40, 43–44, 140, (210–11), A-1
  reflexive 249–50, (314), A-3
  relative 379–81, (423), A-4
punctuation 121, 144, 170, (211), 222, 252, (314), 381, 384

questions
  indirect 385, (426)
  information (28), 45, 122, 143, 385
  yes / no (29), 122, (211), 385

reflexive pronouns 249–50, (314), A-3
reflexive verbs 249–50, (314)
relative clauses 379–81, (423)
relative pronouns 379–81, (423), A-4

sein 7, (28), 61, (104), 119, (209), 298, 301–02, (315, 317), 359, A-5/7
sentence structure
    charts 67, (107), 140, (211), 227, (319), 380, (423)
    commands (29), 170, 193, (208–09, 211), 385, (426)
    coordinate clauses 67, (107)
    indirect speech 384–385, 411–12, (425)
    infinitive phrases and clauses 252, (314)
    modals, position 142–44, 194, (208), 297, (314), 332, 353–54, 359–60
    negation 66–67, (107), 227, (319)
    questions (28–29), 122, (211), 385, (426)
    relative clauses 379–81, (423)
    sentence elements (28), 45–46, (106), 122, 143, 193, (211, 314)
    sequence of adverbs 67, (107), 226–27, (319)
    sequence of objects 87, 140, (211), 250
    statements (28), 45, 143, 193, (209), 385
    subordinate clauses 121–22, 144, 194, (209, 211), (316), 385
    verb complements 66, (106), 241–42
    verb position (28–29), 45, 6, (106), 116, 121–23, 143, 193, (208–09, 211), 298, 331–32, 381, 385, (423)
separable-prefix verbs 193–95, (208–09, 211), 298, (315–16), 332
simple past 296–98, (315–16), A-8
    haben 297, A-5
    irregular t-verbs 297, (315)
    modals 297
    n-verbs 297–98, (315), A-4/5/6/7
    sein 298, A-5/7

strong verbs. See n-verbs.
t-verbs 296, (315)
weak verbs. See t-verbs.
werden 298, A-5/7
sondern vs. **aber** 147, (212)
spelling reform 417
statements (28), 45, 143, 193, (209), 385
stem, verb 40, 116–17, 296, (315)
subject 43–44, 45, (105–06), 140, (210), (317), A-1
subjunctive
    general (or II) 353–56, 359–60, 385, (423–26), A-8
    indirect speech 384–385, 411–12, (425)
    mood 352
    special (or I) 410–12, (423–326), A-8
subordinate clauses 121–22, 144, 194, (209, 211), 300, (316), 385
subordinating conjunctions 121–22, 144, 194, (209, 211), 300, (316), 385
superlative. See comparison.

tenses. See future, present, simple past, present / past perfect.
time
    adverbs 224–26, 226–27, (319)
    dates 111, 225, 232
    days of the week 16
    expressions with accusative 225, (319)
    expressions with dative 225–26
    expressions with genitive 225, (319)
    formal clock 187
    informal clock 20–21
    months 16
    seasons 15
transitive verbs 62–63, 62–63, 166–67
t-verbs 116, (208), 296, (315–16)
two-way prepositions 165–67, (210), 225, 271–72, (317), A-1

verb complements 66, (106), 241–42
verbs
    commands (29), 170, 193, (208–09, 211), 385, (426)

future tense 41, (105), 331–32, 410, (423), A-8
    with **-ieren** 118, (208), (315)
infinitive 40
inseparable-prefix 117–18, 195, (208–09), (315)
intransitive 63, 119, 165–67, (209)
irregular t-verbs 116, (208–09), 296–97, (315–16), 354, A-4/5/6/7
linking 45–46, (105), (210), (317), A-3
modals 142–44, 194, (208), 252, 297, (314), 332, 353–54, 359–60, 385, 406, (423–24, 426)
n-verbs 116–17, 119, (208), 297–98, (315), A-4/5/6/7
passive voice 405–07, 410, (426–27), A-9
past perfect tense 301–02, (315), A-8
position (28–29), 45, 6, (106), 116, 121–23, 143, 193, (208–09, 211), 298, 331–32, 381, 385, (423)
present perfect tense 116–18, 119, 193–94, (208–09), (321–22), A-8
present tense 40–41, 84, (104–05), 226, 331, A-8
principal parts 297–98, (315), A-4/5/6/7
reflexive 249–50, (314)
separable-prefix 193–95, (208–09, 211), 298, (315–16), 332
simple past 296–98, (315–16), A-8
stem 40, 116–17, 296, (315)
strong. See n-verbs.
subjunctive. See subjunctive general (II), subjunctive special (I)
transitive 62–63, 166–67
t-verbs 116, (208), 296, (315–16)
weak verbs. See t-verbs.
with dative 88, (105), 165–67, (210), 271, (317), A-1
with prepositional objects 271–72, (314)

with vowel changes. 84, (104), 170. See also irregular t-verbs, n-verbs.

wann, wenn, als 300–01, (316)
werden
    auxiliary for future 331–32, 410, (423), A-8
    auxiliary for passive 405–07, 410, (426–27), A-9
    full verb 84, (104), 119, (210), (317), 332, 410, (427)
    review of 410, (427)
würde-form 355, 385, 410, (424, 427)
wissen vs. **kennen** 171–72, (208)

wo-compounds 274, (316)
word order. See sentence structure.

zu 252, (314)